RULING
PLANETS

Symbol of the Universal Spirit of Nature.

RULING PLANETS

YOUR ASTROLOGICAL GUIDE TO LIFE'S UPS AND DOWNS

CHRISTOPHER RENSTROM

HarperResource

An Imprint of HarperCollins*Publishers*

RULING PLANETS © 2002 by Christopher Renstrom. Printed in Singapore. No part of this book may be used or reproduced in any manner whatsoever without written permission except in the case of brief quotations embodied in critical articles and reviews. For information address HarperCollins Publishers Inc., 10 East 53rd Street, New York, New York 10022.

HarperCollins books may be purchased for educational, business, or sales promotional use. For information, please write to: Special Markets Department, HarperCollins Publishers Inc., 10 East 53rd Street, New York, New York 10022.

FIRST EDITION

DESIGN AND BOOK LAYOUT: RENATO STANISIC
ART RESEARCHER AND DESIGN CONSULTANT: TINA KLEM

LIBRARY OF CONGRESS CATALOGING-IN-PUBLICATION DATA

Renstrom, Christopher.
    Ruling planets : your astrological guide to life's ups and downs / Christoper Renstrom.—
  1st. ed.
      p. cm.
    ISBN 0-06-019992-X
    1. Astrology.   2.   Planets—Miscellanea.   I.   Title.

  BF1724.R46 2001
  133.5'3—dc21

                                                              2001024078

  02   03   04   05   06   WBC / IM   10   9   8   7   6   5   4   3   2   1

TO MY TWO RULING PLANETS:

Adam and Mom

CONTENTS

PART IV

WORK & PLAY: HOW THE RULING
PLANETS GET ALONG . . . AND WHAT TO
DO WHEN THEY DON'T

ACKNOWLEDGMENTS

Some other stars in the firmament:

LING LUCAS, the agent every author prays for. None of this would have happened without her business savvy, support, and friendship.

TINA KLEM, whose taste, diligence, and vision midwived the look and layout of this book.

MEGAN NEWMAN, for taking a chance on a first-time author.

The entire team at HarperCollins, with a special nod to NICK DARRELL ("point man") and KATHRYN HUCK ("troubleshooter").

Janis Donnaud, Linda Wells, Isaac Mizrahi, Gregory St. John, Dawn Brown, and Gwen Sutton.

CAROLYN ASNIEN, my astrology teacher who first sent me down this path.

INTRODUCTION

Nowadays just about everyone knows his or her zodiac sign. However, the practice of describing oneself as an Aries or a Virgo is actually very recent; in fact, it's not even a hundred years old. Identifying with one's sign is a direct result of the newspaper horoscope column created by the British astrologer R. H. Naylor in 1930. Before then, one would say, "I am a Child of Mars," or "I am a Child of Mercury." Most of us are familiar with the old nursery rhyme describing the qualities of a child born on a particular day of the week:

MONDAY'S CHILD IS FAIR OF FACE,
TUESDAY'S CHILD IS FULL OF GRACE,
WEDNESDAY'S CHILD IS FULL OF WOE,
THURSDAY'S CHILD HAS FAR TO GO,
FRIDAY'S CHILD IS LOVING AND GIVING,
SATURDAY'S CHILD WORKS HARD FOR A LIVING,
BUT A CHILD THAT'S BORN ON THE SABBATH DAY
IS FAIR AND WISE AND GOOD AND GAY.

It was the Romans, the great believers in patrons, who named the days of the week after the planets in the sky. They believed that anyone born on that particular day would inherit both the planet's personality and sponsorship—in effect becoming a "child" of that planet. Monday belonged to the Moon, thus "fair of face" referred to the Moon's silvery complexion. Tuesday was associated with Mars, a planet named after the god of war, who was prized by the Romans for his athletic grace and prowess. Wednesday was identified with Mercury, and the child "full of woe" was the recipient of this planet's quick mind as well as the nervous tendency to worry too much. Thursday was Jupiter's—the planet of long journeys and adventure (as attested to by the wide reach of the Roman Empire). Friday was Venus's, the planet of love and pleasure and revels—which is still commemorated today with the phrase: T.G.I.F ("Thank God it's Friday"). Saturday was Saturn's—the planet of toil and discipline. Finally, the Sabbath was the Sun's day, and we all know that anyone said to possess a "sunny" personality is going to be cheerful and upbeat.

Yet this pantheon of planetary days was itself borrowed by the Romans from an even older astrological tradition that apportioned the calendar year into planetary rulerships. At the heart of the year stood the Sun and Moon—the two brightest and closest "planets." It may be odd to think of the Sun and Moon as planets, but to ancient astronomers, Earth and the heavens were seen as fixed in place, and it was the planets that moved. Sometimes they moved forward. Sometimes they moved backwards. Some were fast. Others were very slow. One night the planets might be spread out across the sky, and on another evening they might be clumped together in one spot. This erratic behavior fostered the belief that there was a greater design to their movement. After all, if observing clouds, tidal flows, and sudden changes in the wind foretold of approaching weather conditions, why wouldn't the same hold true with the planets? Perhaps the planets were somehow trying to communicate something to us through their actions. And if only we could understand them, then we would be that much closer to comprehending how life was supposed to work. Thus it was the planets' movements through the sky that influenced life down here on Earth. The Sun and Moon were seen as exerting their strongest influence in summer, so they ruled the months of July and August, when days are long, nights are warm, and the earth is bursting with life. Mercury ruled the two months flanking July and August, Venus the two months next to those, then Mars and Jupiter. Finally Saturn, the slowest and most distant planet (at least to the naked eye), was assigned rulership of the winter months December and January, when nights are dark, days are cold, and the earth is barren and hard.

Yet the influence of the planets reached beyond the months of the year or a person's disposition. Certain herbs were ruled by planets, as were animals and colors, body parts, professions, love interests, countries—even the sky itself was divided up into domains ruled by each planet, so that when, for instance, Venus was traveling through a part of the sky ruled by Mars she behaved more aggressively (i.e., *martially*) than she did when she was traveling through a part of the sky ruled by the more sedate Moon. It's not unlike the way a woman when traveling in France would dress differently from the way she would if she were traveling in the Middle East. And, of course, whatever affects the planet affects everything that's influenced by it—including its "children."

The emphasis on the Ruling Planet is what's missing from today's astrology books and newspaper columns. Traditionally one's Ruling Planet was regarded as a kind of patron saint, a celestial entity that watched over those born under its influence. Your zodiac sign is static, whereas your Ruling Planet will always describe what's going on in the heavens vis-à-vis you, because it is in constant motion. Is it traveling through a part of the sky that presages difficulty or is it signaling a time when you're shedding old ways and yearning for something new? If you think about it, it's not unlike charting the growth of your mutual fund. Keeping tabs on your Ruling Planet allows you to keep a lookout for what's happening in your life.

HOW TO USE THIS BOOK

The first part of this book is made up of Planetary tables. Simply look up the year you were born and then your birthday to find what Planet you were born under. You can think of it as your Ruling (or Birthday) Planet.

The second part of this book describes the general characteristics, temperaments, and outlook of each Planet's Children. Some readers will have two Ruling Planets. The reason for this is that ancient astrologers knew of only seven planets. As Uranus, Neptune, and then Pluto were discovered, they were partnered with older or "traditional" planets—moving from the farthest planet (Saturn) back toward the Sun. Imagine if you had only seven sheets of paper for a letter you were writing. After filling them up, it would become necessary to write on the back of some of them and in a way that would be comprehensible to the person reading it. At the end of each "Child of . . ." chapter you will find a second set of tables. These will tell you what part of the sky (or zodiac sign) your Planet was traveling through on the day you were born.

Not everyone was born at a time when his or her Ruling Planet was in power. Most people are a blend of Planetary energies. For instance if you are a Child of Venus with Venus in Aries then you will have a strong Mars streak, because Mars rules the constellation Aries. Planets are not the same as zodiac signs. They are much more powerful. Planets are the actors on the stage, while zodiac signs provide the backdrop to the action. These unique blends of energies—along with good (as well as not so good) times of year—will be fully explained in Part III.

Part IV describes how the Children of the Planets get along with one another—and what to do when they don't. There is no such thing as a "perfect" match in astrology. Each of us is drawn to a variety of people for a variety of reasons. Relationships are fluid and not set in stone. Part IV explores this by examining each Planetary combination in relationships ranging from love interest to parent to child to colleague. Not only will you have an opportunity to see how the relationship dynamic changes, but you'll also gain further insight into whomever you're asking about by looking up this person's Ruling Planet and taking a look at things from his or her point of view.

Think of your Birthday Planet as a coach, sponsor, den mother, and guardian angel all wrapped up in one. Moody and at times partial, it nevertheless tells you when it's time to push for what you want and when to cool it. Your Birthday Planet shows you where you're coming from and where you're going. It affects your relationships, helps you to set priorities, and colors just about every decision you'll ever make, but it doesn't tell you what to do or how to live your life any more than the weather does. Think of *Ruling Planets* as your personal guide to that wonderfully creative partnership with your "higher" power up there in the sky. As above, so below.

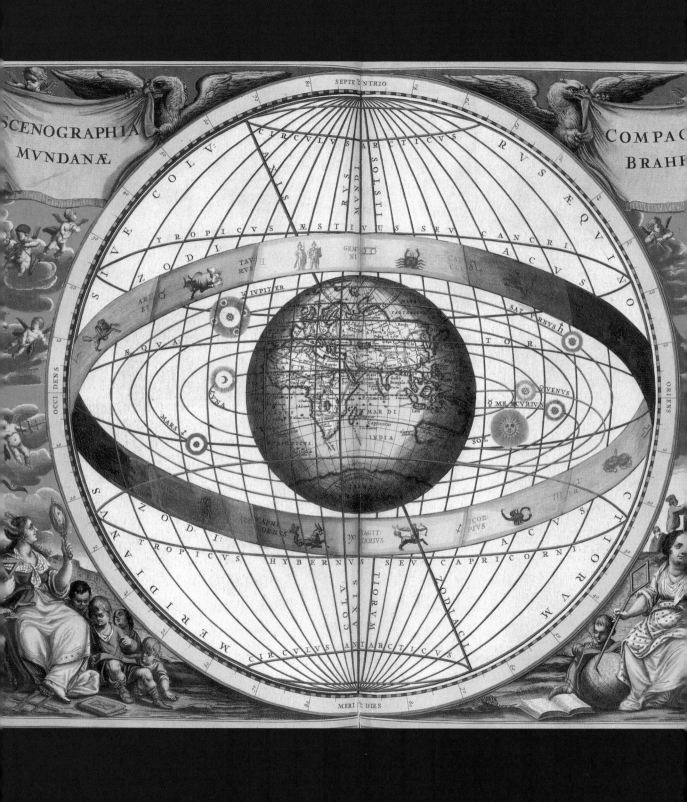

PART I

IF YOU WERE BORN ON...
FINDING YOUR
RULING
PLANET

FINDING YOUR
RULING PLANET

1900

IF YOU WERE BORN ON . . .	YOUR RULING PLANET IS . . .
January 1 to 19	Saturn
January 20 to February 18	Uranus
February 19 to March 20	Neptune
March 21 to April 19	Mars
April 20 to May 20	Venus
May 21 to June 20	Mercury
June 21 to July 22	Moon
July 23 to August 22	Sun
August 23 to September 22	Mercury
September 23 to October 22	Venus
October 23 to November 21	Pluto
November 22 to December 21	Jupiter
December 22 to 31	Saturn

1901

IF YOU WERE BORN ON . . .	YOUR RULING PLANET IS . . .
January 1 to 19	Saturn
January 20 to February 18	Uranus
February 19 to March 20	Neptune
March 21 to April 19	Mars
April 20 to May 20	Venus
May 21 to June 21	Mercury
June 22 to July 22	Moon
July 23 to August 22	Sun
August 23 to September 22	Mercury
September 23 to October 23	Venus
October 24 to November 21	Pluto
November 22 to December 21	Jupiter
December 22 to 31	Saturn

1902

IF YOU WERE BORN ON . . .	YOUR RULING PLANET IS . . .
January 1 to 19	Saturn
January 20 to February 18	Uranus
February 19 to March 20	Neptune
March 21 to April 20	Mars
April 21 to May 21	Venus
May 22 to June 21	Mercury
June 22 to July 22	Moon
July 23 to August 23	Sun
August 24 to September 22	Mercury
September 23 to October 23	Venus
October 24 to November 22	Pluto
November 23 to December 21	Jupiter
December 22 to 31	Saturn

1904

IF YOU WERE BORN ON . . .	YOUR RULING PLANET IS . . .
January 1 to 20	Saturn
January 21 to February 19	Uranus
February 20 to March 20	Neptune
March 21 to April 19	Mars
April 20 to May 20	Venus
May 21 to June 20	Mercury
June 21 to July 22	Moon
July 23 to August 22	Sun
August 23 to September 22	Mercury
September 23 to October 22	Venus
October 23 to November 21	Pluto
November 22 to December 21	Jupiter
December 22 to 31	Saturn

1903

IF YOU WERE BORN ON . . .	YOUR RULING PLANET IS . . .
January 1 to 20	Saturn
January 21 to February 18	Uranus
February 19 to March 20	Neptune
March 21 to April 20	Mars
April 21 to May 21	Venus
May 22 to June 21	Mercury
June 22 to July 23	Moon
July 24 to August 23	Sun
August 24 to September 23	Mercury
September 24 to October 23	Venus
October 24 to November 22	Pluto
November 23 to December 22	Jupiter
December 23 to 31	Saturn

1905

IF YOU WERE BORN ON . . .	YOUR RULING PLANET IS . . .
January 1 to 19	Saturn
January 20 to February 18	Uranus
February 19 to March 20	Neptune
March 21 to April 19	Mars
April 20 to May 20	Venus
May 21 to June 21	Mercury
June 22 to July 22	Moon
July 23 to August 22	Sun
August 23 to September 22	Mercury
September 23 to October 23	Venus
October 24 to November 21	Pluto
November 22 to December 21	Jupiter
December 22 to 31	Saturn

1906

IF YOU WERE BORN ON...	YOUR RULING PLANET IS...
January 1 to 19	Saturn
January 20 to February 18	Uranus
February 19 to March 20	Neptune
March 21 to April 20	Mars
April 21 to May 21	Venus
May 22 to June 21	Mercury
June 22 to July 22	Moon
July 23 to August 23	Sun
August 24 to September 22	Mercury
September 23 to October 23	Venus
October 24 to November 22	Pluto
November 23 to December 21	Jupiter
December 22 to 31	Saturn

1908

IF YOU WERE BORN ON...	YOUR RULING PLANET IS...
January 1 to 20	Saturn
January 21 to February 19	Uranus
February 20 to March 20	Neptune
March 21 to April 19	Mars
April 20 to May 20	Venus
May 21 to June 20	Mercury
June 21 to July 22	Moon
July 23 to August 22	Sun
August 23 to September 22	Mercury
September 23 to October 22	Venus
October 23 to November 21	Pluto
November 22 to December 21	Jupiter
December 22 to 31	Saturn

1907

IF YOU WERE BORN ON...	YOUR RULING PLANET IS...
January 1 to 20	Saturn
January 21 to February 18	Uranus
February 19 to March 20	Neptune
March 21 to April 20	Mars
April 21 to May 21	Venus
May 22 to June 21	Mercury
June 22 to July 23	Moon
July 24 to August 23	Sun
August 24 to September 23	Mercury
September 24 to October 23	Venus
October 24 to November 22	Pluto
November 23 to December 21	Jupiter
December 22 to 31	Saturn

1909

IF YOU WERE BORN ON...	YOUR RULING PLANET IS...
January 1 to 19	Saturn
January 20 to February 18	Uranus
February 19 to March 20	Neptune
March 21 to April 19	Mars
April 20 to May 20	Venus
May 21 to June 21	Mercury
June 22 to July 22	Moon
July 23 to August 22	Sun
August 23 to September 22	Mercury
September 23 to October 23	Venus
October 24 to November 21	Pluto
November 22 to December 21	Jupiter
December 22 to 31	Saturn

1910

IF YOU WERE BORN ON . . .	YOUR RULING PLANET IS . . .
January 1 to 19	Saturn
January 20 to February 18	Uranus
February 19 to March 20	Neptune
March 21 to April 19	Mars
April 20 to May 20	Venus
May 21 to June 21	Mercury
June 22 to July 22	Moon
July 23 to August 23	Sun
August 24 to September 22	Mercury
September 23 to October 23	Venus
October 24 to November 22	Pluto
November 23 to December 21	Jupiter
December 22 to 31	Saturn

1912

IF YOU WERE BORN ON . . .	YOUR RULING PLANET IS . . .
January 1 to 20	Saturn
January 21 to February 18	Uranus
February 19 to March 19	Neptune
March 20 to April 19	Mars
April 20 to May 20	Venus
May 21 to June 20	Mercury
June 21 to July 22	Moon
July 23 to August 22	Sun
August 23 to September 22	Mercury
September 23 to October 22	Venus
October 23 to November 21	Pluto
November 22 to December 21	Jupiter
December 22 to 31	Saturn

1911

IF YOU WERE BORN ON . . .	YOUR RULING PLANET IS . . .
January 1 to 20	Saturn
January 21 to February 18	Uranus
February 19 to March 20	Neptune
March 21 to April 20	Mars
April 21 to May 21	Venus
May 22 to June 21	Mercury
June 22 to July 23	Moon
July 24 to August 23	Sun
August 24 to September 23	Mercury
September 24 to October 23	Venus
October 24 to November 22	Pluto
November 23 to December 21	Jupiter
December 22 to 31	Saturn

1913

IF YOU WERE BORN ON . . .	YOUR RULING PLANET IS . . .
January 1 to 19	Saturn
January 20 to February 18	Uranus
February 19 to March 20	Neptune
March 21 to April 19	Mars
April 20 to May 20	Venus
May 21 to June 21	Mercury
June 22 to July 22	Moon
July 23 to August 22	Sun
August 23 to September 22	Mercury
September 23 to October 23	Venus
October 24 to November 21	Pluto
November 22 to December 21	Jupiter
December 22 to 31	Saturn

1914

IF YOU WERE BORN ON . . .	YOUR RULING PLANET IS . . .
January 1 to 19	Saturn
January 20 to February 18	Uranus
February 19 to March 20	Neptune
March 21 to April 19	Mars
April 20 to May 20	Venus
May 21 to June 21	Mercury
June 22 to July 22	Moon
July 23 to August 23	Sun
August 24 to September 22	Mercury
September 23 to October 23	Venus
October 24 to November 22	Pluto
November 23 to December 21	Jupiter
December 22 to 31	Saturn

1916

IF YOU WERE BORN ON . . .	YOUR RULING PLANET IS . . .
January 1 to 20	Saturn
January 21 to February 18	Uranus
February 19 to March 19	Neptune
March 20 to April 19	Mars
April 20 to May 20	Venus
May 21 to June 20	Mercury
June 21 to July 22	Moon
July 23 to August 22	Sun
August 23 to September 22	Mercury
September 23 to October 22	Venus
October 23 to November 21	Pluto
November 22 to December 21	Jupiter
December 22 to 31	Saturn

1915

IF YOU WERE BORN ON . . .	YOUR RULING PLANET IS . . .
January 1 to 20	Saturn
January 21 to February 18	Uranus
February 19 to March 20	Neptune
March 21 to April 20	Mars
April 21 to May 21	Venus
May 22 to June 21	Mercury
June 22 to July 22	Moon
July 23 to August 23	Sun
August 24 to September 23	Mercury
September 24 to October 23	Venus
October 24 to November 22	Pluto
November 23 to December 21	Jupiter
December 22 to 31	Saturn

1917

IF YOU WERE BORN ON . . .	YOUR RULING PLANET IS . . .
January 1 to 19	Saturn
January 20 to February 18	Uranus
February 19 to March 20	Neptune
March 21 to April 19	Mars
April 20 to May 20	Venus
May 21 to June 21	Mercury
June 22 to July 22	Moon
July 23 to August 22	Sun
August 23 to September 22	Mercury
September 23 to October 22	Venus
October 23 to November 21	Pluto
November 22 to December 21	Jupiter
December 22 to 31	Saturn

1918

IF YOU WERE BORN ON . . .	YOUR RULING PLANET IS . . .
January 1 to 19	Saturn
January 20 to February 18	Uranus
February 19 to March 20	Neptune
March 21 to April 19	Mars
April 20 to May 20	Venus
May 21 to June 21	Mercury
June 22 to July 22	Moon
July 23 to August 22	Sun
August 23 to September 22	Mercury
September 23 to October 23	Venus
October 24 to November 22	Pluto
November 23 to December 21	Jupiter
December 22 to 31	Saturn

1920

IF YOU WERE BORN ON . . .	YOUR RULING PLANET IS . . .
January 1 to 20	Saturn
January 21 to February 18	Uranus
February 19 to March 19	Neptune
March 20 to April 19	Mars
April 20 to May 20	Venus
May 21 to June 20	Mercury
June 21 to July 22	Moon
July 23 to August 22	Sun
August 23 to September 22	Mercury
September 23 to October 22	Venus
October 23 to November 21	Pluto
November 22 to December 21	Jupiter
December 22 to 31	Saturn

1919

IF YOU WERE BORN ON . . .	YOUR RULING PLANET IS . . .
January 1 to 20	Saturn
January 21 to February 18	Uranus
February 19 to March 20	Neptune
March 21 to April 20	Mars
April 21 to May 21	Venus
May 22 to June 21	Mercury
June 22 to July 22	Moon
July 23 to August 23	Sun
August 24 to September 23	Mercury
September 24 to October 23	Venus
October 24 to November 22	Pluto
November 23 to December 21	Jupiter
December 22 to 31	Saturn

1921

IF YOU WERE BORN ON . . .	YOUR RULING PLANET IS . . .
January 1 to 19	Saturn
January 20 to February 18	Uranus
February 19 to March 20	Neptune
March 21 to April 19	Mars
April 20 to May 20	Venus
May 21 to June 20	Mercury
June 21 to July 22	Moon
July 23 to August 22	Sun
August 23 to September 22	Mercury
September 23 to October 22	Venus
October 23 to November 21	Pluto
November 22 to December 21	Jupiter
December 22 to 31	Saturn

1922

IF YOU WERE BORN ON . . .	YOUR RULING PLANET IS . . .
January 1 to 19	Saturn
January 20 to February 18	Uranus
February 19 to March 20	Neptune
March 21 to April 19	Mars
April 20 to May 20	Venus
May 21 to June 21	Mercury
June 22 to July 22	Moon
July 23 to August 22	Sun
August 23 to September 22	Mercury
September 23 to October 23	Venus
October 24 to November 22	Pluto
November 23 to December 21	Jupiter
December 22 to 31	Saturn

1924

IF YOU WERE BORN ON . . .	YOUR RULING PLANET IS . . .
January 1 to 20	Saturn
January 21 to February 18	Uranus
February 19 to March 19	Neptune
March 20 to April 19	Mars
April 20 to May 20	Venus
May 21 to June 20	Mercury
June 21 to July 22	Moon
July 23 to August 22	Sun
August 23 to September 22	Mercury
September 23 to October 22	Venus
October 23 to November 21	Pluto
November 22 to December 21	Jupiter
December 22 to 31	Saturn

1923

IF YOU WERE BORN ON . . .	YOUR RULING PLANET IS . . .
January 1 to 20	Saturn
January 21 to February 18	Uranus
February 19 to March 20	Neptune
March 21 to April 20	Mars
April 21 to May 21	Venus
May 22 to June 21	Mercury
June 22 to July 22	Moon
July 23 to August 23	Sun
August 24 to September 23	Mercury
September 24 to October 23	Venus
October 24 to November 22	Pluto
November 23 to December 21	Jupiter
December 22 to 31	Saturn

1925

IF YOU WERE BORN ON . . .	YOUR RULING PLANET IS . . .
January 1 to 19	Saturn
January 20 to February 18	Uranus
February 19 to March 20	Neptune
March 21 to April 19	Mars
April 20 to May 20	Venus
May 21 to June 20	Mercury
June 21 to July 22	Moon
July 23 to August 22	Sun
August 23 to September 22	Mercury
September 23 to October 22	Venus
October 23 to November 21	Pluto
November 22 to December 21	Jupiter
December 22 to 31	Saturn

1926

IF YOU WERE BORN ON . . .	YOUR RULING PLANET IS . . .
January 1 to 19	Saturn
January 20 to February 18	Uranus
February 19 to March 20	Neptune
March 21 to April 19	Mars
April 20 to May 20	Venus
May 21 to June 21	Mercury
June 22 to July 22	Moon
July 23 to August 22	Sun
August 23 to September 22	Mercury
September 23 to October 23	Venus
October 24 to November 22	Pluto
November 23 to December 21	Jupiter
December 22 to 31	Saturn

1928

IF YOU WERE BORN ON . . .	YOUR RULING PLANET IS . . .
January 1 to 20	Saturn
January 21 to February 18	Uranus
February 19 to March 19	Neptune
March 20 to April 19	Mars
April 20 to May 20	Venus
May 21 to June 20	Mercury
June 21 to July 22	Moon
July 23 to August 22	Sun
August 23 to September 22	Mercury
September 23 to October 22	Venus
October 23 to November 21	Pluto
November 22 to December 21	Jupiter
December 22 to 31	Saturn

1927

IF YOU WERE BORN ON . . .	YOUR RULING PLANET IS . . .
January 1 to 20	Saturn
January 21 to February 18	Uranus
February 19 to March 20	Neptune
March 21 to April 20	Mars
April 21 to May 21	Venus
May 22 to June 21	Mercury
June 22 to July 22	Moon
July 23 to August 23	Sun
August 24 to September 23	Mercury
September 24 to October 23	Venus
October 24 to November 22	Pluto
November 23 to December 21	Jupiter
December 22 to 31	Saturn

1929

IF YOU WERE BORN ON . . .	YOUR RULING PLANET IS . . .
January 1 to 19	Saturn
January 20 to February 18	Uranus
February 19 to March 20	Neptune
March 21 to April 19	Mars
April 20 to May 20	Venus
May 21 to June 20	Mercury
June 21 to July 22	Moon
July 23 to August 22	Sun
August 23 to September 22	Mercury
September 23 to October 22	Venus
October 23 to November 21	Pluto
November 22 to December 21	Jupiter
December 22 to 31	Saturn

1930

IF YOU WERE BORN ON . . .	YOUR RULING PLANET IS . . .
January 1 to 19	Saturn
January 20 to February 18	Uranus
February 19 to March 20	Neptune
March 21 to April 19	Mars
April 20 to May 20	Venus
May 21 to June 21	Mercury
June 22 to July 22	Moon
July 23 to August 22	Sun
August 23 to September 22	Mercury
September 23 to October 23	Venus
October 24 to November 22	Pluto
November 23 to December 21	Jupiter
December 22 to 31	Saturn

1932

IF YOU WERE BORN ON . . .	YOUR RULING PLANET IS . . .
January 1 to 20	Saturn
January 21 to February 18	Uranus
February 19 to March 19	Neptune
March 20 to April 19	Mars
April 20 to May 20	Venus
May 21 to June 20	Mercury
June 21 to July 22	Moon
July 23 to August 22	Sun
August 23 to September 22	Mercury
September 23 to October 22	Venus
October 23 to November 21	Pluto
November 22 to December 21	Jupiter
December 22 to 31	Saturn

1931

IF YOU WERE BORN ON . . .	YOUR RULING PLANET IS . . .
January 1 to 20	Saturn
January 21 to February 18	Uranus
February 19 to March 20	Neptune
March 21 to April 20	Mars
April 21 to May 21	Venus
May 22 to June 21	Mercury
June 22 to July 22	Moon
July 23 to August 23	Sun
August 24 to September 23	Mercury
September 24 to October 23	Venus
October 24 to November 22	Pluto
November 23 to December 21	Jupiter
December 22 to 31	Saturn

1933

IF YOU WERE BORN ON . . .	YOUR RULING PLANET IS . . .
January 1 to 19	Saturn
January 20 to February 18	Uranus
February 19 to March 20	Neptune
March 21 to April 19	Mars
April 20 to May 20	Venus
May 21 to June 20	Mercury
June 21 to July 22	Moon
July 23 to August 22	Sun
August 23 to September 22	Mercury
September 23 to October 22	Venus
October 23 to November 21	Pluto
November 22 to December 21	Jupiter
December 22 to 31	Saturn

1934

IF YOU WERE BORN ON . . .	YOUR RULING PLANET IS . . .
January 1 to 19	Saturn
January 20 to February 18	Uranus
February 19 to March 20	Neptune
March 21 to April 19	Mars
April 20 to May 20	Venus
May 21 to June 21	Mercury
June 22 to July 22	Moon
July 23 to August 22	Sun
August 23 to September 22	Mercury
September 23 to October 23	Venus
October 24 to November 21	Pluto
November 22 to December 21	Jupiter
December 22 to 31	Saturn

1936

IF YOU WERE BORN ON . . .	YOUR RULING PLANET IS . . .
January 1 to 20	Saturn
January 21 to February 18	Uranus
February 19 to March 19	Neptune
March 20 to April 19	Mars
April 20 to May 20	Venus
May 21 to June 20	Mercury
June 21 to July 22	Moon
July 23 to August 22	Sun
August 23 to September 22	Mercury
September 23 to October 22	Venus
October 23 to November 21	Pluto
November 22 to December 21	Jupiter
December 22 to 31	Saturn

1935

IF YOU WERE BORN ON . . .	YOUR RULING PLANET IS . . .
January 1 to 19	Saturn
January 20 to February 18	Uranus
February 19 to March 20	Neptune
March 21 to April 20	Mars
April 21 to May 21	Venus
May 22 to June 21	Mercury
June 22 to July 22	Moon
July 23 to August 23	Sun
August 24 to September 22	Mercury
September 23 to October 23	Venus
October 24 to November 22	Pluto
November 23 to December 21	Jupiter
December 22 to 31	Saturn

1937

IF YOU WERE BORN ON . . .	YOUR RULING PLANET IS . . .
January 1 to 19	Saturn
January 20 to February 18	Uranus
February 19 to March 20	Neptune
March 21 to April 19	Mars
April 20 to May 20	Venus
May 21 to June 20	Mercury
June 21 to July 22	Moon
July 23 to August 22	Sun
August 23 to September 22	Mercury
September 23 to October 22	Venus
October 23 to November 21	Pluto
November 22 to December 21	Jupiter
December 22 to 31	Saturn

1938

IF YOU WERE BORN ON . . .	YOUR RULING PLANET IS . . .
January 1 to 19	Saturn
January 20 to February 18	Uranus
February 19 to March 20	Neptune
March 21 to April 19	Mars
April 20 to May 20	Venus
May 21 to June 21	Mercury
June 22 to July 22	Moon
July 23 to August 22	Sun
August 23 to September 22	Mercury
September 23 to October 23	Venus
October 24 to November 21	Pluto
November 22 to December 21	Jupiter
December 22 to 31	Saturn

1940

IF YOU WERE BORN ON . . .	YOUR RULING PLANET IS . . .
January 1 to 20	Saturn
January 21 to February 18	Uranus
February 19 to March 19	Neptune
March 20 to April 19	Mars
April 20 to May 20	Venus
May 21 to June 20	Mercury
June 21 to July 22	Moon
July 23 to August 22	Sun
August 23 to September 22	Mercury
September 23 to October 22	Venus
October 23 to November 21	Pluto
November 22 to December 20	Jupiter
December 21 to 31	Saturn

1939

IF YOU WERE BORN ON . . .	YOUR RULING PLANET IS . . .
January 1 to 19	Saturn
January 20 to February 18	Uranus
February 19 to March 20	Neptune
March 21 to April 19	Mars
April 20 to May 20	Venus
May 21 to June 21	Mercury
June 22 to July 22	Moon
July 23 to August 23	Sun
August 24 to September 22	Mercury
September 23 to October 23	Venus
October 24 to November 22	Pluto
November 23 to December 21	Jupiter
December 22 to 31	Saturn

1941

IF YOU WERE BORN ON . . .	YOUR RULING PLANET IS . . .
January 1 to 19	Saturn
January 20 to February 18	Uranus
February 19 to March 20	Neptune
March 21 to April 19	Mars
April 20 to May 20	Venus
May 21 to June 20	Mercury
June 21 to July 22	Moon
July 23 to August 22	Sun
August 23 to September 22	Mercury
September 23 to October 22	Venus
October 23 to November 21	Pluto
November 22 to December 21	Jupiter
December 22 to 31	Saturn

1942

IF YOU WERE BORN ON . . .	YOUR RULING PLANET IS . . .
January 1 to 19	Saturn
January 20 to February 18	Uranus
February 19 to March 20	Neptune
March 21 to April 19	Mars
April 20 to May 20	Venus
May 21 to June 21	Mercury
June 22 to July 22	Moon
July 23 to August 22	Sun
August 23 to September 22	Mercury
September 23 to October 23	Venus
October 24 to November 21	Pluto
November 22 to December 21	Jupiter
December 22 to 31	Saturn

1944

IF YOU WERE BORN ON . . .	YOUR RULING PLANET IS . . .
January 1 to 20	Saturn
January 21 to February 18	Uranus
February 19 to March 19	Neptune
March 20 to April 19	Mars
April 20 to May 20	Venus
May 21 to June 20	Mercury
June 21 to July 21	Moon
July 22 to August 22	Sun
August 23 to September 22	Mercury
September 23 to October 22	Venus
October 23 to November 21	Pluto
November 22 to December 20	Jupiter
December 21 to 31	Saturn

1943

IF YOU WERE BORN ON . . .	YOUR RULING PLANET IS . . .
January 1 to 19	Saturn
January 20 to February 18	Uranus
February 19 to March 20	Neptune
March 21 to April 19	Mars
April 20 to May 20	Venus
May 21 to June 21	Mercury
June 22 to July 22	Moon
July 23 to August 23	Sun
August 24 to September 22	Mercury
September 23 to October 23	Venus
October 24 to November 22	Pluto
November 23 to December 21	Jupiter
December 22 to 31	Saturn

1945

IF YOU WERE BORN ON . . .	YOUR RULING PLANET IS . . .
January 1 to 19	Saturn
January 20 to February 18	Uranus
February 19 to March 19	Neptune
March 20 to April 19	Mars
April 20 to May 20	Venus
May 21 to June 20	Mercury
June 21 to July 22	Moon
July 23 to August 22	Sun
August 23 to September 22	Mercury
September 23 to October 22	Venus
October 23 to November 21	Pluto
November 22 to December 21	Jupiter
December 22 to 31	Saturn

1946

IF YOU WERE BORN ON . . .	YOUR RULING PLANET IS . . .
January 1 to 19	Saturn
January 20 to February 18	Uranus
February 19 to March 20	Neptune
March 21 to April 19	Mars
April 20 to May 20	Venus
May 21 to June 21	Mercury
June 22 to July 22	Moon
July 23 to August 22	Sun
August 23 to September 22	Mercury
September 23 to October 23	Venus
October 24 to November 21	Pluto
November 22 to December 21	Jupiter
December 22 to 31	Saturn

1948

IF YOU WERE BORN ON . . .	YOUR RULING PLANET IS . . .
January 1 to 20	Saturn
January 21 to February 18	Uranus
February 19 to March 19	Neptune
March 20 to April 19	Mars
April 20 to May 20	Venus
May 21 to June 20	Mercury
June 21 to July 21	Moon
July 22 to August 22	Sun
August 23 to September 22	Mercury
September 23 to October 22	Venus
October 23 to November 21	Pluto
November 22 to December 20	Jupiter
December 21 to 31	Saturn

1947

IF YOU WERE BORN ON . . .	YOUR RULING PLANET IS . . .
January 1 to 19	Saturn
January 20 to February 18	Uranus
February 19 to March 20	Neptune
March 21 to April 19	Mars
April 20 to May 20	Venus
May 21 to June 21	Mercury
June 22 to July 22	Moon
July 23 to August 23	Sun
August 24 to September 22	Mercury
September 23 to October 23	Venus
October 24 to November 22	Pluto
November 23 to December 21	Jupiter
December 22 to 31	Saturn

1949

IF YOU WERE BORN ON . . .	YOUR RULING PLANET IS . . .
January 1 to 19	Saturn
January 20 to February 17	Uranus
February 18 to March 19	Neptune
March 20 to April 19	Mars
April 20 to May 20	Venus
May 21 to June 20	Mercury
June 21 to July 22	Moon
July 23 to August 22	Sun
August 23 to September 22	Mercury
September 23 to October 22	Venus
October 23 to November 21	Pluto
November 22 to December 21	Jupiter
December 22 to 31	Saturn

1950

IF YOU WERE BORN ON . . .	YOUR RULING PLANET IS . . .
January 1 to 19	Saturn
January 20 to February 18	Uranus
February 19 to March 20	Neptune
March 21 to April 19	Mars
April 20 to May 20	Venus
May 21 to June 20	Mercury
June 21 to July 22	Moon
July 23 to August 22	Sun
August 23 to September 22	Mercury
September 23 to October 22	Venus
October 23 to November 21	Pluto
November 22 to December 21	Jupiter
December 22 to 31	Saturn

1952

IF YOU WERE BORN ON . . .	YOUR RULING PLANET IS . . .
January 1 to 20	Saturn
January 21 to February 18	Uranus
February 19 to March 19	Neptune
March 20 to April 19	Mars
April 20 to May 20	Venus
May 21 to June 20	Mercury
June 21 to July 21	Moon
July 22 to August 22	Sun
August 23 to September 22	Mercury
September 23 to October 22	Venus
October 23 to November 21	Pluto
November 22 to December 20	Jupiter
December 21 to 31	Saturn

1951

IF YOU WERE BORN ON . . .	YOUR RULING PLANET IS . . .
January 1 to 19	Saturn
January 20 to February 18	Uranus
February 19 to March 20	Neptune
March 21 to April 19	Mars
April 20 to May 20	Venus
May 21 to June 21	Mercury
June 22 to July 22	Moon
July 23 to August 22	Sun
August 23 to September 22	Mercury
September 23 to October 23	Venus
October 24 to November 22	Pluto
November 23 to December 21	Jupiter
December 22 to 31	Saturn

1953

IF YOU WERE BORN ON . . .	YOUR RULING PLANET IS . . .
January 1 to 19	Saturn
January 20 to February 17	Uranus
February 18 to March 19	Neptune
March 20 to April 19	Mars
April 20 to May 20	Venus
May 21 to June 20	Mercury
June 21 to July 22	Moon
July 23 to August 22	Sun
August 23 to September 22	Mercury
September 23 to October 22	Venus
October 23 to November 21	Pluto
November 22 to December 21	Jupiter
December 22 to 31	Saturn

1954

IF YOU WERE BORN ON . . .	YOUR RULING PLANET IS . . .
January 1 to 19	Saturn
January 20 to February 18	Uranus
February 19 to March 20	Neptune
March 21 to April 19	Mars
April 20 to May 20	Venus
May 21 to June 20	Mercury
June 21 to July 22	Moon
July 23 to August 22	Sun
August 23 to September 22	Mercury
September 23 to October 22	Venus
October 23 to November 21	Pluto
November 22 to December 21	Jupiter
December 22 to 31	Saturn

1956

IF YOU WERE BORN ON . . .	YOUR RULING PLANET IS . . .
January 1 to 20	Saturn
January 21 to February 18	Uranus
February 19 to March 19	Neptune
March 20 to April 19	Mars
April 20 to May 20	Venus
May 21 to June 20	Mercury
June 21 to July 21	Moon
July 22 to August 22	Sun
August 23 to September 22	Mercury
September 23 to October 22	Venus
October 23 to November 21	Pluto
November 22 to December 20	Jupiter
December 21 to 31	Saturn

1955

IF YOU WERE BORN ON . . .	YOUR RULING PLANET IS . . .
January 1 to 19	Saturn
January 20 to February 18	Uranus
February 19 to March 20	Neptune
March 21 to April 19	Mars
April 20 to May 20	Venus
May 21 to June 21	Mercury
June 22 to July 22	Moon
July 23 to August 22	Sun
August 23 to September 22	Mercury
September 23 to October 23	Venus
October 24 to November 22	Pluto
November 23 to December 21	Jupiter
December 22 to 31	Saturn

1957

IF YOU WERE BORN ON . . .	YOUR RULING PLANET IS . . .
January 1 to 19	Saturn
January 20 to February 17	Uranus
February 18 to March 19	Neptune
March 20 to April 19	Mars
April 20 to May 20	Venus
May 21 to June 20	Mercury
June 21 to July 22	Moon
July 23 to August 22	Sun
August 23 to September 22	Mercury
September 23 to October 22	Venus
October 23 to November 21	Pluto
November 22 to December 21	Jupiter
December 22 to 31	Saturn

1958

IF YOU WERE BORN ON...	YOUR RULING PLANET IS...
January 1 to 19	Saturn
January 20 to February 18	Uranus
February 19 to March 20	Neptune
March 21 to April 19	Mars
April 20 to May 20	Venus
May 21 to June 20	Mercury
June 21 to July 22	Moon
July 23 to August 22	Sun
August 23 to September 22	Mercury
September 23 to October 22	Venus
October 23 to November 21	Pluto
November 22 to December 21	Jupiter
December 22 to 31	Saturn

1960

IF YOU WERE BORN ON...	YOUR RULING PLANET IS...
January 1 to 20	Saturn
January 21 to February 18	Uranus
February 19 to March 19	Neptune
March 20 to April 19	Mars
April 20 to May 20	Venus
May 21 to June 20	Mercury
June 21 to July 21	Moon
July 22 to August 22	Sun
August 23 to September 22	Mercury
September 23 to October 22	Venus
October 23 to November 21	Pluto
November 22 to December 20	Jupiter
December 21 to 31	Saturn

1959

IF YOU WERE BORN ON...	YOUR RULING PLANET IS...
January 1 to 19	Saturn
January 20 to February 18	Uranus
February 19 to March 20	Neptune
March 21 to April 19	Mars
April 20 to May 20	Venus
May 21 to June 21	Mercury
June 22 to July 22	Moon
July 23 to August 22	Sun
August 23 to September 22	Mercury
September 23 to October 23	Venus
October 24 to November 22	Pluto
November 23 to December 21	Jupiter
December 22 to 31	Saturn

1961

IF YOU WERE BORN ON...	YOUR RULING PLANET IS...
January 1 to 19	Saturn
January 20 to February 17	Uranus
February 18 to March 19	Neptune
March 20 to April 19	Mars
April 20 to May 20	Venus
May 21 to June 20	Mercury
June 21 to July 22	Moon
July 23 to August 22	Sun
August 23 to September 22	Mercury
September 23 to October 22	Venus
October 23 to November 21	Pluto
November 22 to December 21	Jupiter
December 22 to 31	Saturn

1962

IF YOU WERE BORN ON . . .	YOUR RULING PLANET IS . . .
January 1 to 19	Saturn
January 20 to February 18	Uranus
February 19 to March 20	Neptune
March 21 to April 19	Mars
April 20 to May 20	Venus
May 21 to June 20	Mercury
June 21 to July 22	Moon
July 23 to August 22	Sun
August 23 to September 22	Mercury
September 23 to October 22	Venus
October 23 to November 21	Pluto
November 22 to December 21	Jupiter
December 22 to 31	Saturn

1964

IF YOU WERE BORN ON . . .	YOUR RULING PLANET IS . . .
January 1 to 20	Saturn
January 21 to February 18	Uranus
February 19 to March 19	Neptune
March 20 to April 19	Mars
April 20 to May 20	Venus
May 21 to June 20	Mercury
June 21 to July 21	Moon
July 22 to August 22	Sun
August 23 to September 22	Mercury
September 23 to October 22	Venus
October 23 to November 21	Pluto
November 22 to December 20	Jupiter
December 21 to 31	Saturn

1963

IF YOU WERE BORN ON . . .	YOUR RULING PLANET IS . . .
January 1 to 19	Saturn
January 20 to February 18	Uranus
February 19 to March 20	Neptune
March 21 to April 19	Mars
April 20 to May 20	Venus
May 21 to June 21	Mercury
June 22 to July 22	Moon
July 23 to August 22	Sun
August 23 to September 22	Mercury
September 23 to October 23	Venus
October 24 to November 22	Pluto
November 23 to December 21	Jupiter
December 22 to 31	Saturn

1965

IF YOU WERE BORN ON . . .	YOUR RULING PLANET IS . . .
January 1 to 19	Saturn
January 20 to February 17	Uranus
February 18 to March 19	Neptune
March 20 to April 19	Mars
April 20 to May 20	Venus
May 21 to June 20	Mercury
June 21 to July 22	Moon
July 23 to August 22	Sun
August 23 to September 22	Mercury
September 23 to October 22	Venus
October 23 to November 21	Pluto
November 22 to December 21	Jupiter
December 22 to 31	Saturn

1966

IF YOU WERE BORN ON . . .	YOUR RULING PLANET IS . . .
January 1 to 19	Saturn
January 20 to February 18	Uranus
February 19 to March 20	Neptune
March 21 to April 19	Mars
April 20 to May 20	Venus
May 21 to June 20	Mercury
June 21 to July 22	Moon
July 23 to August 22	Sun
August 23 to September 22	Mercury
September 23 to October 22	Venus
October 23 to November 21	Pluto
November 22 to December 21	Jupiter
December 22 to 31	Saturn

1968

IF YOU WERE BORN ON . . .	YOUR RULING PLANET IS . . .
January 1 to 19	Saturn
January 20 to February 18	Uranus
February 19 to March 19	Neptune
March 20 to April 19	Mars
April 20 to May 20	Venus
May 21 to June 20	Mercury
June 21 to July 21	Moon
July 22 to August 22	Sun
August 23 to September 21	Mercury
September 22 to October 22	Venus
October 23 to November 21	Pluto
November 22 to December 20	Jupiter
December 21 to 31	Saturn

1967

IF YOU WERE BORN ON . . .	YOUR RULING PLANET IS . . .
January 1 to 19	Saturn
January 20 to February 18	Uranus
February 19 to March 20	Neptune
March 21 to April 19	Mars
April 20 to May 20	Venus
May 21 to June 21	Mercury
June 22 to July 22	Moon
July 23 to August 22	Sun
August 23 to September 22	Mercury
September 23 to October 23	Venus
October 24 to November 22	Pluto
November 23 to December 21	Jupiter
December 22 to 31	Saturn

1969

IF YOU WERE BORN ON . . .	YOUR RULING PLANET IS . . .
January 1 to 19	Saturn
January 20 to February 17	Uranus
February 18 to March 19	Neptune
March 20 to April 19	Mars
April 20 to May 20	Venus
May 21 to June 20	Mercury
June 21 to July 22	Moon
July 23 to August 22	Sun
August 23 to September 22	Mercury
September 23 to October 22	Venus
October 23 to November 21	Pluto
November 22 to December 21	Jupiter
December 22 to 31	Saturn

1970

IF YOU WERE BORN ON . . .	YOUR RULING PLANET IS . . .
January 1 to 19	Saturn
January 20 to February 18	Uranus
February 19 to March 20	Neptune
March 21 to April 19	Mars
April 20 to May 20	Venus
May 21 to June 20	Mercury
June 21 to July 22	Moon
July 23 to August 22	Sun
August 23 to September 22	Mercury
September 23 to October 22	Venus
October 23 to November 21	Pluto
November 22 to December 21	Jupiter
December 22 to 31	Saturn

1972

IF YOU WERE BORN ON . . .	YOUR RULING PLANET IS . . .
January 1 to 19	Saturn
January 20 to February 18	Uranus
February 19 to March 19	Neptune
March 20 to April 18	Mars
April 19 to May 19	Venus
May 20 to June 20	Mercury
June 21 to July 21	Moon
July 22 to August 22	Sun
August 23 to September 21	Mercury
September 22 to October 22	Venus
October 23 to November 21	Pluto
November 22 to December 20	Jupiter
December 21 to 31	Saturn

1971

IF YOU WERE BORN ON . . .	YOUR RULING PLANET IS . . .
January 1 to 19	Saturn
January 20 to February 18	Uranus
February 19 to March 20	Neptune
March 21 to April 19	Mars
April 20 to May 20	Venus
May 21 to June 21	Mercury
June 22 to July 22	Moon
July 23 to August 22	Sun
August 23 to September 22	Mercury
September 23 to October 23	Venus
October 24 to November 21	Pluto
November 22 to December 21	Jupiter
December 22 to 31	Saturn

1973

IF YOU WERE BORN ON . . .	YOUR RULING PLANET IS . . .
January 1 to 19	Saturn
January 20 to February 17	Uranus
February 18 to March 19	Neptune
March 20 to April 19	Mars
April 20 to May 20	Venus
May 21 to June 20	Mercury
June 21 to July 21	Moon
July 22 to August 22	Sun
August 23 to September 22	Mercury
September 23 to October 22	Venus
October 23 to November 21	Pluto
November 22 to December 21	Jupiter
December 22 to 31	Saturn

1974

IF YOU WERE BORN ON . . .	YOUR RULING PLANET IS . . .
January 1 to 19	Saturn
January 20 to February 18	Uranus
February 19 to March 20	Neptune
March 21 to April 19	Mars
April 20 to May 20	Venus
May 21 to June 20	Mercury
June 21 to July 22	Moon
July 23 to August 22	Sun
August 23 to September 22	Mercury
September 23 to October 22	Venus
October 23 to November 21	Pluto
November 22 to December 21	Jupiter
December 22 to 31	Saturn

1976

IF YOU WERE BORN ON . . .	YOUR RULING PLANET IS . . .
January 1 to 19	Saturn
January 20 to February 18	Uranus
February 19 to March 19	Neptune
March 20 to April 18	Mars
April 19 to May 19	Venus
May 20 to June 20	Mercury
June 21 to July 21	Moon
July 22 to August 22	Sun
August 23 to September 21	Mercury
September 22 to October 22	Venus
October 23 to November 21	Pluto
November 22 to December 20	Jupiter
December 21 to 31	Saturn

1975

IF YOU WERE BORN ON . . .	YOUR RULING PLANET IS . . .
January 1 to 19	Saturn
January 20 to February 18	Uranus
February 19 to March 20	Neptune
March 21 to April 19	Mars
April 20 to May 20	Venus
May 21 to June 21	Mercury
June 22 to July 22	Moon
July 23 to August 22	Sun
August 23 to September 22	Mercury
September 23 to October 23	Venus
October 24 to November 21	Pluto
November 22 to December 21	Jupiter
December 22 to 31	Saturn

1977

IF YOU WERE BORN ON . . .	YOUR RULING PLANET IS . . .
January 1 to 19	Saturn
January 20 to February 17	Uranus
February 18 to March 19	Neptune
March 20 to April 19	Mars
April 20 to May 20	Venus
May 21 to June 20	Mercury
June 21 to July 21	Moon
July 22 to August 22	Sun
August 23 to September 22	Mercury
September 23 to October 22	Venus
October 23 to November 21	Pluto
November 22 to December 20	Jupiter
December 21 to 31	Saturn

1978

IF YOU WERE BORN ON . . .	YOUR RULING PLANET IS . . .
January 1 to 19	Saturn
January 20 to February 18	Uranus
February 19 to March 19	Neptune
March 20 to April 19	Mars
April 20 to May 20	Venus
May 21 to June 20	Mercury
June 21 to July 22	Moon
July 23 to August 22	Sun
August 23 to September 22	Mercury
September 23 to October 22	Venus
October 23 to November 21	Pluto
November 22 to December 21	Jupiter
December 22 to 31	Saturn

1980

IF YOU WERE BORN ON . . .	YOUR RULING PLANET IS . . .
January 1 to 19	Saturn
January 20 to February 18	Uranus
February 19 to March 19	Neptune
March 20 to April 18	Mars
April 19 to May 19	Venus
May 20 to June 20	Mercury
June 21 to July 21	Moon
July 22 to August 21	Sun
August 22 to September 21	Mercury
September 22 to October 22	Venus
October 23 to November 21	Pluto
November 22 to December 20	Jupiter
December 21 to 31	Saturn

1979

IF YOU WERE BORN ON . . .	YOUR RULING PLANET IS . . .
January 1 to 19	Saturn
January 20 to February 18	Uranus
February 19 to March 20	Neptune
March 21 to April 19	Mars
April 20 to May 20	Venus
May 21 to June 20	Mercury
June 21 to July 22	Moon
July 23 to August 22	Sun
August 23 to September 22	Mercury
September 23 to October 23	Venus
October 24 to November 21	Pluto
November 22 to December 21	Jupiter
December 22 to 31	Saturn

1981

IF YOU WERE BORN ON . . .	YOUR RULING PLANET IS . . .
January 1 to 19	Saturn
January 20 to February 17	Uranus
February 18 to March 19	Neptune
March 20 to April 19	Mars
April 20 to May 20	Venus
May 21 to June 20	Mercury
June 21 to July 21	Moon
July 22 to August 22	Sun
August 23 to September 22	Mercury
September 23 to October 22	Venus
October 23 to November 21	Pluto
November 22 to December 20	Jupiter
December 21 to 31	Saturn

1982

IF YOU WERE BORN ON . . .	YOUR RULING PLANET IS . . .
January 1 to 19	Saturn
January 20 to February 17	Uranus
February 18 to March 19	Neptune
March 20 to April 19	Mars
April 20 to May 20	Venus
May 21 to June 20	Mercury
June 21 to July 22	Moon
July 23 to August 22	Sun
August 23 to September 22	Mercury
September 23 to October 22	Venus
October 23 to November 21	Pluto
November 22 to December 21	Jupiter
December 22 to 31	Saturn

1984

IF YOU WERE BORN ON . . .	YOUR RULING PLANET IS . . .
January 1 to 19	Saturn
January 20 to February 18	Uranus
February 19 to March 19	Neptune
March 20 to April 18	Mars
April 19 to May 19	Venus
May 20 to June 20	Mercury
June 21 to July 21	Moon
July 22 to August 21	Sun
August 22 to September 21	Mercury
September 22 to October 22	Venus
October 23 to November 21	Pluto
November 22 to December 20	Jupiter
December 21 to 31	Saturn

1983

IF YOU WERE BORN ON . . .	YOUR RULING PLANET IS . . .
January 1 to 19	Saturn
January 20 to February 18	Uranus
February 19 to March 20	Neptune
March 21 to April 19	Mars
April 20 to May 20	Venus
May 21 to June 20	Mercury
June 21 to July 22	Moon
July 23 to August 22	Sun
August 23 to September 22	Mercury
September 23 to October 22	Venus
October 23 to November 21	Pluto
November 22 to December 21	Jupiter
December 22 to 31	Saturn

1985

IF YOU WERE BORN ON . . .	YOUR RULING PLANET IS . . .
January 1 to 19	Saturn
January 20 to February 17	Uranus
February 18 to March 19	Neptune
March 20 to April 19	Mars
April 20 to May 20	Venus
May 21 to June 20	Mercury
June 21 to July 21	Moon
July 22 to August 22	Sun
August 23 to September 22	Mercury
September 23 to October 22	Venus
October 23 to November 21	Pluto
November 22 to December 20	Jupiter
December 21 to 31	Saturn

1986

IF YOU WERE BORN ON . . .	YOUR RULING PLANET IS . . .
January 1 to 19	Saturn
January 20 to February 17	Uranus
February 18 to March 19	Neptune
March 20 to April 19	Mars
April 20 to May 20	Venus
May 21 to June 20	Mercury
June 21 to July 22	Moon
July 23 to August 22	Sun
August 23 to September 22	Mercury
September 23 to October 22	Venus
October 23 to November 21	Pluto
November 22 to December 21	Jupiter
December 22 to 31	Saturn

1988

IF YOU WERE BORN ON . . .	YOUR RULING PLANET IS . . .
January 1 to 19	Saturn
January 20 to February 18	Uranus
February 19 to March 19	Neptune
March 20 to April 18	Mars
April 19 to May 19	Venus
May 20 to June 20	Mercury
June 21 to July 21	Moon
July 22 to August 21	Sun
August 22 to September 21	Mercury
September 22 to October 22	Venus
October 23 to November 21	Pluto
November 22 to December 20	Jupiter
December 21 to 31	Saturn

1987

IF YOU WERE BORN ON . . .	YOUR RULING PLANET IS . . .
January 1 to 19	Saturn
January 20 to February 18	Uranus
February 19 to March 20	Neptune
March 21 to April 19	Mars
April 20 to May 20	Venus
May 21 to June 20	Mercury
June 21 to July 22	Moon
July 23 to August 22	Sun
August 23 to September 22	Mercury
September 23 to October 22	Venus
October 23 to November 21	Pluto
November 22 to December 21	Jupiter
December 22 to 31	Saturn

1989

IF YOU WERE BORN ON . . .	YOUR RULING PLANET IS . . .
January 1 to 19	Saturn
January 20 to February 17	Uranus
February 18 to March 19	Neptune
March 20 to April 19	Mars
April 20 to May 20	Venus
May 21 to June 20	Mercury
June 21 to July 21	Moon
July 22 to August 22	Sun
August 23 to September 22	Mercury
September 23 to October 22	Venus
October 23 to November 21	Pluto
November 22 to December 20	Jupiter
December 21 to 31	Saturn

1990

IF YOU WERE BORN ON . . .	YOUR RULING PLANET IS . . .
January 1 to 19	Saturn
January 20 to February 17	Uranus
February 18 to March 19	Neptune
March 20 to April 19	Mars
April 20 to May 20	Venus
May 21 to June 20	Mercury
June 21 to July 22	Moon
July 23 to August 22	Sun
August 23 to September 22	Mercury
September 23 to October 22	Venus
October 23 to November 21	Pluto
November 22 to December 21	Jupiter
December 22 to 31	Saturn

1992

IF YOU WERE BORN ON . . .	YOUR RULING PLANET IS . . .
January 1 to 19	Saturn
January 20 to February 18	Uranus
February 19 to March 19	Neptune
March 20 to April 18	Mars
April 19 to May 19	Venus
May 20 to June 20	Mercury
June 21 to July 21	Moon
July 22 to August 21	Sun
August 22 to September 21	Mercury
September 22 to October 22	Venus
October 23 to November 21	Pluto
November 22 to December 20	Jupiter
December 21 to 31	Saturn

1991

IF YOU WERE BORN ON . . .	YOUR RULING PLANET IS . . .
January 1 to 19	Saturn
January 20 to February 18	Uranus
February 19 to March 20	Neptune
March 21 to April 19	Mars
April 20 to May 20	Venus
May 21 to June 20	Mercury
June 21 to July 22	Moon
July 23 to August 22	Sun
August 23 to September 22	Mercury
September 23 to October 22	Venus
October 23 to November 21	Pluto
November 22 to December 21	Jupiter
December 22 to 31	Saturn

1993

IF YOU WERE BORN ON . . .	YOUR RULING PLANET IS . . .
January 1 to 19	Saturn
January 20 to February 17	Uranus
February 18 to March 19	Neptune
March 20 to April 19	Mars
April 20 to May 20	Venus
May 21 to June 20	Mercury
June 21 to July 21	Moon
July 22 to August 22	Sun
August 23 to September 22	Mercury
September 23 to October 22	Venus
October 23 to November 21	Pluto
November 22 to December 20	Jupiter
December 21 to 31	Saturn

1994

IF YOU WERE BORN ON . . .	YOUR RULING PLANET IS . . .
January 1 to 19	Saturn
January 20 to February 17	Uranus
February 18 to March 19	Neptune
March 20 to April 19	Mars
April 20 to May 20	Venus
May 21 to June 20	Mercury
June 21 to July 22	Moon
July 23 to August 22	Sun
August 23 to September 22	Mercury
September 23 to October 22	Venus
October 23 to November 21	Pluto
November 22 to December 21	Jupiter
December 22 to 31	Saturn

1996

IF YOU WERE BORN ON . . .	YOUR RULING PLANET IS . . .
January 1 to 19	Saturn
January 20 to February 18	Uranus
February 19 to March 19	Neptune
March 20 to April 18	Mars
April 19 to May 19	Venus
May 20 to June 20	Mercury
June 21 to July 21	Moon
July 22 to August 21	Sun
August 22 to September 21	Mercury
September 22 to October 22	Venus
October 23 to November 21	Pluto
November 22 to December 20	Jupiter
December 21 to 31	Saturn

1995

IF YOU WERE BORN ON . . .	YOUR RULING PLANET IS . . .
January 1 to 19	Saturn
January 20 to February 18	Uranus
February 19 to March 20	Neptune
March 21 to April 19	Mars
April 20 to May 20	Venus
May 21 to June 20	Mercury
June 21 to July 22	Moon
July 23 to August 22	Sun
August 23 to September 22	Mercury
September 23 to October 22	Venus
October 23 to November 21	Pluto
November 22 to December 21	Jupiter
December 22 to 31	Saturn

1997

IF YOU WERE BORN ON . . .	YOUR RULING PLANET IS . . .
January 1 to 19	Saturn
January 20 to February 17	Uranus
February 18 to March 19	Neptune
March 20 to April 19	Mars
April 20 to May 20	Venus
May 21 to June 20	Mercury
June 21 to July 21	Moon
July 22 to August 22	Sun
August 23 to September 21	Mercury
September 22 to October 22	Venus
October 23 to November 21	Pluto
November 22 to December 20	Jupiter
December 21 to 31	Saturn

1998

IF YOU WERE BORN ON . . .	YOUR RULING PLANET IS . . .
January 1 to 19	Saturn
January 20 to February 17	Uranus
February 18 to March 19	Neptune
March 20 to April 19	Mars
April 20 to May 20	Venus
May 21 to June 20	Mercury
June 21 to July 22	Moon
July 23 to August 22	Sun
August 23 to September 22	Mercury
September 23 to October 22	Venus
October 23 to November 21	Pluto
November 22 to December 21	Jupiter
December 22 to 31	Saturn

2000

IF YOU WERE BORN ON . . .	YOUR RULING PLANET IS . . .
January 1 to 19	Saturn
January 20 to February 18	Uranus
February 19 to March 19	Neptune
March 20 to April 18	Mars
April 19 to May 19	Venus
May 20 to June 20	Mercury
June 21 to July 21	Moon
July 22 to August 21	Sun
August 22 to September 21	Mercury
September 22 to October 22	Venus
October 23 to November 21	Pluto
November 22 to December 20	Jupiter
December 21 to 31	Saturn

1999

IF YOU WERE BORN ON . . .	YOUR RULING PLANET IS . . .
January 1 to 19	Saturn
January 20 to February 18	Uranus
February 19 to March 20	Neptune
March 21 to April 19	Mars
April 20 to May 20	Venus
May 21 to June 20	Mercury
June 21 to July 22	Moon
July 23 to August 22	Sun
August 23 to September 22	Mercury
September 23 to October 22	Venus
October 23 to November 21	Pluto
November 22 to December 21	Jupiter
December 22 to 31	Saturn

2001

IF YOU WERE BORN ON . . .	YOUR RULING PLANET IS . . .
January 1 to 19	Saturn
January 20 to February 17	Uranus
February 18 to March 19	Neptune
March 20 to April 19	Mars
April 20 to May 19	Venus
May 20 to June 20	Mercury
June 21 to July 21	Moon
July 22 to August 22	Sun
August 23 to September 21	Mercury
September 22 to October 22	Venus
October 23 to November 21	Pluto
November 22 to December 20	Jupiter
December 21 to 31	Saturn

2002

IF YOU WERE BORN ON . . .	YOUR RULING PLANET IS . . .
January 1 to 19	Saturn
January 20 to February 17	Uranus
February 18 to March 19	Neptune
March 20 to April 19	Mars
April 20 to May 20	Venus
May 21 to June 20	Mercury
June 21 to July 22	Moon
July 23 to August 22	Sun
August 23 to September 22	Mercury
September 23 to October 22	Venus
October 23 to November 21	Pluto
November 22 to December 21	Jupiter
December 22 to 31	Saturn

2004

IF YOU WERE BORN ON . . .	YOUR RULING PLANET IS . . .
January 1 to 19	Saturn
January 20 to February 18	Uranus
February 19 to March 19	Neptune
March 20 to April 18	Mars
April 19 to May 19	Venus
May 20 to June 20	Mercury
June 21 to July 21	Moon
July 22 to August 21	Sun
August 22 to September 21	Mercury
September 22 to October 22	Venus
October 23 to November 20	Pluto
November 21 to December 20	Jupiter
December 21 to 31	Saturn

2003

IF YOU WERE BORN ON . . .	YOUR RULING PLANET IS . . .
January 1 to 19	Saturn
January 20 to February 18	Uranus
February 19 to March 20	Neptune
March 21 to April 19	Mars
April 20 to May 20	Venus
May 21 to June 20	Mercury
June 21 to July 22	Moon
July 23 to August 22	Sun
August 23 to September 22	Mercury
September 23 to October 22	Venus
October 23 to November 21	Pluto
November 22 to December 21	Jupiter
December 22 to 31	Saturn

2005

IF YOU WERE BORN ON . . .	YOUR RULING PLANET IS . . .
January 1 to 18	Saturn
January 19 to February 17	Uranus
February 18 to March 19	Neptune
March 20 to April 18	Mars
April 19 to May 19	Venus
May 20 to June 20	Mercury
June 21 to July 21	Moon
July 22 to August 22	Sun
August 23 to September 21	Mercury
September 22 to October 22	Venus
October 23 to November 21	Pluto
November 22 to December 20	Jupiter
December 21 to 31	Saturn

2006

IF YOU WERE BORN ON . . .	YOUR RULING PLANET IS . . .
January 1 to 19	Saturn
January 20 to February 17	Uranus
February 18 to March 19	Neptune
March 20 to April 19	Mars
April 20 to May 20	Venus
May 21 to June 20	Mercury
June 21 to July 21	Moon
July 22 to August 22	Sun
August 23 to September 22	Mercury
September 23 to October 22	Venus
October 23 to November 21	Pluto
November 22 to December 21	Jupiter
December 22 to 31	Saturn

2008

IF YOU WERE BORN ON . . .	YOUR RULING PLANET IS . . .
January 1 to 19	Saturn
January 20 to February 18	Uranus
February 19 to March 19	Neptune
March 20 to April 18	Mars
April 19 to May 19	Venus
May 20 to June 20	Mercury
June 21 to July 21	Moon
July 22 to August 21	Sun
August 22 to September 21	Mercury
September 22 to October 22	Venus
October 23 to November 20	Pluto
November 21 to December 20	Jupiter
December 21 to 31	Saturn

2007

IF YOU WERE BORN ON . . .	YOUR RULING PLANET IS . . .
January 1 to 19	Saturn
January 20 to February 18	Uranus
February 19 to March 20	Neptune
March 21 to April 19	Mars
April 20 to May 20	Venus
May 21 to June 20	Mercury
June 21 to July 22	Moon
July 23 to August 22	Sun
August 23 to September 22	Mercury
September 23 to October 22	Venus
October 23 to November 21	Pluto
November 22 to December 21	Jupiter
December 22 to 31	Saturn

2009

IF YOU WERE BORN ON . . .	YOUR RULING PLANET IS . . .
January 1 to 18	Saturn
January 19 to February 17	Uranus
February 18 to March 19	Neptune
March 20 to April 18	Mars
April 19 to May 19	Venus
May 20 to June 20	Mercury
June 21 to July 21	Moon
July 22 to August 21	Sun
August 22 to September 21	Mercury
September 22 to October 22	Venus
October 23 to November 21	Pluto
November 22 to December 20	Jupiter
December 21 to 31	Saturn

2010

IF YOU WERE BORN ON . . .	YOUR RULING PLANET IS . . .
January 1 to 19	Saturn
January 20 to February 17	Uranus
February 18 to March 19	Neptune
March 20 to April 19	Mars
April 20 to May 20	Venus
May 21 to June 20	Mercury
June 21 to July 21	Moon
July 22 to August 22	Sun
August 23 to September 22	Mercury
September 23 to October 22	Venus
October 23 to November 21	Pluto
November 22 to December 20	Jupiter
December 21 to 31	Saturn

2012

IF YOU WERE BORN ON . . .	YOUR RULING PLANET IS . . .
January 1 to 19	Saturn
January 20 to February 18	Uranus
February 19 to March 19	Neptune
March 20 to April 18	Mars
April 19 to May 19	Venus
May 20 to June 19	Mercury
June 20 to July 21	Moon
July 22 to August 21	Sun
August 22 to September 21	Mercury
September 22 to October 22	Venus
October 23 to November 20	Pluto
November 21 to December 20	Jupiter
December 21 to 31	Saturn

2011

IF YOU WERE BORN ON . . .	YOUR RULING PLANET IS . . .
January 1 to 19	Saturn
January 20 to February 18	Uranus
February 19 to March 19	Neptune
March 20 to April 19	Mars
April 20 to May 20	Venus
May 21 to June 20	Mercury
June 21 to July 22	Moon
July 23 to August 22	Sun
August 23 to September 22	Mercury
September 23 to October 22	Venus
October 23 to November 21	Pluto
November 22 to December 21	Jupiter
December 22 to 31	Saturn

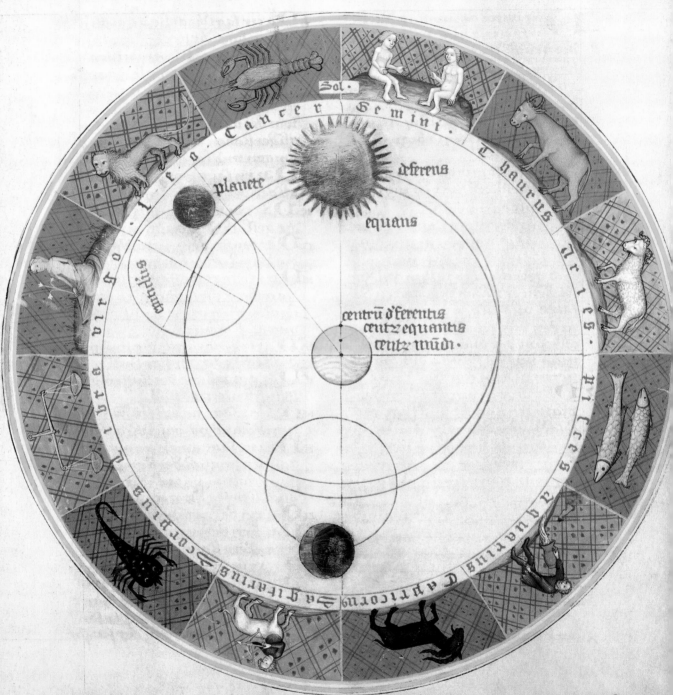

PART II

. . . .

CHILD
OF. ❋ ❋ ❋

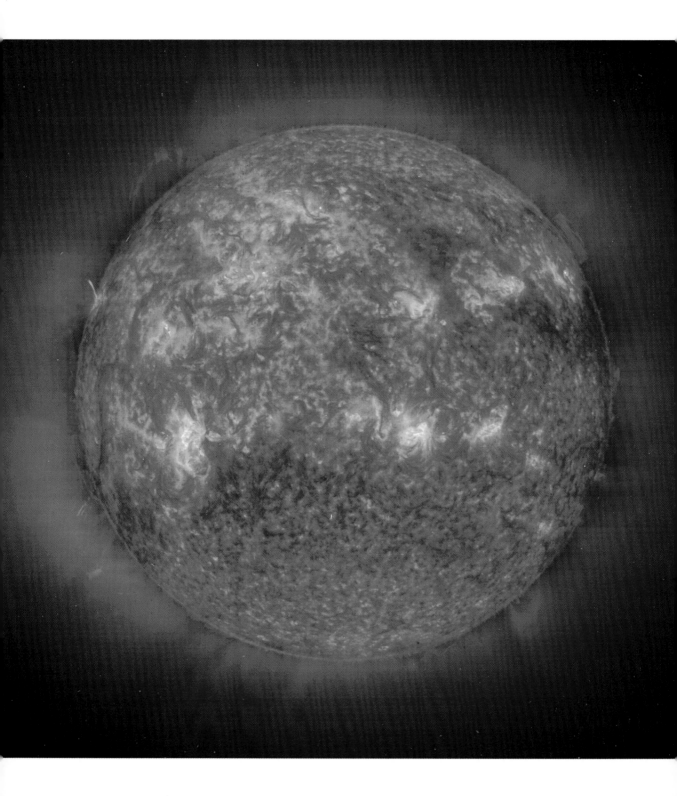

The sunburst pose from Balanchine's ballet Apollo.

CHILD OF THE SUN

Charismatic and inviting, you give off so much energy that people gravitate toward you. They sense the fire burning inside you and want to be near it. As a Child of the Sun, the source of heat and light, you have a natural ability to enliven and excite and to draw people out of themselves. You breathe life into just about everything you do. You are as sincere as the day is long, and you like having a positive effect on people's lives.

The lion, king of the beasts, is one of the animals ruled by your Birth-

KEY WORDS

Heart, light, sight, Dad, healing, the liberal arts, poetry, dance, music, palaces, gold, museums, flight, royalty, fame, youth, public places

NAPOLEON BONAPARTE
August 15, 1769

FIDEL CASTRO
August 13, 1926

MADONNA
August 16, 1958

day Planet, the Sun, as are the crocodile and the falcon. These animals stand at the top of the food chain, just as the Sun stands at the top of the Planetary chain. As a Child of the Sun, you were born with a supreme self-confidence. Naturally you assume that whatever you do is in your (and everyone else's) best interests. For this reason, you are often accused of being self-absorbed and egocentric. But you're not being you just for your benefit. You're being you for the benefit of everyone around you. Your personality is your greatest masterpiece. Think of Jacqueline Kennedy Onassis, Martha Stewart, Lucille Ball, and Julia Child—all Children of the Sun. No one would dispute their talents and abilities, yet it's their personalities that leave the lasting impression.

Audacity is a good word for you. Most people think *audacity* means arrogance—when one is conceited or feels somehow above the rest. Audacity has to do with feeling entitled. Without that basic feeling of privilege, there would be no colorful personalities, noble characters, or outstanding individuals. Everyone's identity would be cookie-cutter cutout. Most people feel they could be something if given half a chance, but often talk themselves out of it by saying, "I'm not that smart" or "He's more talented than I am" or "I'll never be as pretty as she." Even someone who's gifted is in danger of being overlooked unless he or she possesses a certain chutzpah. That would never happen to you. As a Child of the Sun, you were born with a healthy dose of audacity. *Carpe diem* is your motto. You were born to seize the day. And you will—every single one.

You want to become what you were always meant to be. You're not too interested in abstractions like the meaning of life. As long as you're up and running, you're satisfied with how life works. To you, every day contains a high point. You don't know what that high point is or even when it's

going to happen (which is all part of the fun), but you know you'll experience it sometime over the next twenty-four hours. Maybe today's the day you score that big client, lock eyes again with that person who makes your heart flutter, roll around on the floor laughing with your kid, or get out of work early so you can swing by the driving range on the way home or browse through a favorite store.

HIGH FLIERS

ORVILLE WRIGHT
August 19, 1871

AMELIA EARHART
July 24, 1897

NEIL ARMSTRONG
August 5, 1930

**PLAYING FOR
LAUGHS**

MAE WEST
August 17, 1892

BERT LAHR
August 13, 1895

LUCILLE BALL
August 6, 1911

You really do take each day as it comes. If you had a really crummy day at work, you don't sweat it. You go home, see your honey, and get a good night's sleep because you know that things will look brighter in the morning. After all—doesn't the Sun always rise on a new day?

You believe the future will be a brighter place than the past. It comes from that innate sense that you're always moving toward your high point—your noontime zenith. Look at Louis Armstrong and Madonna—two Children of the Sun. There was nothing in their backgrounds to suggest that they would become such popular icons in their own lifetimes. Indeed, the odds were against them. Nevertheless their sights remained fixed on the future. Children of the Sun inevitably take one step ahead of the generation that came before. You might be the first person in your family to make a lot of

money or to build a career instead of having to take a job for the paycheck. If you came from a troubled background, it will be very important for you to set up a healthy home. You may devote yourself to creating the kind of life for your child that you never had. Perhaps you come from a long line of very creative people who never got the chance to express their creativity, and so here you are with an opportunity to express yours. You know your destiny rides piggyback on destinies that fell short or were left unfulfilled. That's why it's so important for you to rise above. Like a king, you must be better than most. You hold yourself to a higher standard. Noblesse oblige.

And like a king, you don't take criticism well. You see nothing "constructive" about someone pointing out your faults. As far as you're concerned, a naysayer just wants to ruin your day. This is when you Children of the Sun can get very imperious. You'll adopt a "take it or leave it" attitude about your performance on the job or at home. You aren't ambitious in the ordinary sense of the word. You see ambition as déclassé. Ambitious people are just out for themselves. Needy, grabby, and hopelessly dissatisfied, they're driven by what's lacking in their lives. You don't see yourself as lacking anything. This isn't to say you're perfectly happy. There are plenty of things you'd like to have or hope to achieve one day. But the difference is that you see yourself as constantly moving toward your golden age. If you don't get what you want today, there's always a chance you'll get it tomorrow. Even when skies are cloudy and gray, your Ruling Planet, the Sun, never deviates from its path.

Because you look at everything in life in terms of who you are, you can

JOIE DE VIVRE

JOHN HAY (JOCK)
WHITNEY
*American multimillionaire
and playboy sportsman*
August 17, 1904

LOUIS ARMSTRONG
August 4, 1901

JULIA CHILD
August 15, 1912

unwittingly place limits on others as well as on yourself. If a certain topic bores you, you assume others will be bored by it, too. If you don't see how you could accomplish a task, you doubt anyone else will be successful. If you don't grasp an idea immediately, you'll skip it . . . *and* expect everyone else to follow suit. A closed mind is never good, but for you it can be a disaster. Like the heart, which is also ruled by your Birthday Planet, the passages need to be open in order for blood and oxygen to circulate freely. Heat and light need to flow into you and out of you. If you close off your mind or harden your heart, then you stop being the benevolent monarch who blesses everyone with your presence, and you become a problem that needs to be taken care of immediately.

However it can be lonely at the top. The only thing that keeps you from getting lonely is your knowledge that you play a central role in others' lives. Watch the way flowers crane their stems as they follow the Sun across the sky or sunbathers as they arrange and rearrange themselves so as to soak up the most rays. People are drawn to you in the same way.

What others don't know is that you make it all look easy. The reality is that you're "on" twenty-four hours a day. Like the lion, the falcon, and the crocodile, you are the ruler of all you survey. And the only way you can maintain that supremacy is to dominate the field. This is where people who aren't Children of the Sun misunderstand you. They may resent you making a spectacle of yourself. They don't like it when you hog all the attention or are overly effusive, theatrical, and play to the crowd—something that former President Clinton (a Child of the Sun) was always being accused of doing. Yet you're not trying to be anything other than what you are. And what you are is BIG. Everything about you is on display for others to see. You're expressive and demonstrative. Like the lion, you live out in the open. But there's a more important reason for you being on display. You want to make your presence known, so that when you're frolicking with loved ones or enjoying a lazy afternoon, jealous rivals and nit-picking critics know better than to mess with you. The reason the people in your life feel happy and safe is because of your watchful gaze. They know that if someone tries to make trouble for them, you'll become a fury of teeth and claws.

Yet as a Child of the Sun, you must try to find the middle course. If you're too involved, the force of your personality can be overwhelming. Remember that when the Sun is out, the other planets are no longer visible. Thus when you're the center of focus, there's no such thing as another point of view. That's when what's majestic about you becomes tyrannical. It's your way or no way. Instead of encouraging life and growth, your Solar fire

begins to burn—feelings dry up and loyalties wilt. If you're too hands-off then situations in your life get too unruly and spin out of control. Loved ones complain of being neglected, and no one's around to make the big decisions that only you can make.

Because you live out in the open, it's very hard for you to admit you made a mistake. Everyone makes mistakes. But as a Child of the Sun, you know copping to a mistake is like walking down a dark alley late at night waving your wallet around for all the predators to see. To you, a mistake is a vulnerability. It invites

ANDY WARHOL
August 6, 1928

JACQUELINE KENNEDY
ONASSIS
July 28, 1929

BILL CLINTON
August 19, 1946

attack, which is why you refuse to recognize them. This blind spot can lead to humiliating scenes in public if you don't try to take care of slipups early on. Approaching mistakes in a good-humored way makes you look more human and elicits sympathy and support.

Your Ruling Planet, the Sun, is the king in astrology. You sit up there on the throne with everyone's eyes on you. You have to be strong, but not too strong-willed. Individual, but not a maverick. An authority, but not a bully. Like a king, you know that you're responsible for the people in your life. It's not the love of recognition that drives you or a deep-seated need to stand out that makes you who you are. It's your job to rule them, love them, and protect them. After all—you see your entire existence as being in service to their happiness.

Even though the Sun rules only one month, a day can't begin or end without it. Just as six o'clock in the morning doesn't look or feel the same as six o'clock in the evening, your Birthday Planet's influence changes during the course of a day. There are certain hours when it burns hot and bright and other hours when it burns cool and low.

An astrological day is measured differently from our normal one. Instead of twenty-four hours it is divided up into twelve parts or "Houses." Each House rules over a particular area of life. As a Child of the Sun you were probably born during daylight saving time, so in order to find your House, you'll have to subtract an hour from your birth time. Your Ruling Planet day reads as follows:

IF YOU WERE BORN BETWEEN . . .	YOUR SUN IS IN THE	IF YOU WERE BORN BETWEEN . . .	YOUR SUN IS IN THE
4–6 A.M.	First House	4–6 P.M.	Seventh House
6–8 A.M.	Twelfth House	6–8 P.M.	Sixth House
8–10 A.M.	Eleventh House	8–10 P.M.	Fifth House
10–12 P.M.	Tenth House	10 P.M.–12 A.M.	Fourth House
12–2 P.M.	Ninth House	12–2 A.M.	Third House
2–4 P.M.	Eighth House	2–4 A.M.	Second House

Part III of this book will show how your Ruling Planet varies its expression according to the time you were born. But first turn to the tables on page 46 to see if you were born during an eclipse. If you were born during an eclipse, you'll want to come back and read the following:

ECLIPSES

A solar eclipse is when the Moon passes in front of the Sun and blocks its rays temporarily. Although a *total* eclipse of the Sun is viewed on only rare occasions, solar eclipses actually take place about two to three times a year, as do lunar eclipses. A lunar eclipse is when the Earth stands between the Sun and the Moon and thus casts its shadow on the Moon. If you're a Child of an Eclipse, you can feel as if you've been singled out. Your gains are bigger, your losses are heavier, stakes are higher, and the decisions you face tend to be much more dramatic. However there is a difference between the effects of a solar eclipse and a lunar eclipse.

Keep in mind that every eight years an eclipse recurs at about the same place in the sky or at the point directly opposite it. That makes the ages of eight, sixteen, twenty-four, thirty-two, forty, etc. critical junctures for you.

CHILD OF THE SUN BORN DURING A SOLAR ECLIPSE

Every eight birthdays you'll feel this compulsion to clear away all the deadwood in your life. No ifs, ands, or buts. It's time for a fresh start. Whatever isn't absolutely necessary will be tossed out. This can be anything from a situation that's outlived its purpose to a relationship or endeavor that hasn't been working out to your express satisfaction.

You're more impetuous than the typical Child of the Sun. You're in a hurry to get things up and running, and this overriding urgency propels you through life. You manifest talents earlier than most and have a quick grasp of situations. However you tend to be high-strung and can suffer from high blood pressure. You are the cause of much of the good—as well as the bad—that happens in your life, so you need to cultivate self-awareness. Always remember to look before you leap or you'll wind up in many a briar patch.

Being a Child of a Solar Eclipse, you'll experience sudden rises and

Sixteenth-century astronomers observing a solar eclipse.

dips in energy. When you're up, you're up. And when you're down—it's like you're moving through molasses. It's doubtful that you'll be able to control these extremes, but you can learn to live with them by moderating your pace. Because your Birthday Planet is blocked by the Moon in a solar eclipse, you have an innate fear of being upstaged and will go to great lengths to call attention to yourself. Subsequently you can run afoul of authority figures (particularly men) if you're not careful, so it's important for you to find your place in the pecking order. You may think you're a maverick, but in truth you believe in upholding the chain of command.

Your blind spot is your emotional life. You're conflicted about how much you depend on loved ones and friends. You rely on them for unconditional love and support; yet you also expect them to be your voice of conscience. This is a tall order for anyone—and you don't make it easy by turning on them when you don't like what they're saying. Learning how to play well with others begins in nursery school and will continue throughout your life.

CHILD OF THE SUN BORN DURING A LUNAR ECLIPSE

As a Child of a Lunar Eclipse, you prefer to leave well enough alone. People should be free to do their own thing, and as long as nobody gets hurt, life is fine. You don't like conflict, however that doesn't mean you'll run from a fight. If anyone can lay down the law instantly and unequivocally, it's you. At times you can have a knee-jerk reaction to controversy and can move too quickly to suppress something that should be allowed to run its course. Remember there's nothing wrong with the boat being rocked once in a while.

People respect you because you're fair and will go the extra mile to do the right thing. You're also consistent and bring stability and equilibrium to most every situation. You don't change (unless you absolutely have to!) and can hold on to things long past the time you should let them go. If you were to go to your refrigerator right now, you'd probably find a number of items that have outlived their expiration date.

Every eight birthdays your Ruling Planet forces you to ask if a life situation is still doing it for you or if it's time to move on. As you can imagine, this sort of decision won't be made in haste. Indeed it may never be made. You have a bad habit of mulling over decisions without making them. This is when you can abdicate control until circumstances force you to act. This isn't good, especially considering your reputation for good judgment. Try to understand that there is no danger in making a bad decision. It's in not deciding at all and then forcing yourself (and others) to live with it that is counterproductive. Think of choices as cards in a card game. Play one hand, and whether you win or lose, you'll certainly be dealt another.

ECLIPSE TABLE
FOR CHILD
OF THE SUN

IF YOU WERE BORN ON . . .	YOU'RE A CHILD OF . . .
August 1–15, 1905	A Lunar Eclipse
July 23–August 4, 1906	A Lunar Eclipse
August 5–20, 1906	A Solar Eclipse
July 24–25, 1907	A Lunar Eclipse
August 8–21, 1914	A Solar Eclipse
July 23–26, 1915	A Lunar Eclipse
July 27–August 10, 1915	A Solar Eclipse
July 23–30, 1916	A Solar Eclipse
July 23–31, 1924	A Solar Eclipse
August 1–14, 1924	A Lunar Eclipse
July 23–August 4, 1925	A Lunar Eclipse
July 23–25, 1926	A Lunar Eclipse
July 23–August 5, 1933	A Lunar Eclipse
August 6–21, 1933	A Solar Eclipse
July 23–26, 1934	A Lunar Eclipse
July 27–August 10, 1934	A Solar Eclipse
July 23–30, 1935	A Solar Eclipse
July 30–August 12, 1942	A Solar Eclipse
July 23–August 1, 1943	A Solar Eclipse
August 2–15, 1943	A Lunar Eclipse
July 22–August 4, 1944	A Lunar Eclipse
August 4–17, 1951	A Lunar Eclipse
July 22–August 5, 1952	A Lunar Eclipse
August 7–20, 1952	A Solar Eclipse

IF YOU WERE BORN ON . . .	YOU'RE A CHILD OF . . .
July 23–26, 1953	A Lunar Eclipse
July 27–August 9, 1953	A Solar Eclipse
July 29–August 11, 1961	A Solar Eclipse
July 23–31, 1962	A Solar Eclipse
August 1–15, 1962	A Lunar Eclipse
August 4–17, 1970	A Lunar Eclipse
July 23–August 6, 1971	A Lunar Eclipse
August 7–20, 1971	A Solar Eclipse
July 22–26, 1972	A Lunar Eclipse
August 9–22, 1979	A Solar Eclipse
July 22–27, 1980	A Lunar Eclipse
July 28–August 10, 1980	A Solar Eclipse
July 22–31, 1981	A Solar Eclipse
August 4–17, 1989	A Lunar Eclipse
July 23–August 6, 1990	A Lunar Eclipse
July 23–26, 1991	A Lunar Eclipse
July 23–August 8, 1998	A Lunar Eclipse
August 9–22, 1998	A Solar Eclipse
July 23–28, 1999	A Lunar Eclipse
July 29–August 11, 1999	A Solar Eclipse
July 22–30, 2000	A Solar Eclipse
July 22–August 1, 2008	A Solar Eclipse
August 2–16, 2008	A Lunar Eclipse
July 22–August 6, 2009	A Lunar Eclipse

CHILD OF THE MOON

❉

It's in your nature to nurture. That's because you were born during the height of summer, when days are long, nights are warm, and the earth is bursting with life. To you life is a cornucopia, a horn of plenty. This isn't to say you won't experience your share of rough spells. But as long as your creature comforts are taken care of, then you know things can never be all that bad. As a Child of the Moon you naturally gravitate to the security of hearth and home. If you have a bad day, then the first thing you do when you get home is reach for the comfort food. It

KEY WORDS

Hearth and home, Mom, body, land, small bodies of water (pools, ponds, and lakes), milk products, childbirth, stomach, womb, breasts, inner life, memory, pictures, aspirin, unconscious, roots

FAMILY VALUES?

KING HENRY VIII
June 28, 1491

CAPTAIN KANGAROO
June 27, 1927

RALPH REED JR.
June 24, 1961

might be a bowl of soup, a cup of hot tea, maybe even a pint of ice cream. After you've had a moment to relax, you'll find you're in a good mood again. As far as you're concerned everything looks better on a full stomach.

The Moon is the brightest "planet" in the night sky, so it's only natural that it governs those deeply personal characteristics you keep hidden or only allow to come out in your private life. Children of the Moon are guided by what they *feel* to be true. You place your trust in your emotions, memories, instincts, and dreams. Indeed, you do some of your best thinking while nodding off. When you wake up again, chances are you'll have the answer you were looking for. Your unconscious acts as your silent partner.

You can't turn off your feelings. They're as much a part of you as breathing. Yet if there's anything you hate, it's being called *over*sensitive. But rather than perceiving your sensitivity as a weakness, you should embrace it as a strength because it's this sensitivity that allows you to work in tandem with the ebb and flow of life. It also gives you your expert sense of timing. You're very good at knowing just when to begin a venture and when to end it. As a Child of the Moon, you never just stop cold. What you'll do is leave something alone if nothing's happening and pursue another activity for a while. Your instinct is to move along with the current of events, not against it. You go wherever it might take you. If you don't get something now, then you believe there's always a chance you'll get it later—when the time is right. You believe that there's a time and a place for everything, and that if you're patient, your time will come.

Nothing changes its appearance in the sky as dramatically as the

Moon. And like the Moon, your fortunes may start out full and bright and then begin to diminish. As time goes on (and burdens weigh heavily on you), your fortunes might wane altogether, even disappear completely from view. But then your fortunes gradually reemerge again until they're once again full and bright. All this can happen in the course of a day or over a span of years. As a Child of the Moon, you understand that this is how life works. It has its ups and downs, but you know that life will provide. This is lost on a lot of people who react to life's ups and downs as if they were happening for the first time. While others have no feel for history and no real sense of cycles, you have the unique ability to roll with life's punches and move on. Your Ruling Planet makes you flexible and adaptable, and that means you can survive just about anything.

Because you see everything in cycles, you know that every ending carries the seeds of a fresh start. Just when you finish one activity you're on to something else. For you, life is constantly being renewed. The future flows into the past in one continuous stream, as F. Scott Fitzgerald writes at the end of *The Great Gatsby*: "so we beat on, boats against the current, borne back ceaselessly into the past." As a Child of the Moon, you believe that the only thing that gives you a true sense of yourself is everything that has come before. Your past. Your history. These are the cornerstones you

REFLECTED GLORY

SIR ROBERT DUDLEY,
EARL OF LEICESTER
Consort to Elizabeth I
June 24, 1532

EMPRESS JOSÉPHINE
Consort to Napoleon
June 23, 1763

PRINCESS DIANA
Consort to Prince Charles
July 1, 1961

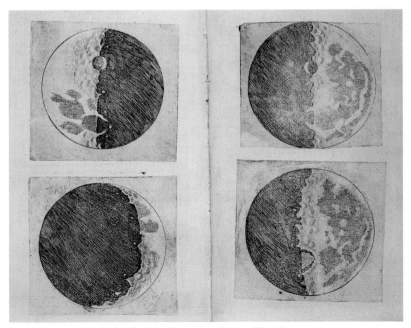

Galileo's studies of the phases of the Moon.

FOUNDING MOTHERS

MARY BAKER EDDY
Founder of Christian Science
July 16, 1821

HARRIET NELSON
Starred in Ozzie and Harriet
July 18, 1909

ROSE FITZGERALD
KENNEDY
Kennedy clan matriarch
July 22, 1890

will build your life's foundation on. But this doesn't make you wistful or nostalgic—although you can get that way on occasion. What it does is make you consistent.

Things don't have to be lost to the past—not when you can recycle. Habits, routines, and traditions are all attempts on the part of your unconscious to recycle what has come before. It's in this way that you, as a Child of the Moon, attempt to navigate and even anticipate the vicissitudes of the future. You side with history over trends.

You were born under the Planet of family values. Whether you agree with that term or not, you probably sympathize with the aim of family values—which is to preserve the hearth and home so that nobody is left out in the cold. You have a strong nesting instinct. Your family is extremely important because it roots you in place. You can travel wherever you like in the world, but you need to know that you have a place to return to. It's interesting to note that the top box office names—Harrison Ford, Tom Cruise, and Tom Hanks—are all Children of the Moon. These are celebrities who are famous for shunning the limelight. As soon as they're done with filming and/or making the publicity rounds, they head straight back to their jealously guarded private lives.

Not all Children of the Moon subscribe to life according to *Leave It to Beaver*. Indeed some of you are just as likely to walk around in combat boots and sport neon green mohawks. After all, your Birthday Planet rules over the things that come out at night. You all have that wild werewolf side, and like the Moon, you'll go through your "phases" when you'll even want

Geodesic dome creator Buckminster Fuller was a Child of the Moon.

to indulge it. Nevertheless your instinct is to provide and protect. Even if your ears are pierced beyond all recognition, you'll still be the one who remembers to run to the store for toilet paper before it runs out or who can't help fretting about the houseplants.

Yet there is a dark side to the Children of the Moon. One of the

PRINCE EDWARD VIII
Duke of Windsor
June 23, 1894

DALAI LAMA XIV
July 6, 1935

NELSON MANDELA
July 18, 1918

things you have to watch out for is that you can be very tribal and will react with great hostility to anyone or anything that you perceive as trespassing on your physical or psychic turf. When you start splitting the world into *us* and *them*, you know you're in trouble. That's when you need to get back in touch with your heart and examine where and when you hardened it.

Another thing that can be difficult for you to handle is your needs. It's ironic that for someone who constantly administers to the needs of others, you regard your own as potential liabilities. It's why you devote so much time to covering them up. The needs that the Moon rules over are primal needs. Childish needs. Your neediest needs. Not socially acceptable needs. When you are in that needy, Lunar mode, then you're not

UNIVERSAL PICTURES
PRESENTS

WOLF MAN

LIZZIE BORDEN
July 19, 1860

JOHN DILLINGER
June 28, 1902

O. J. SIMPSON
July 9, 1947

exactly sensitive to the needs of others. You want whatever it is you want, and you won't be satisfied until you get it. If you've ever seen children begging their mothers for a piece of candy or being carried out of the toy store crying at the top of their lungs—one hand still reaching out for the beloved stuffed animal that's been denied them—then you'll get some idea of how powerful those needs of yours can be. It's not a pretty sight. Yet Lunar needs, like a child's needs, are actually very simple to appease. Give a child some*thing*—anything—and they'll be fine. It's when you deny or repress them that there's hell to pay.

Once you make friends with your needs (which means letting them exist without apology) you'll find that your capacity to love is tremendous. It comes quite naturally and doesn't require any of the Sturm und Drang that others associate with it. You're one of the few people who doesn't really need someone to love you. What you need is someone to love. Your emotional reservoirs are so deep that you have more than enough love to go around. Too much, perhaps. What you want is to belong to someone. It makes you feel secure. It's like the Moon orbiting Earth. That gravitational pull creates a healthy equilibrium. Without it you'd be lost in space.

The world may not always be a summertime paradise, but that won't prevent you from trying to make it one. Much of your life is devoted to the creative act of reshaping your outer circumstances so that they reflect your inner landscape—a place of plenty where no one wants for anything.

The Moon is the fastest-moving "planet." It passes through all twelve zodiac signs in one month. All Children of the Moon are deeply feeling. But since the Moon changes signs practically every two days, the types of feeling and the way that they're dealt with will be different. No other Planet begets such a rich diversity of personalities.

Go ahead and turn to the Moon tables on page 57 to find what sign your Ruling Planet was in on the day you were born. Part III of this book will show how your Ruling Planet varies its expression from sign to sign. If there is a single asterisk (*) next to your birth date, then you were born during a solar eclipse. A double asterisk (**) means you were born during a lunar eclipse. If you were born during an eclipse, you'll want to come back and read the following:

ECLIPSES

A solar eclipse is when the Moon passes in front of the Sun and blocks its rays temporarily. Although a total eclipse of the Sun is viewed on rare occasions, solar eclipses actually take place about two to three times a

REMEMBRANCE OF THINGS PAST

MARCEL PROUST
July 10, 1871

GEORGE EASTMAN
Inventor of Kodak film
July 12, 1854

INGMAR BERGMAN
July 14, 1918

**PHASES OF
THE MOON**

THE SELF-PORTRAITS
OF REMBRANDT
July 15, 1606

year, as do lunar eclipses. A lunar eclipse is when the Earth stands between the Sun and the Moon and thus casts its shadow on the Moon. When you're a Child of an Eclipse, you can feel as if you've been singled out. Your gains are bigger, your losses are heavier, stakes are higher, and the decisions you face tend to be much more dramatic. However there is a difference between the effects of a solar eclipse and a lunar eclipse.

Keep in mind that every eight years an eclipse recurs at about the same place in the sky or at the point directly opposite it. That makes the ages of eight, sixteen, twenty-four, thirty-two, forty, etc., critical junctures for you.

CHILD OF THE MOON BORN DURING A SOLAR ECLIPSE

For you, every eight years something goes kaput. This can be anything from a trusty appliance to a source of revenue. Thankfully this is limited to only one area of your life, so you won't feel like everything's coming apart at the seams. Still, this doesn't mesh well with your need for security and foundation. You don't like surprises. Even though starting again from scratch almost always results in an improvement for you, the wear and tear on your emotional life can be tremendous.

This feeling of being on shaky ground is nothing new. You may have experienced many disruptions when you were younger. Your family may have moved around a lot or experienced boom or bust cycles fairly regularly. Chances are you came from a household where it was laudable to maintain a stiff upper lip while keeping emotions under lock and key. Unfortunately this didn't lessen their potential explosiveness. If anything, life at home may have been analogous to tiptoeing across a psychic minefield.

Unlike other Children of the Moon, you will put off settling down until later in life when you feel more secure about yourself. You have no

interest in reproduc-
ing the sort of tension
you grew up with, and
since most of it was
money based, you'll
want to make sure
finances are in order
before seeking out a
partner or spouse. You
also have little toler-
ance for displays of
temper. If the noise

level in the room gets too loud, you'll remove yourself.

Because it's your Birthday Planet that blocks the Sun's rays in a solar
eclipse, you can't escape this feeling that you're surrounded by possibilities, yet you are unsure that you recognize their true merit. This is why you
always question if you made the most of a given opportunity. Few are as
conscientious about their decision-making as you. Easy access to your
unconscious gives you an almost photographic memory. Preferring to
store information in your head, you may keep sparse files or notes. This
very same meticulousness can lead to overanalyzing, an inability to make
up your mind, and fumbling around with what others regard as perfectly
obvious choices. Relaxation doesn't come easily to you, and you could
suffer from bouts of insomnia. Your conscious mind—even asleep—is
never far from the surface. That's why it's especially important for you to
exercise regularly. Physical exertion is the key to your peace of mind.
Besides, it will keep you in good shape.

CHILD OF THE MOON BORN DURING
A LUNAR ECLIPSE

Every eight years you come to a crossroads in your life where you must
decide either to stick with what you have or cut your losses and move on.
This is a time of intense frustration, and what makes it even more difficult
is that there are no tangible benefits in sight. It really is a choice between
the devil and the deep blue sea. That's why it's important for you to go back
and take a long hard look at the three years leading up to your dilemma. If
things have been on a steady decline, you should fold your cards. How-

ever be on the lookout for an opportunity to finesse that loss into a gain. Remember that it's your Birthday Planet's nature to be cyclical, which means that nothing ever comes to a complete stop. There will always be a way to recoup your losses.

But you need to be absolutely certain that you've given matters enough time. As a Child of a Lunar Eclipse, you can sometimes be in too much of a hurry to draw a line of summation and tally up the figures. Bottom-line thinking is excellent if you're an executive, manager, or supervisor, but it can be counterproductive if you're trying to get something off the ground or want to build on what you already have. It would be analogous to digging up a newly planted seed each day to see if it's sprouted yet. It's best for you to have several irons in the fire at once. Splitting your focus prevents you from getting too fixated and keeps you out of trouble, while it also keeps those creative juices flowing.

WHAT SIGN IS THE MOON IN?

1900

IF YOU WERE BORN ON . . .	YOUR MOON IS IN . . .
June 21	Aries
June 22–23	Taurus
June 24–25	Gemini
June 26–28	Cancer
June 29– 30	Leo
July 1–2	Virgo
July 3–5	Libra
July 6–7	Scorpio
July 8–10	Sagittarius
July 11–12	Capricorn
July 13–14	Aquarius
July 15–16	Pisces
July 17–18	Aries
July 19–20	Taurus
July 21–22	Gemini

1901

IF YOU WERE BORN ON . . .	YOUR MOON IS IN . . .
June 22	Virgo
June 23–25	Libra
June 26–27	Scorpio
June 28–30	Sagittarius
July 1–2	Capricorn
July 3–4	Aquarius
July 5–6	Pisces
July 7–9	Aries
July 10–11	Taurus
July 12–13	Gemini
July 14–15	Cancer
July 16–17	Leo
July 18–20	Virgo
July 21–22	Libra

1902

IF YOU WERE BORN ON . . .	YOUR MOON IS IN . . .
June 22	Capricorn
June 23–25	Aquarius
June 26–27	Pisces
June 28–29	Aries
June 30–July 1	Taurus
July 2–3	Gemini
July 4–5	Cancer
July 6–7	Leo
July 8–10	Virgo
July 11–12	Libra
July 13–14	Scorpio
July 15–17	Sagittarius
July 18–19	Capricorn
July 20–22	Aquarius

* = Solar eclipse   ** = Lunar eclipse

1903

IF YOU WERE BORN ON ...	YOUR MOON IS IN ...
June 22	Taurus
June 23–24	Gemini
June 25–26	Cancer
June 27–28	Leo
June 29– 30	Virgo
July 1–2	Libra
July 3–4	Scorpio
July 5–7	Sagittarius
July 8–9	Capricorn
July 10–12	Aquarius
July 13–14	Pisces
July 15–17	Aries
July 18–19	Taurus
July 20–21	Gemini
July 22–23	Cancer

1905

IF YOU WERE BORN ON ...	YOUR MOON IS IN ...
June 22–23	Pisces
June 24–26	Aries
June 27–28	Taurus
June 29–30	Gemini
July 1–3	Cancer
July 4–5	Leo
July 6–7	Virgo
July 8–9	Libra
July 10–11	Scorpio
July 12–13	Sagittarius
July 14–16	Capricorn
July 17–18	Aquarius
July 19–20	Pisces
July 21–22	Aries

1907

IF YOU WERE BORN ON ...	YOUR MOON IS IN ...
June 22	Scorpio
June 23–24	Sagittarius
June 25–26	Capricorn
June 27–28	Aquarius
June 29–30	Pisces
July 1–3	Aries
July 4–5	Taurus
July 6–8	Gemini
*July 9–10	Cancer
July 11–13	Leo
July 14–15	Virgo
July 16–17	Libra
July 18–20	Scorpio
July 21–22	Sagittarius
July 23	Capricorn

1904

IF YOU WERE BORN ON ...	YOUR MOON IS IN ...
June 21	Libra
June 22–24	Scorpio
June 25–26	Sagittarius
June 27–28	Capricorn
June 29–July 1	Aquarius
July 2–3	Pisces
July 4–6	Aries
July 7–8	Taurus
July 9–10	Gemini
July 11–12	Cancer
July 13–14	Leo
July 15–16	Virgo
July 17–19	Libra
July 20–21	Scorpio
July 22	Sagittarius

1906

IF YOU WERE BORN ON ...	YOUR MOON IS IN ...
June 22–23	Cancer
June 24–25	Leo
June 26–28	Virgo
June 29–30	Libra
July 1–2	Scorpio
July 3–4	Sagittarius
July 5–6	Capricorn
July 7–8	Aquarius
July 9–10	Pisces
July 11–13	Aries
July 14–15	Taurus
July 16–18	Gemini
*July 19–21	Cancer
July 22	Leo

1908

IF YOU WERE BORN ON ...	YOUR MOON IS IN ...
June 21–22	Aries
June 23–24	Taurus
June 25–27	Gemini
*June 28–29	Cancer
June 30–July 2	Leo
July 3–4	Virgo
July 5–7	Libra
July 8–9	Scorpio
July 10–11	Sagittarius
**July 12–13	Capricorn
July 14–15	Aquarius
July 16–17	Pisces
July 18–19	Aries
July 20–21	Taurus
July 22	Gemini

* = Solar eclipse   ** = Lunar eclipse

1909

IF YOU WERE BORN ON . . .	YOUR MOON IS IN . . .
June 22–24	Virgo
June 25–26	Libra
June 27–29	Scorpio
June 30–July 1	Sagittarius
July 2–3	Capricorn
July 4–5	Aquarius
July 6–8	Pisces
July 9–10	Aries
July 11–12	Taurus
July 13–14	Gemini
July 15–16	Cancer
July 17–19	Leo
July 20–21	Virgo
July 22	Libra

1911

IF YOU WERE BORN ON . . .	YOUR MOON IS IN . . .
June 22–23	Taurus
June 24–25	Gemini
June 26–27	Cancer
June 28–29	Leo
June 30–July 1	Virgo
July 2–3	Libra
July 4–6	Scorpio
July 7–9	Sagittarius
July 10–11	Capricorn
July 12–13	Aquarius
July 14–16	Pisces
July 17–18	Aries
July 19–20	Taurus
July 21–22	Gemini
July 23	Cancer

1913

IF YOU WERE BORN ON . . .	YOUR MOON IS IN . . .
June 22	Aquarius
June 23–25	Pisces
June 26–27	Aries
June 28–30	Taurus
July 1–2	Gemini
July 3–4	Cancer
July 5–6	Leo
July 7–8	Virgo
July 9–10	Libra
July 11–12	Scorpio
July 13–15	Sagittarius
July 16–17	Capricorn
July 18–20	Aquarius
July 21–22	Pisces

1910

IF YOU WERE BORN ON . . .	YOUR MOON IS IN . . .
June 22–24	Capricorn
June 25–26	Aquarius
June 27–28	Pisces
June 29–30	Aries
July 1–2	Taurus
July 3–4	Gemini
July 5–7	Cancer
July 8–9	Leo
July 10–11	Virgo
July 12–14	Libra
July 15–16	Scorpio
July 17–19	Sagittarius
July 20–21	Capricorn
July 22	Aquarius

1912

IF YOU WERE BORN ON . . .	YOUR MOON IS IN . . .
June 21–23	Libra
June 24–25	Scorpio
June 26–27	Sagittarius
June 28–30	Capricorn
July 1–2	Aquarius
July 3–5	Pisces
July 6–7	Aries
July 8–10	Taurus
July 11–12	Gemini
July 13–14	Cancer
July 15–16	Leo
July 17–18	Virgo
July 19–20	Libra
July 21–22	Scorpio

1914

IF YOU WERE BORN ON . . .	YOUR MOON IS IN . . .
June 22	Gemini
June 23–24	Cancer
June 25–27	Leo
June 28–29	Virgo
June 30–July 1	Libra
July 2–3	Scorpio
July 4–5	Sagittarius
July 6–7	Capricorn
July 8–10	Aquarius
July 11–12	Pisces
July 13–14	Aries
July 15–17	Taurus
July 18–19	Gemini
July 20–22	Cancer

* = Solar eclipse   ** = Lunar eclipse

1915

IF YOU WERE BORN ON . . .	YOUR MOON IS IN . . .
June 22–23	Scorpio
June 24–25	Sagittarius
June 26–27	Capricorn
June 28–30	Aquarius
July 1–2	Pisces
July 3–4	Aries
July 5–7	Taurus
July 8–9	Gemini
July 10–12	Cancer
July 13–14	Leo
July 15–16	Virgo
July 17–19	Libra
July 20–21	Scorpio
July 22	Sagittarius

1917

IF YOU WERE BORN ON . . .	YOUR MOON IS IN . . .
June 22–23	Leo
June 24–26	Virgo
June 27–28	Libra
June 29–30	Scorpio
July 1–3	Sagittarius
**July 4–5	Capricorn
July 6–7	Aquarius
July 8–9	Pisces
July 10–11	Aries
July 12–13	Taurus
July 14–15	Gemini
*July 16–18	Cancer
July 19–20	Leo
July 21–22	Virgo

1919

IF YOU WERE BORN ON . . .	YOUR MOON IS IN . . .
June 22	Aries
June 23–24	Taurus
June 25–26	Gemini
June 27–28	Cancer
June 29–30	Leo
July 1–3	Virgo
July 4–5	Libra
July 6–8	Scorpio
July 9–10	Sagittarius
July 11–13	Capricorn
July 14–15	Aquarius
July 16–17	Pisces
July 18–19	Aries
July 20–21	Taurus
July 22	Gemini

1916

IF YOU WERE BORN ON . . .	YOUR MOON IS IN . . .
June 21	Pisces
June 22–23	Aries
June 24–26	Taurus
June 27–28	Gemini
June 29–July 1	Cancer
July 2–3	Leo
July 4–6	Virgo
July 7–8	Libra
July 9–10	Scorpio
July 11–12	Sagittarius
**July 13–14	Capricorn
July 15–16	Aquarius
July 17–18	Pisces
July 19–21	Aries
July 22	Taurus

1918

IF YOU WERE BORN ON . . .	YOUR MOON IS IN . . .
June 22–23	Sagittarius
**June 24–25	Capricorn
June 26–27	Aquarius
June 28–29	Pisces
June 30–July 1	Aries
July 2–4	Taurus
July 5–6	Gemini
July 7–8	Cancer
July 9–10	Leo
July 11–13	Virgo
July 14–15	Libra
July 16–18	Scorpio
July 19–20	Sagittarius
July 21–22	Capricorn

1920

IF YOU WERE BORN ON . . .	YOUR MOON IS IN . . .
June 21–22	Virgo
June 23–24	Libra
June 25–27	Scorpio
June 28–29	Sagittarius
June 30–July 2	Capricorn
July 3–4	Aquarius
July 5–6	Pisces
July 7–9	Aries
July 10–11	Taurus
July 12–13	Gemini
July 14–15	Cancer
July 16–17	Leo
July 18–19	Virgo
July 20–21	Libra
July 22	Scorpio

* = Solar eclipse   ** = Lunar eclipse

1921

IF YOU WERE BORN ON . . .	YOUR MOON IS IN . . .
June 21–22	Capricorn
June 23–24	Aquarius
June 25–27	Pisces
June 28–29	Aries
June 30–July 1	Taurus
July 2–3	Gemini
July 4–5	Cancer
July 6–7	Leo
July 8–9	Virgo
July 10–11	Libra
July 12–14	Scorpio
July 15–16	Sagittarius
July 17–19	Capricorn
July 20–21	Aquarius
July 22	Pisces

1923

IF YOU WERE BORN ON . . .	YOUR MOON IS IN . . .
June 22–23	Libra
June 24–25	Scorpio
June 26–27	Sagittarius
June 28–29	Capricorn
June 30–July 1	Aquarius
July 2–3	Pisces
July 4–6	Aries
July 7–9	Taurus
July 10–11	Gemini
July 12–13	Cancer
July 14–15	Leo
July 16–18	Virgo
July 19–20	Libra
July 21–22	Scorpio

1925

IF YOU WERE BORN ON . . .	YOUR MOON IS IN . . .
June 21–22	Cancer
June 23–25	Leo
June 26–27	Virgo
June 28–30	Libra
July 1–2	Scorpio
July 3–4	Sagittarius
July 5–6	Capricorn
July 7–8	Aquarius
July 9–10	Pisces
July 11–12	Aries
July 13–15	Taurus
July 16–17	Gemini
*July 18–20	Cancer
July 21–22	Leo

1922

IF YOU WERE BORN ON . . .	YOUR MOON IS IN . . .
June 22–23	Gemini
June 24–26	Cancer
June 27–28	Leo
June 29–30	Virgo
July 1–2	Libra
July 3–4	Scorpio
July 5–6	Sagittarius
July 7–9	Capricorn
July 10–11	Aquarius
July 12–14	Pisces
July 15–16	Aries
July 17–19	Taurus
July 20–21	Gemini
July 22	Cancer

1924

IF YOU WERE BORN ON . . .	YOUR MOON IS IN . . .
June 21–22	Pisces
June 23–25	Aries
June 26–27	Taurus
June 28–30	Gemini
July 1–2	Cancer
July 3–5	Leo
July 6–7	Virgo
July 8–9	Libra
July 10–11	Scorpio
July 12–13	Sagittarius
July 14–15	Capricorn
July 16–18	Aquarius
July 19–20	Pisces
July 21–22	Aries

1926

IF YOU WERE BORN ON . . .	YOUR MOON IS IN . . .
June 22	Scorpio
June 23–24	Sagittarius
**June 25–26	Capricorn
June 27–28	Aquarius
June 29–30	Pisces
July 1–2	Aries
July 3–5	Taurus
July 6–7	Gemini
*July 8–10	Cancer
July 11–12	Leo
July 13–15	Virgo
July 16–17	Libra
July 18–19	Scorpio
July 20–22	Sagittarius

* = Solar eclipse   ** = Lunar eclipse

1927

IF YOU WERE BORN ON . . .	YOUR MOON IS IN . . .
June 22–23	Aries
June 24–25	Taurus
June 26–27	Gemini
*June 28–30	Cancer
July 1–2	Leo
July 3–4	Virgo
July 5–7	Libra
July 8–9	Scorpio
July 10–12	Sagittarius
July 13–14	Capricorn
July 15–16	Aquarius
July 17–18	Pisces
July 19–20	Aries
July 21–22	Taurus

1929

IF YOU WERE BORN ON . . .	YOUR MOON IS IN . . .
June 21	Sagittarius
June 22–23	Capricorn
June 24–26	Aquarius
June 27–28	Pisces
June 29–30	Aries
July 1–2	Taurus
July 3–4	Gemini
July 5–6	Cancer
July 7–8	Leo
July 9–11	Virgo
July 12–13	Libra
July 14–15	Scorpio
July 16–18	Sagittarius
July 19–20	Capricorn
July 21–22	Aquarius

1931

IF YOU WERE BORN ON . . .	YOUR MOON IS IN . . .
June 22–24	Libra
June 25–26	Scorpio
June 27–28	Sagittarius
June 29–30	Capricorn
July 1–3	Aquarius
July 4–5	Pisces
July 6–8	Aries
July 9–10	Taurus
July 11–12	Gemini
July 13–15	Cancer
July 16–17	Leo
July 18–19	Virgo
July 20–21	Libra
July 22	Scorpio

1928

IF YOU WERE BORN ON . . .	YOUR MOON IS IN . . .
June 21	Leo
June 22–23	Virgo
June 24–26	Libra
June 27–28	Scorpio
June 29–July 1	Sagittarius
July 2–3	Capricorn
July 4–5	Aquarius
July 6–8	Pisces
July 9–10	Aries
July 11–12	Taurus
July 13–14	Gemini
July 15–16	Cancer
July 17–18	Leo
July 19–21	Virgo
July 22	Libra

1930

IF YOU WERE BORN ON . . .	YOUR MOON IS IN . . .
June 22–23	Taurus
June 24–25	Gemini
June 26–27	Cancer
June 28–29	Leo
June 30–July 1	Virgo
July 2–3	Libra
July 4–5	Scorpio
July 6–8	Sagittarius
July 9–10	Capricorn
July 11–13	Aquarius
July 14–15	Pisces
July 16–18	Aries
July 19–20	Taurus
July 21–22	Gemini

1932

IF YOU WERE BORN ON . . .	YOUR MOON IS IN . . .
June 21–22	Aquarius
June 23–24	Pisces
June 25–27	Aries
June 28–29	Taurus
June 30–July 2	Gemini
July 3–4	Cancer
July 5–6	Leo
July 7–8	Virgo
July 9–10	Libra
July 11–13	Scorpio
July 14–15	Sagittarius
July 16–17	Capricorn
July 18–19	Aquarius
July 20–21	Pisces
July 22	Aries

* = Solar eclipse   ** = Lunar eclipse

1933

IF YOU WERE BORN ON . . .	YOUR MOON IS IN . . .
June 21	Gemini
June 22–24	Cancer
June 25–26	Leo
June 27–29	Virgo
June 30–July 1	Libra
July 2–3	Scorpio
July 4–5	Sagittarius
July 6–7	Capricorn
July 8–9	Aquarius
July 10–11	Pisces
July 12–14	Aries
July 15–16	Taurus
July 17–19	Gemini
July 20–21	Cancer
July 22	Leo

1935

IF YOU WERE BORN ON . . .	YOUR MOON IS IN . . .
June 22	Pisces
June 23–24	Aries
June 25–26	Taurus
June 27–29	Gemini
*June 30–July 1	Cancer
July 2–4	Leo
July 5–6	Virgo
July 7–9	Libra
July 10–11	Scorpio
July 12–13	Sagittarius
**July 14–15	Capricorn
July 16–17	Aquarius
July 18–19	Pisces
July 20–21	Aries
July 22	Taurus

1937

IF YOU WERE BORN ON . . .	YOUR MOON IS IN . . .
June 21–22	Sagittarius
June 23–25	Capricorn
June 26–27	Aquarius
June 28–29	Pisces
June 30–July 2	Aries
July 3–4	Taurus
July 5–6	Gemini
July 7–8	Cancer
July 9–10	Leo
July 11–12	Virgo
July 13–15	Libra
July 16–17	Scorpio
July 18–20	Sagittarius
July 21–22	Capricorn

1934

IF YOU WERE BORN ON . . .	YOUR MOON IS IN . . .
June 22–23	Scorpio
June 24–25	Sagittarius
June 26–27	Capricorn
June 28–29	Aquarius
June 30–July 2	Pisces
July 3–4	Aries
July 5–6	Taurus
July 7–9	Gemini
July 10–11	Cancer
July 12–14	Leo
July 15–16	Virgo
July 17–19	Libra
July 20–21	Scorpio
July 22	Sagittarius

1936

IF YOU WERE BORN ON . . .	YOUR MOON IS IN . . .
June 21–22	Leo
June 23–25	Virgo
June 26–27	Libra
June 28–30	Scorpio
July 1–2	Sagittarius
**July 3–5	Capricorn
July 6–7	Aquarius
July 8–9	Pisces
July 10–11	Aries
July 12–13	Taurus
July 14–15	Gemini
July 16–17	Cancer
July 18–20	Leo
July 21–22	Virgo

1938

IF YOU WERE BORN ON . . .	YOUR MOON IS IN . . .
June 22	Aries
June 23–24	Taurus
June 25–26	Gemini
June 27–28	Cancer
June 29–30	Leo
July 1–2	Virgo
July 3–4	Libra
July 5–7	Scorpio
July 8–9	Sagittarius
July 10–12	Capricorn
July 13–14	Aquarius
July 15–17	Pisces
July 18–19	Aries
July 20–21	Taurus
July 22	Gemini

* = Solar eclipse   ** = Lunar eclipse

1939

IF YOU WERE BORN ON . . .	YOUR MOON IS IN . . .
June 22–23	Virgo
June 24–25	Libra
June 26–27	Scorpio
June 28–29	Sagittarius
June 30–July 2	Capricorn
July 3–4	Aquarius
July 5–7	Pisces
July 8–9	Aries
July 10–12	Taurus
July 13–14	Gemini
July 15–16	Cancer
July 17–18	Leo
July 19–20	Virgo
July 21–22	Libra

1941

IF YOU WERE BORN ON . . .	YOUR MOON IS IN . . .
June 21	Taurus
June 22–23	Gemini
June 24–25	Cancer
June 26–28	Leo
June 29–30	Virgo
July 1–2	Libra
July 3–4	Scorpio
July 5–6	Sagittarius
July 7–8	Capricorn
July 9–11	Aquarius
July 12–13	Pisces
July 14–15	Aries
July 16–18	Taurus
July 19–20	Gemini
July 21–22	Cancer

1943

IF YOU WERE BORN ON . . .	YOUR MOON IS IN . . .
June 22–23	Pisces
June 24–25	Aries
June 26–28	Taurus
June 29–30	Gemini
July 1–3	Cancer
July 4–5	Leo
July 6–8	Virgo
July 9–10	Libra
July 11–12	Scorpio
July 13–14	Sagittarius
July 15–16	Capricorn
July 17–18	Aquarius
July 19–20	Pisces
July 21–22	Aries

1940

IF YOU WERE BORN ON . . .	YOUR MOON IS IN . . .
June 21	Capricorn
June 22–23	Aquarius
June 24–26	Pisces
June 27–28	Aries
June 29–July 1	Taurus
July 2–3	Gemini
July 4–5	Cancer
July 6–7	Leo
July 8–9	Virgo
July 10–12	Libra
July 13–14	Scorpio
July 15–16	Sagittarius
July 17–18	Capricorn
July 19–21	Aquarius
July 22	Pisces

1942

IF YOU WERE BORN ON . . .	YOUR MOON IS IN . . .
June 22–23	Libra
June 24–25	Scorpio
June 26–27	Sagittarius
June 28–29	Capricorn
June 30–July 1	Aquarius
July 2–3	Pisces
July 4–5	Aries
July 6–8	Taurus
July 9–10	Gemini
July 11–13	Cancer
July 14–15	Leo
July 16–18	Virgo
July 19–20	Libra
July 21–22	Scorpio

1944

IF YOU WERE BORN ON . . .	YOUR MOON IS IN . . .
June 21–22	Cancer
June 23–24	Leo
June 25–27	Virgo
June 28–29	Libra
June 30–July 1	Scorpio
July 2–4	Sagittarius
**July 5–6	Capricorn
July 7–8	Aquarius
July 9–10	Pisces
July 11–12	Aries
July 13–14	Taurus
July 15–17	Gemini
*July 18–19	Cancer
July 20–21	Leo

*= Solar eclipse   ** = Lunar eclipse*

1945

IF YOU WERE BORN ON . . .	YOUR MOON IS IN . . .
June 21	Scorpio
June 22–24	Sagittarius
**June 25–26	Capricorn
June 27–28	Aquarius
June 29–July 1	Pisces
July 2–3	Aries
July 4–5	Taurus
July 6–7	Gemini
*July 8–9	Cancer
July 10–11	Leo
July 12–14	Virgo
July 15–16	Libra
July 17–19	Scorpio
July 20–21	Sagittarius
July 22	Capricorn

1947

IF YOU WERE BORN ON . . .	YOUR MOON IS IN . . .
June 22	Leo
June 23–24	Virgo
June 25–26	Libra
June 27–29	Scorpio
June 30–July 1	Sagittarius
July 2–4	Capricorn
July 5–6	Aquarius
July 7–9	Pisces
July 10–11	Aries
July 12–13	Taurus
July 14–15	Gemini
July 16–17	Cancer
July 18–19	Leo
July 20–21	Virgo
July 22	Libra

1949

IF YOU WERE BORN ON . . .	YOUR MOON IS IN . . .
June 21–22	Taurus
June 23–25	Gemini
June 26–27	Cancer
June 28–29	Leo
June 30–July 1	Virgo
July 2–3	Libra
July 4–5	Scorpio
July 6–8	Sagittarius
July 9–10	Capricorn
July 11–12	Aquarius
July 13–15	Pisces
July 16–17	Aries
July 18–20	Taurus
July 21–22	Gemini

1946

IF YOU WERE BORN ON . . .	YOUR MOON IS IN . . .
June 22–23	Aries
June 24–25	Taurus
June 26–27	Gemini
*June 28–29	Cancer
June 30–July 1	Leo
July 2–4	Virgo
July 5–6	Libra
July 7–9	Scorpio
July 10–11	Sagittarius
July 12–14	Capricorn
July 15–16	Aquarius
July 17–18	Pisces
July 19–20	Aries
July 21–22	Taurus

1948

IF YOU WERE BORN ON . . .	YOUR MOON IS IN . . .
June 21–22	Capricorn
June 23–25	Aquarius
June 26–27	Pisces
June 28–30	Aries
July 1–2	Taurus
July 3–4	Gemini
July 5–6	Cancer
July 7–8	Leo
July 9–10	Virgo
July 11–13	Libra
July 14–15	Scorpio
July 16–17	Sagittarius
July 18–20	Capricorn
July 21	Aquarius

1950

IF YOU WERE BORN ON . . .	YOUR MOON IS IN . . .
June 21–22	Virgo
June 23–24	Libra
June 25–26	Scorpio
June 27–28	Sagittarius
June 29–30	Capricorn
July 1–2	Aquarius
July 3–4	Pisces
July 5–7	Aries
July 8–9	Taurus
July 10–12	Gemini
July 13–14	Cancer
July 15–17	Leo
July 18–19	Virgo
July 20–21	Libra
July 22	Scorpio

* = Solar eclipse   ** = Lunar eclipse

1951

IF YOU WERE BORN ON . . .	YOUR MOON IS IN . . .
June 22	Aquarius
June 23–24	Pisces
June 25–27	Aries
June 28–29	Taurus
June 30–July 2	Gemini
July 3–4	Cancer
July 5–7	Leo
July 8–9	Virgo
July 10–12	Libra
July 13–14	Scorpio
July 15–16	Sagittarius
July 17–18	Capricorn
July 19–20	Aquarius
July 21–22	Pisces

1953

IF YOU WERE BORN ON . . .	YOUR MOON IS IN . . .
June 21	Libra
June 22–23	Scorpio
June 24–25	Sagittarius
June 26–27	Capricorn
June 28–30	Aquarius
July 1–2	Pisces
July 3–4	Aries
July 5–6	Taurus
July 7–8	Gemini
*July 9–11	Cancer
July 12–13	Leo
July 14–16	Virgo
July 17–18	Libra
July 19–20	Scorpio
July 21–22	Sagittarius

1955

IF YOU WERE BORN ON . . .	YOUR MOON IS IN . . .
June 22–23	Leo
June 24–25	Virgo
June 26–28	Libra
June 29–30	Scorpio
July 1–3	Sagittarius
July 4–5	Capricorn
July 6–8	Aquarius
July 9–10	Pisces
July 11–12	Aries
July 13–14	Taurus
July 15–16	Gemini
July 17–18	Cancer
July 19–20	Leo
July 21–22	Virgo

1952

IF YOU WERE BORN ON . . .	YOUR MOON IS IN . . .
June 21	Gemini
June 22–23	Cancer
June 24–26	Leo
June 27–28	Virgo
June 29–July 1	Libra
July 2–3	Scorpio
July 4–5	Sagittarius
July 6–7	Capricorn
July 8–9	Aquarius
July 10–11	Pisces
July 12–13	Aries
July 14–16	Taurus
July 17–18	Gemini
July 19–21	Cancer

1954

IF YOU WERE BORN ON . . .	YOUR MOON IS IN . . .
June 21–22	Pisces
June 23–24	Aries
June 25–26	Taurus
June 27–28	Gemini
*June 29–July 1	Cancer
July 2–3	Leo
July 4–5	Virgo
July 6–8	Libra
July 9–10	Scorpio
July 11–13	Sagittarius
**July 14–15	Capricorn
July 16–17	Aquarius
July 18–19	Pisces
July 20–22	Aries

1956

IF YOU WERE BORN ON . . .	YOUR MOON IS IN . . .
June 21–22	Sagittarius
June 23–24	Capricorn
June 25–27	Aquarius
June 28–29	Pisces
June 30–July 1	Aries
July 2–4	Taurus
July 5–6	Gemini
July 7–8	Cancer
July 9–10	Leo
July 11–12	Virgo
July 13–14	Libra
July 15–16	Scorpio
July 17–19	Sagittarius
July 20–21	Capricorn

*= Solar eclipse   ** = Lunar eclipse

1957

IF YOU WERE BORN ON ...	YOUR MOON IS IN ...
June 21	Aries
June 22–24	Taurus
June 25–26	Gemini
June 27–28	Cancer
June 29–30	Leo
July 1–2	Virgo
July 3–4	Libra
July 5–7	Scorpio
July 8–9	Sagittarius
July 10–11	Capricorn
July 12–14	Aquarius
July 15–16	Pisces
July 17–19	Aries
July 20–21	Taurus
July 22	Gemini

1959

IF YOU WERE BORN ON ...	YOUR MOON IS IN ...
June 22–24	Aquarius
June 25–26	Pisces
June 27–28	Aries
June 29–July 1	Taurus
July 2–4	Gemini
July 5–6	Cancer
July 7–8	Leo
July 9–11	Virgo
July 12–13	Libra
July 14–15	Scorpio
July 16–17	Sagittarius
July 18–19	Capricorn
July 20–21	Aquarius
July 22	Pisces

1961

IF YOU WERE BORN ON ...	YOUR MOON IS IN ...
June 21–22	Libra
June 23–25	Scorpio
June 26–27	Sagittarius
June 28–29	Capricorn
June 30–July 1	Aquarius
July 2–3	Pisces
July 4–5	Aries
July 6–7	Taurus
July 8–10	Gemini
July 11–12	Cancer
July 13–15	Leo
July 16–17	Virgo
July 18–20	Libra
July 21–22	Scorpio

1958

IF YOU WERE BORN ON ...	YOUR MOON IS IN ...
June 21	Leo
June 22–23	Virgo
June 24–25	Libra
June 26–27	Scorpio
June 28–29	Sagittarius
June 30–July 1	Capricorn
July 2–4	Aquarius
July 5–6	Pisces
July 7–9	Aries
July 10–11	Taurus
July 12–14	Gemini
July 15–16	Cancer
July 17–18	Leo
July 19–20	Virgo
July 21–22	Libra

1960

IF YOU WERE BORN ON ...	YOUR MOON IS IN ...
June 21–22	Gemini
June 23–25	Cancer
June 26–27	Leo
June 28–30	Virgo
July 1–2	Libra
July 3–4	Scorpio
July 5–6	Sagittarius
July 7–8	Capricorn
July 9–10	Aquarius
July 11–12	Pisces
July 13–15	Aries
July 16–17	Taurus
July 18–20	Gemini
July 21	Cancer

1962

IF YOU WERE BORN ON ...	YOUR MOON IS IN ...
June 21	Aquarius
June 22–23	Pisces
June 24–25	Aries
June 26–28	Taurus
June 29–30	Gemini
July 1–2	Cancer
July 3–5	Leo
July 6–7	Virgo
July 8–10	Libra
July 11–12	Scorpio
July 13–14	Sagittarius
**July 15–16	Capricorn
July 17–18	Aquarius
July 19–21	Pisces
July 22	Aries

*= Solar eclipse   ** = Lunar eclipse

1963

IF YOU WERE BORN ON . . .	YOUR MOON IS IN . . .
June 22	Cancer
June 23–24	Leo
June 25–27	Virgo
June 28–29	Libra
June 30–July 2	Scorpio
July 3–4	Sagittarius
**July 5–7	Capricorn
July 8–9	Aquarius
July 10–11	Pisces
July 12–13	Aries
July 14–15	Taurus
July 16–17	Gemini
*July 18–20	Cancer
July 21–22	Leo

1965

IF YOU WERE BORN ON . . .	YOUR MOON IS IN . . .
June 21	Pisces
June 22–23	Aries
June 24–25	Taurus
June 26–27	Gemini
June 28–29	Cancer
June 30–July 1	Leo
July 2–3	Virgo
July 4–6	Libra
July 7–8	Scorpio
July 9–10	Sagittarius
July 11–13	Capricorn
July 14–15	Aquarius
July 16–18	Pisces
July 19–20	Aries
July 21–22	Taurus

1967

IF YOU WERE BORN ON . . .	YOUR MOON IS IN . . .
June 22–23	Capricorn
June 24–25	Aquarius
June 26–28	Pisces
June 29–30	Aries
July 1–3	Taurus
July 4–5	Gemini
July 6–7	Cancer
July 8–10	Leo
July 11–12	Virgo
July 13–14	Libra
July 15–16	Scorpio
July 17–18	Sagittarius
July 19–20	Capricorn
July 21–22	Aquarius

1964

IF YOU WERE BORN ON . . .	YOUR MOON IS IN . . .
June 21	Scorpio
June 22–23	Sagittarius
**June 24–26	Capricorn
June 27–28	Aquarius
June 29–July 1	Pisces
July 2–3	Aries
July 4–5	Taurus
July 6–7	Gemini
*July 8–9	Cancer
July 10–11	Leo
July 12–13	Virgo
July 14–15	Libra
July 16–18	Scorpio
July 19–21	Sagittarius

1966

IF YOU WERE BORN ON . . .	YOUR MOON IS IN . . .
June 21–22	Leo
June 23–24	Virgo
June 25–26	Libra
June 27–28	Scorpio
June 29–30	Sagittarius
July 1–3	Capricorn
July 4–5	Aquarius
July 6–8	Pisces
July 9–10	Aries
July 11–13	Taurus
July 14–15	Gemini
July 16–17	Cancer
July 18–19	Leo
July 20–21	Virgo
July 22	Libra

1968

IF YOU WERE BORN ON . . .	YOUR MOON IS IN . . .
June 21–22	Taurus
June 23–24	Gemini
June 25–27	Cancer
June 28–29	Leo
June 30–July 1	Virgo
July 2–3	Libra
July 4–5	Scorpio
July 6–7	Sagittarius
July 8–9	Capricorn
July 10–12	Aquarius
July 13–14	Pisces
July 15–16	Aries
July 17–19	Taurus
July 20–21	Gemini

* = Solar eclipse   ** = Lunar eclipse

1969

IF YOU WERE BORN ON...	YOUR MOON IS IN...
June 21	Virgo
June 22–24	Libra
June 25–26	Scorpio
June 27–28	Sagittarius
June 29–30	Capricorn
July 1–2	Aquarius
July 3–4	Pisces
July 5–6	Aries
July 7–9	Taurus
July 10–11	Gemini
July 12–14	Cancer
July 15–16	Leo
July 17–19	Virgo
July 20–21	Libra
July 22	Scorpio

1971

IF YOU WERE BORN ON...	YOUR MOON IS IN...
June 22–24	Cancer
June 25–26	Leo
June 27–29	Virgo
June 30–July 1	Libra
July 2–3	Scorpio
July 4–6	Sagittarius
July 7–8	Capricorn
July 9–10	Aquarius
July 11–12	Pisces
July 13–14	Aries
July 15–16	Taurus
July 17–19	Gemini
*July 20–21	Cancer
July 22	Leo

1973

IF YOU WERE BORN ON...	YOUR MOON IS IN...
June 21–22	Pisces
June 23–24	Aries
June 25–26	Taurus
June 27–28	Gemini
*June 29–30	Cancer
July 1–2	Leo
July 3–5	Virgo
July 6–7	Libra
July 8–10	Scorpio
July 11–12	Sagittarius
**July 13–15	Capricorn
July 16–17	Aquarius
July 18–19	Pisces
July 20–21	Aries

1970

IF YOU WERE BORN ON...	YOUR MOON IS IN...
June 21–22	Aquarius
June 23–24	Pisces
June 25–27	Aries
June 28–29	Taurus
June 30–July 1	Gemini
July 2–4	Cancer
July 5–6	Leo
July 7–9	Virgo
July 10–11	Libra
July 12–13	Scorpio
July 14–16	Sagittarius
July 17–18	Capricorn
July 19–20	Aquarius
July 21–22	Pisces

1972

IF YOU WERE BORN ON...	YOUR MOON IS IN...
June 21–22	Scorpio
June 23–25	Sagittarius
June 26–27	Capricorn
June 28–30	Aquarius
July 1–2	Pisces
July 3–4	Aries
July 5–6	Taurus
July 7–8	Gemini
*July 9–10	Cancer
July 11–12	Leo
July 13–15	Virgo
July 16–17	Libra
July 18–20	Scorpio
July 21	Sagittarius

1974

IF YOU WERE BORN ON...	YOUR MOON IS IN...
June 21	Cancer
June 22–23	Leo
June 24–25	Virgo
June 26–27	Libra
June 28–30	Scorpio
July 1–2	Sagittarius
July 3–5	Capricorn
July 6–7	Aquarius
July 8–10	Pisces
July 11–12	Aries
July 13–14	Taurus
July 15–16	Gemini
July 17–18	Cancer
July 19–20	Leo
July 21–22	Virgo

* = Solar eclipse   ** = Lunar eclipse

1975

IF YOU WERE BORN ON . . .	YOUR MOON IS IN . . .
June 22	Sagittarius
June 23–24	Capricorn
June 25–27	Aquarius
June 28–29	Pisces
June 30–July 2	Aries
July 3–4	Taurus
July 5–7	Gemini
July 8–9	Cancer
July 10–11	Leo
July 12–13	Virgo
July 14–15	Libra
July 16–17	Scorpio
July 18–19	Sagittarius
July 20–22	Capricorn

1977

IF YOU WERE BORN ON . . .	YOUR MOON IS IN . . .
June 21	Leo
June 22–23	Virgo
June 24–25	Libra
June 26–27	Scorpio
June 28–29	Sagittarius
June 30–July 1	Capricorn
July 2–3	Aquarius
July 4–5	Pisces
July 6–8	Aries
July 9–10	Taurus
July 11–13	Gemini
July 14–15	Cancer
July 16–18	Leo
July 19–20	Virgo
July 21	Libra

1979

IF YOU WERE BORN ON . . .	YOUR MOON IS IN . . .
June 21–23	Gemini
June 24–25	Cancer
June 26–28	Leo
June 29–30	Virgo
July 1–3	Libra
July 4–5	Scorpio
July 6–7	Sagittarius
July 8–9	Capricorn
July 10–11	Aquarius
July 12–13	Pisces
July 14–15	Aries
July 16–18	Taurus
July 19–20	Gemini
July 21–22	Cancer

1976

IF YOU WERE BORN ON . . .	YOUR MOON IS IN . . .
June 21	Aries
June 22–23	Taurus
June 24–26	Gemini
June 27–28	Cancer
June 29–30	Leo
July 1–2	Virgo
July 3–4	Libra
July 5–7	Scorpio
July 8–9	Sagittarius
July 10–11	Capricorn
July 12–13	Aquarius
July 14–16	Pisces
July 17–18	Aries
July 19–21	Taurus

1978

IF YOU WERE BORN ON . . .	YOUR MOON IS IN . . .
June 21	Capricorn
June 22–23	Aquarius
June 24–26	Pisces
June 27–28	Aries
June 29–30	Taurus
July 1–3	Gemini
July 4–5	Cancer
July 6–8	Leo
July 9–10	Virgo
July 11–13	Libra
July 14–15	Scorpio
July 16–17	Sagittarius
July 18–19	Capricorn
July 20–21	Aquarius
July 22	Pisces

1980

IF YOU WERE BORN ON . . .	YOUR MOON IS IN . . .
June 21–22	Libra
June 23–24	Scorpio
June 25–26	Sagittarius
June 27–29	Capricorn
June 30–July 1	Aquarius
July 2–3	Pisces
July 4–5	Aries
July 6–7	Taurus
July 8–9	Gemini
July 10–12	Cancer
July 13–14	Leo
July 15–16	Virgo
July 17–19	Libra
July 20–21	Scorpio

*= Solar eclipse   ** = Lunar eclipse*

1981

IF YOU WERE BORN ON . . .	YOUR MOON IS IN . . .
June 21	Aquarius
June 22–23	Pisces
June 24–26	Aries
June 27–28	Taurus
June 29–30	Gemini
July 1–2	Cancer
July 3–4	Leo
July 5–6	Virgo
July 7–9	Libra
July 10–11	Scorpio
July 12–14	Sagittarius
**July 15–16	Capricorn
July 17–18	Aquarius
July 19–21	Pisces

1983

IF YOU WERE BORN ON . . .	YOUR MOON IS IN . . .
June 21	Scorpio
June 22–24	Sagittarius
**June 25–26	Capricorn
June 27–29	Aquarius
June 30–July 1	Pisces
July 2–4	Aries
July 5–6	Taurus
July 7–8	Gemini
July 9–10	Cancer
July 11–12	Leo
July 13–14	Virgo
July 15–16	Libra
July 17–18	Scorpio
July 19–21	Sagittarius
July 22	Capricorn

1985

IF YOU WERE BORN ON . . .	YOUR MOON IS IN . . .
June 21–22	Leo
June 23–24	Virgo
June 25–26	Libra
June 27–28	Scorpio
June 29–30	Sagittarius
July 1–2	Capricorn
July 3–5	Aquarius
July 6–7	Pisces
July 8–10	Aries
July 11–12	Taurus
July 13–15	Gemini
July 16–17	Cancer
July 18–19	Leo
July 20–21	Virgo

1982

IF YOU WERE BORN ON . . .	YOUR MOON IS IN . . .
June 21–22	Cancer
June 23–24	Leo
June 25–26	Virgo
June 27–29	Libra
June 30–July 1	Scorpio
July 2–4	Sagittarius
**July 5–6	Capricorn
July 7–9	Aquarius
July 10–11	Pisces
July 12–13	Aries
July 14–16	Taurus
July 17–18	Gemini
*July 19–20	Cancer
July 21–22	Leo

1984

IF YOU WERE BORN ON . . .	YOUR MOON IS IN . . .
June 21–22	Aries
June 23–25	Taurus
June 26–27	Gemini
June 28–29	Cancer
June 30–July 1	Leo
July 2–3	Virgo
July 4–6	Libra
July 7–8	Scorpio
July 9–10	Sagittarius
July 11–12	Capricorn
July 13–15	Aquarius
July 16–17	Pisces
July 18–20	Aries
July 21	Taurus

1986

IF YOU WERE BORN ON . . .	YOUR MOON IS IN . . .
June 21	Sagittarius
June 22–23	Capricorn
June 24–25	Aquarius
June 26–27	Pisces
June 28–29	Aries
June 30–July 2	Taurus
July 3–4	Gemini
July 5–7	Cancer
July 8–9	Leo
July 10–12	Virgo
July 13–14	Libra
July 15–16	Scorpio
July 17–18	Sagittarius
July 19–20	Capricorn
July 21–22	Aquarius

* = Solar eclipse   ** = Lunar eclipse

1987

IF YOU WERE BORN ON ...	YOUR MOON IS IN ...
June 21–22	Taurus
June 23–24	Gemini
June 25–27	Cancer
June 28–29	Leo
June 30–July 2	Virgo
July 3–4	Libra
July 5–6	Scorpio
July 7–8	Sagittarius
July 9–10	Capricorn
July 11–12	Aquarius
July 13–15	Pisces
July 16–17	Aries
July 18–19	Taurus
July 20–22	Gemini

1989

IF YOU WERE BORN ON ...	YOUR MOON IS IN ...
June 21–22	Aquarius
June 23–25	Pisces
June 26–27	Aries
June 28–29	Taurus
June 30–July 1	Gemini
July 2–3	Cancer
July 4–5	Leo
July 6–8	Virgo
July 9–10	Libra
July 11–13	Scorpio
July 14–15	Sagittarius
July 16–18	Capricorn
July 19–20	Aquarius
July 21	Pisces

1991

IF YOU WERE BORN ON ...	YOUR MOON IS IN ...
June 21–23	Scorpio
June 24–25	Sagittarius
**June 26–28	Capricorn
June 29–30	Aquarius
July 1–3	Pisces
July 4–5	Aries
July 6–7	Taurus
July 8–9	Gemini
*July 10–11	Cancer
July 12–13	Leo
July 14–15	Virgo
July 16–17	Libra
July 18–20	Scorpio
July 21–22	Sagittarius

1988

IF YOU WERE BORN ON ...	YOUR MOON IS IN ...
June 21	Virgo
June 22–23	Libra
June 24–26	Scorpio
June 27–28	Sagittarius
June 29–30	Capricorn
July 1–2	Aquarius
July 3–4	Pisces
July 5–6	Aries
July 7–8	Taurus
July 9–11	Gemini
July 12–13	Cancer
July 14–16	Leo
July 17–18	Virgo
July 19–21	Libra

1990

IF YOU WERE BORN ON ...	YOUR MOON IS IN ...
June 21	Gemini
June 22–23	Cancer
June 24–25	Leo
June 26–28	Virgo
June 29–30	Libra
July 1–3	Scorpio
July 4–5	Sagittarius
July 6–8	Capricorn
July 9–10	Aquarius
July 11–12	Pisces
July 13–14	Aries
July 15–17	Taurus
July 18–19	Gemini
*July 20–21	Cancer
July 22	Leo

1992

IF YOU WERE BORN ON ...	YOUR MOON IS IN ...
June 21–22	Pisces
June 23–24	Aries
June 25–26	Taurus
June 27–28	Gemini
*June 29–30	Cancer
July 1–2	Leo
July 3–5	Virgo
July 6–7	Libra
July 8–9	Scorpio
July 10–11	Sagittarius
July 12–14	Capricorn
July 15–16	Aquarius
July 17–19	Pisces
July 20–21	Aries

* = Solar eclipse   ** = Lunar eclipse

1993

IF YOU WERE BORN ON . . .	YOUR MOON IS IN . . .
June 21	Cancer
June 22–23	Leo
June 24–25	Virgo
June 26–27	Libra
June 28–29	Scorpio
June 30–July 2	Sagittarius
July 3–4	Capricorn
July 5–6	Aquarius
July 7–9	Pisces
July 10–11	Aries
July 12–14	Taurus
July 15–16	Gemini
July 17–18	Cancer
July 19–20	Leo
July 21	Virgo

1995

IF YOU WERE BORN ON . . .	YOUR MOON IS IN . . .
June 21	Aries
June 22–24	Taurus
June 25–26	Gemini
June 27–29	Cancer
June 30–July 1	Leo
July 2–3	Virgo
July 4–6	Libra
July 7–8	Scorpio
July 9–10	Sagittarius
July 11–12	Capricorn
July 13–14	Aquarius
July 15–16	Pisces
July 17–18	Aries
July 19–21	Taurus
July 22	Gemini

1997

IF YOU WERE BORN ON . . .	YOUR MOON IS IN . . .
June 21	Capricorn
June 22–24	Aquarius
June 25–26	Pisces
June 27–28	Aries
June 29–30	Taurus
July 1–2	Gemini
July 3–5	Cancer
July 6–7	Leo
July 8–10	Virgo
July 11–12	Libra
July 13–15	Scorpio
July 16–17	Sagittarius
July 18–19	Capricorn
July 20–21	Aquarius

1994

IF YOU WERE BORN ON . . .	YOUR MOON IS IN . . .
June 21–22	Sagittarius
June 23–24	Capricorn
June 25–26	Aquarius
June 27–29	Pisces
June 30–July 1	Aries
July 2–4	Taurus
July 5–6	Gemini
July 7–8	Cancer
July 9–11	Leo
July 12–13	Virgo
July 14–15	Libra
July 16–17	Scorpio
July 18–19	Sagittarius
July 20–21	Capricorn
July 22	Aquarius

1996

IF YOU WERE BORN ON . . .	YOUR MOON IS IN . . .
June 21–22	Virgo
June 23–25	Libra
June 26–27	Scorpio
June 28–29	Sagittarius
June 30–July 1	Capricorn
July 2–3	Aquarius
July 4–5	Pisces
July 6–7	Aries
July 8–10	Taurus
July 11–12	Gemini
July 13–15	Cancer
July 16–17	Leo
July 18–20	Virgo
July 21	Libra

1998

IF YOU WERE BORN ON . . .	YOUR MOON IS IN . . .
June 21–22	Gemini
June 23–25	Cancer
June 26–27	Leo
June 28–29	Virgo
June 30–July 2	Libra
July 3–4	Scorpio
July 5–7	Sagittarius
July 8–9	Capricorn
July 10–11	Aquarius
July 12–13	Pisces
July 14–16	Aries
July 17–18	Taurus
July 19–20	Gemini
July 21–22	Cancer

* = *Solar eclipse*   ** = *Lunar eclipse*

1999

IF YOU WERE BORN ON . . .	YOUR MOON IS IN . . .
June 21–22	Libra
June 23–24	Scorpio
June 25–27	Sagittarius
June 28–29	Capricorn
June 30–July 2	Aquarius
July 3–4	Pisces
July 5–6	Aries
July 7–8	Taurus
July 9–10	Gemini
July 11–12	Cancer
July 13–14	Leo
July 15–17	Virgo
July 18–19	Libra
July 20–22	Scorpio

2001

IF YOU WERE BORN ON . . .	YOUR MOON IS IN . . .
*June 21–22	Cancer
June 23–24	Leo
June 25–26	Virgo
June 27–28	Libra
June 29–July 1	Scorpio
July 2–3	Sagittarius
**July 4–5	Capricorn
July 6–8	Aquarius
July 9–11	Pisces
July 12–13	Aries
July 14–15	Taurus
July 16–17	Gemini
July 18–19	Cancer
July 20–21	Leo

2003

IF YOU WERE BORN ON . . .	YOUR MOON IS IN . . .
June 21–23	Aries
June 24–25	Taurus
June 26–28	Gemini
June 29–30	Cancer
July 1–2	Leo
July 3–5	Virgo
July 6–7	Libra
July 8–9	Scorpio
July 10–11	Sagittarius
July 12–13	Capricorn
July 14–15	Aquarius
July 16–17	Pisces
July 18–20	Aries
July 21–22	Taurus

2000

IF YOU WERE BORN ON . . .	YOUR MOON IS IN . . .
June 21	Aquarius
June 22–23	Pisces
June 24–26	Aries
June 27–28	Taurus
June 29–30	Gemini
*July 1–2	Cancer
July 3–4	Leo
July 5–6	Virgo
July 7–8	Libra
July 9–11	Scorpio
July 12–13	Sagittarius
**July 14–16	Capricorn
July 17–18	Aquarius
July 19–21	Pisces

2002

IF YOU WERE BORN ON . . .	YOUR MOON IS IN . . .
June 21	Scorpio
June 22–23	Sagittarius
**June 24–25	Capricorn
June 26–28	Aquarius
June 29–30	Pisces
July 1–3	Aries
July 4–5	Taurus
July 6–8	Gemini
July 9–10	Cancer
July 11–12	Leo
July 13–14	Virgo
July 15–16	Libra
July 17–18	Scorpio
July 19–20	Sagittarius
July 21–22	Capricorn

2004

IF YOU WERE BORN ON . . .	YOUR MOON IS IN . . .
June 21–22	Leo
June 23–24	Virgo
June 25–26	Libra
June 27–28	Scorpio
June 29–30	Sagittarius
July 1–2	Capricorn
July 3–4	Aquarius
July 5–6	Pisces
July 7–9	Aries
July 10–11	Taurus
July 12–14	Gemini
July 15–16	Cancer
July 17–19	Leo
July 20–21	Virgo

*= Solar eclipse   ** = Lunar eclipse

2005

IF YOU WERE BORN ON . . .	YOUR MOON IS IN . . .
June 21	Sagittarius
June 22–23	Capricorn
June 24–25	Aquarius
June 26–27	Pisces
June 28–29	Aries
June 30–July 1	Taurus
July 2–4	Gemini
July 5–6	Cancer
July 7–9	Leo
July 10–11	Virgo
July 12–14	Libra
July 15–16	Scorpio
July 17–18	Sagittarius
July 19–20	Capricorn
July 21	Aquarius

2007

IF YOU WERE BORN ON . . .	YOUR MOON IS IN . . .
June 21	Virgo
June 22–24	Libra
June 25–26	Scorpio
June 27–28	Sagittarius
June 29–July 1	Capricorn
July 2–3	Aquarius
July 4–5	Pisces
July 6–7	Aries
July 8–9	Taurus
July 10–11	Gemini
July 12–14	Cancer
July 15–16	Leo
July 17–18	Virgo
July 19–21	Libra
July 22	Scorpio

2009

IF YOU WERE BORN ON . . .	YOUR MOON IS IN . . .
June 21	Gemini
June 22–23	Cancer
June 24–25	Leo
June 26–27	Virgo
June 28–30	Libra
July 1–2	Scorpio
July 3–5	Sagittarius
**July 6–7	Capricorn
July 8–10	Aquarius
July 11–12	Pisces
July 13–14	Aries
July 15–17	Taurus
July 18–19	Gemini
*July 20–21	Cancer

2006

IF YOU WERE BORN ON . . .	YOUR MOON IS IN . . .
June 21–22	Taurus
June 23–24	Gemini
June 25–26	Cancer
June 27–29	Leo
June 30–July 1	Virgo
July 2–4	Libra
July 5–6	Scorpio
July 7–8	Sagittarius
July 9–10	Capricorn
July 11–12	Aquarius
July 13–15	Pisces
July 16–17	Aries
July 18–19	Taurus
July 20–21	Gemini

2008

IF YOU WERE BORN ON . . .	YOUR MOON IS IN . . .
June 21–22	Aquarius
June 23–25	Pisces
June 26–27	Aries
June 28–29	Taurus
June 30–July 1	Gemini
July 2–3	Cancer
July 4–5	Leo
July 6–7	Virgo
July 8–10	Libra
July 11–12	Scorpio
July 13–15	Sagittarius
July 16–17	Capricorn
July 18–20	Aquarius
July 21	Pisces

2010

IF YOU WERE BORN ON . . .	YOUR MOON IS IN . . .
June 21–22	Scorpio
June 23–25	Sagittarius
**June 26–27	Capricorn
June 28–30	Aquarius
July 1–2	Pisces
July 3–5	Aries
July 6–7	Taurus
July 8–9	Gemini
*July 10–11	Cancer
July 12–13	Leo
July 14–15	Virgo
July 16–17	Libra
July 18–19	Scorpio
July 20–21	Sagittarius

*= Solar eclipse   ** = Lunar eclipse

2011

IF YOU WERE BORN ON ...	YOUR MOON IS IN ...
June 21–22	Pisces
June 23–24	Aries
June 25–27	Taurus
June 28–29	Gemini
*June 30–July 1	Cancer
July 2–4	Leo
July 5–6	Virgo
July 7–8	Libra
July 9–10	Scorpio
July 11–12	Sagittarius
July 13–14	Capricorn
July 15–17	Aquarius
July 18–19	Pisces
July 20–22	Aries

2012

IF YOU WERE BORN ON ...	YOUR MOON IS IN ...
June 20–21	Cancer
June 22–23	Leo
June 24–25	Virgo
June 26–27	Libra
June 28–29	Scorpio
June 30–July 1	Sagittarius
July 2–4	Capricorn
July 5–6	Aquarius
July 7–8	Pisces
July 9–10	Aries
July 11–13	Taurus
July 14–16	Gemini
July 17–18	Cancer
July 19–20	Leo
July 21	Virgo

* = Solar eclipse   ** = Lunar eclipse

CHILD OF MERCURY

✳

C hildren of Mercury are smart. You're fast talkers, quick thinkers, and sharp dressers. Your mind is always racing ahead of the conversation. In the time it takes most people to formulate a thought, you've already come up with three ideas, worked out the pros and cons, and probably even decided which one makes the most sense. Because you have so many theories and insights at your disposal, you have no problem discarding one in favor of another. Like a gatekeeper with an enormous ring of keys, you will try them all until you find the one

CAN WE TALK?

DR. RUTH WESTHEIMER
June 4, 1928

JOAN RIVERS
June 8, 1933

BILL MOYERS
June 5, 1934

that works. You love exercising your brain and unlocking mysteries. As far as you're concerned, solving a problem is much more fun than having an answer.

Curiously enough, Children of Mercury usually make very poor students. No doubt there are some of you who behaved at school (probably because doing what you were

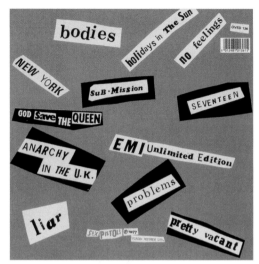

told provided the quickest access to what you wanted), but on the whole Children of Mercury get bored easily. You love to talk. And chances are you were often reprimanded for chatting with a neighbor or passing notes during class. Your intention isn't to disrupt. It's just that you get antsy if you're forced to stay put for too long.

The information you crave needs to be *alive*. Memorizing facts and dates is deadening. Few things give you as much pleasure as finding something no one else can find or combining two ideas in a way that's original and innovative. You tend to fall in love with new things. You want to be the first to name them. Children of Mercury are the ones who can spot the next trend. You see the fashion in the freakishness. You champion the avant-garde before it becomes chic. Is it any wonder that your Birthday Planet rules journalists, writers, advertisers, talent scouts, agents, critics, and media commentators? You want to be one step ahead of the game—"up and coming," never "after the fact."

Mercury has always been an elusive planet. Because it travels so close to the Sun, it can only be viewed at certain times of the year when its orbit moves outside the Sun's rays—either directly following a sunset or just before sunrise. This peekaboo, "now-you-see-me-now-you-don't" quality suits your Ruling Planet's namesake, the god of swift communication and thought. In mythology, Mercury (or Hermes) was the messenger of the gods. A gifted pathfinder, only Mercury could travel freely from heaven to Earth to hell and back again. That's because he knew all the ins and outs. Mercury was familiar with the necessary information—like secret passwords, who to slip a tip to, and which underlings to boss around—simply because that was the only way to get things done.

In the same way, your Birthday Planet serves as a pathfinder in your life. Few people can read a map as expertly as you. You have an amazing ability to open up an instruction manual and zero in on just the information you're looking for. You have a gift for languages whether they be foreign dialects, software codes, musical notes, or stock tips. But one doesn't always travel in a straight line from point A to point B. Sometimes what you're looking for lies off the beaten path. For this reason your Birthday Planet rules over accidental discoveries, coincidences, slips of the tongue, and instant recall. He also rules over inexplicable lapses of memory—like when you're about to say something but can't remember what it is, though it's on the tip of your tongue.

Mercury loves to play, and being a Child of Mercury, life is a game. Yet games don't always sit well with people because many associate game playing with mind games, frivolity, or being swindled. Games are mischievous. However, the very first set of rules we learn in life are rules of a

FOLLOW MY LEAD

DANTE ALIGHIERI
Self-proclaimed Child of Mercury

DOROTHY LEIB
HARRISON WOOD EUSTIS
Established The Seeing Eye, Inc., which trains guide dogs for the blind
May 30, 1886

LANCE ARMSTRONG
Tour de France champion
September 18, 1971

LET'S MAKE A DEAL

HENRY KISSINGER
May 27, 1923

DONALD TRUMP
June 14, 1946

MONTY HALL
August 25, 1923

game. A baby understands right away the rules of peekaboo without needing them to be explained. Games come before language, that's why we're drawn to them. For Children of Mercury game playing is serious business. It's how you make a place for yourself at the table when all the best seats have been taken.

To achieve their objectives some people set a goal and focus all their energy on attaining it. Others make sacrifices in hopes that their luck might turn and favor them one day. You on the other hand trade up. You'll find someone who has something you want and then convince that person to give it to you in exchange for what you have. Because you have this talent for being in the right place at the right time chances are whatever you're peddling is as good as gold—for that moment. Maybe you happen to know a certain person a potential client would love to meet. Or you possess just the item someone needs to complete a valuable collection. Or, like Tom Sawyer, you have a knack for making whitewashing look fun so that everyone on the block wants to come do your chores. As the real estate mogul Donald Trump (a Child of Mercury) once said: "I play to people's fantasies. People may not always think big themselves, but they can still get very excited by those who do. That's why a little hyperbole never hurts."

But you don't look to have fun at someone else's expense—although it can sometimes seem that way to people who don't know you very well. Game playing is the way you make friends. Anyone who's traveled in the Middle East knows how important haggling is to just about any exchange. Merchants will even make a point of inflating prices, just to get a customer to start bargaining. Entering a shop and plunking down money for merchandise is practically an insult. Where's the fun in that? One needs to inspect the wares, look at this and that, throw out a price you know the other party won't accept. Argue, banter, throw out another price, then act like you're leaving. Let yourself be lured back. It may seem like the object of the game is to get the best deal, but the reality is you're *playing* with each other, matching wits and having some fun while you're at it. This is very different from an athletic competition or a contest where one must beat out an opponent for the top prize. However a game's only fun if you're playing with (and against) someone who's on your level. You only make friends or fall in love with people whom you know will make worthy opponents.

Your love of games makes you adept at speculation. It also makes you adept at reading people. You aren't too picky about who you fraternize with. Indeed, your address book is filled with names from all walks of life.

The Mercurial Chinese Conjurer from the dadaist ballet Parade.

MARQUIS DE SADE
Author of Justine
June 2, 1740

HARRIET BEECHER
STOWE
Author of Uncle Tom's Cabin
June 14, 1811

SALMAN RUSHDIE
Author of The Satanic Verses
June 19, 1947

You enjoy the very special privilege of having entrée into every level of society. Because of this skill you converse just as easily with the down-and-out as you can with the well-to-do.

Your mind needs constant stimulation, which means you'll jump from one tangent to another or talk on the phone while flipping through a magazine with the TV on in the background. People may make fun of your short attention span or even gibe you about being a social butterfly. What they don't understand is that you're always on the lookout for words. Words to you are like paints to an artist. Words are how you bring your thoughts to life.

As a Child of Mercury, you have a way of putting things and will practice getting the best spin. Hence your love of a good debate. You revel in argument for argument's sake. A battle of wits allows you to practice your verbal jousts and parries. Wordplay is one of your favorite forms of recreation, and you'll say just about anything if it's a good line. Unfortunately, not everyone shares your fondness for witty repartee. Because you tend to treat conversations like a game, you can be genuinely bewildered when someone takes offense. Often you learn discretion the hard way as you find out that using people's words against them or pointing out their inconsistencies in an argument doesn't always score points.

YASIR ARAFAT
August 24, 1929

AUNG SAN SUU KYI
June 19, 1945

JACK KEVORKIAN
May 26, 1928

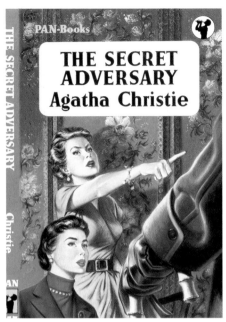

You need to be surrounded by buzz. In fact, you practically invite interruption. Part of it comes from the intensity of your concentration. You can only keep it up for short periods of time—and part of it comes from the fact that you never know when you might hear (or even overhear) something that could prove useful. Besides, there's nothing like a good interruption to get those mental wheels rolling or for leading you down an avenue you might not have otherwise pursued. Nothing is random or too far-fetched, like the stream-of-consciousness writing that was popular in 1920s Paris. A seemingly nonsensical mix of words might contain the makings of an extraordinary thought or phrase. One need only listen to the songs of Cole Porter, Bob Dylan, and Alanis Morissette (all Children of Mercury) to marvel at how a pun becomes surprisingly poignant or a complex idea is rendered in the simplest lines.

Some people may regard you as meddlesome. Others will respond to you as a breath of fresh air. A situation is invariably changed because of your involvement. You can't help it. It's simply impossible for you to leave anything alone. Consider Sherlock Holmes and Hercule Poirot—creations of Children of Mercury Sir Arthur Conan Doyle and Agatha Christie. These detectives are famous for getting on people's nerves. They're always digging deeper and poking holes in everyone else's easy answers. Improvements often result from your helpful suggestions, your pointed question left hanging in the air, or even a derisive chuckle that alerts everyone to the fact that the emperor is parading around in his birthday suit. You don't set out to be a revolutionary or a reformer. You're too moment to moment to let yourself get lost in theorizing. You don't have much patience for abstractions. Words and thoughts are meant to solve riddles, to get you from one place to the other. It's not unlike bees (which are ruled by Mercury) and the role they play in pollination. A garden of delights may spring up as a result of your comings and goings, but as far as you're concerned you were just out collecting nectar for honey. Raising a point or introducing the opposite point of view is part of your ongoing mental process.

You're also very good with your hands. You use them when you speak and have excellent eye-to-hand coordination. It can even be said that your hands have a mind all their own. Miles Davis, Charlie Parker, and Wynton Marsalis—all jazz musicians famous for their improvisational dexterity—are Children of Mercury. And certainly no one would dispute the lightning reflexes of Steffi Graf and Venus Williams—two other Children of Mercury.

You have no problem getting your hands dirty. You like to fiddle and fuss and tinker. While others page through coffee table books wistfully admiring pictures of gardens, interiors, and exquisitely prepared dinners, you're eager to see if you could do it yourself. You want to be out there transplanting the rosebushes, renovating a room in the house, or learning the intricacies of a new dish. You have a love for craftsmanship and are a great admirer of handiwork.

There is only one cardinal sin: to come up empty-handed. You will find an answer—even if you have to make one up on the spot. You have no problem with quick fixes, because you know there will always be time afterward to find a more permanent solution. That's why you Children of Mercury have no patience for people who flip out if some-

Children of Mercury involved in their crafts: painting, divination and diagnosis, commerce, building musical instruments, scribes, and image making.

thing isn't exactly perfect. You know that the illusion of perfection can be achieved much more quickly . . . and for about half the cost.

As a Child of Mercury, you're always playing out one-half of the equation. Like the bicameral mind, it's either going to be the left side of the brain or the right side of the brain with you. If you tend to think in ideas and images, you may be drawn to someone who can help implement them. If you're the brainy type, you may be attracted to more wildly illogical personalities. Everyone knows that opposites attract, but that doesn't mean they'll stay together—which is a lesson you Children of Mercury are constantly learning. You can't go and find a mirror opposite and then expect it to stay on its side of the looking glass.

Friends, colleagues, and loved ones may not like having one side of their personality played up so that it "mirrors" yours. Though you pride yourself on being open-minded, you can be very quick to pigeonhole people—sizing up their complex natures with easy-to-read captions. You end up underestimating who you're dealing with. That's why you really only learn when someone turns the tables on you or beats you at your own game. But then again, what else would one expect from the Planet of the mind—wherein the right side of the brain rules the left side of the body and vice versa? Is it any wonder that things might get a bit mixed up with

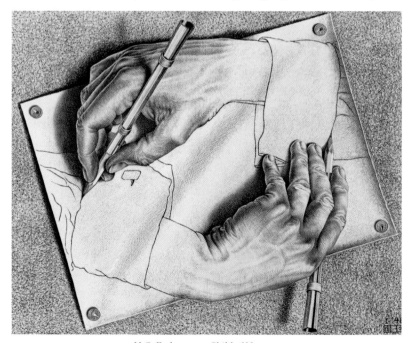

M.C. Escher was a Child of Mercury.

you? Luckily, like the story of the prince who trades places with the pauper, what starts off as a lark often leads to a profound experience. Sometimes it's only when the shoe's on the other foot that you begin to appreciate another person's point of view.

The very qualities that make it easy for you to move about in life—your ability to blend in, to coax your way out of situations, to fascinate, bamboozle, and entertain—can also make it hard for others to get to know you. In truth, you may not always have the clearest idea of who you are either. That's because your life unfolds like one of those "road pictures." Your fortunes rise and fall with every bend or twist. This isn't to say you'll spend your days living out of a suitcase. There are plenty of Children of Mercury who never leave the neighborhood where they were born. However, intellectually, it's a different matter. You're quick to seize an opportunity when you spot it. And by going from opportunity to opportunity, you rewrite the rules as you go. It doesn't much matter how you started out or where you end up. What's important is what happens along the way.

As a Child of Mercury you will feel the need to change *something* about your life every three to four months. You may rearrange the furniture, embark on a new project, or reorganize your desk and files. This corresponds with your Birthday Planet's eighty-eight-day orbit.

Once every six to seven birthdays, Mercury returns to where it was in the sky when you were born. Subsequently the ages of six or seven, twelve or fourteen, eighteen or twenty-one, twenty-four or twenty-seven, etc., are going to be very important to you.

Because your Ruling Planet is associated with ephemeral change and you are more than happy to work with whatever comes your way, it's hard to remember that at some point all these tangents you love to explore must lead somewhere. Thus every six to seven years you will arrive at your destination. But because you've been sidetracked so many times, you may have difficulty recognizing the place you arrive at as the place you originally set your sights on. Like a college student who changes her major or an entrepreneur who starts out in one field only to wind up doing something else, you're not too picky about game plans. However there is a running theme if you care to look for it, and if you want to, you can even use these six- or seven-year turning points to help you plot a course.

Go ahead and turn to the Mercury tables on page 88 to find what sign your Ruling Planet was in on the day you were born. Part III of this book will show how your Ruling Planet varies its expression from sign to sign. If there is an asterisk (*) next to your birth date, then you were born during a retrograde. If so, you'll want to come back and read the following:

CHILD OF MERCURY RETROGRADE

Retrograde refers to a backward motion. The planet Mercury doesn't actually reverse direction. That's just the way it looks to us. It's an optical illusion that occurs periodically from Earth's viewpoint, giving the impression of a planet moving backward against the setting of constellations in the sky. When a planet is retrograde, its energy becomes the opposite of what it is when it's direct. Since Mercury is the Planet of thought and communication, that's what gets turned inside out.

When Mercury is retrograde (which is three times every year), people are plagued by misunderstandings, slips of the tongue, and technological glitches ranging from crossed phone lines to uncooperative ATM machines. It's not unlike adding up a column of numbers and getting a different answer every time. Obviously something's wrong—but what? This was something that took on an eerie relevance during the United States presidential election of 2000, when Mercury was at the height of its retrograde. First the state of Florida was called for the Democratic candidate Al Gore, then for the Republican candidate George W. Bush. This vacillation between the two sides continued for weeks. Indeed the very legality of

the vote recount itself forced the U.S. Supreme Court to step in and announce a winner. That incident raised many questions that still remain unanswered today.

But what's hurly-burly for most is business as usual for you. This isn't to say that if you're a Child of Mercury Retrograde you're dazed and confused or just plain wacky. For most people the mind shuts down when faced with an unexpected twist to an anticipated result. Yet for you Children of Mercury Retrograde, this is when your unique intelligence kicks in. You tend to have a more cautious and skeptical approach to life. You know how things can inexplicably get crazy. This attitude doesn't make you pessimistic; it makes you shrewd and analytical.

Because words and thoughts don't come as easily for you—you may have difficulty with speech, reading, or perhaps you were taught at school to communicate in a language different from the one spoken at home— you really have to develop those mental skills. The result may be an extensive vocabulary, a highly tuned ear, keen eye-to-hand coordination, or a "sixth sense" for reading between the lines. Your Birthday Planet also rules over the five senses, so for those of you who were born with Mercury Retrograde, you may find that if one sense is "blocked" then another one compensates or may even prove superior. The gifted musician Ray Charles is a Child of Mercury Retrograde.

WHAT SIGN IS MERCURY IN?

IF YOU WERE BORN ON . . .	YOUR MERCURY IS IN . . .
May 21–25, 1900	Taurus
May 26–June 8, 1900	Gemini
June 9–20, 1900	Cancer
August 23–September 2, 1900	Leo
September 3–17, 1900	Virgo
September 18–22, 1900	Libra
May 21–31, 1901	Gemini
June 1–21, 1901	Cancer
August 23–24, 1901	Leo
August 25–September 10, 1901	Virgo
September 11–22, 1901	Libra
May 22–28, 1902	Gemini
May 29–June 10, 1902	Cancer
*June 11–21, 1902	Cancer
August 24–September 3, 1902	Virgo
September 4–22, 1902	Libra
*May 22–June 14, 1903	Gemini

IF YOU WERE BORN ON . . .	YOUR MERCURY IS IN . . .
June 15–21, 1903	Gemini
August 24–28, 1903	Virgo
August 29–September 19, 1903	Libra
*September 20–23, 1903	Libra
*May 21–25, 1904	Taurus
May 26–June 13, 1904	Taurus
June 14–20, 1904	Gemini
August 23–27, 1904	Virgo
August 28–September 1, 1904	Libra
*September 2–6, 1904	Libra
*September 7–22, 1904	Virgo
May 21–June 7, 1905	Taurus
June 8–21, 1905	Gemini
*August 23–September 7, 1905	Virgo
September 8–22, 1905	Virgo
May 22–30, 1906	Taurus
May 31–June 13, 1906	Gemini

* = retrograde

IF YOU WERE BORN ON . . .	YOUR MERCURY IS IN . . .
June 14–21, 1906	Cancer
August 24–September 6, 1906	Leo
September 7–22, 1906	Virgo
May 22, 1907	Taurus
May 23–June 5, 1907	Gemini
June 6–21, 1907	Cancer
August 24–30, 1907	Leo
August 31–September 15, 1907	Virgo
September 16–23, 1907	Libra
May 21–29, 1908	Gemini
May 30–June 20, 1908	Cancer
August 23–September 6, 1908	Virgo
September 7–22, 1908	Libra
May 21–June 1, 1909	Gemini
*June 2–21, 1909	Gemini
August 23–31, 1909	Virgo
September 1–22, 1909	Libra
*May 21–31, 1910	Gemini
*June 1–6, 1910	Taurus
June 7–11, 1910	Taurus
June 12–21, 1910	Gemini
August 24–26, 1910	Virgo
August 27–September 12, 1910	Libra
*September 13–22, 1910	Libra
May 22–June 12, 1911	Taurus
June 13–21, 1911	Gemini
August 24–26, 1911	Virgo
*August 27–September 17, 1911	Virgo
September 18–23, 1911	Virgo
May 21–June 4, 1912	Taurus
June 5–18, 1912	Gemini
June 19–20, 1912	Cancer
*August 23–31, 1912	Leo
September 1–9, 1912	Leo
September 10–22, 1912	Virgo
May 21–27, 1913	Taurus

IF YOU WERE BORN ON . . .	YOUR MERCURY IS IN . . .
May 28–June 9, 1913	Gemini
June 10–21, 1913	Cancer
August 23–September 3, 1913	Leo
September 4–19, 1913	Virgo
September 20–22, 1913	Libra
May 21–June 2, 1914	Gemini
June 3–21, 1914	Cancer
August 24–26, 1914	Leo
August 27–September 11, 1914	Virgo
September 12–22, 1914	Libra
May 22–28, 1915	Gemini
May 29–June 13, 1915	Cancer
*June 14–21, 1915	Cancer
August 24–September 4, 1915	Virgo
September 5–23, 1915	Libra
May 21–24, 1916	Gemini
*May 25–June 17, 1916	Gemini
June 18–20, 1916	Gemini
August 23–28, 1916	Virgo
August 29–September 21, 1916	Libra
*September 22, 1916	Libra
*May 21–28, 1917	Taurus
May 29–June 13, 1917	Taurus
June 14–21, 1917	Gemini
August 23–25, 1917	Virgo
August 26–September 4, 1917	Libra
*September 5–13, 1917	Libra
*September 14–22, 1917	Virgo
May 21–June 9, 1918	Taurus
June 10–21, 1918	Gemini
*August 23–September 10, 1918	Virgo
September 11–22, 1918	Virgo
May 22–June 1, 1919	Taurus
June 2–15, 1919	Gemini
June 16–21, 1919	Cancer
*August 24, 1919	Leo

* = retrograde

IF YOU WERE BORN ON . . .	YOUR MERCURY IS IN . . .
August 25–September 8, 1919	Leo
September 9–23, 1919	Virgo
May 21–23, 1920	Taurus
May 24–June 6, 1920	Gemini
June 7–20, 1920	Cancer
August 23–30, 1920	Leo
August 31–September 15, 1920	Virgo
September 16–22, 1920	Libra
May 21–30, 1921	Gemini
May 31–June 20, 1921	Cancer
August 23–September 8, 1921	Virgo
September 9–22, 1921	Libra
May 21–31, 1922	Gemini
June 1–4, 1922	Cancer
*June 5–9, 1922	Cancer
*June 10–21, 1922	Gemini
August 23–September 1, 1922	Virgo
September 2–22, 1922	Libra
*May 22–June 9, 1923	Gemini
June 10–21, 1923	Gemini
August 24–26, 1923	Virgo
August 27–September 15, 1923	Libra
*September 16–23, 1923	Libra
May 21–June 12, 1924	Taurus
June 13–20, 1924	Gemini
August 23–28, 1924	Virgo
*August 29–September 19, 1924	Virgo
September 20–22, 1924	Virgo
May 21–June 5, 1925	Taurus
June 6–19, 1925	Gemini
June 20, 1925	Cancer
*August 23–26, 1925	Virgo
*August 27–September 3, 1925	Leo
September 4–10, 1925	Leo
September 11–22, 1925	Virgo
May 21–28, 1926	Taurus

IF YOU WERE BORN ON . . .	YOUR MERCURY IS IN . . .
May 29–June 11, 1926	Gemini
June 12–21, 1926	Cancer
August 23–September 4, 1926	Leo
September 5–20, 1926	Virgo
September 21–22, 1926	Libra
May 22–June 3, 1927	Gemini
June 4–21, 1927	Cancer
August 24–27, 1927	Leo
August 28–September 13, 1927	Virgo
September 14–23, 1927	Libra
May 21–27, 1928	Gemini
May 28–June 15, 1928	Cancer
*June 16–20, 1928	Cancer
August 23–September 4, 1928	Virgo
September 5–22, 1928	Libra
May 21–27, 1929	Gemini
*May 28–June 20, 1929	Gemini
August 23–29, 1929	Virgo
August 30–September 22, 1929	Libra
*May 21–31, 1930	Taurus
June 1–13, 1930	Taurus
June 14–21, 1930	Gemini
August 23–25, 1930	Virgo
August 26–September 7, 1930	Libra
*September 8–19, 1930	Libra
*September 20–22, 1930	Virgo
May 22–June 10, 1931	Taurus
June 11–21, 1931	Gemini
*August 24–September 13, 1931	Virgo
September 14–23, 1931	Virgo
May 21–June 1, 1932	Taurus
June 2–15, 1932	Gemini
June 16–20, 1932	Cancer
*August 23–26, 1932	Leo
August 27–September 8, 1932	Leo
September 9–22, 1932	Virgo

* = retrograde

IF YOU WERE BORN ON . . .	YOUR MERCURY IS IN . . .
May 21–24, 1933	Taurus
May 25–June 7, 1933	Gemini
June 8–20, 1933	Cancer
August 23–September 1, 1933	Leo
September 2–17, 1933	Virgo
September 18–22, 1933	Libra
May 21–31, 1934	Gemini
June 1–21, 1934	Cancer
August 23–24, 1934	Leo
August 25–September 9, 1934	Virgo
September 10–22, 1934	Libra
May 22–28, 1935	Gemini
May 29–June 8, 1935	Cancer
*June 9–19, 1935	Cancer
*June 20–21, 1935	Gemini
August 24–September 2, 1935	Virgo
September 3–22, 1935	Libra
*May 21–June 11, 1936	Gemini
June 12–20, 1936	Gemini
August 23–26, 1936	Virgo
August 27–September 17, 1936	Libra
*September 18–22, 1936	Libra
*May 21–23, 1937	Taurus
May 24–June 12, 1937	Taurus
June 13–20, 1937	Gemini
August 23–31, 1937	Virgo
*September 1–22, 1937	Virgo
May 21–June 7, 1938	Taurus
June 8–21, 1938	Gemini
*August 23–September 2, 1938	Virgo
*September 3–5, 1938	Leo
September 6–9, 1938	Leo
September 10–22, 1938	Virgo
May 21–30, 1939	Taurus
May 31–June 12, 1939	Gemini
June 13–21, 1939	Cancer

IF YOU WERE BORN ON . . .	YOUR MERCURY IS IN . . .
August 24–September 6, 1939	Leo
September 7–22, 1939	Virgo
May 21–June 3, 1940	Gemini
June 4–20, 1940	Cancer
August 23–28, 1940	Leo
August 29–September 13, 1940	Virgo
September 14–22, 1940	Libra
May 21–28, 1941	Gemini
May 29–June 18, 1941	Cancer
*June 19–20, 1941	Cancer
August 23–September 5, 1941	Virgo
September 6–22, 1941	Libra
May 21–30, 1942	Gemini
*May 31–June 21, 1942	Gemini
August 23–30, 1942	Virgo
August 31–September 22, 1942	Libra
*May 21–25, 1943	Gemini
*May 26–June 4, 1943	Taurus
June 5–13, 1943	Taurus
June 14–21, 1943	Gemini
August 24–26, 1943	Virgo
August 27–September 10, 1943	Libra
*September 11–22, 1943	Libra
May 21–June 10, 1944	Taurus
June 11–20, 1944	Gemini
August 23, 1944	Virgo
*August 24–September 15, 1944	Virgo
September 16–22, 1944	Virgo
May 21–June 3, 1945	Taurus
June 4–17, 1945	Gemini
June 18–20, 1945	Cancer
*August 23–29, 1945	Leo
August 30–September 9, 1945	Leo
September 10–22, 1945	Virgo
May 21–26, 1946	Taurus
May 27–June 9, 1946	Gemini

* = retrograde

IF YOU WERE BORN ON . . .	YOUR MERCURY IS IN . . .
June 10–21, 1946	Cancer
August 23–September 2, 1946	Leo
September 3–18, 1946	Virgo
September 19–22, 1946	Libra
May 21–June 1, 1947	Gemini
June 2–21, 1947	Cancer
August 24–25, 1947	Leo
August 26–September 10, 1947	Virgo
September 11–22, 1947	Libra
May 21–27, 1948	Gemini
May 28–June 10, 1948	Cancer
*June 11–20, 1948	Cancer
August 23–September 2, 1948	Virgo
September 3–22, 1948	Libra
May 21–22, 1949	Gemini
*May 23–June 15, 1949	Gemini
June 16–20, 1949	Gemini
August 23–27, 1949	Virgo
August 28–September 20, 1949	Libra
*September 21–22, 1949	Libra
*May 21–26, 1950	Taurus
May 27–June 13, 1950	Taurus
June 14–20, 1950	Gemini
August 23–26, 1950	Virgo
August 27–September 3, 1950	Libra
*September 4–9, 1950	Libra
*September 10–22, 1950	Virgo
May 21–June 8, 1951	Taurus
June 9–21, 1951	Gemini
*August 23–September 8, 1951	Virgo
September 9–22, 1951	Virgo
May 21–30, 1952	Taurus
May 31–June 13, 1952	Gemini
June 14–20, 1952	Cancer
August 23–September 6, 1952	Leo
September 7–22, 1952	Virgo

IF YOU WERE BORN ON . . .	YOUR MERCURY IS IN . . .
May 21–22, 1953	Taurus
May 23–June 5, 1953	Gemini
June 6–20, 1953	Cancer
August 23–29, 1953	Leo
August 30–September 14, 1953	Virgo
September 15–22, 1953	Libra
May 21–29, 1954	Gemini
May 30–June 20, 1954	Cancer
August 23–September 7, 1954	Virgo
September 8–22, 1954	Libra
May 21–June 2, 1955	Gemini
*June 3–21, 1955	Gemini
August 23–31, 1955	Virgo
September 1–22, 1955	Libra
*May 21–June 6, 1956	Gemini
June 7–20, 1956	Gemini
August 23–25, 1956	Virgo
August 26–September 12, 1956	Libra
*September 13–22, 1956	Libra
May 21–June 11, 1957	Taurus
June 12–20, 1957	Gemini
August 23–26, 1957	Virgo
*August 27–September 18, 1957	Virgo
September 19–22, 1957	Virgo
May 21–June 4, 1958	Taurus
June 5–19, 1958	Gemini
June 20, 1958	Cancer
*August 23–September 1, 1958	Leo
September 2–10, 1958	Leo
September 11–22, 1958	Virgo
May 21–27, 1959	Taurus
May 28–June 10, 1959	Gemini
June 11–21, 1959	Cancer
August 23–September 4, 1959	Leo
September 5–20, 1959	Virgo
September 21–22, 1959	Libra

* = retrograde

IF YOU WERE BORN ON . . .	YOUR MERCURY IS IN . . .
May 21–June 1, 1960	Gemini
June 2–20, 1960	Cancer
August 23–26, 1960	Leo
August 27–September 11, 1960	Virgo
September 12–22, 1960	Libra
May 21–27, 1961	Gemini
May 28–June 13, 1961	Cancer
*June 14–20, 1961	Cancer
August 23–September 3, 1961	Virgo
September 4–22, 1961	Libra
May 21–25, 1962	Gemini
*May 26–June 18, 1962	Gemini
June 19–20, 1962	Gemini
August 23–28, 1962	Virgo
August 29–September 22, 1962	Libra
*May 21–29, 1963	Taurus
May 30–June 13, 1963	Taurus
June 14–21, 1963	Gemini
August 23–25, 1963	Virgo
August 26–September 5, 1963	Libra
*September 6–15, 1963	Libra
*September 16–22, 1963	Virgo
May 21–June 8, 1964	Taurus
June 9–20, 1964	Gemini
*August 23–September 10, 1964	Virgo
September 11–22, 1964	Virgo
May 21–June 1, 1965	Taurus
June 2–15, 1965	Gemini
June 16–20, 1965	Cancer
*August 23–24, 1965	Leo
August 25–September 7, 1965	Leo
September 8–22, 1965	Virgo
May 21–23, 1966	Taurus
May 24–June 6, 1966	Gemini
June 7–20, 1966	Cancer
August 23–31, 1966	Leo

IF YOU WERE BORN ON . . .	YOUR MERCURY IS IN . . .
September 1–16, 1966	Virgo
September 17–22, 1966	Libra
May 21–30, 1967	Gemini
May 31–June 21, 1967	Cancer
August 23, 1967	Leo
August 24–September 8, 1967	Virgo
September 9–22, 1967	Libra
May 21–28, 1968	Gemini
May 29–June 5, 1968	Cancer
*June 6–12, 1968	Cancer
*June 13–20, 1968	Gemini
August 23–31, 1968	Virgo
September 1–21, 1968	Libra
*May 21–June 9, 1969	Gemini
June 10–20, 1969	Gemini
August 23–26, 1969	Virgo
August 27–September 15, 1969	Libra
*September 16–22, 1969	Libra
*May 21, 1970	Taurus
May 22–June 12, 1970	Taurus
June 13–20, 1970	Gemini
August 23–29, 1970	Virgo
*August 30–September 21, 1970	Virgo
September 22, 1970	Virgo
May 21–June 6, 1971	Taurus
June 7–20, 1971	Gemini
June 21, 1971	Cancer
*August 23–28, 1971	Virgo
*August 29–September 4, 1971	Leo
September 5–10, 1971	Leo
September 11–22, 1971	Virgo
May 20–28, 1972	Taurus
May 29–June 11, 1972	Gemini
June 12–20, 1972	Cancer
August 23–September 4, 1972	Leo
September 5–20, 1972	Virgo

* = retrograde

IF YOU WERE BORN ON . . .	YOUR MERCURY IS IN . . .
September 21, 1972	Libra
May 21–June 3, 1973	Gemini
June 4–20, 1973	Cancer
August 23–27, 1973	Leo
August 28–September 12, 1973	Virgo
September 13–22, 1973	Libra
May 21–28, 1974	Gemini
May 29–June 16, 1974	Cancer
*June 17–20, 1974	Cancer
August 23–September 5, 1974	Virgo
September 6–22, 1974	Libra
May 21– 28, 1975	Gemini
*May 29–June 21, 1975	Gemini
August 23–29, 1975	Virgo
August 30–September 22, 1975	Libra
*May 20–June 1, 1976	Taurus
June 2–12, 1976	Taurus
June 13–20, 1976	Gemini
August 23–24, 1976	Virgo
August 25–September 7, 1976	Libra
*September 8–20, 1976	Libra
*September 21, 1976	Virgo
May 21–June 9, 1977	Taurus
June 10–20, 1977	Gemini
*August 23–September 13, 1977	Virgo
September 14–22, 1977	Virgo
May 21–June 2, 1978	Taurus
June 3–16, 1978	Gemini
June 17–20, 1978	Cancer
*August 23–27, 1978	Leo
August 28–September 8, 1978	Leo
September 9–22, 1978	Virgo
May 21–25, 1979	Taurus
May 26–June 8, 1979	Gemini
June 9–20, 1979	Cancer
August 23–September 1, 1979	Leo

IF YOU WERE BORN ON . . .	YOUR MERCURY IS IN . . .
September 2–17, 1979	Virgo
September 18–22, 1979	Libra
May 20–30, 1980	Gemini
May 31–June 20, 1980	Cancer
August 22–23, 1980	Leo
August 24–September 9, 1980	Virgo
September 10–21, 1980	Libra
May 21–27, 1981	Gemini
May 28–June 8, 1981	Cancer
*June 9–20, 1981	Cancer
August 23–September 1, 1981	Virgo
September 2–22, 1981	Libra
*May 21–June 12, 1982	Gemini
June 13–20, 1982	Gemini
August 23–27, 1982	Virgo
August 28–September 18, 1982	Libra
*September 19–22, 1982	Libra
*May 21–24, 1983	Taurus
May 25–June 13, 1983	Taurus
June 14–20, 1983	Gemini
August 23–28, 1983	Virgo
August 29–September 1, 1983	Libra
*September 2–5, 1983	Libra
*September 6–22, 1983	Virgo
May 20–June 6, 1984	Taurus
June 7–20, 1984	Gemini
*August 22–September 6, 1984	Virgo
September 7–21, 1984	Virgo
May 21–29, 1985	Taurus
May 30–June 12, 1985	Gemini
June 13–20, 1985	Cancer
August 23–September 5, 1985	Leo
September 6–21, 1985	Virgo
September 22, 1985	Libra
May 21, 1986	Taurus
May 22–June 4, 1986	Gemini

*= retrograde

IF YOU WERE BORN ON . . .	YOUR MERCURY IS IN . . .
June 5–20, 1986	Cancer
August 23–29, 1986	Leo
August 30–September 14, 1986	Virgo
September 15–22, 1986	Libra
May 21–29, 1987	Gemini
May 30–June 20, 1987	Cancer
August 23–September 6, 1987	Virgo
September 7–22, 1987	Libra
May 20–30, 1988	Gemini
*May 31–June 20, 1988	Gemini
August 22–29, 1988	Virgo
August 30–September 21, 1988	Libra
*May 21–27, 1989	Gemini
*May 28–June 4, 1989	Taurus
June 5–11, 1989	Taurus
June 12–20, 1989	Gemini
August 23–25, 1989	Virgo
August 26–September 10, 1989	Libra
*September 11–22, 1989	Libra
May 21–June 11, 1990	Taurus
June 12–20, 1990	Gemini
August 23–24, 1990	Virgo
*August 25–September 16, 1990	Virgo
September 17–22, 1990	Virgo
May 21–June 4, 1991	Taurus
June 5–18, 1991	Gemini
June 19–20, 1991	Cancer
*August 23–30, 1991	Leo
August 31–September 9, 1991	Leo
September 10–22, 1991	Virgo
May 20–25, 1992	Taurus
May 26–June 8, 1992	Gemini
June 9–20, 1992	Cancer
August 22–September 2, 1992	Leo
September 3–18, 1992	Virgo
September 19–21, 1992	Libra

IF YOU WERE BORN ON . . .	YOUR MERCURY IS IN . . .
May 21–June 1, 1993	Gemini
June 2–20, 1993	Cancer
August 23–25, 1993	Leo
August 26–September 10, 1993	Virgo
September 11–22, 1993	Libra
May 21–27, 1994	Gemini
May 28–June 11, 1994	Cancer
*June 12–20, 1994	Cancer
August 23–September 3, 1994	Virgo
September 4–22, 1994	Libra
May 21–23, 1995	Gemini
*May 24–June 16, 1995	Gemini
June 17–20, 1995	Gemini
August 23–28, 1995	Virgo
August 29–September 21, 1995	Libra
*September 22, 1995	Libra
*May 20–26, 1996	Taurus
May 27–June 12, 1996	Taurus
June 13–20, 1996	Gemini
August 22–25, 1996	Virgo
August 26–September 3, 1996	Libra
*September 4–11, 1996	Libra
*September 12–21, 1996	Virgo
May 21–June 7, 1997	Taurus
June 8–20, 1997	Gemini
*August 23–September 9, 1997	Virgo
September 10–21, 1997	Virgo
May 21–31, 1998	Taurus
June 1–14, 1998	Gemini
June 15–20, 1998	Cancer
August 23–September 7, 1998	Leo
September 8–22, 1998	Virgo
May 21–22, 1999	Taurus
May 23–June 6, 1999	Gemini
June 7–20, 1999	Cancer
August 23–30, 1999	Leo

* = retrograde

IF YOU WERE BORN ON . . .	YOUR MERCURY IS IN . . .
August 31–September 15, 1999	Virgo
September 16–22, 1999	Libra
May 20–29, 2000	Gemini
May 30–June 20, 2000	Cancer
August 22–September 6, 2000	Virgo
September 7–21, 2000	Libra
May 20–June 3, 2001	Gemini
*June 4–20, 2001	Gemini
August 23–31, 2001	Virgo
September 1–21, 2001	Libra
*May 21–June 7, 2002	Gemini
June 8–20, 2002	Gemini
August 23–25, 2002	Virgo
August 26–September 13, 2002	Libra
*September 14–22, 2002	Libra
May 21–June 12, 2003	Taurus
June 13–20, 2003	Gemini
August 23–27, 2003	Virgo
*August 28–September 19, 2003	Virgo
September 20–22, 2003	Virgo
May 20–June 4, 2004	Taurus
June 5–18, 2004	Gemini
June 19–20, 2004	Cancer
*August 22–24, 2004	Virgo
*August 25–September 1, 2004	Leo
September 2–9, 2004	Leo
September 10–21, 2004	Virgo
May 20–27, 2005	Taurus
May 28–June 10, 2005	Gemini
June 11–20, 2005	Cancer
August 23–September 3, 2005	Leo
September 4–19, 2005	Virgo
September 20–21, 2005	Libra
May 21–June 2, 2006	Gemini
June 3–20, 2006	Cancer
August 23–26, 2006	Leo

IF YOU WERE BORN ON . . .	YOUR MERCURY IS IN . . .
August 27–September 11, 2006	Virgo
September 12–22, 2006	Libra
May 21–28, 2007	Gemini
May 29–June 14, 2007	Cancer
*June 15–20, 2007	Cancer
August 23–September 4, 2007	Virgo
September 5–22, 2007	Libra
May 20–25, 2008	Gemini
*May 26–June 18, 2008	Gemini
June 19–20, 2008	Gemini
August 22–28, 2008	Virgo
August 29–September 21, 2008	Libra
*May 20–30, 2009	Taurus
May 31–June 13, 2009	Taurus
June 14–20, 2009	Gemini
August 22–24, 2009	Virgo
August 25–September 6, 2009	Libra
*September 7–17, 2009	Libra
*September 18–21, 2009	Virgo
May 21–June 9, 2010	Taurus
June 10–20, 2010	Gemini
*August 23–September 11, 2010	Virgo
September 12–22, 2010	Virgo
May 21–June 1, 2011	Taurus
June 2–15, 2011	Gemini
June 16–20, 2011	Cancer
*August 23–25, 2011	Leo
August 26–September 8, 2011	Leo
September 9–22, 2011	Virgo
May 20–23, 2012	Taurus
May 24–June 6, 2012	Gemini
June 7–19, 2012	Cancer
August 22–31, 2012	Leo
September 1–15, 2012	Virgo
September 16–21, 2012	Libra

* = retrograde

CHILD OF VENUS

❋

Your most valuable resources are the people in your life. Many of the things you cherish—like your financial security, status, and good times—are directly linked to who you know and how well you get along. Few people cultivate relationships as easily (and numerously) as you. You never do anything yourself. Not if you can help it. What's the point of running after what you want when, if you ask nicely, you can get someone else to run and fetch it for you? As a Child of Venus, you turn "asking nicely" into a refined art.

KEY WORDS

Art, culture, beauty, voice, partners, balance, breasts and buttocks, diplomacy, sweets, fashion, presentation, salons, bedrooms, fine dining, finishing schools, mirrors, settees, parks and gardens, cosmetics

Fabergé, a Child of Venus, is synonymous with luxury and beauty.

Venus rules what we value. Not moral value, but *value* as in how much one is willing to pay. Named after the goddess of love and beauty, beauty is certainly something we all treasure in our lives. Who decides what's in and what's out? What's high end and what's bargain basement? The Children of Venus. You understand the subtleties of packaging. Is it appealing? Does it jump off the shelf and say "buy me," or does it have an understated "come hither" look? One can see your Ruling Planet at work in advertising campaigns, with their emphasis on look, placement, and color. It's not the product that's important; it's the image. If consumers like what they see, then they'll pay top dollar for it. Admittedly you tend to emphasize style over substance, but given your natural good taste people don't seem to mind. Children of Venus can be found in music, the arts, and the fashion industry, as well as auction houses, museums, and marketplaces where luxury items are bought and sold. Venus rules culture, which if you think about it is the ultimate expression of what a society values because it finds those things most attractive. We have the Children of Venus to thank for transforming all of us from a band of Neanderthals ready to clobber one another for a juicy chunk of mastodon into the millions of consumers who have turned Ralph Lauren and Donna Karan into household names.

Your Ruling Planet works her magic through the people you attract in life. What this means is you do everything through someone else. Think of it as sitting at the dining table and asking your neighbor if he would be so kind as to pass the salt. There are many kinds of partnerships in life. Venus isn't exclusive to romance and marriage. She rules over all collaborations, allegiances, mergers and acquisitions. When two people combine forces, for whatever reason, they do it in the spirit of Venus. Subsequently, partnering is very important to you. Usually this means you'll have a partner for every walk of life. What you would ask of a mate isn't going to be the

same thing you would ask of a colleague. The contexts are different, so your wants and needs are different. You may turn to a certain friend for help with your computer, but that might not be the same person you confide in when going through rough times. You like having different partners. Each gives according to his or her means. It could even be said that you conduct your life as if it were an enormous casting call—matching people with the roles you expect them to play. It's not unlike figuring out the seating for a dinner party. Who would get along with whom and what would make for the most stimulating conversation is a project that could occupy you for hours.

An elegant soirée.

MIGHTY APHRODITE

C ATHERINE THE G REAT
Empress of Russia
April 21, 1729

M ARIA T HERESA
*Empress of the Holy Roman
Empire*
May 13, 1717

G OLDA M EIR
*A founder and fourth prime
minister of Israel*
May 3, 1898

Your focus is on the world outside the home. You're very conscientious about how you come across in society. It's not enough to make an impression. What you want to do is make the *right* impression with the *right* set of admirers. You expand your influence through liaisons. You flirt with words, facts, and figures just as easily as you flirt with gestures. The great misunderstanding about Children of Venus is that it's assumed you do everything for pleasure. There's no denying you love having a good time, but a truer description is that you're well versed in the art of giving pleasure. Like a geisha, an escort, or a courtesan you get ahead in the world by making someone else feel good or smart or cultivated. You aim to please.

For most people, the focus is on *me* and *what do I want*. For you the focus is on *you* and *what do you want*. Now this isn't because you're particularly selfless or accommodating. As a Child of Venus, you prefer to conduct the interview. Getting someone to open up puts a person at ease. Yet it also allows you to learn all sorts of things while revealing very little about yourself. Barbara Walters, a Child of Venus, made the celebrity interview an art form. Simple questions like "How do you see yourself accomplishing this?" prompt the other party to explain while you take stock of what's being said. Children of Venus are always running background checks. You familiarize yourself with each person's likes and dislikes, assess strengths, and make note of the weaknesses. Sigmund Freud, the founder of psychoanalysis, was a Child of Venus. He made a career of inviting patients to lie back on the couch and divulge all their troubles.

You know how to play to people. It's easy. You simply give them what they want. And what most people want is to feel charming, attractive, and interesting. If you want to win over a critic, you never argue. Simply agree with everything he has to say. Tell him how bright and insightful he is. Massage his ego, and you'll soon see an adversary rhapsodizing about your intelligence and praising you for your excellent taste. You know the value of keeping your friends close, but your enemies closer. A friend won't always tell you what you need to hear. Who wants to upset someone as positive and charming as yourself? That's why you'll make a point of checking in with those people you know *don't* like you, just to get a balanced view of matters. An enemy can know you just as intimately, but where a friend protects your interests and defends your weaknesses, an enemy will exploit them. This is where Children of Venus get their reputation for intrigues. Your success at keeping the peace depends on how good you are at anticipating those who want to upset it and stopping them in their tracks. If you can prevail on someone else to fight your battles for you—it's even better.

A rare photograph of Freud next to his couch.

FEELING LIKE A WOMAN, LOOKING LIKE A MAN

DIVINE
October 19, 1945

GRACE JONES
May 19, 1952

DENNIS RODMAN
May 13, 1961

Combining business with pleasure is practically your m.o. If you want to do business right, then you have to do it with finesse. You need to ditch the conference calls, notepads, and cold coffee and meet some-place classy. A place with ambience, where you know the service is excellent and the food divine. As a Child of Venus, you understand the benefits of setting the right mood and tone. You will put as much time and energy into courting a prospective client or employer as you would a potential suitor. A good example of this would be Cleopatra. She brought not only one, but two Caesars to their knees. Queen Cleopatra wanted to restore her Egypt to its glory days but knew her armies were no match for the legions of Rome. So she did what she knew how to do best and soon had Marc Antony—one of the most powerful men in the Ancient World—eating figs out of her hand. And Egypt was made great again. Not bad for the queen of an occupied country. All of this goes to show that for a Planet often associated with vanity and pleasure, luxury and frivolity, Venus knows how to make it in a man's world. As long as a whiff of perfume or a glimpse of leg can still turn a fellow's head, you'll use it. That goes for men who are Children of Venus, too—as evidenced in the recent rise of men's fitness and fashion magazines. Knowing the right type of wine to go with dinner can say more about your success than how much money you make. Why use force when there's persuasion?

Yet you'll rarely let your attractions run away with you. You know it's better to be desired than to be the one who desires. The object of affection has the upper hand. You could be enamored of someone, even swept away by the moment, but you'll still want to know what he or she does for a living. Romance is great, but you also know it can be fleeting and you want something more secure. You will always do your level best to keep your partner's interest. Children of Venus are the ones who make a point of staying in shape and keeping up with both the latest fashion *and* financial trends. Money is a big deal to you. Not just because you need it to finance your lifestyle (which can be lavish), but also because you know that if love won't keep you together, money will. You cover all the bases.

Staying together is the most important thing to you. Once you've cho-

And Love's own, flower the blushing Rose,
The Queen of all the garden close:

SHAKESPEARE IN LOVE

WILLIAM SHAKESPEARE
April 26, 1564

SERGEY PROKOFIEV
Composer of the ballet
Romeo and Juliet
April 23, 1891

GWYNETH PALTROW
September 28, 1972

sen a partner, you will do what it takes to make that relationship work. You were born under the Planet of peace and harmony. It's your job to rectify the imbalances, to bridge the gaps, and to find some way for everyone to get along. Subsequently personal feelings often take a backseat to what you believe should be done to make a relationship work. As a Child of Venus, you regard the relationship as an entity unto itself—unique to the two people involved and existing only as long as they remain together. Your Birthday Planet rules over betrothals. In fact the word *betroth* means to "be true." This is why pledges are so important and why you don't enter into them quickly. Giving your word is like giving your bond. Venus, for all intents and purposes, symbolizes a covenant.

You're into making love, not war, so it's only natural for you to want people to be happy. Instead of taking sides, you'll try to appease both parties in a dispute. It's very diplomatic of you, but diplomacy also requires a show of force in order to be effective. You'd rather duck out than confront, which can sometimes give the impression of stringing people along. Saying what someone wants to hear may smooth over ruffled feathers in the moment, but it could lead to complications later on when that person's sentiments change and you end up contradicting yourself. A difficulty that many Children of Venus face is that keeping the peace can be a full-time job. You're the object of affection. You're the one who's got the other person hooked. Others are looking to you for the green light. But as a Child of Venus, you're waiting for them to go first. Like in the comedy routine where one performer holds the door open and says "after you" and the other performer replies "oh, no after you" and then the first performer protests: "Oh no, no. I insist: after you"—the niceties can wind up causing more harm than good. This is when the best of intentions pave the way to a hellish situation.

Yet where would we be without the courtesy and tact you Children of Venus espouse? Your belief that there are two sides to every story and insistence that both be heard is what gives you your reputation for fairness

ELEANOR ROOSEVELT
October 11, 1884

KATHARINE HEPBURN
May 12, 1907

CORETTA SCOTT KING
April 27, 1927

THROUGH THICK AND THIN

Fourteenth-century fresco of Venus, goddess of harmony, resolving a dispute.

and objectivity. Law and judgment don't allow for the gray areas. This is why mediation is so important to you. As far as you're concerned, the best resolution to any dispute isn't in determining who's right and who's wrong. It's in finding a way for both sides to leave with something.

Once every eight birthdays, Venus returns to where it was in the sky when you were born. The ages of eight, sixteen, twenty-four, thirty-two, forty, etc., are going to be very important to you. Relationships will undergo a sea change. You may start running with a different crowd, set your sights on a more exclusive clientele, or someone new enters your life—showing you what you've been missing. It's the perfect time to be out and about. Even if you are already in a relationship, there's nothing wrong with reminding your partner to keep an eye on the store. As a Child of Venus, you refuse to be taken for granted.

Go ahead and turn to the Venus tables on page 109 to find what sign your Ruling Planet was in on the day you were born. Part III of this book will show how your Ruling Planet varies its expression from sign to sign. If there is an asterisk (*) next to your birth date, then you were born during a retrograde. If so you'll want to come back and read the following:

CHILD OF VENUS RETROGRADE

Retrograde refers to a backward motion. The planet Venus doesn't actually reverse direction. That's just the way it looks to us. It's an optical illusion that occurs periodically from Earth's viewpoint, giving the impression of a planet moving backward against the setting of constellations in the sky. When a planet is retrograde, its energy becomes the opposite of what it is when it's direct. Since Venus is the Planet of love and beauty, then that's what gets turned inside out.

Venus has always had two faces. This is in keeping with her cyclical appearances as evening star and morning star—something that was observed and recorded by ancient astrologers in both Mesoamerica and Babylon. What's intriguing is that two such geographically separate civilizations would interpret her celestial influence in the exact same way. Venus's appearance as an evening star (i.e., after sunset) was auspicious for lovemaking, whereas her appearance as a morning star (i.e., before

sunrise) was an omen of war and peril. Venus is retrograde when she appears as a morning star.

When Venus is retrograde (once every two years), people are plagued by betrayals (usually involving women), breakups, feuds, indiscretions, and even public scandal. It was during a particularly powerful Venus retrograde that the affair between President Clinton and Monica Lewinsky came to light.

This isn't to say that if you're a Child of Venus Retrograde you're a born troublemaker. What it implies is that you are no stranger to conflict. You see the best— and the worst—that people have to offer, and you don't romanticize anything. There's nothing wrong with this except that being a Child of Venus, you still believe you won't be able to get what you want without the assistance of someone else. You're afraid that if you're too independent, you'll wind up alone; but, if you're too accommodating, then you're just asking to be used. Therefore it may take several relationships

**GIVE PEACE A
CHANCE**

GANDHI
October 2, 1869

ALFRED NOBEL
*Creator of the Nobel Peace
Prize (also invented dynamite)
October 21, 1833*

JOHN LENNON
October 9, 1940

to figure out what works for you. It might be hard to tell at times whether it's truly a bad choice in partners that bedevils you or an assumption that people always leave that prevents you from lowering your guard. Yet as with any retrograde, it's these ongoing dilemmas that allow your own special genius to emerge. Because you expect to be self-sufficient, you may partner later on in life. When you do, you and the other person will be coming together as individuals rather than as two halves looking to be a whole. You won't try to fit into the other person's life any more than you'd expect that person to fit into yours. You will truly be meeting as equals. You believe in what the poet Kahlil Gibran once said: "let there be spaces in your togetherness."

Children of Venus Retrograde are keen observers of humanity—which makes for political savvy, wit, and an innate sense for what's unspoken but understood. Moreover your tastes and aesthetics aren't dependent on others' opinions. You never confuse life with lifestyle. Life will always come first. The actress Audrey Hepburn was a Child of Venus Retrograde. Raised in war-torn Europe, she experienced starvation and extreme hardship early on. When she became a movie star, the epitome of glamour, she could have easily turned her back on all that unpleasantness. Instead she devoted the latter part of her life appealing to those with plenty to provide shelter and aid to children whose lives had been devastated by war and famine. Children of Venus Retrograde can reach into the heart of despair and draw out the beauty within.

WHAT SIGN IS VENUS IN?

IF YOU WERE BORN ON . . .	YOUR VENUS IS IN . . .
April 20–May 4, 1900	Gemini
May 5–20, 1900	Cancer
September 23–October 7, 1900	Leo
October 8–22, 1900	Virgo
April 20–21, 1901	Aries
April 22–May 16, 1901	Taurus
May 17–20, 1901	Gemini
September 23–October 11, 1901	Scorpio
October 12–23, 1901	Sagittarius
April 21–May 6, 1902	Pisces
May 7–21, 1902	Aries
September 23–October 6, 1902	Virgo
October 7–23, 1902	Libra
April 21–May 12, 1903	Gemini
May 13–21, 1903	Cancer
*September 24–October 8, 1903	Virgo

IF YOU WERE BORN ON . . .	YOUR VENUS IS IN . . .
October 9–23, 1903	Virgo
April 20–May 6, 1904	Aries
May 7–20, 1904	Taurus
September 23–29, 1904	Libra
September 30–October 22, 1904	Scorpio
*April 20–May 8, 1905	Taurus
*May 9–17, 1905	Aries
May 18–20, 1905	Aries
September 23–26, 1905	Leo
September 27–October 20, 1905	Virgo
October 21–23, 1905	Libra
April 21–May 1, 1906	Taurus
May 2–21, 1906	Gemini
September 23–October 8, 1906	Scorpio
October 9–23, 1906	Sagittarius
April 21–26, 1907	Pisces

*= retrograde

IF YOU WERE BORN ON . . .	YOUR VENUS IS IN . . .
April 27–May 21, 1907	Aries
September 24–October 15, 1907	Libra
October 16–23, 1907	Scorpio
April 20–May 4, 1908	Gemini
May 5–20, 1908	Cancer
September 23–October 7, 1908	Leo
October 8–22, 1908	Virgo
April 20–21, 1909	Aries
April 22–May 15, 1909	Taurus
May 16–20, 1909	Gemini
September 23–October 11, 1909	Scorpio
October 12–23, 1909	Sagittarius
April 20–May 6, 1910	Pisces
May 7–20, 1910	Aries
September 23–October 5, 1910	Virgo
October 6–23, 1910	Libra
April 21–May 12, 1911	Gemini
May 13–21, 1911	Cancer
*September 24–October 5, 1911	Virgo
October 6–23, 1911	Virgo
April 20–May 6, 1912	Aries
May 7–20, 1912	Taurus
September 23–29, 1912	Libra
September 30–October 22, 1912	Scorpio
*April 20–May 1, 1913	Taurus
*May 2–15, 1913	Aries
May 16–20, 1913	Aries
September 23–25, 1913	Leo
September 26–October 20, 1913	Virgo
October 21–23, 1913	Libra
April 20–30, 1914	Taurus
May 1–20, 1914	Gemini
September 23–October 9, 1914	Scorpio
October 10–23, 1914	Sagittarius
April 21–26, 1915	Pisces
April 27–May 21, 1915	Aries

IF YOU WERE BORN ON . . .	YOUR VENUS IS IN . . .
September 24–October 14, 1915	Libra
October 15–23, 1915	Scorpio
April 20–May 4, 1916	Gemini
May 5–20, 1916	Cancer
September 23–October 6, 1916	Leo
October 7–22, 1916	Virgo
April 20, 1917	Aries
April 21–May 15, 1917	Taurus
May 16–20, 1917	Gemini
September 23–October 10, 1917	Scorpio
October 11–22, 1917	Sagittarius
April 20–May 5, 1918	Pisces
May 6–20, 1918	Aries
September 23–October 5, 1918	Virgo
October 6–23, 1918	Libra
April 21–May 11, 1919	Gemini
May 12–21, 1919	Cancer
*September 24–October 3, 1919	Virgo
October 4–23, 1919	Virgo
April 20–May 5, 1920	Aries
May 6–20, 1920	Taurus
September 23–28, 1920	Libra
September 29–October 22, 1920	Scorpio
*April 20–24, 1921	Taurus
*April 25–May 13, 1921	Aries
May 14–20, 1921	Aries
September 23–25, 1921	Leo
September 26–October 19, 1921	Virgo
October 20–22, 1921	Libra
April 20–30, 1922	Taurus
May 1–20, 1922	Gemini
September 23–October 9, 1922	Scorpio
October 10–23, 1922	Sagittarius
April 21–25, 1923	Pisces
April 26–May 20, 1923	Aries
May 21, 1923	Taurus

* = retrograde

IF YOU WERE BORN ON . . .	YOUR VENUS IS IN . . .
September 24–October 14, 1923	Libra
October 15–23, 1923	Scorpio
April 20–May 5, 1924	Gemini
May 6–20, 1924	Cancer
September 23–October 6, 1924	Leo
October 7–22, 1924	Virgo
April 20, 1925	Aries
April 21–May 14, 1925	Taurus
May 15–20, 1925	Gemini
September 23–October 10, 1925	Scorpio
October 11–22, 1925	Sagittarius
April 20–May 5, 1926	Pisces
May 6–20, 1926	Aries
September 23–October 4, 1926	Virgo
October 5–23, 1926	Libra
April 21–May 11, 1927	Gemini
May 12–21, 1927	Cancer
*September 24–October 1, 1927	Virgo
October 2–23, 1927	Virgo
April 20–May 5, 1928	Aries
May 6–20, 1928	Taurus
September 23–28, 1928	Libra
September 29–October 22, 1928	Scorpio
*April 20–May 10, 1929	Aries
May 11–20, 1929	Aries
September 23–24, 1929	Leo
September 25–October 19, 1929	Virgo
October 20–22, 1929	Libra
April 20–29, 1930	Taurus
April 30–May 20, 1930	Gemini
September 23–October 11, 1930	Scorpio
October 12–23, 1930	Sagittarius
April 21–25, 1931	Pisces
April 26–May 20, 1931	Aries
May 21, 1931	Taurus
September 24–October 13, 1931	Libra

IF YOU WERE BORN ON . . .	YOUR VENUS IS IN . . .
October 14–23, 1931	Scorpio
April 20–May 5, 1932	Gemini
May 6–20, 1932	Cancer
September 23–October 6, 1932	Leo
October 7–22, 1932	Virgo
April 20–May 14, 1933	Taurus
May 15–20, 1933	Gemini
September 23–October 10, 1933	Scorpio
October 11–22, 1933	Sagittarius
April 20–May 5, 1934	Pisces
May 6–20, 1934	Aries
September 23–October 4, 1934	Virgo
October 5–23, 1934	Libra
April 21–May 10, 1935	Gemini
May 11–21, 1935	Cancer
*September 23–28, 1935	Virgo
September 29–October 23, 1935	Virgo
April 20–May 4, 1936	Aries
May 5–20, 1936	Taurus
September 23–27, 1936	Libra
September 28–October 22, 1936	Scorpio
*April 20–May 8, 1937	Aries
May 9–20, 1937	Aries
September 23–24, 1937	Leo
September 25–October 18, 1937	Virgo
October 19–22, 1937	Libra
April 20–28, 1938	Taurus
April 29–May 20, 1938	Gemini
September 23–October 12, 1938	Scorpio
October 13–23, 1938	Sagittarius
April 20–24, 1939	Pisces
April 25–May 19, 1939	Aries
May 20, 1939	Taurus
September 23–October 13, 1939	Libra
October 14–23, 1939	Scorpio
April 20–May 5, 1940	Gemini

* = retrograde

IF YOU WERE BORN ON . . .	YOUR VENUS IS IN . . .
May 6–20, 1940	Cancer
September 23–October 5, 1940	Leo
October 6–22, 1940	Virgo
April 20–May 13, 1941	Taurus
May 14–20, 1941	Gemini
September 23–October 9, 1941	Scorpio
October 10–22, 1941	Sagittarius
April 20–May 5, 1942	Pisces
May 6–20, 1942	Aries
September 23–October 3, 1942	Virgo
October 4–23, 1942	Libra
April 20–May 10, 1943	Gemini
May 11–20, 1943	Cancer
*September 23–26, 1943	Virgo
September 27–October 23, 1943	Virgo
April 20–May 3, 1944	Aries
May 4–20, 1944	Taurus
September 23–27, 1944	Libra
September 28–October 21, 1944	Scorpio
October 22, 1944	Sagittarius
*April 20–May 5, 1945	Aries
May 6–20, 1945	Aries
September 23, 1945	Leo
September 24–October 18, 1945	Virgo
October 19–22, 1945	Libra
April 20–28, 1946	Taurus
April 29–May 20, 1946	Gemini
September 23–October 15, 1946	Scorpio
October 16–23, 1946	Sagittarius
April 20–24, 1947	Pisces
April 25–May 19, 1947	Aries
May 20, 1947	Taurus
September 23–October 12, 1947	Libra
October 13–23, 1947	Scorpio
April 20–May 6, 1948	Gemini
May 7–20, 1948	Cancer

IF YOU WERE BORN ON . . .	YOUR VENUS IS IN . . .
September 23–October 5, 1948	Leo
October 6–22, 1948	Virgo
April 20–May 13, 1949	Taurus
May 14–20, 1949	Gemini
September 23–October 9, 1949	Scorpio
October 10–22, 1949	Sagittarius
April 20–May 4, 1950	Pisces
May 5–20, 1950	Aries
September 23–October 3, 1950	Virgo
October 4–22, 1950	Libra
April 20–May 10, 1951	Gemini
May 11–20, 1951	Cancer
*September 23–24, 1951	Virgo
September 25–October 23, 1951	Virgo
April 20–May 3, 1952	Aries
May 4–20, 1952	Taurus
September 23–26, 1952	Libra
September 27–October 21, 1952	Scorpio
October 22, 1952	Sagittarius
*April 20–May 3, 1953	Aries
May 4–20, 1953	Aries
September 23, 1953	Leo
September 24–October 17, 1953	Virgo
October 18–22, 1953	Libra
April 20–27, 1954	Taurus
April 28–May 20, 1954	Gemini
September 23–October 22, 1954	Scorpio
April 20–23, 1955	Pisces
April 24–May 18, 1955	Aries
May 19–20, 1955	Taurus
September 23–October 12, 1955	Libra
October 13–23, 1955	Scorpio
April 20–May 7, 1956	Gemini
May 8–20, 1956	Cancer
September 23–October 5, 1956	Leo
October 6–22, 1956	Virgo

* = retrograde

IF YOU WERE BORN ON . . .	YOUR VENUS IS IN . . .
April 20–May 12, 1957	Taurus
May 13–20, 1957	Gemini
September 23–October 9, 1957	Scorpio
October 10–22, 1957	Sagittarius
April 20–May 4, 1958	Pisces
May 5–20, 1958	Aries
September 23–October 2, 1958	Virgo
October 3–22, 1958	Libra
April 20–May 9, 1959	Gemini
May 10–20, 1959	Cancer
September 23–24, 1959	Leo
September 25–October 23, 1959	Virgo
April 20–May 2, 1960	Aries
May 3–20, 1960	Taurus
September 23–26, 1960	Libra
September 27–October 20, 1960	Scorpio
October 21–22, 1960	Sagittarius
*April 20–May 1, 1961	Aries
May 2–20, 1961	Aries
September 23–October 17, 1961	Virgo
October 18–22, 1961	Libra
April 20–27, 1962	Taurus
April 28–May 20, 1962	Gemini
September 23–October 22, 1962	Scorpio
April 20–23, 1963	Pisces
April 24–May 18, 1963	Aries
May 19–20, 1963	Taurus
September 23–October 11, 1963	Libra
October 12–23, 1963	Scorpio
April 20–May 8, 1964	Gemini
May 9–20, 1964	Cancer
September 23–October 4, 1964	Leo
October 5–22, 1964	Virgo
April 20–May 11, 1965	Taurus
May 12–20, 1965	Gemini
September 23–October 8, 1965	Scorpio

IF YOU WERE BORN ON . . .	YOUR VENUS IS IN . . .
October 9–22, 1965	Sagittarius
April 20–May 4, 1966	Pisces
May 5–20, 1966	Aries
September 23–October 2, 1966	Virgo
October 3–22, 1966	Libra
April 20–May 9, 1967	Gemini
May 10–20, 1967	Cancer
September 23–30, 1967	Leo
October 1–23, 1967	Virgo
April 20–May 2, 1968	Aries
May 3–20, 1968	Taurus
September 22–25, 1968	Libra
September 26–October 20, 1968	Scorpio
October 21–22, 1968	Sagittarius
*April 20–28, 1969	Aries
April 29–May 20, 1969	Aries
September 23–October 16, 1969	Virgo
October 17–22, 1969	Libra
April 20–26, 1970	Taurus
April 27–May 20, 1970	Gemini
September 23–October 19, 1970	Scorpio
*October 20–22, 1970	Scorpio
April 20–22, 1971	Pisces
April 23–May 17, 1971	Aries
May 18–20, 1971	Taurus
September 23–October 10, 1971	Libra
October 11–23, 1971	Scorpio
April 19–May 9, 1972	Gemini
May 10–19, 1972	Cancer
September 22–October 4, 1972	Leo
October 5–22, 1972	Virgo
April 20–May 11, 1973	Taurus
May 12–20, 1973	Gemini
September 23–October 8, 1973	Scorpio
October 9–22, 1973	Sagittarius
April 20–May 3, 1974	Pisces

* = retrograde

IF YOU WERE BORN ON . . .	YOUR VENUS IS IN . . .
May 4–20, 1974	Aries
September 23–October 1, 1974	Virgo
October 2–22, 1974	Libra
April 20–May 8, 1975	Gemini
May 9–20, 1975	Cancer
September 23–October 3, 1975	Leo
October 4–23, 1975	Virgo
April 19–May 1, 1976	Aries
May 2–19, 1976	Taurus
September 22–25, 1976	Libra
September 26–October 19, 1976	Scorpio
October 20–22, 1976	Sagittarius
*April 20–26, 1977	Aries
April 27–May 20, 1977	Aries
September 23–October 16, 1977	Virgo
October 17–22, 1977	Libra
April 20–26, 1978	Taurus
April 27–May 20, 1978	Gemini
September 23–October 17, 1978	Scorpio
*October 18–22, 1978	Scorpio
April 20–22, 1979	Pisces
April 23–May 17, 1979	Aries
May 18–20, 1979	Taurus
September 23–October 10, 1979	Libra
October 11–23, 1979	Scorpio
April 19–May 11, 1980	Gemini
May 12–19, 1980	Cancer
September 22–October 3, 1980	Leo
October 4–22, 1980	Virgo
April 20–May 10, 1981	Taurus
May 11–20, 1981	Gemini
September 23–October 8, 1981	Scorpio
October 9–22, 1981	Sagittarius
April 20–May 3, 1982	Pisces
May 4–20, 1982	Aries
September 23–October 1, 1982	Virgo

IF YOU WERE BORN ON . . .	YOUR VENUS IS IN . . .
October 2–22, 1982	Libra
April 20–May 8, 1983	Gemini
May 9–20, 1983	Cancer
September 23–October 4, 1983	Leo
October 5–22, 1983	Virgo
April 19–May 1, 1984	Aries
May 2–19, 1984	Taurus
September 22–24, 1984	Libra
September 25–October 19, 1984	Scorpio
October 20–22, 1984	Sagittarius
*April 20–24, 1985	Aries
April 25–May 20, 1985	Aries
September 23–October 15, 1985	Virgo
October 16–22, 1985	Libra
April 20–25, 1986	Taurus
April 26–May 20, 1986	Gemini
September 23–October 14, 1986	Scorpio
*October 15–22, 1986	Scorpio
April 20–21, 1987	Pisces
April 22–May 16, 1987	Aries
May 17–20, 1987	Taurus
September 23–October 9, 1987	Libra
October 10–22, 1987	Scorpio
April 19–May 16, 1988	Gemini
May 17–19, 1988	Cancer
September 22–October 3, 1988	Leo
October 4–22, 1988	Virgo
April 20–May 10, 1989	Taurus
May 11–20, 1989	Gemini
September 23–October 7, 1989	Scorpio
October 8–22, 1989	Sagittarius
April 20–May 3, 1990	Pisces
May 4–20, 1990	Aries
September 23–30, 1990	Virgo
October 1–22, 1990	Libra
April 20–May 8, 1991	Gemini

* = retrograde

IF YOU WERE BORN ON . . .	YOUR VENUS IS IN . . .
May 9–20, 1991	Cancer
September 23–October 5, 1991	Leo
October 6–22, 1991	Virgo
April 19–30, 1992	Aries
May 1–19, 1992	Taurus
September 22–24, 1992	Libra
September 25–October 18, 1992	Scorpio
October 19–22, 1992	Sagittarius
*April 20–21, 1993	Aries
April 22–May 20, 1993	Aries
September 23–October 15, 1993	Virgo
October 16–22, 1993	Libra
April 20–25, 1994	Taurus
April 26–May 20, 1994	Gemini
September 23–October 12, 1994	Scorpio
*October 13–22, 1994	Scorpio
April 20–21, 1995	Pisces
April 22–May 15, 1995	Aries
May 16–20, 1995	Taurus
September 23–October 9, 1995	Libra
October 10–22, 1995	Scorpio
April 19–May 19, 1996	Gemini
September 22–October 3, 1996	Leo
October 4–22, 1996	Virgo
April 20–May 9, 1997	Taurus
May 10–20, 1997	Gemini
September 22–October 7, 1997	Scorpio
October 8–22, 1997	Sagittarius
April 20–May 2, 1998	Pisces
May 3–20, 1998	Aries
September 23–29, 1998	Virgo
September 30–October 22, 1998	Libra
April 20–May 7, 1999	Gemini
May 8–20, 1999	Cancer
September 23–October 6, 1999	Leo
October 7–22, 1999	Virgo

IF YOU WERE BORN ON . . .	YOUR VENUS IS IN . . .
April 19–30, 2000	Aries
May 1–19, 2000	Taurus
September 22–23, 2000	Libra
September 24–October 18, 2000	Scorpio
October 19–22, 2000	Sagittarius
April 20–May 19, 2001	Aries
September 22–October 14, 2001	Virgo
October 15–22, 2001	Libra
April 20–24, 2002	Taurus
April 25–May 19, 2002	Gemini
May 20, 2002	Cancer
September 23–October 9, 2002	Scorpio
*October 10–22, 2002	Scorpio
April 20, 2003	Pisces
April 21–May 15, 2003	Aries
May 16–20, 2003	Taurus
September 23–October 8, 2003	Libra
October 9–22, 2003	Scorpio
April 19–May 16, 2004	Gemini
*May 17–19, 2004	Gemini
September 22–October 2, 2004	Leo
October 3–22, 2004	Virgo
April 19–May 9, 2005	Taurus
May 10–19, 2005	Gemini
September 22–October 7, 2005	Scorpio
October 8–22, 2005	Sagittarius
April 20–May 2, 2006	Pisces
May 3–20, 2006	Aries
September 23–29, 2006	Virgo
September 30–October 22, 2006	Libra
April 20–May 7, 2007	Gemini
May 8–20, 2007	Cancer
September 23–October 7, 2007	Leo
October 8–22, 2007	Virgo
April 19–29, 2008	Aries
April 30–May 19, 2008	Taurus

* = retrograde

IF YOU WERE BORN ON . . .	YOUR VENUS IS IN . . .
September 22–23, 2008	Libra
September 24–October 17, 2008	Scorpio
October 18–22, 2008	Sagittarius
April 19–23, 2009	Pisces
April 24–May 19, 2009	Aries
September 22–October 13, 2009	Virgo
October 14–22, 2009	Libra
April 20–24, 2010	Taurus
April 25–May 19, 2010	Gemini
May 20, 2010	Cancer
September 23–October 7, 2010	Scorpio

IF YOU WERE BORN ON . . .	YOUR VENUS IS IN . . .
*October 8–22, 2010	Scorpio
April 20, 2011	Pisces
April 21–May 14, 2011	Aries
May 15–20, 2011	Taurus
September 23–October 8, 2011	Libra
October 9–22, 2011	Scorpio
April 19–May 14, 2012	Gemini
*May 15–19, 2012	Gemini
September 22–October 2, 2012	Leo
October 3–22, 2012	Virgo

* = retrograde

Indra, the Aryan god of war and fertility.

CHILD OF MARS

You look to yourself. Others may depend on a parent, spouse, or Providence to see them through hard times, but not you. You are independent, uncompromising, and heroic—traits that are too often in short supply but always in demand. Not only do you rely on yourself, but you assume others will rely on you as well. You even welcome it. The last thing you would ever do is let someone down.

You are driven to burst onto the scene. You may not know exactly what kind of scene you're bursting onto (or why you're there), but that's beside

KEY WORDS

The head, muscles, sex, passion, willpower, contests, fire, ovens, weapons, tools, metalwork, factories, soldiers, alchemists, surgeons, tailors, cooks, carpenters, fevers, spicy foods

BIG BREAKTHROUGHS

BENITO JUÁREZ
First Mexican of Indian descent to become president of Mexico
March 21, 1806

SANDRA DAY O'CONNOR
First woman appointed to the U.S. Supreme Court
March 26, 1930

COLIN POWELL
First African-American to be U.S. secretary of state
April 5, 1937

the point. You will make the most of any opening or opportunity that comes your way. What's important is that you take action. You feel compelled to get things up and running *immediately*. It's only when you're convinced you're safely past the delicate stage where a project can be nipped in the bud or a love affair fades as quickly as it flowered that you even think to take stock of your situation.

As a Child of Mars you gravitate to situations that match your intensity, which is why you're always undergoing a crisis, reaching a turning point, or staring down an opponent. You like cliffhangers where tensions and tempers run high. These are the times when you feel most alive. If you're simply frustrated with a situation, you're loud and blustery. However if there's a lot at stake—you're cool and focused. You see what needs to be done and are ready to jump in and do it because if you don't, nobody else will. If you could just go from crisis to crisis, you'd be in seventh heaven. Others may accuse you of looking for trouble, but the truth is you hate to be sidelined. You really are the spark of life popping out of the fire and looking to make a go of it in a world that seems cold, bleak, and in desperate need of heat and action.

You like getting riled up. The angrier you get, the more impassioned you become. It could even be said that anger is a real turn-on. Getting angry gives you an adrenaline rush. You feel your power and your force. Like a flame, your anger burns hot and fierce in the moment. But afterward, it's gone. This can be puzzling for people who aren't as comfortable with it as you. That's because they try to hold their temper in check. Not you. Getting angry is like laughing at a joke or yelling at a friend to hurry up and get a move on. You're just expressing what you're feeling in the moment. It's impossible for you to sit on your feelings. If something bothers you, then you need to get it off your chest—and you expect others to do the same. However others aren't quite as bold as you. And when they try to broach a subject gingerly, you can get very impatient. You may even feel that they're trying to rein you in.

You like flexing your muscles and will seek to gain the upper hand in any situation you face. You want to be on top and you embrace every challenge as a test of strength and ability. The harder you're pushed, the harder you'll push back. You are the epitome of the Olympic spirit—disciplined, able-bodied, and ready to go the distance.

Children of Mars are also "closet" intellectuals. You have a lot of brainpower to go along with that brawn. Yet because you always see yourself as just starting out, you may regard yourself as a perennial amateur.

RENÉ DESCARTES
Coined the phrase "I think therefore I am"
March 31, 1596

FERDINAND VON LINDEMANN
Proved the number pi is transcendental
April 12, 1852

SAMUEL BECKETT
April 13, 1906

You often apologize for not being bright enough or will make jokes at your own expense—which is surprising for people who push themselves as hard as you do. More often than not, it's a Child of Mars who will actually go and look up the meaning of the word that everyone else pretends to know. You look forward to testing your knowledge, you enjoy a battle of wits. If there's anything you love as much as a test of strength, it's a provocative conversation. Mars is the Planet of combat after all and thrives on friction.

Phrases like "pull yourself up by your bootstraps," "when the going gets tough, the tough get going," and "no pain, no gain" are your everyday mantras. You make no bones about the fact that we live in a competitive society. You love it when someone goes up against impossible odds and snatches a last-minute victory from the jaws of defeat. It was Thomas Jefferson, a Child of Mars, who wrote: "all men are created equal, that they are endowed by their Creator with certain unalienable Rights, that among these are Life, Liberty, and the pursuit of Happiness." You believe that everyone is equal in the arena and should have the opportunity to rise to the occasion of his or her talents and ambitions. This isn't an easy position to take and will often put you at the center of controversy. It requires a certain amount of grit to be a Gloria Steinem or an Erica Jong—two Children of Mars intent on leveling the playing field between men and women. It takes a lot of guts to be openly gay in a public forum like the entertainer Elton John and politician Barney Frank. But your Birthday Planet, Mars, isn't about keeping a stiff upper lip. It was Child of Mars Betty Ford who

BUTTING HEADS

BETTE DAVIS
April 5, 1908

JOAN CRAWFORD
March 23, 1908

GLORIA STEINEM
March 25, 1934

HUGH HEFNER
April 9, 1926

THOMAS JEFFERSON
April 13, 1743

JOHN ADAMS
October 30, 1735
*These two feuding American
revolutionaries both died
on the same day: the
Fourth of July*

had the courage to go public about her alcoholism and instead of stoically hiding it showed everyone that the greater battle was in struggling to overcome it. Mars, the red and angry Planet, isn't just about machismo.

Your Ruling Planet puts you in situations where you have to prove your mettle. Contests are very important to you, and Mars pushes you to realize your high standards of excellence. To you, the only way to be a multimillionaire athlete, one of the fifty most beautiful people, or a member of the Fortune 500 is to compete. You want to win the most coveted position, get the most eligible bachelor or bachelorette, and be outstanding in your field. You are the epitome of the self-made man or woman. However as a Child of Mars you know that in order to get what you want, someone else is going to be deprived of something they

DICK FRANCIS
October 31, 1920

JACKIE CHAN
April 7, 1954

LUCY LAWLESS
March 29, 1968

wanted. Your gain results in someone else's loss. Therefore you know all about jealousy and strife and are prepared to defend what belongs to you.

The best among us sits uneasily on the shoulders of all the near misses, runners-up, and honorable mentions. You know it doesn't take much for people to turn from supporting a winner when he's up to forgetting he exists when he's down. One slipup is all it takes to be dumped unceremoniously into the dustbin of history.

While your ambition is to stand in the winner's circle, it should also be your ambition to be courteous about it. You can afford to be generous if your good fortune makes it so. Besides, it's the classy thing to do. Good sportsmanship isn't just about taking setbacks in stride. It's also about

Lancelot rescuing Guinevere.

showing the proper grace and humility when you come out on top. To the victor go the spoils, but if the victor doesn't give something back—like rewarding those who helped make success possible—then the mood can turn nasty rather quickly. This is something that Child of Mars Ken Lay, former Enron chairman, learned to his own chagrin. When rivals grumble and adversaries flash their frozen smiles, make a point of thanking them earnestly and sincerely. After all, if it weren't for them, you wouldn't be on top of the heap. And if you want to stay on top, then it's a good idea to have them *for* you rather than *against* you.

You're often willing (perhaps even too willing) to give up creature comforts in order to get ahead. This is the secret pact you have with fate. You'll go through the fire if need be to show you've got what it takes, as long as you're rewarded with something that will make it all worthwhile. Now most people have an objective in mind at the outset of any venture, but being a Child of Mars, your objective isn't always clear. Indeed there are times when you haven't the foggiest notion of what it might be. You pursue whatever catches your fancy or tell yourself you'll know what you're looking for when you find it. There can be a lot of aimless wandering in your life or signing up for causes that make sense in the heat of the moment but leave you scratching your head later.

As a Child of Mars, you always have to ask yourself if you *truly* want what you're after. Sometimes you can pursue something just because it's withheld from you—it's a prize to be won. Then again you may stick with an obstacle out of force of habit because it gives you a reason for being, a reason to keep fighting and competing. The worst thing that can happen to desire isn't for it to be thwarted—frustration actually rekindles your fire. The worst thing that can happen is for you to get what you want, because

then it leaves you asking: is that all there is?

Desire seems like a straightforward emotion, but it's actually very complicated. It can be aroused by lust, hunger, and jealousy, yet the desire to better oneself can also inspire you to rein in passions and serve a higher good. Chivalry was designed so that the strong wouldn't abuse the weak. Over time it evolved into a code of honor that serves as the cornerstone for the armed forces as well as our police, firefighters, and emergency rescue units—which are all ruled by Mars. We're familiar with the idea that might makes right. Chivalry glorified the ideal that it takes a lot of might to do right.

Not just anyone cuts mustard with you. That person has to show the right qualities—smarts, ambition, humor, and grace under pressure. Prestige helps. Once someone convinces you that he or she possesses these traits, then that person receives an exclusive membership into your life. What does this person get in return? Undying devotion. Children of Mars are always there for the people they care about. It doesn't matter if you're in the middle of a shower. If someone needs you, you'll drop what you're doing and race to that person's side. A Child of Mars is one of the best friends one can hope to have. If someone is down on their luck, you'll give that person a place to stay, food on the table, or money—no questions asked. However

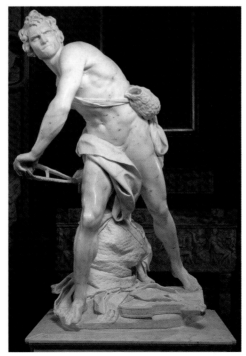

David taking aim at Goliath.

PILLOW TALK

CASANOVA
April 2, 1725

DORIS DAY
April 3, 1924

SARAH JESSICA PARKER
March 25, 1965

you do believe in self-sufficiency, and your aim is to get someone back up on their feet. But if this person happens to be the apple of your eye, well, you'll positively spoil him or her with heroic deeds and riches.

You love to fall in love. The suspense of whether or not this person feels the same keeps you on edge. The longer the separations—or better yet, the more complicated the circumstances—the more ardent you become. For a creature of impulse, however, you can be very selective. You will zero in on those qualities you like while ignoring anything that doesn't gel with how you see the object of your desire. Little things like faults or even warning signs are pushed to one side. In some cases, it may even be your new love's personality that's perceived as getting in the way. As you can imagine, this can make getting together quite complicated. But then again, you believe it's better to pursue happiness than to attain it. Part of you believes that not having what you want makes you stronger, whereas getting it makes you weaker. It's not unlike athletes who—in order to ensure a peak performance—will abstain from sex before the big game.

You can spend a lot of time reinventing the wheel when it comes to relationships. You may say it's because you haven't found anyone who can keep your interest or you were misled into believing you had something special. Perhaps the biggest problem you Children of Mars can have is that although you're built for gallantry, your strongest ties are to your comrades-in-arms. In other words, it's not romance that inspires you but the romantic quest itself. Finding a lover or spouse who shares your love for the quest would be truly fulfilling . . . almost as fulfilling as that quest never coming to an end.

Mars returns to where it was in the sky when you were born approximately every fifteen birthdays. What this means is that the ages fifteen to seventeen, thirty to thirty-two, forty-five to forty-seven, sixty to sixty-two, etc. are going to be very important to you. These are the times when you feel compelled to break out on your own or to take back the power in your life if you've lost direction. These will undoubtedly be peak experiences, when everything feels like it's do or die, but given that you are a Child of Mars, you'll also be in your element.

Go ahead and turn to the Mars tables on page 127 to find what sign your Ruling Planet was in on the day that you were born. Part III of this book will show how your Ruling Planet varies its expression from sign to sign. If there is an asterisk (*) next to your birth date, then you were born during a retrograde. If so, you'll want to come back and read the following:

CHILD OF MARS RETROGRADE

Those born when Mars is retrograde tend to start out slow and then pick up speed as they go along. *Retrograde* refers to a backward motion. The planet Mars doesn't actually reverse direction. That's just the way it looks to us. It's an optical illusion that occurs periodically from Earth's viewpoint, giving the impression of a planet moving backward against the setting of constellations in the sky. When a planet is retrograde, its energy

becomes the opposite of what it is when it's direct. Since Mars is the Planet of gumption and drive, then that's what gets turned inside out. This isn't to say that those born with Mars retrograde are meek and mild or hopeless when it comes to tossing a baseball. But Mars retrograde can mean difficulty dealing with male authority figures, fear of rejection, an inability to know when enough is enough, and problems with anger. In extreme examples it can also bring self-sabotage and duplicity (usually involving men).

A feeling that the game has been fixed haunts many Children of Mars Retrograde. You believe in competition and will always put your best foot forward, but when your Birthday Planet is retrograde it's almost as if an invisible hand is tipping the hurdle just as you're about to spring over it. Being a Child of Mars you won't call foul at first, but as you see your peers bolt forward while you have to clamber over obstacles it's only natural that you would ask: what gives? Another unfortunate side effect to being born with Mars retrograde is that—given your flair for controversy—you can end up becoming the target of others' ire. A position you champion is so unpopular or so incendiary that it can end up looking as if you instigated the trouble. Rodney King, the motorist whose beating at the hands of the Los Angeles police set off a wave of race riots, is a Child of Mars Retrograde.

Things don't come easily for Children of Mars Retrograde, but where others burn out early or fold their cards, you will keep on pushing—no matter how impossible the odds. Eventually you will succeed, as long as you don't wallow in the sour grapes. It's a tall order, admittedly, but to be born under a retrograde planet is to be assigned a special kind of fate. Your actions may often backfire or be ill timed, but they have an ironic way of vindicating you in the end. If there's anyone who can come up from behind in the last minute and win an unexpected victory—it's a Child of Mars Retrograde.

WHAT SIGN IS MARS IN?

IF YOU WERE BORN ON . . .	YOUR MARS IS IN . . .
March 21–April 7, 1900	Pisces
April 8–19, 1900	Aries
October 23–November 21, 1900	Leo
*March 21–April 3, 1901	Leo
April 4–19, 1901	Leo
October 24–November 21, 1901	Sagittarius
March 21–April 20, 1902	Aries
October 24–November 22, 1902	Virgo
*March 21–April 18, 1903	Libra
*April 19–20, 1903	Virgo
October 24–November 2, 1903	Sagittarius
November 3–22, 1903	Capricorn
March 21–April 5, 1904	Aries
April 6–19, 1904	Taurus
October 23–November 19, 1904	Virgo
November 20–21, 1904	Libra

IF YOU WERE BORN ON . . .	YOUR MARS IS IN . . .
March 21–April 1, 1905	Scorpio
*April 2–19, 1905	Scorpio
October 24–November 17, 1905	Capricorn
November 18–21, 1905	Aquarius
March 21–April 20, 1906	Taurus
October 24–29, 1906	Virgo
October 30–November 22, 1906	Libra
March 21–31, 1907	Sagittarius
April 1–20, 1907	Capricorn
October 24–November 22, 1907	Aquarius
March 21–April 6, 1908	Taurus
April 7–19, 1908	Gemini
October 23–November 21, 1908	Libra
March 21–April 8, 1909	Capricorn
April 9–19, 1909	Aquarius
October 24–November 19, 1909	Pisces

* = retrograde

IF YOU WERE BORN ON . . .	YOUR MARS IS IN . . .
November 20–21, 1909	Aries
March 21–April 19, 1910	Gemini
October 24–November 5, 1910	Libra
November 6–22, 1910	Scorpio
March 21–April 20, 1911	Aquarius
*October 24–November 22, 1911	Gemini
March 20–April 4, 1912	Gemini
April 5–19, 1912	Cancer
October 23–November 21, 1912	Scorpio
March 21–29, 1913	Aquarius
March 30–April 19, 1913	Pisces
October 24–November 21, 1913	Cancer
March 21–April 19, 1914	Cancer
October 24–November 10, 1914	Scorpio
November 11–22, 1914	Sagittarius
March 21–April 15, 1915	Pisces
April 16–20, 1915	Aries
October 24–November 22, 1915	Leo
*March 20, 1916	Leo
March 21–April 19, 1916	Leo
October 23–November 21, 1916	Sagittarius
March 21–25, 1917	Pisces
March 26–April 19, 1917	Aries
October 23–November 1, 1917	Leo
November 2–21, 1917	Virgo
*March 21–April 19, 1918	Virgo
October 24–November 10, 1918	Sagittarius
November 11–22, 1918	Capricorn
March 21–April 14, 1919	Aries
April 15–20, 1919	Taurus
October 24–November 22, 1919	Virgo
*March 20–April 19, 1920	Scorpio
October 23–November 21, 1920	Capricorn
March 21–24, 1921	Aries
March 25–April 19, 1921	Taurus
October 23–November 5, 1921	Virgo

IF YOU WERE BORN ON . . .	YOUR MARS IS IN . . .
November 6–21, 1921	Libra
March 21–April 19, 1922	Sagittarius
October 24–29, 1922	Capricorn
October 30–November 22, 1922	Aquarius
March 21–April 15, 1923	Taurus
April 16–20, 1923	Gemini
October 24–November 22, 1923	Libra
March 20–April 19, 1924	Capricorn
October 23–November 21, 1924	Pisces
March 21–23, 1925	Taurus
March 24–April 19, 1925	Gemini
October 23–November 12, 1925	Libra
November 13–21, 1925	Scorpio
March 21–22, 1926	Capricorn
March 23–April 19, 1926	Aquarius
*October 24–November 22, 1926	Taurus
March 21–April 16, 1927	Gemini
April 17–20, 1927	Cancer
October 24–25, 1927	Libra
October 26–November 22, 1927	Scorpio
March 20–April 6, 1928	Aquarius
April 7–19, 1928	Pisces
October 23–November 11, 1928	Cancer
*November 12–21, 1928	Cancer
March 21–April 19, 1929	Cancer
October 23–November 17, 1929	Scorpio
November 18–21, 1929	Sagittarius
March 21–April 19, 1930	Pisces
October 24–November 22, 1930	Leo
March 21–29, 1931	Cancer
March 30–April 20, 1931	Leo
October 24–29, 1931	Scorpio
October 30–November 22, 1931	Sagittarius
March 20–April 2, 1932	Pisces
April 3–19, 1932	Aries
October 23–November 12, 1932	Leo

* = retrograde

IF YOU WERE BORN ON . . .	YOUR MARS IS IN . . .
November 13–21, 1932	Virgo
*March 21–April 11, 1933	Virgo
April 12–19, 1933	Virgo
October 23–November 18, 1933	Sagittarius
November 19–21, 1933	Capricorn
March 21–April 19, 1934	Aries
October 24–November 21, 1934	Virgo
*March 21–April 20, 1935	Libra
October 24–27, 1935	Sagittarius
October 28–November 22, 1935	Capricorn
March 20–31, 1936	Aries
April 1–19, 1936	Taurus
October 23–November 13, 1936	Virgo
November 14–21, 1936	Libra
March 21–April 13, 1937	Sagittarius
*April 14–19, 1937	Sagittarius
October 23–November 10, 1937	Capricorn
November 11–21, 1937	Aquarius
March 21–April 19, 1938	Taurus
October 24, 1938	Virgo
October 25–November 21, 1938	Libra
March 21–April 19, 1939	Capricorn
October 24–November 18, 1939	Aquarius
November 19–22, 1939	Pisces
March 20–31, 1940	Taurus
April 1–19, 1940	Gemini
October 23–November 19, 1940	Libra
November 20–21, 1940	Scorpio
March 21–April 1, 1941	Capricorn
April 2–19, 1941	Aquarius
*October 23–November 9, 1941	Aries
November 10–21, 1941	Aries
March 21–April 19, 1942	Gemini
October 24–31, 1942	Libra
November 1–21, 1942	Scorpio
March 21–April 16, 1943	Aquarius

IF YOU WERE BORN ON . . .	YOUR MARS IS IN . . .
April 17–19, 1943	Pisces
October 24–27, 1943	Gemini
*October 28–November 22, 1943	Gemini
March 20–27, 1944	Gemini
March 28–April 19, 1944	Cancer
October 23–November 21, 1944	Scorpio
March 20–24, 1945	Aquarius
March 25–April 19, 1945	Pisces
October 23–November 10, 1945	Cancer
November 11–21, 1945	Leo
March 21–April 19, 1946	Cancer
October 24–November 5, 1946	Scorpio
November 6–21, 1946	Sagittarius
March 21–April 10, 1947	Pisces
April 11–19, 1947	Aries
October 24–November 22, 1947	Leo
*March 20–28, 1948	Leo
March 29–April 19, 1948	Leo
October 23–November 21, 1948	Sagittarius
March 20, 1949	Pisces
March 21–April 19, 1949	Aries
October 23–26, 1949	Leo
October 27–November 21, 1949	Virgo
*March 21–27, 1950	Libra
*March 28–April 19, 1950	Virgo
October 23–November 5, 1950	Sagittarius
November 6–21, 1950	Capricorn
March 21–April 9, 1951	Aries
April 10–19, 1951	Taurus
October 24–November 22, 1951	Virgo
March 20–24, 1952	Scorpio
*March 25–April 19, 1952	Scorpio
October 23–November 20, 1952	Capricorn
November 21, 1952	Aquarius
March 20–April 19, 1953	Taurus
October 23–31, 1953	Virgo

*= retrograde

IF YOU WERE BORN ON . . .	YOUR MARS IS IN . . .
November 1–21, 1953	Libra
March 21–April 11, 1954	Sagittarius
April 12–19, 1954	Capricorn
October 23–November 21, 1954	Aquarius
March 21–April 9, 1955	Taurus
April 10–19, 1955	Gemini
October 24–November 22, 1955	Libra
March 20–April 13, 1956	Capricorn
April 14–19, 1956	Aquarius
October 23–November 21, 1956	Pisces
March 20–April 19, 1957	Gemini
October 23–November 7, 1957	Libra
November 8–21, 1957	Scorpio
March 21–April 19, 1958	Aquarius
*October 23–28, 1958	Gemini
*October 29–November 21, 1958	Taurus
March 21–April 9, 1959	Gemini
April 10–19, 1959	Cancer
October 24–November 22, 1959	Scorpio
March 20–April 1, 1960	Aquarius
April 2–19, 1960	Pisces
October 23–November 19, 1960	Cancer
*November 20–21, 1960	Cancer
March 20–April 19, 1961	Cancer
October 23–November 12, 1961	Scorpio
November 13–21, 1961	Sagittarius
March 21–April 18, 1962	Pisces
April 19, 1962	Aries
October 23–November 21, 1962	Leo
March 21–April 19, 1963	Leo
October 24, 1963	Scorpio
October 25–November 22, 1963	Sagittarius
March 20–28, 1964	Pisces
March 29–April 19, 1964	Aries
October 23–November 5, 1964	Leo
November 6–21, 1964	Virgo

IF YOU WERE BORN ON . . .	YOUR MARS IS IN . . .
*March 20–April 18, 1965	Virgo
April 19, 1965	Virgo
October 23–November 13, 1965	Sagittarius
November 14–21, 1965	Capricorn
March 21–April 16, 1966	Aries
April 17–19, 1966	Taurus
October 23–November 21, 1966	Virgo
*March 21–30, 1967	Scorpio
*March 31–April 19, 1967	Libra
October 24–November 22, 1967	Capricorn
March 20–26, 1968	Aries
March 27–April 19, 1968	Taurus
October 23–November 8, 1968	Virgo
November 9–21, 1968	Libra
March 20–April 19, 1969	Sagittarius
October 23–November 3, 1969	Capricorn
November 4–21, 1969	Aquarius
March 21–April 17, 1970	Taurus
April 18–19, 1970	Gemini
October 23–November 21, 1970	Libra
March 21–April 19, 1971	Capricorn
October 24–November 5, 1971	Aquarius
November 6–21, 1971	Pisces
March 20–26, 1972	Taurus
March 27–April 18, 1972	Gemini
October 23–November 14, 1972	Libra
November 15–21, 1972	Scorpio
March 20–25, 1973	Capricorn
March 26–April 19, 1973	Aquarius
*October 23–28, 1973	Taurus
*October 29–November 21, 1973	Aries
March 21–April 19, 1974	Gemini
October 23–27, 1974	Libra
October 28–November 21, 1974	Scorpio
March 21–April 10, 1975	Aquarius
April 11–19, 1975	Pisces

= retrograde

IF YOU WERE BORN ON . . .	YOUR MARS IS IN . . .	IF YOU WERE BORN ON . . .	YOUR MARS IS IN . . .
October 24–November 5, 1975	Cancer	March 28–April 19, 1986	Capricorn
*November 6–21, 1975	Cancer	October 23–November 21, 1986	Aquarius
March 20–April 18, 1976	Cancer	March 21–April 4, 1987	Taurus
October 23–November 19, 1976	Scorpio	April 5–19, 1987	Gemini
November 20–21, 1976	Sagittarius	October 23–November 21, 1987	Libra
March 20–April 19, 1977	Pisces	March 20–April 5, 1988	Capricorn
October 23–25, 1977	Cancer	April 6–18, 1988	Aquarius
October 26–November 21, 1977	Leo	*October 23–27, 1988	Pisces
March 20–April 9, 1978	Cancer	October 28–31, 1988	Pisces
April 10–19, 1978	Leo	November 1–21, 1988	Aries
October 23–November 1, 1978	Scorpio	March 20–April 19, 1989	Gemini
November 2–21, 1978	Sagittarius	October 23–November 3, 1989	Libra
March 21–April 6, 1979	Pisces	November 4–21, 1989	Scorpio
April 7–19, 1979	Aries	March 20–April 19, 1990	Aquarius
October 24–November 18, 1979	Leo	*October 23–November 21, 1990	Gemini
November 19–21, 1979	Virgo	March 21–April 2, 1991	Gemini
*March 20–April 5, 1980	Leo	April 3–19, 1991	Cancer
April 6–18, 1980	Leo	October 23–November 21, 1991	Scorpio
October 23–November 21, 1980	Sagittarius	March 20–27, 1992	Aquarius
March 20–April 19, 1981	Aries	March 28–April 18, 1992	Pisces
October 23–November 21, 1981	Virgo	October 23–November 21, 1992	Cancer
*March 20–April 19, 1982	Libra	March 20–April 19, 1993	Cancer
October 23–30, 1982	Sagittarius	October 23–November 8, 1993	Scorpio
October 31–November 21, 1982	Capricorn	November 9–21, 1993	Sagittarius
March 21–April 4, 1983	Aries	March 20–April 13, 1994	Pisces
April 5–19, 1983	Taurus	April 14–19, 1994	Aries
October 23–November 17, 1983	Virgo	October 23–November 21, 1994	Leo
November 18–21, 1983	Libra	*March 21–23, 1995	Leo
March 20–April 4, 1984	Scorpio	March 24–April 19, 1995	Leo
*April 5–18, 1984	Scorpio	October 23–November 21, 1995	Sagittarius
October 23–November 14, 1984	Capricorn	March 20–23, 1996	Pisces
November 15–21, 1984	Aquarius	March 24–April 18, 1996	Aries
March 20–April 19, 1985	Taurus	October 23–29, 1996	Leo
October 23–26, 1985	Virgo	October 30–November 21, 1996	Virgo
October 27–November 21, 1985	Libra	*March 20–April 19, 1997	Virgo
March 20–27, 1986	Sagittarius	October 23–November 8, 1997	Sagittarius

* = retrograde

IF YOU WERE BORN ON . . .	YOUR MARS IS IN . . .
November 9–21, 1997	Capricorn
March 20–April 12, 1998	Aries
April 13–19, 1998	Taurus
October 23–November 21, 1998	Virgo
*March 21–April 19, 1999	Scorpio
October 23–November 21, 1999	Capricorn
March 20–22, 2000	Aries
March 23–April 18, 2000	Taurus
October 23–November 3, 2000	Virgo
November 4–21, 2000	Libra
March 20–April 19, 2001	Sagittarius
October 23–26, 2001	Capricorn
October 27–November 21, 2001	Aquarius
March 20–April 12, 2002	Taurus
April 13–19, 2002	Gemini
October 23–November 21, 2002	Libra
March 21–April 19, 2003	Capricorn
October 23–November 21, 2003	Pisces
March 20, 2004	Taurus
March 21–April 18, 2004	Gemini
October 23–November 10, 2004	Libra
November 11–20, 2004	Scorpio
March 20–April 18, 2005	Aquarius
*October 23–November 21, 2005	Taurus

IF YOU WERE BORN ON . . .	YOUR MARS IS IN . . .
March 20–April 13, 2006	Gemini
April 14–19, 2006	Cancer
October 23–November 21, 2006	Scorpio
March 21–April 5, 2007	Aquarius
April 6–19, 2007	Pisces
October 23–November 14, 2007	Cancer
*November 15–21, 2007	Cancer
March 20–April 18, 2008	Cancer
October 23–November 15, 2008	Scorpio
November 16–20, 2008	Sagittarius
March 20–April 18, 2009	Pisces
October 23–November 21, 2009	Leo
March 20–April 19, 2010	Leo
October 23–27, 2010	Scorpio
October 28–November 21, 2010	Sagittarius
March 20–April 1, 2011	Pisces
April 2–19, 2011	Aries
October 23–November 10, 2011	Leo
November 11–21, 2011	Virgo
*March 20–April 13, 2012	Virgo
April 14–18, 2012	Virgo
October 23–November 16, 2012	Sagittarius
November 17–20, 2012	Capricorn

* = retrograde

Child of Jupiter Mark Twain's Huckleberry Finn.

CHILD OF JUPITER

Your life is a grand adventure. You never know what lies beyond the next bend. The most extraordinary things just seem to happen. That's why you can't wait to see what opportunities tomorrow might bring. But as a Child of Jupiter, you also know that there's a greater purpose at work. It's in your nature to dream the impossible dream. Where would our civilization be if everyone accepted their limits and decided to huddle safely within bounds? There would be no outstanding art, no great inventions, no mind-boggling discoveries. It's the Children of

KEY WORDS

Adventure, voyages, storms, blood, temperament, humor, good fortune, thigh, wisdom, morals, cities, politics, philosophy, religion, justice, philanthropy, publishers, higher education, imports/exports, textiles, state lotteries

JONATHAN SWIFT
Author of Gulliver's Travels
November 30, 1667

JACK KEROUAC
Author of On the Road
March 12, 1922

DOUGLAS ADAMS
Wrote Hitchhiker's Guide
to the Galaxy
March 11, 1952

Jupiter we have to thank for broadening both our physical and metaphysical horizons. Your restless search for greener pastures enriches everyone's lives.

Your love for exploring anything new lends itself to different ideas, fresh perspectives, and ultimately, more enlightened ways of living. When you go to places you haven't been before or meet people you wouldn't usually talk to, you increase your knowledge and your wisdom. You open your world. Instead of relating life to what you already know, you expand on

what you know so you can embrace more of life. Few people live life as fully as you do or revel in its profound diversity.

Your Ruling Planet instills in you a perpetual sense of wonder. Without that, anything different is bizarre at best, threatening at worst. You Children of Jupiter are the ones who can look at something completely alien to your background and say: "Hey, maybe these Amazon rain forest Indians are on to something. Perhaps these plants and herbs really do have medicinal value." Look at how popular Buddhism and yoga are in the United States. Think of the powerful influence Japan has had on the way we do business. Jupiter rules over this unique cross-fertilization. Instead of conquering another country, wiping out everything that's there, and then building a parking garage, some governments have gradually learned to take what they see and incorporate it into their own cultures—thus expanding and reinventing their own societies. Children of Jupiter assimilate new experiences every day. What initially appears exotic or foreign becomes a part *of* you, rather than being seen as apart *from* you.

Your Ruling Planet also acts like a call to adventure. And that call can come in a variety of ways. It might be accepting an invitation to live abroad, or falling in love with someone from an entirely different background, or going to a job interview on a lark only to discover you stumbled onto what you've been looking to do all your life. But you don't have to travel to the far corners of the world for your horizons to be expanded. A shake-up in your belief system can do this, as can the shocking realization that an injustice has taken place.

When you answer your Birthday Planet's call to adventure, you don't answer with your intellect. You answer with your spirit. It can even be said that Jupiter rules the spirit, because it's your spirit that seeks to transcend its limitations and connect with a higher purpose. Just when you come to the end of one journey, you start wondering when the next one will begin. You can't stand to stay in one place too long.

Jupiter is the Planet of wanderlust—with accents on *wander* and *lust*.

LIVE! LIVE! LIVE!

CHRISTINA, QUEEN OF SWEDEN
Abdicated her throne to pursue cultural interests
December 8, 1626

MARIA CALLAS
December 2, 1923

SAMMY DAVIS JR.
December 8, 1925

**EXPLORE YOUR
WORLD**

SIR RICHARD BURTON
*Famed British explorer
and adventurer*
March 19, 1821

WILLIAM F. CODY
Aka "Buffalo Bill"
February 26, 1846

MARGARET MEAD
Author of Coming of Age
in Samoa
December 16, 1901

In mythology, Jupiter (or Zeus) is always sneaking out the back door of Mount Olympus so he can go frolic among the mortal folk. Unlike other father gods in world religions, Zeus is not aloof or distant. Zeus takes a very active role in the creative process. With equal ardor, he impregnates queens, princesses, shepherdesses, goddesses, and various sundry nymphs. Now it could be said that Zeus is a philanderer, but then again, if it weren't for his many escapades, we would never have had all the great gods and goddesses, heroes, and thinkers that sprang up as a result. By commingling the immortal with the mortal, Zeus brings a bit of heaven down to earth.

Admittedly what makes for a romantic metaphor may prove hard to explain to someone you're dating. Which is why, as a Child of Jupiter, you should put off settling down

Jupiter, in the form of a cloud, seducing Io.

until *after* you've sown your wild oats. Nevertheless there is a "share the wealth" tendency to your Birthday Planet. This comes from a generosity of spirit. Jupiter may have been the patron god of Roman emperors, but he was equally protective of those who could not fend for themselves. The poet Ovid tells a charming story about Jupiter and Mercury visiting a town incognito. They are turned away from every door but one. An elderly couple, barely able to feed themselves, invites the two strangers in to share a meal. As they wait upon their guests, miraculous things begin to happen. The wine pitcher refills itself. Olives and figs reappear as soon as they've been eaten. Eventually it dawns on the couple that these are no ordinary strangers, and the gods reveal their true identities. Impressed with the couple's hospitality, they honor the mortals by making them guardians of a magnificent temple. The rest of the town is destroyed unceremoniously. Years later when the man and wife are on the verge of death, they are transformed into trees that stand forever entwined in each other's embrace. And that's pretty much how your Ruling Planet works. It's the opportunity that comes knocking—disguised and unannounced.

However, Jupiter is more than just a stroke of good fortune. It also serves a higher purpose. Many people can have lucky things happen to

them, but it doesn't necessarily mean they'll do anything constructive with it. They might hoard their good fortune, squander it, or just never recognize a break when they see it—even if it is staring them in the face. Jupiter may be the Planet of good fortune, but that doesn't mean you'll always recognize the true value of what comes your way—just like the neighbors of the elderly couple who didn't recognize the gods they turned away from their door. That's why as a Child of Jupiter you'll always extend the benefit of the doubt. You may not like what's happening, but you believe that there's a higher purpose being served and in time you'll come to understand it. Your unique talent is in gleaning the hidden meaning. What takes the sting out of a disappointment is if you can walk away from it having learned something new. You have something positive to build on for the future. You believe that there's a moral to the story instead of a

King Solomon reading the Torah.

gripe—whatever happens in life is somehow meant to be. A life without purpose would be like digging to the bottom of the Cracker Jack box only to discover there's no toy surprise inside.

Your Birthday Planet rules over government, justice, philosophy, and spiritual beliefs. You believe in a higher power. You also believe in the essential goodness of people, which is why you will try to bring everyone together under one roof without stifling anyone's freedom or individuality. As a Child of Jupiter, you'll bend over backward in order to main-

C. COLLODI
Author of Pinocchio
November 24, 1826

CHARLES SCHULZ
Creator of Peanuts
November 26, 1922

C. S. LEWIS
Wrote Chronicles of Narnia
November 29, 1898

tain the very dynamics that make people creative in the first place. You believe that questions and debates expand a person's horizons just as much as a sense of wonder and a need to explore the world. This is what freedom means to you. It isn't the freedom *from*, but the freedom *to do*.

You're concerned with metaphysical values like—what do I believe in? Am I doing the right thing? Does bumping into this person I haven't seen in a dog's age serve some kind of higher purpose? As a Child of Jupiter, you recognize the potential in something and seek to bring it out in some way—like Michelangelo (a Child of Jupiter), who first saw his *David* in a massive block of marble, or a reformer who recognizes the heart of a saint beneath the skin of a sinner. You possess enough faith to cultivate the potential of something sight unseen.

Needless to say, not everyone shares your confidence that there's a higher purpose at work. Indeed they may even feel that life with you is like being handcuffed to Pollyanna—or even shanghaied by Auntie Mame— you're so insistent that everything will work out in the end.

You *need* to believe in what you do. If you can't get behind it, then your enthusiasm will fall flat, and no amount of coaxing or cajoling in the world will change it. However if the spirit moves you, your zeal is like a roaring fire. This is what makes you Children of Jupiter such natural cheerleaders and rabble-rousers. The downside, however, is in your tendency to dress things up. You believe in a moral universe. You don't believe in accidents or happenstance, nor do you believe in such a thing

I HAVE IT ON A HIGHER AUTHORITY

CARRY NATION
Champion of prohibition
November 25, 1846

WILLIAM BLAKE
*English painter, poet,
and mystic*
November 28, 1757

TAMMY FAYE BAKKER
*Famed television evangelist
and singer*
March 7, 1942

as a fight for fight's sake. A fight is something you do in the name of justice—for your country, God, or whatever higher power you believe in—just so long as it's *justified*. Jupiter was the god of justice, and being a Child of Jupiter, you can justify just about anything when push comes to shove. This can come across in some of your more far-fetched interpretations for why things happen the way they do. The Enlightenment philosopher Voltaire (another Child of Jupiter) satirized this unabashed optimism in his masterpiece *Candide*—which chronicles the misadventures of its hero whose experience of violence, rape, disaster, and tragedy is matched only by the ridiculous extent to which he will go to find the thinnest lining in the darkest cloud—even if he has to make it up.

Thankfully your Birthday Planet is famous for its good humor and bonhomie. A natural mimic, you love to play the clown, and one of the first people you'll make fun of is yourself. Child of Jupiter Woody Allen has turned self-parody into an art form. In the classic film *Manhattan*, a character asks Allen: "Who do you think you are? God?" And Allen responds: "Well, I have to model myself after someone."

There are two types of fortune that are ruled by Jupiter—dumb luck and divine guidance. Dumb luck is just something you fall into. Maybe you do something with it, maybe you don't. Yet because there's this feeling that it's something that could have happened to anyone, you don't feel too much remorse when it leaves again. The overall sentiment is: Easy come, easy go. However divine guidance is different. With divine guidance, you feel like good fortune is happening to you for a reason. It's more than just a reward for a job well done, it's like a calling card from your higher purpose. Do you just make a grab for what you can get while the getting's good or do you invite good fortune into your life? If you can recognize the value of what your Ruling Planet gives you vis-à-vis a lucky break, a misadventure, or an impossible dream, then you'll be able to make out the vague outlines of something else at work. You warm to the notions of generosity, optimism, and that uniquely jovial sentiment: we're all in it together. Good begets good. The more good you put out there, the greater good you receive. Just like the wine pitcher that refills itself and the olives and figs that rematerialize as soon as they're eaten. It's a participation thing where you give something back to the world instead of always taking something away. You enter into a reciprocal relationship with life. This is how your Birthday Planet transforms you into the instrument of its higher purpose. Jupiter, Planet of philanthropy, is symbolic of the Divine's love affair with humanity.

MICHELANGELO
March 6, 1475

LUDWIG VAN BEETHOVEN
December 17, 1770

GUSTAVE EIFFEL
Built the Eiffel Tower
December 15, 1832

Once every twelve birthdays, Jupiter returns to where it was in the sky when you were born. The ages of twelve, twenty-four, thirty-six, forty-eight, etc., are going to be very important to you.

Zeus was the only Greek god who could generate new gods from his own body. After he swallowed the titaness Metis, Athena, the goddess of wisdom, sprang full grown from his head. When his mortal lover Semele is killed, Zeus has the fetus she's carrying sewn up in his thigh. He later gives birth to the god Dionysus. These myths illustrate how your Ruling Planet incorporates disparate elements to create new forms.

Every twelve years something emerges full blown into your life. It could be a talent, a calling, or a dramatic change in circumstances. But what appears so utterly new and different is the outgrowth of what came before. Jupiter is about the process of taking something embryonic into yourself and it reemerging as a potential fully realized, therefore every twelve years something old will fall away in order to make room for something fresh and dynamic.

Go ahead and turn to the Jupiter tables on page 144 to find what sign your Ruling Planet was in on the day you were born. Part III of this book will show how your Ruling Planet varies its expression from sign to sign. If there is an asterisk (*) next to your birth date, then you were born during a retrograde. If so, you'll want to come back and read the following:

CHILD OF JUPITER RETROGRADE

Retrograde refers to a backward motion. The planet Jupiter doesn't actually reverse direction. That's just the way it looks to us. It's an optical illusion that occurs periodically from Earth's viewpoint, giving the impression of a planet moving backward against the setting of constellations in the sky. When a planet is retrograde, its energy becomes the opposite of what it is when it's direct. Since Jupiter is the Planet of good fortune and higher purpose, that's what gets turned inside out. This isn't to say that if you're a Child of Jupiter Retrograde you can't win at anything—even a coin toss. What it implies is that you regard fate as fickle and accepted long ago that it's up to you to make your own luck.

Like Saturn, Jupiter is a teacher of life lessons. The difference is that Saturn withholds while Jupiter gives. As a Child of Jupiter Retrograde, you may feel that the cosmos is always playing the same kind of practical joke. Just when you get loaded up with all sorts of goodies and you feel like your life is just starting to go somewhere, the plug is inexplicably pulled and things come to a standstill. Yet as with anything having to do with your

Birthday Planet, there is a purpose behind it. The purpose is to see if you're worthy.

The only time when anyone truly looks past their good fortune to see if there is such a thing as a higher purpose is when that good fortune *stops* coming their way. This causes a crisis in faith, when people curse their luck or scold themselves for having been so gullible. As a Child of Jupiter Retrograde, you're no stranger to fortune's fits and starts. But because Jupiter rules the experiences that enrich—and more importantly how you interpret those experiences—you're very familiar with the fine line between belief and faith. To believe in something is to accept it as true—no matter how fantastic. This applies to Noah's ark, alien abductions, and whether or not there really will be such a thing as Social Security when you retire. Faith implies a certain willingness on your part to make something *come* true. Crises of faith bring out the adventurer in you. Do you turn your back on those aspirations that went up in smoke or do you go and take a running leap into the unknown—trusting that some sort of higher power will guide you to where you need to be in the end? The latter, obviously.

You may have more mixed blessings than lucky breaks, but your Ruling Planet Retrograde will still endow you with character, conscience, and a benevolent spirit. Considering how good fortune is apt to bring out the worst in someone as well as the best, these qualities may be all you need to make something of yourself.

PHILANTHROPY

SAINT JOHN OF GOD
*Patron saint of hospitals
and the sick*
March 8, 1495

JOSEPH II
*"Enlightened despot" and
Holy Roman Emperor
(1765–1790)*
March 13, 1741

SAMUEL PUTNAM AVERY
March 17, 1822

BARON DE HIRSCH
December 9, 1831

ANDREW CARNEGIE
November 25, 1835

J. PAUL GETTY
December 15, 1892

WALTER H. ANNENBERG
March 13, 1908

CAROLINE KENNEDY
SCHLOSSBERG
November 27, 1957

WHAT SIGN IS JUPITER IN?

IF YOU WERE BORN ON . . .	YOUR JUPITER IS IN . . .
February 19–March 20, 1900	Sagittarius
November 22–December 21, 1900	Sagittarius
February 19–March 20, 1901	Capricorn
November 22–December 21, 1901	Capricorn
February 19–March 20, 1902	Aquarius
November 23–December 21, 1902	Aquarius
February 19, 1903	Aquarius
February 20–March 20, 1903	Pisces
November 23–December 22, 1903	Pisces
February 20–29, 1904	Pisces
March 1–20, 1904	Aries
*November 22–December 14, 1904	Aries
December 15–21, 1904	Aries
February 19–March 6, 1905	Aries
March 7–20, 1905	Taurus
*November 22–December 3, 1905	Gemini

IF YOU WERE BORN ON . . .	YOUR JUPITER IS IN . . .
*December 4–21, 1905	Taurus
February 19–March 8, 1906	Taurus
March 9–20, 1906	Gemini
*November 23–December 21, 1906	Cancer
*February 19–24, 1907	Cancer
February 25–March 20, 1907	Cancer
November 23–30, 1907	Leo
*December 1–21, 1907	Leo
*February 20–March 20, 1908	Leo
November 22–December 21, 1908	Virgo
*February 19–March 20, 1909	Virgo
November 22–December 21, 1909	Libra
*February 19–March 20, 1910	Libra
November 23–December 21, 1910	Scorpio
February 19–28, 1911	Scorpio
*March 1–20, 1911	Scorpio

*= retrograde

IF YOU WERE BORN ON . . .	YOUR JUPITER IS IN . . .
November 23–December 9, 1911	Scorpio
December 10–21, 1911	Sagittarius
February 19–March 19, 1912	Sagittarius
November 22–December 21, 1912	Sagittarius
February 19–March 20, 1913	Capricorn
November 22–December 21, 1913	Capricorn
February 19–March 20, 1914	Aquarius
November 23–December 21, 1914	Aquarius
February 19–March 20, 1915	Pisces
November 23–December 21, 1915	Pisces
February 19–March 19, 1916	Aries
*November 22–December 19, 1916	Aries
December 20–21, 1916	Aries
February 19–March 20, 1917	Taurus
*November 22–December 21, 1917	Gemini
February 19–March 20, 1918	Gemini
*November 23–December 21, 1918	Cancer
*February 19–March 1, 1919	Cancer
March 2–20, 1919	Cancer
November 23–December 4, 1919	Leo
*December 5–21, 1919	Leo
*February 19–March 19, 1920	Leo
November 22–December 21, 1920	Virgo
*February 19–March 20, 1921	Virgo
November 22–December 21, 1921	Libra
*February 19–March 20, 1922	Libra
November 23–December 21, 1922	Scorpio
February 19–March 4, 1923	Scorpio
*March 5–20, 1923	Scorpio
November 23, 1923	Scorpio
November 24–December 21, 1923	Sagittarius
February 19–March 19, 1924	Sagittarius
November 22–December 17, 1924	Sagittarius
December 18–21, 1924	Capricorn
February 19–March 20, 1925	Capricorn
November 22–December 21, 1925	Capricorn

IF YOU WERE BORN ON . . .	YOUR JUPITER IS IN . . .
February 19–March 20, 1926	Aquarius
November 23–December 21, 1926	Aquarius
February 19–March 20, 1927	Pisces
November 23–December 21, 1927	Pisces
February 19–March 19, 1928	Aries
*November 22–December 21, 1928	Taurus
February 19–March 20, 1929	Taurus
*November 22–December 21, 1929	Gemini
February 19–March 20, 1930	Gemini
*November 23–December 21, 1930	Cancer
*February 19–March 6, 1931	Cancer
March 7–20, 1931	Cancer
November 23–December 8, 1931	Leo
*December 9–21, 1931	Leo
*February 19–March 19, 1932	Leo
November 22–December 21, 1932	Virgo
*February 19–March 20, 1933	Virgo
November 22–December 21, 1933	Libra
*February 19–March 20, 1934	Libra
November 22–December 21, 1934	Scorpio
February 19–March 9, 1935	Scorpio
*March 10–20, 1935	Scorpio
November 23–December 21, 1935	Sagittarius
February 19–March 19, 1936	Sagittarius
November 22–December 1, 1936	Sagittarius
December 2–21, 1936	Capricorn
February 19–March 20, 1937	Capricorn
November 22–December 19, 1937	Capricorn
December 20–21, 1937	Aquarius
February 19–March 20, 1938	Aquarius
November 22–December 21, 1938	Aquarius
February 19–March 20, 1939	Pisces
*November 23, 1939	Pisces
November 24–December 19, 1939	Pisces
December 20–21, 1939	Aries
February 19–March 19, 1940	Aries

* = retrograde

IF YOU WERE BORN ON . . .	YOUR JUPITER IS IN . . .
*November 22–December 20, 1940	Taurus
February 19–March 20, 1941	Taurus
*November 22–December 21, 1941	Gemini
February 19–March 20, 1942	Gemini
*November 22–December 21, 1942	Cancer
*February 19–March 11, 1943	Cancer
March 12–20, 1943	Cancer
November 23–December 12, 1943	Leo
*December 13–21, 1943	Leo
*February 19–March 19, 1944	Leo
November 22–December 20, 1944	Virgo
*February 19–March 19, 1945	Virgo
November 22–December 21, 1945	Libra
*February 19–March 20, 1946	Libra
November 22–December 21, 1946	Scorpio
February 19–March 13, 1947	Scorpio
*March 14–20, 1947	Scorpio
November 23–December 21, 1947	Sagittarius
February 19–March 19, 1948	Sagittarius
November 22–December 20, 1948	Capricorn
February 18–March 19, 1949	Capricorn
November 22–29, 1949	Capricorn
November 30–December 21, 1949	Aquarius
February 19–March 20, 1950	Aquarius
November 22–30, 1950	Aquarius
December 1–21, 1950	Pisces
February 19–March 20, 1951	Pisces
*November 23–29, 1951	Aries
November 30–December 21, 1951	Aries
February 19–March 19, 1952	Aries
*November 22–December 20, 1952	Taurus
February 18–March 19, 1953	Taurus
*November 22–December 21, 1953	Gemini
February 19–March 20, 1954	Gemini
*November 22–December 21, 1954	Cancer
*February 19–March 15, 1955	Cancer

IF YOU WERE BORN ON . . .	YOUR JUPITER IS IN . . .
March 16–20, 1955	Cancer
November 23–December 17, 1955	Virgo
*December 18–21, 1955	Virgo
*February 19–March 19, 1956	Leo
November 22–December 12, 1956	Virgo
December 13–20, 1956	Libra
*February 18, 1957	Libra
*February 19–March 19, 1957	Virgo
November 22–December 21, 1957	Libra
*February 19–March 19, 1958	Scorpio
*March 20, 1958	Libra
November 22–December 21, 1958	Scorpio
February 19–March 17, 1959	Sagittarius
*March 18–20, 1959	Sagittarius
November 23–December 21, 1959	Sagittarius
February 19–29, 1960	Sagittarius
March 1–19, 1960	Capricorn
November 22–December 20, 1960	Capricorn
February 18–March 14, 1961	Capricorn
March 15–19, 1961	Aquarius
November 22–December 21, 1961	Aquarius
February 19–March 20, 1962	Aquarius
November 22–December 21, 1962	Pisces
February 19–March 20, 1963	Pisces
*November 23–December 4, 1963	Aries
December 5–21, 1963	Aries
February 19–March 19, 1964	Aries
*November 22–December 20, 1964	Taurus
February 18–March 19, 1965	Taurus
*November 22–December 21, 1965	Gemini
February 19–March 20, 1966	Gemini
*November 22–December 21, 1966	Leo
*February 19–March 20, 1967	Cancer
November 23–December 21, 1967	Virgo
*February 19–26, 1968	Virgo
*February 27–March 19, 1968	Leo

* = retrograde

IF YOU WERE BORN ON . . .	YOUR JUPITER IS IN . . .	IF YOU WERE BORN ON . . .	YOUR JUPITER IS IN . . .
November 22–December 20, 1968	Libra	February 18–23, 1982	Scorpio
*February 18–March 19, 1969	Libra	*February 24–March 19, 1982	Scorpio
November 22–December 15, 1969	Libra	November 22–December 21, 1982	Scorpio
December 16–21, 1969	Scorpio	February 19–March 20, 1983	Sagittarius
*February 19–March 20, 1970	Scorpio	November 22–December 21, 1983	Sagittarius
November 22–December 21, 1970	Scorpio	February 19–March 19, 1984	Capricorn
February 19–March 20, 1971	Sagittarius	November 22–December 20, 1984	Capricorn
November 22–December 21, 1971	Sagittarius	February 18–March 19, 1985	Aquarius
February 19–March 19, 1972	Capricorn	November 22–December 20, 1985	Aquarius
November 22–December 20, 1972	Capricorn	February 18–19, 1986	Aquarius
February 18–22, 1973	Capricorn	February 20–March 19, 1986	Pisces
February 23–March 19, 1973	Aquarius	November 22–December 21, 1986	Pisces
November 22–December 21, 1973	Aquarius	February 19–March 1, 1987	Pisces
February 19–March 7, 1974	Aquarius	March 2–20, 1987	Aries
March 8–20, 1974	Pisces	*November 22–December 14, 1987	Aries
November 22–December 21, 1974	Pisces	December 15–21, 1987	Aries
February 19–March 17, 1975	Pisces	February 19–March 7, 1988	Aries
March 18–20, 1975	Aries	March 8–19, 1988	Taurus
*November 22–December 9, 1975	Aries	*November 22–29, 1988	Gemini
December 10–21, 1975	Aries	*November 30–December 20, 1988	Taurus
February 19–March 19, 1976	Aries	February 18–March 10, 1989	Taurus
*November 22–December 20, 1976	Taurus	March 11–19, 1989	Gemini
February 18–March 19, 1977	Taurus	*November 22–December 20, 1989	Cancer
*November 22–December 20, 1977	Cancer	*February 18–23, 1990	Cancer
*February 19, 1978	Gemini	February 24–March 19, 1990	Cancer
February 20–March 19, 1978	Gemini	November 22–29, 1990	Leo
November 22–24, 1978	Leo	*November 30–December 21, 1990	Leo
*November 25–December 21, 1978	Leo	*February 19–March 20, 1991	Leo
*February 19–27, 1979	Leo	November 22–December 21, 1991	Virgo
*February 28–March 20, 1979	Cancer	*February 19–March 19, 1992	Virgo
November 22–December 21, 1979	Virgo	November 22–December 20, 1992	Libra
*February 19–March 19, 1980	Virgo	*February 18–March 19, 1993	Libra
November 22–December 20, 1980	Libra	November 22–December 20, 1993	Scorpio
*February 18–March 19, 1981	Libra	February 18–27, 1994	Scorpio
November 22–26, 1981	Libra	*February 28–March 19, 1994	Scorpio
November 27–December 20, 1981	Scorpio	November 22–December 8, 1994	Scorpio

*= retrograde

IF YOU WERE BORN ON . . .	YOUR JUPITER IS IN . . .
December 9–21, 1994	Sagittarius
February 19–March 20, 1995	Sagittarius
November 22–December 21, 1995	Sagittarius
February 19–March 19, 1996	Capricorn
November 22–December 20, 1996	Capricorn
February 18–March 19, 1997	Aquarius
November 22–December 20, 1997	Aquarius
February 18–March 19, 1998	Pisces
November 22–December 21, 1998	Pisces
February 19–March 20, 1999	Aries
*November 22–December 19, 1999	Aries
December 20–21, 1999	Aries
February 19–March 19, 2000	Taurus
*November 22–December 20, 2000	Gemini
February 18–March 19, 2001	Gemini
*November 22–December 20, 2001	Cancer
*February 18–28, 2002	Cancer
March 1–19, 2002	Cancer
November 22–December 3, 2002	Leo
*December 4–21, 2002	Leo
*February 19–March 20, 2003	Leo
November 22–December 21, 2003	Virgo

IF YOU WERE BORN ON . . .	YOUR JUPITER IS IN . . .
*February 19–March 19, 2004	Virgo
November 21–December 20, 2004	Libra
*February 18–March 19, 2005	Libra
November 22–December 20, 2005	Scorpio
February 18–March 3, 2006	Scorpio
*March 4–19, 2006	Scorpio
November 22–23, 2006	Scorpio
November 24–December 21, 2006	Sagittarius
February 19–March 20, 2007	Sagittarius
November 22–December 17, 2007	Sagittarius
December 18–21, 2007	Capricorn
February 19–March 19, 2008	Capricorn
November 21–December 20, 2008	Capricorn
February 18–March 19, 2009	Aquarius
November 22–December 20, 2009	Aquarius
February 18–March 19, 2010	Pisces
November 22–December 20, 2010	Pisces
February 19–March 19, 2011	Aries
*November 22–December 21, 2011	Taurus
February 19–March 19, 2012	Taurus
*November 21–December 20, 2012	Gemini

* = retrograde

"You're gonna make it after all!" Child of Saturn Mary Tyler Moore.

CHILD OF SATURN

❊

Children of Saturn age backward. Born old, you grow younger in both appearance and spirit with each passing year. By the time you reach middle age, you look as if you've hardly a care in the world. You've outpaced all the jocks who gave you such a hard time in school and surpassed the "in" crowd that made you feel so out of it. People may marvel at your "good fortune," but they don't know how much hard work went into making that prosperity happen. There's always a price to pay for a Child of Saturn. And that price is usually paid at a time

KEY WORDS

Melancholy, history, hard work, lasting accomplishments, bones, skin, old age, CEOs, banks, libraries, endowments, rules, teachers, farmers, judges, clocks and schedules, tests, limits, material plane, irony, comebacks.

BREAKING THROUGH THE BARRIER

MARTIN LUTHER
KING JR.
January 15, 1929

LOUIS BRAILLE
*Created the "Braille"
system for the blind*
January 4, 1809

CHUCK YEAGER
*First pilot to break the
sound barrier*
February 13, 1923

when everyone's supposed to be feeling young and carefree. If there was a hard way to do something, you found it. You were probably the last one chosen when the kids were picking teams for softball. It took you forever to muster up the courage to speak in front of the class or ask someone out on a date. Yet it's your perseverance and strength in the face of setbacks and stumbling blocks that ultimately leads to your great achievements and sense of self-fulfillment.

Saturn, the last planet visible to the naked eye, symbolized the very opposite of the Sun, the hottest and brightest of the planets. In the mind of the ancients, Saturn, cold and remote, came to be regarded as the Planet of age and experience. That's why you were born an old soul and tend to be a late bloomer. It's also why you're drawn to people much older than you. You've always respected your elders. You know that if you pay close attention to them, you're bound to get advice from someone who has been down the road you're traveling. Even if this person isn't familiar with what you do *exactly*, chances are they've survived something similar. Instead of waiting to benefit from your own hindsight, you can always make things a little easier by benefiting from someone else's.

Saturn is also regarded as the Planet of time and matter. That's why time is very precious to you and you hate it when somebody wastes it by being late or talking endlessly about trivialities. Faced with living in a

Saturn teaching the Lombards how to sickle.

ROBERT BURTON
His Anatomy of Melancholy
*was the first book on how
to treat depression*
February 8, 1577

SIR ISAAC NEWTON
Formulated the law of gravity
December 25, 1642

HUMPHREY BOGART
Film "noir" star
December 25, 1899

world where nothing lasts forever, the Children of Saturn are acutely aware that the clock is ticking and will struggle to make the most of their material resources. Not many people think this way, but you do. It's what gives you your melancholy nature. You are no stranger to depression. However, your dark moods also give you depth and profundity—along with a wicked sense of humor. The comedians Jim Carrey and Chris Rock are both Children of Saturn. Ironically their *spontaneous* performances stem from years of repetition and fine-tuning. Others may talk about all the things they'd like to do if circumstances allowed. You will actually put your shoulder to the wheel and make it happen. Industrious and hard-working, you will build castles out of toothpicks.

Saturn is the Planet of trials and tribulations, which means that you see your destiny as a series of challenges—each one steeper than the next. And only by surmounting these challenges will you find lasting success. But what drives you isn't ambition or even hope. What drives you are your anxieties and fears. The Samuel Beckett line "I can't go on, I'll go on" is your motto. You can't arrive at a solution without going through the problem first. That, in essence, is how your Birthday Planet functions in your life. It also pushes you to do more than you thought you could. The end result is a mastery over your life.

**TURNING
SETBACKS INTO
STRIDES**

SAMUEL SMILES
*Wrote the first self-help book,
called* Self-Help
December 23, 1812

MADAME DE POMPADOUR
*Daughter of a black
marketeer, she became Louis
XV's mistress*
December 29, 1721

RICHARD M. NIXON
January 9, 1913

Saturn acts as both conscience and nemesis, seemingly keeping you away from what you want the most. Yet for all the hassles, Saturn will take you only as far as you want to go. Saturn tests your desires, abilities, and even motives.

For most people when they come up against an obstacle, their hopes and dreams are stopped short. When they don't get what they want right away, they will tell themselves it wasn't meant to be or perhaps they weren't all that serious about it in the first place. They go back the way they came or go on to something else that's easier for them to do. But being a Child of Saturn you see obstacles as a crossroad. There's so much at stake. You *have* to go after what you see before you, because you don't know if you'll ever get this opportunity again. Yet you also see how you could fall flat on your face. In some ways it would be easier if these dilemmas could be resolved quickly. But that's not the way life works for a Child of Saturn. With Saturn, things take twice as long to come together *and* twice as long to fall apart, which means you have plenty of time to question what you're doing. Your Ruling Planet is famous for making you slog through all sorts of delays, postponements, and things falling through at the last minute. This is why Saturn symbolizes a rite of passage.

Saturn will thwart, obstruct, withhold, and maybe even change the rules when you're not looking; however, you will become all the better for it. Wrestling with obstacles teaches you to persevere, to think twice, to live with doubts rather than false hopes. To cop to your insecurities rather than cower from them, to prove your mettle. Saturn will test you, and this test determines whether or not you're ready to transcend a limit, to cross a boundary. It will tell you whether you're ready to leave behind what's comfortable and familiar and go to the next level. It's as old as the twelve labors of Hercules and as current as the latest PlayStation.

Saturn is the Planet of authority in astrology. He symbolizes all those things you have to do when you occupy a position of responsibility—like rising to the challenge or agonizing over tough decisions. Your Birthday Planet also rules over the nagging doubts that come along with excerising authority. After all, once you've stepped into that kind of position in your life, there's no passing the buck. It's all up to you. And if you've ever been responsible for people other than yourself, then you know the kinds of doubts that come with it. Doubts like: did I do everything I could have done? Did I handle things in the right way? Do I even know what I'm doing? And it's these doubts that either push you to do more or end up paralyzing your best efforts.

Now it may sound like being a Child of Saturn doesn't exactly lend itself to fun and laughter. It's true that you tend to take things seriously.

Jacob wrestling with the angel.

BUMPING THE GRINDSTONE

ELVIS PRESLEY
January 8, 1935

GYPSY ROSE LEE
January 9, 1914

RICKY MARTIN
December 24, 1971

You're sensitive to rejection and will cultivate an aloof facade so that you appear indifferent or blasé. Saturn's remoteness and steadiness can give his Children a stodgy, skeptical, been there/done that jadedness. You always keep your eye on the faults and are constantly aware of what's lacking. But that doesn't mean you wouldn't be ready to throw it all off at a moment's notice.

You will always take things more seriously than the people around you, which is why you're drawn to warm, cheery, upbeat types. If you're rigid—which Saturn is known to be at times—then your partner may be more easygoing. If you're always serious and focused, then your child might be lighthearted or rebellious. Perhaps you're always composed and classic in appearance, so your colleagues or friends may be a bit wild and crazy. If a lover is noncommittal, that person isn't in your life to make you feel abandoned and miserable. Chances are, if commitment's an issue (and being a Child of Saturn, commitment is always an issue), this person is there to introduce some flexibility: to move you away from what's *supposed* to make you happy and closer to a relationship you might actually enjoy. A child's lightheartedness is meant to remind you of your own delight. Rebelliousness in another prompts you to reexamine truths you hold to be self-evident. Your natural attraction to people who are warm and gushing gets you to open up. Fear certainly isn't the only color in your emotional palette. There are lighter hues, ones that are often introduced by the people who make you smile and laugh.

Saturn is a great editor. He gets rid of anything you don't need anymore. If you've ever had to clean out your closets, then you know how important a great editor can be. Saturn asks the tough questions like: Do you need this? Are you ever going to use it? Or is it just taking up valuable space? Saturn gets you to consolidate your resources. Instead of being spread out all over the place, your resources are gathered in one spot where they can anchor and support you. Saturn gives you a no-nonsense, disciplined, and what's the bottom-line approach to life: weeding out the things that don't do anything for you while focusing more energy on what truly makes you happy.

Saturn also brings wisdom, patience, and compassion. Saturn is the Planet of longevity. Relationships that are blessed by Saturn will last. Projects and enterprises you take on will reap great profits. If you move, get promoted, or receive a raise, it will have staying power and strides you make will not be easily erased. It's kind of like the Energizer bunny: whatever is blessed by your Ruling Planet will just keep on going and going.

Saturn and the fruits of labor.

HORATIO ALGER
The original "rags-to-riches" story
January 13, 1832

MADAME C. J. WALKER
First African-American businesswoman to become a millionaire
December 23, 1867

HAROLD GRAY
Creator of Little Orphan Annie
January 20, 1894

Like the tortoise in the race with the hare, you may start out slow and behind, but in the end you'll wind up sitting pretty.

Seven-year cycles are very important in your life. The ages of seven, fourteen, twenty-one, and twenty-eight to thirty will probably stand out in your life as being very significant. After thirty, it moves in two-year brackets, like thirty-five to thirty-seven, forty-two to forty-four, etc. These are the ages when your Ruling Planet tests your mettle. Now not every Child of Saturn gets the same test at the same age. The area of life that gets tested will correspond to where Saturn is situated in the sky at that time. One Child of Saturn may be tested in his home life when he's seven, whereas another Child of Saturn may be tested in her home life when she's twenty-eight.

When Saturn is testing you, it applies pressure to the weak points in your life until they begin to give way. What can be disconcerting is that the things you thought would never change are the first to collapse. It may have to do with the foundation of a relationship, the security of a job, or a home or family matter. As Saturn applies pressure to the weak points in your life, it tests the strength of the structure to see if it's sound. And as things begin to sway and crumble, you start to recognize the false securities for what they are.

Yet Saturn does have a kinder, gentler side. Saturn is more than just a necessary evil. Once you've gone through your rite of passage, it's a safe bet that you'll be set for life. That's because your Birthday Planet rules over all those things that stand the test of time. Things like being a pillar of your community, being tops in your field, having the love of family and friends, a good marriage, and reaping the benefits of experience.

Go ahead and turn to the Saturn tables on page 160 to find what sign your Ruling Planet was in on the day you were born. Part III of this book will show how your Ruling Planet varies its expression from sign to sign. If there is an asterisk (*) next to your birth date, then you were born during a retrograde. If so, you'll want to come back and read the following:

CHILD OF SATURN RETROGRADE

"Retrograde" refers to a backward motion. The planet Saturn doesn't actually reverse direction. That's just the way it looks to us. It's an optical illusion that occurs periodically from Earth's viewpoint, giving the impression of a planet moving backward against the setting of constellations in the sky. When a planet is retrograde, its energy becomes the opposite of what it is when it's direct. Since Saturn is the Planet of trials and tribulations, then that's what gets turned inside out. This isn't to say that if you're a Child of Saturn Retrograde you'll have a worry-free existence. If anything, it's your avoidance of obstacles that leads to your greatest problems and—ironically—your most magnificent triumphs.

When Saturn is direct, it restricts or limits what you do by acting as a resistance against your best efforts. If you've ever worked out with a phys-

ROBERT RIPLEY
Founder of Ripley's Believe It or Not!
December 26, 1893

MARION DAVIES
Second-rate actress whose affair with William Randolph Hearst was immortalized in the film Citizen Kane
January 3, 1897

ROD SERLING
Creator of The Twilight Zone
December 25, 1924

ical trainer, then you know it's not the lifting of the weights that builds muscles. It's the resistance to lowering them. So in a very real way, Saturn makes you stronger by making things difficult. When Saturn is retrograde, however, it acts *against* your progress. What was resistant in a constructive way can become oppressive or overbearing. This often takes the form of an inescapable dilemma.

In mythology, when it is prophesied that Saturn, the king of the gods, is to be overthrown by one of his own children, he orders his wife, Rhea, to bring him each child as soon as it's born. Having overthrown his own father, Saturn isn't eager to suffer the same fate. Rhea obeys and can only look on helplessly as her husband swallows her children one by one. However, Rhea hides the youngest, Zeus, with friends so that he can grow up one day to rescue his brothers and sisters. Saturn knows that prophecies are never wrong, but he hopes that by swallowing his children he'll be able to buy time. It's a false security, but a security nonetheless.

Another person who tries to outwit fate is Jonah. When God commands his prophet to go to Nineveh and urge its citizens to repent, Jonah promptly boards a ship heading in the opposite direction. Jonah regards Nineveh as a lost cause—hardly worth the effort. His deliberate disobedience of God's will lands him in the belly of a whale (who happens to be swimming back the way Jonah just came). Like Saturn, Jonah tries to forestall the inevitable by taking preventive measures only to wind up stumbling into the very fate he was trying to avoid.

As a Child of Saturn Retrograde, you will have to live through long periods of dormancy when you will feel imprisoned and stifled and like you're dangling on the horns of a dilemma. Like the mythological Saturn, who by imprisoning his children also imprisons himself, and Jonah, who knows that if he wants to escape the whale, he's going to have to do what he's told, you can find yourself stuck in a similar no-win situation. Faced with equally undesirable outcomes, it only makes sense that you would get depressed and feel like all is for naught.

Predicaments often carry the clues to their own solution. Just as what you thought was right ends up being wrong, *ironically* (and in true Saturn fashion) it may be that very same wrong thinking that ultimately proves right in the end. As a Child of Saturn Retrograde, deliverance lies in learning to cope with your limited circumstances.

It's the special genius of you Children of Saturn Retrograde to make "all" out of the "naught." You have a natural sympathy for what's been rejected or overlooked—having experienced it yourself. Just because something's labeled "refuse" doesn't mean it's garbage. Indeed it may have hidden potentials that others have never dreamed of. The physicist Stephen W. Hawking is a wonderful example of a Child of Saturn Retrograde. Not only does he have to contend with a debilitating illness that's left him virtually imprisoned within his own body, but he's also done this while establishing himself as one of the greatest scientists of the twentieth century precisely for his work on the physics of black holes, which were regarded as literally "nothing" until he came along. While barely moving a muscle Hawking has reshaped how we look at our universe and time. He also has the singular distinction of writing a best-seller that nobody could understand.

Eventually Zeus comes of age, rescues his brothers and sisters, and overthrows his father—as foretold. Yet in perhaps the most ironic twist of all, Zeus decides against punishing Saturn and sets him up with a palace of his own on the Isle of the Blessed (a sort of mythological version of retiring to Florida), where the sun never sets and perfumed breezes blow in off the ocean. In a similar vein, Jonah upon reaching Nineveh succeeds (despite his misgivings) in immediately getting the entire city to repent.

Like anything having to do with your Birthday Planet, progress in life may be slow and cumbersome, but you'll recognize its value with hindsight. That's why it's so very important that you work with whatever comes your way (even if it does look like an exercise in futility) and to not be too quick to write anything off as a lost cause. It may wind up being the key to your salvation.

WHAT SIGN IS SATURN IN?

IF YOU WERE BORN ON . . .	YOUR SATURN IS IN . . .
January 1–20, 1900	Sagittarius
January 21–February 18, 1900	Capricorn
December 22–31, 1900	Capricorn
January 1–February 18, 1901	Capricorn
December 22–31, 1901	Capricorn
January 1–February 18, 1902	Capricorn
December 22–31, 1902	Capricorn
January 1–18, 1903	Capricorn
January 19–February 18, 1903	Aquarius
December 23–31, 1903	Aquarius
January 1–February 19, 1904	Aquarius
December 22–31, 1904	Aquarius
January 1–February 18, 1905	Aquarius
December 22–31, 1905	Aquarius
January 1–7, 1906	Aquarius
January 8–February 18, 1906	Pisces

IF YOU WERE BORN ON . . .	YOUR SATURN IS IN . . .
December 22–31, 1906	Pisces
January 1–February 18, 1907	Pisces
December 22–31, 1907	Pisces
January 1–February 19, 1908	Pisces
December 22–31, 1908	Aries
January 1–February 18, 1909	Aries
December 22–31, 1909	Aries
January 1–February 18, 1910	Aries
*December 22–31, 1910	Aries
*January 1, 1911	Aries
January 2–19, 1911	Aries
January 20–February 18, 1911	Taurus
*December 22–31, 1911	Taurus
*January 1–14, 1912	Taurus
January 15–February 18, 1912	Taurus
*December 22–31, 1912	Taurus

*= retrograde

IF YOU WERE BORN ON . . .	YOUR SATURN IS IN . . .
*January 1–27, 1913	Taurus
January 28–February 18, 1913	Taurus
*December 22–31, 1913	Gemini
*January 1–February 10, 1914	Gemini
February 11–18, 1914	Gemini
*December 22–31, 1914	Gemini
*January 1–February 18, 1915	Gemini
*December 22–31, 1915	Cancer
*January 1–February 18, 1916	Cancer
*December 22–31, 1916	Cancer
*January 1–February 18, 1917	Cancer
*December 22–31, 1917	Leo
*January 1–February 18, 1918	Leo
*December 22–31, 1918	Leo
*January 1–February 18, 1919	Leo
December 22, 1919	Virgo
*December 23–31, 1919	Virgo
*January 1–February 18, 1920	Virgo
December 22–31, 1920	Virgo
January 1–3, 1921	Virgo
*January 4–February 18, 1921	Virgo
December 22–31, 1921	Libra
January 1–16, 1922	Libra
*January 17–February 18, 1922	Libra
December 22–31, 1922	Libra
January 1–28, 1923	Libra
*January 29–February 18, 1923	Libra
December 22–31, 1923	Scorpio
January 1–February 10, 1924	Scorpio
*February 11–18, 1924	Scorpio
December 22–31, 1924	Scorpio
January 1–February 18, 1925	Scorpio
December 22–31, 1925	Scorpio
January 1–February 18, 1926	Scorpio
December 22–31, 1926	Sagittarius
January 1–February 18, 1927	Sagittarius

IF YOU WERE BORN ON . . .	YOUR SATURN IS IN . . .
December 22–31, 1927	Sagittarius
January 1–February 18, 1928	Sagittarius
December 22–31, 1928	Sagittarius
January 1–February 18, 1929	Sagittarius
December 22–31, 1929	Capricorn
January 1–February 18, 1930	Capricorn
December 22–31, 1930	Capricorn
January 1–February 18, 1931	Capricorn
December 22–31, 1931	Capricorn
January 1–February 18, 1932	Capricorn
December 22–31, 1932	Aquarius
January 1–February 18, 1933	Aquarius
December 22–31, 1933	Aquarius
January 1–February 18, 1934	Aquarius
December 22–31, 1934	Aquarius
January 1–February 13, 1935	Aquarius
February 14–18, 1935	Pisces
December 22–31, 1935	Pisces
January 1–February 18, 1936	Pisces
December 22–31, 1936	Pisces
January 1–February 18, 1937	Pisces
December 22–31, 1937	Pisces
January 1–13, 1938	Pisces
January 14–February 18, 1938	Aries
December 22–31, 1938	Aries
January 1–February 18, 1939	Aries
*December 22–27, 1939	Aries
December 28–31, 1939	Aries
January 1–February 18, 1940	Aries
*December 21–31, 1940	Taurus
*January 1–8, 1941	Taurus
January 9–February 18, 1941	Taurus
*December 22–31, 1941	Taurus
*January 1–22, 1942	Taurus
January 23–February 18, 1942	Taurus
*December 22–31, 1942	Gemini

* = retrograde

IF YOU WERE BORN ON . . .	YOUR SATURN IS IN . . .
*January 1–February 5, 1943	Gemini
February 6–18, 1943	Gemini
*December 22–31, 1943	Gemini
*January 1–February 18, 1944	Gemini
*December 21–31, 1944	Cancer
*January 1–February 18, 1945	Cancer
*December 22–31, 1945	Cancer
*January 1–February 18, 1946	Cancer
*December 22–31, 1946	Leo
*January 1–February 18, 1947	Leo
*December 22–31, 1947	Leo
*January 1–February 18, 1948	Leo
*December 21–31, 1948	Virgo
*January 1–February 17, 1949	Virgo
December 22–29, 1949	Virgo
*December 30–31, 1949	Virgo
*January 1–February 18, 1950	Virgo
December 22–31, 1950	Libra
January 1–11, 1951	Libra
*January 12–February 18, 1951	Libra
December 22–31, 1951	Libra
January 1–23, 1952	Libra
*January 24–February 18, 1952	Libra
December 21–31, 1952	Libra
January 1–February 4, 1953	Libra
*February 5–17, 1953	Libra
December 22–31, 1953	Scorpio
January 1–February 16, 1954	Scorpio
*February 17–18, 1954	Scorpio
December 22–31, 1954	Scorpio
January 1–February 18, 1955	Scorpio
December 22–31, 1955	Scorpio
January 1–11, 1956	Scorpio
January 12–February 18, 1956	Sagittarius
December 21–31, 1956	Sagittarius
January 1–February 17, 1957	Sagittarius

IF YOU WERE BORN ON . . .	YOUR SATURN IS IN . . .
December 22–31, 1957	Sagittarius
January 1–February 18, 1958	Sagittarius
December 22–31, 1958	Sagittarius
January 1–4, 1959	Sagittarius
January 5–February 18, 1959	Capricorn
December 22–31, 1959	Capricorn
January 1–February 18, 1960	Capricorn
December 21–31, 1960	Capricorn
January 1–February 17, 1961	Capricorn
December 22–31, 1961	Capricorn
January 1–2, 1962	Capricorn
January 3–February 18, 1962	Aquarius
December 22–31, 1962	Aquarius
January 1–February 18, 1963	Aquarius
December 22–31, 1963	Aquarius
January 1–February 18, 1964	Aquarius
December 21–31, 1964	Pisces
January 1–February 17, 1965	Pisces
December 22–31, 1965	Pisces
January 1–February 18, 1966	Pisces
December 22–31, 1966	Pisces
January 1–February 18, 1967	Pisces
December 22–31, 1967	Aries
January 1–February 18, 1968	Aries
December 21–31, 1968	Aries
January 1–February 17, 1969	Aries
*December 22–31, 1969	Taurus
*January 1–2, 1970	Taurus
January 3–February 18, 1970	Taurus
*December 22–31, 1970	Taurus
*January 1–16, 1971	Taurus
January 17–February 18, 1971	Taurus
*December 22–31, 1971	Gemini
*January 1–9, 1972	Gemini
*January 10–30, 1972	Taurus
January 31–February 18, 1972	Taurus

* = retrograde

IF YOU WERE BORN ON . . .	YOUR SATURN IS IN . . .
*December 21–31, 1972	Gemini
*January 1–February 12, 1973	Gemini
February 13–17, 1973	Gemini
*December 22–31, 1973	Cancer
*January 1–6, 1974	Cancer
*January 7–February 18, 1974	Gemini
*December 22–31, 1974	Cancer
*January 1–February 18, 1975	Cancer
*December 22–31, 1975	Leo
*January 1–13, 1976	Leo
*January 14–February 18, 1976	Cancer
*December 21–31, 1976	Leo
*January 1–February 17, 1977	Leo
*December 21–31, 1977	Virgo
*January 1–4, 1978	Virgo
*January 5–February 18, 1978	Leo
December 22–23, 1978	Virgo
*December 24–31, 1978	Virgo
*January 1–February 18, 1979	Virgo
December 22–31, 1979	Virgo
January 1–5, 1980	Virgo
*January 6–February 18, 1980	Virgo
December 21–31, 1980	Libra
January 1–17, 1981	Libra
*January 18–February 17, 1981	Libra
December 21–31, 1981	Libra
January 1–30, 1982	Libra
*January 31–February 17, 1982	Libra
December 22–31, 1982	Scorpio
January 1–February 11, 1983	Scorpio
*February 12–18, 1983	Scorpio
December 22–31, 1983	Scorpio
January 1–February 18, 1984	Scorpio
December 21–31, 1984	Scorpio
January 1–February 17, 1985	Scorpio
December 21–31, 1985	Sagittarius

IF YOU WERE BORN ON . . .	YOUR SATURN IS IN . . .
January 1–February 17, 1986	Sagittarius
December 22–31, 1986	Sagittarius
January 1–February 18, 1987	Sagittarius
December 22–31, 1987	Sagittarius
January 1–February 12, 1988	Sagittarius
February 13–18, 1988	Capricorn
December 21–31, 1988	Capricorn
January 1–February 17, 1989	Capricorn
December 21–31, 1989	Capricorn
January 1–February 17, 1990	Capricorn
December 22–31, 1990	Capricorn
January 1–February 5, 1991	Capricorn
February 6–18, 1991	Aquarius
December 22–31, 1991	Aquarius
January 1–February 18, 1992	Aquarius
December 21–31, 1992	Aquarius
January 1–February 17, 1993	Aquarius
December 21–31, 1993	Aquarius
January 1–27, 1994	Aquarius
January 28–February 17, 1994	Pisces
December 22–31, 1994	Pisces
January 1–February 18, 1995	Pisces
December 22–31, 1995	Pisces
January 1–February 18, 1996	Pisces
December 21–31, 1996	Aries
January 1–February 17, 1997	Aries
December 21–31, 1997	Aries
January 1–February 17, 1998	Aries
*December 22–28, 1998	Aries
December 29–31, 1998	Aries
January 1–February 18, 1999	Aries
*December 22–31, 1999	Taurus
*January 1–11, 2000	Taurus
January 12–February 18, 2000	Taurus
*December 21–31, 2000	Taurus
*January 1–23, 2001	Taurus

* = retrograde

IF YOU WERE BORN ON . . .	YOUR SATURN IS IN . . .
January 24–February 17, 2001	Taurus
*December 21–31, 2001	Gemini
*January 1–February 7, 2002	Gemini
February 8–17, 2002	Gemini
*December 22–31, 2002	Gemini
*January 1–February 18, 2003	Gemini
*December 22–31, 2003	Cancer
*January 1–February 18, 2004	Cancer
*December 21–31, 2004	Cancer
*January 1–February 17, 2005	Cancer
*December 21–31, 2005	Leo
*January 1–February 17, 2006	Leo
*December 22–31, 2006	Leo
*January 1–February 18, 2007	Leo
*December 22–31, 2007	Virgo

IF YOU WERE BORN ON . . .	YOUR SATURN IS IN . . .
*January 1–February 18, 2008	Virgo
December 21–30, 2008	Virgo
*December 31, 2008	Virgo
*January 1–February 17, 2009	Virgo
December 21–31, 2009	Libra
January 1–12, 2010	Libra
*January 13–February 17, 2010	Libra
December 21–31, 2010	Libra
January 1–25, 2011	Libra
*January 26–February 18, 2011	Libra
December 22–31, 2011	Libra
January 1–February 6, 2012	Libra
*February 7–18, 2012	Libra
December 21–31, 2012	Scorpio

*= retrograde

Toppled statue of Lenin following the collapse of communism.

CHILD OF URANUS

KEY WORDS

Ideals, air, mathematics, science, eternity, revolution and change, birds, outer space, platinum, World Wide Web, architects, unions, artificial intelligence, nervous system, biotechnology, electricity, genius, iconoclasm, extended family, mavericks

I f you're a Child of Uranus, then you're one of the few people who have two Birthday Planets! Not only are you a Child of Uranus, but you are also a Child of Saturn. Go and read the section on Saturn first, then come back here to get the rest of the story.

You were born different. There are many people who choose to be different. They enjoy going against the grain or revel in tipping sacred cows. Yet after their fling with rebellion is over, they return to the status quo— often embracing it more powerfully than they did before. You, on the other

BRAVE NEW WORLD

SIR THOMAS MORE
Coined the term "Utopia"
February 7, 1477

FREDERICK DOUGLASS
*This ex-slave fought for his
people's freedom*
February 7, 1817

FRANKLIN DELANO
ROOSEVELT
*His "New Deal" redefined
American society*
January 30, 1882

The Wheel of Fortune.

hand, never really felt like you belonged. There may have been a lot of upsets in your early upbringing. Perhaps your family moved around a lot or there were times when one or maybe even both parents had to be away for extended periods. Then again you might have come on the scene a little too early or too late to enjoy the comfort and security of a stable environment. There is an out-of-sync quality built into your psyche. An unsettling restlessness makes you uncertain as to whether you should stay or go. Loved ones may chide you, saying you just don't know what you want. Friends might make light of your tendencies to "rock the boat." Yet what drives you isn't so much a profound dissatisfaction as it is an innate sense that you're just not getting *it*. There must be something more to what you're looking at. You can't help feeling like you're poring over the small corner of a far bigger picture.

As the Planet of revolution and change, your Ruling Planet is famous for upsetting one's best-laid plans. Uranus introduces all sorts of unseen elements into the mix. He's connected with sudden swings, surprise breaks, reversals of fortune, and last-minute victories. As a Child of Uranus, you're no stranger to taking a wild spin on the wheel of fortune. What's up one day can be down the next. You've seen things you gave up on long ago suddenly pop back into the picture. With Uranus as your Birthday Planet, life can be kooky and unpredictable. Then again: what else would you expect from the only planet in our solar system that spins on its side?

Uranus was discovered in 1781, a time of immense social upheaval. America had just declared its independence from Britain. France hovered on the brink of a bloody revolution. The discovery of Uranus (which could only be seen through a telescope—thus giving it rulership over all modern technology) destroyed the traditional lineup of planets that had defined our solar system for centuries. It also raised the prospect that there might be more planets out there somewhere. Everything that was familiar had been thrown into chaos. But then, that's progress—which is practically Uranus's middle name.

There's more to Uranus than havoc. It is also the Planet of revelation: after all, Uranus had always been there in the sky. It didn't just suddenly pop into existence one day. Uranus is often erroneously perceived as being chaotic when all it really does is change your frame of reference. In an instant it shows you that what you've been looking at is a painting hung upside down. Your Ruling Planet is the great debunker and liberator in astrology. Children of Uranus like to turn arguments on their head. This isn't the same thing as wordplay, which is a favorite pastime for Children

DON'T START THE REVOLUTION WITHOUT ME

THOMAS PAINE
Author of The Rights of Man
January 29, 1737

ANGELA DAVIS
January 26, 1944

RONALD REAGAN
February 6, 1911

MARTIN BUBER
Author of I-Thou
February 8, 1878

SIMONE WEIL
*French philosopher
and mystic*
February 3, 1909

MICHAEL "AIR" JORDAN
February 17, 1963

of Mercury. Children of Mercury have a dash of the trickster in them and sometimes delight in leading people on. For a Child of Uranus, questioning beliefs and challenging assumptions is done in pursuit of an open mind.

The truth is very important to you. Yet the truth that fascinates and inspires you isn't simply made up of facts. To you a fact is merely stating the obvious. There's nothing uplifting or enlightening about something that's as plain as the nose on your face. Facts don't further your understanding or growth as a person. The Truth you yearn for is connected to something higher and more profound. It's an Ideal.

But not everyone is ready to see the Truth, nor do they agree on how to look at it. Which is where, as a Child of Uranus, you can run into trouble. You know that the Truth is multifaceted. There are many sides to an argument, and everyone's point of view should be taken into account. You—more than most—will go to great lengths to do this. And like most farsighted people, you tend to trip over the things under your nose. What is also hard for you is the concept that the people in your life are not so willing to give up *their* truths to see the bigger one.

People tend to identify with a variety of things in their lives, such as their job, relationships, the way they were raised—even their belongings. But what you have a hard time swallowing is when someone identifies with his limitations. It's one thing when someone doesn't have the money, power, or capability to change his circumstances; it's quite another when that person won't do it because he's so invested in his frustration, pain, and despair. Your natural inclination is to talk this person out of it, to reveal the falsehoods and misconceptions. This is where your insistence that someone get some perspective on his problems and see the bigger picture can come across as being insensitive and even condescending. This is where you, as a Child of Uranus, can lose the person for the cause.

For someone who's so open-minded, you can be fixated and stubborn. That's because you insist on getting it right. This isn't the same as being right. You don't believe that anyone's right—least of all yourself. Indeed you can even go a bit overboard with the self-criticism. That's why it hurts when people accuse you of being bossy or self-righteous. You don't understand what they mean. As far as you're concerned, you're in service to an ideal. But the problem with ideals is that they're perfect and we're not.

As a Child of Uranus, you can be relentless in your pursuit of the ideal. You can have enormous expectations. There's a part of you that insists that the material world conform to the perfect model, which is why so many Children of Uranus become ballet dancers, scientists, architects, and engineers. Form should emulate the ideal, not the other way around. You're keenly aware of the split between the spiritual and the material—the *real* thing and the facsimile. You have an ideal in mind, and you will make yourself be it. If you have to reshape your body or suppress those yearnings that distract you—like need, desire, exhaustion, and pain—then so be it. People should live up to high standards, to be the very best that they can be and not take the easy way out and opt for compromises and quick fixes.

Sometimes this works, like with Child of Uranus Abraham Lincoln

**AHEAD OF THEIR
TIMES**

JACKIE ROBINSON
*First African-American
to play in major league
baseball*
January 31, 1919

FRANÇOIS TRUFFAUT
New Wave filmmaker
February 6, 1932

ROSA PARKS
February 4, 1913

who made America endure a bitter Civil War so that all its people could be free. Sometimes this can have catastrophic effects, like with Boris Yeltsin, another Child of Uranus, who plunged Russia into dismal chaos in order to liberate her from communism. As you can imagine, it's not always easy to tell if you're doing the right thing, or if you're doing the right thing but just at the wrong time. This is an ongoing paradox for you. You're constantly trying to judge if you've seized on an idea that's ahead of its time or an idea whose time has come. An idea that's ahead of its time might get noticed at first for being odd or eccentric, but for the most part it's ignored or squashed. It's too way-out or impractical, whereas an idea whose time has come may be the very thing that transforms a woman like Oprah Winfrey, yet another Child of Uranus, into one of the most powerful forces in the entertainment industry.

There will be times when you'll feel that things aren't happening as fast as they should or that you're constantly being held back by people who just don't get what you're about. Then again there will be times when you get quick glimpses of the way things could be, and you might be overwhelmed by what you see and wonder how you could ever bring that about. There will be times when you may want to give up. Then suddenly something in your life gives way. A major shift occurs. That's how your Birthday Planet works. It acts as a sort of cosmic rectification. It's a catalyst for change in your life, but these changes aren't just accidental or haphazard. They happen in order for you to get it right, so that your life is aligned with the workings of the Higher Plan, rather than at odds with it. How radical the changes will be depends on how close you already are to the way things are supposed to be working out for you.

Capitalist dinner with forces of revolution in the background.

The conversion of St. Paul is considered a Uranian example of a dramatic about-face.

Although Uranus is the Planet of revolution and change, it still takes seven years to pass through one zodiac sign. For the most part, you will experience Uranus as a low-level restlessness that occasionally flares up. Like people who live near fault lines, you grow accustomed to the rumbling and shaking after a while. Yet you do have to keep an eye out for when your Ruling Planet changes signs. It will change signs again in 2003.

When your Birthday Planet changes signs, you can expect a surprise upset in that area of life that corresponds to where Uranus is situated in the sky. But if you remember that a revolution refers not only to the overthrow of old structures that have outlived their purpose but also to something coming around full circle thus fulfilling and redeeming itself, then you'll come to understand how Uranus is always trying to get you to be true to yourself. In your own unique way, you are rebuilding that stairway to heaven, so you can get back to where everything will be good and beautiful and true.

CHILD OF SATURN AND URANUS

When your Ruling Planet was discovered in 1781, astrologers had to accommodate this new find. Uranus, not Saturn, was the farthest planet from the Sun, so it was only fitting that it be given rulership of that time of year when the Sun is weakest—late January and February. Up to this point every Ruling Planet (with the exception of the Sun and Moon) had

LEWIS CARROLL
Wrote Alice in Wonderland
January 27, 1832

GERTRUDE STEIN
February 3, 1874

YOKO ONO
February 18, 1933

ARTISTIC GENIUS

WOLFGANG AMADEUS
MOZART
January 27, 1756

GEORGE BALANCHINE
*Choreographer and founder
of NYC Ballet*
January 22, 1904

BERTOLT BRECHT
February 10, 1898

had two months. Now Saturn would have to share one of its months with its neighbor Uranus.

Being a Child of two Planets can get a little complicated. It's not unlike having two sets of parents. In your case, Saturn and Uranus have a bit of history between them. And it's not altogether pretty.

The planet Uranus was named after the sky god Ouranos, whose name means "heaven." In Greek mythology, Uranus is the prime mover who gets the ball rolling when he made love to Gaia, goddess of the earth. At first Gaia gave birth to mountains and springs and forests and deserts. But it's when she sired one-eyed Cyclopes and hairy giants with hundreds of arms that things went awry. These weren't exactly the creatures Uranus had in mind for offspring. They offended his senses, so what Uranus did was put them back inside Gaia and then sealed up her womb. As you can imagine, this was a rather unpleasant experience. Gaia begged her children for help, and her son Saturn volunteered. Gaia gave Saturn a sickle—a blade shaped in the form of a half moon—and under the cover of darkness Saturn crept up on Uranus and castrated him. Pushing apart his father and mother, Saturn, the god of time, separated heaven (eternity) from earth (the material plane).

This split between heaven and earth—or the shiny ideal versus the day-to-day reality—lies at the crux of who you are. You can't heed the pull of one direction without feeling the grip of the other. As soon as your Uranian side flies up into space and begins contemplating the infinite realm of ideas and possibilities, that Saturn side brings you crashing back down to earth again with practical questions like: how are you going to make it happen? Whenever you try to conform to convention and live within the bounds—like any good Child of Saturn seeks to do—that Uranian side just erupts forth and knocks aside any of the people or situations it believes are trying to control you or hold you back. As a Child of Uranus, you are always struggling to understand your place in the order of things. You believe that your actions have an effect on the lives of others and that theirs have an effect on you. Your Saturn side will help you in your struggle to do what's right. Together, they make you reach for a wonderful place where what's right by you has to include what's right by others.

It's not hard to imagine this split playing out in your relationships. You may be drawn to stodgy controlling types so that they can provoke you into action. Then again you may find yourself constantly picking up after the crazy sibling or lover who goes spinning through your life like a runaway twister. Chances are you'll experience both. With two Planetary

Rulers, you're not so much a split personality as a pendulum that swings back and forth between extremes.

If a relationship feels like it's gone too far in the direction of *control*, then you'll feel hemmed in and start to believe that things are controlling you. This will then make you want to swing back the other way toward total *freedom*. But if you start to feel like you're too out there and that there isn't anything for you to latch onto, then you'll swing back in the direction of *control*—thus starting the whole cycle over again. Yet there's nothing like a smart paradox to open your mind. There is a way to incorporate both Ruling Planets in your life. You honor both equally. Know that Uranus gives you the ideas and Saturn provides you with the means to implement them. You can learn to get past that initial opposition of the two natures and work with them to your benefit.

Go ahead and turn to the Uranus tables on page 176 to find what sign Uranus was in on the day that you were born. Part III of this book will show how your Ruling Planet varies its expression from sign to sign. If there is an asterisk (*) next to your birth date, then you were born during a retrograde. If so, you'll want to come back and read the following:

CHILD OF URANUS RETROGRADE

Plus ça change, plus c'est la même chose is French for "the more things change, the more things remain the same." As a Child of Uranus Retrograde, you can relate to this. *Retrograde* refers to a backward motion. Uranus doesn't actually reverse direction. That's just the way it looks to us. It's an optical illusion that occurs periodically from Earth's viewpoint,

Saturn castrating his father, Uranus, and separating Earth from Sky.

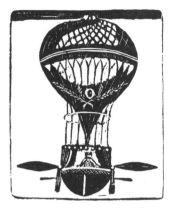

giving the impression of a planet moving backward against the setting of constellations in the sky. When a planet is retrograde, its energy becomes the opposite of what it is when it's direct. Since Uranus is the Planet of revolution and change, then that's what gets turned inside out. This isn't to say that if you're a Child of Uranus Retrograde your life will be static and uneventful. What it means is that you see things come and go on such a regular basis that you're in danger of becoming jaded. Change is less about progress and more akin to a hamster on an exercise wheel getting nowhere fast.

What often happens to Children of Uranus Retrograde is that you can start out making a series of changes only to find yourself back where you began, scratching your head and asking: what did I miss? That's because a revolution literally refers to the turn of a wheel. When something comes full circle, it returns, but it can also revert. Consider the French Revolution, which coincided with Uranus's discovery. The citizens of France overthrew their king and queen, wheeled out a guillotine, chopped off a lot of heads, went to war with their European neighbors, and for what? So Napoleon Bonaparte could come promenading down the Champs Élysées and proclaim himself emperor. And with the French people's blessing! Even the recent technological "revolution" has run true to form. Computers may bring innovation and progress, but the result is longer working hours than ever before while the rich still get richer and the poor get poorer. It's the same old, same old. New doesn't always mean different—which is something that you Children of Uranus Retrograde are keenly aware of. It's also why you tend to agonize over your actions and decisions.

For every point you can immediately anticipate a counterpoint. Your mind is so lightning fast that it catalogs all the possible causes and effects before you've even taken action. Subsequently you become overly involved with Byzantine maneuvers and can miss the through line. This can make you look as if you needlessly complicate things or are even trying to talk your way out of doing something that needs to be done. This locking of the mental wheels is hardly an agreeable experience. In Jonathan Swift's *Gulliver's Travels* the Laputians are a race of intellectuals whom Gulliver visits on their floating island. Years of theorizing have resulted in the Laputians having one eye turned inward while the other is cocked upward. Thus they are forced to hold their heads askew in order to avoid running into one another. Although meant as a parody, Jonathan Swift still conveys the ridiculous extremes people are forced to go to when they refuse to take the simplest course.

That's why it's so important that you *apply* yourself. Even if you don't see what there is to gain, you're better off acquiring experience. Not only will you discover that *doing* can be very different from *thinking*, but your thought process also changes once you actually engage the different quotients and variables. Foresight isn't always conducive to discovery. In some ways, it works against it. Hands-on experience gives you more control and maneuverability—transforming a wheel from something fickle into a device you can steer. Hands-on experience also keeps your head from getting lost in the clouds.

WHAT SIGN IS URANUS IN?

IF YOU WERE BORN ON . . .	YOUR URANUS IS IN . . .
January 20–February 18, 1900	Sagittarius
January 20–February 18, 1901	Sagittarius
January 20–February 18, 1902	Sagittarius
January 21–February 18, 1903	Sagittarius
January 21–February 19, 1904	Sagittarius
January 20–February 18, 1905	Capricorn
January 20–February 18, 1906	Capricorn
January 21–February 18, 1907	Capricorn
January 21–February 19, 1908	Capricorn
January 20–February 18, 1909	Capricorn
January 20–February 18, 1910	Capricorn
January 21–February 18, 1911	Capricorn
January 21–29, 1912	Capricorn
January 30–February 18, 1912	Aquarius
January 20–February 18, 1913	Aquarius
January 20–February 18, 1914	Aquarius

IF YOU WERE BORN ON . . .	YOUR URANUS IS IN . . .
January 21–February 18, 1915	Aquarius
January 21–February 18, 1916	Aquarius
January 20–February 18, 1917	Aquarius
January 20–February 18, 1918	Aquarius
January 21–February 18, 1919	Aquarius
January 21, 1920	Aquarius
January 22–February 18, 1920	Pisces
January 20–February 18, 1921	Pisces
January 20–February 18, 1922	Pisces
January 21–February 18, 1923	Pisces
January 21–February 18, 1924	Pisces
January 20–February 18, 1925	Pisces
January 20–February 18, 1926	Pisces
January 21–February 18, 1927	Pisces
January 21–February 18, 1928	Aries
January 20–February 18, 1929	Aries

* = retrograde

IF YOU WERE BORN ON . . .	YOUR URANUS IS IN . . .	IF YOU WERE BORN ON . . .	YOUR URANUS IS IN . . .
January 20–February 18, 1930	Aries	*January 20–February 18, 1958	Leo
January 21–February 18, 1931	Aries	*January 20–February 18, 1959	Leo
January 21–February 18, 1932	Aries	*January 21–February 18, 1960	Leo
January 20–February 18, 1933	Aries	*January 20–February 17, 1961	Leo
January 20–February 18, 1934	Aries	*January 20–February 18, 1962	Leo
January 20–February 18, 1935	Aries	*January 20–February 18, 1963	Virgo
January 21–February 18, 1936	Taurus	*January 21–February 18, 1964	Virgo
January 20–February 18, 1937	Taurus	*January 20–February 17, 1965	Virgo
January 20–February 18, 1938	Taurus	*January 20–February 18, 1966	Virgo
*January 20–21, 1939	Taurus	*January 20–February 18, 1967	Virgo
January 22–February 18, 1939	Taurus	*January 20–February 18, 1968	Virgo
*January 21–25, 1940	Taurus	*January 20–February 17, 1969	Libra
January 26–February 18, 1940	Taurus	*January 20–February 18, 1970	Libra
*January 20–29, 1941	Taurus	*January 20–February 18, 1971	Libra
January 30–February 18, 1941	Taurus	January 20–22, 1972	Libra
*January 20–February 2, 1942	Taurus	*January 23–February 18, 1972	Libra
February 3–18, 1942	Taurus	January 20–26, 1973	Libra
*January 20–February 6, 1943	Gemini	*January 27–February 17, 1973	Libra
February 7–18, 1943	Gemini	January 20–31, 1974	Libra
*January 21–February 11, 1944	Gemini	*February 1–18, 1974	Libra
February 12–18, 1944	Gemini	January 20–February 4, 1975	Scorpio
*January 20–February 14, 1945	Gemini	*February 5–18, 1975	Scorpio
February 15–18, 1945	Gemini	January 20–February 9, 1976	Scorpio
*January 20–February 18, 1946	Gemini	*February 10–18, 1976	Scorpio
*January 20–February 18, 1947	Gemini	January 20–February 13, 1977	Scorpio
*January 21–February 18, 1948	Gemini	*February 14–17, 1977	Scorpio
*January 20–February 17, 1949	Gemini	January 20–February 18, 1978	Scorpio
*January 20–February 18, 1950	Cancer	January 20–February 18, 1979	Scorpio
*January 20–February 18, 1951	Cancer	January 20–February 18, 1980	Scorpio
*January 21–February 18, 1952	Cancer	January 20–February 16, 1981	Scorpio
*January 20–February 17, 1953	Cancer	February 17, 1981	Sagittarius
*January 20–February 18, 1954	Cancer	January 20–February 17, 1982	Sagittarius
*January 20–February 18, 1955	Cancer	January 20–February 18, 1983	Sagittarius
*January 21–27, 1956	Leo	January 20–February 18, 1984	Sagittarius
*January 28–February 18, 1956	Cancer	January 20–February 17, 1985	Sagittarius
*January 20–February 17, 1957	Leo	January 20–February 17, 1986	Sagittarius

* = retrograde

IF YOU WERE BORN ON . . .	YOUR URANUS IS IN . . .
January 20–February 18, 1987	Sagittarius
January 20–February 14, 1988	Sagittarius
February 15–18, 1988	Capricorn
January 20–February 17, 1989	Capricorn
January 20–February 17, 1990	Capricorn
January 20–February 18, 1991	Capricorn
January 20–February 18, 1992	Capricorn
January 20–February 17, 1993	Capricorn
January 20–February 17, 1994	Capricorn
January 20–February 18, 1995	Capricorn
January 20–February 18, 1996	Aquarius
January 20–February 17, 1997	Aquarius
January 20–February 17, 1998	Aquarius
January 20–February 18, 1999	Aquarius

IF YOU WERE BORN ON . . .	YOUR URANUS IS IN . . .
January 20–February 18, 2000	Aquarius
January 20–February 17, 2001	Aquarius
January 20–February 17, 2002	Aquarius
January 20–February 18, 2003	Aquarius
January 20–February 18, 2004	Pisces
January 19–February 17, 2005	Pisces
January 20–February 17, 2006	Pisces
January 20–February 18, 2007	Pisces
January 20–February 18, 2008	Pisces
January 19–February 17, 2009	Pisces
January 20–February 17, 2010	Pisces
January 20–February 18, 2011	Pisces
January 20–February 18, 2012	Aries

* = retrograde

CHILD OF NEPTUNE

KEY WORDS

Ocean, exotic cultures, pearls, body fluids, trends, icons, the collective unconscious, film, photography, fantasy, wine, mysticism, self-sacrifice, empathy, addictions, hallucinogens, redemption, ships, illusion/disillusionment

If you're a Child of Neptune, then you're one of the few people who have two Birthday Planets! Not only are you a Child of Neptune, but you are also a Child of Jupiter. Go and read the section on Jupiter first, then come back here to get the rest of the story.

What you show the world is an infinitesimal part of who you really are. When people say you look like you're off in some dreamworld, they don't know the half of it. You're not just walking around in a dreamworld. You're walking around in a dream universe. Your inner life is so rich and alluring

DIVINE MADNESS

VASLAV NIJINSKY
*Brilliant ballet dancer and
choreographer who went mad*
February 28, 1889

DIANE ARBUS
*Influential photographer of
what was considered at the
time to be bizarre;
took her own life*
March 14, 1923

KURT COBAIN
*Lead singer of Nirvana
who committed suicide
at height of fame*
February 20, 1967

Ansel Adams was a Child of Neptune.

it's no wonder you'd rather be there than here. And if others could see what you see—chances are they'd dive in and join you.

Three-quarters of Earth's surface is submerged in water. This should give you some idea of how vast your psychic life is. When you think of all the sea creatures that scientists are still discovering—the giant squids that no one's actually seen alive, and how a prehistoric fish, the coelacanth (long thought extinct), resurfaced alive and well—then you'll begin to grasp how mysterious your unconscious truly is. People often think of the unconscious in terms of their feelings, dreams, and memories. But that would be like equating the ocean with what we see at the seashore. The unconscious, like the ocean, slides out past the shoals and rocks and down into a murky realm that has nothing to do with the world we live in. Your inner life is a barely tapped resource.

Neptune rules the imagination—which is why you Children of Neptune are all image makers. Indeed Neptune's discovery coincided with the advent of photography. Your ability to paint a picture with words, music, color, film, and even theorems (Child of Neptune Albert Einstein's $E = MC^2$ is probably one of the most famous invocations known) holds others spellbound. What you say, do, or create resonates on such a psychic level that people respond as if it were a God-given truth. Unfortunately you may not always know what you're setting loose. There are times when you may feel more like a vessel than a person. Having easy access to your imagination doesn't necessarily mean you control it. It takes a lifetime to learn how to swim in these uncharted waters without getting pulled down.

Neptune is the planet of glamour and illusion. The word *glamour* didn't always imply something high profile and fabulous. In medieval times glamour referred to an enchantment—like a magic spell. Music and film (both ruled by Neptune) are good examples of modern-day magic wherein people can get so swept up in the moment that they forget themselves. One can sit down at the movie theater in a dreadful mood and ninety minutes later depart feeling elated and inspired. Although it's impossible to predict what makes a hit, everyone certainly recognizes it when it materializes. Suddenly that one song on the radio is being dedicated by millions of fans to millions of their sweethearts or a

Narcissus gazing at his reflection.

FAR-OUT NOTIONS

ALEXANDER
GRAHAM BELL
Inventor of the telephone
March 3, 1847

FRITZ STRASSMANN
February 22, 1902
AND OTTO HAHN
*Together discovered
nuclear fission*
March 8, 1879

COPERNICUS
*Famous Polish astrologer who
theorized that the planets
orbited the Sun*
February 19, 1473

SYRENS

ANAÏS NIN
February 21, 1903

ELIZABETH TAYLOR
February 27, 1932

VANESSA WILLIAMS
March 18, 1963

character from a film takes on a life of his or her own—reappearing in merchandise, impersonations, hairstyles, and commercials—sometimes long after the actor has passed away. Lines of dialogue like "make my day" snake their way into the popular vernacular.

The effect of glamour is analogous to sipping a love potion and falling so desperately in love with the *image* of something that you want to become it—or at least be a part of it. Advertising campaigns thrive on this. They deliberately blur the lines between fantasy and reality so that millions of consumers believe that if they send away for that exercise machine then they really will have fabulous abs! Movie stars bank on it. Countries go to war because of it. An image or a symbol is extremely powerful. Think of a cross, a flag, or even a gang's colors and then consider how upset people become when they feel that something they identify with has been desecrated. A symbol isn't just a metaphor. It provokes an immediate and overwhelming response.

Like a symbol, you have an innate ability to stir the unconscious waters in just about everyone you meet. Have you ever noticed how often

people come up to you and ask if you've met before? You may remind them of someone, but they can't quite recollect who. That's your Ruling Planet's glamour at work. As a Child of Neptune you are a natural screen for others' projections. When they look at you, they

see the embodiment of their hopes and
wishes. Like the Syrens of myth, you become
the ideal partner, friend, love interest, or
employee. This is wonderful if you happen
to be a fashion model or spokesperson,
because what your Birthday Planet does is
transform you into a psychic billboard.
You're the perfect whatchamacallit. It's very
seductive to play into someone else's vision
of who you could be. It's also not such a bad
idea. Sometimes it's other people's dreams
and fantasies, rather than your own, that
enable you to make something of yourself.

The downside is that what others proj-
ect on to you may have very little (if anything) to do with who you are. Like
Eliza Doolittle in *My Fair Lady*, you can allow yourself to be transformed
into the toast of upper-class society—only to be dumped in the gutter the
next day. You can wind up feeling like an imposter in your own life if
you're not careful. Performers have to deal with this all the time, which is
why they'll create a third-person relationship to their own public persona.
That public persona is something they can put on and take off—like
makeup. However, if you're not a performer, you'll have to introduce some
of your own self-awareness into the picture. A clear line of demarcation
needs to be drawn between when you're on and when you're off or you will

Neptune rules hypnosis.

always be on call to other people's wants, needs, and desires. You become a figment of *their* imaginations—which, if you think about it, isn't much of a life. *No* may very well be the most valuable word you ever learn to use.

As a Child of Neptune, you believe that everyone comes from the same source—the sea. Just as the ocean gave birth to life billions of years ago, you believe that it's the emotions—the waters of life—that give birth to the person. It doesn't matter if you were born in New York City or Tehran. Everyone knows what it's like to *feel*. Regardless of what language you speak or culture you spring from everyone falls in love, suffers a broken heart, experiences ecstasy, and dreads agony. People may not feel to the same degree or even express themselves in the same way, but feelings are still universal. They provide the sympathy that links one psyche to another.

You're one of the few people capable of unconditional love. Unconditional love, by its very definition, must include every shade and glimmer. Darker currents like self-hate and despair run beneath lighter sentiments like mercy and self-sacrifice. You span the full gamut—sometimes within the space of a moment. It's very hard for you to be judgmental because you're always aware of "there but for the grace of God go I." There are few things you cannot imagine yourself doing. However, just because you can imagine yourself doing something doesn't mean you'll do it. You're well aware of the difference between a fancy and an action. Yet your empathy comes from an innate understanding that few people are driven to do harm for the fun of it. If someone inflicts pain on others it stems from having suffered it in their own lives. It's how that person learned to cope. You see cruelty as an extreme that some people—often victims themselves—are driven to. Therefore the solution isn't to punish but to rehabilitate.

To you everyone deserves a second chance. Water has always been associated with a fresh start. Out of the flood that carried Noah's ark a new world rises. Baptism—a sacrament integrally connected to water—signifies a spiritual birth. Forgiveness is your way of wiping the slate clean. Under the healing waters of Neptune, grudges lose their shape and grievances their force so that all that emotional energy is recycled—like water

evaporating into air. Forgiveness is a strength, not a weakness. And it's your particular challenge, as a Child of Neptune, to practice something that others will often deride. Forgiveness has its roots in our imperfections, not our perfections. Your sympathies lie with the underdogs and outcasts. There—*and with* the grace of God—go you.

When you experience love as unconditionally as you do, it's important to remember that *that* love is generic. Being a Child of Neptune, you don't make distinctions. The waves that swell in Antarctica are the same ones that loll ashore in Tahiti. In other words, your emotions are so fluid and changeable that the love you feel for a lover is going to be the same love you feel for a sunny day or a favorite pet. You can switch from one to the next,

Return of the Prodigal Son.

**WIPING THE SLATE
CLEAN**

EDWARD KENNEDY
February 22, 1932

LIZA MINNELLI
March 12, 1946

DREW BARRYMORE
February 22, 1975

like a kaleidoscope changing designs with every turn of the wheel. Love is what's most important. Objects of affection—like shorelines—are interchangeable. It's important to keep in mind that most people tend to measure love in the opposite way. That's why they can find it off-putting when you suddenly interrupt an intensely personal discussion to rhapsodize about last night's game or observe the play of light on the wall from the afternoon sun. Since you are an endless stream of consciousness, it's perfectly natural to free-associate; but not everyone channel surfs emotions like you.

As a Child of Neptune, you're out there holding people's hands, providing a strong shoulder for them to lean on, and imparting words of wisdom and encouragement. Yet sometimes you can end up going through the motions—the *emotional* motions—practiced countless times in the past. This is when you might wonder: what's in it for me? Relationship isn't the same as love. Although the two often complement each other, they are totally separate domains—like land and sea.

When two people fall in love they yearn to be together, to merge as one. Physically we can't do that, but emotionally we can. Emotions seek to dissolve differences, to mix and blend. A relationship, however, begins with the understanding that no two people experience the same thing at the same time. Each person has a personality, a history, likes and dislikes. Therefore a relationship is based on the understanding that there will always be some misunderstanding, because there is no possible way for one person to *really* know what another person thinks, much less feels. You can share mutual interests and even want the best for each other, but there will always be that separateness. Relationship emphasizes cooperation and teaches us to respect people's differences.

This is something that you, as a Child of Neptune, have a hard time accepting. When someone says he or she doesn't feel the same way you do, you must learn to respect that as a boundary. It's hard to do, because on an emotional level it's impossible to *not* know what someone else is feeling. After all, don't we all spring from the same emotional source? However, in the interests of your own psychic survival you must learn to take people at their word. Even if you can sense the undertones of attraction or resentment, you need to respect the face that people choose to show. It's not your job to do their emotional homework for them.

Yet being born empathetic doesn't mean you have to feel lost at sea. Sympathizing with life's victims doesn't require you to become one. With sensitivity comes the confidence to accept someone for who he or she is.

Your compassion is so strong that you needn't feel hurt when people can't reciprocate your feelings. But you have needs, too. Instead of searching emotional wrecks looking for something to salvage, why not relax in your element? That way you end up attracting someone who really appreciates you for who you are—and has no trouble matching you stroke for stroke.

Once every thirteen years, Neptune changes zodiac signs. It will change signs again in 2011.

Neptune glamourizes whatever astrological sign it passes through. Your Ruling Planet has to do with imaging, so you'll see its effect in popular trends like beliefs, politics, and fashion. When Neptune was in conservative Capricorn (the astrological sign of big business) from 1984 to 1998, wealth and status were the popular fixation. Television shows like *Dynasty* gave viewers a peek into the lifestyles of the rich and famous, and suddenly everyone was dressing up for success. When Neptune entered independent-minded Aquarius (the astrological sign of brotherhood and equality) in 1998, the myth shifted from climbing the corporate ladder to the benefits of synergy. Visions of a global village linked by a World Wide Web appeared. Start-up companies replaced trickle-down economics, and the home office made the big hair, bold makeup, and armored shoulder pads look of the 1980s a thing of the past.

VICTOR HUGO
Author of Les Miserables
and The Hunchback of
Notre-Dame
February 26, 1802

Although sensitive to the vicissitudes of your Birthday Planet, its effects won't be immediately apparent. Like the tide, it will move in slowly. When Neptune is about halfway through a sign, you'll find yourself completely immersed in what has let loose. Then the tide goes back out again so that when it departs there's very little value or meaning in what seemed so pervasive. But if you wait long enough, what was once fashionable comes back in a retro sort of way—which is only fitting, since your Birthday Planet rules nostalgia.

MAXIM GORKY
Wrote The Lower Depths
March 16, 1868

CHILD OF JUPITER AND NEPTUNE

Neptune's discovery was the result of what can only be called a "fishing expedition." It was theorized that something was pulling Uranus out of its predicted orbit, and the only reasonable explanation was the presence of another planet. Unfortunately, no one had been able to spot it. Using Newtonian principles, the Cambridge graduate John Adams was able to calcu-

JOHN STEINBECK
Author of The Grapes of Wrath
February 27, 1902

late the orbit of this spectral eighth planet. When Adams presented his findings to the royal astronomer, they were met with skepticism. How fitting that the first results of a study that would have led to Neptune's discovery were treated like the figment of someone's imagination!

At about the same time (and without Adams's knowledge) the French scientist Le Verrier was also engaged in predicting the orbit of an undiscovered planet using Newtonian principles. Coincidence or synchronicity? In any case the illusory planet was finally observed and confirmed in 1846 based on Le Verrier's formula. Seeing as Le Verrier was a Child of Neptune, it's only appropriate that he be the discoverer—though ultimately both men would share the credit. However, in true Neptunian fashion, the calculated orbit didn't even match the actual one. Its discovery was a lucky accident. If the search had taken place at any other time, the existence of Neptune might have remained a mystery.

When your Ruling Planet was discovered in 1846, astrologers had to accommodate this new find. Since Uranus (the first of the "new" planets) had already been partnered with Saturn, it seemed only natural to link Neptune with his brother Jupiter.

Things can get complicated when you're a Child of two Planets. It's not unlike having two sets of parents. Luckily for you, Jupiter and Neptune are similar in temperament (in fact, it's impossible to tell the two gods apart in classical art without the telltale thunderbolt or trident). Neptune, like Jupiter, rules over his own domain. Neptune's domain is the sea and Jupiter's is the sky. Like Children of Jupiter, you are in love with the world. However, you may not always be too sure *which* world you're talking about.

Children of Jupiter are in love with *this* world. For Children of Jupiter, there are always places to go and people to meet. They tend to see life as just getting up on its feet, and all anyone (or any*thing*) needs is a healthy push in the right direction. Your Jupiter side is what gives you your love of other lands and cultures as well as an enthusiasm about helping people become everything they can be.

Your Neptune side is in love with the spiritual world standing right behind the material one we all live in. For that side of you, the real world is the one that's yet to come. That's why you're willing to sacrifice and suffer as much as you do, because you know deep inside that everything will be made right in the end. The wicked will be punished and the meek shall inherit the earth. Your Neptune side allows you to commiserate and sympathize—but it can also manifest in Chicken Little–type hysteria where you run around crying out that the sky is falling. Despite your dread of things falling apart,

(M. Adams cherchant la planète de M. Leverrier.)

(M. Adams découvrant la nouvelle planète dans le rapport de M. Leverrier)

*Nineteenth-century French lampoon of the British astronomer Adams watching
Le Verrier discover the Planet Neptune.*

there's a secret part of you that actually looks forward to endings because
they put you that much closer to the way things are *supposed* to be.

As you can imagine, this split focus can divide your loyalties. Do you
choose Jupiter's world—the one that lies beyond the blue horizon? Or do
you choose Neptune's world—the one that's yet to come? Why not the *best*
of all possible worlds—which is the one that exists in your imagination?
Imagination is responsible for our creative genius. Without imagination,
we wouldn't be able to conceive of things as being any different from the
way they appear. Imagination—as much as time and nature—has shaped
the world we live in. It was Constantine the Great's vision of the holy cross

that inspired him to convert to Christianity and move the Roman Empire east—thus radically altering the face of the Ancient World. The imagination of Nicolaus Copernicus reconfigured our picture of the heavens by demonstrating that the planets revolved around the Sun, and it was the genius of Galileo that proved it. Ferdinand II had the foresight to send Columbus on his ocean voyage to the New World. George Washington fought for the American dream—literally. W. E. B. Du Bois's refusal to accept second-class citizenship and his subsequent cofounding of the NAACP laid the foundation for the civil rights movement in this country. Mikhail Gorbachev was responsible for Glasnost, F. W. de Klerk helped deconstruct apartheid, and Itzhak Rabin gave his life to further the Mideast peace process. All these were Children of Jupiter and Neptune. Part mystic, part adventurer, they were either reforming pioneers or they pioneered reform. As you can see—the imagination is not a force to be taken lightly or hidden away. As the writer Iris Murdoch once said: "Man is a creature who makes pictures of himself, and then comes to resemble the picture." The world, for you Children of Jupiter and Neptune, is truly what you make of it.

Go ahead and turn to the Neptune tables on page 192 to find out what sign your Ruling Planet was in on the day that you were born. Part III of this book will show how your Ruling Planet varies its expression from sign to sign. If there is an asterisk (*) next to your birth date, then you were born during a retrograde. If so, you'll want to come back and read the following:

CHILD OF NEPTUNE RETROGRADE

Neptune rules illusion *and* disillusionment. You need illusion. If you didn't have a dream of how you envisioned things coming together one day, then why get out of bed? When you're a child, you need to believe that you could grow up to become president. You need to feel as if your parents will always be there and that bad things will never happen. Not only does this give you hope, but it also puts your imagination to work on making your dreams a reality. But no one remains a child forever. And if it weren't for disillusionment, you wouldn't be able to adjust that vision. You'd still be trying to live life according to what you learned in nursery school. Although rarely a pleasant experience, disillusionment isn't just about feeling disappointed when things don't turn out the way you expected.

Disillusionment can also be that sinking feeling that follows any accomplishment or success. It's the sensation of waking from a really good dream. Yet it also permits you to roll over and dream anew.

Retrograde refers to a backward motion. Neptune doesn't actually reverse direction. That's just the way it looks to us. It's an optical illusion that occurs periodically from Earth's viewpoint, giving the impression of a planet moving backward against the setting of constellations in the sky. When a planet is retrograde, its energy becomes the opposite of what it is when it's direct. Since Neptune is the Planet of glamour and illusion, that's what gets turned inside out. This isn't to say that if you're a Child of Neptune Retrograde, you're a wallflower or will develop a jaded outlook because you've been burned so many times. What it means is you tend to see through things right away and can often anticipate the current of events.

The difficulty with seeing something before anyone else does is that by the time they recognize it, it's after the fact. Which does you no good. Hence your double bind. Do you follow your vision—which can make you sound deluded and hysterical—like some modern-day Cassandra? Or do you turn your back on what could have been and force yourself to ignore the phantom possibilities?

Many of us are taught to think of illusions as being negative. But since one can't always tell the difference between illusion and truth, it's sometimes better to adopt a more flexible attitude. Imagine someone lost in the desert. This person sees an oasis shimmering on the horizon. Believing himself saved, he crawls to that oasis only to realize he was fooled by a mirage. Frustrated, he curses his misfortune until he spots another oasis shimmering on the horizon. Now what should he do? Should he stay where he is, because this is probably just another trick of the mind? Or should he get up and go see for himself if this is truly a mirage or not? As a Child of Neptune Retrograde you know all too well how illusions work for and against. They can inspire you when you wouldn't have tried otherwise, just as much as they can lead you down the garden path. In any case, the only way to tell if you'll find what you're looking for is to seek it out.

WHAT SIGN IS NEPTUNE IN?

IF YOU WERE BORN ON . . .	YOUR NEPTUNE IS IN . . .
*February 19–March 4, 1900	Gemini
March 5–20, 1900	Gemini
*February 19–March 7, 1901	Gemini
March 8–20, 1901	Gemini
*February 19–March 9, 1902	Gemini
March 10–20, 1902	Gemini
*February 19–March 12, 1903	Cancer
March 13–20, 1903	Cancer
*February 20–March 13, 1904	Cancer
March 14–20, 1904	Cancer
*February 19–March 15, 1905	Cancer
March 16–20, 1905	Cancer
*February 19–March 18, 1906	Cancer
March 19–20, 1906	Cancer
*February 19–March 20, 1907	Cancer
*February 20–March 20, 1908	Cancer

IF YOU WERE BORN ON . . .	YOUR NEPTUNE IS IN . . .
*February 19–March 20, 1909	Cancer
*February 19–March 20, 1910	Cancer
*February 19–March 20, 1911	Cancer
*February 19–March 19, 1912	Cancer
*February 19–March 20, 1913	Cancer
*February 19–March 20, 1914	Cancer
*February 19–March 20, 1915	Cancer
*February 19–March 18, 1916	Leo
*March 19, 1916	Cancer
*February 19–March 20, 1917	Leo
*February 19–March 20, 1918	Leo
*February 19–March 20, 1919	Leo
*February 19–March 19, 1920	Leo
*February 19–March 20, 1921	Leo
*February 19–March 20, 1922	Leo
*February 19–March 20, 1923	Leo

* = retrograde

IF YOU WERE BORN ON . . .	YOUR NEPTUNE IS IN . . .
*February 19–March 19, 1924	Leo
*February 19–March 20, 1925	Leo
*February 19–March 20, 1926	Leo
*February 19–March 20, 1927	Leo
*February 19–March 19, 1928	Leo
*February 19–March 20, 1929	Leo
*February 19–March 20, 1930	Virgo
*February 19–March 20, 1931	Virgo
*February 19–March 19, 1932	Virgo
*February 19–March 20, 1933	Virgo
*February 19–March 20, 1934	Virgo
*February 19–March 20, 1935	Virgo
*February 19–March 19, 1936	Virgo
*February 19–March 20, 1937	Virgo
*February 19–March 20, 1938	Virgo
*February 19–March 20, 1939	Virgo
*February 19–March 19, 1940	Virgo
*February 19–March 20, 1941	Virgo
*February 19–March 20, 1942	Virgo
*February 19–March 20, 1943	Libra
*February 19–March 19, 1944	Libra
*February 19–March 19, 1945	Libra
*February 19–March 20, 1946	Libra
*February 19–March 20, 1947	Libra
*February 19–March 19, 1948	Libra
*February 18–March 19, 1949	Libra
*February 19–March 20, 1950	Libra
*February 19–March 20, 1951	Libra
*February 19–March 19, 1952	Libra
*February 18–March 19, 1953	Libra
*February 19–March 20, 1954	Libra
*February 19–March 20, 1955	Libra
*February 19–March 11, 1956	Scorpio
*March 12–19, 1956	Libra
*February 18–March 19, 1957	Scorpio
*February 19–March 20, 1958	Scorpio

IF YOU WERE BORN ON . . .	YOUR NEPTUNE IS IN . . .
*February 19–March 20, 1959	Scorpio
*February 19–March 19, 1960	Scorpio
*February 18–March 19, 1961	Scorpio
*February 19–March 20, 1962	Scorpio
*February 19–March 20, 1963	Scorpio
*February 19–March 19, 1964	Scorpio
February 18, 1965	Scorpio
*February 19–March 19, 1965	Scorpio
February 19–21, 1966	Scorpio
*February 22–March 20, 1966	Scorpio
February 19–23, 1967	Scorpio
*February 24–March 20, 1967	Scorpio
February 19–26, 1968	Scorpio
*February 27–March 19, 1968	Scorpio
February 18–27, 1969	Scorpio
*February 28–March 19, 1969	Scorpio
February 19–March 2, 1970	Sagittarius
*March 3–20, 1970	Sagittarius
February 19–March 4, 1971	Sagittarius
*March 5–20, 1971	Sagittarius
February 19–March 6, 1972	Sagittarius
*March 7–19, 1972	Sagittarius
February 18–March 8, 1973	Sagittarius
*March 9–19, 1973	Sagittarius
February 19–March 10, 1974	Sagittarius
*March 11–20, 1974	Sagittarius
February 19–March 13, 1975	Sagittarius
*March 14–20, 1975	Sagittarius
February 19–March 14, 1976	Sagittarius
*March 15–19, 1976	Sagittarius
February 18–March 17, 1977	Sagittarius
*March 18–19, 1977	Sagittarius
February 19–March 19, 1978	Sagittarius
February 19–March 20, 1979	Sagittarius
February 19–March 19, 1980	Sagittarius
February 18–March 19, 1981	Sagittarius

* = retrograde

IF YOU WERE BORN ON . . .	YOUR NEPTUNE IS IN . . .
February 18–March 19, 1982	Sagittarius
February 19–March 20, 1983	Sagittarius
February 19–March 19, 1984	Capricorn
February 18–March 19, 1985	Capricorn
February 18–March 19, 1986	Capricorn
February 19–March 20, 1987	Capricorn
February 19–March 19, 1988	Capricorn
February 18–March 19, 1989	Capricorn
February 18–March 19, 1990	Capricorn
February 19–March 20, 1991	Capricorn
February 19–March 19, 1992	Capricorn
February 18–March 19, 1993	Capricorn
February 18–March 19, 1994	Capricorn
February 19–March 20, 1995	Capricorn
February 19–March 19, 1996	Capricorn
February 18–March 19, 1997	Capricorn

IF YOU WERE BORN ON . . .	YOUR NEPTUNE IS IN . . .
February 18–March 19, 1998	Aquarius
February 19–March 20, 1999	Aquarius
February 19–March 19, 2000	Aquarius
February 18–March 19, 2001	Aquarius
February 18–March 19, 2002	Aquarius
February 19–March 20, 2003	Aquarius
February 19–March 19, 2004	Aquarius
February 18–March 19, 2005	Aquarius
February 18–March 19, 2006	Aquarius
February 19–March 20, 2007	Aquarius
February 19–March 19, 2008	Aquarius
February 18–March 19, 2009	Aquarius
February 18–March 19, 2010	Aquarius
February 19–March 19, 2011	Aquarius
February 19–March 19, 2012	Pisces

* = retrograde

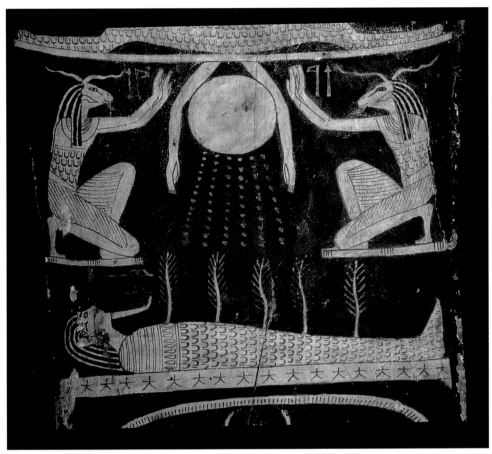

Ancient Egyptian rendition of seedlings from the mummified body of Osiris representing resurrection and new life.

CHILD OF PLUTO

❈

I f you're a Child of Pluto, then you're one of the few people who have two Birthday Planets! Not only are you a Child of Pluto, you are also a Child of Mars. Go and read the section on Mars first, then come back here to get the rest of the story.

Many people have a sense that their true nature is buried deep inside. They might attend workshops, go on spiritual retreats, or follow a specific regimen in hopes of connecting to that core self. You never had that problem. You've always known who you are—in your gut. You may not be able

KEY WORDS

The underworld, the soul, guts, obsession, secrets, other people's money, precious metals, petroleum, grain, surgery, cryogenics, laboratories, "hermetically sealed" or controlled environments, caves, geologists, archaeology, microbiologists, antibiotics, ancestors

Odysseus in the Underworld.

to describe it (much less explain it), but you know it's in there urging you, compelling you to live a complete and realized life. But this doesn't come as a result of good habits and healthy living. Crisis plays an active role in your psychic development. Pluto is the Planet of ordeals and the remarkable transformations that arise from them.

You don't flinch when it comes to looking at life's underside. What else would one expect from someone whose Birthday Planet is named after the god of the Underworld? In mythology, Pluto was the god of the dead. He ruled over that invisible realm beneath our feet, a subterranean world of rank and decay. Pluto rules over all those things that have died *and* are waiting to be born. Prehistoric cultures buried their dead in fetal positions. They believed that being buried in the earth was like being returned to the womb. You were put back in, so you could be born again. It's not too strange if you think of a seed. A seed is planted in the soil then sprouts, takes root, grows to full maturity, produces new seeds, then withers away and dies. The following year at about the same time, that same plant pops up again with maybe a few relatives in tow. Reincarnation doesn't seem so exotic or mysterious if you think of it in agricultural terms. It's why Eastern religions treat reincarnation like a mundane fact of life.

Psychologically speaking, as a Child of Pluto you "die" and are "born again" throughout your life. It can even be said you pack several lifetimes into one. Who you are at eight is very different from who you are at eighteen or twenty-eight, but underneath it all, you are still essentially the same person. You may grow into something much wilder than you would have thought—or thicker. Perhaps you branch out in all directions then flower, fade, and flower again. Nevertheless the essence of you is still the same. Pluto rules that essential essence, the seed that is you. And as a Child of Pluto, you will protect and relentlessly pursue who you were always meant to be.

As lord of the Underworld, Pluto was also the god of riches. Metals are dug up from the earth, as well as precious stones and "black gold"—oil. The name Pluto comes from *Pluton*, which means "giver of wealth." Yet the wealth originally referred to may have been a different kind of gold— grain. Grain is responsible for our daily bread, which nowadays can mean anything from food to money. Clearly your Birthday Planet has to do with the mining of riches—both literally and figuratively. But you have to be willing to go down into the depths to find them.

Pluto was discovered in 1930—right at the midpoint between the beginning of World War I and the end of World War II. Those years bore witness to the darkest humanity had to offer. Ironically, it was two attributes of Pluto that brought the overall conflict to an end—petroleum (which means "rock oil") and plutonium (which was named after your Ruling Planet). Possession of the world's oil reserves along with the atom bomb ensured an Allied victory. However, in true Pluto fashion, there is a dark side to all this. It's the specter of complete annihilation that serves to keep the peace.

BORN AGAIN

CHRISTIAAN BARNARD
The first doctor to perform a heart transplant
November 8, 1922

BILLY GRAHAM
Evangelist
November 7, 1918

BRAM STOKER
Creator of Dracula
November 8, 1847

TELLING IT LIKE IT IS

LARRY FLYNT
Founder of Hustler *magazine
and free speech activist*
November 1, 1942

ROBERT MAPPLETHORPE
Censored photographer
November 4, 1946

ROSEANNE
Comedienne and feminist
November 3, 1952

Justice and Divine Vengeance pursuing Crime.

You operate on a more instinctive level than most. You know when something's amiss. It might come across as a whiff of intrigue or an averted glance. You have a sixth sense for what's been left *unsaid*. You believe everyone has a hidden agenda—whether they're aware of it or not. You don't like secrets (although you're excellent at keeping them), and you can't stand lies—not even white ones. If you feel that someone has lied to you, or isn't being particularly forthcoming, you will pursue a line of inquiry with all the zeal of a grand inquisitor. Senator Joe McCarthy, whose name has become synonymous with witch hunts, was a Child of Pluto. Even if the person finally breaks down and divulges all, it still takes you a while to put on the brakes. The truth is very important to you. But this isn't some abstract, spiritual truth. What you're after is the dirty-little-secret truth.

As a Child of Pluto, you know all about the darker corners of the human psyche. Dependency, obsession, compulsion, fear of abandonment, rage, lust, and greed are like old friends. Most people are afraid of these characteristics and will try to distance themselves from them or at least pawn them off on others. You know that's impossible. The dark side is most dangerous when it's kept buried, because that's when it bubbles up through the cracks and plays havoc with your life. This is something celebrities and politicians have to deal with constantly when the skeletons in their closets come out to play. Children of Pluto, however, are rarely caught with their pants down. That's because you would never have compromised yourself to begin with. Owing up to your dark side keeps you honest.

People like to unburden their souls to you. It doesn't matter if someone is a perfect stranger, within moments of striking up a conversation, you'll hear all about the sordid details of this person's life—whether you wanted to or not. Somehow everyone knows that you *know* what it's like. Yet being a confidant gives you a peculiar status. You're the first person everyone seeks out when going through a rough patch, but you may also be the first person they avoid when they emerge safely on the other side. It's almost as if they identify you with the problem, and continued exposure to you might bring it back. That's why it's so important (for your own mental health) to understand that there's a difference between life on the surface and life in the lower depths.

You don't do "lite." It's not in your Birthday Planet's vocabulary. You're too intense. You may have gone through periods (especially when you were younger) when you felt ashamed for reacting the way you do. Perhaps you even tried to cover it up. In time you've come to accept you're not everyone's cup of tea. You may know a lot of people, but you have very few friends. And you like it that way. You rely on your inner circle. It's the only place (other than when you're by yourself) where you open up. In those moments of soul-searching—when you descend into the very depths of your being—you want to know you can do that without having to worry about being too intense for the people around you. You don't have much patience for people who live "surface" lives, but you may also come to realize that not everyone has to reach your depth of feeling to be a friend. Someone can react to a situation coolly or pragmatically, but it doesn't mean that person doesn't care.

Pluto's season falls in autumn after the crops have been harvested. The Sun grows distant and cold and Mother Nature, who was so rich

MARIE-ANTOINETTE
November 2, 1755

HILLARY RODHAM
CLINTON
October 26, 1947

BILL GATES
October 28, 1955

and bountiful in summer, looks like she's gathered up her things and gone home. Everything goes to seed in the fall. You can't escape this pervasive feeling that you arrived just when everyone else left—as if somehow you "missed out." That's why you have such a strong reaction to being short-changed or offered sloppy seconds. You refuse to make do. You want what you should have gotten in the first place—a seat at the table. Children of Pluto are born with a chip on their shoulder, and whatever bumps and lumps follow in life only reinforces the conviction that you were handed the short end of the stick to begin with. Someone will always be smarter, better looking, richer, or further along in the game than you. But you don't begrudge anyone their success—if they earned it. What you can't stand is when someone gets a free ride.

Outrage is the source of your power. The more rejections you experience, the more persistent you become. The more you fall short, the more determined you are to get even. You never roll over and take it. You always fight back—but not necessarily in the moment. As a Child of Pluto, you bide your time. Resentments can go underground and remain very hot—like burning coals—for years. That need to get even can keep you going when everything looks hopeless.

The downside to this is you can get hooked into a vicious cycle. If your willpower is fueled by pain and rejection, then it only makes sense that you continue to feel hurt if you want to stay willful. Your survival can become invested in your always feeling victimized. Even if it's not true, your survival instinct may feel it's in your best interest to perceive life that way. This can get into some pretty tricky territory wherein you will nurse a grudge rather than move past it.

As a Child of Pluto you know what it's like to fixate on one thing to the exclusion of anything else. Everyone goes through periods when they feel like they have to have something in their lives—or else! Yet unlike most people, your obsessions can last for months, even years. That's because your obsession is based on seeing the world as a place of scarcity, not plenty. When you're obsessed you say "I have to be in love with *this* person" or "I have to get *this* job—nothing else will do." Yet an obsession is psychically designed to keep you from getting what you want. It's the frustration, pain, and despair—not fulfillment—that keep you coming back for more.

These are dark passions. You may have noticed how friends and loved ones refuse to "go there" after a while, because there's just no reasoning with you when you're like that. Part of you knows you don't make for the

Charles Atlas was a Child of Pluto.

most pleasant company when you're obsessed, but another part of you knows that seeds take root in the dark, and that in a very organic way you can draw upon your dark passions for sustenance. They provide the energy and strength to break out of the ground and grow into the light. As the philosopher Spinoza once said: "There is no hope without fear and no fear without hope."

Although Pluto is the Planet of obsessions, it's also the very Planet

**ORPHEUS
DESCENDING**

SYLVIA PLATH
October 27, 1932

DYLAN THOMAS
October 27, 1914

ANNE SEXTON
November 9, 1928

that forces you to realize that you can—and must—live without them. That's why it's the Planet of ordeals and the transformations that arise from them. Only by descending into the Underworld will you reemerge stronger and more vital than you were before.

Your Ruling Planet's ordeals have to do with loss—loss of belongings, loss of control, loss of your better senses—such as when you're obsessed with something you can't have. If an obsession continues unchecked, it will drain the life from you, like an addiction. Pluto insists that you face your fears, because it's only by facing your fears that you can truly call upon your life force. But facing your fears doesn't mean mastering them. Facing your fears is about realizing you're beat and there's nothing left to lose. It's the moment of supreme desperation, or despair, that allows you to do something you would never do on your own—which, by the way, is the very thing necessary to rise again from the depths. No one really knows what that's like—unless they've been there. And what that answer means to you may be completely meaningless to someone else. However as a Child of Pluto you can tell when someone you meet has gone through that experience. There's something in that person's demeanor that sets him or her apart from all the rest.

Yet not all Underworld journeys are dreadful—like not all obsessions are bad. Sometimes Pluto beckons you to follow a path that leads away from what is considered healthy, normal, or productive. These Underworld journeys may be perceived as bad by others—why are you leaving a wonderful relationship to run off with a bum? Or do you really have to quit your high-profile job in order to write poetry full-time? These are perfectly valid choices, but they might not make a lot of sense to anyone but you. In order to follow through with these decisions, you have to be single-

minded, which makes you appear unreasonable or even . . . *obsessed*. It's
a fine line between an attraction to something you feel you can't live without and an attraction to something you feel completes you as a person.
This distinction between the two is only discovered after you've been
through the worst. Yet your Ruling Planet rewards those who brave its crucible. Life after a Pluto ordeal is always rich and fulfilling. The transformation of self into something greater is your life work. When you think of
the very deep and soulful journeys of St. Augustine, Martin Luther,
Mahalia Jackson, and Sylvia Plath (all Children of Pluto) you begin to
appreciate the full measure of your planetary legacy. The power of their
personalities and the confessional intimacy of their work still give us solace in our troubles and inspiration to rise from the depths. The artist Pablo
Picasso (another Child of Pluto) believed that his work would keep him
alive. When one reflects on the power and enormity of his output, who
would argue?

Because Pluto has such an eccentric orbit (at one point it crosses Neptune's path and actually moves *closer* to the Sun) it can take anywhere from
twelve to thirty-one years to pass through one astrological sign, which
means you can spend a long time in one holding pattern. However when

Resurrection of the Dead.

PARACELSUS
*First person to link chemistry
to medicine*
November 11, 1493

MARTIN LUTHER
November 10, 1483

MARIE CURIE
*First woman to receive
Nobel Prize*
November 7, 1867

Pluto changes signs you'll experience a dramatic shift in energies. It won't happen all at once. You may even feel the vibrations approaching as much as two or three years before the actual change of sign. Like anything to do with Pluto, the developments start out small and then build in intensity. Your Ruling Planet will change signs again in 2008.

It's this very orbital eccentricity that has led some astronomers to say that Pluto is not a planet at all, but a comet. This makes poetic sense in that Pluto would go from being the smallest planet to the largest of the Kuiper Belt objects (where it's believed that comets originate from)—essentially making it king of the comets. Given the reputation of comets as omens or messengers from beyond, it would certainly be in keeping with your Birthday Planet's status as lord of the Underworld. Edmond Halley, the discoverer of Halley's Comet, was a Child of Pluto.

CHILD OF MARS AND PLUTO

When Pluto was discovered in 1930, astrology once again had to accommodate a new planet. Saturn, the last of the ancient planets, had already been partnered with Uranus, and Jupiter with Neptune, so it only made sense that Mars (being third from the last) be paired with Pluto.

Things can get complicated when you're a Child of two Planets. It's not unlike having two sets of parents. Yet few could imagine what it's like to contend with your pair of extremes. In no other Child of the Planets are the forces of life and death (Eros and Thanatos) so utterly entwined. Mars, whose season is the spring, propels you forward into life while Pluto, whose season is autumn, shows that loss leads to gain. A sitcom featuring Mike Brady marrying Morticia Addams might give you some idea of the incongruity at play.

Mars identifies with the winner. It's the part of you that refuses to give up no matter

Children of Pluto can have a fiendish intensity.

what. It prevails upon you to score (and score big!) and to hell with the consequences. Yet the Pluto side of you knows that for every action there is an opposite and equal reaction. One can say to hell with the consequences in the moment but that doesn't preclude the fact that eventually there will be hell to pay. You're acutely aware of the ratio of winners to losers. Winners are in the minority. Fear of retaliation can make you come on too strong—Children of Mars and Pluto are famous for the preemptive strike. Then there will be times when, because you were too timid, you didn't act decisively and thus lost your advantage. Tempering your strengths is a lifelong discipline.

However Mars and Pluto also bestow one of the most passionate and creative temperaments one can ever hope to have. There's no such thing as apathy or world-weariness. Admittedly few things pique your interest, but when aroused, you will pour all your time and energy into pursuing what fascinates you. This can make you obstinate in love—which may be a turnoff for people who don't get it, but a turn-on for the few who do. When it comes to choosing between quality and quantity, you go for quality. Love affairs may be few and far between, but that's because lovemaking is something sacred to you. When you bond, it's on a very deep and soulful level. Passion is your eternal flame.

Go ahead and turn to the Pluto tables on page 207 to find what sign your Ruling Planet was in on the day you were born. Part III of this book will show how your Ruling Planet varies its expression from sign to sign. If there is an asterisk (*) next to your birth date, then you were born during a retrograde. If so, you'll want to come back and read the following:

CHILD OF PLUTO RETROGRADE

Those born when Pluto is retrograde tend to keep their dark side under wraps. *Retrograde* refers to a backward motion. Pluto doesn't actually reverse direction. That's just the way it looks to us. It's an optical illusion that occurs periodically from Earth's viewpoint, giving the impression of a planet moving backward against the setting of constellations in the sky. When a planet is retrograde, its energy becomes the opposite of what it is when it's direct. Since Pluto is the Planet of ordeals and the transformations that arise from them, that's what gets turned inside out. This isn't to say that if you're a Child of Pluto Retrograde, you'll live an ordeal-free existence. What it means is that you will go out of your way to avoid trouble, and by

END OF THE LINE

CHARLES II
Last monarch of the Spanish Hapsburg dynasty
November 6, 1661

BAHADUR SHAH II
Last Mughal emperor of India
October 24, 1775

VICTOR EMMANUEL III
Last king of Italy
November 11, 1869

GUSTAV VI
Last king of Sweden to hold real political power
November 11, 1882

MANUEL II
Last king of Portugal
November 15, 1889

PRAJADHIPOK
Last absolute king of Siam
November 8, 1893

ALEKSANDR VASILYEVICH KOLCHAK
Supreme ruler of Russia . . . for a year
November 4, 1874

MOHAMMAD REZA SHAH PAHLAVI
The deposed Shah of Iran
October 26, 1919

doing so, you could inadvertently make things harder on yourself.

Things often appear hopelessly out of reach, so you'll hug the side of the pool rather than dive down into the depths. There's nothing wrong with that except you can't help feeling you should be doing more. You may choose to repress certain talents because you don't think you're good enough. You undercut yourself before somebody else can get the chance. You don't act on an attraction because you're afraid of being rejected, or you live a "double-life" where you're wildly creative in private but like to appear unassuming in public. Then again you may neglect certain parts of yourself simply because it never occurred to you to do anything with them in the first place.

There are only two occasions when you'll question what you're doing with your life. The first is when you're forced to—with, for example, a crisis. And the second is when something deep inside says this is the right time for it. You may go through fallow periods, but when the time comes for those hidden parts of yourself to emerge, you'll know it.

To be born under a retrograde Planet is to be assigned a special kind of fate. You may have to wait a long time before anything happens, but when it does, that transformation will be powerful and dramatic. It will provide a rich and rewarding experience that proves well worth the wait.

Beatitude by Ben Shahn, 1952

WHAT SIGN IS PLUTO IN?

IF YOU WERE BORN ON . . .	YOUR PLUTO IS IN . . .
*October 23–November 21, 1900	Gemini
*October 24–November 21, 1901	Gemini
*October 24–November 22, 1902	Gemini
*October 24–November 22, 1903	Gemini
*October 23–November 21, 1904	Gemini
*October 24–November 21, 1905	Gemini
*October 24–November 22, 1906	Gemini
*October 24–November 22, 1907	Gemini
*October 23–November 21, 1908	Gemini
*October 24–November 21, 1909	Gemini
*October 24–November 22, 1910	Gemini
*October 24–November 22, 1911	Gemini
*October 23–November 21, 1912	Gemini
*October 24–November 21, 1913	Cancer
*October 24–November 22, 1914	Cancer
*October 24–November 22, 1915	Cancer

IF YOU WERE BORN ON . . .	YOUR PLUTO IS IN . . .
*October 23–November 21, 1916	Cancer
*October 23–November 21, 1917	Cancer
*October 24–November 22, 1918	Cancer
*October 24–November 22, 1919	Cancer
*October 23–November 21, 1920	Cancer
**October 23–November 21, 1921	Cancer
*October 24–November 22, 1922	Cancer
*October 24–November 22, 1923	Cancer
*October 23–November 21, 1924	Cancer
*October 23–November 21, 1925	Cancer
*October 24–November 22, 1926	Cancer
*October 24–November 22, 1927	Cancer
*October 23–November 21, 1928	Cancer
*October 23–November 21, 1929	Cancer
*October 24–November 22, 1930	Cancer
*October 24–November 22, 1931	Cancer

* = retrograde

IF YOU WERE BORN ON . . .	YOUR PLUTO IS IN . . .
October 23, 1932	Cancer
*October 24–November 21, 1932	Cancer
October 23–25, 1933	Cancer
*October 26–November 21, 1933	Cancer
October 24–26, 1934	Cancer
*October 27–November 21, 1934	Cancer
October 24–28, 1935	Cancer
*October 29–November 22, 1935	Cancer
October 23–29, 1936	Cancer
*October 30–November 21, 1936	Cancer
October 23–30, 1937	Leo
*October 31–November 21, 1937	Leo
October 24–November 1, 1938	Leo
*November 2–21, 1938	Leo
October 24–November 3, 1939	Leo
*November 4–22, 1939	Leo
October 23–November 3, 1940	Leo
*November 4–21, 1940	Leo
October 23–November 5, 1941	Leo
*November 6–21, 1941	Leo
October 24–November 7, 1942	Leo
*November 8–21, 1942	Leo
October 24–November 9, 1943	Leo
*November 10–22, 1943	Leo
October 23–November 10, 1944	Leo
*November 11–21, 1944	Leo
October 23–November 11, 1945	Leo
*November 12–21, 1945	Leo
October 24–November 13, 1946	Leo
*November 14–21, 1946	Leo
October 24–November 15, 1947	Leo
*November 16–22, 1947	Leo
October 23–November 16, 1948	Leo
*November 17–21, 1948	Leo
October 23–November 18, 1949	Leo
*November 19–21, 1949	Leo

IF YOU WERE BORN ON . . .	YOUR PLUTO IS IN . . .
October 23–November 20, 1950	Leo
*November 21, 1950	Leo
October 24–November 22, 1951	Leo
October 23–November 21, 1952	Leo
October 23–November 21, 1953	Leo
October 23–November 21, 1954	Leo
October 24–November 22, 1955	Leo
October 23–November 21, 1956	Virgo
October 23–November 21, 1957	Virgo
October 23–November 21, 1958	Virgo
October 24–November 22, 1959	Virgo
October 23–November 21, 1960	Virgo
October 23–November 21, 1961	Virgo
October 23–November 21, 1962	Virgo
October 23–November 21, 1963	Virgo
October 24–November 22, 1963	Virgo
October 23–November 21, 1964	Virgo
October 23–November 21, 1965	Virgo
October 23–November 21, 1966	Virgo
October 24–November 22, 1967	Virgo
October 23–November 21, 1968	Virgo
October 23–November 21, 1969	Virgo
October 23–November 21, 1970	Virgo
October 24–November 21, 1971	Libra
October 23–November 21, 1972	Libra
October 23–November 21, 1973	Libra
October 23–November 21, 1974	Libra
October 24–November 21, 1975	Libra
October 23–November 21, 1976	Libra
October 23–November 21, 1977	Libra
October 23–November 21, 1978	Libra
October 24–November 21, 1979	Libra
October 23–November 21, 1980	Libra
October 23–November 21, 1981	Libra
October 23–November 21, 1982	Libra
October 23–November 4, 1983	Libra
November 5–21, 1983	Scorpio

* = retrograde

IF YOU WERE BORN ON . . .	YOUR PLUTO IS IN . . .
October 23–November 21, 1984	Scorpio
October 23–November 21, 1985	Scorpio
October 23–November 21, 1986	Scorpio
October 23–November 21, 1987	Scorpio
October 23–November 21, 1988	Scorpio
October 23–November 21, 1989	Scorpio
October 23–November 21, 1990	Scorpio
October 23–November 21, 1991	Scorpio
October 23–November 21, 1992	Scorpio
October 23–November 21, 1993	Scorpio
October 23–November 21, 1994	Scorpio
October 23–November 9, 1995	Scorpio
November 10–21, 1995	Sagittarius
October 23–November 21, 1996	Sagittarius
October 23–November 21, 1997	Sagittarius

IF YOU WERE BORN ON . . .	YOUR PLUTO IS IN . . .
October 23–November 21, 1998	Sagittarius
October 23–November 21, 1999	Sagittarius
October 23–November 21, 2000	Sagittarius
October 23–November 21, 2001	Sagittarius
October 23–November 21, 2002	Sagittarius
October 23–November 21, 2003	Sagittarius
October 23–November 20, 2004	Sagittarius
October 23–November 21, 2005	Sagittarius
October 23–November 21, 2006	Sagittarius
October 23–November 21, 2007	Sagittarius
October 23–November 20, 2008	Sagittarius
October 23–November 21, 2009	Capricorn
October 23–November 21, 2010	Capricorn
October 23–November 21, 2011	Capricorn
October 23–November 20, 2012	Capricorn

* = *retrograde*

WHAT SIGN IS MY RULING PLANET IN?

CHILD OF THE SUN ...

You were born near dawn when your Ruling Planet was just peeking over the horizon. Subsequently, life comes to you, you don't have to go to it. Ever since you can remember, you've been treated like someone special. Loved ones couldn't help fawning over you. Kids at school wanted you to join their circle of friends. Teachers always favored you and—if you happened to be too much of a hellion—let you off with a light rap on the knuckles. Your presence makes faces light up when you walk into a room—even when you're not trying to. You are the ray of hope everyone's been looking for, the youthful promise of a new day.

In many ways your childhood extends throughout your entire life. You will never grow jaded or bitter. Life won't let you. There will always be the promise of a fresh romance or exciting endeavor just around the next bend. This doesn't make you immune to life's disappointments, but emotional scars tend to heal quickly. Though you are romantic and theatrical, there's a secret part of you that wouldn't mind being more melancholic at times—breathing heavy sighs and thinking profound and mysterious thoughts. But no one takes you seriously when you do, it just isn't you. A pat on the back or a funny face is all it takes to make that sunny smile of yours come back out again.

Because of the Sun's position at the time you were born, you're one of the lucky few who gets to do what you love for a living. Your Birthday Planet rules entertainment, leisure, and recreation—as well as the arts and sciences. Even if all you do is scribble theorems all day, there's something about the sheer pleasure of your expression that makes others wish they could trade places with you—even if they haven't the foggiest notion of what you do. A First House Sun is an excellent position for anyone who has to be on the scene—like a lawyer, doctor, athlete, or performer—in order for the job to get done. It also gives you a keen mind. However, the difficulty with things coming easily when you're young is that you may grow into the habit of ignoring anything that doesn't. Crossing your arms and refusing to budge may bolster you in the moment, but in the long run you only shortchange yourself.

Obviously you want to be seen in your best

WITH SUN IN FIRST HOUSE

light. You're concerned about leading with your strengths and not your weaknesses, but you can't be right all the time. Not only is it impossible, but how will you ever learn from your mistakes if you don't acknowledge them? Few people will tell you this. In part because they don't want to upset someone as charming as yourself, but also because after a certain age it becomes easier to accommodate you than to contradict you. If you don't want to find yourself in the same predicament as the emperor parading about in his "new clothes" it's best that you develop a healthy self-awareness to go along with that strong personality of yours.

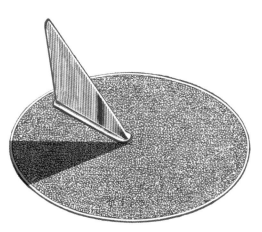

Like a thoroughbred, you're good for short fast sprints and should never be saddled with doing something long and tedious. Your talent is in the "attack." You come on the scene with such a burst of energy that you immediately steal all the attention with the first move you make or remark you utter. You're a hard act to follow. However you don't have a strong follow-through, which means you need to get in and out quickly. You do best with short-term projects—especially ones that require you to absorb what's going on in the moment and then act on it. Your best times of the year are near the equinoxes and solstices—which means on or around the twentieth of March, June, September, and December. If you can time it so that you're either starting out or finishing up around then, you'll meet with success. Paradoxically, your own birthday month is a lackadaisical time for you. Since it often follows on the heels of a busy period, the only thing you feel like doing is sprawling out for an afternoon catnap.

CHILD OF THE SUN ...

You are unabashedly possessive. Possessiveness is a universal emotion that most people pretend not to feel. Yet it's borne from self-preservation. If you could rope off your own little corner of the world and hang up a sign that reads NO TRESPASSING—you would. For you, maintaining clearly marked boundaries is the secret to peaceful coexistence. But this territorial instinct is hardly rooted in selfishness. Self-sufficiency is your credo, and you, more than most, will go the extra distance to help someone get set up. As a Child of the Sun with the Sun in the Second House you are naturally drawn to the business of financing—anything from entrepreneurship to helping young homeowners purchase their first house. You believe it's always better to teach someone the ropes than to foster dependency with handouts.

You look at money the same way you look at food and shelter. It's a staple. You need it in order to survive. You're also extremely sensitive to the fact that nothing lasts forever—food spoils, clothes fall apart, the house needs remodeling. This is why you pinch those pennies for every cent they're worth and stretch those dollars like they were rubber bands. You want to make sure you will always be able to provide for yourself and your loved ones.

In truth money is an extremely complex and sensitive topic. You can go through periods where you won't think twice about laying out an enormous sum but will feel scandalized if an item costs fifty cents more in one store than it does in another. You are always taken aback when people discuss their finances in public. Not only is it gauche, but they also remind you of hungry grasshoppers eating through their savings during the golden days of summer while foolishly ignoring the wintry days ahead. However you are still a Child of the Sun. You have a genuine love of beautiful things, and though you will always keep an eye out for sales, you won't deny yourself either. You're a firm believer in positive thinking. Give yourself what you want now and you'll work hard to maintain it. Deny yourself the luxuries and you'll gradually settle for second best.

Sometimes the price of upkeep can be too high, and instead of your possessions belonging to you, you can wind up belonging to your possessions. This can get especially complicated,

WITH SUN IN SECOND HOUSE

considering your need for emotional security. Financial security is pretty straightforward, because it's all about money. But emotional security is based on how you *feel*. And, as any financier will tell you, mixing figures with feelings is never a good idea. Because of the Sun's position at the time of your birth, you will dole out a lot in order to feel

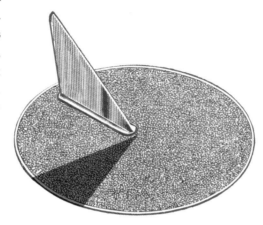

emotionally secure. You will pay whatever you *feel* you need to if it means keeping worries and fears at bay. You may stay in a job you don't want, a relationship that has lost any relevance, or slavishly maintain a lifestyle aimed at keeping up with the Joneses—even if you surpassed the Joneses a long time ago. This is when it's important to remind yourself that money really is *just* a staple. It's meant to ensure your survival—not dominate it. Too much focus on money, like too much absorption with anything, leads to fixation, not fulfillment. In your quest to be self-sufficient you don't want to develop a dependency.

Late April through mid-May, late August through mid-September, and late December through mid-January are your most prosperous times. You work very hard, and these are the periods when you reap the rewards you so richly deserve. Late October through mid-November is tough, since more money is going out rather than coming in. It may be a typical trend, but you still won't be happy about it. Nevertheless it's a necessity and actually works to drain off any excess. Late February through March is the best time to expand your field of operations or clientele. It's when you're feeling especially enthusiastic and vigorous. It's also a wonderful time for romance, as you're feeling just a little full of yourself—which, on you, is always attractive.

CHILD OF THE SUN ...

You were born in the wee hours of the morning and like a seed sprouting in the fresh dark earth, you're eager to establish yourself as soon as possible. When you're a Child of the Sun with the Sun in the Third House, urgency colors just about everything you do. But this isn't the urgency that accompanies crisis, it's urgency borne of haste. Most people tend to follow events as they gradually unfold over weeks or months. You pack as much as you can into one day. A single morning—if need be.

Because there are never enough hours in the day you go right to the heart of the matter. Some people may be put off by your familiarity, but most respond positively to your Solar charm and "let's-not-beat-around-the-bush" candor. Your earnestness leaves people feeling that what they have to say is very important. You're a rapt listener. You have a keen mind and absorb things quickly. Everything interests you and if sufficiently fascinated, you'll immerse yourself completely—and to the total exclusion of anything else. You will read everything you can about a certain topic or teach yourself the rudiments of a technique until you acquire some mastery of it.

You have extraordinary powers of concentration and an ironclad self-discipline. However your interest also tends to burn out quickly, and when it does it's unlikely you'll ever return to what enthralled you again.

Hurry-scurry is so ingrained that it's like going through psychic withdrawal if you're kept out of the loop for too long. You live and breathe work, but not because you're a workaholic. You're drawn to professions where things are highly charged and ephemeral—like journalism, advertising, buying and selling shares, or even food catering—where a great deal of fuss is made over something that's over in an hour or two. The shelf life may be short, but the moments are intense and all-consuming.

It's easy to get caught up in the hectic pace of your day-to-day life. This can lead to burning the candle at both ends if you're not careful. Given your tendency to fixate on anything *new* (and with your insatiable curiosity, there will *always* be something new and interesting), you can exhaust yourself with constant excitement and anticipation. You need downtime to counterbalance your "up" time or you'll fizzle.

WITH SUN IN THIRD HOUSE

Because of the Sun's position at the time of your birth, you come into your own later on in life. One wouldn't think it, considering how early you develop, but as a child you were forced to contend with ever changing circumstances—and these bouts of unpredictability would have frustrated rather than emboldened you. One of these circumstances may

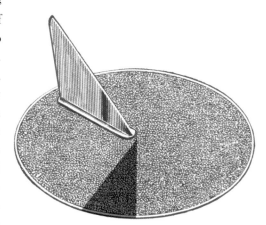

have been a problematic relationship with a sibling. A brother or sister may have stolen much of the attention when you were growing up (either in a positive or a negative way), and you might have felt more like a second thought than a primary focus. This could leave you with a lingering ambivalence when it comes to your family as well as mixed feelings about settling down with a partner or working closely with a colleague. It might very well take until your early thirties to develop a self-confidence that isn't easily undermined as well as the capacity to share the limelight without fear of being overshadowed.

Late May through mid-June as well as August through September are active times for you. If you aren't taken up with professional concerns then you're tending to your equally busy social life. Friendships are very important, as are relationships with clients and customers—who inevitably become friends. You bring a personal dimension to work as well as a no-nonsense approach to your private life. Late January through February is when you tend to feel overextended, so make a point of slowing down then. This also happens to be your most romantic time of year, but love is fleeting unless you make a conscious effort to sustain it. You tend to put your paramour's needs on the back burner and may be mystified when the phone stops ringing. Make this person a priority and you'll learn there's more to love than a passing infatuation.

CHILD OF THE SUN ...

You were born in the last hours of the day, when one is thankful for that basic feeling of stability that comes with having a roof over your head and a bed to call your own. As a Child of the Sun with the Sun in the Fourth House, the impulse to provide and protect runs deep. Like a night watchman patrolling city streets, you check to make sure that everything is in its place and that no one wants for anything. Even if business demands that you be away for an extended period, you will call to make sure that everybody's all right and that the day-to-day regimen is still being followed like clockwork. You're never so happy as when you can return home and relax in the company and comfort of loved ones.

Family comes first with you. Even if there are relatives or in-laws you can't abide, you will still be there for them with love, money, or a couch to sleep on if things are tense for them at home. You've always been parental—even when you were a kid. You possess a quiet authority that makes people trust you with their secrets, property, and big life choices. And like any good parent, you don't tell anyone what to do. You will listen thoughtfully, ask judicious questions, and really try to help whomever you're talking to get to the root of the problem. Your advice is as soothing and reassuring as a glass of warm milk before bed.

That benign vigilance you exude in private also carries over to work. You gravitate toward positions where you are the "keeper of the keys." You may be in charge of human resources, the person who authorizes funds, or the head of production. Whenever there's any talk of a new project or endeavor, colleagues and supervisors check in with you first to see if it's doable. If they get a thumbs-up, it's full steam ahead. If they meet with a frown or a shake of the head, then they know better than to proceed. You're the unofficial official expert. Even if you genuinely have no opinion—one way or the other—the simple fact that you're not completely sold is enough to send them back to the drawing board or make them postpone plans until things look more certain. Inevitably there will be those who won't accept your say-so. But you don't fight with them nor will you try to win them over. You just go about your business. In a short time, they get the drift and life will return to normal.

WITH SUN IN FOURTH HOUSE

The Sun's position at the time you were born gives you a feeling of being "old." It's not so much that you look older than you are, as it is how you carry yourself. Perhaps it's an articulate way of speaking, a manner of dress, or an unquestioned sense of duty that makes you appear a little old-fashioned. You have a great love of history—whether it's antiques or antiqui-

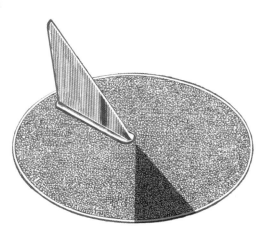

Your nature is to ensure that life runs smoothly. This isn't to say you'd fold your cards at the first sign of trouble. You're made of stern stuff. But the likelihood of you being surprised is rare because you're so good at anticipating the probable course of events and nipping potential problems in the bud. In any case the equinoxes and solstices (on or around the twenti-

ties—and sometimes you may even wonder if you were born two or three generations too late. But the lessons of history never lose their relevance, and in a similar vein "old-fashioned" shouldn't be confused with conservative. Loved ones and friends know you are capable of outlandish ideas that would make even the most forward-thinking blush. Yet your wildest notions are still firmly grounded in an emotional pragmatism.

eth of March, June, September, and December) are critical junctures for you. You can always expect to have to take a firmer hand in matters. June and December are when you need to get things up to speed, while March and September are when you should pull in the reins. Your own birthday month is a marvelous time, because you can take things at a leisurely pace and bask in the lazy days of summer.

CHILD OF THE SUN ...

Your spirit is like a lantern burning in the night. Some people are born depressed, and some, like you, happen to come by their joy naturally. When you're a Child of the Sun with the Sun in the Fifth House, you never outgrow your childlike exuberance. You may have inherited this joyful nature from your father. Creative and fun-loving, you can't help but accent the positive. And like that lantern you're there to light the way and even help those whose flame is burning low to rekindle their own joie de vivre.

As far as you're concerned, people spend too much time worrying. So much energy is devoted to trying to get to a place in life where they'll be happy that they don't realize that when they get there, they'll be too worn out and jaded to enjoy it. You don't fret a lot about the future. You'll deal with it when it comes. You have more than enough good humor to go around, but that doesn't mean you're oblivious to the troubles and worries that surround you.

You were born in the early evening after sunset. This time of day has always been associated with recreation. It's when most people are finished with work and are looking for a way to unwind before bed. There's a reason why television networks call it "prime time." There's an audience of millions looking to be entertained. Your Birthday Planet rules the business of fun. Subsequently you may be the events coordinator in charge of throwing that black-tie gala, the actor appearing nightly in a play, or the person producing it. And since recreation is hardly exclusive to the hours of eight through ten, you may radiate your own special warmth as a massage therapist, personal trainer, or yoga teacher. It's your job to make people feel good again.

This inevitably leads to conversations with others who don't respect what you do for a living. It looks like fun and games to them. You know it isn't, that what you do is hard work, but that's not the point. What's really at issue is your positive approach to life. The difficulty with being optimistic isn't that you have to strain to keep it up or are afraid of it being taken away. Your spirit is inextinguishable. The difficulty with being a bright light is that you tend to attract a lot of bugs.

There are some people who just aren't happy

WITH SUN IN FIFTH HOUSE

unless they're making others miserable. You have an unfortunate tendency to attract this type, and after you learn that you can't *really* do anything for them, then you will wisely choose to stick to neutral topics—or even avoid their company altogether. You only need to brighten your own corner of the world; you don't have to save it.

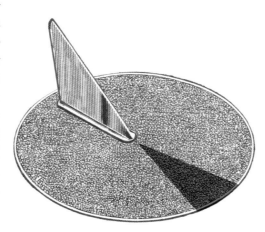

You love children and identify with them, but not in a wistful, sentimental way. You see their spirits as little flames that need tending so that they're not abruptly snuffed out by the pressures of adulthood. You'll either have children of your own or be involved with your friends' kids or your nephews and nieces. Because you want to strengthen their spirits and not quash them, you're likely to be very sensitive about their education. You exert a positive influence in their lives—through activities such as art therapy, after-school coaching, or volunteering as a tutor. Making sure kids have a golden childhood *now* is your way of guaranteeing that the future will be a better place.

You do best during the "fiery" times of year, which are late March through mid-April, late July through mid-August, and late November through mid-December. These months also correspond with school breaks and holidays—which is when people need entertaining. They are your busy and lucrative seasons. You don't do so well in February and March (except for Valentine's Day: you're very romantic!) and September. These are periods when you may feel especially susceptible to criticisms as well as colds and flus. Make a point of resting up and you'll be bright-eyed and bushy-tailed for when you need to be "on."

CHILD OF THE SUN ...

You take great pride in your work. And given the level of expertise and commitment you bring to it, bosses, colleagues, and clients can all sleep at night, knowing you're on the job. Not only do you get things done on time and with a minimum of fuss, but there's also a little extra something you manage to add that nobody ever thought of before—a signature detail that's undeniably you, yet which somehow feels as if it belonged there all along. You subtly raise the bar with everything you do.

You're more likely to think of yourself as a technician than an artist—even if what you do is connected to the arts (which is highly possible, given your Birthday Planet's proclivities). Being a Child of the Sun with the Sun in the Sixth House gives you excellent eye-to-hand coordination. Indeed the speed and dexterity with which you manipulate your fingers create the impression that they've a mind all their own. You can handle the most minuscule instruments or delicate material with a relaxed confidence. It's all in the technique. You put your faith in discipline and repetition. This isn't to say you're not sponta-

neous—few people live so fully in the moment. If anyone's prepared to take advantage of a flash of inspiration—it's you. But you prefer to make progress one step at a time. This way you always know exactly what you can and cannot do. Continually honing your skills gives you greater control over what you produce.

The downside to this extraordinary work ethic of yours is that the same intensity of focus you bring to perfecting details also causes you to block out anything that isn't relevant to what you're doing. Keeping yourself busy is a favorite form of procrastination. The more work you have in front of you, the less you need to think about what lies farther down the road. All you want is to find a place to set up shop and go to work, which is why you may take the first job that comes along or accept the initial price you're offered. Subsequently you often wind up in positions that are beneath you. You believe your work speaks for itself and that your efforts will eventually be rewarded. Yet it's ironic that for someone who insists on being specific you would be so willing to trust your career to vagaries.

Because you were born at the time of day

WITH SUN IN SIXTH HOUSE

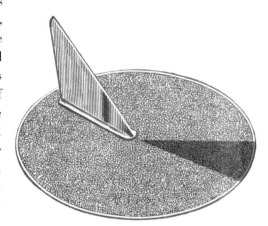

when the last of the Sun's rays trail on the horizon, you often feel like you've arrived too late and should settle for what's left. This same feeling of tardiness may also be reflected in where you fall in your family lineup or the fact that your parents were "older" when you were born. The instinct to accommodate is built-in. This is all well and good, but sometimes you need to be more Solar.

Status is something your Ruling Planet knows all about. Status isn't just puffing up your chest and pretending to be more important than you are. It's about carrying yourself with the kind of authority that immediately commands respect. One of the ways our society understands status is price. The price you ask for says just as much—if not more—about you than the work you do. When you cheapen your price, you lower your status.

But when you hold out for what you're worth, then you automatically move to the level where you should be operating. The work *you* do is of such superior quality that it only makes sense that you command top price for it.

For the most part, you like to be left alone in peace to do what you do. Late April through mid-May, late August through mid-September, and late December through mid-January are when you can expect to work without interruption. But despite your isolating tendencies, you are still a Child of the Sun—which means that people are inevitably drawn to you. You can expect to be inundated with phone calls, invites, and drop-by chats throughout June, October, early December, and late January. You may resent the constant small talk, but it's really for your own good. It keeps you from becoming a curmudgeon.

CHILD OF THE SUN . . .

You're the person who brings people together, the one irreplaceable link everyone has in common. After all, if it weren't for you then that up-and-coming talent would still be down-and-out; that kid genius everyone ignored at work would never have gotten the chance to strut his stuff and save the company. It's your vote of confidence or stamp of approval that opens doors and makes things happen. But you have more than just an eye for talent. You can also spot trouble when it's still a faint trail of smoke on the horizon. When you're a Child of the Sun with the Sun in the Seventh House, you have a *proactive* rather than a *reactive* approach to life. Your philosophy is to never burn a bridge (there may come a time when you need to cross back over it), and if things don't work out and you have to show somebody the door, you will find a way for that person to depart wearing a smile instead of a frown.

Relationships are your lifeblood—which is why you never form just one. But no two people play the same role in your life. There is only *one* love interest, *one* confidant, *one* major client, etc. at any given time. You treat each with the same degree of importance. It can get a little peculiar when, for instance, you fret about letting down your dry cleaner because you won't be able to pick up your shirts when you said you would. Nevertheless you find a way to smooth out the wrinkles. Anyone admitted into your inner circle will immediately see you're absolutely loyal, but they will have to learn to share you. Your open-door policy is an essential ingredient in your formula for success.

You enjoy middle management positions. That way you're not too high (you don't want to be away from all the action and fun) and you're not too low (you're nobody's errand boy or girl Friday). Though you're often found at the heart of a group, you do all your decision making, brainstorming, and even the occasional dressing-down one-on-one, which is why you take the time to cultivate trust and rapport. You know that what someone says in a group can be very different from what would be expressed out of earshot or "off the record." Your *entre nous* approach not only reverses negative trends, but it also gives you the opportunity to input your own ideas through the grapevine.

WITH SUN IN SEVENTH HOUSE

Because of the Sun's position at the time of your birth, you're happiest when you're in a partnership. You'll find it's a slow go if you have to do something on your own. But once in proximity to someone who's brilliant and dynamic, then your Solar fire roars to life. Suddenly you're full of ideas, questions, plans, and inspiration. You need someone to bounce ideas off of and to dialogue with. Your excitement gets them excited. The only things you ask for in return are loyalty and respect. You don't mind if someone hogs all the credit. You know that you sit at the center of everyone's social orbit, and the only reason people make those important connections is because you had a hand in it. However if you find out that someone you championed turns on you, then all that golden sweetness and light gets shut down. And no amount of apologizing, pleading, and begging will turn it back on again.

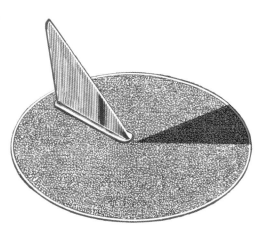

One of the reasons you go to such lengths to keep the peace is because you know forgiveness isn't in your nature. Once someone has crossed the line, then it's as if the earth swallowed him or her whole.

You do best during the "airy" times of year, which are late January through mid-February, late May through mid-June, and late September through mid-October. This is when you make the rounds—picking up new protégés, making valuable contacts, and reveling in the productive collaborations you so enjoy. Ironically, it's during the "fiery" months (April, August, and December) when you run into the most trouble. These are the times when you may have to lay down the law with all those colorful personalities you're drawn to. Thankfully a brief exchange is usually all it takes to get things back on track.

CHILD OF THE SUN . . .

When your Ruling Planet is in the Eighth House, you possess a "sixth" sense for what's going on behind the scenes. This doesn't necessarily make you psychic, but like a detective in an old movie, you have a gut feeling for when the pieces don't fit. It's often up to you to discover what went wrong and to put it right. But you don't come by this desire to "do the right thing" naturally. Your Solar tendency is to steer clear of anything too dark and heavy. Nevertheless adventure will inevitably come looking for you. This is why you stumble into so many emotionally wrought and deeply complicated situations—especially in your twenties and early thirties. And the bait almost always involves love or money.

If it's a romantic interest, then all the attractive and wonderful things about this person are put on show for you. If it's a job interview, then the company will make a point of emphasizing all the perks and benefits you can expect from being on a winning team. However when you're a Child of the Sun with the Sun in the Eighth House, what you see is often a far cry from what *you get*—which are all the things that *weren't* discussed at the first meeting or date. Certain details may be glossed over, like a previous marriage, family secrets, or the fact that what looked good on paper is barely held together by spit and glue. Every partnership has its downside. Yet it's this very downside that becomes the catalyst for change and growth in your life. Rather than breaking up the relationship, it often empowers it.

It's as old as the Brothers Grimm. Every fairy tale contains a catch. You don't get to marry the prince or dig up that pot of gold for nothing. There's usually some sort of puzzle you have to solve first or a spell you need to break. As a Child of the Sun, you tend to focus on the bright side of life. And there's nothing wrong with that, but that's not how life works all the time. Just because the Sun sets at the end of the day doesn't mean it stops being the source of energy and life. If it did, we'd all be in a lot of trouble. In many ways it's your destiny to bring light to the dark corners—or to unearth what's been buried so that it sees the light of day. It isn't easy. You could learn things about yourself that may be unflattering and not exactly showy, but this increases your capacity to live and love—it does not diminish it. In the end

WITH SUN IN EIGHTH HOUSE

these experiences transform you into the hero you always felt you could be but didn't exactly know how to become.

Because of the Sun's position at the time of your birth, you will be drawn to professions that deal with life-and-death matters. This can range from vocations infused with urgency (like emergency services or medicine) to ones that require

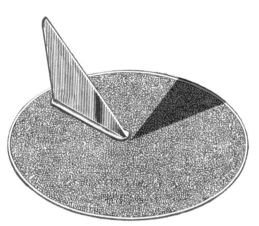

split-second timing (like stunt work or handling dangerous materials). But since most people regard love and/or money as being a matter of life and death, you may be drawn to something more along the lines of wedding planning or marriage counseling as well as managing others' investments or estates. The success of just about anything you do depends on bonding with your associate or client so that you can really get inside this person's skin.

Late February through mid-March, late June through your own birthday month, and late October through mid-November are auspicious times. This is when you're most in tune with others and don't have to think twice about making a request or bringing up a delicate matter. These are also the months when people make resources available to you. January and September aren't so good, and mid-April through May is like trying to pull teeth. Doors are closed and everyone's feeling extremely territorial. It would be a good idea to reschedule projects for another time. Even if people say everything's ready to go, your "sixth" sense will tell you otherwise and it will be right.

CHILD OF THE SUN ...

You put your trust in a *higher* power. It makes no difference if that power can be described in religious terms or philosophical ones; whether it resides in the will of the people or the mysteries of nature. When your Birthday Planet is in the Ninth House, you believe that everything in life happens for a reason. Always intrigued by the question of *why*, the answer for you doesn't lie in identifying the cause and effect. To you there's a moral to every story, and if we can only grasp it, then our lives will be greatly enriched.

You have a tremendous love of learning, which is why you don't think twice about visiting an out-of-the-way place or going on a date with someone sight unseen. You never know when you might stumble on a moment that could change your entire outlook. You are drawn to ideas and experiences that open the mind and broaden your horizons. Most people regard an experience as something they've already done. They might say, "I've been to that place or met that person." But you embrace an experience as a moment that never stops happening—it continues to shape and influence you long after you've lived it. Every time you invoke it as a story or share it as a cautionary tale, you glean something new. Knowledge isn't a destination you arrive at. Knowledge is what you accrue through all the things that happen to you along the way.

You are a born storyteller. You know how to draw in your audience with a good opening line and possess a performer's instinct for dramatic build. Anyone can relate a series of facts, but not everyone knows how to weave them into a compelling argument or fascinating lecture. You can look at a complete hodgepodge of information and then suddenly recognize the figure in the carpet. People come to you for your "take" on events. A Ninth House Sun is an excellent placement for anyone who has to explain a complicated matter in easy-to-understand terms (like a lawyer, a teacher, or a magazine editor) as well as for people who have to address truths that can't be proved factually but nevertheless resonate within all of us (like a writer, a religious leader, or politician).

Because of the Sun's position at the time of your birth, it's impossible for you to be impartial. You were born at the time of day when your Rul-

WITH SUN IN NINTH HOUSE

ing Planet burns hottest and brightest. You have a strong personality, and because you believe it's better to have an opinion than not to have one, you may give the impression that what you're saying is the only way to look at things. Sometimes you call into question how things are done or make the people turning to you for advice uncomfortable. You must be prepared to

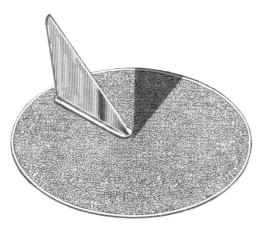

ask yourself if your judgment call is right. Do you *really* believe in it? Is it worth turning into a cause célèbre, or is it best left as a question hanging in the air? Again this is where your performer's instincts serve you best. You want to hook your audience but not provoke them to storm the stage. There's a fine line between pricking people's conscience and inflaming it. If you always infuse what you have to say with humor and humanity, then you'll bring light, not heat, to any situation.

Mid-March through April is perhaps your best time of year. This is when your Ruling Planet is in its exaltation—thus ensuring all eyes are focused on you, with everyone eagerly anticipating what you'll say and do next. But this is not a time for acting impulsively. Rivals will be ready to pounce on the slightest slipup—taking advantage of any opening you might give them. July and August—as well as the early weeks of December—are wonderful times for pursuing what you want, but the timbre of the energy is more private than public. February is often an unpredictable time, as is mid-May through June. If you make a point to think through what you say during these periods (and perhaps tone it down a bit), you'll breeze through them fine.

CHILD OF THE SUN ...

You are driven to be outstanding. It doesn't matter if your aim is to be CEO of your company or a great artist, you will focus your Solar energies on rising through the ranks until you've gone as high as you can go. And when you reach your zenith (as you eventually will), then you'll cast about for a way to climb higher still. You are the classic over-achiever. When you're a Child of the Sun with the Sun in the Tenth House, you want to make a lasting impact that won't be forgotten.

But ambition isn't the driving force behind what you do. Love is. And for you there's only one great love in your life: your chosen area of expertise. What you do isn't a job, it's a career and careers operate by a different set of rules. A career requires you to make choices that go beyond the weekly paycheck. You may have to break up with someone you're seeing in order to relocate, resign a prosperous position because it's a dead end and the only way to move forward is to start again at a lower level, or maybe you spend years working a number of *other* jobs to support you until you get that big break. If this isn't passion, what is?

Because you are so focused on your career, it makes perfect sense that the person you fall in love with—as well as the friendships you form—will somehow be linked to what you do. You don't mind intermingling the professional with the personal. In many ways you prefer it. Loyalties are rarely in question, and you can always rely on others to come through. The downside is your life can get too insular. Even if you're surrounded by the most fascinating and talented people imaginable, seeing the same faces at home that you do at work can eventually lead to a narrowing of the margins. This can become deadening after a while, which is why every few years someone controversial will enter your life. Yours is a creative and vital spirit, and like a fire, it needs to be stoked in order to burn bright. Regardless of whether this person becomes your best friend or bitter rival, the aim is to get you crackling again.

Because of the Sun's position at the time of your birth, you will experience many peaks and valleys in your life. In part, this is a reflection of your father's fortunes and temperament—which may have vacillated between ecstatic highs and

WITH SUN IN TENTH HOUSE

despondent lows. More importantly, it is a reflection of the love you feel for what you do, which never stops growing, though sometimes you wish it would. You are more than a perfectionist. You really do feel that your mission in life is to realize the potential you carry inside. You won't stop—even when you've seemingly reached the end of the road. There's

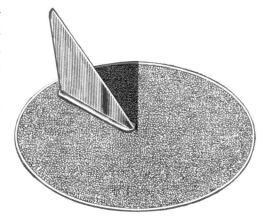

always more you can do. This is why being told to relax and take it easy never really makes sense to you. Nevertheless there are times when you need to take a break. Not only because you'll run yourself ragged if you don't, but also because you never know when something seen in an altogether different quarter may cast a new light on what you do.

The best time to begin anything is at the spring equinox (around March 20). This is when you feel most invigorated and ready to take on enormous challenges—which is good, considering how often you're drawn to them. The summer months are when you feel lethargic and enervated. Given that it's your least productive season, you may want to schedule a retreat or vacation. Your energy returns with the beginning of the fall. The winter solstice (around December 20) may very well be the best time of all. This is when you reap the fruit of the preceding year's labors. It's also when you have the clearest idea of what still needs to be done. It's important that you assess matters reasonably. It's wonderful to have a life passion, but sometimes the constant prodding to do more can rob you of your greatest pleasure—which is your own sense of fulfillment.

CHILD OF THE SUN ...

Yours is the spirit of cooperation. When your Ruling Planet is in the Eleventh House, you're drawn to the hustle and bustle of big groups. Perhaps you grew up in a large family or lived in a neighborhood where everyone's kids fraternized with one another. With so many personalities competing for attention, you learned to share and share alike—whether you wanted to or not. You're used to interruptions and can drop what you're doing to attend to something else completely different—and then pick up again where you left off without missing a beat. Jostling for position taught you to take setbacks in stride, so you've never been traumatized by rejection or afraid to speak your mind. You're up front and candid and expect others to be as well. If someone has a problem, you want to hear about it. Maybe you can take care of it, maybe you can't, but as far as you're concerned—it never hurts to ask.

You put the overall good of the group ahead of any one person's—including yourself. This may seem contrary to your Birthday Planet's nature; however, the Sun rules identity, and when you *identify* with a group, then that's where you'll focus your Solar energies. You have no patience for anyone you believe is conceited or selfish. You appreciate how much your life affects and in turn depends on the actions of others—how fortunes are integrally linked. If you think about it, it's not unlike a karmic ecosystem. One person's good acts (or bad) can't help but have a ripple effect on everyone else. Everything that happens—for better or for ill—is interrelated. You feel personally responsible for others' happiness and, in turn, will hold them accountable for yours. This may sound a little intense, but when you consider how much a surgeon depends on her nurses or a firefighter on his backup, then it isn't so hard to understand. You are a team player and will take it upon yourself to ensure that the team acts as one. Even on the odd occasion when you are reprimanded in front of everyone for making a mistake, you will accept it stoically. You are constantly aware of needing to set an example for others.

Ironically you don't like being singled out for praise and recognition. Should your gain result in somebody else's loss, or you get promoted before a colleague, you may be tempted to go in the

WITH SUN IN ELEVENTH HOUSE

opposite extreme—which is to deny yourself a reward you richly deserve. This can create a predicament where, by *not* taking what's rightfully yours, you risk throwing everything into turmoil. It would be like King Arthur pulling the sword out of the stone and deciding not to tell anyone about it or Cinderella refusing to try on the glass slipper even though she knows

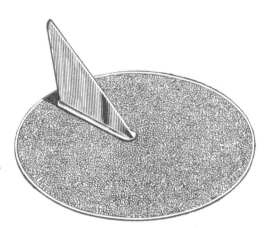

it's hers. You have to take that step forward. Ultimately you'll do what's right, but not without agonizing over it.

Because of the Sun's position at the time of your birth, good things come to you through the people you know. It may be a loved one, a friend, or even a friend of a friend who opens an important door for you. But you can't go after anything "cold." Reading about a job in the paper and calling up for an interview just won't work because you don't do

well in situations where you have to prove yourself or win someone over. It's hard to prove that you're a team player without a team. Your strengths are in your ability to coordinate everybody and get them to work together.

Your best times of year are January and February, mid-May through June, and mid-September through October. Though fiery by nature, it's usually during the "fiery" months (April, August, and December) that you clash with strong personalities. Even if you're working for the overall good of the group, it's still *your* idea of what's in everyone's best interests. You don't always understand how your own strong personality can contribute to a rise in tensions. That's why it's best to strive for some perspective during these times. Thankfully you're surrounded by good friends and always respect their feedback.

CHILD OF THE SUN ...

When you are born with your Ruling Planet in the Twelfth House, life may not start out easily, but your energy grows warmer and stronger as you go along. It takes a while for your fire to catch. At first it can barely be seen beneath obstacles and responsibilities. But it's in there, smoking. And at a time when other Children of the Sun are beginning to burn low, you suddenly roar to life—burning bright and strong—the obstacles and responsibilities becoming the fuel for your brilliant spirit.

A family legacy may cast a long shadow in your life. Perhaps it's a piece of property or a sum of money that's passed down to you. Then again genius or a hidden talent may be in your genetic makeup. The very thing that makes you special will also be the very thing you have to live up to. But you know there are strings attached. Your family legacy could also include some psychic loose ends that need tying up. What isn't settled in one generation tends to get carried on over to the next. Nobody knows why this happens. It's as old as Greek drama and as current as Disney's *The Lion King*. Perhaps heartbreak lies some-where in the back of your family closet or a simple matter of somebody doing somebody else wrong. Through the years it morphs into an outlook on life or even an ingrained behavior. You are the inheritor—and hopefully redeemer—of what has come before. When you're a Child of the Sun with the Sun in the Twelfth House, the buck stops with you.

This isn't your Birthday Planet's ideal way to go through life. As a Child of the Sun, you want to be you. You don't want to be stuck lugging family baggage. Which is why you will find a way to distance yourself from it. You may leave home at an early age, hook up with a partner who has an even more colorful family history, or—if you're the shy, retiring type—take a job that will keep you busy every waking hour of the day. Even if you're a galley slave, it's your oar to row. The Sun rules identity. Since you only get one, you don't want yours to be overshadowed by anyone else's.

Everyone inherits a "legacy." No matter who we are, each of us will travel the same path our parents did at some point in our lives. It could be something as typical as raising a child or deeply personal—like battling substance abuse. Yet it's

WITH SUN IN TWELFTH HOUSE

only when you travel this same path that you begin to appreciate where your parents have been and the choices they made. You may not agree with them. You may even be bent on leading a totally different lifestyle, but consider what it means to see, touch, and feel what your mother or father went through—albeit in the context of your own life. This realization lib-

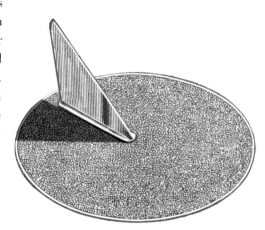

erates you by allowing you to empathize with your parents. And if things were difficult growing up, it even helps you to forgive them. All it takes is one choice to change an outcome. By embracing your family legacy you won't lose your identity, you'll grow into it.

Because of the Sun's position at the time you were born, you go through "purging" cycles every seven or twelve years. This is when your life gets turned upside down, things unravel, and you find yourself standing on the threshold of a new beginning. Though this can sometimes prove inconvenient, the real purpose is to stoke your inner flames so that they grow brighter, not dimmer. Being a Twelfth House Sun, you may have had a shaky start (perhaps you were ill a lot as an infant), so these disruptions are meant to rejuvenate you.

Your best times of year are March, July, and November. This is when you're feeling inspired and you don't have to struggle to see the road in front of you. September, however, is always a bit of a bummer. It probably stems from the fact that you're a child of the summer and autumn puts you in mind of having to go back to school. Always one to take on enormous responsibilities, you still bristle when forced to do something against your will.

CHILD OF THE MOON ...

Mars rules the zodiac sign Aries. Subsequently you Children of the Moon with Moon in Aries have a powerful Mars streak. Mars quickens the pulse and pushes you to act in the heat of the moment. For Mars whatever is happening *now* is of utmost importance. This doesn't always blend well with your cyclical Lunar energy. Your belief that if something doesn't work out now it will later is thrown off balance by Mars's impatience. You're often conflicted about when is the right time to act. Though you are constantly checking your impulses, whatever's driving you will win out. At times you can get easily agitated, edgy, and are prone to unexpected eruptions. You don't like feeling uncomfortable in your own skin. But once the Mars energy peaks, much like a fever that breaks (fevers are ruled by Mars), you will revert to your calm, peace-loving self.

Because of the Moon's position at the time of your birth, it often feels like you're arriving on the scene at the eleventh hour. This isn't to say you're chronically tardy (though you tend to put things off till the last minute), but you may go through life feeling like you never have enough time to prepare and must constantly improvise. This puts you in a *reacting* rather than an *initiating* position. You yearn for a time when you can just sit down and put everything in order. But somehow someone always needs you, and you're forced to drop what you're doing and come running. Well-meaning friends and loved ones advise you to set boundaries and make time for yourself. But when you're a Child of the Moon ruled by Mars, there's a secret part of you that can't bear being away from the action. You like it when you're in the thick of things. You need to feel needed.

You're the person everyone calls on to clean up after someone's mess. The Mars part of you intuits solutions quickly and will implement them without a second thought, while the Lunar part of you will check to make sure nobody's feet are stepped on in the process. Even in the most pressured circumstances, you never lose your sympathy for others. But you don't wear your heart on your sleeve. Your Mars streak gives you a "pull-yourself-up-by-your-bootstraps" spunk. You don't ask for breaks and you won't give any either. However if someone is committed to going

WITH MOON IN ARIES

the distance, then you'll support that person all the way.

Mars likes life fast and furious. He delights in noise and commotion. Subsequently, you're drawn to situations or vocations where the competition is fierce and your time is short. However your Birthday Planet ensures that the intensity won't be constant. Like the tides (which are ruled by the Moon), the level of intensity can rise, abate, and then rise again on a regular basis. For example you might work at an ER where life-and-death decisions are commonplace, or you could be a short-order cook who knows that every weekday at twelve the lunch crowd descends and you won't be able to think straight until they go back to work at one. You like a good rush, but as a Child of the Moon, it's up to you to bring peace and calm to the situation.

With the Moon so fiery, chances are your mother is a very powerful figure in your life. She might not have been the most concerned or sensitive parent, but she probably grew on you as you got older. Around her, you may still feel like nothing you do is good enough, but it's important to remember that little of that has to do with you. It is more a reflection of the way your mother sees the world—an arena where one is constantly battling for one's place. She may have infuriated you with her inability to change or adapt, but at the same time you inherited her fighting spirit and code of honor.

Late September through October and late December into January are stressful times for you. These are the times when your Ruling Planet is at its lowest ebb and you're most prone to burnout. You need to conserve your energy during these periods and push yourself less. Late March through April and late June through July are when you feel most in your element.

CHILD OF THE MOON ...

Venus rules the zodiac sign Taurus. Subsequently you Children of the Moon with Moon in Taurus have a Venusian love of beauty, sensuality, and creature comforts. Venus rules over our aesthetics and tastes. One's tastes can *influence* what others think, which is how Venus works her particular magic. Whenever millions of men decide to sport goatees or women emulate a celebrity's hairstyle, then that's a sign of Venus at work. And with Venus as ruler of your Moon, you have one eye on your presentation and the other on its effect.

One of your chief aims in life is to feather your nest. As a Child of the Moon you want to make sure you and your loved ones will never be deprived of anything. You won't settle for anything less than the best. You may admire a beautiful piece of art for its appeal, but there's a voice in the back of your head constantly asking: how much is it worth? You often wonder if you're getting the best value for your dollar or if sitting next to an influential person at a dinner party will lead to more profitable contacts in the future. That Venusian part of you is always looking to add to your collection of valuables. It could be jewelry, property, or phone numbers of people you meet at parties. You don't acquire just to have. Almost everything you own is earmarked for the time when it matures in value and you can trade it in for something better. You may be nostalgic, but you're not sentimental. At the end of the day what matters most is what you can weigh in the palm of your hand.

You delight in people's company and will naturally seek out groups. This runs contrary to your Birthday Planet's nature—which is to be private. But since the company you keep is made up of those who come from a similar background, it is easy for you to regard them as your extended family. Your easygoing nature makes you a joy to be around. Content to drift along the current of conversation, you drink in all the stories, problems, and passions that people share with one another. Their concerns are your concerns. Their victories are your victories. You're a good listener. And because you have an innate ability to make everyone feel at ease, your unique combination of Lunar sympathy and Venusian persuasion plants the seeds of loyalty with just about everyone you meet.

WITH MOON IN TAURUS

However, you are no great fan of conflict. Because of the Moon's position at the time of your birth, you tend to toe the party line and frown on anyone who threatens to rock the boat. Your ability to blend into the woodwork of any group you join makes you the person most likely to be appointed club treasurer. People just inherently trust you. Yet it's your

Birthday Planet's very sensitivity to those who have been left out (or taken advantage of) that also causes you to buck the herd instinct on occasion. You can't help having a conscience. These are times of great emotional unrest, when you have to ask yourself how far you're willing to go *not* to make waves.

Female relatives—particularly the ones on your mother's side of the family—play a supportive role in your life. They may intercede on your behalf, cull resources to make something you want possible, or simply live near the place you're planning to relocate to for school or work. In any case, you'll want to always show them the proper appreciation and respect. You don't ever want to get on the bad side of these ladies.

Late April through mid-May and late August through mid-September are the best times for you. The end of summer is when you really feel like you're ready to take on life with renewed gusto. Late December through mid-January is okay, however June, October, and February are off times. November (with the exception of Thanksgiving weekend!) hardly ever goes well and is the time of year when you're most prone to feeling out of sorts. Chances are this is brought on by the advent of holiday shopping, when more money's going out than coming in . . . which never puts you in a good mood. Just keep telling yourself this is payback time for all the good that people have done for you throughout the year.

CHILD OF THE MOON ...

Mercury rules the zodiac sign Gemini. Therefore you Children of the Moon with Moon in Gemini possess Mercury's quick thinking, shrewd analysis, and ability to anticipate what's about to be said before it's voiced. You are adept at reading signals. In some cases you're better at articulating a position than the person presenting it. Sometimes you can cut people off in midsentence. You don't mean to be rude, it's just that you want them to get to the point, so that you can address the one you already see forming.

Because your Birthday Planet rules the body (especially the stomach), you pick up information viscerally. You feel the energy spike when someone fascinating enters the room, just as the hairs on the back of your neck will rise when you're around somebody who's up to no good. Sometimes your body responds before your mind does. A feeling you think is all in your head could very well be your body trying to warn you that something's up.

It's the Mercury part of you that prompts you to make the acquaintance of people outside your social circle. Normally, Children of the Moon seek the company of those who make them feel at ease. Yet in mythology, Mercury was known as "the companion of man"— always willing to help people find what they're looking for. Because Mercury is powerful for you, communication, travel, and commerce will factor strongly in your life. That could manifest as traveling for business, being in the business of travel, or engaging in transactions that take place over distances by phone, fax, or the Internet. Camaraderie comes easily and acquaintances enter and exit your life as if they were moving through a revolving door. And like a revolving door, there's always a good chance you'll bump into them again.

However, what engages you one moment can bore you the next. That's because the Moon and Mercury are the swiftest moving planets. This often gives the impression you run hot and cold. Since you yourself aren't too sure which one you'll be, you prefer to make short-term plans that can be reviewed every few weeks or months. You like to know you have the option of moving on to something else if you want to. It's like the difference between reading a collection of short stories and a

WITH MOON IN GEMINI

novel. You prefer succinct episodes to one ongoing narrative—even if both books add up to the same number of pages. Therefore you prefer employment that guarantees a constant change of scene or where you're dealing with matters that are time sensitive.

Your restless mind is hungry for new information and stimulating conversation. However you are still a Child of the Moon. Where the Mercury part of you sizes up people and situations on the spot (perhaps giving too much credence to first impressions), the Lunar part of you keeps an eye out for what might come in handy later. You have a long memory and can summon up the most obscure detail. You keep tabs on everyone you meet. Others may lose touch with past chums, but chances are you still send old friends cards each year.

All this mental wheel turning can be exhausting. And as a Child of the Moon, you need your time-outs. It's a good idea to have a special place you can go to where no one can reach you. If a monastery isn't immediately available, you can always settle for a weekend getaway. These times of self-imposed isolation are necessary for recharging the psychic batteries.

Because of the Moon's position at the time of your birth, you can experience lots of false starts and endings. For instance, in your enthusiasm, you can jump into a situation before you're ready; then again, if you're frustrated about not being able to master something immediately you may give up prematurely. This could be a holdover from a competitive relationship with a sibling. This is a blind spot you may never master, so it's best to have two or three people you trust to turn to for advice.

February, June, and October are when you feel most in sync with events. However, in those couple of days that precede a new moon, every month, you will experience a sudden drain of energy or inability to see straight. These are times of vulnerability when it's better to wait than push on.

CHILD OF THE MOON ...

The Moon rules the zodiac sign Cancer. You Children of the Moon with the Moon in Cancer have the good fortune of being born during a new Moon—one of the most dynamic times possible. The world is your oyster. Literally. Life, to you, is chock full of opportunities and you're willing and able to get out there and live according to your inner vision. You're extremely creative, but the creative process, as you've surely experienced for yourself, is hardly complacent. You need a little grit to make a pearl.

Events don't shape you, you shape events. This is done not by the force of your personality but by your quiet strength. You prefer to work in sympathy with events—biding your time until it's the right moment to ask a question or introduce a plan. Not only does this give you a greater success rate, but you also accomplish what you want without calling undue attention to yourself. That's why whatever you do is just a little bit different from what's come before, but familiar enough not to scare anyone. You know it's the subtle changes in a course that will be accepted, not the radical shifts.

However you are not as cool and composed as you seem. You constantly fret over variables that most people wouldn't even think of. What doesn't help is the innate feeling that your private wants and needs are somehow transparent. You're afraid that even the most casual stranger can peer right down into the depths of your soul, which is why you will go to great lengths to cover your tracks. As a Child of the Moon you approach goals indirectly. The more you want something, the more uninterested you'll appear as you circle round it and then snatch it before anyone's the wiser. There's a reason why the Moon was associated with Diana, goddess of the hunt.

If you were to ask friends to describe you, they would probably talk about the role you play in their lives. The irony is that for all your fear of exposure, most people haven't the slightest idea what makes you tick. This is beneficial if you happen to occupy a position of authority, like a business executive, advisor, or counselor. But for more intimate associations, it's up to you to clue them in. Being a Lunar person, you assume a lot that's unspoken. Others simply aren't as deeply

WITH MOON IN CANCER

feeling as you. You can remedy these misunderstandings by making a conscious effort to communicate what you feel.

When you're a Child of the Moon with the Moon powerful, you're the *mothering* type . . . regardless of sex. It could be anything from helping your spouse get dressed in the morning to micromanaging all the unruly brats at work. The Moon is a sheltering, nourishing Planet. She rules the body, the house, land, and legacies. But along with the support and encouragement comes a reluctance to explore anything new or different. The life lesson you're constantly learning is that we do not all hail from the same tribe. This is where your private concerns often conflict with social expectations. It isn't easy to recognize the line between private and public sectors. For you each relationship is meaningful, so you can't help worrying about the people in your life . . . including the dry cleaner.

Because of the Moon's position at the time of your birth, you're most comfortable taking the initiative. You don't like being under anyone's thumb, and though you yearn to be a team player, it rarely works out to your liking. You embody what you do, which means that your job or task is so singular that it won't take place unless you are physically present. It's not unlike a mom, if you think about it. There may be millions of mothers in the world, but for a child in need there's only one Mom, which is how people look at you.

You are a true child of the summer. June, July, and August are peak times for you. December, January, and February are when you instinctively go into psychic hibernation. You may put on some weight or have difficulty getting up in the morning, but once April rolls around, your energy picks up and you'll start getting that body of yours in shape for bathing suit season.

CHILD OF THE MOON . . .

The Sun rules the zodiac sign Leo. Subsequently you Children of the Moon with the Moon in Leo possess a fiery charisma and majesty. You're the sort of person others can't help noticing. You don't have to do anything to call attention to yourself, you just attract it.

Although the Solar part of you exudes good humor, confidence, and sincerity, it's the Lunar part that leaves the lasting impression. Not many people get asked back as often as you do. It might be a callback, a second date, or the next round of job interviews. There's something about you that people want more of in their lives. They're drawn to you the way cold and exhausted travelers gather around the warmth of a fire. And like a hearth at night, the longer people relax in your presence, the more reluctant they are to leave. This suits you fine. You like being the center of attention.

The downside is you can't get away with anything—not even the slightest peccadillo. Others can bend a rule or indulge a whim, but not you. Your very noteworthiness guarantees you'd get caught and even be made an example of.

The Sun and Moon symbolize opposites. The only time they both appear in the sky is when one is rising and the other is setting (unless it's during an eclipse—then everything is out of whack). One must be stronger than the other. As a Child of the Moon, you will allow someone else to play the central role in your life. Belonging to someone makes you feel secure and rooted.

However this can be an area of conflict for you. Although the Lunar part of you is happy to let someone else do the driving, you still have a powerful Solar streak. And that part of you doesn't want to be taken for granted any more than it wants to be seen as an extension of someone else—no matter how dynamic this person may be. Torn between a need for security and a fear of being eclipsed, you may strike a bargain with that luminary you happen to be reflecting. You expect a partner to share the wealth or support you when it's your turn to shine. You may have to go through a number of partners before you find the right give-and-take. When you do, this will be a relationship that lasts a lifetime.

Being a Child of the Moon with the Sun strong, you're naturally drawn to performance—like theater, movies, and music. If you're going to

WITH MOON IN LEO

pursue the arts, however, it's important to make that commitment early on, because the Moon rules over habits. Anything you practice over a period of time will be eventually mastered. However, creative impulses could take a backseat to your material needs. You are not the starving artist type. You like the good things in life too much to risk sacrificing in vain. Even if you decide not to pursue a career in the arts, that won't keep you from being surrounded by creative people or beautiful things. You will always seek an individual niche where you can shine.

Because of the Moon's position at the time of your birth, you will find that things tend to develop very quickly when you're starting out. The early stages of a venture are easier to handle than when things are winding down. Both the Moon and Sun are known for their creative impetus. But because their orbits are fixed (they don't change direction like the other planets do), you expect life to follow a certain course. Your time for experimenting is in your teens and twenties. When you hit thirty, you want everything in its place.

You shine from mid-July to mid-September. These are the times of year when you will feel most in your element. Mid-January to mid-March is when you feel like you're out of it and just can't be bothered. However, being a trouper, you'll never let that grouchy side show. April is invigorating, and December is good for harvesting the fruits of your labors.

CHILD OF THE MOON ...

Mercury rules the zodiac sign Virgo. You Children of the Moon with the Moon in Virgo posses all the dexterity and skill associated with this accomplished Planet. You enjoy fixing your surroundings. This can be anything from renovating a room to figuring out a way to make a procedure run more smoothly. Nothing gets your creative juices flowing quite like a problem. The fact that life can be a mess is a source of secret delight. It ensures you'll never run out of things to do.

You are more into craft than art. Others can look at an empty canvas and see a masterpiece waiting to be painted. You look at an empty canvas and get a big headache. That's why you prefer to be *assigned* things to do. Your imagination works in tandem with your problem-solving abilities. If you know you have a certain number of days to complete a task and limited resources with which to complete it, it's remarkable how inventive you become. The stricter the parameters, the better job you do.

The downside to this is you can deny yourself any opportunity to experiment. Being a Child of the Moon, you are constantly aware of those day-to-day concerns like paying bills and putting food on the table. The more jobs you take on, the more money comes in. Which is why you may choose a profession where you can work on consignment—thus allowing you to juggle several clients at once. At the very least, you'll work two, maybe even three jobs. You have a fear of being without money. You don't do anything on a lark. However the real reason why you avoid initiating something on your own is that both the Moon and Mercury are *responsive* Planets. They need something to play off. Left to your own devices, you could come up with a number of possibilities, but with no guidelines to direct you, you wouldn't be able to choose one over another. You like repetition. It's familiar and consistent. It also allows you to hone your skills.

Being a Child of the Moon with Mercury prominent, it makes perfect sense that you would be drawn to professions involving meticulous and repetitive work. You're not interested in producing something that's one-of-a-kind (where's the profit in that?), but in finding a way to reproduce something that's one-of-a-kind over and over again. This is the difference between someone

WITH MOON IN VIRGO

who discovers or invents something and the person who patents it and finds a way to market it. When you consider that Mercury is the patron Planet of buyers and sellers, it should be clear where your inclinations lie.

Because of the Moon's position at the time of your birth, you have the advantage of being able to access both your conscious (Mercury) and unconscious (Moon). This gives you a perseverance when it comes to researching minute details, as well as an excellent memory for facts and figures. However, the Moon and Mercury are the most swiftly moving planets in the sky, which means that you don't have much patience for abstractions or explanations that take a long time. Yet if you're physically involved—such as working out the details of an intricate design or rehearsing an instrument—then hours fly like seconds. You never grow tired of perfecting your craft. Indeed when your mind becomes overloaded, there's nothing like busywork to relax those stressed-out brain cells.

Female siblings will play a strong supportive role in your life. They may have even filled in for a parent who was away. You'll still have your fair share of squabbles, but things work themselves out eventually. Mercury is at his most helpful when he rules the Moon. Mutual interests are emphasized over differences.

You tend to build on what's come before, so the weeks immediately preceding an equinox or solstice are best for you. Therefore late February to early March, late May to early June, late August to early September, and late November to early December are when you're at the height of your powers. Admittedly, February thru March is challenging, but it's okay because you're also very busy. The weeks following a change of season (March 20, June 20, September 20, and December 20) are often disorienting. You're extremely sensitive to shifts in temperature.

CHILD OF THE MOON ...

Venus rules the zodiac sign Libra. Therefore you Children of the Moon with the Moon in Libra enjoy the allure, charm, and powers of persuasion associated with the Planet of love and beauty. Being the Planet of partnership, Venus expands her influence through liaisons. Hooking up with the right person opens doors that might otherwise have remained closed. You progress faster and double your take by putting mutual interests ahead of personal ones.

Venus rules mirrors. Is it any wonder that you would reflect whatever the prevailing opinion happens to be? But you don't do this because you've no mind of your own. You're actually very controlling. You're just subtle about it. You, more than most, know how fickle people can be. Sometimes they're easily satisfied and sometimes there's no pleasing them. By keeping your finger on the pulse of events and listening before you act, you often know exactly what to do to bring people back in line again. This is what makes you so good at management. You have an innate feel for when to apply pressure and when to be accommodating. It's a balancing act.

This balancing act is mirrored in your very own personality. The Moon and Venus rule over potentially conflicting spheres of life. The Moon is connected to hearth and home. She rules over the family and things that you inherit from your family like money and property, as well as physical and psychological tendencies. Because the Moon wants to reproduce, nurture, and provide, she symbolizes motherly love.

Venus rules over the *other* kind of love. After all—people have to get married to start a family and you're not going to find a suitable partner as long as you're tied to the apron strings. But there's more to Venus than that. She is responsible for the ties that bind *outside* the jurisdiction of the family. In other words: anything that *isn't* a blood tie—like a contract, pledge, or betrothal. Venus rules over marriage and love affairs as well as arbitration, corporate mergers, and peace treaties. If the Moon's concerns are for family, then Venus's concerns are purely social—which can sometimes split your allegiances right down the center.

You take longer than most to make up your mind. Yet what looks like chronic vacillating is

WITH MOON IN LIBRA

actually you letting the other side do all the coaxing and cajoling. You believe in keeping options open, and you're in no hurry to exercise one in case a better one comes along. You're also a big believer in damage control, and you do what's necessary to make the disappointed party feel better about taking a setback in stride.

It isn't easy being a people pleaser. Just the thought of alienating someone can tie your stomach up in knots. You may suffer from digestive trouble when you're mulling over pros and cons, but after you've made your decision, you'll find that things return to their normal ease and flow. Too much digestive trouble is a sign that you're holding on to tensions.

Because of the Moon's position at the time of your birth, you often feel like you're being pushed out into the world before your time. You like to build from the bottom up and want to be sure your foundation is solid. However, given your druthers, you could take forever to put plans into action, which is why events and people sometimes have to force your hand. You resent feeling pressured in the moment, but later on you'll come to appreciate that pushiness.

Late September through December are your peak months. This is the time when people are returning from their summer vacations and are in need of redirection and grounding. You'll find them receptive to suggestions, recommendations, and compromises. It's also the season of family get-togethers and holiday socializing. This sets the stage for your particular brand of networking. You'll find you also do well during the months when Venus is powerful, like March and May. Late December through mid-April (with the exception of Valentine's Day!) is slow going as far as you're concerned, because everyone's either paying off Christmas or battening down the hatches for tax season.

CHILD OF THE MOON ...

Both Mars and Pluto rule the zodiac sign Scorpio. Therefore you Children of the Moon with the Moon in Scorpio experience the gumption of Mars combined with the concentration of Pluto. You never say never and will relentlessly pursue what you want. Unlike other Children of the Moon, your feelings never change. Or if they do, you will deliberately bring them back in line to where they should be. Your willpower stems from your emotions. You remain focused on the prize long after others have given up.

Your challenge is to find a way to harness the energies of both Mars and Pluto. Mars urges you to get out in the world and make something of yourself. It embraces risk. Pluto, on the other hand, sees the world as a place where nothing lasts forever. Named after the god of the Underworld, Pluto regards all outcomes as final. A do-or-die intensity infuses just about everything you do. When you're a Child of the Moon ruled by Mars and Pluto, you're no stranger to separation and loss. You want to grab what you can while you can—and never let go.

This gives you a thick skin, which is impor-

tant, since you are drawn to situations that test your personal and spiritual mettle. Pluto is the Planet of ordeals and the transformations that arise from them. Where other Children of the Moon would go out of their way to avoid anything unsettling, you have no problem braving the crucible. You're often faced with life decisions that make people's blood run cold. It could be anything from leaving a secure job with no guarantees for the future to standing by someone everyone else has turned their backs on. This isn't to say that you go out looking for trouble, but you are an intense person. And intense people naturally seek situations that match their intensity. If there are times when you have to pitch everything, then so be it. Pluto is the Planet of death and rebirth. From the ashes of the old comes the impetus for the new. You are strengthened by ordeals.

You are a solitary figure and need a lot of elbowroom. It's a good idea to seek the type of employment where you can make your own hours. Neither Mars nor Pluto is known for taking orders well. You're happiest being your own boss. However, you're not misanthropic. When you're done

WITH MOON IN SCORPIO

for the day, you'd love nothing more than to socialize.

Your Birthday Planet and Pluto both share a love for the past, so you may be drawn to activities like restoration, archiving, or research. The Moon rules the night. Pluto's domain is what lurks beneath the surface. This gives you a fascination with mysteries and secrets, ranging from mundane to religious and scientific. You may also notice that people tend to trust you with their property for safekeeping. You dote over objects—particularly if they have a long history. Few things pain you like the sight of a neglected antique. You know that whoever made it poured his heart and soul into it or it was the treasured item of someone who passed away. These daily reminders of mortality are never far from your thoughts. Call it morbid or romantic, but your psychic connection to history is what gives you your extraordinary empathy. It's almost impossible for you to look at a homeless person and not be reminded that at one time this man or woman

was a child, with a child's hopes for the future.

Because of the Moon's position at the time of your birth, you find it easy to express what you feel. There's nothing shy or vacillating about your opinions, and the Lunar Mars flavor gives you the courage of your convictions. You don't wait for things to come to you. This is an extremely dynamic position, as you will work hard to make your dreams materialize. Your parents' parents are bound to be influential in some way—particularly a grandmother.

You love warm, dark places and come to life when the Sun goes down. You enjoy summer nights but are no great fan of long hot days. The autumn months—September, October, and November—are most auspicious, as well as the months preceding the spring—like March and early April. August isn't easy nor is early June. Perhaps they bring up memories of your mother harping on you to go outside and play when you were perfectly happy reading indoors.

CHILD OF THE MOON ...

Jupiter rules the Zodiac sign Sagittarius. Therefore you Children of the Moon with the Moon in Sagittarius are blessed with the generosity of spirit and optimism associated with this magnanimous Planet. You open your doors to just about everyone you meet—which makes sense, considering that the Moon rules the hearth and Jupiter is the Planet of hospitality. You see people in their best light. This doesn't make you a stranger to downsides, you just believe in emphasizing the positive.

When you're a Child of the Moon with Jupiter powerful, your concept of hearth and home expands to include the area where you live. You believe in community service and have great civic pride. You know all your neighbors, the merchants of the stores you patronize, and maybe even the mayor. You are friends with the people you work with and believe in a relaxed and open office atmosphere. You don't like job titles. You think it makes people uppity. You believe that if you treat coworkers with respect, they'll respect you in return.

You're a staunch believer in homegrown industry. You have nothing against "globalization" per se. If anything, you're fascinated by other cultures. But as far as you're concerned the world is a big enough place with plenty to go around. Why should one country or community compete with another when each has something unique to offer? You believe that helping and encouraging people to develop their own resources will result in everyone bringing something to the table and in sharing the wealth.

Philosophies we work out for *ourselves* don't necessarily apply to everyone. And when you're a Child of the Moon with Jupiter prominent, you can get impatient with people who don't readily support your munificence—especially if you perceive them to be cynical or cheap. You take immediate offense, and your response can sometimes be over the top. Jupiter was named for the god of storms, and you can be just as loud and thunderous when you don't get your way. Thankfully neither your Ruling Planet nor Jupiter are known for holding a grudge. Sooner or later the rainbow comes out and everything is harmonious again. But even if you agree to disagree, you still believe you're in the right.

WITH MOON IN SAGITTARIUS

Your folksy approach to life makes you popular with young people as well as the average Joe. You don't even have to be the person in charge to be in charge. It's a given that you have the support of most people in a group, so anyone looking to lead will need to win you over first. You may be gentle and nonassuming, but you're still a force to be reckoned with.

Your devotion to your community also extends to love of the land where you live. Environmental concerns will be as important as cultural ones, maybe even more so, given your fondness for the outdoors. There's no such thing as compartmentalization with you. Everything is interconnected.

Because of the Moon's position at the time of your birth, you have an ability to represent others' concerns as vigorously as your own. Many feel forced to choose between the two, but the scope of your personality is big enough to incorporate both. You would prefer to combine them, of course, but you'll champion others' interests, even if you disagree with their position. Your sense of fair play is that big. Although you will always have strong feelings and opinions, you know when to tone them down to make room so other voices can be heard.

March and April, July and August, as well as December are when you feel most confident and secure. These are times when you have the clearest idea of what you have and don't need to think so much about what needs to be done. However, you do tend to get irritable during those couple of days that precede the full Moon. You have a problem saying no, and given that full Moons are when tensions come to the surface, these can be rough spots for you. Even the most generous spirits can have off days, so it's a good idea to give loved ones and friends fair warning.

CHILD OF THE MOON ...

Saturn rules the zodiac sign Capricorn. Subsequently you Children of the Moon with the Moon in Capricorn have the fortitude and persistence associated with the Planet that rules the school of hard knocks. Things take longer to come together than they do for most people, and just about every step forward can bring some sort of complication. However, when you do eventually reap the fruits of your labors, it's an extraordinary harvest. Not only does it replenish diminished stores, but it also redeems all the hardship.

You believe in good, solid hard work. As far as you're concerned there's no finer investment than the blood, sweat, and tears you pour into an enterprise. You like to talk about accomplishments in terms of personal cost and effort. If you didn't suffer for something, then it just isn't that valuable to you—no matter how impressive it might look to others.

Interestingly enough, you haven't always been the responsible type. Being a Child of the Moon with Saturn dominant gives you a very earthy nature. You like to eat, drink, and be merry—and often to excess. You may even go through a period of full-bodied licentiousness. But bacchanalias can take a toll. At some point—perhaps in your late twenties or early thirties—a life-changing experience will cause you to get your act together. There is a dramatic break between your youth and your adulthood. Indeed people who knew you when you were young may have a hard time reconciling the before and after pictures.

The Moon's position at the time of your birth makes you very results oriented. This is good, because your Birthday Planet tends to behave as if the shortest distance between two points is a circle. Yet you can get very impatient with your own process. Being a Child of the Moon, your mind likes to wander. Which makes perfect sense, because the Moon rules the unconscious. Saturn, however, is the Planet of time. It always keeps an eye on the clock and isn't satisfied unless it has something to show for itself at the end of the workday. Be patient when things don't come as easily or quickly as you would like. "Everything in its own time" is a very good motto for you.

WITH MOON IN CAPRICORN

You enjoy being everyone's Rock of Gibraltar. Shouldering responsibility keeps you from feeling adrift. As a Child of the Moon with Saturn strong, you are no stranger to depression. Dark moods every now and again are fine, but yours can get debilitating if you aren't grounded. That's why you follow such a set routine in your life. It's not just because you're disciplined. People's expectations serve as your psychic mooring points.

You feel like you have something to contribute to society at large. You want to make a difference and will work as tirelessly for a stranger as you would for a best friend. You consider it a moral duty to pass on to others what someone once passed on to you. Saturn is the patron Planet of mentors. Perhaps an older relative or friend of the family believed in your potential when others didn't. It was this person's support and encouragement that made a difference at a time when you needed it. You want to do the same for someone else.

Expect in-laws or a partner's relatives to play a prominent role in your life. This pattern of adopting someone else's family started in childhood and carries on to this day. It isn't a negative reflection on your own family. It may just be that a friend's mother had a better-stocked refrigerator.

Strangely enough, your birthday season isn't always the easiest time of year for you. Summers are supposed to be relaxed, but somehow it never seems to work out that way. You may find the same to be true of the winter holidays. You—more than most—need to schedule annual getaways. You work very hard and can only relax when you're in a totally different environment. March, May, and September are very good months. March is especially favorable. That's when opportunities come knocking, and you want to be home for that.

CHILD OF THE MOON ...

Both Saturn and Uranus rule the zodiac sign Aquarius. Therefore you Children of the Moon with the Moon in Aquarius have the exacting qualities of Saturn combined with the idealism of Uranus. For you, the way things *should* be is more important than the way they are. This makes you tireless in your quest for perfection. Asking tough questions and revealing inconsistencies is all part of your campaign for improvement. You're both a practical and a logical thinker, and the combination of the two ensures you'll get your way most of the time. Unfortunately these very same qualities also make you intolerant of people's foibles. You're benevolent toward those you're trying to help, but demanding and brusque toward those who work for or with you. Subsequently you can be very warm and open to people you hardly know and oddly impersonal toward those who should matter most. In truth this is a reflection of your own deeply complex nature.

Your Ruling Planet takes everything personally, while Saturn and Uranus tend to react coolly to any emotional display. Saturn regards feelings as potential liabilities, while Uranus sees them as just getting in the way. That's why you may rely on formulas or principles to judge what's right. If you're reacting to what you perceive to be a gross injustice or a popular misconception, you can become very adamant and heated. It's easier to respond to others' pain than it is to express your own. You're more comfortable debating than sitting through a heart-to-heart session of hand-holding. However there's something about your earnestness that betrays some kind of personal investment. This makes people ask why you care so much. Expecting a candid moment, they're puzzled when you begin quoting facts and figures.

The difficulty with having three Planets at work in your life is that you have to juggle them all. Admittedly this can make for awkward moments—especially if someone catches you in midargument with yourself. However, this psychic peanut gallery can also make life dynamic and exciting, because you're constantly evolving as a person. There are times when you need to be Lunar (personal), when you need to be Saturnine (professional), and when you need to be Uranian (principled). Sometimes these happen all at once,

WITH MOON IN AQUARIUS

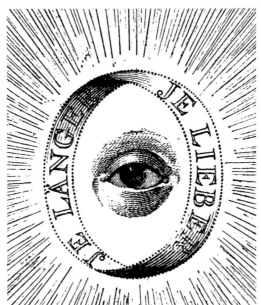

and sometimes you'll go for years wearing one hat and then another. That's why it wouldn't be surprising if you spent your youth as an emotional mess only to emerge as a button-down type, or if you traded in your lab coat one day for a tie-dye T-shirt and a pair of Birkenstocks. You need to play with different roles. Squeezing yourself into one self-definition would be a disaster, but life gets easier as you grow older.

Despite all this restless energy (or perhaps because of it) you are drawn to regimented professions because Saturn is the Planet of rules and Uranus is the Planet of systems. Your Birthday Planet rules fluctuations. You continually prove and disprove the assumptions we all live by in order to get at the truth. This is something scientists do all the time—as do investigators, academics, and policy makers. Like them, you benefit from the meticulous standards of a format. Sometimes the truth isn't in what's apparent, but in what's missing.

Because of the Moon's position at the time of your birth, you'll find yourself professionally involved in other people's private business. This isn't because you're nosey, it's just that the answers you need lie in their recollections, possessions, bank accounts, or even bodies. It's your job to remain objective while pursuing what could turn into an intensely private line of questioning. Yet you are careful not to impose on them anything you wouldn't be willing to impose on yourself. You're both impartial and sensitive.

The times when you're culling resources are different from the times when you're required to make something of them. Therefore the days following a full Moon are best for gathering information or finding whatever ingredients you may require. You'll want to pay particular attention to when the full Moon falls in February, June, and October. These times of year yield the best results or are key for the success of any long-range plan.

CHILD OF THE MOON ...

Both Jupiter and Neptune rule the zodiac sign Pisces. You Children of the Moon with the Moon in Pisces possess the high-mindedness of Jupiter as well as the soulful depth of Neptune. You have an extraordinary psychic life and see reality as the interplay between your inner and outer worlds.

Jupiter is perhaps the most humanitarian of the Planets. It rules over our moral code as exemplified in religion, philosophy, and justice. It speaks to the spirit that seeks a higher purpose in life. Jupiter marvels at the world and is always falling in love with faraway places and exotic ideas. Jupiter wants to *dive* into things. Neptune, on the other hand, wants to *delve* into things. Like the sea god it's named for, Neptune is a realm all its own. It rules over our dreams, fantasies, and artistic impulses. Although your Birthday Planet rules the unconscious, it's Neptune that rules what Carl Jung called "the Collective Unconscious." Our dreams may be individual, but their vocabulary is not. Neptune rules the well where all of our imaginations go to drink.

When you're a Child of the Moon with Jupiter and Neptune powerful, everything about you is big. You have big hopes, dreams, and expectations. You're no stranger to disappointment, but you have an extraordinary ability to rebound. If one dream doesn't work out, you can always go on to another. The wonderful thing about Neptune's influence is that your imagination will never run dry.

Neptune rules over seas and oceans. Your Birthday Planet rules smaller bodies of water—like ponds, streams, and lakes. Streams and lakes feed into the sea, and likewise you can sometimes feel like you're being drained by your inner life. The Neptune part of you isn't too happy with the state of the world you live in. After all, if you have the ability to visualize things to the extent of almost touching them, it can be dispiriting when you're held back by mundane day-to-day obstacles. That Neptune part of you can turn its back on the world and say, "Not for me. I'd rather live in my dreams."

Thankfully the Jupiter part of you refuses to accept resignation. The Planet of journeys, Jupiter will go just about anywhere for the experience. It's this insistence that there's a higher purpose that keeps you climbing back up out of your

WITH MOON IN PISCES

steepest pitfalls. Being a Child of the Moon, you know (more than most) that life moves in cycles. If something doesn't come together now, there's always a chance it will later.

Words and pictures are very important to you, so it would make perfect sense for you to be drawn to film, television, or publishing. You may also be attracted to teaching, coaching, as well as rehabilitation—which appeals to both your spiritual and spirited sides.

Because of the Moon's position at the time of your birth, you are continually drawn to the world beyond your stoop. This serves as a wonderful counterbalance to the natural tendency of your Ruling Planet, which is to nest. However the Moon's position indicates that you'll be doing more than collecting frequent-flier miles in your future. You could find purpose in a culture or lifestyle very different from the one you were raised in. Moreover other people's plights or issues can capture your imagination and heart and become deeply meaningful.

Late November through December as well as late February through March are wonderful times of the year for you. These are the periods when your imagination is the most fertile and your enthusiasm is heightened. July is particularly favorable; the change of climate that accompanies May through June as well as September through October can be difficult. Your mood tends to reflect the ups-and-downs in temperature, and your sensitive nature is susceptible to colds and allergies. Be especially wary around the Ides of May and the Ides of October—that's the fifteenth of those months.

CHILD OF MERCURY ...

Venus rules the zodiac sign Taurus. Subsequently you Children of Mercury with Mercury in Taurus have a down-to-earth approach to life. When the Planet of the senses (Mercury) meets the Planet of sensuality (Venus), then you have to be able to see something, touch it, and even smell it. Your deductive reasoning is based on keen observation of physical details. You'll dab your finger in a boiling pot to get a quick taste or take apart a piece of machinery just so that you can get a "feel" for how it works. Unlike other Children of Mercury, you have little patience for theories and abstractions. Indeed you even make fun of them. If someone can't explain himself simply, chances are that person's got something to hide. To you, everything must be provable.

This can sometimes give the impression that you are too set in your ways. In truth, you're discriminating. Venus, the Planet of beauty, influences your tastes. You have very high and exacting standards. Moreover Venus is not easily seduced any more than Mercury—the Planet of quick thinking—is likely to be bamboozled. It would be like trying to kid a kidder. Few people can spot a fake or shoot down a flimsy argument as precisely and efficiently as you. But you've a talent for more than just debunking. As a Child of Mercury with Venus powerful, you're a persuasive communicator. Your ability to sell an idea is unrivaled.

You're both arty and artful. You can exaggerate for effect just as easily as you can downplay your smarts. Your Birthday Planet rules all forms of communication—whether it's words, musical notes, or numbers. Venus rules over anything we find aesthetically pleasing. This could make you a gifted writer, performer, or musician as well as an eloquent speaker or advocate. Since Mercury rules sales and Venus rules packaging, you might be attracted to advertising, design, or image consulting. There's a very strong commercial side to both Mercury and Venus. Where your Ruling Planet's focus is on finding ways to make a whim a reality, Venus's objective is to expand her area of influence through the people she knows. For example, it isn't enough to build a client base. You want to build the *right* client base—which means attracting the interests of people with money and prestige, so that you can increase your

WITH MERCURY IN TAURUS

status and fill your coffers. Mercury may be more into the gaming aspect of making money, but that Venus part of you has expensive tastes. You don't lift a finger unless the price is right. However, once engaged, you will do whatever it takes to meet a deadline or get the job done. Those exacting standards of beauty translate into you producing high-quality workmanship.

Because of Mercury's position at the time of your birth, you come into your own later on. It's tempting to say you're a late bloomer, but the truth is you tend to wander from one thing to another when you're young. That Venusian side of you loves to have a good time. The rowdier the better, as far as you're concerned. But pursuit of pleasure isn't the only thing on your mind. Being a Child of Mercury with Venus strong, few things are sexier than a rousing game of cat and mouse.

This can involve you in love triangles or overly complicated affairs. You may waste a lot of opportunities before you decide to actually do something with the talents you've been given. But all that means is you'll just be hitting your stride right when others are running out of gas. The older you get, the more likely it is that you will be able to realize your full potential.

February and March are when you're at the height of your mental powers. Prospects are jumping, and it's easy for you to get in doors that might otherwise remain closed. You should never commit to anything in November or December. This is the time of year when you're likely to feel at loose ends. It's also when you're the most susceptible to getting embroiled in people's soap operas.

CHILD OF MERCURY ...

Mercury rules the zodiac sign Gemini. Therefore you Children of Mercury with Mercury in Gemini are chock-full of ideas. Like a circus juggler who has to split his focus to keep all the balls in the air, you can't become preoccupied with one or you'll lose control of all of them. This is the particular dilemma of a Child of Mercury with Mercury strong. You have more ideas than you know what to do with. And because your mind darts in one direction and then another, you may be incapable of developing any one of them past its initial concept—unless of course you can find someone to lend you a helping hand.

You're convinced your "other half" is out there somewhere. Your dream is to meet, discover you have everything in common, and successfully reunite two parts that belong together as a whole. Unfortunately you can't expect someone else to fill the blanks in your personality. People aren't extensions of you. They have personalities of their own. Not even the mind, with its left and right hemispheres, is divided into two neatly defined camps—both sides work in unison. Once you jettison the expectation that someone else is supposed to complete you as a person then a relationship invites more of you into play, rather than only a few select traits.

Mercury's position at the time of your birth makes you precocious. From an early age, you've been able to grasp concepts quickly and apply them. You rose swiftly through the ranks and perhaps even graduated ahead of time or were singled out for special recognition and honors. But there's a downside to catching on to things so easily—it's hard to imagine encountering something you don't get. And when you do, all of that ingenuity becomes focused on how to get out of a fix or around an obstacle rather than on progressing to the next level of expertise. Hopefully you had a very wise parent or teacher who prevented you from wiggling out of these predicaments so easily. More often than not, Children of Mercury with Mercury strong can charm their way out of having to work their mental muscles, and the result is you don't move past a certain point. That's why when you face a problem that you'd rather just avoid, it's best to challenge yourself to master it. This way you can develop the discipline

WITH MERCURY IN GEMINI

that will augment your facility.

The need to develop is very important for you. Plans don't spring fully hatched from your mind. You'll begin with a quick sketch, and only as you play with it does a fuller picture emerge. Many Children of Mercury with Mercury powerful are involved in graphic design—from layouts to illustrating to coloring and framing. Your Birthday Planet is the patron Planet of artisans. This is very different from an artist who relies on vagaries such as inspiration. You like to know exactly what you're dealing with.

Late May to mid-June, late September to mid-October, and late January to mid-February are wonderful for you. These are the "airy" times of year when ideas, information, and interesting people circulate freely. As a Child of Mercury with Mercury powerful, you like it when there's a steady flow of events pouring into your life. That's why August is rarely fun (you've had about all you can take of your summer-share friends) not to mention November and December—especially if you have to celebrate the holidays with your family. As a Child of Mercury, you're hardwired for sibling rivalry, and all it takes is a couple of days around your family to transform you from a coolly sophisticated adult into a six-year-old fighting over who gets the TV remote.

CHILD OF MERCURY . . .

The Moon rules the zodiac sign Cancer. You Children of Mercury with Mercury in Cancer have a rich inner life. Your memories and dreams move fluidly through your consciousness, and you could while away the hours absorbed in reverie. The Moon's nature is contemplative, so you don't need to communicate your emotions verbally. You *feel*.

You have an intuitive sense for what's *not* being said. You take in the body language, pitch of the voice, even the way eyes meet or avoid another's gaze. For you subtext is as important (maybe even more so) than what you're actually discussing. Most people don't appreciate how powerful words are. You choose yours with the scrutiny of a poet.

You're an avid reader and moviegoer, so it wouldn't be surprising if you were drawn to writing and filmmaking. You're also extremely sensitive to aromas. Since the Moon rules the memory, your powers of recall are tremendous. But this is more than a good head for names and dates. You can watch someone perform a task and then repeat it with astonishing ease. That, combined with the improvisational talents of your Birthday Planet, transform a gift for mimicry into something uniquely yours.

As a Child of Mercury with the Moon strong, your unconscious is an active part of your life. You do a lot of thinking in your sleep. Your creative process might begin with a catnap, a daydream, or simply vegging out. All you need is a few minutes of downtime. When you wake up again, you're energized—and will have the answer you're looking for.

The erratic nature of your Ruling Planet combined with your waxing/waning emotional life make you hard to understand . . . even to yourself. You can be warm and engaging one moment, cool and abrupt the next. People wonder if they said something to offend you, yet it's more likely that your mind has simply wandered off. You can wear a wistful, even profound expression—almost as if you were looking right through a person and in fact, you are. But while people might believe you're peering into the depths of their very souls, you may simply be mulling over your lunch order.

You are very attached to your roots, your family, and your people. The Moon rules over hearth

WITH MERCURY IN CANCER

and home. Subsequently your mother (as well as your mother's side of the family) plays an influential role in your life. You love family. Even if you weren't raised in the most nurturing of environments, you'll still invite people into your life and give them a place at your table. You have a strong sense of community and a social conscience.

There is a marked difference between who you are when you're young and who you are when you reach adulthood. Most people can recognize the seeds of the man or woman in the child, but for you there's an about-face that occurs sometime in your late twenties. If outgoing as a child, you'll become introverted; if you were shy—more gregarious. For many Children of Mercury with the Moon powerful, childhood was restless and even inse-cure. Your adult years give you an opportunity to treat yourself to the childhood you never felt you had.

April and May are when you feel most in sync with the current of events. This is the best time of year to either initiate a project or bring it to fruition. You have until July to take care of all the details—anytime after that and progress will be sluggish. Mid-December through January is not favorable. With the exception of the holidays (which always brings out your warm and cozy side), you'll feel lethargic. You and cold weather don't mix well, so it's best to move to warmer climates if you can. Also beware of your tendency to "dry out" during the winter. You'll want to drink plenty of water, invest in a good humidifier, and use moisturizers.

CHILD OF MERCURY ...

The Sun rules the zodiac sign Leo. Therefore you Children of Mercury with Mercury in Leo possess a noble spirit and sincerity that few would question. Everything you say and do comes straight from the heart. Since the dawn of civilization the heart has been equated with the Sun. The heart is the seat of our affections. All our joy, thrills, humor, and pleasure emanate from this source of heat and life. There's a warmth that generates from deep inside you. Your analysis of any given situation is enlightening and upbeat.

The Sun's brilliance is more showy than cerebral. You're more comfortable lecturing or performing than you are debating. However you are still a Child of Mercury, which means you're cunning and think nothing of using your Solar charm and magnanimity to get out of a tight spot. On its own, the Sun can get haughty; your Birthday Planet is irreverent. But together these two energies give you the ability to find the humor in almost any predicament. You're wry without being caustic, self-deprecating rather than condescending. This is a disarming combination. People enjoy you because even when you're naughty, you're nice.

Nevertheless that Solar side of you still feels a sense of entitlement. You won't downplay your successes. You will advertise yourself aggressively—which can get on the nerves of those who live and work with you. Sometimes they feel shortchanged. But because it's your personality they rally around or your charisma that brings in business—they'll sit on their gripes. You are a lightning rod of good fortune. Happy coincidences and unexpected windfalls follow wherever you go. Even surprise upsets tend to work out in your favor.

When you're a Child of Mercury with the Sun strong, you rely on intuitive flashes more than intellect. You'll still come up with the right answer, but when pressed for an explanation you may be at a loss as to how you arrived at it. Unfortunately you're too sincere to just make something up (as other Children of Mercury would), so you can spend a lot of time backtracking over your thought process. This is why you get peevish when someone questions your judgment—even if it's only rhetorical.

As a general rule, Mercury's Children don't take anything on faith. Their need to question is

WITH MERCURY IN LEO

just too strong. However it's the Sun's nature to promote growth, to enliven, and to inspire. Your entire life is in service to this golden optimism. This is what makes you heroic. You will go to great lengths to bring out the best in people. Your belief in someone can make all the difference when it comes to success or failure. You teach by the example of your own life. Rather than get too preachy or philosophical, you will show how you overcame similar obstacles. Ironically this is the only time when you play fast and furious with the facts. You're not above stretching the truth if it makes for a dramatic life story that sells.

Because of Mercury's position at the time of your birth, it takes a while for you to develop into who you really are. You may start out very modest and humble, forcing yourself to blend into the background. But as time passes and you begin to realize you're more on the ball than most people you meet, you'll let that Solar side of you peek out from behind the clouds. The older you get, the younger you become, which is in keeping with your innate conviction that the best is yet to come.

The end of spring is always associated with life in full bloom, so May and June are marvelous months for you. You feel most connected to your vital spirit and can give of yourself without feeling drained. Moreover, you're surrounded by people who are uppers, not downers. Although your personality is too strong to be dominated by others for very long, it helps to have them supporting you rather than dragging their heels. February and March are when you're apt to feel unsupported and ignored. This is the time of year when loved ones and colleagues are self-absorbed, so you should lower your expectations.

CHILD OF MERCURY . . .

Mercury rules the zodiac sign Virgo. You Children of Mercury with Mercury in Virgo are always eager to help out in a pinch. You're just the person people come to when they need information, a sounding board, or simple practical advice. You know how to get the job done, but this isn't just humble service. Your Ruling Planet was named after the Greek god of trade and commerce, so you're a firm believer in "I scratch your back, you scratch mine."

By volunteering to take on mundane tasks—like household chores or managing someone's accounts—you make yourself invaluable. Everyone—from loved ones to clients—will come to depend on you. You become associated in their minds with the norm, the way things should be done. Routines are powerful, because once set in motion, they're difficult to stop. And you know this. By ensuring that the business of people's everyday lives runs like clockwork, you get to set the agenda.

Familiarizing yourself with what bossy types want keeps you one step ahead of the game. You know exactly what to say and do, and though you make it appear as if you're doing others' bidding, you are actually laying a trail of bread crumbs that leads straight to the conclusion you want them to make. You have a tireless eye for detail and are often better informed than the people in charge. Subsequently you know just what adjustments to make in order to avoid a fiasco. You learned a long time ago it's not the one up on the throne who's in charge, but the person behind it.

You both disdain and identify with the underdog. If there's anything you can't stand it's a victim, and you don't suffer fools gladly. At the same time you will go to great lengths to help people who wind up with the short end of the stick. Few would suspect that beneath that skeptical veneer lies a powerful social conscience.

Highly sensitive, you try to run your own emotional life like you would a bureaucracy. Unfortunately the psyche doesn't work like that. It's why you can be so self-conscious at the most intimate moments. Your Birthday Planet rules the bicameral brain, so you're of two minds when it comes to getting close. Part of you would love to get lost in someone else, but then your fear of being used kicks in. There's a big difference

WITH MERCURY IN VIRGO

between being a servant and a slave. Deep down inside you're afraid of giving so much of yourself that you'll disappear altogether. Making yourself unattainable in some way guarantees that you come first. You truly believe that your survival depends on it.

Mercury's position at the time of your birth makes you self-sufficient—perhaps too self-sufficient for your own good. Some of this stems from your mother. She may have had a terrible fear of being penniless—either because she was or the women in her family had a history of being abandoned. In all likelihood you inherited this anxiety. Even if you couldn't care less about money, there's still a part of you that believes you should never trade in your autonomy, because once you do you will be under someone else's control. Thankfully sisters, friends, aunts, and grandmothers also play important roles. Early relationships with women may reinforce some of your mother's negative beliefs, but that will change as you mature and begin rewriting the rules for yourself.

Late April to mid-May, late August to mid-September, and late December to mid-January are wonderful for you. These are the "earthy" times of year when work is plentiful, money is flowing, and you really apply yourself. As a Child of Mercury with Mercury powerful, you like to be busy, and you get antsy when forced to sit on your hands. February and March can be exasperating. This is a fickle time of year, when for every step forward there are three steps backward. You can create a lot of extra aggravation for yourself if you're not careful. Take your own good advice: don't sweat the small stuff.

CHILD OF MERCURY ...

Venus rules the zodiac sign Libra. Although you have a critical mind (along with definite opinions and tastes), your allegiance to rules and laws is stronger. You Children of Mercury with Mercury in Libra are committed to finding a way for everyone to get along. When Venus influences your Birthday Planet, everything you do is in service to relationships. You're happy only if the people in your life are happy. This raises the sights of your Birthday Planet (which can be a little mercenary) and sets it on the higher path of bringing people together. Diplomatic and fair, you believe there's another side to the story and will naturally extend the benefit of the doubt.

Often cast in the role of go-between, you have to run back and forth between two camps. Now most Children of Mercury would simply report the salient points of each side, but the Venus part of you wants to find their common ground and lead them to it. By *mirroring* what each party has to say (Venus rules mirrors), they begin to hear themselves and figure out where the problems in their thinking may be. Of course a little coaxing and cajoling helps—Venus and Mercury are both master flatterers. In no time at all you build a bridge where a divide used to be, and without calling undue attention to yourself. Is it any wonder that so many people flock to you for advice and input?

But making your happiness contingent on the happiness of others can be exhausting, if not self-defeating. Especially if, in the interests of keeping the peace, being true to yourself winds up taking a backseat to being true to others. By keeping your own feelings in check or only doling out as much truth as you think is palatable, you can appear to be disingenuous. This makes it hard for others to get a sense of the "real" you. That's why they treat you warily or only deal with you according to the role you play in their lives. This can leave you feeling lonely in a room full of your twenty-five closest friends.

When you're this well designed for politics and public relations, it's hard to be personal. You will suppress any of your own concerns and needs if you regard them as getting in the way of your being there for others. Unfortunately, if you're not careful, you can get caught up in a vicious cycle: the more you suppress a desire, the more it takes hold. Your body is the first place you register signs of trouble. Sometimes it can be a rash or an

WITH MERCURY IN LIBRA

allergy. Sometimes it can be more overwhelming—like an eating disorder or sexual compulsion. It's a good idea to give your own concerns airplay, even if it feels awkward at first.

Because of Mercury's position at the time of birth, your focus is on the world around you. You want to create a place for yourself, and the best way to do this is to identify what's missing and then fill it in. You're a shrewd observer of people and a strict adherent to protocol. There's no excuse for bad manners, and you won't tolerate abuse. As you get older (perhaps as you approach middle age) you begin to see that you are more than just a spokesperson for others. This could be a potentially upsetting time—especially if you haven't seen to your own concerns. You may find that your inner life isn't as developed as your public one. It's like overexercising one muscle at the expense of another. Give yourself time to bring your private life up to speed and you'll establish a healthy balance.

June and July are when you feel most centered. This is the time of year when you can see for yourself how all the pieces come together and are able to make whatever adjustments are necessary. It's a time of satisfaction and when you can indulge in more relaxed pursuits. You love to be kept busy, but there's a difference between being industrious and being hectic. March and April (and quite possibly August) are when you feel most at others' beck and call. No matter what you do to try to organize their affairs and timetables, they never seem to get around to doing what needs to be done—which leaves you having to make up for their lost time.

CHILD OF VENUS...

Both Jupiter and Neptune rule the zodiac sign Pisces. You Children of Venus with Venus in Pisces possess all the wisdom of Jupiter combined with the empathy of Neptune. You are extremely generous and self-sacrificing. You feel everyone's pains and joys, and it's this immense compassion that draws people to you. Your ability to find the moral in a setback and to rise above disappointments sets a high standard for others to follow. Is it any wonder that people tend to put you on a pedestal?

In truth, you are a reluctant saint. Your Birthday Planet isn't built for selfless love. Her domain is one-on-one relationships. Jupiter rules over community affairs, whereas Neptune influences what's best described as "popular movements"—that spontaneous gathering of people around a charged political or social issue. Subsequently these two Planets push you to get on out there in the world. But you are still a Child of Venus. At some point you will ask: what's in it for me?

Some people are born with a sense of purpose. You encounter your purpose through the person you fall in love with. Venus is her most romantic when colored by Jupiter (ruler of the skies) and Neptune (ruler of the seas). You want to live and love adventurously. But as is the case with all great romances—they're starcrossed. This isn't to say yours will be ill fated, but great sacrifices will have to be made, and your choice of lover will send a shock wave through the rest of your life. This person might hail from a different background, follow a more liberal or conservative religion, or espouse a set of beliefs that turns yours on end. You're apt to be split in your allegiances and won't feel comfortable on either side of the divide. Everyone (but the two of you) will question the wisdom and appropriateness of the match. But it's important to keep in mind that Venus's allegiance is to the world *outside* the home. And when you remember that the purpose of both Jupiter and Neptune is to expand your horizons, you'll gain more confidence in your choice.

You could be drawn to community or civic affairs. Jupiter is the Planet of justice, and you may want to help or defend those who find themselves on the wrong side of the law. This would certainly satisfy any cravings for adventure. On

WITH VENUS IN PISCES

the other hand, Neptune's domain is the imagination. Since Venus is the Ruling Planet of beauty and culture, you may pursue a career in the arts, arts education/arts therapy, or work in imports/exports. Then again you may be in the business of luxury items—such as perfume, jewelry, textiles, or gourmet foods. Given Neptune's bacchanalian nature, you'd make a superb events coordinator.

who you are before you can commit to someone else. Nevertheless you will eventually wind up in a respectable match— usually around the time when your family has given up all hope.

Because of Venus's position at the time of your birth, there's a lot of experimenting with who you are in the first half of your life. You will go through a number of dramatic transformations. You will have many romances. This is less about your capricious nature and more about finding the proper balance between your private and public selves. It would be a good idea to wait to marry. It's especially important to be comfortable with

Late February to mid-March and late April through May are the best times of year for you. This is when you celebrate your own personal "New Year's," because you're sloughing off the old skin and looking at the world with fresh perspective. Moreover, the Neptunian part of your nature enjoys the rainy season. September and November are when you're in a winding-down cycle. These are periods when you should be conservative with investments, store away extra earnings, and take care of any unfinished business. This is not the time for protracted negotiations or deals. Bring them to a close— even if you have to cut your losses.

CHILD OF VENUS . . .

Mars rules the zodiac sign Aries. Therefore you Children of Venus with Venus in Aries possess all the determination and focus of this headstrong Planet. When you have Mars powerful, you are drawn to conflict and crisis. The more critical a situation becomes, the more intensely that Mars fire burns in your veins. Nothing is more exhilarating than to snatch a last-minute victory from the gaping jaws of defeat. When it comes down to the wire: it's all up to you.

This is not the way your Birthday Planet is put together. As a Child of Venus, you want to make things nice, not go looking for trouble. The Venus/Mars dynamic can set up a push/pull dichotomy, where it becomes difficult to gauge if you're trying too hard—or not hard enough. Mars is the Planet of willpower. He pursues. Venus is the Planet of beauty. She attracts. When you have both coaching from the sidelines, you can wind up receiving (and sending) some very mixed messages.

It can be difficult to bond with someone else—though that is what you want most of all. The Venus side of your nature may insist on downplaying your Mars energy by suppressing your own wants and needs in the interests of peace and making a partnership work; whereas the Mars side of you may regard a partner as draining away the vital energy you need to accomplish the things you want to do in life. Relationships—in both your private and professional spheres—can become intense battlegrounds. But this isn't about egos, pride, or even control. It's actually about *sustaining* conflict. Unrest is your creative dynamo.

Mars needs an open-ended challenge—someplace to direct its energies. With Mars, the drive to improve is more important than the improvement itself. Therefore you need a quest. Given that Venus influences aesthetic taste, you could focus your energies on trying to attain the unattainable—the ideal good, the perfect beauty.

Trying to attain the unattainable isn't as lofty or futile as it sounds. Athletics provides a good example. Competition (Mars) may be fierce, but it is also framed within a certain etiquette (Venus). One is expected to honor an opponent—no matter how desperate things get in the heat of the game. Another example is the courtroom, where the law

WITH VENUS IN ARIES

encourages both the prosecution and the defense to aggressively pursue their case—while always observing protocol. You may be drawn to medicine or one of the other physical or psychological therapies where you are fighting to heal your patient. You may win, lose, then win again. This keeps your inner fire burning. Given an ongoing conflict to sink its teeth into, your Mars energy has a healthy outlet—thus leaving the Venus side of you in peace to cultivate the things it enjoys most, like harmony.

Venus's position at the time of your birth shows that the early part of your life was anything but harmonious. You were no stranger to disruptions and may even have been the unwitting object of a dispute. As an adolescent you may have been intolerant toward anything that might upset the balance of your life, or you became a figure of controversy by consciously (or unconsciously) mixing it up among loved ones and friends. With each passing year you grow more adept at harnessing these two opposing energies, rather than being run by them. It's natural for you to gravitate toward positions of responsibility, and you're the one others trust most to step into the breach. You have a talent for fashioning effective compromises and also understand when you have to lose a battle to win a war.

April and May are the best months for you. This is when Venus and Mars are most simpatico, and you can get a lot accomplished without having to step on too many toes. It's also a very romantic time—unlike October and November, which can be counterproductive. Like the spring, your passions can heat up and cool down a little too quickly. You need to hook up with a partner who mirrors your inherent feistiness, one who can return your affection and your fire, if need be, barb for barb.

CHILD OF VENUS...

Venus rules the zodiac sign Taurus. As a Child of Venus with Venus in Taurus, you can't help but be attractive and alluring. Your beauty is down-to-earth and approachable. There is nothing off-putting about you. After all— your Birthday Planet aims to please, not to intimidate. Just about everything you say and do looks good, sounds appealing, and is meant to arouse the interest and attention of anyone you come across.

You truly want to make the world a more beautiful place . . . or at least your corner of it. All your actions are aimed at accomplishing this. You won't just settle anywhere. It has to be the right space with the right light (or address). But your desire for beauty goes beyond your surroundings. You also want to live a beautiful life. You are a very physical person. You have strong desires and cravings and want them fulfilled. Therefore you will go about acquiring those things you need to feel comfortable and secure— like a good job, a beautiful partner, and a solid financial plan—in the belief that once that's settled, you can start living the life you like. Some-

times though the result can be the opposite. You want to be careful that your life doesn't wind up being in service to that expensive car or couture wardrobe. You don't want to be left feeling cornered in your own beautiful corner.

When you're a Child of Venus with Venus this strong in your life, you can't help but excite passion in others. It's important to understand that you're putting out signals even if you don't think you are. This is why people tend to act as if you mean yes when you say no. Attractions also come in a variety of expressions. The jealousy of others can be a form of attraction, just as much as their hostility or desire to imitate everything you do. You may find yourself scratching your head, trying to figure out how you came to be at the center of a turf war or stormy love affair.

The way you see it, it's your job to keep the people in your life happy. However once you begin fanning their expectations, they're going to want you to keep on fanning them. And if you don't, then all that admiration, loyalty, and love you worked so hard to attain deteriorates into disappointment and even outright resentment. Sometimes it can feel like you're living life in a

WITH VENUS IN TAURUS

fishbowl. Many celebrities have had to learn this lesson the hard way. You can't walk out on your public—if you don't want your public to walk out on you. There's a part of you that will always belong to someone else. Beauty may have the power to calm the savage Beast, but take Beauty away— for even an instant—and that cuddly behemoth starts gnashing his teeth all over again.

Because of Venus's position at the time of your birth, you will experience a constant tug-of-war between what you feel you owe others versus what you feel you owe yourself. This creates a blind spot when it comes to accurately assessing the give-and-take of life. You have a deep-rooted fear of giving and not getting back. This can come up primarily around lending—be it money, clothing, or a favorite video. There's a part of you that can't help asking when you'll get it back. This is why partnership is so important to you. A partner teaches you how to share while keeping your feet planted firmly on the ground.

Late April to mid-May, late August to mid-September, and late December to mid-January are wonderful for you. These are the "earthy" times of year when money is flowing, and you can really take on those projects and ventures aimed at improving the quality of your life. As a Child of Venus with Venus powerful, physical comfort and feelings of security are a must. You don't do well when forced to work long hours or when you have to break up your normal routine. Late October to mid-November is not a great time for you. This is when you're apt to feel most overwhelmed by demands. But just because you're at your physical nadir doesn't make you a sitting duck. A relaxing massage or visit to a day spa may be exactly what's needed to perk you up.

CHILD OF VENUS...

Mercury rules the zodiac sign Gemini. As a Child of Venus with Venus in Gemini, your head rules your heart—but not in a stuffy, cerebral way. You have a very active mind and are always curious about what others are doing. Part of this comes from a lively interest in their affairs and part of it is based on the fact that you do some of your best thinking while conversing. Like a stand-up comic or a satirist, you're always taking in the goings-on around you. People provide both your inspiration and your audience.

Unlike other Children of Venus, you don't wait on people. You're far too impatient. If you don't like what you hear then you'll get a second opinion. If you happen to come across a better offer, you'll use it to coax the first party to lower their price. When the Planet of seduction and intrigue (Venus) meets the Planet of wheeling and dealing (Mercury), just about everything is fair game. Your Birthday Planet is at her most playful when colored by Mercury, and outsmarting the competition is one of your favorite sports.

But not everyone shares your love of game playing. Indeed some people can feel duped or insulted. Even those who like being egged on sometimes just aren't in the mood. Like a performer, you need to read the audience you're playing for. Thankfully both Venus and Mercury are quick-thinking Planets. If anyone can switch gears, it's you.

Loved ones and friends may regard you as being a "split personality," and there is some truth to this. If there's anything consistent about you, it's your inconsistency. Mercury rules the bicameral mind. Venus rules mirrors. So you're always playing out one half of an equation. Being drawn to opposites is an ongoing theme in your life. If you tend to be visual, you will be attracted to verbal types; whereas if you're logical, you may enjoy being around wildly impulsive people. But you're never consistently one or the other. You change according to who you hook up with. That's why someone accustomed to you acting ditsy may be astonished to overhear you reciting Shakespeare. Truth to tell, you enjoy being a constant surprise—even to yourself.

Because of Venus's position at the time of your birth, you'll experience a big turnover of people, places, and maybe even vocations. You're

WITH VENUS IN GEMINI

not fickle, it's just that you have to try something on in order to get a feel for it. Although you show a lot of promise early on (and may even be encouraged to develop a particular talent), it takes you longer than most to find a comfortable fit. Chances are it's because you're good at more than just one thing. This could result in you going from one career to another until you get to a place in life where you can comfortably wear a number of hats all at once.

Friends may rib you about your *paramour du jour*, but it's important for you to know that a potential partner can keep up intellectually. If someone isn't good at witty repartee, then that association won't get past the introductory conversation. The same holds true for anyone you do business with. You need to be stimulated mentally or you'll move on. Yet you should also know that you've a built-in competitive streak. While

your Ruling Planet likes to make nice, the Mercury side of you can give the impression that you need to have the last word. In reality, you're just verbalizing all your thoughts. Remember that Venus, the Planet of good taste, is also the Planet of discretion. A little extra editing will keep that Mercury side of you in check.

May and June are when you feel most that you get back what you put in—maybe even more so. This is a congenial time of year when it's not too hot or wet and people are in a relaxed, sunny mood. You enjoy being out and about and have little tolerance for "controlled" climates. Your body temperature never seems to be in sync with the office heater or air-conditioner. That's why extreme times of year—like midsummer or midwinter—never mix well with you. September is a good month for new loves and pursuits.

CHILD OF VENUS...

The Moon rules the zodiac sign Cancer. As a Child of Venus with Venus in Cancer, you have a very strong mothering instinct—even if you're a guy. You're patient, supportive, and trust that if things don't come together now, they will eventually. For you, everything moves in cycles. The reason the first calendars were based on the Moon is because all one needed to do to keep track of time was look up in the sky and see what phase she was in. The Moon is changeable but consistent. She rules over routines and the ebb and flow of our day-to-day lives. Like the Moon, you come and go—but people know you're always there for them.

Your Birthday Planet's peace-loving nature is augmented by the Moon's nurturing and sympathetic qualities. You have an ability to make someone feel at ease and that anything said will be held in complete confidence. As a Child of Venus, you can always count on turning people's heads. The Moon's attraction works differently. Tides rise and fall according to the Moon's pull, and you will find that people's emotions respond to you in kind. You bring out their softer side.

There's a fine line between cultivating interest and fostering dependency. And you can wind up with more than you bargained for if you're not careful. Your Ruling Planet and the Moon are both highly agreeable— but, again, for different reasons. Venus is reluctant to shun anyone's interest (you never know what that person might bring to the table), and your highly sensitive Lunar nature doesn't want people's feelings to be hurt. Subsequently, you can find it hard to say no. However saying yes is equally—if not more—difficult. You can't possibly please all the people all the time without getting drained in the process. Putting people at ease without taking on their problems is an ongoing exercise.

Thankfully you were born under a Planet famous for her discriminating nature. The goddess of beauty doesn't just load up her shopping cart and make a beeline for the checkout counter. She's a very choosey customer. This is good, because it forces you to winnow down your purchases. In other words, relationships and associations will go through periods of review when you decide whether they are worth continuing or not.

WITH VENUS IN CANCER

Those that are appealing stay in the cart while those that don't make the grade go back on the shelf. It takes a while to develop this kind of an eye. The Lunar part of you is extremely sentimental, and its need to belong can be just as strong as Venus's need to please. However when you've been overtaxed enough times (and find yourself weighed down by too many obligations and commitments), you'll learn to be pickier. It saves everyone a lot of trouble.

People always come first with you. Not only is this a characteristic of your Ruling Planet, but it's also reflected in her position at the time of your birth. The Moon rules over the body, the house, land, and legacies. Therefore you may be drawn to the health profession, real estate, or being a financial consultant. Being a Child of Venus, there's bound to be a beautifying element—like interior decorating, renovation, or working at a spa or salon. With Venus and the Moon prominent, you may find your niche in a profession catering to women and/or children. But even though you are involved in the intimate affairs of others, your own loved ones may regard you as absentee. This can result in "everyone's got shoes, but the shoemaker's children" syndrome. You will often have to rectify the balance between your public and private lives.

May through July is a wonderful season for you. You love the Sun (but not when it's too hot) and revel in that feeling of abundance that follows the first blooming cycle. Nothing quite compares with those late spring days when you just want to be outside. Not surprisingly, you lose much of that luster from late October through January. This is a dormant period for you, when you don't have much vitality and so you'll want to conserve energy. Once February arrives, things pick up again. There are lots of new beginnings and intriguing overtures, but wait until after April 15 to commit to any of them.

CHILD OF VENUS...

The Sun rules the zodiac sign Leo. Born under a golden Venus, you possess the Midas touch. Even if fortune turns against you, its impact will be soft and you will easily find a way to rise again. Your buoyant spirit can't be kept down. You are truly sun-kissed. When you're a Child of Venus with Venus in Leo, all the elegance and glamour of your Birthday Planet mixes freely with the radiance and playfulness of the Sun. Not only do you command attention when you walk into a room, but you also can't get from the door to the host or hostess without collecting an entourage along the way.

When the Sun is out all the other planets are invisible. So, like the Sun, you become the shining standard that others emulate. You set the tone for how a conversation should take place or how business will be transacted. Etiquette is very important to you. You believe people should be on their best behavior at all times, and you have zero tolerance for rudeness. Sophistication has always been equated with prestige; vulgarity shows lack of self-control. By refusing to lower yourself, you banish all prospects of an ugly episode. Conversations must stay light and breezy or they won't take place. This iron-hand-in-a-velvet-glove approach suits you well.

As a Child of Venus, you're always interested in improving yourself. You want to improve your mind, your looks, and most of all—your station in life. Your Solar side, however, feels a sense of entitlement. You want to rise to what you feel is your proper place, which is the highest point in the sky—or society (which is ruled by Venus). This is where you can make trouble for yourself if you're not careful. Your Birthday Planet's m.o. is all about hooking up with someone. But when it's colored by the Sun, you're always keeping an eye out for something better to come along. This can lead to a chronic dissatisfaction, where you're racing to keep up with the Joneses—despite the fact that you overtook them long ago.

Because of Venus's position at the time of your birth, you can always rely on others to lend a hand—particularly those who are better off. People take a real interest in your welfare and progress. And a simple smile from you is enough to make their day. The downside is it takes you longer than most to figure out what's really in your

WITH VENUS IN LEO

own best interests. Accustomed to making most decisions by committee, you may not emerge as a personality in your own right until your thirties or even forties. All Children of Venus resist becoming too independent. It stems from a fear that if you can do everything yourself, then you won't be in a partnership. As you mature, you'll realize that the best partnerships are the ones that grow right alongside you.

This is why friendships, especially old ones, play such an important role in your life. Not only do friends remind you of where you came from (always a humbling experience), but they also serve as your collective voice of conscience. They prompt you to question more than you would on your own, and to figure out the most politic way of negotiating an awkward situation. But more importantly, they get you to laugh at yourself when you get too self-important. When a romantic partner becomes as near and dear to you as one of your best friends, then you'll know you and this person truly belong together.

The end of summer through the fall is a wonderful season for you. The quality of light that accompanies the autumnal equinox always puts you in a romantic mood. You prefer the golden browns and ruddy oranges of harvest to the waif-like greens of spring. Late January through February (with the exception of Valentine's Day!) as well as late March through April don't really appeal to you. There isn't much of a social season to speak of, and even if you do go out, there's always a lot of sloshing around in the snow or rain. For a fashionista like you, it's an annual nightmare!

CHILD OF VENUS...

Mercury rules the zodiac sign Virgo. You Children of Venus with Venus in Virgo look for ways to improve on what you see. When Mercury, the Planet of craft, mingles with Venus, the Planet of art, then it only makes sense that you would switch from being an admirer of beauty to someone who creates it. Whether it's absent-minded doodling or concentrated needlework, the intricate construction of instruments or the playing of them, you like to keep your hands busy. It might even be said you have a hands-on approach to life. Discerning and critical, you get frustrated when you have to explain yourself. That's because a good part of your thinking takes place not in your head but in your fingers. You prefer to show by example—or better yet, because you want the job done right, you'll do the work yourself.

Venus is at her most industrious when colored by Mercury, so your mind and body need to be in constant motion. It's when you do your best thinking. Sitting only makes you fret. Unlike other Children of Venus, you happily apply yourself to arduous tasks—as long as your mind is engaged. You think nothing of putting in the extra hours to get the details right—constantly editing and refining so that what emerges is as close to perfection as possible.

Learning to keep your hands to yourself, however, is a running theme throughout your life. Despite your Birthday Planet's pursuit of peace and harmony, the Mercury side of you finds it hard to refrain from picking apart what others are doing. That's because for every action, you see a myriad of possibilities spring into view. You're curious about what would happen if you tried this or took away that. Mercury has a student's zeal to improve, so you will always learn from your mistakes.

Yet what you consider helpful and thought provoking could sometimes come across as being interfering and counterproductive. Nine out of ten people simply can't keep up with how fast your mind works. Which is why it's always a good idea to spell things out, and if you don't have the time to explain yourself, then let it go. Another potentially problematic area is romance. You have an uncanny knack for captivating the attention of other people's dates. This is all right when

WITH VENUS IN VIRGO

you're younger—when everyone's falling in and out of love haphazardly—but it could create a bad rep if it continues into adulthood.

Because of Venus's position at the time of your birth, you are no stranger to rivalries—particularly with women. This could result from a stormy relationship with a sister or your mother, who may have consciously or unconsciously compared herself to you. Yet many of your close relationships are with women. If you're a man, that sibling competition may follow you into your romantic relationships—causing you to be too exacting or deferential. If you're a woman, you may exaggerate the trustworthiness or treachery of each female friend. As you grow older, you will come to see relationships with women in light of your current circumstances rather than as an outgrowth of what came before.

You may even come to a fuller understanding of why that rivalry existed in the first place.

September and October are when you are at the height of your discriminating powers. This is the perfect time to streamline priorities and weigh the value of obligations. You're reflective without being solemn and expectant without being anxious. In true harvest fashion, you're able to separate the wheat from the chaff. This is in direct contrast to March and April, when you tend to overcommit yourself. The holiday season—particularly late November through January—is a good time for romance. This is when you're forced to socialize, and since you often combine work with pleasure, you stand a good chance of meeting someone with similar interests—as well as a schedule that won't conflict with yours.

CHILD OF VENUS...

Venus rules the zodiac sign Libra. You Children of Venus with Venus in Libra are people magnets. You take great care with your appearance and strive to put a positive spin on everything you say. But that's not the reason why you're so popular. It's your ability to disarm with a flattering comment or a perceptive inquiry that invites friend and foe alike to relax in your presence. You have a unique talent for saying exactly what's on everyone's mind, but you put it in such a way that no one could possibly take offense. Even the most taciturn types just naturally open up around you. Fair-minded but never cloying, you make everyone you meet feel as if you have their best interests at heart. And you do.

But you will also keep in mind the best interests of the other party. Born under the Planet of beauty and harmony, you have an innate sense of symmetry. What's good for the goose is good for the gander and vice versa. You preach the gospel of compromise and cooperation. And for the most part your message prevails. In classical mythology, Venus was always superior to Mars, the god of war. She let him believe he was top dog, but by the time she was through with him, he was sweetly napping like a baby while she smiled her quiet smile of triumph. Like Venus, you never vanquish, insult, or humiliate. You learned a long time ago that affability always wins out over hostility.

You're rarely on the opposite end of a dispute. More often than not, you're at the center of it. You might be the prize being fought for or you may be the one entrusted with finding a viable solution. In any case, you are a fair judge. You will insist that the victor concede something so that the losing side saves face. And you will convince the one who's lost that it's in his best interests to make some kind of conciliatory gesture to show there are no hard feelings. Yet the real secret to your success lies in the subtle way you win both sides over to *your* side—and with neither of them knowing it. By prevailing upon them to adopt your compromise, you emerge the victor of the field.

But because of Venus's position at the time of your birth, you have a blind spot when it comes to you. Your Birthday Planet rules mirrors, so your natural focus is on mirroring others. Because you aim to please, you spend a lot of time figuring out

WITH VENUS IN LIBRA

what others want and how to make them happy. This is a full-time job and doesn't leave much energy to contemplate your side of the looking glass. This is why whenever you need to do some real hard thinking, you will go off by yourself for a while. You require peace of mind to get to the heart of what you truly feel. You want to avoid ever being in a position where you have to explain yourself without giving matters proper thought beforehand. Your desire to make others happy can sometimes outweigh your better judgment, and your efforts to accommodate them could lead to you contradicting yourself and making yourself vulnerable.

Late January through February, late May through June, and late September through October are wonderful for you. These are the "airy" times of year when reason prevails; everyone is committed to focusing on the best that situations have to offer, and the squeaky wheels in your life are well greased and running smoothly. Late March through April and late August through September are not so good, because these are the times of year when you are most likely to be taken by surprise—which is never a good thing with you. When in doubt, you should always stop what you're doing and wait for a time when you can think clearly again. When you possess the ability to influence public opinion, it's crucial that you be confident of your own.

CHILD OF VENUS...

Both Mars and Pluto rule the zodiac sign Scorpio. Therefore you Children of Venus with Venus in Scorpio love deeply and powerfully—perhaps more than you really want to. The passion of Mars combined with the obsession of Pluto doesn't mix easily with your Birthday Planet. Venus is a Planet of harmony, not strife. She doesn't like it when things get too heavy, and she will go out of her way to avoid any unpleasantness. Being a Child of Venus, you want order and symmetry in your life and care very much about appearances. However when you are a Child of Venus colored by Mars and Pluto, you can't help taking a walk on the wild side.

Ambivalence shadows your attractions. That's because your need for security—particularly *emotional* security—runs counter to your desires. Your idea of who you should be with rarely matches who you end up with—at first. As a Child of Venus, you prefer to be the object of desire rather than the person who does the desiring. You're a natural hook for people who can't live without you, and you like it that way. In classical myth, Venus always dominated Mars (ruler of desire), so you have no problem keeping that side of you under wraps. Being a Child of Venus gives you the upper hand in matters of the heart, and since you naturally trust your judgment more than your partner's, you're the designated driver when it comes to love. You always keep a cool head.

But Mars isn't the only Planet you have to contend with. There's Pluto. And Pluto plays by a very different set of rules. Pluto is an intense Planet that only becomes active at certain times. But when it does, you'll know it. Pluto stirs up the undesirable aspects of our desires—the parts we know are there but don't want to have anything to do with—and fans them into a flame. What results is something you might never do in your right mind but can't help doing nonetheless. Pluto rules over those dark parts of ourselves like obsession, lust, and envy. But it also rules your soul's survival instinct. From those dark corners comes a strength you didn't know you had or a superhuman endurance to see you through a grueling passage. The Planet of Underworld journeys, Pluto compels you to descend down into the darkness for the purpose of unlocking that part of yourself

WITH VENUS IN SCORPIO

you'll need for the next stage of your growth as a person.

Because of Venus's position at the time of your birth, you pledge allegiance first—then ask questions later. This can lead to making a lot of promises that are difficult to keep. This is hardly a unique predicament— Children of Venus hate to be alone and will hook up with someone until something better comes along. What makes you different is that your Mars side will insist you keep your word. And because Pluto instills tenacity, you can force yourself to remain in a highly unsatisfactory situation. It may even be a point of pride with you. This could prove a burden in your younger years. However Pluto takes those difficulties and spins a cocoon out of them, so when it's time for you to reemerge, you will be dramatically transformed!

When you're a Child of Venus with Mars and Pluto powerful, your capacity to love will always be deeper than you know. Love, for you, isn't about finding the right person or fretting about staying attractive. Love is your life force. And as you go on in life, it grows stronger and fuller—like an eternal flame.

Late February through mid-March, late June through July, and October through November are when you're in your prime. These are the months when you feel most centered in yourself and less worried about what others think. They're also the times when others spontaneously give to you. April and May don't sit well with you. It's a season when resources fall a bit short—no matter how well you plan ahead of time. But two off months out of the year isn't so bad. And in typical Mars-Pluto fashion, you'd rather get them out of the way in one fell swoop than waste precious energy fretting.

CHILD OF VENUS . . .

Jupiter rules the zodiac sign Sagittarius. In classical mythology, Jupiter was no slouch when it came to love. He spent just as much time (if not more!) as Venus occupied in romantic pursuits. But where Venus was mostly concerned with the "arts of love" (i.e., getting two people together), Jupiter's purpose was to mix the immortal with the mortal. By modern standards, Jupiter would be considered a philanderer. Yet in ancient times, he was seen as a benevolent force because his many amours produced offspring that benefited civilization as a whole—making it more divine. Jupiter, father of the gods, quite literally brought a little bit of heaven down to earth. When you're a Child of Venus with Venus in Sagittarius, you aim to do the same.

A Jupiter Venus makes you more adventurous and speculative than the typical Child of Venus. Jupiter is the Planet of fortune, and you aim to achieve yours by hooking up with the right person. But it's not just any person you set your sights on. You have an almost evangelical belief that if you could only get in to meet that Big Name—be it a client, agent, or sponsor—then that person will recognize what you have to offer, happily combine forces, and then the two of you will go on to make your fame and fortune, enriching your lives as well as the lives of those around you. It's a very romantic dream, but there is a grain of truth in it. The reason you're such a people person is that, like Jupiter, you don't really know what you're capable of producing until you get around the right person. It's your interaction with others that brings to light your talents and gifts. By yourself, those potentials might remain unrealized. You were built for collaboration.

However this can also produce an "I was meant for better things" snobbishness if you're not careful. Venus has a roving eye, and Jupiter is always falling in love with greener pastures. You could make the mistake of taking certain people in your life for granted. Moreover the Jupiter side of you can be a little too gullible when it comes to name dropping. Although appearances matter a great deal to you (you have a weakness for status symbols), you still have an ability to laugh at yourself. You'll never get so self-important that you forget to honor the contribution others make

WITH VENUS IN SAGITTARIUS

to your prosperity and happiness. Good fortune is a two-way street with you. If someone helped you out or gave you a hand, you will always return the favor—no matter how long it takes.

Venus's position at the time of your birth makes you outgoing and open to new ideas. Being involved with others on a day-to-day basis is a must, and you would do well in a public relations setting, promotions, or as a team/events coordinator. The "sum is greater than its parts" is a truism that resonates with you. Your ability to get everyone to work together to achieve a common good is one of your great talents. You're not big on personal recognition, you just like being around beautiful, gregarious people. One of the things you'll come to realize is how much they want to be around you.

Mid-February through early March and all of December are the best times of year for you. Your creative juices are flowing, people are at their most cooperative, and work is so enjoyable that it feels more like play than something you have to do for a living. These are also auspicious times for finalizing deals. July is particularly good for making investments and purchasing property. The mood changes in late March through April, however, and you may find yourself suddenly at odds with those working for or with you. For some reason this is a stormy time of year, when people feel compelled to challenge your authority. You prefer to be sweetness and light. You're a lover, not a fighter. However you'll flex your muscles if pressed, and opponents will soon learn not to mess with you again.

CHILD OF MARS . . .

Mars rules the zodiac sign Aries. You Children of Mars with Mars in Aries are quick on the uptake and decisive. You're the person everyone turns to when they want something done. You believe the only way to make things happen is to take action, any action. Even if it's wrong, it's better to find out right away than waste precious time and energy debating pros and cons. As a result you accomplish a lot in a short period of time.

However, you're only as good as the direction you're given. For someone who exhibits obvious leadership qualities, you're more comfortable being second-in-command. The reason is twofold: you have no patience for building consensus (you'd prefer to show by doing rather than try to sell people on what you're after), and you're not so good at follow-up. People often require more coddling than you're willing to give. Sometimes you assume that what's important to you is as important to them and are baffled by their lack of attention and support. The truth is, no matter how showy your results, people still have pursuits of their own. However if it's your job to whip them into shape as a team or to spearhead an endeavor, then you'll do fine. As a Child of Mars with Mars strong, you're much better at marshaling the forces than calling the shots.

Sympathy isn't always one of your strong points. You equate it with being weak and permissive. This doesn't mean you're cruel and unfeeling. Few are as loyal and devoted as you. But because your Birthday Planet's nature is hot and dry, you can be more sensational than sensitive. Sensation responds to stimulus. Things that are *sensational* excite interest and quicken the pulse. Sensation is hot. Sympathy, on the other hand, is about feeling others' joys and pains. It requires you to lower your guard and to commiserate. You don't want to hang out holding hands and having heart-to-heart talks when you can be out and about making things happen. Sympathy cools the inner fire you rely on to keep you up and running. That's why you avoid it.

It's not until someone tries and fails under your coaching that you begin to ask if you're being too tough. Although you can sometimes be as aggressive in your self-reproach as you are in your pursuit of excellence, a little mortification

WITH MARS IN ARIES

goes a long way. As a Child of Mars with Mars strong, you always learn from your mistakes. It may take a while to recognize you made one, but once the lightbulb goes off, you will do everything in your power to rectify it and make amends.

Because of Mars's position at the time of your birth, you see yourself as caring more about life than most people you meet. Even if you don't express it, you feel like you're in the right and others just aren't as willing to do what's required to make things happen. It takes years to learn that yours isn't the only means to accomplishing an end and that occasionally you even have to lose a battle to win the war. That's why life gets easier as you grow older. If you're a Child of Mars born in October or November, you tend to let others off the hook too easily and blame yourself for not trying harder.

You may think this is noble, but sometimes it can invite them to pin their mistakes on you. Learning to tolerate your own shortcomings while leaving others to get themselves out of their own fixes will help a great deal.

Late March through mid-April, late July through August, and November through December are powerful times for you. These are the "fiery" months when you feel most emboldened by the support of those around you. Late September through October is not very good, and the same can be said for early March. You may feel like you're on slippery ground and that it's nearly impossible to make headway. Moreover people's feelings are particularly sensitive, and you may feel manipulated by them. Late December through January is perfect for launching projects and making bold strides.

CHILD OF MARS ...

Venus, Planet of love and beauty, rules the zodiac sign Taurus. Often portrayed as the companion to Mars, she's actually the flip side of the same coin. If Mars is desire then Venus is the object of that desire. She could care less about going on the warpath. Her domain is the runway where models play to the cameras. She doesn't attack, but attract. When you're a Child of Mars with Venus prominent, all of that aggressive energy is channeled into creating order out of disorder—and then keeping the peace. You don't like upsets and will work hard to ensure they don't happen. This can give you a conservative bent, wherein your focus is on maintaining the status quo. You preserve and protect your interests rather than push the envelope. But at no point is that Mars side of you put to bed. Like a napping dog, you always keep an eye out for anything that might disturb the balance you fought so hard to establish. One unexpected move or surprise knock at the door and you will defend your turf—tooth and claw.

Your Birthday Planet tends to attack things head-on. Seized by the urgency of the moment, Mars does whatever it takes to get the job done *immediately*. But Venus is built for comfort, not speed. Having strains of both can be difficult because you'll veer one way then the other. Languorous one moment, you can suddenly be up on your feet ready to go the next. Likewise if you feel like you've given your all and there's nothing left to give, you'll haughtily announce you've had enough and depart. Thankfully, Venus and Mars prefer to work in concert, and the result is that you are both industrious and scrupulous. Feisty and temperamental, peace loving and gracious—clients and colleagues often don't know what to make of you. But if anything's certain, it's that you won't settle for second best.

You work hard and play harder. You have healthy appetites and passions and love to have a good time. You also have expensive tastes. Part of the reason you work as hard as you do is because you can spend money as if maxing out credit cards was an Olympic event. Fortunately the Venus side of you is good at wheeling and dealing. She may be the force behind your conspicuous consumption (Children of Mars tend to be more

WITH MARS IN TAURUS

spartan), but she also has a sixth sense for profitable investments.

Because of Mars's position at the time of your birth, your business is other people's business. Partnerships, collaborations, and forming strategic alliances are key to your advancement and success. Indeed you have a special knack for fund-raising, and if anyone can persuade tightwads to open their wallets—it's you. Working for *mutual* interests will always be more profitable than pursuing your own. Nevertheless because you're so good at what you do—and often have something nice to show for it—jealous rivals may accuse you of being self-serving. Nothing gets your dander up more than someone implying you're a cheat. And as a Child of Mars, it's hard not to take out your best one-liner and verbally slap an opponent across the face. But resist the temptation. More often than not, it's others who benefit from you losing your temper—which is something that you Children of Mars born in October and November must keep in check. Don't let a little matter like name-calling get under your skin.

Late winter through midspring is an excellent quarter for you. Indeed your energy builds as you move toward May. This is when you feel most able-bodied and optimistic. August through October is when you're likely to be at odds with your surroundings—tempers are peaked and pledges and agreements stomped on. You feel more like an enforcer than a protector, which isn't quite as heroic as you like. November is an especially auspicious time. It's good for investments and renegotiating any long-term loans. It's also a good time to consolidate those credit cards.

CHILD OF MARS . . .

Mercury rules the zodiac sign Gemini. Therefore you Children of Mars with Mars in Gemini possess keen minds, sharp tongues, and love to play the devil's advocate. You consider complacency to be a sign of laziness, and you will take it upon yourself to mix things up. You're just as likely to poke holes in conventional wisdom as you are to champion the downtrodden. Provocative and opinionated, you believe a battle of wits is the only way to get at the truth. Nothing gets your pulse racing like a good debate. It almost doesn't matter which side wins. But consensus doesn't sit well with you. You will automatically begin looking for the faults in the logic—even if it happens to be your own point of view!

As a Child of Mars with a strong Mercury streak, you have a love of wordplay. Like in fencing, words should be wielded artfully and cleverly. One would no more take them personally than one would actually try to harm an opponent. Unfortunately when the person you're bantering with bursts into tears, you're truly at a loss for words. This may appear disingenuous to those who don't know you well, but the simple fact is: you don't know how matters got so out of hand. You were playing a game. It's not *real* life.

This is why you need to develop an ability to read your opponent that extends beyond the adversarial. Just as you have an intuitive sense of where the weaknesses are in an argument, you should also be able to detect when someone's getting hurt. Athletes—especially those in contact sports—do this all the time. We may be surprised to see opponents fraternize with one another, but this is their way of assuring themselves that what they're doing is still a game. Ironically it's not the ferocity of combat that creates a peak performance—it's the camaraderie. Free of the fear of retaliation, they can increase the level of competition, knowing that they're not antagonizing as much as they're raising the stakes. The more you can exhibit good humor and show that there are "no hard feelings," the more others will be eager to play with you—which is what you wanted all along.

Nevertheless, it's still your job to ask the tough questions. Like the practice of using fire to burn away the underbrush so new life can grow,

WITH MARS IN GEMINI

your aim is to clear out hackneyed ideas and false assumptions. These sound like the skills of a critic or social commentator, but they're also skills used by anyone who investigates, examines, or is expected to render a judgment. Giving someone the "third degree" isn't bad. It's constructive. Besides, as far as you're concerned, anyone who can't stand the heat should get out of the kitchen.

Because of Mars's position at the time of your birth, friendships often emerge from rivalries . . . or deteriorate into them. Paradoxically, it's the people you fight with on first meeting who end up becoming mainstays. This may reflect an off-again, on-again relationship you have with a sibling—perhaps an older brother. It's important to turn a potential opponent into a sparring partner whenever you can. This isn't easy, as you're drawn to chip-on-the-shoulder types. But not

every antihero is a good guy who's just been misunderstood. That's why you need to watch out for people who really are as cynical as they sound. Children of Mars born in October and November should be particularly wary of the friend/rival about-face.

Late May through June and late September through October are wonderful times for you. You enjoy interacting with people, and these are the months when you're making new acquaintances and adding to that already crowded roster of friends and associates. More importantly, you're at the height of your intellectual powers—unlike mid-March, when you're feeling moody and confused. Late January and February is a time of reckoning. You'll want to put ideas to the test and see which ones are worth pursuing. Sometimes what you come up with is as much a surprise to you as it is to everyone else.

CHILD OF MARS ...

The Moon rules the zodiac sign Cancer. Therefore you Children of Mars with Mars in Cancer are deeply sensitive and tend to consider the consequences before you act. This is due to the calming nature of the Moon. The Moon is queen of the night, and when she's out, even the blistering heat of the desert cools under her influence. Yet another reason for self-restraint is you don't want to give away the fact that you're easily hurt. The Moon makes you sympathetic. You register others' disappointment or joy in everything you do. Sometimes you resent caring so much, but it's this very Achilles' heel that makes you so complex.

The Moon rules over the watery realm of the unconscious, which houses your dreams and memories. Lunar emotions are what you feel on the inside, like when you long for something that's hard to put into words or are wistful and nostalgic. Unlike fire, water can be languid and heavy. It holds on to feelings. This can make you sulky, but it's also tremendously creative. Many painters and writers are Lunar in temperament. They draw sustenance and inspiration from the rich soil of their interior landscape. You do, too, but you're not as comfortable with it. Mars is active. It wants to be alert and awake. The Moon is responsive. It needs time to mull things over—maybe even sleep on it. You want to believe in your watery feelings, but you're also afraid of your inner fire being extinguished.

As a Child of Mars with the Moon strong, your past and family ties are very important to you. As are your attachments to things that make you feel rooted and secure. Knowing you have a certain amount of money in the bank allows you to sleep at night, or perhaps you need to be married with children before you can even think about what to do with your life. You're more akin to a lord in a castle than you are to a crusading knight. Instead of going out into the world, you want to fortify your position in it.

What you have to watch out for is taking on responsibilities before you're ready for them. The Lunar side of you wants to belong. It will look for anything stable to attach itself to—like the Moon orbiting Earth. Yet if you settle down before the Mars side of you has had a chance to strut its stuff (or prove itself) then you could be asking for trouble. Your Birthday Planet doesn't like to be short-

WITH MARS IN CANCER

changed or held back. It will fight and stir up a ruckus in order to be free.

Your Lunar and Martial natures aren't as irreconcilable as you might think. It's simply a matter of working with this unique blend of temperaments. You Children of Mars born in the spring need to develop a conscious appreciation for what your emotional side has to offer. For you Children of Mars born in the autumn, it's the Moon's fluidity that can be hard to accept. That's because stoking the furnace of your hurt feelings fuels your willpower. You're not eager to get over anything, because what will you use as an alternative energy source?

Nevertheless Mars's position at the time of your birth (regardless of season) shows you will move away from your birth family—either physically or philosophically. What may seem like an arbitrary break is actually your Mars side assert-ing itself. You need psychological distance so you can grow into your own person. You want the decisions you make to be the result of conscious choice, not force of habit.

For you Children of Mars born in the spring, March through July is your peak season. For you Children of Mars born in the fall, it's October through February. Neither of you does well in the other one's time of year. You're liable to feel enervated, as if you just can't muster up the willpower to get things done. This is especially important to keep in mind for you Lunar Mars Children who form relationships with other Children of Mars born at the opposite time of year. You can save yourself a lot of aggravation by remembering that you operate on different seasonal "clocks"—not unlike a morning person in a relationship with a night person.

CHILD OF MARS ...

The Sun rules the zodiac sign Leo. When you're a Child of Mars with Mars in Leo, then nothing short of your personal best will do. You will do everything in your power to exceed expectations. It doesn't matter if you're running for president or competing in a Bake-Off. If you can think of a way to improve your performance, you'll immediately put it into action. You don't wait to see what others think, and you're not always big on listening to advice. You have little patience for angling and maneuvering. Why settle for progressing inch by inch, when you can score a big touchdown or a home run? Indeed, given your love of excitement, the more down-to-the-wire things get, the better.

Mars and the Sun are both fiery Planets. Each feeds off the heat generated by the other. The Sun fuels Mars's boldness while Mars fans the Sun's excitement. They urge each other on constantly, not unlike buddies engaged in a friendly rivalry. Subsequently you can sustain an effort or a level of concentration for longer than most. While others throw up their hands in sheer frustration (or exhaustion), you're one of those people who can appear bright-eyed and bushy-

tailed even after pulling an all-nighter. Once you begin something you won't stop until you've seen it through to the end. The complexity of a problem refuels your interest and your drive. But you aren't built for multitasking. If a priority isn't front and center, it can suffer from neglect. You may tell yourself that once you're done with whatever happens to be absorbing your attention, you'll swoop in at the last minute and make up for all the lost time in an instant. Unfortunately a loved one, colleague, or client may have other ideas. You'll realize, as you get older, people are less likely to sit around and wait.

It's in your nature to come to the rescue when you're a Child of Mars. And with the Sun powerful, you want to make people proud and impress them with your efforts. However, because you generate your own heat, it's not always easy to figure out the role someone else is supposed to play in your life—other than that of prize to be won or victim to be saved.

If you need to be needed then a peaceful existence is not what you're after—despite your insistence otherwise. This could explain your attraction to emotionally demanding people. You

WITH MARS IN LEO

thrive on heat and excitement—the source of which is friction. What can be difficult to acknowledge is how much you need some people in your life to be *impossible*. Drama isn't generated by everyone getting along famously. It's fueled by hot tempers, incendiary words, and inflammatory actions. It may be strange to think of it this way, but you may seek out people who you know will prove to be unbearable for the purpose of keeping passions burning. It may even be a turn-on!

As a Child of Mars with the Sun strong, you're drawn to professions that show off what you do best. There's no such thing as taking a job for the paycheck. You need a ladder to climb and a prize to shoot for. Clearly you have high standards of excellence, but you're in no hurry to reach them. If anything, you keep finding ways to raise the stakes. That's because striving will always be more important than arriving. However you should remember that the Solar part of you does need to feel appreciated and recognized. There's no harm in letting yourself enjoy the spoils of an occasional victory. It also prevents burnout.

Late March through April, late July through August, and late November through December are invigorating times for you. These are the months when you feel engaged and motivated. Late September through mid-October is when you're feeling lackluster and even a bit wishy-washy. Obviously you can't be chipper all the time, but enthusiasm is an essential ingredient in your formula for success. Therefore you'll want to avoid reckless actions or disputes around the autumnal equinox. Thankfully you only have to wait until the end of October for your energy to perk up again.

CHILD OF MARS ...

Mercury rules the zodiac sign Virgo. You Children of Mars with Mars in Virgo are great at fixing things. Not only are you handy around the house (you're one of the few people who actually *understands* an instruction manual), but you're also just as adept at negotiating red tape and handling particularly thorny standoffs. You have a referee's objectivity and can remain impartial in the most embroiled circumstances. You take great pride in your supreme self-control. But this mastery doesn't come easily. It comes from years of slipups and near misses. Thanks to the unique combination of Mercury (wits) and Mars (fortitude), you always learn from your mistakes.

When you're a Child of Mars with Mercury strong, you have to get used to living with different endeavors in various stages of development. This isn't simple, as your Mars nature wants to finish what it has started. Yet Mercury doesn't share your Birthday Planet's single-mindedness. It likes to channel surf from one interesting topic to another. Some might criticize this as a lack of direction, but in reality your mind craves tremendous stimulus. What could be livelier than several things transpiring at once? Not only does this make your mental reflexes lightning fast, but it also improves your physical ones, too.

Mercury questions. Mars seeks new quests. Together these two Planets give an inexhaustible drive for self-improvement. You are attracted to intellectual and/or physical disciplines that demand extraordinary levels of concentration. You want to hone your skills so that they are as sharp as can be. Left alone, Mercury and Mars energies would run roughshod over your life. The restlessness of Mercury would make you flighty, while the irritability of Mars would make you contentious. Yet harnessed, you can repeat a routine any number of times and still find something fresh and new. This is the sort of commitment that athletes and dancers, as well as writers, musicians, and researchers, make every day of their professional lives. When you're a Child of Mars with Mercury powerful, you practice to perfect.

In mythology, Mercury, messenger of the gods, was also known as "the companion of man." He was the one you appealed to when you needed

WITH MARS IN VIRGO

help finding your way. In this same vein, you make yourself available to the people around you. You don't think twice about lending a helping hand. And given your ability to remain cool under pressure, you're no stranger to guiding loved ones, friends, or even clients through dire straits. Too often associated with combat, your Birthday Planet also rules those bonds that are forged between people who have faced an ordeal together. Ask any soldier or police officer. Nothing quite compares to the loyalty they feel for a comrade-in-arms.

Although your Ruling Planet's inclination is to be a lone wolf, Mars's position at the time of your birth indicates you like to run in packs. This is less about socializing and more about joining forces to achieve a common goal. Your most intense relationships involve people you work with, yet paradoxically, you may know very little about their private lives. This isn't bad, but it does reveal a certain blind spot. You can wind up living for work if you're not careful. That's why it's so important that you develop a life for yourself outside of work. However, given the time and energy you pour into your vocation, it only makes sense that you would become personally involved with someone who works side by side with you—or at least hails from a similar field of interest.

Late December through January and late August through September are your optimal times of year. These are the months when you harvest the fruit of your labors. Not only does this bestow a clear sense of accomplishment, but it also gives you some idea of what remains to be done. You need to assess achievements on a semiregular basis. If not, you can wind up feeling like a hamster on an exercise wheel—running hard but getting nowhere fast. For you Children of Mars born in the spring, you will experience your lowest ebb in October, whereas you Children of Mars born in the fall will feel it in May. Pace yourself accordingly and try to avoid initiating anything during these times. Though always one to rise to a challenge, there is something to be said for timing your actions so that they work to your maximum benefit.

CHILD OF MARS ...

Venus, Planet of relationships, rules the zodiac sign Libra. Therefore cooperation is the key to your success. Everything you do is a collaboration. Admittedly, this is a tall order for you Children of Mars. Usually it's "my way or no way." Nevertheless, you will embrace the Venusian ideal of teamwork with gusto. Because you are motivational and upbeat, people are drawn to your heroic vision. You get them to go beyond what they're capable of by challenging them to challenge themselves. Your relentless pursuit of high standards creates an aura of exclusivity. And it's your reputation for demanding only the best that induces others to join your ranks.

A Venus Mars makes you decisive as well as calculated in your approach. You carefully weigh all options before acting—adding or subtracting until you achieve the perfect balance. This makes you a canny judge of character. You can size up someone's capabilities quickly and accurately predict who is reliable versus who spells trouble. If you have to part with something or compromise on a certain issue to get what you want, you'll do it—regardless of sentiment. To you the sum is always greater than its parts. Venus rules aesthetics. She is drawn to the beauty of theories. This is bolstered by your Martial urge to get on with the business at hand. You will always choose order over chaos and black and white answers to fuzzy gray.

You're a very good listener, but if someone is trying to discuss *your* behavior, the criticisms (no matter how constructive) may fall on deaf ears. Because you have a preconceived idea of the way things should be, you hear only what you want to hear. This is where your own self-confidence can mislead you if you're not careful. You project such certainty that you attract a lot of yes-men. However with your Birthday Planet, everything is still open to debate. You rely on close friends and loved ones to tell you the things about yourself others won't. You will question and argue, coax and cajole. If there's anything you respect it is the strength of someone's convictions. The Venusian side of you may be drawn to symmetry and order, but you are still a Child of Mars. While it isn't easy for you to hear criticism, the force of argument will always impress you.

Because of Mars's position at the time of

WITH MARS IN LIBRA

birth, you will often find yourself struggling to impose order on a chaotic situation. When you were young, you may have felt buffeted about by circumstances beyond your control, but as you grew older you learned to harness strong and disparate personalities and then get them to pull together as a team. This is a terrific Planetary position for a teacher, coach, director, or producer. Though conscientious, you aren't too self-reflective. The reason for that is Venus. With Venus, everything needs to be done through another person—including self-discovery. You need a partner to bounce ideas off of or to fight and argue with. For someone who gets people to see themselves in a more positive light, it's poetic that the only way to realize your own potential is through your dealings with people. More often than not, this is done through some kind of friction. The idol of many, you may have a hard time hooking up with that person who truly understands you.

For you Children of Mars born in the fall, late February through March and late June through July are dynamic times for you. This is when your sensitivity and drive work best together. You have a sixth sense for which toes to avoid stepping on as you boldly go about accomplishing what you want. Your difficult period is April and May. Both your judgment and timing are off, so postpone big decisions if you can. For you Children of Mars born in the spring, December through mid-February is the season when you're at the height of your powers. You'll have no problem gaining people's interest and enlisting their support. Things begun during this time go on to yield terrific results. Your difficult period is the fall. False starts and hidden agendas will plague you, so postpone endeavors until late November. Regardless of whether you're a fall or spring Child of Mars, February is the perfect month for a budding romance.

CHILD OF MARS ...

Both Mars and Pluto rule the zodiac sign Scorpio. As a Child of Mars, if you see something you want, you jump up and run after it. No ifs, ands, or buts. You'll give an endeavor your best shot, and if it doesn't work out, you tell yourself you'll try harder next time. However when Pluto mixes with your Birthday Planet's energy, there's no such thing as "next time." Aims and objectives take on a life-or-death urgency. This gives you an edge, because you're completely invested in doing what it takes to realize your goals.

Named after the god of the Underworld, Pluto rules over everything that takes place under the surface of our lives. This can be anything from a fault line running beneath your house to a genetic predisposition toward high blood pressure or a seductive game of footsie. Pluto is the Planet of secrets. When you are a Child of Mars with Pluto strong, you are keenly aware of what's *not* immediately apparent. There's no such thing as "out of sight, out of mind" with you. Indeed, you see yourself as standing guard against all the things that could happen if the people in your life aren't careful. For the most part you're content to leave loved ones, friends, and clients to their peaceful grazing. But when it comes time to sound the alarm, you won't hesitate to cut through all the niceties and do what needs to be done. This is why it often falls on you to break the bad news or to ask the tough questions. You keep a cool head when everyone around you is losing theirs. You also know how to rouse that hidden trait each of us carries around inside. You have a talent for jump-starting the soul's survival mechanism.

People treat you seriously and with respect. They recognize your authority on a gut level. Yet without meaning to, you can also be intimidating and arouse suspicion. You are no stranger to controversy and have probably found yourself in a number of situations where others project their anxieties and fears onto you. This has a certain dark appeal, but it's best to move past it. There's a difference between being notorious and being celebrated.

Because of Mars's position at the time of your birth, you will be drawn to professions that have to do with getting to the bottom of things. A Pluto

WITH MARS IN SCORPIO

Mars is excellent for scientific or detective work. You have the capacity to peer into the heart of darkness without wincing. Your love of deciphering secrets makes you a great researcher. Your perseverance in the face of despair makes you a compassionate counselor or doctor. What makes people trust your analysis is that you tell it like it is. You also exude the feeling of having been down a similar road before—and survived to tell about it.

When you're a Child of Mars with Pluto powerful, then your mother plays a strong role in your life. Much of your fortitude and resourcefulness comes from her as well as your possessiveness and refusal to adapt. Colorful figures are always controversial, and as you go through alternating periods of admiration and resentment, you will eventually arrive at a healthy respect for the differences between you as well as a profound appreciation for the seeds she planted in your life—seeds that you, in turn, will go on to sow in someone else's.

Late October through March is a marvelous time for you. There's something about the leaves turning and the late afternoon smell of neighbors' fireplaces that makes you happy and content. Even if you live in a part of the world that doesn't show much change in seasons, you will still respond as if it does. Being a Child of Mars with Pluto strong, you like dark, hot places. You think nothing of closing the windows tight, piling on the blankets, and burying your head beneath a mound of pillows. Late April through May isn't a very good time. Although you enjoy the spring, there's something about the character of the season that's too capricious for you. As you get older, July becomes a pleasurable month—although sunscreen should never be far from reach.

CHILD OF MARS ...

Jupiter, Planet of long journeys and higher education, rules the zodiac sign Sagittarius. You Children of Mars with Jupiter powerful often leave home at an early age. But you don't just set off on your own for parts unknown. You do so under the auspices of a higher institution. Indeed if it weren't for this kind of "divine" intervention, you would stay put. Perhaps it's a scholarship that allows you to study abroad or you earn your college education while stationed on foreign shores serving your country. Jupiter symbolizes the world and the worldliness that comes with experience. Not only does Jupiter give you a higher purpose in life, but it also helps you grow as a person along the way.

These adventures you embark on improve your material fortunes as well as your status in society. Since ancient times, those who went to sea, fought in wars, set off as missionaries, or regularly braved the trade routes, returned home dramatically changed—if they came back at all. At a time when people didn't travel very far from their own town, these were the only opportunities available to reinvent oneself. The world may have become a smaller place since then, but the lure of greener grass on the other side of the fence is still there. When Jupiter colors your Birthday Planet, you have a speculator's fearless optimism. Subsequently your fortunes dip and rise with every new bend in the road. As far as you're concerned, this is all part of the adventure.

Your boldness and enthusiasm make you a formidable presence. Once you jump up on your soapbox, critics might as well surrender the field. If anyone can rally the disenfranchised and convert the jaded, it's you. You don't believe that anyone is born better than anyone else. What makes us noble are our acts, not our rank. You are committed to helping people help themselves. Because you came from humble beginnings (or believe it would have been better if you had), you will give special attention to those who have had the deck stacked against them since day one.

The downside is in how quickly a situation deteriorates when you're not around. Your vision, which gave others such hope, vanishes, and you can even wind up being blamed for inspiring them in the first place. This is a lesson that is constantly being learned (and relearned) by anyone

WITH MARS IN SAGITTARIUS

who advocates, coaches, or teaches. You may be tempted to chuck the burden of moral responsibility. You enjoy the devotion but can get impatient with the hand-holding that comes along with it. Yet these experiences lead you to eventually develop patience and compassion—not typical Mars and Jupiter traits. By learning to punctuate those motivational speeches with practical tips and investing the time necessary to cultivate self-sufficiency, you will encourage and enable those eager to follow your positive example.

Because of Mars's position at the time of your birth, money isn't hard to come by. You have an uncanny knack for picking the winning horse. However speculators make poor investors. Your intuition lacks a calculated indifference and you're often swayed by hopes and sympathies. Since you can't separate your sentiments from your talent, it's useless trying to reform them. You'll always make back what you lose, and as long as you stay in the game, you won't be side-lined for long. But be sure to salt away a portion of your gains—you'll never regret it.

Late March through mid-April, late July through August, and November through December are prime. This is when you feel most confident and energized. If you can, make a point of scheduling impossible tasks for these times. You're most likely to succeed. Avoid risky undertakings in May and October—particularly around the ides, which is the fifteenth of those months. Not only is your judgment off, but jealous rivals also have the upper hand. It's important to remember that you can generate controversy without meaning to—especially when you're in the service of doing what's right rather than appeasing the status quo. Thankfully your natural bonhomie keeps people from feeling burned for too long. The adage "if you can't beat 'em, join 'em" was probably meant to describe someone like you.

CHILD OF MARS . . .

Saturn, Planet of commitment and endurance, rules the zodiac sign Capricorn. Mars is exalted when colored by Saturn, so *surrender* isn't a word uttered in your presence. Your determination is ironclad. Yet unlike other Children of Mars, you look before you leap. You invest a lot of time and energy scoping out parameters and will run through all the worst-case scenarios before signing on to anything. Your calculations are rarely off, but because they tend to be so down to the wire, they are not for the faint of heart. Many people who support you at the outset of a venture wind up feeling anxious and panicky near the end. When you're a Child of Mars with Saturn strong, the only goal worth aiming for is one that nobody in his or her right mind would go near.

Yet you aren't fearless. Clients and colleagues might be surprised to discover you're full of doubts and worries. Loved ones and close friends know this side of you all too well. They're used to playing sounding board while you review an action over and over again. The conflict between your Birthday Planet's need to act and Saturn's insistence that you be absolutely certain (not unlike driving with one foot on the accelerator and the other on the brake) creates the friction that's so essential to realizing the great things you want to do. It just doesn't make for a smooth ride.

Although you don't like having a boss, you do your best work when there's a bane to your existence. Lack of recognition, fear of rejection, and the burning need to "show 'em all" pushes you to go further than you would on your own. Mars is lost without an opponent. Saturn can't think straight outside of strict limitations. You need someone to give you a hard time until you develop the necessary self-motivation and discipline.

Because of Mars's position at the time of your birth, you often want to do a better job than those around you. This can create some sticky predicaments if you aren't careful. Volunteering to take on Herculean tasks that haven't been assigned to you could result in associates dumping their work on you—while taking all the credit for it. You don't want to generate a lot of thankless work for yourself. You also don't want to create enmity in the workplace by acting too aggressively. You have to find a way to shine without being obvious.

WITH MARS IN CAPRICORN

This is where Saturn's innate respect for propriety can help. There is a time and *pace* for everything. Saturn's motto is "slow and steady wins the race." By preventing you from moving up the ranks too fast, Saturn forces you to make the most of your opportunities on an *as per needed* basis. It may take you a little longer to reach that position of authority, but when you do you'll have earned everyone's respect and loyalty along the way.

When you're a Child of Mars with Saturn powerful, then your father plays a significant role. Like any other figure of authority in your life, he is someone you admire but also resent. You want to love him unconditionally, however you can't help feeling like you're competing with his other interests. Not all fathers do their best parenting in childhood. Yours may be one who has more to give as you grow into an adult. In any case, you're bound to recognize some of his shortcomings in yourself, and given time (and humor) you'll leave past slights behind.

If you're a Child of Mars born in the spring, then mid-April through June, mid-August through September, and mid-January through February are wonderful times for you. For you Children of Mars born in autumn, mid-February through March, mid-June through July, as well as your own birthday month will be the most propitious and enlivening. Regardless of whether you're spring or autumn, mid-December through January is when you're at your peak. Just about everything you apply yourself to turns out well. It's also the perfect time for getting your life back on course if you feel like you've lost your way, because your willpower is indomitable.

CHILD OF MARS . . .

Both Saturn and Uranus rule the zodiac sign Aquarius. Saturn symbolizes laws. Since you Children of Mars already trust that there's a right way to do things, it's only natural for you to follow Saturn's lead and embrace an orderly existence. You believe in discipline, regimen, and uniformity. It isn't hard to curb your appetites and desires. You're proud of your self-control and look upon it as a test of will. Uranus (which means "heavenly") symbolizes those eternal truths that are the basis for the laws we live by. However an ideal game plan doesn't always translate easily into reality. Nevertheless you will pursue this with gusto. Much of your life's journey will be concerned with holding yourself up to impossibly high standards while making the most of what you have to work with.

But this isn't a journey you make on your own. You are drawn to like-minded individuals and have an uncanny knack for finding them in the strangest places. It's easy for you to make friends, and you enjoy fraternizing with people from all walks of life. You couldn't care less about someone's background or credentials. What's most important are the interests you and this person have in common. This is how the "universalness" of Uranus's ideals transcends the boundaries imposed by culture, society, or even physical circumstances.

But universal laws don't just serve you or the group of individuals you happen to be aligned with. They are meant to serve everybody. Your Birthday Planet is its most chivalric when colored by Saturn and Uranus. You truly believe that helping others helps you and that the success of a company or community depends on everyone pitching in.

With much of your energy focused on accomplishing a goal (Mars), doing it by the book (Saturn), and in a way that serves the overall good (Uranus), it's easy to overlook those people who don't immediately fit into your scheme of things. The conundrum of politics is how to build a consensus while leaving as few people as possible out in the cold. And given that some are bound to be disappointed, how will you make it up to them afterward? There is nothing consistent or predictable about a group. Dynamics shift according to who enters and leaves. But this

WITH MARS IN AQUARIUS

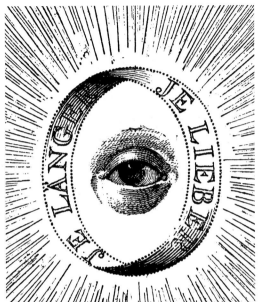

is actually a wonderful life lesson for you. Your Ruling Planet isn't naturally accommodating. In moments of uncertainty you will fall back on the Mars maxim "might makes right." Subsequently learning to deal with others' constantly changing needs and priorities makes you more flexible. The result is a unique blend of decisiveness and sensitivity.

Because of Mars's position at the time of your birth, friends—as well as the families of friends—play a very important role in your life. They may even overshadow your own blood ties. This could stem from having been raised in two households or being sent to live with a parent's relatives while they were busy elsewhere. This rootlessness may be the basis for your cosmopolitan interests, however it also impacts your personal life. You don't like it when people get too close. Traveling in connection with work or maintaining a long-distance relationship isn't strange for you. But with the right partner it makes your time together all the more intimate and precious.

If you're a Child of Mars born in the spring, then mid-January through February, mid-May through June, and mid-September through October are when you feel vigorous and inspired. People are most likely to follow your lead, so this is a good time to set the agenda for what needs to be done. For Children of Mars born in the autumn, your fortunes are more integrally linked to those you ally yourself with. How you fare depends on how well they're doing. Mid-April through May and mid-August through September may not be idyllic for you, but it will be marvelous for them—which, in turn, is good for you. Thankfully April and late July through early August are all yours. Regardless of whether you were born in the spring or autumn, mid-December through January is a fortuitous time of year.

CHILD OF MARS ...

Both Jupiter and Neptune rule the zodiac sign Pisces. You Children of Mars with Mars in Pisces possess all the magnanimity of Jupiter mixed with the selflessness of Neptune. You have big hearts and souls and stand by people who can't stand up for themselves. You recognize potential when you see it and go to great lengths to sponsor and protect those whom you feel will one day go the distance. You make a point of rescuing those seeds that have fallen on barren ground and then transplanting them to fertile soil.

Your mind is full of images, plans, and fresh variations on old themes. You have a unique ability to inspire. Once you get talking about your latest *big* idea, people become enraptured by your vision of how things could be. You have a way of making the phantasmal appear as if it's in easy reach. Unfortunately many aspirations have a hard time making the transition from what's envisioned by your mind's eye to a tangible result. Your ingrained resistance to tackling mundane matters (you hate filling out forms, standing in lines, making phone calls, etc.) often results in you abandoning the field, leaving many of your brilliant creations half-finished.

Your own Birthday Planet bears some responsibility. Patience isn't exactly a strong suit. However the real reason for the long string of incompletes may lie with the "otherworldliness" of Neptune. Neptune, named after the god of the sea, is the Planet of imagination. But its most perfect expression is visualization. Which begs the question: if what you can imagine is purer and superior to anything you could possibly construct, then why ruin it? The realm of the imagination, like the sea, is different from the world we live in. It's mysterious and invisible. It also has a very powerful undercurrent. You go to it. It doesn't have to go to you.

Fuzzy-headedness, meandering thoughts, and sudden loss of vitality are how Neptune protects his watery domain. As a Child of Mars, you may feel as if your actions are often watered down and that you must do constant battle with your own feelings of futility. Thankfully, Neptune isn't the only Planetary influence. Jupiter has a fondness for *this* world, and it's his energy that prevents you from feeling lost at sea. Named after the god of fellowship, Jupiter brings you into contact

WITH MARS IN PISCES

with a supportive group or community. Without a context, you meander— but given a place in society where you're surrounded by people who both require things of you *and* have something to contribute, you'll find your niche and flourish. It's this experience of working with others that leads you to eventually realizing your own potential. What seemed convoluted when you were younger becomes clearer as you mature. Don't be surprised if you begin cultivating hidden talents later in life.

Most people experience obstacles spread out over time. Yours tend to dog you early on and for what feels like an unduly long period. This is due to Mars's position at the time of your birth. Thankfully life gets easier once you're into your mid- to late twenties. Though being a true Child of Mars toughens rather than breaks you, you can still have extremely powerful reactions to every downward spiral as you get older. Instead of fighting the current of events, calmly tread water until you can make your way back to solid ground.

Late February through mid-March, late June through August, and late November through December are optimum times of year for you. Being an extremely sensitive person, it's important that you feel in sync with your surroundings. If your environment is thriving, then you're thriving. You Children of Mars born in the spring will feel most out of sorts in September, whereas you Children of Mars born in the fall will experience April as a low ebb. Given that Jupiter rules the ides, you'll want to be particularly careful around the thirteenth of those months. Remember that no matter how gloomy things may look, a conversation with a loved one or a visit with a neighbor is all it takes to buoy your spirits. You have the good fortune to be surrounded by people who love and admire you.

CHILD OF JUPITER...

Mars rules the zodiac sign Aries. Therefore you Children of Jupiter with Jupiter in Aries are fierce individualists. You believe everyone has the right to choose their own path and, with proper support and encouragement, will go on to become the best they can be. You don't like people being pigeonholed, however they must be given guidelines. Your own success is the result of self-determination. You are your own best example that anyone can make it if they try. Individuality is one of humanity's most precious gifts. Like the element of chance, it's what keeps our expectations from drifting into the formulaic. But that individual spark requires constant attention and should never be allowed to go out.

You're not too interested in changing the world. You'd rather go off and start something new on your own than try to fix a system that doesn't work. Moreover you prefer small groups where you can interact one-on-one. As a Child of Jupiter with Mars strong, you are drawn to like-minded types who are already up to your level—or, hopefully, higher. Mars is the Planet of contests. It seeks to hone its skills through constant trial. You prefer to focus your energies on achieving a high standard of excellence than to waste them on wishy-washy types who will just bring everyone else down. You have nothing against them per se. It's just that there are people who get it and people who don't. The only thing you ask of the people who don't get it is that they step out of the way so that the people who do get it can make something of themselves.

Now if you happen to be an athletics coach or work with kids who have special needs, then this sort of outlook will be understood and even encouraged. But it can provoke trouble in other areas if you're not careful. Get too exclusive and people become uneasy. Thanks to your Birthday Planet, however, you possess a wonderful affability and love to talk about what you do. Bearing in mind that a closed door is always more fascinating than an open one, you have no problem opening up your books, giving an impromptu lecture, or inviting outsiders to a weekend workshop. A little time and attention is all it takes to put them at ease.

At some point you will break with convention—and may have to pay for it. Jupiter often

WITH JUPITER IN ARIES

outgrows situations in life, and Mars isn't known for playing it safe. Nothing bores you more than money for money's sake. It doesn't matter how ennobling a job or a responsibility might be— if you're not into it, then the money tree is bare. Interestingly enough it's not until you're forced to stand up for what you believe in that money starts flowing your way.

Because of Jupiter's position at the time of your birth, it may take a while to find your true vocation. This is due in part to the up-and-down nature of your finances early in life—which may have interfered with (yet stimulated) your growth as an individual. It's also because you're so groundbreaking. The difficulty with being innova-tive is that you rarely get things right at the outset. You have to experiment. If you keep in mind that every tangent serves a pur-pose, you'll never waver.

Late March through April, late July through August, and late Novem-ber through December are enlivening periods for you. Your faith is strong and your spirit bright. You're apt to feel out of sorts and like you just can't rally the forces in late May and June. Everyone needs a little downtime—especially someone as generous as you. This is the perfect time for a vacation or a retreat. For Children of Jupiter born in the late winter, July is a particularly auspicious month. For you Children of Jupiter born in the late fall, January is when fortunes look brightest.

CHILD OF JUPITER...

Venus, Planet of love and harmony, rules the zodiac sign Taurus. Jupiter is the Planet of government, so it's only fitting that you'd be cast in the role of peacekeeper. This isn't something you go looking for. You're not the bossy type. Oftentimes it's the disputing parties who seek your help in settling a quarrel amicably. People find it hard to argue with your laid-back, down-to-earth approach. You make everything sound so humorous and reasonable. That's because as a Child of Jupiter with Venus strong, you're like a divining rod when it comes to finding ways for everyone to get along. You know that when push comes to shove most people don't want to be inconvenienced. It's easier to make up than break up.

Venus rules both material and aesthetic values. She gives you your love for the finer things in life and belief that it's better to be a sophisticate than a brute. Even if your idea of a good time is hanging out at tailgate parties, there's something about the clothes you wear or the car you drive that's a cut above the rest. Jupiter rules your moral and philosophical values. He gives you your sense of fair play and the underlying conviction that doing good works is not only right, but also a calling to each and every one of us to make the world a better place. Venus's values do not contradict Jupiter's. Indeed they're wonderfully complementary. What emerges from this mix of Planets is an outlook based on plenty. As far as you're concerned, there's more than enough of what people want to go around. And the sooner they get their fair share of the pie, the better.

But you don't believe in handouts. You champion the old-fashioned work ethic. Give a man a fish and he'll eat for a day. But *teach* him how to fish—and he'll eat forever. You have a lot of faith in business. To you, money isn't the root of all evil. Greed is. You want well-to-do types to understand that there's a material, as well as spiritual, value in helping people to help themselves. Nobody buys when they're poor. They scrimp. Create an atmosphere of equal opportunity and you're in business.

Yet not everyone will conform to your ready-made plan for success. And given your Venusian tendency to pooh-pooh critics, as well as your Ruling Planet's high-handedness when contra-

WITH JUPITER IN TAURUS

dicted, you may not real-
ize what a drawback this
can be. It's important to
remember that you don't
like to be inconvenienced
either. And perhaps in
your effort to make all the
pieces fit, you may be
unwittingly forcing a
square peg into a round
hole. Just because you
mean well doesn't always
mean you listen. It's the
inevitable shortcoming of
anyone who has a life phi-

losophy. It's inconceivable to you how someone
can have a problem with a belief system that
works for everyone else. This is why developing
tolerance for—and perhaps even learning from—
the exceptions to the rule can be so rewarding.
You may even find it's the nuisance, not the disci-
ple, who has the most to offer in return.

Jupiter's position at the time of your birth
shows you were probably raised in comfortable
but modest circumstances. Security, order, and
making the most of your resources are very important to you. "Waste not, want not" is a childhood

value you still subscribe to.
This won't be easy to teach
someone—like a child
or new employee—who's
always known you as a success. It doesn't mesh with
the picture of prosperity
you present. You may have
to impose artificial limits
just to get your point
across. Though denying a
loved one anything goes
against your Jupiterian
nature, it may be exactly
what's needed to teach the
more valuable lesson of self-sufficiency.

For Children of Jupiter born in late winter,
the months May, July, and January are wonderful
times for you. If you want endeavors to work out
favorably, then schedule them as close to the fifteenth of May and July as you can. Those days
belong to your Birthday Planet, so prospects are
strongest. For Children of Jupiter born in late
autumn, May and January are also good, but September and October are especially favorable.
Indeed October 15 is the perfect time to pursue a
courtship or clinch a deal.

CHILD OF JUPITER...

Mercury, Planet of thought and communication, rules the zodiac sign Gemini. Thanks to this Planetary influence, you will never grow bored with life or assume you've learned everything there is to know. The world will always amaze and intrigue you. Others grow more set in their ideas as they get older, but the more you learn, the more you realize how much you've missed, which in turn sends you back to the library, the classroom, or off to some exotic locale. As soon as you latch onto an exciting sentence or phrase, you'll want to put it to use. This may explain, in part, the holes in your own education. You don't sit still long enough to read something all the way through. Hence your tendency to mispronounce words or use them interchangeably. Nevertheless a Mercury Jupiter is still the sign of a highly original and inventive thinker.

You'd rather kick around an idea than prove it. Which is why you're not as personally invested in your beliefs as other Children of Jupiter. You want to see how your idea will play. Is it something that just sounded good in the moment or does it have real merit? This is why you're drawn to collaboration and group feedback. Running a thought or proposal by others fleshes out its color and adds dimension. A disagreement or critique may identify that missing secret ingredient.

Besides, you need an audience. A natural clown, you enjoy getting a rise out of everybody. You love people. It doesn't always come across when you're making fun of them, but people are your source of inspiration, humor, and wisdom. Thankfully your ego doesn't bruise easily, and you can take gibes as well as dish them out. You're often the first to laugh at yourself. But just because you're irreverent doesn't make you a goofball. When it's time to focus on the matter at hand, you get down to business instantly. The grace and speed with which you weave a jumble of thoughts and words into a cohesive plan is one of your great hidden talents. Like any good clown, you like to keep them guessing.

As a Child of Jupiter with Mercury prominent, you follow your interests rather than your needs. This isn't to say you're not deeply feeling. You are. Indeed you have more feeling than you know what to do with. You just don't like all the

WITH JUPITER IN GEMINI

clinging and cloying that accompanies relationships that are supposed to be serious and deep. Therefore you can give the impression of *not* wanting to be tied down, when actually the opposite is true. What you want is a mate—in the "buddy" sense, not a ball and chain. There's a difference between someone sitting around waiting for you to come home at the end of the day and someone who's just as busy and active as yourself—someone with whom you can compare notes and share laughs, along with the occasional tears.

Because of Jupiter's position at the time of your birth, the first half of your life will be dramatically different from the latter—especially for those of you born in late fall. It takes a while to discover your true calling, but once you do, your circumstances will immediately change to accommodate it. But because everything you do contributes to this—including ill-advised investments, misadventures, and questionable liaisons—there isn't really anything you can do to avoid the pitfalls. Just chalk them all up to experience because yours is the sort of life that works itself out as you go along.

For Children of Jupiter born in late autumn, mid-January through February and mid-September through October are pivotal for you. Your interests are tied up with the interests of others, so these are the times when you'll find the necessary backing and support for what you want to do. You're better off laying low from mid-May through June. For Children of Jupiter born in late winter, your endeavors are most likely to succeed when launched around your birthday or in early May or December. The Sun is too hot in late August and September for you to expect to accomplish much. Given your Neptunian side, you fare much better at cooler times.

CHILD OF JUPITER...

The Moon, Planet of emotions and memory, rules the Zodiac sign Cancer. No matter how many ups and downs you experience, you will always remain the same sympathetic, good-natured person. It takes a lot for you to get bent out of shape. That's because the Moon's nature is to accommodate, while Jupiter's is to incorporate. This combination makes you adaptable and resilient. You always bounce back. Though your appearance and circumstances will often change dramatically, you never lose touch with who you are.

Being a Child of Jupiter with the Moon strong is wonderfully creative, because you have a rich and varied inner life to go along with that wild thirst for adventure. But you don't head off to the far corners of the world just to take in the sights. You want to immerse yourself totally in the experience. You practically *drink in* your surroundings—filling up on all the sensations, details, and local color. You approach any endeavor you're excited about with the same enthusiasm and devotion. Buying every book written on a topic or loading up on more supplies than necessary is your way of getting absorbed in what you do. But

you're hardly fastidious. Even something as simple as repapering the kitchen shelves will somehow result in your being covered in paper and glue. Making a mess is your way of bonding with what you do. Nevertheless you always find a way to tie it all together successfully in the end.

Although the Moon and Jupiter have much in common—both are generous, hospitable, and mindful of community responsibilities—there is a basic difference. The Moon is introverted, while your Birthday Planet is extroverted. Most people never see this private side, given your ease with strangers and willingness to open your home at a moment's notice. It's hard for them to imagine someone as candid and effusive as you withholding anything. Which is exactly what you want them to think. You go to great lengths to keep your public and personal lives separate. Part of this stems from wanting to put your best foot forward (many people depend on you to be positive and upbeat—and you won't let them down), and part of it comes from you having to guard your downtime. It's a rare moment when you get to relax and just be you. Introspective and inventive, you can while away the hours

WITH JUPITER IN CANCER

with favorite hobbies and pursuits.

Because of Jupiter's position at the time of your birth, you will experience two major changes in direction during your life. The first will be in your mid to late thirties, and the second will be in your mid to late fifties. These are the ages when you reevaluate who you are and what you're really about. Sometimes your Lunar side is too willing to make concessions in order to get along, and when too many are made in the name of "convenience," then the Jupiter side of you can start to get antsy—and may even kick over the traces to go looking for its life purpose. Conversely, if you've spent too much time wandering from place to place (or relationship to relationship), then these are the ages when you will feel compelled to honor your Lunar urge to settle down and nest build. Despite your Ruling Planet's gypsy leanings, you weren't meant to live life out of a suitcase.

Late February through March, late June through July, and late October through November are fertile periods for you. These are times when just about any seed planted will immediately sprout and take root. Since you're drawn to gathering and collecting (either as a vocation or hobby), these are perfect times for finding an elusive quarry, getting an insider's price, or convincing a client to entrust you with the sale or upkeep of a valuable piece of property. Late December through most of January is a dormant period for you. Since you like to play as hard as you work, this gives you plenty of time to recover from holiday revels.

CHILD OF JUPITER...

The Sun, source of heat and light, rules the zodiac sign Leo. When you're a Child of Jupiter with Jupiter in Leo, Solar energy kindles your Birthday Planet's sense of higher purpose, so that you become the shaping force in your own life. It's not up to fate or circumstances to determine what you make of yourself. It's up to you. You feel a moral responsibility to realize your potential—whether it's a talent, resources, or a simple opportunity. But you're not doing this just for yourself. You're doing it because you know deep down inside that you play a pivotal role in people's lives.

More often than not, this is a humbling rather than an aggrandizing experience. Few people are born with the innate conviction that they are *meant* to make a difference. Your fulfillment lies in playing the role you were meant to play all along. It doesn't matter if it's leading man or bit player, because if you don't play it, then you—along with a lot of other people—will be sorely disappointed. It's not unlike the realization that the character George Bailey comes to in Frank Capra's classic film *It's a Wonderful Life*. George may not have thought too much of his accomplishments, but for the people whose lives he touched, he was irreplaceable. It's not until George is treated to a view of the world without him in it that he learns to appreciate the enormous difference he makes.

Because you are the active ingredient in your own formula for success, it isn't easy to step back and look at yourself objectively. Like a performer who feels a responsibility to her audience or a star athlete who knows that all eyes are on him, you're under a lot of pressure to deliver. You regard almost everything you do as being in service to others. This can lead you to vacillate between feeling self-important and feeling taken for granted. Loved ones and friends are reluctant to offer a helping hand, because you give the impression that this is definitely *your* show. That's why it's up to you *not* to lose yourself in the role. Identifying with a higher purpose isn't the same as saying "the world revolves around me." Clarifying that distinction for yourself and keeping it uppermost in mind will allow you to leave work at the end of the day and go home to enjoy some peace and quiet.

WITH JUPITER IN LEO

You possess the rare gift of leadership. But it isn't bossy or flashy. Yours is more akin to that of a governor or a minister. Jupiter's position at the time of your birth shows you will naturally gravitate to positions of authority—but you won't be allowed to act as you see fit. Every decision you make must be submitted to others for approval. You can't do anything without their support. However you must also have the wherewithal to uplift and inspire, to encourage when colleagues, employees, and even clients are confused or doubtful. When they disagree, you will have to win them over. When they're eager to do something you don't think is right, you will have to pull rank. When you are in the wrong, you will have to possess the good sense (and humor) to concede. Although the Solar part of you wants to be outstanding (it's the Sun's nature to outshine everything else in the sky), it's ultimately your Ruling Planet that interweaves your interests with the interests of those around you. All for one and one for all.

Mid-July through August and mid-November through December are when you feel like you have the full cooperation of everyone in your life. January and February are not so good for you Children of Jupiter born in the late winter. This is when you're apt to feel most frustrated and exploited, so you should postpone any major decisions until after your birthday. For you Children of Jupiter born in the late fall, it's the month *prior* to your birthday that's most troublesome. It's a time of infighting and backbiting. Rather than get involved, leave people alone to settle their own differences. Regardless of whether you were born in the winter or fall, mid-March through April is marvelous, because the Sun is in its exaltation. Just about anything you touch will turn to gold.

CHILD OF JUPITER . . .

Mercury, Planet of craft and ingenuity, rules the zodiac sign Virgo. As a Child of Jupiter, you may recognize a situation's inherent potential, but that doesn't always mean you know how to develop it or put it to good use. It's the Mercury side of you that prompts you to roll up your sleeves and start tinkering with a problem—looking for possibilities, testing each one, tirelessly mixing and matching them until you come up with a viable solution. This unique combination of cleverness (Mercury) and insight (Jupiter) makes you both inventive and practical. Yours is a utilitarian approach to life. Something is valuable only if it serves a particular function. However, being a Child of Jupiter, that function—in turn—must also serve a higher purpose.

You know people like their answers quick and to the point, so you'll say what you need to in short, easy-to-understand sentences. However that terseness doesn't quite mask your Jupiter side, which always sees past the immediate and considers how circumstances *could* play out in the long run. Mercury may rule connections, but it's your Birthday Planet that rules the way those connections run together. It is like the difference between playing connect the dots and intuiting the greater design at work. As a Child of Jupiter you are naturally oriented toward the larger—and potentially more complicated—view of matters. You can't help but be concerned about how everything will turn out in the end. That's why you're often torn between doing only what's expected—which is often the expedient thing to do—and going above and beyond the call of duty in order to do what's "right." You won't waste time and effort on an enterprise that will come to nothing in the end, so you force yourself to stay within certain prescribed limits. You don't want to start down a road with no clear destination in sight.

Yet it's the expertise of your work that betrays your conscientiousness. Perhaps it's the beautifully crafted prose that makes your report stand out from all the rest, your gift for detail that captures the attention of anyone viewing your handiwork, or maybe something as simple as your repair job being a marked improvement over what was originally installed. Of course if someone points this out, you'll shrug it off. The reason you

WITH JUPITER IN VIRGO

avoid praise is because it's your work that makes you happy, not recognition for a job well done. You are your harshest critic and, in private, the one who's most proud of what you do.

You enjoy being part of a group effort. Given Jupiter's position at the time of your birth, you're drawn to institutions that serve important causes. However the Mercury part of you isn't too comfortable with anything ostentatious. An important cause shouldn't call attention to itself. For example, a church, school, or hospital is there to serve people, not the other way around. You will look for a place in an organization where you can fulfill a particular, yet indispensable, function. You prefer your interactions to be hands-on and enjoy running back and forth getting things done. You also have a talent for building on what you see. All you require is the freedom to develop an idea and the means to apply it. Knowing you contribute to the greater good fills you with a personal sense of pride and purpose.

April, August, and December are good times to initiate an action—although you'll have to wait about ten months to see the results. The wheels of bureaucracy move slowly, and since you're a team player, much of your timing depends on other people coming through on their end. This doesn't really bother you, because you're not in much of a hurry to get anywhere. It's not that you're free of deadline pressures—March, June, September, and mid-December are usually intense periods for you—but for the most part you steer away from jobs or projects that require urgency. You don't like slapdash. You prefer to take your time, so that you can do the best job possible. What you make is built to last.

CHILD OF JUPITER...

Venus, Planet of betrothals, rules the zodiac sign Libra. You were born under the Planet of oaths and treaties, so it makes perfect sense that you be the one to negotiate a contract or draft the law that enforces it. Then again, given your fairness and wisdom, you may even rise to a position of authority where what you say—goes. When you're a Child of Jupiter with Venus strong, you have excellent judgment and acute political instincts. You're savvy about people and know how to soft-pedal a request. But that doesn't necessarily mean you should pack your bags and head off to Washington, D.C. You'd be just as happy being town mayor, frat president, union organizer, or local matchmaker. What counts most with you is bringing people together.

You find people utterly fascinating. You could watch them all day—scrutinizing, speculating, and discerning what would be in their best interests. This isn't done to satisfy voyeuristic tendencies. You really see yourself as an invisible agent in their affairs. Given Venus's philosophy of letting people decide matters for themselves, you always limit yourself to asking questions (albeit *leading* ones) and will never tell anyone what to do—until the time has come. Books and movies are full of characters like you. You're the "deus ex machina" ("god in the machine"), the person who arrives just in the nick of time to set things right. Maybe you're the only one who believes in a friend's talent, and thanks to you, this person goes on to become a great success. Or it's because of you that a colleague decides not to leave her husband and to give her marriage another chance. Perhaps you're the anonymous donor who writes the check that keeps an arts organization from slipping into bankruptcy. If volunteering your time, energy, and resources makes people happy, then you'll do it—no questions asked.

But you aren't always so altruistic. Venus and Jupiter may rule betrothals and oaths, but they also have a great fondness for intrigue and seduction. You will always be true—in your fashion. But you can't help seeing if you can maneuver your way around the technicalities. This makes you an expert strategist—and given the charm and persuasion of Venus—a formidable opponent, since people often underestimate your

WITH JUPITER IN LIBRA

guile. However if loved ones allow you the room to spread your feathers and parade around like a peacock, then they've nothing to fear. The fun isn't in getting away with something. It's in knowing that you *could* have if you wanted to.

You are no fan of routine. You require a great deal of stimulation or your interest wanders. This is a bit of a tall order given Jupiter's position at the time of your birth. You need certain things to be locked into place before you can feel comfortable. You'll single-mindedly pursue emotional *and* financial security as well as an attractive partner with social connections. When you have Venus and Jupiter strong like you do, you can't get away from mixing the romantic with the politic. There's nothing wrong with this except that in your haste to set things up, you could settle into a job (or a marriage) without really taking into account how quickly you might outgrow it. One of the hardest things for you is to consciously choose to do *with-out*, but if you can postpone these decisions until your late twenties, then you're likely to find a more suitable and lasting fit.

Late April through May and late September through October (especially around the fifteenth) are marvelous times for you. These are Venus's months, and because she always brings you good fortune through others, it's the perfect time to network, entertain, or flirt up a storm. The first three weeks of March are outstanding—not only because they belong to your Birthday Planet, but it's also when Venus's influence is exalted. You Children of Jupiter born in late winter should conserve you energies during August and September, while you Children of Jupiter born in late fall might want to moderate your pace during May and June. These are capricious and unpredictable months when you may have the attention of someone one moment only to lose it the next. Save your wiles for when they'll be fully appreciated.

CHILD OF JUPITER...

Both Mars and Pluto rule the zodiac sign Scorpio. Mars is the Planet of valor. It always seeks new challenges. Ennobled by your Birthday Planet's sense of higher purpose, you feel duty bound to come to the rescue of a damsel in distress or lost soul. Pluto is the Planet of ordeals and the transformations that arise from them. You are drawn to people whose inner anguish or despair matches your own supreme trust in Providence. You are no stranger to tests of faith and courage. But rather than break you, these dark nights of the soul empower you.

You're not out to convert the world or even discover the hidden meaning of life. With you, good works speak louder than words. If someone benefits from your sagacity, then you're only too happy to have helped out. One of your great gifts is to tell it like it is. This includes copping to a mistake when you've made it. Not everyone has that kind of courage. Yet it's this candor and humor that make you all the more trustworthy.

As a Child of Jupiter with Mars and Pluto powerful, you are often put in charge of others' fortune and fortunes. You carry great responsibil-ity, and it's up to you to either make things happen or put a stop to them. Financiers often find themselves in such pivotal positions, as do spiritual leaders, doctors, policy makers, and administrators.

People respect your judgment, but that won't prevent them from trying to influence it. Sometimes you're the lone moral voice in the wilderness. Adding to your dilemma is that little comes from your own independent efforts. The combination of Mars and Pluto puts you in awkward situations where somebody else's loss results in your gain. It may be money you inherit, a position you take over due to a superior's abrupt departure, or a situation you never asked for that winds up in your lap. Not only do you have to prove that you're up to the task at hand (adversity is Mars's m.o.), but there's also something inherent in this transfer of responsibility that has all the makings of an ongoing moral dilemma, a thorny predicament meant to prick your conscience and drive you to grapple with the larger questions. Whatever it is, it has the power to change your life so that you become the embodiment of your beliefs rather than pay lip service to them. Pluto may be the Planet of

WITH JUPITER IN SCORPIO

ordeals, but he also rewards those who brave them.

Jupiter's position at your birth shows that most of your family drama had played itself out by the time you arrived on the scene. But turn back the page one generation and you will find embroiled conflicts and painful sacrifices. How you were raised was meant to counteract this, which is why ambiguous matters were often treated with commonsense answers. You may find that the theme of your life picks up where a grandparent's (or even great-grandparent's) left off. Perhaps you will be able to realize a talent this person couldn't or find the happiness that always remained elusive. What you make of life is your own, but sometimes knowing the "back story" helps fill in the blanks.

Children of Jupiter born in the late winter thrive from mid-February through March, mid-June through July, and mid-October through November. These are "watery" times of year, and your Neptunian nature enjoys the powerful undercurrent of emotions. These are perfect occasions for partnering (romantically as well as professionally) and drawing upon resources, as they are full to brimming. Your "dry spell" is August and September. You Children of Jupiter born in late fall do best from mid-summer through the autumn. July is especially favorable. This is the perfect time for buying and selling property or for mergers and acquisitions. Pluto's month (mid-October through mid-November) is not very good. Your judgment is off, and you may feel like you're in over your head. Brothers in mythology, Jupiter and Pluto also possessed the good sense to steer clear of each other's stomping ground. Likewise you should wait until November 23, when you'll be able to pick up again where you left off—and without missing a beat.

CHILD OF JUPITER...

Jupiter, king of the gods in classical mythology, rules the zodiac sign Sagittarius. Jupiter symbolizes the light at the end of the tunnel. After the violent conflicts that preceded his rise to the Olympian throne, Jupiter is the only one who can bring the warring deities together under a single roof. He doesn't do this by dominating them, but by giving shape to their many influences. Each god is assigned a unique part to play in the scheme of things, so that Jupiter's reign becomes an ongoing creative process, a group effort where everyone works in concert. As a Child of Jupiter with Jupiter powerful, you are the shaping force in people's lives. This is why they come to you with their ideas and problems, their hopes and their concerns. Not only because you get them to lighten up and believe everything will turn out for the best (you exude enormous confidence and optimism; you are everyone's safe harbor), but they also trust in your vision of how things *should* proceed. You are more than a problem solver, morale booster, or zealous advocate. You put things right.

Your own journey, however, hasn't been an easy one. Your Birthday Planet was named after the god of storms, so you have weathered your fair share of emotional tempests—especially early on in life. Perhaps your father was tossed about on the turbulent seas of fortune, or both parents clashed—like thunder and lightning—on a semi-regular basis. Though by no means pleasant, it didn't exactly traumatize you either. You have a naturally dramatic personality and would have resonated with the emotional cacophony. After all, you can scream and holler with the loudest of them. But as soon as you were old enough to go your own way—you did.

Whatever road you take automatically leads to bigger and better things. You might start out as a waiter and end up becoming a celebrity chef with his own television show. Or an impassioned speech at a PTA meeting becomes your first unknowing step toward a career in the United States Senate. Even your misadventures somehow work to get you off a road leading nowhere and onto the fast track where you want to be. Yet you may never know the true impact you have. Like a drop falling on the quiet surface of a pond, you send out ripples that expand in all directions;

WITH JUPITER IN SAGITTARIUS

but by the time they reach their full scope, you're long gone.

Because of Jupiter's position at the time of your birth, your purpose in life is not always knowable. It's constantly unfolding, and reinventing itself. Since it's larger than you, you will be sharing it with a number of people. As a Child of Jupiter with Jupiter powerful, everyone's your best friend— the greatest love of your life or the canniest businessperson you ever met. You don't really differentiate. And given your charisma and appeal, everyone will take your word for it—which could lead to trouble if you aren't careful. Loved ones will have to learn to share you unconditionally. You are not a one-on-one type of personality. Everything is a group effort. Bear in mind that not everyone is up to such a tall order, so you may have to go through a few trial runs before you hit

on the real thing. You work from the outside in, so it's no surprise that you wind up developing a private life only after you've established your public one.

For Children of Jupiter born in late autumn, the months between August and January are when things move speedily toward their completion. Anything begun early in the year (like late February or March) ripens at this time. The August-to-January quarter is also when you are in the strongest position to influence the outcome. For you Children of Jupiter born in late winter, this culminating period lies between November and April. If a project or endeavor isn't ready to go by late July, then it's best to wait a year before initiating it. When you're a Child of Jupiter with Jupiter strong, there is no such thing as a missed opportunity. Just consider it one you haven't gotten to yet.

CHILD OF JUPITER...

Saturn, Planet of authority and discipline, rules the zodiac sign Capricorn. Therefore you Children of Jupiter with Jupiter in Capricorn often find yourselves in supervisory positions where you oversee many people, and the success (or failure) of a venture rests squarely on your shoulders. Even if aims are modest and you're low man on the totem pole, associates and colleagues will still seek your advice and approval. Bosses automatically treat you like an equal; clients feel safest only when you're on board. In a way, you don't really have to be ambitious. The opportunity to advance always comes to you. There's no hiding your integrity or old-fashioned work ethic. When people think of the right person for the job, your name tops everyone's short list.

You and great expectations are like old friends. Indeed you've been struggling under the weight of them for years. Saturn rules old age, so you always seem more experienced than you are. This is more than precociousness. In some ways you were born fully developed. Perhaps it was your sophisticated interests that first betrayed the adult trapped inside the kid or a talent that was far too accomplished. Your childhood was run like a training camp for the adult you were expected to be. It was important to your family (especially your father) that you realize your remarkable potential. And given the confluence of support and pressure, you were also in a hurry to grow up.

Thankfully it's in your Birthday Planet's nature to think *big*. And though an extraordinary accomplishment usually results in weightier expectations, the truth is you thrive in this kind of environment. The Saturn side of you is proud of the blood, sweat, and tears that go into making something happen. You don't do anything small or halfhearted. What makes you different from other Children of Jupiter, though, is that you're not content to describe what you would like to see and then hand it over to someone else to carry out. Saturn is the Planet of matter. You must be the one to give your ideas form. The fact that you're doing this while being in charge of a group tests your ability to delegate authority and to coordinate efforts. Ironically these additional obligations increase your productivity rather than diminish it.

However growing up in a hurry doesn't

WITH JUPITER IN CAPRICORN

necessarily mean you've matured. Like a gifted child, the desired facilities may be developed while everything else is ignored. Given your Ruling Planet's penchant for incorporating disparate—and sometimes even contradictory elements—you will eventually reconcile the life you live with the one you *could be* living. Indeed the realization that there's more to life than meeting expectations as they're doled out leads to one of your most dramatic growth spurts—which, because of Jupiter's position at the time you were born, takes place in your forties.

At an age when contemporaries are just catching up to your level of seriousness and commitment, you may suddenly put everything at risk to pursue a torrid romance. Or perhaps you walk out on the business you built from scratch to join a monastery or go fly-fishing. It may seem like a delayed adolescence, but there are greater forces at play here than you just becoming one more person with a midlife crisis. These episodes of rebellion give you an opportunity to break out of the mold you've been in so that you can live a well-rounded existence. They allow you to reshape what you do so that it reflects your tastes rather than somebody else's.

Late April through mid-May, late August through mid-September, and late December through January are wonderful times of year. These are the "earthy" months when whatever resources (or funding) you require are put at your disposal. These are amazingly fertile and productive periods for you. October through November is good for networking, but you can prove resistant. With Saturn powerful, you tend to get so absorbed in work that it's impossible to tear you away. Unfortunately hard work doesn't always speak for itself, and you need to be out and about refreshing old contacts and generating new ones. Once you get talking about what you do, however, your enthusiasm shines through and you invariably win over your audience—while even having some fun in the process.

CHILD OF JUPITER...

Saturn, Planet of concrete reality, and Uranus, Planet of infinite possibility, both rule the zodiac sign Aquarius. When you're a Child of Jupiter with Jupiter in Aquarius, you appreciate the breadth of infinite possibilities but also understand they're ultimately useless unless something's done with them. That technical ability to make the most of one's raw materials falls under the rulership of Saturn. But just as you recognize practical necessity, you also recognize that a strictly material view of life is limited. The line from Shakespeare's *Hamlet* "there are more things in heaven and hell than are dreamt of in your philosophy" sizes up your point of view. Finding a way to stay true to your ideal *and* make it work without selling out is a life purpose that challenges and inspires you.

You have a unique ability to keep volatile situations from falling apart. This stems from your genuine interest in people's grievances as well as a solid conviction that all the pieces can be made to fit. You are perhaps the most humanitarian of the Children of Jupiter because you recognize that each of us has a part to play in a greater plan.

But that plan may be unknowable. Which is why you will work to change the framework itself, rather than try to force a square peg into a round hole. This may sound revolutionary, but actually your approach is through reform.

It takes a lot of people to make big dreams come true, so you are drawn to large organizations. But you don't get lost in them. You rise swiftly through the ranks to a position of influence and authority. However you may resist taking on a leadership role, preferring instead to be a subtle but firm guiding hand. Colleagues assume this is because you want to maintain "hands-on" control. Although partially true, the real reason has to do with an underlying ambivalence toward authority—much of which may be colored by your father's beliefs.

Your father might be highly principled or extremely practical. If idealistic, then his head is in the clouds—making him a brilliant yet unreliable (or even absent) parent. If his thinking is rooted in reality, then he may resemble an ostrich with its head in the sand, refusing to consider anything outside his own field of expertise. Respect and admiration for your father's lofty

WITH JUPITER IN AQUARIUS

principles inspire you, but they also serve as a constant reminder of what's been left undone. Adopting your father's down-to-earth approach could reveal bottom-line solutions for larger-than-life problems, but leave you feeling like you're only treating symptoms without addressing causes. In true Jupiterian fashion, this ongoing conflict prompts you to look beyond the either/or and to seek your answers in uncharted waters.

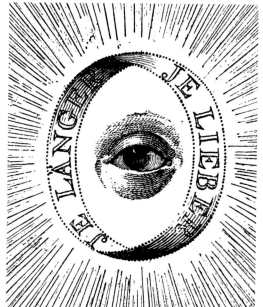

Because of Jupiter's position at the time of your birth, you are drawn to organizations that offer some kind of life plan. This could range from environmental protection to urban planning; providing seed money for start-up companies or fixing the education system. You want to reform without intruding upon or invalidating structures already in place. Utopian principles like equality, freedom, social responsibility, and justice really do mean something to you. As a Child of Jupiter with Saturn and Uranus strong, you are truly committed to realizing the highest we have to offer.

For Children of Jupiter born in late autumn, your busy periods are January through February and September through October. From May 20 through June 20 you will feel like you just aren't on top of things. However you can utilize this period by being open to input. Much of your creativity is in taking a rough idea and turning it into a polished concept. By August you start to feel like yourself again. For Children of Jupiter born in late winter, your off weeks are January 20 through February 20. This is when situations may unravel or fall apart. Let them. Once into May, you're back on solid ground. Productive periods are June, October, and especially December. But try to wrap things up by year's end. The first two months of any new year are traditionally "dark." This is when thoughts and ideas incubate. Though it may not seem like much is happening on the surface, your dream life is extremely active.

CHILD OF JUPITER...

Both Jupiter and Neptune rule the zodiac sign Pisces. As a Child of Jupiter, you're eager to get out in the world so you can experience every facet of it. The idea that you never know when you might meet someone who will have an extraordinary impact on your life makes you look forward to each day. When Neptune suffuses your Birthday Planet's energy, the emphasis changes ever so subtly from the outer perspective to the inner one. Neptune's approach to life is more soulful than spirited. The Planet of the imagination, Neptune rules over the hopes and dreams that stream through us all. The reason we can understand one another—regardless of language, race, or nationality—is because we all draw from the same emotional reservoir. One person's joy—or tears—has the power to move another without a single word being spoken.

When you're a Child of Jupiter with Jupiter and Neptune strong, you experience dramatic highs and lows. Jupiter is named after the god of the sky while Neptune is named after the god of the sea. Yours is what used to be called a *romantic* personality back in the 19th century. Romantics were profoundly creative, very moral, and extremely deep. But just because agonies are entwined with ecstasies doesn't make you an emotional wreck. Think about how water evaporates into air, accumulates into clouds, and then returns to the sea as rain. Our entire atmosphere works like an enormous recirculating fountain. In its own way, your emotional life does, too.

Neptune rules the mysterious *other* world that speaks to us through our art and music, our religions and our myths. Subsequently you may be drawn to institutions—like the church, academia, and the arts—that house, nurture, and shape our culture. In an age when something said yesterday is considered ancient history, you make a point of invoking the past to enrich the present. You may pursue a career as a teacher, minister, curator, historian, or performer. These occupations may seem diverse, but they share an underlying purpose—which is to strengthen the bonds between our social world and our spiritual one. The wonderful thing about culture is that it is open to everybody—and you never tire of sharing that with loved ones and friends. You are constantly dragging them off to an exhibit or prevail-

WITH JUPITER IN PISCES

ing upon them to read a book that will broaden their horizons. At a time when education is practically synonymous with on-the-job training, you are like the fabled Irish monks of the Middle Ages who preserved the literary treasures of the past in order to remind and inspire future generations. To you it is a terrible thing to waste a mind, particularly a creative one.

Because of Jupiter's position at the time of your birth, you don't really relax into who you are until your forties and fifties. Jupiter and Neptune are both named after storm gods, and given your powerful emotional life, you can get loud and tempestuous. This is not for the meek and mild mannered, and it takes you a while to realize that you may be scaring people away without meaning to. Yet you are drawn to the company of others. The interplay of people's lives with your own alleviates emotional pressures. It puts those watery feelings into circulation so that they don't amass and grow too dark and heavy.

For Children of Jupiter born in late autumn, the time between November and April is when you feel most creative and inspired. May through August is your "gestation" period, when you're absorbing everything you've taken in over the preceding months. Though you may feel your energy is low, this half-awake state is actually when your mind sketches out all the insights that will seemingly appear "out of nowhere" later on. For you Children of Jupiter born in late winter, the quarter between August and January is particularly busy. Drawn to long-term projects and endeavors, this is the season when you're making preparations for what comes next. It's an excellent time for locking in funding, organizing particulars, and culling resources. If you can, try to work with two-year plans. That way you'll always have something in the works and can take full advantage of your "lucky" four-year cycles.

CHILD OF SATURN...

Mars, Planet of action, rules the zodiac sign Aries. You Children of Saturn with Saturn in Aries feel an enormous responsibility to do what's right. You never do anything on impulse—it's too unpredictable, and passing the buck or walking away is simply not an option. Whether it's a personal dilemma or a professional judgment call, you know that when it comes right down to it—everything hinges on what you do next. Thankfully your Saturn side can block out the surrounding tension and focus squarely on the matter. Others may get frustrated with how long it takes you to actually *do* something, but you refuse to let circumstances force your hand. You will wait until the moment presents itself. When it does, you act swiftly and decisively.

Yet you didn't come by your coolness under pressure easily. As a young adult, you may have been very meek and apologetic—often calling attention to your faults. Being a Child of Saturn, you naturally focus on what's wrong, but it would have been the Mars side of you that sought to strengthen your willpower by attracting adversity. You may have practically "invited" peers to antagonize you by dressing provocatively, championing controversial causes, or being particularly touchy and argumentative. This was Mars's way of forcing you to develop a thick skin. Not the healthiest approach to strengthening psychic muscles, but it's not all that different from the self-punishment athletes willingly endure when in training. This would have outfitted you for steeper obstacles yet to come.

You have extraordinary powers of endurance. And given your ability to "go it alone" you may seek a profession where you work long hours by yourself or spearhead a small team that answers only to itself. Autonomy is very important to you. You can't think straight if you feel as if somebody's looking over your shoulder. When you're a Child of Saturn with Mars strong, you are drawn to situations where the obstacles are awesome and the benefits are hard to glean—at first. But you won't back down. In time the equation reverses itself so that you wind up reaping tremendous rewards with what looks to be a modicum of effort.

It isn't your intention to be a trailblazer or an innovator (indeed your Ruling Planet prefers to

WITH SATURN IN ARIES

keep a low profile), but you inevitably wind up challenging the status quo—either because you're the only one willing to make an unpopular decision or you realize that the only way to move forward is by scrapping the way things are traditionally done. You are often the one who lays the foundation for a new way of doing things. And thanks to that thick skin you developed, you will always stand your ground.

Yet Saturn's position at the time of your birth indicates a deep ambivalence toward assuming authority. This probably reflects your own feelings about your father. Because you will end up surpassing him, you may experience a lingering guilt—like somehow what you do undermines the significance of his accomplishments or calls into question the choices he made. Obviously your accomplishments don't have to invalidate his, but it does betray a deeper fear of not wanting to be surpassed yourself. Finding ways to join the old

with the new, so that one doesn't have to be in conflict with the other, is something that will play out repeatedly in your life as you make the transition from child to parent or employee to employer. Do it enough times and you'll gradually see that setting up something new doesn't necessarily mean having to throw out *everything* that came before.

The January-to-April quarter is your most productive and personally fulfilling period. This is when you're energized, focused, and can accomplish a lot in a short amount of time. Life slows down between late May and early September. Though you will always stay busy, you won't feel very enthusiastic. This isn't a good time for making any crucial decisions, as your judgment is hazy and your reaction time is off. After autumn begins, however, you'll feel revitalized. November is a particularly powerful month. This is when seeds sown in spring suddenly burst to life.

CHILD OF SATURN...

Venus, Planet of beauty, rules the zodiac sign Taurus. Therefore you Children of Saturn with Saturn in Taurus are blessed with refined taste, a discriminating eye, and can often spot the diamond in the rough. Whether it's a ramshackle piece of property or a business plan that has everything thrown in but the kitchen sink, you will roll up your sleeves and go to work—peeling off the layers, polishing and refurbishing until what emerges is a vision of beauty. Not only does it scarcely resemble what you started out with, but you will increase its value as well. In truth you only brought out what you saw there all along. The line from Psalms "the stone which the builders refused is become the head stone of the corner" might very well be the key to your particular aesthetic. Finding a way to work with what's problematic is the first step in your creative process.

But this remarkable insight does not come naturally. Indeed when you were younger your personal tastes probably ran toward the parochial. Much of this would have been due to the awkward relationship between Venus and Saturn. Venus is all about *connecting*, whereas your Ruling Planet is all about *limiting*. In a way this makes them opposites, because where Venus reaches out, Saturn holds back. The Venus side of you is drawn to things you find pleasing and attractive, while the Saturn side of you wants to peek under the hood to see where the imperfections lie. This inner tug-of-war is also reflected in feelings of attraction doing battle with your fears of rejection. This can create a psychic deadlock wherein you wind up making a series of "safe" choices that might meet with everyone else's approval while leaving you feeling vaguely dissatisfied.

It requires maturity and sophistication to give each side its due, and because of Saturn's position at the time of your birth, it may take until your thirties for you to start feeling comfortable in your own skin. This "breakthrough" could come in the form of an unusual assignment at work, an "unlikely" romantic match, or even a creative whim. Once you see that you can actually make something out of what others would happily pass over, then your perceptions change. Instead of trying to fit in with the prevailing taste, you become the person who influences it.

WITH SATURN IN TAURUS

Another deep and abiding conflict that may not be so easy to reconcile is that Venus is the Planet of partnerships. She does everything in tandem. What this means is you rarely initiate anything on your own. This isn't to say you can't. But prospects for success automatically improve when you combine efforts. The drawback is you often have to wait on others and are forced to deal with matters they bring to the table. Their business becomes your business—whether you want it to or not. Moreover there's the question of ownership and recognition. Because you will be working with ideas and resources that have their genesis with someone else, but are uniquely transformed by you into something of value, there's always a blurry line about what belongs to you and what belongs to the other person. Needless to say, these sorts of complications aren't much to your liking. As a Child of Saturn you strive to be self-sufficient. Venus adds a polit-ical dimension to your personal and financial relationships. These enforced collaborations may make you feel insecure and edgy, but over time they actually get you to open up around people. This counteracts your Saturnine tendency toward isolation and withdrawal.

Late April through mid-May, late August through mid-September, and late December through January are your best times for networking. This is when you're rubbing shoulders with people who are in a position to back what you want or whose say-so can open doors. April and November are when you want to be on guard. This is when people are feeling territorial (you included), and there can be a lot of turf wars if you aren't careful. It will be up to you to handle matters firmly and diplomatically. Late September through October is perfect for a different type of partnership—one that's closer to your heart.

CHILD OF SATURN . . .

Mercury, Planet of the intellect, rules the zodiac sign Gemini. Therefore you Children of Saturn with Saturn in Gemini have sharp and penetrating minds. You question everything. Though you may come across as just a doubting Thomas, you truly believe there's more going on than what meets the eye. It drives you crazy how the simplest things can get muddled in claptrap. You disdain theoretical explanations that only make sense to a theorist. And you will unerringly set your sights on debunking the latest UFO conspiracy or get-rich-quick scheme. Thankfully the combination of Mercury and Saturn tinges everything you say with wit and humor, so that people are often left smiling at themselves while grudgingly relinquishing some of their more cherished notions.

In your youth you may have been particularly susceptible to betrayals and double crosses, as friends who were initially drawn to your company left to go hang out with the more popular crowd. Then again, given Mercury's ability "to pass," you yourself may have dumbed things down in order to gain acceptance. In any case, one doesn't become the astute observer you are by coloring inside the lines or by rejecting convention. When you're a Child of Saturn with Mercury strong, your sense of irony makes you too honest (and complex) to accept anything as black or white. You want to be able to travel in a variety of social circles, so that you can examine a situation from a myriad of angles.

It's only natural that you're drawn to professions where your sharp analysis can be put to use. Isolating a problem is easy, but searching for the solution challenges you to use your mind in a constructive way. Because Mercury hates to be out of the loop, you will be drawn to issues that are current and relevant. You may analyze and advise on information as short-lived as today's fluctuating markets or struggle with the ongoing problem of righting social wrongs. Invariably communication plays a strong role in your life. Given your Birthday Planet's penchant for turning faults into merits, there may also be a hidden motive at work. A Mercury Saturn usually indicates something problematic in the way you communicate (anything ranging from a thick accent to a reading disorder) that either inspires you to pursue your particular pro-

WITH SATURN IN GEMINI

fession or is the thing you constantly struggle with as you try to master whatever it is you do.

Because of Saturn's position at the time of your birth, life becomes easier as you grow older. This is good news, as your childhood may have had some rough edges to it. Money could have been tight or your parents were too preoccupied with holding everything together to give you much attention. Moreover a sibling may have been a particular thorn in your side—either this person bullied you physically and/or emotionally or was a drain on everyone's energies. In any case, the need to stand on your own two feet is very strong, as is your drive to distinguish yourself intellectually. Keep in mind, however, that the seeds of adulthood are sown in childhood and—in your efforts to escape where you came from—you could inadvertently stumble into circumstances similar to what your parents once faced (especially your father). As with your ability to examine a problem, it's not enough to isolate a single thread. You also have to find a way to weave it back into the tapestry of surrounding circumstances. You can't go wrong cultivating a tolerance and acceptance that's in proportion to your more critical facilities.

Late January through mid-February, late May through mid-June, and late September through mid-October are your best times of year. This is when things flow smoothly in your life and you're free to pick and choose among the items that intrigue and fascinate you. It's also a busy time—which you always complain about (but secretly enjoy). Late November through December gets tense as business slows down and the prospect of family politics rears its head. Deciding whom to spend the holidays with, refereeing loved ones and in-laws, as well as dealing with unresolved issues from when you were three doesn't always make for the coziest of get-togethers—however it does provide you with plenty of material for future anecdotes.

CHILD OF SATURN...

The Moon, Planet of family ties, rules the zodiac sign Cancer. But this doesn't mean you're a homebody. Indeed you've been packing and unpacking suitcases since you can remember, and travel (no matter how much you dread it) may even be a requirement of your profession. Nevertheless you Children of Saturn with Saturn in Cancer have a unique ability to set up house wherever you hang your hat. You won't sheepishly enter a new situation or linger outside the door waiting to be invited in. You establish yourself promptly. And as long as no one interferes with what you do, then there will never be cause for complaint or worry. Work will be done efficiently and on time.

Yet underneath that button-down demeanor is a wonderful sense of the absurd. You have your own peculiar take on things, and people are often surprised by how silly and lighthearted you can be. That's because by itself the Moon doesn't have a strong motivation to express what it feels. It simply reacts and responds privately. It's your Saturn side that will try to fish something out of the deep well of your imagination and turn it into some-thing tangible by generating a piece of writing, some photography, or maybe even music. These spontaneous expressions of creativity and flair show that there's more happening on the inside than you let on.

You are deeply mixed about letting people see this hidden side of you—mostly because you enjoy your hobbies and don't want anyone ruining your fun with criticisms. This is why you are very selective about what you take on—whether it's a date or a job—and will cut short an endeavor you don't see as going anywhere. You edit impulses so that they stay safely within the circumference you've drawn for yourself. People may think you're tightly wound, but it's actually a form of self-preservation.

When you're a Child of Saturn with the Moon powerful, you can't turn off your feelings even if you try. That's why you want people to think you have a thick skin, because in truth, it's very permeable. You may have learned how to erect these barriers from your own mother. And like her, you can get so good at masking all traces of feeling that people will simply take you at face value and not assume that you have much emotional depth.

WITH SATURN IN CANCER

If you don't want to wind up living in a psychic suit of armor then you need to find a way to lower the drawbridge or, like Rapunzel, to let down your hair so that a would-be love interest can climb the golden stair. A little vulnerability never hurt anyone.

Because of Saturn's position at the time of your birth, you may go through long "plateau" periods where it doesn't seem like much is going on in your life. This can be deceptive. Because the Moon is the Planet of the unconscious, most of what's really going on with you takes place beneath the surface—which is why you tend to attract people with such colorful and hectic lives. Although you are meant, in part, to provide them with a haven or framework, it's also important to remember that you are not the cleanup crew. By dealing with people who are emotionally needy or who spend a lot of time running in circles, you begin to discover that nothing awful is going to happen if you lower your guard.

The spring and autumnal equinoxes (around March 20 and October 20) are pivotal for you. Either you're racing the clock to complete something or you're launching a new project or relationship. The summer and winter solstices, however, can be very stressful. Because you were born when your Birthday Planet was retrograde, these are the times when you feel most under pressure and least like you're in control. There's nothing you can really do, but learn to go with the flow. There are just going to be certain times of year—like certain periods in your life—when you can't alter the course of events. But remember—as a Child of Saturn with the Moon powerful, what doesn't work out now eventually will one day.

CHILD OF SATURN ...

The Sun, source of light and life, rules the zodiac sign Leo. As a Child of Saturn with Saturn in Leo, you exude a warm paternal authority that people appreciate and respect. Even you female Children of Saturn tend to be more *fatherly* than motherly in your advice. You won't coddle, placate, or overprotect. You believe that when push comes to shove, most people will rise to the occasion, and that only by encouraging them to step up to the plate will they discover the strengths and abilities they wouldn't have otherwise. It does a person good to be held accountable—which is why you make it a point to always deliver on a promise and will promptly accept responsibility if things don't pan out. It isn't easy holding yourself to a higher standard. But then again, you are no pretender to the throne. You are the genuine article.

Your Solar side is an optimist. Full of exuberance and charisma, it believes that the best is yet to come. Your Saturn side, however, is a pessimist. It pokes holes in your hopes and wonders (aloud) about what you got yourself into. One would think these Planetary energies contradict each other, but they eventually dovetail nicely.

Your Ruling Planet gives you perseverance. No matter the setback, you will pick yourself up, dust yourself off, and start again. But without the Sun's glowing optimism, you would be yet another hard-luck story. Just like without Saturn's hard-won experience and ability to learn from its mistakes, the Solar part of you would merrily skip down the garden path—only doing the things it wants while ignoring anything unpleasant. Your Solar and Saturnine sides together recognize the fulfillment in every challenge and that obstacles, although troublesome, are the very things that promote growth. "Tough love" is deeply ingrained. But then again, your loyalty and trust don't come cheap. Going through a rough patch is character-building. This is why you won't really open up to anyone new until you've undergone some kind of difficulty together. If the relationship falls apart—it wasn't meant to be. But if it stands up under pressure, then you know you've forged a bond with this person that will last a lifetime.

Because of Saturn's position at the time of your birth, money won't be easy to come by at first. Indeed, it may take until your forties for you

WITH SATURN IN LEO

to feel like you're making what you're worth. This may just be the price you have to pay in order to pursue a particular vocation; however, given that both the Sun and Saturn symbolize the father, there's a good chance he may have inadvertently colored your outlook. Perhaps money was scarce when he was growing up, or if it wasn't, it might have been used as a means of discipline and control. Then again, your father may have been unable to realize a heart's desire, so he instilled in you a penny-earned-is-a-penny-saved pragmatism to spare you similar disappointment.

The Sun rules gold. Your Birthday Planet rules safekeeping, so it wouldn't be surprising for you to be drawn to the financial sector. Other people's money—their property and their welfare—will be integrally connected to what you do. Yet other people's welfare isn't exclusive to their private property. It could refer to things that are put aside for everyone's benefit—like endowments, public works, landmarks, or national parks. Your Birthday Planet teaches you to turn a possession into a resource.

The fall quarter—late September through December—is when your "storehouses" are full and resources are brimming. It's a time of plenty, and you feel both confident and generous. It's not until this season that you can relax and allow yourself to coast a bit on your momentum. The groundwork for this is laid down in the previous spring quarter—which is when you're busiest. The summer—particularly July and August—is when you feel like you're struggling just to keep things on track. Schedule important business for either the spring or fall and you'll be fine. Winter—particularly your birthday month—is when you bask in the company of loved ones—the smiles on their faces serve as a radiant reminder of why you work as hard as you do.

CHILD OF SATURN . . .

Mercury rules the zodiac sign Virgo. You Children of Saturn with Saturn in Virgo are precise and exacting. The phrase "God is in the details" is your personal motto. Others may be content to settle for vague truths and tired maxims, but you Children of Saturn with Mercury strong will spend hours combing over seemingly trivial minutiae—convinced that they hold the clues to a greater design at work. And they do. Whether it's by patiently analyzing statistics, sifting through old bills, or simply discerning someone's intent in the midst of a rambling monologue, you will eventually discover the chain that links all the random associations. But you won't stop there. Anyone can present a list of facts. Not everyone can interpret it. Your unique blend of cleverness and wit (Mercury) combined with a depth firmly rooted in common sense (Saturn) allows you to bring these tidbits of information to life in a way that's both revealing and rich. In an instant you transform what was unclear and confusing into a deduction as plain as the nose on someone's face.

You love history and old things and may even amass a collection of obscure memorabilia or eccentric knickknacks. You don't regard the past as dead and buried. To you, it's every bit as contemporary as the present but just packaged differently. You'd love to say your preoccupation with days gone by is based on gleaning valuable lessons, but in truth you love it for its quirkiness. You're constantly amused and intrigued by the way people think and all the crazy things they come up with. This comes in handy with your day-to-day dealings because you're naturally curious about how others view matters. You may have a reputation for "thinking too much" or "reading into" a situation, but you were born with an extremely active mind. Thankfully your willingness to pursue a tangent (no matter how far-fetched) usually results in a revealing explanation and, on some occasions, an opportunity to address a problem when it's still a symptom and before it becomes a full-fledged crisis. Your commitment to get to the bottom of things is what makes you the problem solver extraordinaire.

Because of Saturn's position at the time of your birth, you may be drawn to professions in

WITH SATURN IN VIRGO

higher education, government, publishing, or advertising. Mercury rules communication and information, and the Saturn side of you likes to know that what you do is important and will have an impact on society at large. But because of the heavy volume of traffic, you will be kept on a tight schedule, where you have to juggle a number of different tasks at once. This fits in with your active mind and blends well with your Mercury/Saturn energy—especially since Mercury likes to do things quickly and Saturn always frets about wasting precious time. However, you may be haunted by a chronic sense of things left hanging. You may even feel like you never get to go into matters as deeply as you'd like or that just when you're beginning to put all the pieces together, you have to move on to another project. It's good to remember in times like these that you are part of a larger organization. You are not a cog in the machine. You may not always see the results right away, but trust that your actions acquire a cumulative effect over time.

Your best times of year are late April through mid-May, late August through mid-September, and late December through January. This is when aims are clearest and you can take care of business in a timely fashion. As a Child of Saturn, you need to have set parameters—dealing with nebulous terms or being forced to second-guess what the other party wants drives you nuts. That's why late February through March and late November to mid-December can be so trying. There's much too much hemming and hawing and it takes forever to pin down specifics. Romantic cycles are strongest just before or after the summer. Since you're almost always at work, you'll want to keep an eye open. You never know who may be secretly pining away for you in the cubicle next door.

CHILD OF SATURN ...

Venus, Planet of harmony, rules the zodiac sign Libra. You were born under the Planet of rules, so it often falls to you to keep the peace or ensure that an obligation will be met. Whether it's running a household or a multinational corporation, you almost always get your way. Most people don't handle supervisory positions well. They get too preoccupied with who's boss. However the unique combination of Venus and Saturn gives you a gracious and subtle executive ability. Indeed a "laissez-faire" approach colors just about every decision you make. If someone comes to you with a problem, you won't rack your brain searching for an answer. Trusting that this person probably knows more about what's going on than you (but just can't see straight), you will ask neutral questions aimed at getting this person to rethink the thinking. In moments a frown turns into a smile as a realization dawns and the solution emerges. But you can also be tough when you need to be. Colleagues and clients know better than to force your hand with a confrontation or ultimatum. You have no problem ignoring threats, because you've already checked the rule book and know that the responsibility will ultimately fall on their shoulders, not yours. The secret to preserving your authority is in steering clear of situations that would compromise it.

This can sometimes give the impression that all you do is wash your hands clean of problems as they arise—that you don't really have a mind of your own. Actually, it takes an enormous amount of self-discipline to put aside sympathies and uphold the rules in place. Rules are there for a reason, and one of them is to provide guidance when tempers flare and everyone is focused on short-term gains rather than on long-term consequences. But you do more than play policeman. You believe that a rule, like a limit, forces people to draw on resources they didn't know they had. In this spirit you will concentrate on supporting and encouraging them to reach for the highest in themselves. And when they've reached that, to reach higher still. Indeed, if it weren't for your firm yet benevolent presence, many people you've stood behind wouldn't have accomplished the things they have. But you don't need them to know that. Like a rule, you don't call attention to yourself.

WITH SATURN IN LIBRA

Because of Saturn's position at the time you were born, you will naturally focus on being impartial and fair while overlooking that you have a life—with your own wants and needs, moods and feelings. Understandably you want to keep your professional and private concerns separate, but nowadays with the rise of home offices and flexible work hours, one blends into the other. This can leave you feeling like you have to maintain your composure twenty-four hours a day—which is psychologically impossible. Just as others know they can rely on you as a sounding board, you need to allow loved ones and friends to do the same for you. But don't expect them to be neutral. Indeed, they may have no compunction about telling you what to do. That's their way of balancing *your* energy. They're not in your life to help you control emotions but to *feel* them. They may get under your skin from time to time, but you won't ever doubt that you have strong views of your own.

Your best times are late February through mid-March, late May through mid-June, and late September through mid-October. This is when you have a healthy give-and-take with others and your rapport is strongest. Paradoxically, your own birthday month is not a very auspicious time. This is when you're apt to feel most under the gun and stressed out. Whatever you can do to find breaks in the day—whether it's a quick catnap or workout at the gym—would be a good idea. It doesn't take much to restore your energy. But you do need to replenish it. Although partnerships are always uppermost in your mind (after all, you have a very strong and powerful Venus), the opportunities for romance are especially ripe in the fall.

CHILD OF SATURN ...

Mars, Planet of will, and Pluto, Planet of obsession, both rule the zodiac sign Scorpio. Together they are a force to be reckoned with, and as a Child of Saturn with Mars and Pluto powerful, you have your work cut out for you. Left to its own devices, your Mars side would pursue what it wants with no thought for future consequences, while your Pluto side, if sufficiently provoked, will sacrifice everything just in order to win. As you can imagine, this doesn't exactly jibe with your preference for taking things slow and building from the ground up. Thankfully your Birthday Planet gives you the presence of mind and persistence to rein in these two potentially hooligan energies, so that what emerges is the best of all three—an unflagging resolve, an ability to keep your cool under pressure, as well as a "gut" feel for how things will play out. You may never shed your recklessness and passion, but your actions won't be foolhardy.

When you possess a combination like this, the simple life is not for you. Despite your leanings toward an orderly existence, you crave depth and intensity. As a Child of Saturn, you'll instinc-tively choose the most difficult route from point A to point B. It's your way of turning an obstacle into an object lesson. But where Saturn is about mastery, Pluto is about growth through catharsis. With Pluto involved, that difficulty you face becomes heated and dramatic, because it's meant to activate a chain reaction deep within you. Pluto, the Planet of obsession, is also the Planet of ordeals and the transformations that arise from them—so in a way, it actually goes looking for trouble. But there are different ways of channeling Pluto energy without having to lurch from crisis to crisis. For instance, you can be drawn to vocations where urgent matters are dealt with on a day-to-day basis. This could range from working as a paramedic to being a therapist, social worker, or pursuing a career in criminal justice. Then again, because of your love of the past (Saturn) and secrets (Pluto), your energies might be equally engaged in research and study.

Given Saturn's position at the time of your birth, your crowning successes will come later—probably after you turn forty. There's a lot of work that needs to be done beforehand, and most of it

WITH SATURN IN SCORPIO

has to do with reversing two potentially detrimental traits. Mars and Pluto give you an extremely penetrating mind. You are always convinced there is more going on than meets the eye. But sometimes your gut instinct for what lies underneath doesn't take into account another person's right to privacy. It's especially important for someone as perceptive as yourself to develop a healthy respect for boundaries. The second thing you need to cultivate is an accurate understanding of when enough is enough. Your Saturn side tends to focus more on what's missing rather than on what you have—and with Mars and Pluto always willing to push things to the brink, you could get hooked into a vicious cycle where every achievement *has* to outshine the previous one, and you wind up being in competition with yourself. Thankfully, this is where your Ruling Planet's pragmatism can come in handy, but it's still up to you to put on the brakes.

Mars rules the beginning of spring and Pluto rules midautumn, so these are the seasons when you thrive. Likewise your energy is strongest at the outset of a venture and again when you have to bring it to a close. The only time it wanders is in between. This is when you have to continually bring your focus back to the matter at hand. Summer is when you may feel like you're on automatic pilot—and though you will still put your shoulder to the wheel, you need to take things at a relaxed pace so you can "refuel" along the way. Your own birthday month is a peak time of year. This is when you're feeling most can-do. But make certain you settle old business and tie up loose ends before taking on anything new.

CHILD OF SATURN...

Jupiter, Planet of beliefs, rules the zodiac sign Sagittarius. You don't have to be an especially religious person to believe that there's a higher purpose to life. You might seek it in the pursuit of knowledge, serving the common good, or by helping people to realize their own hidden potential. Jupiter rules justice, philosophy, and wisdom. These aren't abstract principles to you. You believe that they are there to lift our sights so that we can look past the limits and contemplate the possibilities. But you're not into searching for new and clever ways to bring these higher principles down to earth. You believe that people already have a pretty clear idea of what's good for them. When you're a Child of Saturn with Jupiter strong, you will devote yourself to the infinitely more arduous task of lifting the earth up to the level of these principles.

Oftentimes doing what's right doesn't square with other people's idea of the right thing to do. And you may even have paid the price—especially when you were younger—by parting company with a loved one, a circle of friends, or even a job because of a clash of values. But you won't get a chance to make your corner of the world a better place if you keep breaking up or getting canned. At some point you need to turn the tables. And the best way to reverse the equation is by tapping into your Jupiter side.

"If you can't beat 'em, join 'em" is Jupiter's m.o. It may sound like taking the easy way out, but prospects automatically improve once you get yourself inside that closed door you keep banging your head against. As a Child of Saturn, you're predisposed to living *without*. Jupiter is all about working *with*. Its creative process is based on weaving something into what's already in motion. Following your Jupiterian instinct (e.g., developing a potential) allows you to put the horse back where it belongs—in front of the cart. That way, your Saturn side can do what it does best—which is steer and direct.

Because of Saturn's position at the time of your birth, you will go through a number of boom-and-bust cycles. As a Child of Saturn you can't help but learn things the hard way. Thankfully, Jupiter is the Planet of fortune—which means you will always land on your feet. No matter how rough things get, you will find your way through to

WITH SATURN IN SAGITTARIUS

the other side. After the age of forty, things work themselves out and fortunes solidify. At this point you will probably find your way to being part of a larger organization—so that you're not just some lone voice in the wilderness. Jupiter likes to do things big, and the sorts of causes you take on are simply too enormous for one person to handle alone. But you won't fade into the woodwork. Your Saturn side is too conscientious—and your judgment calls are too savvy—for that to happen. You may never see all your hopes realized—after all, the world can always be improved—but you will see how important and valuable your contributions are. And that will be worth all the hard work that goes into them.

Money is an important ingredient in what you do, and in order to generate it, you'll need to be on good terms with backers and clients. Therefore your best times of year are mid-March through April, mid-July through August, and mid-November through December. This is when resources are flush and you'll be able to tap them without having to go through a song and dance. However, these periods may often coincide with you feeling down or just not up to the task at hand. Part of this is the way your psychic clock is put together, and part of it results from the natural ambivalence you feel about turning to anyone for help. You may never resolve that for yourself, but one look at all the good you do in your life should be enough to settle any qualms you may have.

CHILD OF SATURN . . .

Saturn rules the zodiac sign Capricorn. You Children of Saturn with Saturn in Capricorn are quite familiar with the weight of the world (you've carried it on your shoulders often enough) and secretly pride yourself on your ability to withstand punishment. Few people have experienced so many ups and downs. But rather than dispirit you, your travails empower you. An accomplishment just isn't worth it unless you can point out all the blood, sweat, and tears you poured into it. Although you preach the gospel of work and will underscore the value of prudent investments and safe choices, there's still a part of you that enjoys wrestling with the angels.

Fear is a driving force for you. But living in Job-like terror gets old. Life for you Children of Saturn with Saturn strong changes once you begin to rethink a couple of fundamental questions. The first is: how can people who don't spend a fraction of the time you do fretting make it to the top with hardly a gray hair? Secondly: how is it you can work as hard as you do and still not have much to show for it? These sober yet telling realizations pop up sometime in your thirties and again in your sixties. These are the times when you realize that too much fear is as foolhardy as too much bravado. And that in your effort to master every single detail you can lose the forest for the trees. Thankfully you were born under an extremely pragmatic Planet. You may never get over your fears and anxieties (and why should you—they're the things that prod you on to do the great things that you do), but when you realize that there's a difference between working hard and working hard at working hard, then your outlook changes dramatically. Ironically you learn that you get further when you don't fuss as much.

It only took a few years in childhood for you to don that psychic armor you wear so tightly. But it will take most of your adult life to remove it— and even then it only comes off one piece at a time. Nevertheless you have an extraordinary ability to inspire loyalty and support. You know what it's like to do grunt work, and that makes you instantly recognizable to people who have faced similar obstacles. You never get cocky. And though you will experience great success in whatever you choose to do, you never forget where you came from.

WITH SATURN IN CAPRICORN

Because of Saturn's position at the time of your birth, your father casts a long shadow over your life. Getting his approval wasn't easy, and this might have colored many of your relationships with authority. Instead of trying to win a boss's approval, you may have cultivated an air of indifference in order to show you didn't really need it. Your Birthday Planet hides what it perceives to be a weak spot—little knowing that it often does it too well. As you grow older you may be surprised to learn that your father doesn't have the same view of your relationship with him as you do. In fact he may have simply been too preoccupied with matters of his own. This can get a little complicated, because you may have needed to feel rejected in order to go the extra distance. However you don't have to stick with that point of view. Debunking it won't bring down your whole raison d'être. It may even bring peace to a side of you that's been restless for too long.

The summer and winter solstices (around June 21 and December 21) are important. These are your turning points, when you're just rounding the bend or getting over the hump. Circumstances feel like they're finally under control. The spring and autumnal equinoxes, however, are more "dramatic." These are the times when the most unlikely things happen and you're never quite certain if you're going to be experiencing a breakthrough or a breakdown. Romance has less to do with the seasons and more to do with where you feel you are in your life. If you're feeling too vulnerable, things won't really come together. But if you're feeling confident, then your love life will blossom. You don't like relying on others and feel most comfortable when they can lean on you.

CHILD OF SATURN...

Saturn, Planet of the material plane, and Uranus, Planet of the immaterial one, both rule the zodiac sign Aquarius. When you're a Child of Saturn with these two locked in a continuous tug-of-war (your Saturn side striving to establish the bottom line while your Uranus side explores *all* of the possibilities) then you are accustomed to living life in fits and starts. You may go through slow periods where you're forced to struggle, only to experience a big breakthrough overnight that redefines everything you do. You may go from one short-lived job to the next before realizing that they can all be combined into one, creating the dream career you've been looking for. Uranian energy always gives a flash of pure brilliance. Unfortunately these insights aren't that consistent or predictable, which leads your Saturn side to not depend on them too much. Nevertheless you have to make allowances for their surprise appearances and be ready to accommodate them—like unexpected guests—at a moment's notice.

Things always happen to you in twos. First comes an event—like buying a wonderful piece of property or going on a fantastic date—and then comes the "twist." Usually it's some sort of chaotic element thrown in out of nowhere or an unforeseen string attached that winds up testing both your dedication and your ingenuity. Most people can't cope with this roller-coaster ride on the wheel of fortune. But being a Child of Saturn, you are no stranger to setbacks. Indeed, you've learned to cultivate your own special blend of wariness and appreciation for the absurd. More often than not, if something falls through it's because there's something better that's on its way.

Saturn's position at the time you were born shows you will never be at loose ends for long. Despite all the upheavals in your life, you're actually very good at finding stable situations. But just because a situation looks conventional doesn't necessarily mean that the people connected to it are. You enjoy fraternizing with maverick types—people who don't fit in with the mainstream set of expectations. You yourself may have flirted with an "alternative" lifestyle when you were younger, but after a while you would have grown annoyed with its limited means. You want to work—to

WITH SATURN IN AQUARIUS

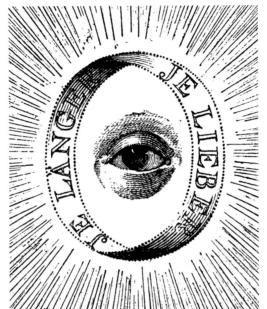

make things happen. You thrive in a group atmosphere. Uranus rules groups of people—from labor unions to bowling leagues. Like the stars that make up a single constellation, a group or corporation shines only as brightly as the people who form it. This appeals to your Uranian side—which enjoys politics and politicking—as well as your Saturn side, which wants to do *important* things. Your knack for handling chaos makes you the ideal bridge between powerfully creative personalities and the dreams they want to realize.

As a Child of Saturn with both Saturn and Uranus strong, you will be drawn to positions that sit at the hub of activity. You may supervise a number of projects, manage different departments, or be the person in charge of coordinating everyone so that they work cohesively as a team. You're not quite the big boss (you don't want a figurehead position, you need constant stimulus) nor are you one of many "chiefs" (you don't want anyone going over your head). It's a pretty good bet that what you do evolved naturally from a number of different activities and may be custom-made for the company you work for. There's always something traditional yet up-to-date about your Birthday Planet and Uranus.

Your best times of year are late January through February, late May through June, and late September through October. These are the times when you can switch back and forth between Saturn's need for structure and conformity and Uranus's insistence that you try something new. During the other months of the year you may tend to be a little too controlling while everyone else is acting nutty or vice versa. This may be especially true during late July and August, when you're apt to feel at cross-purposes. Thankfully these Planetary energies are too dynamic to leave you hanging, and even though nothing goes off without a hitch, you can always count on all the twists and turns to work themselves out in the end.

CHILD OF SATURN . . .

Jupiter, Planet of the spirit, and Neptune, Planet of the psyche, both rule the zodiac sign Pisces. These may sound similar, but they're actually quite different. Jupiter has always been associated with that higher power at work in our lives. Its zeal empowers you. All you need is to *believe* and you can make just about anything happen in life. Neptune rules the realm of the imagination and illusion. It represents that dream of a perfect world that exists within every one of us and which we constantly seek in our hopes and wishes. When you're a Child of Saturn with Jupiter and Neptune strong, it's up to you to make something concrete out of these extraordinary forces. You have more belief and imagination than anyone could ask for, but along with these come doubts and a pervading sense of futility and hopelessness. You often wonder if you have what it takes to make your dreams a reality. And if they do materialize, what's to keep them from dissolving again? Spurred on by your vision of the way things *could* be, it's hard for you to recognize the beauty in your own handiwork.

Many artists are driven by a vision or a compulsion to create. They feverishly try to capture this on their canvases or in their writing, dance, or music. More often than not, they're left feeling dissatisfied—either because they feel that they fell short of what they were after, or if they exceed expectations, they're afraid that the best work they'll ever do is behind them. Although the artist may not know it, what he or she leaves behind is an extraordinary body of work. The painting a painter can't stand to look at anymore may be a masterpiece, or that book a writer fears is a flash in the pan may be a classic that readers never tire of returning to time and time again. As a Child of Saturn with Jupiter and Neptune strong, you may carry a similar blind spot when it comes to assessing the work you do. Continually frustrated by all the unrealized possibilities, you may never treasure what you do as much as others will. This is why it's so important for you to accept their gratitude and appreciation. Belief in yourself is rooted in their belief in you.

Saturn's position at the time of your birth shows you will eventually rise to the top of your profession. Given your Jupiter zeal and Neptun-

WITH SATURN IN PISCES

ian empathy, you may be in charge of others who look to you for leadership, inspiration, or to intervene on their behalf. But you need to be careful, because if you are too dismissive of your merits (or forthcoming with your insecurities) then others may take advantage of your openness. That's why your Saturn side will seek to rein in those Jupiter impulses to make jokes at your own expense and that Neptunian tendency to commiserate a bit too deeply. You don't want to saddle yourself with the expectation that you always have something to show for your efforts either, or you will lose touch with your imaginative side. You have to allow yourself the flexibility and freedom to make mistakes and to stumble upon those accidental discoveries that you would never have found otherwise.

Late September through November is a wonderful time for you. This is when you feel most inspired and motivated. Subsequently you may feel like you're at your lowest ebb in July and August. This is when you're apt to fall prey to frustrations and anxieties. Be careful about giving in to self-defeating tendencies. Neptune is "otherworldly" by nature. It doesn't feel a strong allegiance to this world and thinks nothing of walking out on a job or commitment. Thankfully Saturn makes you honor your obligations, so that if you do decide to pull up stakes, you'll leave through the front door and not down the back stairs. Late February through March is your most romantic time of year. This is when you can expect to meet someone you'll bond with on a deep and profound level.

CHILD OF URANUS . . .

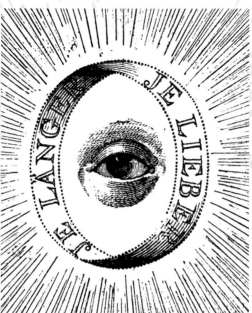

Mars rules the zodiac sign Aries. You Children of Uranus with Uranus in Aries have penetrating minds and indomitable wills. You won't accept no for an answer if you think you deserve better. Little things like a waiting list, proper credentials, or the fact that the person you're infatuated with is already attached will never stand in your way. You reach your objective through sheer force of personality. Given your relentlessness and drive, it's very hard for anyone to resist you. However there is often a telling difference between what you see and what you get. What you end up with rarely matches the ideal you had in mind. Yet being a Child of Uranus with Mars strong, you will always stand by your commitments. Instead of dropping a disappointment like a hot potato, you will struggle to make the best of the situation. And this is when the *real* adventure in your life begins.

You could probably save yourself a lot of trouble if you looked before you leaped. But that's not Mars's style. Mars, the Planet of gumption and drive, would rather be *in* the game than cooling its heels on the sidelines. It's that part of you that just

knows you can single-handedly turn things around for the better if given half a chance. And considering your spirit and determination: who would argue? A cautious approach to life doesn't really fit your Birthday Planet's profile either. As a Child of Uranus, you don't put much faith in a "right" answer. You trust that there is a higher design at work in everything you do, and because you believe that its scope dwarfs your ability to understand it, you're willing to live with a certain suspension of disbelief when it comes to upheavals and setbacks. After all, what's to say they might not turn out to be blessings in disguise? It's this kind of open-mindedness and resourcefulness that allows you to make the most of every opportunity that comes your way.

When you're a Child of Uranus with Mars strong, then "accidents" happen all the time. You've bumped into so many walls that you're probably on a first-name basis with them by now. But along with the garden-variety accidents come the happy ones as well. Chance meetings, unlikely coincidences, and surprise windfalls are commonplace. Which only validates what you

WITH URANUS IN ARIES

already believe to be true—if you don't really know how something's going to turn out, it's best to say yes to everything and *not* to make any assumptions, especially negative ones.

Because of Uranus's position at the time of your birth, you are drawn to communications, design, and the pursuit of knowledge. But it has to be done in your own way and on your own terms. The Mars side of you wants something to push against while your Uranian side needs to shake off what it perceives to be blinders. This may have led you to rebel against certain rules and disciplines when you were younger. But given your Ruling Planet's turn-of-the-wheel nature, it wouldn't be surprising if you find your way back to these very same belief systems when you're older. Acceptance, however, doesn't come with the knowledge that they were right all along. Acceptance comes with you hav-

ing acquired the necessary experience and skills to make them your own.

Late March through mid-April, late July through August, and November through December are dynamic times of the year for you. These are the months when you feel most in sync with events and that your life has direction. Late September through October and the first half of January are when you feel like you're wandering or even at loose ends. It doesn't help that this is when others' concerns weigh heaviest on you, and you often have to wait for them to get their acts together before you can get on with whatever it is you need to do. It's best not to push during these times of year, as you're apt to upset them, which will only result in more delays. Go blow off steam at the gym. Physical exertion always relaxes you and clears the mind.

CHILD OF URANUS...

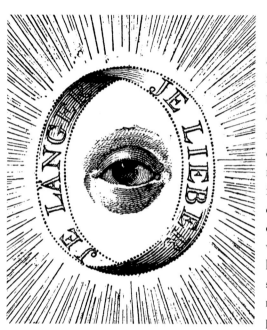

Venus rules the zodiac sign Taurus. You Children of Uranus with Uranus in Taurus have distinctive tastes, colorful opinions, and naturally think you're on to something that everyone else should know about. Many people consider trends and fashions to be fickle and silly. Why invest anything in these fly-by-night, what's-here-today-is-gone-tomorrow whims? But that's not how you see things. Given your Birthday Planet's penchant for foresight, you can see that what's here today might be gone tomorrow, but then—what's to say it won't come back again next year? Whoever influences public opinion is ultimately the person who can direct the values of a society. And where values go, money and power are sure to follow. But you understand that there's only so much lecturing, proselytizing, and finger waving that people can take. As a Child of Uranus with Venus strong, you know that a spoonful of sugar makes the medicine go down.

One could look at today's pop culture and see nothing more than shallow, sensational entertainment aimed at the couch-potato set. But look a little closer, and you see suburban kids learning about the plight of their inner-city counterparts through rap and hip-hop, and life-*threatening* illnesses becoming the cause for life-*affirming* marathons. For you nothing is cheap or frivolous; everything has some level of value. Regardless of whether you're motivated by fun and profit or a transcendent vision of how to make the world a better place, as a Child of Uranus with Venus strong, your medium (whatever it may be) is your means to an end; it's your way of getting the word out there.

If not for Venus, you might voice whatever comes to mind and not really care if people take it or leave it. Venus is, at her core, a *social* Planet, which means that there's a side to you that wants to connect to people, and so you will make the necessary adjustments (or compromises) to ensure that you do. This need of yours to connect is also mirrored in many of your relationships. Though you may cultivate the appearance and demeanor of a maverick and a renegade, you'll be drawn to people who are more traditional and perhaps even conservative in their outlook and dress. Subsequently if you tend to be formulaic in what you do, you may have a talent for spotting

WITH URANUS IN TAURUS

original and innovative personalities. At first glance your choice of love interest or business partner may seem wildly incongruous, but for relatives and friends who know you, they understand that you're looking for someone not only to balance your energies, but also to help you stay in touch with the world around you.

As a Child of Uranus, you have no compunction about knocking over whatever's in place. Uranus *is* the Planet of revolution and change after all. However, because of Uranus's position at the time of your birth, you must then replace what you uprooted or debunked. Venus insists that you create something out of the rubble. You are, in your heart, a builder.

Late winter through midspring is an excellent quarter for you. Not only do ideas spring fully hatched from your head, but you also immediately see how to put them to work. Because Venus is powerful during these months, you should have no trouble securing the sponsorship or clientele for what you want. August through November is more dubious. This is when every step forward results in three steps back. Although still progress (after a fashion), it's not the kind you like or want. Nevertheless curb the impulse to do something radical—like scrap what you're working on. Persevere and know that circumstances will straighten themselves out as you approach December.

CHILD OF URANUS...

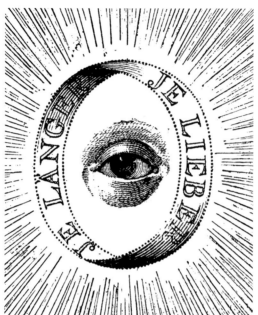

Mercury rules the zodiac sign Gemini. When you're a Child of Uranus with Uranus in Gemini, then your mental wheels turn twenty-four hours a day. You are always processing information, experimenting with new ideas, and contemplating their many possibilities, so it's a wonder you can sleep at all. Mentally and physically restless, you're always on the go.

Change is ingrained in both Planets, but there is a difference. Mercury rules over the changes that take place *now*. Subsequently it symbolizes *ephemeral* information. For instance today's weather or market figures are the sort of "up-to-the-minute" information that's important in the present moment. But once that moment has passed, it's practically useless. After all, who really cares about what the weather was like three days ago? Your Birthday Planet, however, rules over changes that take place in the grand scheme of things. The Planet of revolution, it symbolizes upheavals, but rectifications, too. Like a gyroscope it keeps your day-to-day life on track and up-to-date with the workings of the higher plan. When you're a Child of Uranus with Mercury powerful, you live with this split focus between what's happening in the moment and how you see it all playing out in the big picture. In some ways this makes you uncannily prescient. It can also lead you to trip over your own feet.

Mercury rules the mind as well as the tricks that the mind can play. You're able to follow the line of logic in just about any conversation, and possess the wherewithal to question even your own thought process. Mercury is both cerebral and street-smart, which is why it's the shrewdest of all the Planets. It would be nice if your own Ruling Planet were as flexible (or adaptable) in its thinking, but it tends to be relentless in its pursuit of the truth—as well as adamantly refusing to bend it in the least. If you're a Child of Uranus with Mercury strong, then this can lead to some dramatically mixed results. There's a tendency to misjudge some situations, so that instead of being on top of the game, you wind up holding the smoking gun or waving a red flag in front of a stampeding herd.

Mercury and Uranus love controversy. Your Mercury side enjoys a good debate, and your Uranus side believes that any difference of

WITH URANUS IN GEMINI

opinion carries the potential for insight. This is why you are drawn to media and writing, as well as politics. Whether a professional or amateur speaker, you love a good soapbox. Unfortunately what both Planetary energies fail to take into account is how volatile people's feelings and reactions can get when stirred up. Not everyone shares your high regard for free speech or embraces argument as a form of vigorous intellectual exercise. Not only will some people take offense, but they might even get quite forceful about putting you in your place. Being a Child of Uranus, you won't take this sitting down. Before you know it, you can find yourself becoming the cause célèbre rather than the person commenting on it.

Because of Uranus's position at the time of your birth, you will always find safe passage through the storm—no matter how bad things get. You have Mercury, the pathfinder, to thank for

this. Since controversy will always be a part of your life, you need to be careful about the kinds of people you attract. They might mistake you for a troublemaker or a rabble-rouser, when in truth you're not. You don't like heated debates. Luckily you tend to form intimate attachments to people who make good chaperones.

Your own birthday month is a marvelous time of year. This is always a galvanizing period for you and is excellent for doing heavy mental work. Late May through mid-June as well as September and October are also invigorating. But you want to be careful during April, August, and December. This is when people are on edge, and one incendiary remark from you is all it takes to provoke a hullabaloo. By no means muzzle your opinions. Just remember that there's a difference between intellectual exchanges that inspire and taking part in a verbal Punch-and-Judy show.

CHILD OF URANUS...

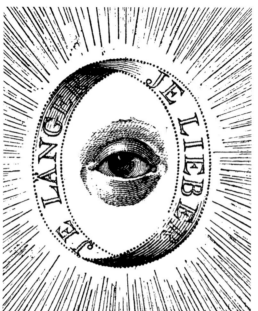

The Moon rules the zodiac sign Cancer. As a Child of Uranus with Uranus in Cancer, you run the full range of emotions in a fraction of the time it takes most people to experience just one. When first meeting someone you can instantly tell if you want that person in your life or not, which friend you'll form a lasting bond with, and who will inevitably turn out to be a disappointment. Many people might question how you can possibly *know* these things. What makes you so sure that you aren't just superimposing your initial impressions—creating a sort of self-fulfilling prophecy—rather than giving yourself a chance to get to know someone? The Moon is an extraordinary barometer when it comes to reading people's inner nature. Ruler of the unconscious, the Moon gives you an instinctual sense for what lies behind the facade. Given that your own Birthday Planet has a pretty strong grasp on how things will play out in the long run, these two make a formidable pair. This is what makes you such a good judge of character—and why you will excel at anything that engages people psychologically, whether it's fiction writing or working in human

resources. If there's a misstep, it won't be the result of you being taken by surprise. It will be because you didn't heed your instincts in the first place.

However this ability to jump ahead of the game—to anticipate how someone is going to act (or react)—doesn't make life easy. You're still a person, after all, with feelings, needs, and desires that take place in real time and not on fast-forward time. What that means is you're going to have to find a way to reconcile the bird's-eye view of life with the one you live on a daily basis. It's not unlike the difference between reading a book and scanning the plot synopsis. Just because you can recount what happens doesn't mean you've absorbed the ambiance or even know why the characters make the choices they do. Every story has its dimensions. Foresight isn't the same as experience. There's only one way to gain experience, and that's by living your life. Even if something still doesn't turn out the way you expect, chances are you'll be enriched by the episode, not deprived.

Because of Uranus's position at the time of your birth, it's unlikely that you were raised in a "typical" home. Your early life probably took

WITH URANUS IN CANCER

some peculiar twists. You and your mother may have been separated (physically or even psychologically) for a period of time, or someone other than she might have raised you. This would have had a strong influence on the way you form attachments. The Moon is the Planet of the family, roots, and tradition; Uranus is the Planet of upheaval and change. Yet when you're a Child of Uranus with the Moon powerful, a family is whatever you make of it. Blood ties don't really matter all that much to you. You can form intimate bonds with people from wildly different backgrounds, and it wouldn't be unusual for you to eventually settle halfway across the world from where you were born.

There can be a split between your mind (Uranus) and your body (the Moon). As a Child of Uranus, it's easy to rise above what you're feeling and even shut it out. Yet the body has its own way of registering when something's amiss. You need to pay attention to what it has to say because you don't want to be sideswiped by an illness or condition that you could have prevented if you had simply heeded your body's signals.

Since your Ruling Planet was retrograde when you were born, it only makes sense for the opposite times of year to be the best for you. Therefore the summer is when you feel most comfortable with yourself physically and emotionally. Your own birthday month may not be particularly good. Indeed you can swing between extremes of feeling agitated and nervous to drowsy and apathetic. Keeping yourself physically fit and active is a surefire way to balance these mood shifts. You have a special rapport with Children of the Sun, Moon, and Mercury.

CHILD OF URANUS...

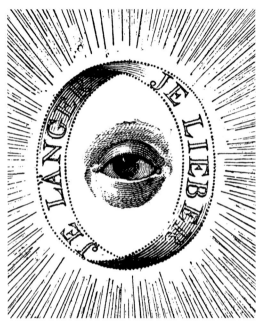

The Sun rules the zodiac sign Leo. When you're a Child of Uranus with Uranus in Leo, then you know you make *all* the difference. This isn't an ego thing. It's an *energy* thing—like an engine or a battery. You don't have to do anything to stand out. You just do. The strength of your convictions motivates people. You smile, and everyone laughs. You look perplexed, and colleagues fall over themselves searching for what went wrong. If you believe something can be done, others will want to make it happen—just on the power of your say-so.

Life would be so much easier if you really were a Child of the Sun. You would be perfectly comfortable with all this. However you are a Child of Uranus, which means that you just can't help feeling a bit—inauthentic. The difference between the Sun and Uranus is like the difference between one star and a sky full of constellations. This tension between Big Picture (Uranus) and Big Personality (Sun) is something you struggle with your entire life.

As a Child of Uranus, you have a vision of the way things play out in the greater scheme of things. But where other Uranian Children are content just knowing there's a higher order to the events in their lives, you can't help but wonder what would happen if you were to change this or get rid of that. When you're a Child of Uranus with the Sun strong, then you want to do something with that enormous personality you've been given. The Sun gives you the confidence (some might even say audacity) to turn those ideas of yours into reality. You know that nothing innovative will ever be reached by consensus. It's takes the power of one personality—an individual vision—to make it happen.

Yet your Solar side, which naturally sees itself as the center of its Universe, isn't all that comfortable with your Uranian side. Uranus's Big Picture can be a bit too broad and impersonal. It doesn't take into account the personal triumphs and the crowning glories. Stellar moments tend to lose their luster when judged according to their historical significance or lasting impact. The Sun, generator of heat and light, wants to feel connected to life, to stand out in a crowd—not apart from it or out of reach.

This need to stay in touch can lead to some

WITH URANUS IN LEO

curious twists in your life, where you will actually slow (or perhaps even work against) your own progress. If your Solar side feels like you're losing touch with the things that matter to you *personally* (like a relationship, your home life, or the way you're used to seeing yourself), then it will slam on the brakes. This won't be a conscious choice but will take the form of a misguided business decision, a peculiar choice of partner, or simply turning left when you should have gone right. This is your way of moderating your speed until you feel that you've grown into this new thing you're asking of yourself.

Because of Uranus's position at the time of your birth, you will experience a major change of direction when you reach middle age. If you've been struggling, you'll suddenly arrive. If you've been career and/or relationship hopping, you'll find what you're looking for and settle down. Conversely, you could also discover that the lifestyle you thought you wanted no longer has any value—causing you to pull up stakes and try something new. This is most likely to happen if you feel like you've become a "big fish in a small pond." As a Child of Uranus with the Sun powerful, you need to feel that the best is yet to come. You were born under the Planet of progress, and the Sun believes that it is continually rising and evolving.

Because you were born when your Birthday Planet was retrograde, summer is the season when you thrive. Indeed January and February may be when you feel most at cross-purposes or like you're being pressured to make decisions before you're ready. Yet six months after your birthday things couldn't be clearer. August is a very romantic time. Instead of weighing pros and cons, you'll have no problem getting right to the heart of the matter.

CHILD OF URANUS...

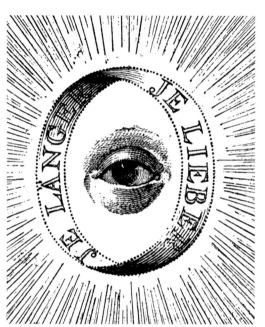

Mercury, the Planet of speed and skill, rules the zodiac sign Virgo. When you're a Child of Uranus with Uranus in Virgo you think quick and act faster. Mercury rules the mind as well as the five senses, so mental and physical reflexes are already heightened. Add your Birthday Planet to the mix and it's everything you can do to sit still long enough to hear what someone wants. Although you always appear nonchalant, behind that cool facade mental processes are already busy working out the quickest way to do what's being asked while dropping off your dry cleaning, picking up something for dinner, checking in on the kids, and getting back to the office before your boss even knows you're gone. You were built for multitasking. You can get three times as much done in the time it takes most people to just get started. Indeed, you can't think straight unless you have a number of things all pressing at the same time.

Thoughts fly in and out of your head so rapidly that you're lucky if you can remember half of them. This accounts for that mildly distracted, preoccupied air. In mid-sentence you may hesitate when speaking or suddenly forget what you were talking about. This may even have been misunderstood as a learning problem when you were younger, because of your tendency to read ahead or transpose words or numbers just to see how they'd work combined differently. However, for all your inventiveness, you need to find a constructive way to harness those remarkable mental powers. But that won't happen as a result of you trying to slow down or even focus on just one thing at a time. Your Ruling Planet was retrograde when you were born, which means that your approach is going to have to be as unorthodox as the thinking itself.

When you're a Child of Uranus Retrograde with Mercury strong, then interruptions are a daily occurrence. It's almost as if you were born with a psychic buzzer that keeps telling you to drop what you're doing and come tend to something totally unrelated. Most people automatically shut out distractions. You, however, do your best problem solving when your mind is focused on something utterly different. You can be right in the middle of adding up a column of numbers (or even ordering lunch) when the mental clouds will

WITH URANUS IN VIRGO

suddenly part—revealing the answer you've been looking for. Of course you only have seconds to jot it down before it disappears again. That's why it's best to always keep your Palm Pilot handy.

As you can imagine, all this activity can run you ragged. And it does. Both Mercury and Uranus are "mental" Planets, which means that when they're on-line, you're up and running. And when they're off-line, you're left to collapse into an exhausted heap. Just as you need to be kept busy with a number of activities (if you're not, you become high-strung), you also need to factor your physical needs into the equation. You may have to make a mental note to eat (even if you're not feeling hungry) and sleep (even if you're not tired). The body has its up-and-down cycles, too, and those won't always correspond to your mental ones.

Because of Uranus's position at the time of your birth, you may have dual careers, or succeed in one business, opt for early retirement, and then come back to succeed again in a totally different field. You have a knack for marketing and do very well with parlaying finances into fortunes. However, given Uranus's nature, you can expect a lot of dips and rises. Also inheritances figure strongly in your life—whether it's money, property, or simply taking over a position left vacant by someone else.

As a Child of Uranus Retrograde, the summer, rather than the winter, will be the best time of year for you. But don't expect to get much work done. Indeed, because you're constantly working at a breakneck pace, the summer is when you can finally catch up on your personal life. Although you enjoy lounging around the pool as much as the next person, that idyll only lasts so long before you get antsy. Thankfully loved ones and friends are always game for whatever you have in mind.

CHILD OF URANUS...

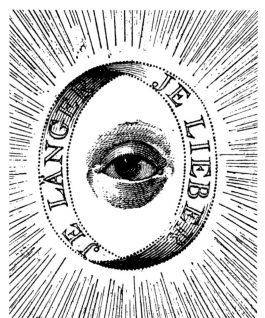

Venus, the Planet of love and beauty, rules the zodiac sign Libra. When you're a Child of Uranus with Uranus in Libra, then your ideals rule your heart. You have such strong views of what's attractive, how everyone should get along, and what would constitute the "perfect" existence that anything less just won't cut it. As far as you're concerned, the reason why the world is in such a sorry state is because everyone's grown so accustomed to quick fixes that they've stopped demanding anything of quality from society—or themselves. Expectations have naturally been defined by the lowest common denominator because there are always so many more failures to point to than successes. But where would our civilization be if we settled for (or even applauded) the cheap, the disposable, and the convenient? As a Child of Uranus with Venus strong, you are guided by the desire for something better.

Venus is more than the Planet of elegance and refinement. She also rules relationships. This creates an interesting dichotomy, because on one hand she stimulates those pristine ideals of yours—Venus rules over the "right" schools, high society, and $5,000-a-plate dinners, so she can be quite elitist—yet Venus is also the very agency that brings you into contact with people with whom you wouldn't usually associate. Your Venus side needs to feel *connected*, so it will naturally seek a counterbalance by attracting people who will disagree with your views, introduce ideas of their own, and maybe even prevail upon you to question some familiar assumptions. This creates a kind of psychic symmetry, because without that Venusian side, you might be very uncompromising—perhaps even militant in your approach. Needless to say, the parade of colorful personalities in and out of your life can get very interesting.

Because of Uranus's position at the time of your birth, you will be drawn to the public arena. Venus is an arbiter of taste, so it makes sense for you to pursue a career in public relations, fashion, advertising, publishing, or popular entertainment. However, Venus has an equally strong political knack. You might consider running for office, but it's more likely that you would work for a special interest group that's responsible for

WITH URANUS IN LIBRA

shaping public opinion. You could just as easily lobby for big business, as you could sound the clarion call for social reform. It all depends on the message you want to send.

You yourself may not always be clear on what that message is supposed to be. Just because you can see the ideal doesn't mean you have the necessary means to make it happen. Moreover, because Venus rules partnerships, you won't get as far on your own steam as you would by joining forces with someone else. Your huge successes, big breaks, and giant leaps forward will be due, in part, to the efforts of other people. There will always be some kind of a trade-off involved. And sometimes that trade-off may require you to stand behind things that don't exactly measure up to your standards of excellence.

Although your Venus side wants to feel connected and accepted, you are still a Child of Uranus—which means there will be periods when everything you believe to be fair and good is suddenly turned on its head. Your Birthday Planet keeps you from getting too "agreeable." Just as your Venus side keeps you connected to people, your Uranian side keeps you independent. Whenever you're on the verge of lapsing into docility, you can always rely on a bolt out of the blue to upset some of those alliances that have gotten a bit too "political."

Your own birthday month, as well as late May through mid-June and late September through mid-October are wonderful times of year for you. These are the months when those glistening ideals of yours are in easy reach. But act on them, because late June through early September are when they could disappear just as quickly. The month before your own birthday is also a time when you want to be especially careful. The rest of the year is spent either preparing for big to-dos or recovering from them. Given how single-minded you can get during your "peak" seasons, you'll be grateful for the more civilized pace.

CHILD OF URANUS...

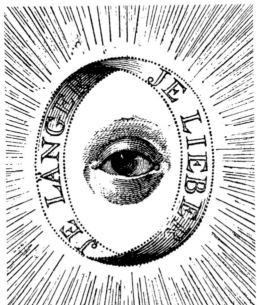

Mars, Planet of gumption and drive, and Pluto, Planet of obsession, both rule the zodiac sign Scorpio. When you're a Child of Uranus with Uranus in Scorpio then you are a unique blend of passion and disinterest. There are times when you will take things *very* personally (Mars loves to act in the heat of the moment, while Pluto relies on insults and slights to fuel its willpower), and then there are times when you let the most difficult things simply wash right over you. Not only do you remain coolly focused under the most extraordinary pressures, but you also have the remarkable ability to keep on going, even if your body is past the point of exhaustion. You know what you want and you won't stop until you get it.

When Mars and Pluto set their sights on a goal they will pursue it to the ends of the earth. It could be the love of your life or righting a terrible wrong—it doesn't really much matter. Your own Birthday Planet rules ideals—those perfect models of truth, beauty, and justice that lie eternally beyond our grasp. In a sense, there is no *real* end to be reached. The pursuit could go on ad infinitum.

Given that Mars and Pluto would rather chase than catch, you could find yourself going from one infatuation to another (or one outrage to the next) without ever getting satisfaction. Then again, given the turn-of-the-wheel character of your Birthday Planet, you may be constantly bedeviled by near misses or last-minute reversals.

In some ways this can actually be good. Born under Uranus, the Planet of progress, you need something to strive for, and with Mars and Pluto strong you may be drawn to industries or careers that are constantly reinventing themselves—like technology, scientific research, or athletics. These are never-ending pursuits because one is always striving to outdo what has come before. Every scientific breakthrough will eventually be surpassed by another, in the same way that winning a gold medal sets a new standard for others to measure themselves against as well as a target to shoot for. This drive to outdo even yourself resonates with all three Planetary energies.

Yet for all this, you rarely get what you want. Some might say it's because you're too much of a perfectionist; that nothing but the absolute best

WITH URANUS IN SCORPIO

will do. Uranus's position at the time you were born makes you extremely driven. Perhaps too driven. As soon as you get within reach of what you want, you begin to feel that you don't want it anymore. This is when you do an about-face and go from pursuing to fleeing in the opposite direction. In truth, you may not really want to get what you're after. After all, if you were to get it, then your life would come to a complete stop. And then what would you do with yourself?

But if you don't want to end up like Sisyphus in the Underworld—continually heaving a boulder up to the top of the hill only to watch it slip from his grasp and roll back down to the bottom again—then you need to work out a truce between your passions and your expectations. If you find yourself continually rejecting things like a career, a relationship, or even your social status as "not good enough," then you may have to ask yourself if it's really not good enough, or if rejecting them just keeps you searching.

Your peak time of year is late October through November. Your low point is late April through May. The most important times of year, however, are actually late February through March and late June through July. These are very emotional times, when you will feel softer, weaker, and maybe even a bit lonely. This is very good for you. Acceptance doesn't come easily. Either you adopt a stoic approach (Mars and Pluto) or you take a more "existential" view (which is Uranus and also a bit Pluto as well). The best form of acceptance, however, is the down-to-earth kind. There's nothing wrong with taking the defect with the perfect, the need with the want. Not only does it make you more humane—but it will also do wonders for your love life.

CHILD OF URANUS...

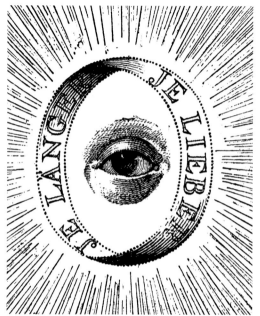

Jupiter, Planet of long journeys, rules the zodiac sign Sagittarius. When you're a Child of Uranus with Uranus in Sagittarius, then you're a restless spirit. This doesn't necessarily mean you're fond of travel. In fact you may be very attached to your daily routine. However Jupiter and Uranus are both Planets that like to paint on a larger canvas. Jupiter symbolizes the world beyond your doorstep, and Uranus symbolizes the big picture we know is always there but that we can only comprehend in stages. At some point you will either outgrow your surroundings or—given the revolutionary nature of your Birthday Planet—your surroundings may send you packing. When you're a Child of Uranus with Jupiter strong, you will often feel that there isn't just one place to call your own, that you are indeed a true "citizen of the world."

What others might regard as a calamity, you consider the first fumbling steps in your adventure. Your Jupiter side believes there's a higher purpose in everything you do. Your Uranian side puts its trust in the workings of the higher plan. You're convinced that there's always an opportu-nity in the changes that life throws your way. You just need to figure out what it is.

However, the experience of being shaken loose from the tree is something that will occur repeatedly at different points in your life—perhaps once every twelve years. It may come as a result of circumstances beyond your control or in the form of a "calling." This is your Ruling Planet's way of saying it's time for you to move on to the next stage of your development. This won't be easy to explain to loved ones and friends, who naturally want you to stay put. Especially since what you're saying is: I can't do what I want here.

Thankfully the Jupiter side of you is good at maintaining relationships as well as forming new ones wherever you go. Jupiter may be the Planet of long journeys, but he's also the Planet of hospitality. One of the most important customs in ancient civilizations was guest-friendship. Guest-friendship was based on the idea that if a stranger showed up at your door or was washed up on the beach tired and hungry, you didn't just toss him into prison or offer him up as sacrifice to the local gods. That was just bad form. What you did was

WITH URANUS IN SAGITTARIUS

invite him inside and treat him like a member of your family. After all, you never know when you yourself might be in need of similar hospitality one day.

Because of Uranus's position at the time you were born, you will find that people automatically trust you. Wherever you go, they will open their doors or take out their pocketbooks. They want to do what they can to help out. But this isn't about taking what you can get where you can get it. You must give something back in return. In the old days it used to be a story or perhaps a secret recipe known only in your part of the world. Nowadays it's apt to be information. When you're a Child of Uranus with Jupiter strong, you may be drawn to professions that "trade" in or exchange information. You yourself may be a gifted interpreter, teacher, or simply the one who came up with the business model or proposal in the first place. Therefore you may be the person who's sent to another division in the company (or perhaps the overseas office) to show them just how things are done back home.

Your best times of year are late March through mid-April, late June through August, and late November through mid-December. These are the months when you feel most animated and inspired. Expect to be very busy, and though it's tempting to let yourself get carried away, don't. You really need to pace yourself so that your energy doesn't flag. Being a Child of Uranus with Jupiter strong, you will also have family concerns to see to. Loved ones will only put up with so much absence before they feel neglected. Those principles of guest-friendship apply to them as well. Make a point of spending extra time with them in February and March.

CHILD OF URANUS...

As a Child of Uranus, you're no stranger to upheaval. Indeed there's a part of you that has no problem starting again from scratch if that's what it takes to bring your life up to speed with the workings of the higher plan. However when you're a Child of Uranus with Uranus in Capricorn, then you have to honor your *other* Ruling Planet—Saturn. Saturn rules the zodiac sign Capricorn, so there's no such thing as starting again from scratch. You must build on what's come before.

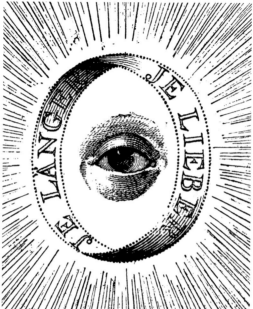

Saturn is the Planet of tradition. It says that no matter how modern or attractive contemporary ideas may be, they stand on the shoulders of history. Knock that down and you lose your foundation. Uranus is the Planet of progress. It regards history as old baggage that prevents us from realizing the best that humanity has to offer by continually reminding us of the worst. Uranus wants nothing more than to rewrite the script so that the outcome is ennobling rather than depressing. You are continually pulled back and forth between these two Planetary impulses. You don't want old ways of doing things to bog down what you've got

in mind, anymore than you want to make a change for change's sake. After all—if it ain't broke, why fix it.

As a Child of Uranus with Saturn strong you are a fierce blend of optimism and angst. Uranian ideals may lift your sights, but it's Saturn's fears that fuel your strengths. You don't like change. Just the thought of it can make your palms sweaty. Whenever you make a change in your life—even if it's altering your daily routine by a hair—you can't help feeling that you've violated some kind of taboo. This stems from a fear of *not* knowing what the rules are and being punished for doing something you didn't know was wrong. This may be a residual effect from a shake-up in the home when you were a child (perhaps you blamed yourself for circumstances that were beyond your control). However given Uranus's position at the time of your birth, it's more likely that there was a disruption in one of your parent's (or even grandparent's) childhoods that got transmitted to you in the form of an abiding anxiety.

Life with Saturn can be like a never-ending game of Simon says, wherein obedience promises advancement. This appeals to the side of you that

WITH URANUS IN CAPRICORN

wants to color inside the lines, dutifully fulfill expectations, and never stray off course. But this doesn't leave much room for personal evolution, independent thinking, and invention—all qualities ruled by Uranus.

Every fourteen years your life goes through an enormous upheaval where everything you believed to be true is turned upside down. These periods are always dramatic, but instead of frightening you, these crises actually *galvanize* you. Catastrophe has the strange effect of making you more courageous. Sometimes things take a turn for the worse. Sometimes they take a turn for the better. Yet it's up to you to maintain a tradition. Maybe you're one of the few who stand by your floundering company while everyone else abandons ship. Or, given Saturn's tendency to rise to positions of leadership, you may have to stand firm on a matter of principle while everyone else pressures you

to yield to the current of events. When you're a Child of Uranus with Saturn strong, you're often thrust into the very revolutionary position of safeguarding values that are considered outmoded or backward. Given the turn-of-the-wheel nature of your Birthday Planet, you know that what looks irrelevant today may be pertinent tomorrow.

Saturn rules the winter, so late December through mid-March is your best time of year. This is when you have a firm grasp on the reins and you are guiding events. The summer season, however, is not so favorable. This is when things work against you and you will encounter more than the usual obstacles and delays. Rather then press on, you would do better to take things at a leisurely pace—or maybe take time off altogether. Given the drive and focus you exhibit during the rest of the year, you could use a breather.

CHILD OF URANUS . . .

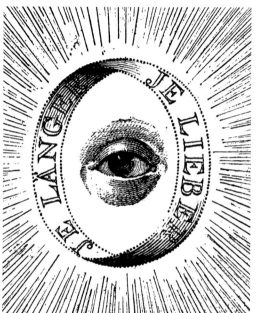

Both Saturn and Uranus rule the zodiac sign Aquarius. This is an extremely volatile and forceful combination, as they happen to also be your Birthday Planets. People enter and exit your life in the blink of an eye. Events fly past in a blur. Decisions are made, unmade, and made again so rapidly that they almost appear to be standing still. It can sometimes feel as if you're riding the buzzer on one of those game show lightning rounds. You don't really have much time to think. You have to trust in your reflexes and hope for the best. And thankfully, more often than not, your reflexes are right.

When you're on, you're on and can see things so clearly. While everyone else stands around scratching their heads, you can connect the dots no one else can visualize and reveal a design where there was only a blank slate. You make the incomprehensible easy to understand. But you don't just carry these ideas around in your head. They were all there to begin with. When you're a Child of Uranus with Uranus strong, then you see everything in life as being interconnected—no matter how obvious or accidental. Indeed you see through-lines crisscrossing all around you. It's why you never dismiss an idea as stupid or harebrained. Just because something doesn't make sense now doesn't mean it won't at some time in the future.

The downside to this kind of brilliance is a chronic impatience with how *long* it takes for people to get a clue. Furthermore you don't have much respect for physical limitations. When you can see things as clearly as you do, then you believe that circumstances should bend to fit the ideal. Ideals shouldn't have to yield to circumstances. Unfortunately that's not how physical reality works—which you often discover for yourself when the resources you were counting on run out, a situation you saw as having infinite potential comes up short, or a boss pulls the plug on your pet project. An unstoppable force is only unstoppable until it encounters its first immovable object.

Because of Uranus's position at the time of your birth, this may be a lesson you have to learn over and over again until you're well into your forties. That may sound like a long time, but given how fast your life moves, you'll be there before

WITH URANUS IN AQUARIUS

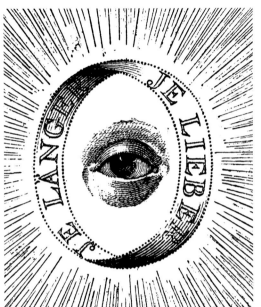

you know it. It's important to remember that though you are committed to serving the universal ideal (this can range from a career in music or science to social reform), you are still human, which means you can get petulant when you don't get your way. This is something that many people will put up with, because you happen to be brilliant. They see how you recognize the greater design at work and can so clearly explain the way things should be. Yet they also see something you don't—which is that for someone who can show others where they fit into the grand scheme of things, you often don't have the slightest idea as to where you belong.

Thankfully Uranus isn't the only Planetary energy at work within you. There's also Saturn. Saturn always turns a fault into a merit, and it's your Saturn side that teaches you to develop a tolerance for the imperfect, because for all your striving and yearning, the imperfect is all you have. You can conceive of the most magnificent ideas in the world, but you'll still be transcribing them with pencils that break and on paper that deteriorates. Instead of looking at life as an exercise in futility, flip the equation on its head and enjoy life for what it is.

Your best times of year are late December through February, late May through June, and all of October. These are the times when you're making those brilliant connections and go from one brainstorm to the next. However you'll have to exercise a different set of mental muscles from late April to mid-May and late August to mid-September. This is when concerns that are more material, like finances and other people's priorities, pop up in the picture. Although it always grates on you to have to divert your focus, these mundane concerns keep both your feet firmly planted on the ground.

CHILD OF URANUS...

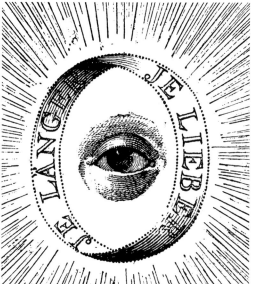

Both Jupiter and Neptune rule the zodiac sign Pisces. You Children of Uranus with Uranus in Pisces possess all the benevolence of Jupiter mixed with the charity of Neptune. But as with your own Birthday Planet combination, these two have a dynamic all their own.

Jupiter is the Planet of philanthropy. It believes that each of us possesses all the resources and abilities necessary to make the world a better place. All we need to do is develop our potential. Named after the god of hospitality and justice, Jupiter symbolizes that part of the human spirit that believes there's a place at the table for everyone. Help your fellow man and you help yourself.

Neptune has a different worldview. The Planet of empathy and self-sacrifice, Neptune relates more to the have-nots. Not everyone starts out in life on an equal footing. Many are hampered by physical or economic handicaps. It's nice to believe that people should be given a seat at the table—but whose table is it anyway? And why can't everyone be free to make their own tables? Neptune believes that the best way to service humanity is to get away from the table

altogether and to give of oneself.

The pull between doing good *by* people and doing good *for* them infuses just about every one of your relationships. And being a Child of Uranus, you're naturally going to have your own unique take on this. Though you may not face such global concerns as figuring out the politics of humanitarian aid or deciding when to intervene in another government's affairs, you will face similarly complicated issues on a more intimate scale, such as: is it right to stand by a loved one who you don't feel is making the right choice? Or do you pipe up and risk alienating this person? How far do you go to help a friend who's on a downward spiral? Or does this person have to bottom out before things can get better?

In many ways, Uranus's position at the time you were born has prepared you for navigating moral dilemmas. You yourself are no stranger to calamity. You've weathered many a boom-and-bust cycle—most likely when you were younger. You're used to packing up your things in a hurry. You take life one day at a time. Perhaps it's because things never felt that secure to begin with

WITH URANUS IN PISCES

that you shied away from forming certain expectations. When something falls apart in your life, you don't ask yourself what the meaning of it all is. You look for a way to land on your feet.

As a Child of Uranus, you place your trust in a higher order. Born under the Planet of progress, you are predisposed to seeing the future as a better place. It doesn't matter if you fail to understand the higher purpose (or don't even much like it), you still believe that whatever happens is for the best. Everything will work out in the end. You take the long view. Subsequently it may be hard to convince the people in your life how much you care. You do care—and very deeply. But you won't wring your hands over every disappointment or pound your chest in grief. Your brand of compassion isn't for everyone. Indeed it may strike some people as a bit stark or cold, but that doesn't make it any less benevolent or charitable. If anything, it's the most humanitarian.

Your best times of year are your birthday month through February and late October through December. You're apt to feel most fragmented in June and September and can even begin second-guessing and picking apart what you've put together. You want to be especially careful during these times because you're easily irritable and darkly self-critical. It would be a good idea to check with someone whose opinion you trust to see if things are as bad off as they appear to you. Chances are they aren't. July is a very special month. It's when you feel emotionally comfortable and secure within yourself. It's a good time to pursue a romance, because you're not so overburdened with everyone else's concerns.

CHILD OF NEPTUNE...

Mercury, Planet of the mind, rules the zodiac sign Gemini. When you're a Child of Neptune with Neptune in Gemini, then you believe that most limits in life are self-imposed. One's capacity to shortchange oneself—just by virtue of negative thinking—is greater than anything the outside world could do. That's why you're so careful about what you put *into* your mind. You might make a point of looking up a new word when you hear it, refrain from watching the news before bedtime (so you don't go to sleep worried or depressed), or read a few lines of inspirational text on a daily basis. Just as someone with high cholesterol should watch what he eats, you believe that most people should watch how they think.

You aim to improve your mind (and your life) by tapping into its latent power so that it becomes inventive, rather than receptive; active rather than susceptible. If you can do that, then you could turn the tables on life. Instead of circumstances having you by the tail, it's you who can direct the outcome of events. When Mercury, Planet of the mind, combines with Neptune, Planet of the imagination, then you believe that each of us possesses the creative capacity to reshape our lives by reshaping our minds.

Mercury was named after the god of roads and tangents, so you like it when you can follow a sequence of words, numbers, or formulas to their logical conclusion. Indeed with Mercury powerful, you can intuit the gist of a text just by glancing at it or recall with almost photographic precision an episode that occurred years ago. Your mind is that sharp. However you are still a Child of Neptune—which means you have an extraordinary imagination. You may extol the virtues of rational thinking, but you won't be able to resist those wild leaps of fancy.

Mercury is sequential in its thinking, whereas your Birthday Planet is associative. In other words, it's not the facts that get your creative juices flowing—it's the sound of a word, a particular shade of color, or how a shape puts you in mind of something you once saw somewhere else. Neither Mercury nor Neptune are known for doing things by the book. Mercury may rule the mind, but he also rules the tricks of the mind as well. And given your Neptunian imagination,

WITH NEPTUNE IN GEMINI

you're not going to let a little thing like an unsubstantiated fact or bit of inconsistent logic prevent you from making a brilliant realization—no matter how far-fetched.

People who regard you as the epitome of good sense and logic might be surprised to discover that your thought process has less to do with deductive reasoning and is more akin to reading shapes in clouds. But that same eloquence you employ to make the far-fetched sound reasonable also comes in handy when you need to cover your tracks under a veil of hastily constructed explanations.

Because of Neptune's position at the time of your birth, you may have experienced your childhood home as an undependable place—but not your neighborhood. Indeed your fondest memories may be of hanging out at the corner store or of spending time with your best friend's family. You like to have structure in your life and feel most secure when you know what your parameters are. It's important for you to follow a regimen. You would do well working in a corporate environment, for a government agency or, given your mental aptitude, a think tank.

Your best times of year are late May to mid-June, late September through mid-October, and late January through mid-February. This is when there's a steady flow of people running through your life, and conversations ranging from the profound to the trivial offer boundless inspiration. Subsequently early May, early September, and early January are sluggish. These are times when there aren't a lot of diversions and you may find yourself holed up somewhere doing a lot of tedious work by yourself. Although this provides the perfect setting for getting things done, you sorely miss those newsy conversations or bits of gossip that provide just the offbeat impetus needed to get your mental wheels turning.

CHILD OF NEPTUNE...

If everyone had a place to call home, knew that they could count on the company of loved ones and friends, and went to bed at night with a full stomach, then there would be nothing to worry about. All of life's problems would be solved. The Moon, Planet of hearth and home, rules the zodiac sign Cancer. When you're a Child of Neptune with Neptune in Cancer, then you don't believe in big solutions to big problems. Tend to people's mundane concerns—like food, shelter, and love—and everything else will fall into place.

It galls you that anyone should have to go hungry, considering all the technology and resources that are available nowadays. Regardless of whether it's a homeless person on the corner or a child in some war-torn country, you can't stand to see anyone do without. Yet for all your empathy—which truly knows no bounds—there is also a part of you that knows (and *insists*) that each of us makes the bed we sleep in. In the end we can only live our lives as best we can—and put our trust in the ripple effects that our day-to-day actions have in the lives of others.

But drawing that line isn't so easy. As a Child of Neptune, you can't simply choose to block out the spill of feeling that comes seeping under the door. You soak up people's moods like a sponge. It's an involuntary reaction. But unlike your Birthday Planet, which rules the vastness of oceans, the Moon rules over shorelines and smaller bodies of water, like ponds and pools. What this does is let you feel the bottom beneath your feet. Where other Children of Neptune have difficulty distinguishing their feelings from the general atmosphere of the room, your Lunar side can instantly recognize the emotions you came in with—not unlike the way animals or birds living in enormous communities can immediately pick out their offspring from the hundreds of look-alikes. You will safeguard your "psychic" turf.

As a Child of Neptune with the Moon strong, many people will see you as their safe harbor. Your depth of understanding provides solace, while your earthy pragmatism gives them the gentle prodding necessary to get back on their feet. You believe people should fend for themselves, and you will always take time out to show them what needs to be done. But you are in someone's

WITH NEPTUNE IN CANCER

life to get him or her up and running, so once past the initial stages, you fully expect this person to be self-sufficient. You won't indulge, placate, or fuss over anyone—no matter how much you care.

Neptune's position at the time of your birth gives you a powerful interior life—along with an equally powerful means of expressing it. This may lead to a career in public life—which is not exactly agreeable to Neptune or the Moon. Both Planets treasure their privacy and enjoy their time alone. But that may not prove to be the case with you. Maybe it's a piece of your writing or a musical composition that finds its way into the mainstream—bringing with it notoriety and recognition. Or perhaps it's your involvement with someone else that leads—in a roundabout fashion—to the spotlight being shined on you.

Neptune rules scandals as well as selfless acts, so you can never be too choosy when picking friends.

Late February through mid-March, late April through mid-May, and late October through mid-November are enriching periods for you. When the people in your life do well, you do well—and since these are propitious times for loved ones and friends, you will flourish. August through October is not such a good time. Your Neptunian nature doesn't do well when the season is too hot or too dry, so this is when you'll feel weakest. Conserve your energy and your strength and be there only for people you know won't drain you. Late June through mid-July is a marvelous time for you. This is when you can forget all about your obligations and just romp around like a kid.

CHILD OF NEPTUNE...

The Sun rules the zodiac sign Leo. When you're a Child of Neptune with Neptune in Leo then it's your personality—with all its talents and gifts, temperaments and quirks—that is the single most valuable thing you can bring to the table. The Sun is the Planet of kings and queens, but as any public figure can tell you, once you accept that crown and scepter your life stops being your own. Your first responsibility is to the people who look to you for inspiration. When Neptune, Planet of glamour, combines with the Sun, source of heat and light, then you can't help being a hook for others' imagination and fascination. Somehow things just seem more special or important when you do them. When you're a Child of Neptune with the Sun strong, your wish is *apparently* everyone's command.

Your Ruling Planet gives you direct access to the collective unconscious. What you say and do reverberates in the imaginations of the people around you. It will be copied, mimicked, and discussed. Yet as much as you captivate people's attention and imagination, you are also in an extremely vulnerable position. Ask anyone who's spent time in the public eye. That adulation carries more than just a hint of envy and hostility. Neptune may be the Planet of unconditional love, but unconditional love, by its very definition, must contain *all* aspects of love. Not only will you attract the highest that love has to offer but you will also attract the less than desirable aspects as well.

This is where you need to be careful. By itself, your Ruling Planet can make you feel like you don't have the right to say no. If unconditional love knows no bounds, then why should you? When combined with the Sun's need for approval, this can keep you hooked into people's wants and needs regardless of their importance in your life. If ninety-nine out of a hundred people like what you're doing, then you'll feel miserable about having disappointed that one person. In a peculiar way others' adulation can become a form of servitude for you.

Without the Sun, we wouldn't exist. It stands at the top of the Planetary chain, just as the lion (which it rules) stands at the top of the food chain, and the heart (which the Sun also rules) is the most important organ in the human body. The Sun gives you that necessary self-centeredness you

WITH NEPTUNE IN LEO

need in order to carry the weight of all those hopes and expectations, projections and assumptions that are heaped on you. Without it, you wouldn't have a life. You'd just be a cipher. It's your Solar side that gives you the confidence to pursue your own unique vision—that feeling of privilege that prevents you from being immobilized by others' expectations, and the audacity that keeps you ahead of the pack and that also keeps the pack from turning on you.

Your Birthday Planet influences "popular movements"—those spontaneous gatherings of people around charged political or social issues. This would certainly come in handy for a career in entertainment or advertising, but you should also know you have a flair for trade and marketing. Neptune's position at the time of your birth gives you a talent for spotting (and influencing) financial as well as cultural trends. Despite the glam-our and prestige of what you do, it will still be hard work. You will be constantly reminded that you serve the interests of those who elected you or funded and sponsored you in the first place. You'll need every ounce of the Solar specialness just to survive in such a high-pressured environment.

Because you were born when your Ruling Planet was retrograde, midsummer through early fall is when you thrive. Indeed your own birthday month could be a time when you feel too overwhelmed by external events or awash in people's demands and expectations. Yet six months after your birthday things couldn't be more together. Late March through mid-April is a wonderful period for you financially. This is the best time for launching an endeavor or selling off property or assets. You're sure to make a profit.

CHILD OF NEPTUNE...

Mercury, Planet of wiles, rules the zodiac sign Virgo. When you're a Child of Neptune with Mercury strong, then you believe most of us have the ability to improve our lives, but we're spoiled. No one who is able-bodied should be waiting around for some guardian angel (or government agency for that matter) to come to the rescue. People won't help themselves if you make it easy. Throw them back on their own resources and they will develop the wherewithal, savvy, and skill to find their way.

Life to you is a work in progress. There's no such thing as a final product. Even milestones like success, marriage, or your first child are things you strive to make better. Life is truly what you make of it. Some may think that's frightening (they want guarantees), but you find it liberating. It means you have to use your imagination—not save it for a rainy day or waste it on daydreams and reveries. Most people never get around to using their imaginations. They're too quick to believe it when someone says you can't do this or it's impossible to do that. But for those who are resourceful, being told you can't do something is really an invitation to look for a way that you can.

You didn't come by your own resourcefulness naturally. Indeed you may have started out shamefully gullible. Your Ruling Planet was retrograde when you were born, so disillusionment is going to play an active role in your development as a person. For most people, when something falls apart in their lives, they either justify it according to their beliefs or—if it's a particularly difficult period—they might turn their back on their beliefs altogether. For you, disillusionment actually introduces you to your potential and prompts you to do something creative with it. That's why setbacks and heartbreaks that would have stopped most others short actually have the strange effect of fulfilling you as a person. This isn't to say you like them or even go out looking for them. You don't. But you also recognize somewhere inside that when they happen they're presenting you with an opportunity to do something more with your life. And inevitably, you do.

You are no stranger to sacrifice. Indeed once every twelve years you find yourself faced with a painful choice: stay true to yourself and risk los-

WITH NEPTUNE IN VIRGO

ing someone's love and approval or stand by this person and forgo something you'd like to pursue? It's because of these crossroads, which appear regularly (but are never the same), that you won't assume that an answer that worked once will necessarily work again. You treat each decision as if you were making it for the first time.

Neptune's position at the time of your birth shows that partnership plays a strong role in your life. This is interesting, because given your druthers you'd rather do things on your own. You may marry young (and possibly more than once), or you will go into business with someone older. Bringing people together—like playing mediator or go-between—could be a big part of what you do, or with your eye for potential, you may be very good at spotting talent or identifying companies to be bought or sold. Your pen-

chant for one-on-one dealings would also make you an excellent consultant, therapist, or counselor.

As a Child of Neptune retrograde, late summer rather than late spring will be the best season for you. It's your chance to get reacquainted with loved ones and friends and the things that matter to you personally. Because so much of what you do is focused on other people and their concerns, you get very little time for yourself. Thankfully work thins out in the late summer, which gives you an opportunity to vacation. People who work so hard often get antsy when left with so much free time, but not you. Being a Child of Neptune, you'd love nothing more than to while away the hours on the beach, by a lake, or lounging by the pool, catching up on your reading.

CHILD OF NEPTUNE...

Venus, Planet of partnership, rules the zodiac sign Libra. When you're a Child of Neptune with Neptune in Libra, then you believe that two people together can accomplish more than anyone alone. This is why you are so choosy about the company you keep and will only hook up with that special person (or persons) you know will bring out the best in you—and vice versa. Lost causes, emotional wrecks, and thankless obligations need not apply. If someone is not up to snuff, then you will show this person the door. You are guided by a vision of beauty and harmony and are looking for just the right people who are going to make that happen.

Though named after the goddess of love and beauty, Venus is more interested in forming relationships than she is in love for love's sake. This is very different from your Birthday Planet, which looks to love for inspiration, solace, and redemption. As a Child of Neptune, you believe that love is (and should be) unconditional. All aspects are permissible—both the dark and the light. Indeed you can't appreciate one without the other. For you, love is everything. Yet when you're a Child of

Neptune with Venus strong, then you must also honor your Venusian side. Venus believes that harmony is everything. Too much empathy, like too much passion or too much selfishness, will upset the balance of any relationship. It isn't easy for two people to get along. It requires a great deal of give-and-take. Just as one respects a boundary by not trespassing, you also need to claim the turf on your side of the fence— otherwise you will *invite* trespassing. This is the subtle yet essential difference between Neptune and Venus. Neptune would rather just erase the boundaries altogether—trusting in the waters of love that flow through us all to create a world of peaceful coexistence. Venus recognizes that the world is never going to work like that, which is why she puts her trust in laws and boundaries to keep the peace. Good fences make good neighbors.

Venus, Planet of balance, works her magic through the people she brings into your life. Your Venus side needs to feel *connected*, so it will naturally seek a counterbalance in relationships— whether personal or professional. If you are too trusting and forgiving, then Venus may bring peo-

WITH NEPTUNE IN LIBRA

ple who will trample on your visions of a peaceful garden, thus forcing you to take action on your own behalf. If you tend to be too political in your approach to relationships and are willing to sacrifice your feelings in order to make a good match, then Venus will bring people who will open your heart in new and unexpected ways. Extremes prompt you to find a balance in your life that will allow you to fulfill your part of a relationship while insisting that your partner fulfill his or hers.

Neptune's position at the time of your birth shows that your need to feel *emotionally* secure could lead to making love decisions based on money rather than feelings. But this doesn't necessarily mean "marrying up" or seeking jobs where you hope to make a profit. A fear of being without money could just as easily inspire you to renounce it altogether—declaring all materialism is base. Neptune also rules what Germans call *Zeitgeist*, or "spirit of the times." Combined with Venus's penchant for fashion, you have a "sixth" sense for trend spotting—whether it's a look or an investment. This would be particularly useful for work in advertising, film, or music as well as dealing in luxury items, antiques, designing interiors, or managing others' financial portfolios.

Since your Ruling Planet was retrograde when you were born, it only makes sense for the opposite time of year to be the best for you. Therefore late summer is when you feel that relationships are balanced and everything is running smoothly. Your own birthday month may be a time when you feel that more is going out—emotionally or financially—than is coming in. This is a time when you need to reinforce your personal boundaries and not let others' concerns overwhelm you. You have a special rapport with Children of the Sun, Mercury, and Venus.

CHILD OF NEPTUNE...

Mars, Planet of desire, and Pluto, Planet of compulsion, both rule the zodiac sign Scorpio. When you're a Child of Neptune with Neptune in Scorpio then you are drawn to emotionally charged situations that teeter on the edge. But you're neither a thrill seeker nor do you do anything just for kicks (though you have been known to get carried away in the moment from time to time). You were born under the Planet of unconditional love, which means you are meant to experience love in all its aspects—the light along with the dark. When you're dealing with Mars and especially Pluto, then the tendency, at first, may be for more dark than light. Pluto is the Planet of ordeals and the transformations that arise from them. As a Child of Neptune with Mars and Pluto strong, you will be drawn to situations that not only test your mettle but may even cause you suffering. But the suffering isn't meant to defeat you. It will actually empower (Mars) and enliven (Pluto). Your capacity to love is much fuller than most people's, because you won't stop at heartbreak. It's by going down into the depths that you rise again—fuller and stronger than you

could ever have imagined.

Neptune, Planet of selfless acts, is also the Planet of scandal. This hails from the phrase that the road to hell is often paved with good intentions—something you may be able to attest to from personal experience. Regardless of whether you're misguided or misunderstood, there will be certain times when you will find yourself in dire straits. Given the nature of Pluto, it may involve sex, death, and/or other people's money. No matter how noble or heroic, you will wind up being blamed for what transpired. But where others would humble themselves or do whatever's required in order to save face—you won't. Mars, Planet of fortitude, won't bow to anyone, and if you have to suffer public derision, then it's that Mars side of you that will do it with head held high. Yet it's these circumstances that set the stage for your greatest triumph.

A moral victory rarely upholds beliefs that are already in place. More often than not it rocks our most precious beliefs to the core by revealing their shortcomings and shining a light on their hypocrisy. It's as old as feeding Christians to the

WITH NEPTUNE IN SCORPIO

lions and as recent as the murder of Matthew Shepherd. But you are no martyr and you are no victim. Where the Neptune side of you might be tempted to let go (Neptune always feels a stronger pull to the *other* world than it does to this one), your Mars and Pluto side still wants the satisfaction of toughing it out, being redeemed, and shaming those who heckled you the loudest. This is the part of you that won't give up or give in. You will rise again—no matter what.

Because of Neptune's position at the time of your birth, you may feel drawn to work for one of the many humanitarian organizations that have sprung up in recent years—like Doctors Without Borders—or you might concentrate on more local concerns like education, outreach, or human services. Although you may not start out being political, it's likely that a personal incident will transform you from bystander to player. You don't

have to necessarily drop what you're doing and become an activist, but politics has its roots in people—not in elected officials. Conversely, a small act in your own life may send ripple effects moving in unforeseen directions. One can never judge the repercussions of events—especially nowadays.

Your own birthday month, late June through mid-July, and late October through mid-November, are your strongest times of year. This is when you're feeling emotionally vital and at the height of your creative powers. But this can also be the time when you could get into trouble, as your inner waters are flowing so strongly and powerfully that they could flood their banks. Make a point of always holding back a little before following a generous impulse. It will cut down on the slipups and allow you to judge more sensibly the current of the times.

CHILD OF NEPTUNE...

Your *other* Birthday Planet, Jupiter, rules the zodiac sign Sagittarius. When you're a Child of Neptune with Neptune in Sagittarius then you see your entire life as being in service to the potential you carry inside you. But there's more at stake than talent, a gift, or realizing a dream. You feel a personal link to those who have come before. Maybe it's a parent or grandparent whose sacrifice and hard work resulted in the unique opportunities you enjoy today. Perhaps you pick up where a predecessor of yours left off by carrying on with his or her work. Then again you may feel such a powerful connection to those who once practiced a religion or philosophy you espouse that following in their footsteps is an almost palpable experience. For you history isn't something you learn about in school or that takes place in somebody else's neck of the woods. History is unfolding in your life—now. You're aware that everything you do is meant to have a great impact. You don't see yourself as special. You just see yourself as someone living during very special times.

But sometimes that "specialness" can become a burden all its own. If you are too beholden to what someone has done or if you feel like what's come before is so sacred that anything you do will just bring it down, then you can, in effect, become immobilized by your own reverence. Neptune is *otherworldly* by nature. It will always invest more importance in dreams than in reality. As a Child of Neptune, you're already predisposed to thinking that what you conceive of in your imagination is far better than anything you will ever reproduce through your own efforts. And, without knowing it, this *glamourization* of history can work along similar lines. It can make you feel that you're under an obligation to live up to what's come before or that you have to stay true to some legacy. As a result, feelings of expectation and disappointment can start eroding your confidence in an endeavor before you've even undertaken it.

Thankfully Jupiter is more in love with this world than with the other one. And it's the Jupiter side of you that will push to make something your own. How can you even think straight if you're constantly comparing your actions to what's already been done? Not surprisingly, your first

WITH NEPTUNE IN SAGITTARIUS

step may be to walk out on all these expectations you've been glorifying. Given Neptune's tendency to "wipe the slate clean" this wouldn't be so unusual—especially around the ages of twenty-four and maybe even thirty-six.

Because of Neptune's position at the time of your birth, you won't really come into your own until your early forties. This isn't to say your life is on hold till then. Indeed you could have a precocious childhood where a particular talent or aptitude develops early. But then you'll go through a period where you lose touch with it—either because you lose faith in your ability or you don't feel as if you can do what you want, given the circumstances. This is when you enter a very creative and profound process of making this calling or legacy your own. You are meant to be more than the custodian of someone's memory or the obedient servant of

some cause or belief. You have your own unique contribution to make—but you have to go outside the lines and be willing to break with convention in order to find it.

Late March through April, late June through August, and late November through mid-December are your best times of year. This is when you're the most open-minded and willing to explore a new tangent or perspective. It's important to keep that spirit of adventure burning—especially during your "low" periods, which tend to be around June and September. There's a part of you that can lapse into "do it by the book" behavior, and when that happens it's often a sign that you're feeling insecure or overtaxed. July is a wonderful time for romance. It's when you're feeling flush and can go ahead and show a paramour a good time without having to keep close tabs on the bank balance.

CHILD OF NEPTUNE...

Saturn, Planet of law and order, rules the zodiac sign Capricorn. When you're a Child of Neptune with Neptune in Capricorn then your values tend to be conservative and your love—tough. You believe each person is responsible for making his or her own way in life. But you aren't hard or unfeeling. In fact you're quite the opposite. You're one of the few people who are actually concerned about preserving something for future generations. Because Saturn rules the winter solstice, it tends to see the world as a dark and barren place where resources are in short supply. Indeed you may feel like you were born at a time when a lot went to waste because people let their appetites and desires get the better of them. When your Birthday Planet is colored by Saturn, you believe that there are more takers than givers in life and that the best way to even the score is by bringing everyone firmly into line.

People need an authority they can respect. And your father may have played such a role in your own life. If not, then you would have transferred all of that loyalty and obedience to an uncle, teacher, or spiritual mentor. Hard work has

always been your credo, and you will gladly make whatever sacrifices are necessary in order to create a place for yourself and loved ones that is stable and secure.

Neptune is the Planet of imagination. Without imagination, we wouldn't be able to conceive that things can be any different from the way that they appear. It's this creative faculty that allows you to hold the image of something in your mind so that you can seek to become it. Though your truest ambition may be to leave the world a better place than you found it, an aspiration—no matter how decent and honest—is still something you made up. What you may not be paying enough attention to is the undercurrent running through that aspiration. This undercurrent may very well be a slavish devotion to what others think, a cultivation of friends and contacts for the purpose of promoting your own interests, or even an aggressive hostility toward anyone you feel is trying to rock the boat and spoil things for everyone else. In your efforts to be benevolent, you may be surprised to find you have the potential to turn into a tyrant.

As a Child of Neptune, it's seductive to hand authority over to a "parent" figure. You don't have

WITH NEPTUNE IN CAPRICORN

to think for yourself. Even when you become a parent, you can still pledge allegiance to something larger than yourself, like a family tradition, a set of beliefs, or proper conduct. But there's no passing the buck with Saturn. At some point you will find yourself in a situation where those values of yours are put to the test—perhaps in your late twenties, early forties, or even late fifties—and though they may be found wanting, you won't be. This paves the way to your ultimately discovering the authority within yourself.

Neptune's position at the time of your birth shows that you're naturally drawn to groups of people. You like hierarchy and feel most comfortable when everything is arranged in proper rank and file. You may be attracted to a career in the armed forces or law enforcement, but the loosely designed structure of a corporation or a small firm would suit you just as well. Whatever organization you join just has to be well thought-out and tailor-made for your need to achieve and to have something tangible to show for your efforts.

Late December through mid-March is your best time of year. This is when you feel like you're moving with the current of events rather than struggling against it. The summer season is not so favorable, as this is when you experience the most conflict and resistance from colleagues and even loved ones. The nice thing about being a Child of Neptune with Saturn strong is that you mellow with age. While others grow more intolerant, you actually become more receptive and self-reflective. Once into your fifties and sixties you may be amazed by how many of your closest friends are young people.

CHILD OF NEPTUNE...

Saturn, Planet of bounds, and Uranus, Planet of everything that lies outside them, both rule the zodiac sign Aquarius. When you're a Child of Neptune with Neptune in Aquarius, then you have the unique ability to stand both *inside* and *outside* a situation. You bring a personal dimension to abstract concerns as well as an objective criterion to the most intimate and sensitive issues. You know that words and feelings don't always flow together—just like rules don't always guide behavior and social concerns don't always respect individual freedoms. Your ability to find a way for the impersonal and the personal to get along—to entwine the two—is one of your great talents. Instead of siding with one over the other or imposing some artificial compromise, you will coordinate both, and by doing so you will create something new and innovative.

You were born at a time when so many ideals seemed within easy reach. Technological revolutions redefined the way people looked at the world—from currency and communication to medical therapies. Uranus rules the ideals—like liberty, freedom, and equality—that society has always strived to embrace. Given Neptune's penchant for glamorizing whatever Planetary energy it gets near, it makes perfect sense that the prevalent myth would have been the Global Village. And just as soon as that myth sprung up, Saturn, Planet of limitations, began cutting it down to size by exposing ethnic hatreds, wild economic disparities, and the fact that certain nations were not going to tolerate the political equivalent of a "hostile bid." This was the spirit of the times you were born into, and that spirit continues to emanate through your life.

Being a Child of Neptune with Saturn and Uranus strong makes you a natural bridge builder. By themselves, Saturn and Uranus would retreat to opposite corners. Uranus is idealistic, while Saturn is pragmatic. You often struggle with this deep split. There will be times when you can see the way things should be but lack the means to bring it about, and there will be times when you have the means but you're so bogged down with obligations and responsibilities that you can't get to the things you'd like to do. But you will never stop configuring and reconfiguring ideas in your imagination. As a Child of Neptune, your well

WITH NEPTUNE IN AQUARIUS

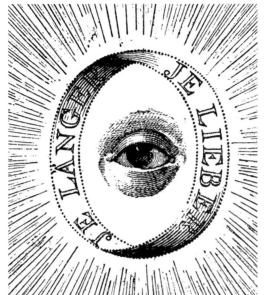

of inspiration never runs dry.

Neptune's position at the time of your birth shows you will be drawn to areas of life that require your particular form of "bridge building." Both Saturn and Uranus rule building and engineering—as well as technology and science—so you may be interested in these fields. But you also have all the makings of a mediator or arbitrator. Uranus gives you the ability to decipher where the problems lie, Saturn gives you the sort of common sense that naturally appeals to people in distress, while Neptune provides the persuasion and élan that get them to listen. You may simply be repeating what people have heard before (or even already know to be true), but somehow it just *sounds* better coming from you. As a Child of Neptune with Uranus and Saturn strong, you can't help having a wide variety of roving interests. You're proficient at a number of different things, but whoever said "Jack of all trades; master of none" obviously wasn't living in the twenty-first century. The secret to your inventiveness lies in your ability to synthesize a hodgepodge of elements rather than be stymied by them.

Your own birthday month is a wonderful time of year, as is late May through mid-June and late September through mid-October. These are when all three Planetary energies are working in unison, and you will benefit from their ingenuity, steadfastness, and acuity. It's the period in between—late June through mid-September—that can be problematic. You attract a lot of strong personalities in your life, and this is the time when they're being the most demanding or self-involved. It might be preferable to just tune them out, but they won't let you—and that's actually good. As a Child of Neptune your head tends to be up in the clouds, and it's these wonderfully dramatic (and exasperating) personalities that keep your feet planted on the ground.

CHILD OF PLUTO...

Mercury, Planet of the mind, rules the zodiac sign Gemini. When you're a Child of Pluto with Pluto in Gemini, then you pick up on subtleties most people miss. Perhaps it's the way the topic changes whenever a certain issue is brought up, or maybe it's an inconsistency that strikes you as odd the second time you hear a story. It doesn't take much to set off those psychic alarm bells of yours, and if sufficiently intrigued then your curiosity (Mercury) and suspicion (Pluto) are aroused. You need to find out what is going on. Most people prefer to leave well enough alone, but as a Child of Pluto with Pluto in Gemini, your experience has proven the opposite: it's what you don't know that *can* hurt you.

Growing up, we are told that life is played by certain rules. If you always do the right thing then you will never have cause for shame or regret. But as you get older, you realize that the rules you were told about when you were younger rarely apply to the game of life as everyone else plays it. The world is far more competitive and complex, and a certain amount of finessing is required. As a Child of Pluto, you can't help but attract the occa-

sional "hard time." It's what makes you grow as a person. If everyone else is speeding on the freeway, chances are you'll be the one who gets pulled over. At different points in your life you will experience firsthand the discrepancy between the game that was outlined in the rule book and the game as it's played in the *real* world. Mercury rules the mind, but it rules the tricks of the mind as well. Named after the Greek god of commerce, Mercury was as much the patron god of shopkeepers and merchants as he was the favorite of swindlers and cheats. To this day we are more likely to forgive (or even applaud) someone who "pulls a fast one," while we look down on the person who was duped. You may start out gullible, but after being burned once or twice, it's hard not to want to keep a trick or two up your sleeve, just in case.

But once you bend a rule (or even break it), it's hard to go back to the way the game was played before. Why go through the hassle when there's an easier way to get what you want? Besides, you can always justify your actions by saying that this is the way of the world; you didn't make up the rules, you just play by them. You can

WITH PLUTO IN GEMINI

even blame harsh circumstances for leading you astray. But the crucible of Pluto isn't in its harsh circumstances (anyone can point a finger and say "this is what drove me to it"); the crucible of Pluto is in rising above those harsh circumstances, which only happens when you come face-to-face with your dark side and decide *not* to go down that path. This is when Pluto empowers you.

Because of Pluto's position at the time of your birth, you may be drawn to buying and selling, as well as the handling (and safeguarding) of other people's property. Plugging into your own "dark side" makes you incredibly vigilant and savvy. No one's going to hoodwink you. Mercury's love of riddles, combined with your Birthday Planet's fascination for anything mysterious, also makes you a perfect candidate for detective work, medical research, or anything to do with mapping, surveying, and geology.

Since your Ruling Planet was retrograde when you were born, it only makes sense for the opposite time of year to be the best for you. Therefore the spring is when you feel like you're on solid ground and finances are secure. Your own birthday month may be when you feel that times are lean. Be very careful, because this is when you're apt to be most tempted. A true master of the game is someone who knows how to play by the rules so expertly that he or she can manipulate an opponent's maneuvers. When you understand the game of life to that extent, then you will never have to worry about getting fleeced again. Fortune will always play into your hands.

CHILD OF PLUTO . . .

The Moon, Planet of roots, rules the zodiac sign Cancer. When you're a Child of Pluto with Pluto in Cancer, then you draw sustenance and strength from your past. But this isn't to say you're nostalgic or miss your childhood. As a Child of Pluto, your "past" is your family tree, the land where your family (or your people) hail from, and the history that is bred in your bone. Whether it's psychological or cultural, you are proud of your heritage. You turn to it for inspiration, solace, and vitality. You believe that the apple doesn't fall far from the tree—even if that tree happens to reside in another town or country. You will never forsake your past. Where others may want to move on or reinvent themselves, you will never forget. You invoke your past on a daily basis in your stories, your jokes, and your philosophy. You carry it all inside of you.

Yet despite your need for roots, you may live a restless and somewhat nomadic existence. No other Planet changes its appearance as dramatically as the Moon, and in keeping with its waxing and waning phases, you may be coming and going constantly. As prospects brighten then darken then brighten again, your life can feel like one long transition—punctuated by periods of stability.

But this is where you need to be careful. You were born under the Planet of ordeals *and* the transformations that arise from them. There's a part of your psyche that needs hard times in order to grow. Although arduous, these hard times fill you with purpose and vitality. In their own way they can also be very difficult to leave behind. But the very Planet that brings you down into the crucible is the very Planet that insists you rise again. And in order to do this, you may have to relinquish your hold on that "past" you credit with keeping you going. It's hard to think of the past as being fluid. We're used to thinking of it as being fixed. But it's just as changeable as our memories and our perceptions. This isn't to say the past is bad. But your personal investment in it could be getting in the way of you creating a place for yourself. Just like birth, rebirth isn't easy.

In ancient times women prayed to the Moon for safe passage through the dangers and rigor of childbirth. The very act of giving life robbed many of them of theirs. As a Child of Pluto you are drawn

WITH PLUTO IN CANCER

to life's dark moments—not as a bystander, but as someone who—having *been* delivered—can now turn around and help with the deliver*ing*. As a Child of Pluto with the Moon strong, you midwife people's progeny—be they children, aspirations, projects, or even souls.

Pluto's position at the time of your birth makes you, in essence, a keeper of the flame. It may be up to you to keep a certain art form or tradition alive—through practice or daily observance. This may lead to a career in education, with your house of worship, or cultural anthropology—which is as much about preserving traditions as recording them. In a similar vein, preservation and restoration may be themes that run throughout your life, as might be a powerful devotion to the safeguarding of human welfare—especially the welfare of children.

Late February through March, late June through July, and your own birthday month are your most vital times of year. Finances are secure, your body is strong, and your prospects are good. December through late January, however, is a particularly challenging time. Even if there's nothing wrong with your life, you will still experience a drop in energy and a depression that's hard to shake. As a Child of Pluto, you need to go on those periodic descents into your own lower depths. They reinvigorate you. However, adopting a more "Lunar" approach to them (the Moon passes through all its phases in just one month) may serve to remind you that dark periods don't last forever, and just as you feel compelled to go down into them, you are equally compelled to resurface from them.

CHILD OF PLUTO . . .

The Sun, source of heat and light, rules the zodiac sign Leo. When you're a Child of Pluto with Pluto in Leo, then you have an extremely powerful presence. You don't even have to smile or frown and the temperature in the room will rise or drop according to your mood. This isn't always easy for you to understand, much less accept. That's because your Birthday Planet was named after the Greek god of the Underworld, who also happened to be the god of invisibility. When you're a Child of Pluto with the Sun strong, then getting to know your own strength is a lifelong endeavor.

The Sun, Planet of kings and queens, rules public figures. It needs to be out in the open and on show for all to see. When you have strong Solar energy like you do, then people will naturally turn to you—as they would toward the Sun. They look to you for leadership and approval, and they will eagerly follow your example. However nothing could be more contrary to your nature. As a Child of Pluto, you shun the spotlight. You don't like feeling that you're under a microscope, nor are you eager to put yourself in a position where you have to worry about what people think. Truth be told: you don't trust people. You know how fickle they can be.

Yet Pluto's position at the time of your birth shows that you will rise to some level of prominence—whether it's at work, in your community, or even in your own family. You are built for leadership. But you were also born under the Planet of ordeals and the transformations that arise from them. Subsequently, you draw as much negative attention as positive. Controversy follows you wherever you go.

By never wanting to let anyone see you sweat you can come across as being arrogant and proud. In your effort to cover up your weaknesses, you may inadvertently invite people to search for them. And as they take a swipe at you with a critical remark or a malicious barb, you, in Child of Pluto fashion, will retaliate in kind until the whole thing becomes a vicious circle. By lowering your status, you empower those who didn't have it.

But just because you lose one round doesn't mean you lose the game. Indeed you may go through these episodes on a semiregular basis for the express purpose of getting it right. But getting

WITH PLUTO IN LEO

it right doesn't mean becoming hardened. The very Planet that sets the stage for this is the very Planet that demands you move past it. And the way to move past it isn't by hardening your heart, but by opening it.

As a Child of Pluto, you respond hotly to anything you perceive to be a slight or an outrage. This gave you a volatile temperament when you were younger, so you learned to mask what you felt. Since your Solar side naturally generates warmth, humor, and optimism, you may have decided to cultivate a casual—so what?—nonchalance. Given that the Sun rules the father, you may have modeled this after him. And when you're comfortable, this is exactly what comes out because it's what you feel anyway. However when you're *uncomfortable*, there may be a certain edge to your voice or incongruity in your manner that sends the message that something isn't quite right. This inadvertently triggers a flight-or-fight response in those around you. Get rid of the mask and you'll find that your feelings and expressions flow a lot easier. You'll also hold on to your power because you won't be inviting people to come take it away.

You do very well in the summer months. You love the heat. Even if you have to be careful about lying out in the sun (Children of Pluto tend to burn easily), you still relish being outdoors as much as possible. January and February are not great times of the year for you. This is when you tend to get moody and depressed. Your Solar battery is running low. Thankfully it doesn't last long, because late March through mid-April is always reinvigorating. Spring brings out your romantic side.

CHILD OF PLUTO...

Mercury, Planet of expertise, rules the zodiac sign Virgo. Named after the Greek god of crafts, Mercury was the patron of artisans, who because of their unique abilities, were free to move about as they pleased. Farmers had to work the land, kings had to stay put on their thrones, but Mercury's Children could set up shop wherever they wanted to—not unlike today's independent contractors. All they needed were their tools and their talent.

As a Child of Pluto with Mercury strong, you will spend hours pursuing a favorite craft, hobby, or field of interest. You read, analyze, and collect everything you can find on your beloved subject. When you're passionate about something, you are totally absorbed. Most people dream of getting *away* from work. You dream of being able to immerse yourself full-time in what you want to do. But doing what you want *and* making a living at it don't dovetail. You firmly believe that you have to do something *else* in order to eke out a living.

That Mercury side of you knows that specialization is key. By honing your skills for a particular market or creating a position for yourself by figuring out what the need is and then filling it, you know how to make yourself invaluable. You could probably have your pick of opportunities and prospects. But that's not the way you see it. Your chronic fear of being without money often drives your decision making more than your desires and aspirations do.

You were born under the Planet of ordeals and the transformations that arise from them. Your psyche requires some amount of hardship in order to grow. But the hardship you're afraid of may not be the same one your Ruling Planet has in mind. Indeed it may be your *need* for financial security, more than the lack of it, that leads you down all those blind alleys. Every time you resolve to go your own way, you find yourself being lured back into your gilded cage by a hefty sum waved under your nose, or you're confronted by a debt dangling menacingly overhead.

Nevertheless, the Planet that brings you down into this crucible is also the very Planet that insists you transcend it. And, not surprisingly, that may entail walking out on a cushy job. After all, if you waited for the circumstances to be just right or the conditions to align themselves just so,

WITH PLUTO IN VIRGO

then it would probably be time for retirement. What may lie underneath all this is that Plutonian belief that you can't possibly have what you yearn for. And in typical Pluto fashion, you'll never know unless you go ahead and take the plunge.

Pluto's position at the time of your birth shows that you feel most comfortable in a group atmosphere and can only think straight when there's a strict schedule or regimen to adhere to. This is rather atypical for Children of Pluto, who usually prefer to be by themselves. Ironically, your talent for zeroing in on one thing and then tailoring your abilities so that they fill that niche to perfection works against you becoming the independent agent you could be. Once you see yourself as being able to do what you want in a variety of situations and venues, then you'll figure out that it's not too hard to make money in your chosen field. After all—you were born under the Planet of wealth. Your skills and talents are like the tools and instruments that craftsmen used to carry with them from town to town. Change the mindset and you'll realize for yourself that you can set up shop wherever you like.

Late summer and fall through to the winter solstice (which begins around December 21) is your best time of year. This is when you're most industrious and your sixth sense for finances is working at full capacity. Any sort of negotiating, bargaining, or wheeling and dealing should be done during this period. You'll always come out on top. Late winter through spring is not such a good time. This is when you're short on both money and patience. Don't make any major decisions, because they're either too emotional or you're just reaching for another quick fix. Early summer is always relaxed.

CHILD OF PLUTO...

Venus, Planet of love and marriage, rules the zodiac sign Libra. When you're a Child of Pluto with Pluto in Libra, then you can't wait to hook up with that special person who's going to help make your life complete. But you are incredibly selective. Everyone you have dealings with gets the same thorough inspection—be it a potential spouse, business partner, or the person who cuts your hair. You take your commitments seriously. You give your best and naturally expect the same in return. When you're a Child of Pluto with Venus powerful, these bonds are meant to last a lifetime.

This doesn't seem like a terribly tall order. And given your scintillating combination of Venusian allure and Plutonian magnetism, you'll have no shortage of takers. People will vigorously compete for your hand and/or business. The problem, however, always seems to start *after* you've made the commitment. That transition from what looked good on paper to day-to-day reality is often a bumpy one. But then that's why you make only long-term commitments. You're convinced that the kinks can be worked out. But people aren't static. They change. And what began as a match made in heaven winds up resembling one of those fugitives-from-justice movies where the protagonists are handcuffed to each other. So what's wrong with this picture?

Pluto's position at the time of your birth implies that your parents' marriage might have been going through a rough spell when you arrived on the scene, or one of them may have been facing hard times because of business. One of your grandparents might have faced similar circumstances at the outset of raising a family. Pluto rules ancestors, and sometimes the plight of one generation is visited on the next. In any case that fear of being left in the lurch lies at the very core of your being.

Although the Venusian side of you just wants to find the right person to hook up with and can't figure out why you wind up with all these lemons, it's your Birthday Planet that keeps creating the difficult circumstances. But there's more than just bum luck at work. You were born under the Planet of ordeals and the transformations that arise from them. You need hardship in order to grow. Ironically, those people who disappoint on a

WITH PLUTO IN LIBRA

Venusian level actually happen to be doing their job on a Plutonian level. Your search for the right partner—and your insistence that he or she stay put—may have nothing to do with that person and everything to do with placating your anxieties. The very Planet that generates this obsession is also the Planet that forces you to move past it. Bending over backwards to make a relationship work or paying out through the nose to keep a business afloat may be exactly what it takes for you to reabsorb that power from the person you've pinned so many hopes on and to begin seeing yourself as a full person rather than merely half an equation.

Given how relationships are such a prevalent theme, you may be drawn to vocations that deal with partnerships. You would make an excellent counselor, mediator, or broker. Pluto rules other people's money, so you might be involved in their estates or investments. Venus, the Planet of love and harmony, gives you excellent taste and a love of beauty. You would do well in the arts—particularly music or dance—as well as the business of art. If anyone can tell the difference between what's hype and what's real—it's you.

Late February through mid-March, late May through mid-June, and late September through mid-October are your best times of year. This is when you have the clearest sense of what's going on beneath the surface, and your assessment of matters is spot-on. Negotiations made during this time will go smoothly, and you may even get a little something extra for your efforts. Late March through mid-April, however, is not a good time, as it's when you feel most vulnerable and tend to give away your power. Obviously this isn't the season for making long-range plans or commitments. August is when you're at your most charming and charismatic and admirers come out of the woodwork—which never fails to please your Venusian side.

CHILD OF PLUTO...

Mars, Planet of combat, and Pluto, Planet of empowerment, both rule the zodiac sign Scorpio. When you're a Child of Pluto with Pluto in Scorpio, then you are drawn to situations that not only test your mettle but also forge it into something stronger than it was before. The hotter the fire, the closer you hold your feet to it. You always push the envelope—at work and in your personal life. But you don't do this carelessly or recklessly. You only do it until the other party cries uncle. Your tolerance for pain and ability to withstand pressure is greater than most people's and subsequently your opponent will fold long before you do. As a Child of Pluto with both Mars and Pluto strong, you strive to maintain the upper hand.

Most Children of Pluto go out of their way to avoid a confrontation. Your Birthday Planet was named after the god of the Underworld, so it's only natural to hug the shadows. However, it's your Mars side that wants to ensure nobody messes with you. And the best way to do this is to appear tough. This is why you always look people straight in the eye or speak with a slight edge in your voice. But not everyone reacts well to a show of force. Even if your intention is to keep the peace, you can come across as if everything you do is a fait accompli. Instead of nipping a problem in the bud, you may inadvertently sow the seeds of dissent.

You were born under the Planet of ordeals and the transformations that arise from them. You need hardship in order to grow. You attract (or are attracted to) incendiary situations aimed at transforming your life. You may *say* you're not looking for trouble, but you won't back down either. Which is why you end up drawing so much negative fire. There's no disputing that this can be exhausting and at times unfair. But it may be the appeal of conflict that keeps drawing you into these clashes. It's easy (not to mention seductive) to just spin from crisis to crisis. The intensity takes on a thrill all its own and can keep you from actually *living* your life.

Nevertheless the Planet that fans the flames is also the very Planet that insists you walk through them. And the way Pluto does this is by letting you bottom out. You could literally "burn out," or you may find yourself in a situation where you're fighting the good fight, but because you've

WITH PLUTO IN SCORPIO

brawled so many times before no one takes your side anymore. This makes you look like a trouble-maker, so your company lets you go or the person you're in love with walks out. These aren't pleasant experiences, but some-times the only way to stop an obsession is by pulling the plug. Pluto is about empowerment. And that's not going to happen if you're locked in a vicious cycle where you keep throwing gasoline on the fire.

Yours is a creative, shaping energy, so you need a career or vocation where you can tackle new challenges, but where the intensity comes and goes. The ideal would be a job where you have episodes of tremendous concentration that are bro-ken up by periods of relaxation. Seasonal employ-ment or working on individual projects would be good. You may be attracted to more "combative"

occupations—like law or advocacy or even emer-gency services. But make sure you don't get hooked into a nonstop revolving door. You're not good at moderating your pace and could burn out.

Late October through mid-January is your best time of year. This is when you feel strong and most at ease with yourself. As a Child of Pluto you like it when it's dark outside and warm inside—just like a cave. Late April through mid-July is not so good. Your focus is fuzzy and the change in surroundings (or daily schedule) puts you on edge. You may not be a big fan of rou-tine, but you can get bent out of shape if life lacks a certain regularity. You like things and people to stay put. Nevertheless a little flexibility can't hurt, and by the time you get to August you're feeling sufficiently relaxed to think about more romantic pursuits.

CHILD OF PLUTO . . .

Jupiter, Planet of fortune, rules the zodiac sign Sagittarius. When you're a Child of Pluto with Pluto in Sagittarius, you have a prospector's instincts for zeroing in on that precious find. Whether it's a business plan, a relationship, or a ramshackle piece of property that needs fixing up, you will commit all your resources to transforming its potential into a reality. You know that when you finally hit pay dirt, you will not only make back everything you invested, but you'll also be set for life.

Jupiter, Planet of fortune, is also the Planet of higher purpose, so there's a side of you that believes there's more at work than chance or luck. When good things start to happen in your life, you regard this as living proof that the universe is on your side. When you're a Child of Pluto with Jupiter strong, then physical gains work in tandem with your beliefs. Everything you do is either an expression of your spiritual philosophy or a response to it.

Jupiter is an incorporating Planet, so you won't think twice about trying to convert others to your way of thinking. And because Pluto sees everything in terms of the soul's survival, it's easy to become convinced that it's up to you to save a friend or colleague. But not everyone wants to be "saved," or they may have other ideas of how that will be done. This can result in broken hearts or severed ties. And if you feel that an aspiration or talent conflicts with what you hold dear, then it will go by the wayside, too. Born under the Planet of ordeals and the transformations that arise from them, you require some measure of hardship in order to grow. It isn't pleasant, but if sacrifices need to be made, so be it.

However your idea of hardship may not be exactly what your Ruling Planet has in mind. Just as Pluto is the Planet that introduces these moral quandaries, Pluto is also the Planet that insists you resolve them in ways you haven't explored before. What's at stake may not be the rightness or wrongness of your beliefs at all. Indeed the underlying purpose of being drawn to people whose outlook differs from yours may be to expand your horizons, not limit them. The truest test of your beliefs could have nothing to do with faith and everything to do with developing the tolerance and compassion to respect others' beliefs—to live and let live.

WITH PLUTO IN SAGITTARIUS

Pluto's position at the time of your birth shows that you are territorial. But you want to do more than just accrue; you also want to take what you find and make it better. You may build a highly successful business from scratch or dramatically transform your field of expertise. You're extremely gifted at recognizing the potential in almost any situation. Your vitality and inspiration allow you to breathe new life into something that's been long neglected or to take the bare outline of an idea and flesh it out into a concept that is dynamic and compelling. The combination of Jupiter and Pluto makes you prudent, wise, and insightful—qualities that would be invaluable for a real estate developer, buyer for a store, entrepreneur, minister, or even a judge.

Your best times of year are late February through mid-March, late June through mid-July, and late October through all of November. These are times when you are feeling both confident and open-minded. You have a nice rapport with the people in your life and won't feel like you have to come on strong or talk them out of their positions. Late April through mid-June is an iffy time, as prospects feel uncertain. What's required is a delicate touch, so you need to curb that tendency of yours "to draw the line." Sometimes you can cut yourself out of the action by getting too impatient or exasperated. This is a time when leaving a situation alone may work to your benefit. People want to include you in things and believe they'll do much better with you in their corner. No one's going to make a big decision without running it by you first.

CHILD OF PLUTO...

Saturn, Planet of time, rules the astrological sign Capricorn. When you're a Child of Pluto with Pluto in Capricorn, then timing is everything to you. You'll obsess over the right moment to close a deal, fret about whether you've been given enough lead time to prepare, and carefully study any relationship or association you're thinking of pursuing in terms of how you see it working out in the long run. There is no such thing as living in the moment for you. You would never be so foolhardy as to leave anything to chance. But you're not stilted either. Your love of history and trends gives you a rich understanding as well as intuitive feel for how and why things take place. You're very good at predicting what will happen next.

However beneath that appearance of cool confidence is a nervous impatience that can eat away at you. Like anyone ruled by the clock, you're acutely aware of time running out. Yet with Saturn prevalent, things will take twice as long to come together and twice as long to fall apart. Moreover you will go through long plateau periods where not much of anything is going on. Saturn can be mulish and slow. And all the pushing and shoving in the world won't make you progress any faster. In fact, you may wind up sabotaging your own best efforts.

What makes this even more difficult is that in your late teens and twenties you will be presented with a banquet of opportunity—but you won't be allowed to eat. Saturn is the Planet of tests, so you can expect complications to arise right when you're within reach of what you want. There will be so many close calls and also-rans that you won't know whether to cry—because it's so frustrating—or laugh—because it's so ridiculous. It's never easy being sidelined when you show so much promise, but that's because Saturn has bigger plans in store for you. Yours will be more than a fly-by-night success. Your accomplishments are meant to last, to stand the test of time.

But this won't always be easy to keep uppermost in mind. Born under the Planet of ordeals and the transformations that arise from them, you require some measure of hardship in order to grow. With Saturn added to the mix, you can expect that hardship to be overbearing and that growth to be achingly slow and incremental. But

WITH PLUTO IN CAPRICORN

you won't give up. You are a Child of Pluto. No matter how many times your hopes are leveled or you cross the finish line only to discover it's really just another starting mark, you will persevere. And given Saturn's discipline and tenacity, you will master your circumstances. At a time when most of the people you grew up with are nestled comfortably in their lifestyles, you will just be coming into your own.

Pluto's position at the time of your birth shows a talent for commerce as well as media. This offers a wide variety of possibilities ranging from systems analyst to movie mogul. Writing— and nonverbal forms of communication like music or drawing—may come easier than speaking, and given your resistance toward anything extemporaneous, these may be especially appealing. You also do very well when governed by strict parameters. It could even be said that the more rigid the format, the more inventive you become. It wouldn't be surprising for you to take a hackneyed feature or conventional formula that's been around for years and turn it into something smart, new, and sophisticated.

Late April through May, early September through October, and late December through January are your best times of year. This is when you feel sturdy, resolute, and your ideas will easily translate into reality. Part of the reason things take so long to come together (don't expect any big strides before thirty) is because there's a certain level of accomplishment you need to be operating at before you can establish yourself. Given the enormous role the rank and file plays in your success, don't expect much action between Memorial Day and Labor Day. Not only is this your weakest time of year Planetary-wise, but it also happens to coincide with vacation season.

PART IV

WORK & PLAY

HOW THE RULING PLANETS GET ALONG ... AND WHAT TO DO WHEN THEY DON'T

✺

CHILD OF THE SUN

.... ❋ ....

WITH CHILD OF THE SUN

You can spot a fellow Sun Child in an instant. Maybe it's the laugh, the gleam in the eye, or the regal pose of the head. It could even be a mannerism you both share. Before long the two of you are horsing around like old chums. Every time you get together (even if you haven't seen each other for years) it will feel like you're picking up right where you left off.

LOVE INTEREST

This makes for a powerful attraction and is a frequent pairing. Many people will respond to you as the "perfect couple." However your Solar energies don't necessarily interlink unless you're both looking to settle down. Otherwise you could just as easily be friends or business partners.

MATE

So who gets top billing? Each of you needs a chance to shine, and since neither is particularly flexible (you can forget about taking turns), you're better off divvying up the domain from the start. For instance, if your mate likes to cook and you excel at entertaining, then you can go ahead and be the life of the party while your spouse gets to show off by serving a sumptuous dinner. This tag team approach will serve you well—until it's time to do the dishes.

CHILD

Your Sun child is your pride and joy. Nothing makes you happier than to bask in each other's radiance—however it might be a good idea to include the rest of the family on occasion.

PARENT

Everything's fine until you hit adolescence. Trying to get a Sun parent to treat you like an adult is an exercise in futility. It might take until your mid- to late twenties to realize that your Sun parent wasn't trying to patronize you. He or she simply didn't know how to deal with you while you were "finding" yourself. As a Child of the Sun, you can appreciate the need to know where everything fits in the descending order of things. Once you have a child—or even a pet—you'll see your Sun parent treat you like an equal, because then you'll both have something to fawn over.

SIBLING

For the most part, your relationship will follow the pecking order. If you're the younger sibling, you'll show respect; if you're the older one—you'll insist on it. As Children of the Sun, you take pride in your pride and will swiftly close ranks against anyone who tries to mess with it.

FRIEND

One of you is the goof and the other is the straight man—always rolling the eyes at the latest harebrained scheme, but going along with it anyway. Tempestuous and stubborn, you'll go through times when you're not talking to each other, but in the end you always fall into each other's arms—full of apologies and pledging undying friendship.

ENEMY

It's hard to make an enemy of a fellow Sun Child, but if it happens, there's bound to be good reason for it. If so, one of you will exit the scene before too long. Your personalities are too strong to share the same turf.

BOSS

There can be only one person in charge, and if you aren't given your own special niche in which to shine, then this Solar Child's personality will grate on you. Even if he or she is popular with everyone, you will inevitably find something to criticize. Though not pretty, you need this kind of friction to urge you on to greater heights—but you may have to go elsewhere to realize your ambitions.

COLLEAGUE

You like to bond with the people you work with, but it's important to remember why you're together in the first place. There will be times when you'll have to put your feelings aside and concentrate on the job at hand. Always keep a little space between you, so that you can pull rank when you need to.

CHILD OF THE SUN

########## ❈ ....

WITH CHILD OF THE MOON

There's a naturally flowing rapport between the two of you. A Child of the Moon can intuit what you need right when you need it. This person knows just when to push and when to back off. The only thing missing is a clear idea of what he or she really thinks and feels. Unlike you, a Child of the Moon isn't especially forthcoming with what's going on and will change the subject rather than pursue a sensitive matter.

LOVE INTEREST

You want to be with this person but aren't always sure if this person wants to be with you. It's important to give your Lunar love interest plenty of breathing room. Chances are much of the emotional vagary has nothing to do with you. If you want this person to be in your life then you need to respect his or her need for privacy.

MATE

You can always rely on a Lunar mate for support and encouragement. Indeed, this person is much more comfortable playing the backcourt while you play the net. Just don't allow yourself to get lost in the shuffle. A Moon Child will focus so much on day-to-day affairs that you can become just another item on the to-do list if you're not careful. Occasional time spent away from home is key to keeping the relationship alive and fresh.

CHILD

The Moon reflects the Sun, so it only makes sense that your Lunar child will want to be all the things you expect. But you want to invite this little Moon to explore things on his or her own. Don't introduce things for the sake of introducing them. You'll only confuse matters. Just encourage those natural expressions of individuality as they begin to appear.

PARENT

Because it's the Moon's nature to nurture, your Lunar parent will always be concerned about your welfare. It doesn't matter what kind of existential problems you face, this Moon mom or dad just wants to know if there's enough food in the refrigerator and money in the bank. Don't expect him or her to embrace your spouse. Nobody's good enough for you.

SIBLING

You'll never figure out how your Lunar sibling got away with so many things. The two of you could have grown up sharing the same room and you still won't be able to fathom this mysterious Child of the Moon. One thing you should know for certain is that this person will always be there for you—no matter what.

FRIEND

Chances are the two of you met through a mutual friend. And though you may have started off socializing as part of a group, you would have quickly established your own friendship. A Child of the Moon is one of the best people to pal around with, because you can spend a whole day together doing nothing and still have loads of fun.

ENEMY

Children of the Moon are so surreptitious that you may never know you made an enemy—until somebody spills the beans. Forget about trying to figure out why. The Moon rules the emotions and memory, so it could very well be that you remind this person of an ex or a childhood rival. Just ignore it and stand your ground. Lunar Children hate confrontation, and this person will go out of his or her way to avoid having to deal with you.

BOSS

A Lunar boss is generous with praise, but cheap with the money. That's why you need to negotiate aggressively *before* you're hired. After you're on board, it's cost-of-living raises for the duration of the time you're there.

COLLEAGUE

You can always rely on a Child of the Moon to remember what you forgot. Indeed this person is so in sync with what you do that he or she can complete your sentences and even forge your signature. Given that—keep a close watch on things.

CHILD OF THE SUN

❊

WITH CHILD OF MERCURY

You can always depend on a Child of Mercury to keep you up-to-date with what's going on. This person has his or her fingers in just about everything. If you want to know the latest stats or trends, just give a call. Born under the Planet of the mind, this clever wit can run intellectual circles around most people you know. The only problem is you can't always tell if you're in on the joke or the butt of it. The fact that this person will tell you it's all in your head doesn't help matters.

LOVE INTEREST

You are completely enamored with how this person's mind works. But sometimes the incessant restlessness can get on your nerves. Unlike Children of Mercury, you don't need to be on the go twenty-four hours a day. You're more than happy to hang out. However if you're going to hook up with a Mercury Child, then you'll have to accept that there are going to be some changes. Ask yourself if you're willing to be brought up to speed. You can't expect a Child of Mercury to slow down.

MATE

One of the biggest frictions you'll experience in your relationship is your Mercury mate's need to rearrange your surroundings every three to six months. One thing you need to tell your mate right off the bat is: keep your hands off my stuff. Once that's clear, then you don't much care what color scheme you end up living with or whether the furniture is Mission style or retro kitsch.

CHILD

Get used to the fact that your kid will eventually end up being smarter than you. This isn't easy for most parents, because they'll respond as if their authority is being undermined. Thankfully, you're more relaxed about that. However there is a difference between smart and smart aleck. Encourage intelligence, but curb the back talk. Your Mercury child will thank you later.

PARENT

One of the most difficult things to figure out about a Mercury parent is the peculiar combination of exacting standards and short attention span. A Mercury parent thinks nothing of pointing out a fault and then moving on to the next interesting topic. Once you begin to understand that all things are equal—criticism doesn't undercut love and vice versa—then you'll save on therapy costs.

SIBLING

Mercury siblings are intensely competitive, but don't expect them to admit it. Just tell your brother or sister that they're number one and leave it at that. There can't be a contest if you refuse to play.

FRIEND

One thing you'll have to get used to with your Mercury friend is the periodic conversations where he or she just gets contrary for contrary's sake. Listen attentively but don't volunteer anything more than a yes or no. Eventually this person will tire of running around in mental circles and move on to something more fun.

ENEMY

Not a good idea. Either make peace as soon as you can or avoid at all costs. These Children of Mercury can be as relentless as yellow jackets buzzing over a jar of jam.

BOSS

You won't have to stand on ceremony when you work for a Mercury boss. He or she will treat you as one of the gang. However keeping this person's interest is another matter. Make a point of introducing new ideas and you'll never have to worry. You'll get tuned out if you keep chewing over the same old same old.

COLLEAGUE

Sidekick—not unlike Robin to your Batman or Gabrielle to your Xena. You can always rely on this person to be there at your elbow. But there will be times when you'll have to come running to the rescue. Mercury Children just can't help getting themselves into trouble from time to time.

CHILD OF THE SUN

.... ❋ ....

WITH CHILD OF VENUS

A Child of Venus will take what you have and make it better. It doesn't matter if it's your wardrobe or your investments; there is always room for improvement as far as this arbiter of taste is concerned. And more often than not, you are the ultimate beneficiary of this person's expert advice and shrewd judgment. However it doesn't come cheap. If you thought you had extravagant tastes, you'll soon learn they pale in comparison.

LOVE INTEREST

No one but a Child of Venus can make you feel so loved and adored. This person enjoys being out in public as much as you and will always bring the conversation back to praising your virtues and accomplishments. A Child of Venus loves to show off his or her partner. You'll find it's not unlike traveling around with your own backup band.

MATE

Don't expect domesticity. Children of Venus just aren't good at it. This isn't to say that your Venus mate is immune to household upkeep. But it has to be something fabulous, like learning a trendy new dish or remodeling the kitchen. If you're expecting room service (or even this person to pick up after him or herself)—forget it. Hire a maid.

CHILD

It can sometimes feel as if your Venus child is preprogrammed to ask to sign up for the most expensive classes possible. Whether it's ballet or horseback riding, you can expect to pay a lot for your kid's "refinement." As a Sun Child you'll do it. You hate to disappoint. But it's worth it. It doesn't much matter if you end up with the next Baryshnikov or not; the payoff will be the kind of polish that commands the big bucks.

PARENT

If your Venus parent took an interest in you growing up, then it would have been in order for you to accomplish something beautiful and good. You couldn't ask for a more earnest promoter when it came to education, the arts, or even athletics—although more "Venusian" sports might have been encouraged like baseball, running, or swimming. If not, then you were left to your own devices while your Venus parent pursued his or her own interests. Thankfully, your relationship improves with age.

SIBLING

Children of Venus make wonderful siblings. If older, then you would have been taken under wing. If younger, however, you would have been followed around without fail. Even if you were bratty, your Venus sibling would have forgiven you. A Venus Child will always stay in touch.

FRIEND

Few friendships will be as valuable and reliable, however there's just one catch. A Venus friend will be every bit as demanding (if not more so) as a lover. This may take some explaining to whomever you happen to be dating (or married to), but once over the initial hump, your Venus friend will begin to share. Who knows? You may be consigned to the background while your Venus friend becomes best buddies with your spouse.

ENEMY

Never underestimate a Venus enemy. They are much more political than you and far better at covering their tracks. That said, they were still born under the Planet of peace and harmony—which means the door is always open for a truce.

BOSS

Your relationship will be complicated, because your Venus boss thinks nothing of coming to you for ideas and then claiming all the credit for them. After all, this Child of Venus pays the bills, and that's what you're there for—to make him or her look good. If that is an agreeable arrangement, then you'll be fine. If not, go elsewhere; but don't worry. Your references will be glowing. Children of Venus never burn a bridge.

COLLEAGUE

Careful not to say anything you wouldn't mind being repeated ad infinitum. Although a Child of Venus will always make you feel like everything said is *"entre nous"* they're incorrigible gossips. They just can't help it.

CHILD OF THE SUN

.... ✳ ....

WITH CHILD OF MARS

A Child of Mars will always give your life direction. You may not know you were in need of any, but afterward you'll discover your convictions are that much stronger and your standards that much higher. Admittedly, Mars intensity can be a bit much (as a Child of the Sun you prefer a more laid-back approach), but there's no denying the extra oomph you feel when you're around one of these energy dynamos.

LOVE INTEREST

You're romantic. A Child of Mars is passionate. At first that might seem like the same thing, but you'll soon learn there's an enormous difference. You enjoy occasional candlelit dinners and silly jokes. Your Mars love interest will always want to know what you *really* feel. Don't be glib, if you know what's good for you. In time your Solar lightheartedness will get this Mars Child to unwind.

MATE

Mars mates love to fight. It's their way of blowing off steam—and checking to see if you still care. Think of it as going a few rounds at the gym. Introduce politics and world events into the conversation—it may even be worth it to occasionally adopt the opposite point of view. That way frustrations get vented and you'll stay away from breakable things—like feelings.

CHILD

This is one active kid, and the sooner you get him or her into athletics or dance, the better. You'll also want to encourage some kind of group activity. Your Mars child needs to learn how to share, take setbacks in stride, and use basic amenities like "please" and "thank you."

PARENT

When you have a Mars parent, your personal best is never enough. Others can shrug it off, but being a Child of the Sun you might have taken it hard—especially if you have a Mars father. It may not be easy to understand that this is your parent's way of being in your life. But look at it this way—if you actually accomplished what your Mars parent wanted, then you'd have nothing to talk about.

SIBLING

Your Mars sibling may not even notice you exist until after all the contests are won and the trophies collected. He or she was probably always coming home late from practice or getting up early to do some last-minute cramming. However you couldn't ask for a better friend once you get into adulthood.

FRIEND

This is the person you call in a crisis. It doesn't much matter if it's a physical one or an emotional one, your Mars friend will be right over. But don't expect much hand-holding. A Mars friend likes to "tell it like it is." Sometimes the analysis can be hard to take, but like any good medicine, it will cure what ails.

ENEMY

Mars may be the god of war, but Children of Mars are rarely vindictive. If you and this person don't get along, you may never know it, because a Child of Mars simply won't talk to you.

BOSS

Nothing but the best will do for this Mars boss—and what you consider to be "best" doesn't count. That said, you may feel more like poor Sancho Panza trotting off after Don Quixote as he takes aim at the next windmill. It's hard to figure out exactly what a Mars boss wants, but there's never a dull moment. And you'll always learn something new.

COLLEAGUE

How you get along all depends on the group atmosphere. If things are tense and everyone has to watch what's being said, then don't expect to do any fraternizing. This Child of Mars will be coolly professional—minding his or her own business and expecting you to do the same. However if you happen to work in a job where everyone is inspired to do their utmost, then you'll marvel at this person's inexhaustible enthusiasm and can-do spirit.

CHILD OF THE SUN

············ ❊ ············

WITH CHILD OF JUPITER

A Child of Jupiter will broaden your horizons. As a Child of the Sun, you tend to focus too much on your own little corner, whereas this adventurous spirit always aims to explore something new. This person's idea of getting out to see the world can range from a weekend jaunt to some exotic locale to dragging you off to the local art house to watch movies with subtitles. With a Jupiter Child, you'll get to do all the wonderful things that most people just talk about.

LOVE INTEREST

A Child of Jupiter loves to have a good time. It doesn't much matter if it's a round of darts at the sports bar or a glamorous night at the opera—your Jupiter love interest is game. There are only two things you need to watch out for—keeping up with this person's boundless energy, and the tab. That last round of drinks you thought was on the house may very well have been charged to you.

MATE

It's a good thing you like children, because you'll have quite a brood—even if they're not all yours. Expect to inherit many strays and neighborhood kids who have decided that your home is the cool place to hang. Your Jupiter spouse believes in an open-door policy, so don't be surprised to find lots of people in your TV room whom you've never met before.

CHILD

You'll need eyes in the back of your head just to keep tabs on your Jupiter child. There's a tendency to wander off. Outfit the kid with a cell phone so you can contact him or her anytime or anywhere. This will come in handy, especially during adolescence.

PARENT

Your Jupiter parent is fair and just. Even on those occasions when he or she had to discipline you, you knew it was for the best. A winsome smile always let you know that there were no hard feelings, that this was all part of the job. Yet a Jupiter parent never outgrows his or her inner child—which is perfect, since you don't outgrow yours either.

SIBLING

In a strange way, your Jupiter sibling always seems to be heading in the opposite direction. When you were in your stay-at-home phase, he or she was out and about. When you entered your "independent" period, this sibling began hassling you about family loyalty and showing up on time for holidays. Don't try figuring it out. The truth is you're just on different psychic clocks.

FRIEND

You and your Jupiter friend share just about everything—which may even include an ex. This Child of Jupiter always accents the positive, and though you are an optimist as well, you find that he or she can get too carried away—which is why it often falls to you to be the voice of reason. You never tire of each other's company and make great shopping and/or fishing buddies.

ENEMY

A difference of opinion is all it takes to draw a dividing line between you and a Child of Jupiter. However this person's investment is more ideological, whereas yours tends to be just plain stubborn. Of the two, it will be up to you to be accommodating. Stay away from potentially incendiary topics like religion and politics.

BOSS

You couldn't ask for a more relaxed boss. But don't take advantage of his or her easygoing nature. If this Child of Jupiter gets wind of you trying to pull a fast one, it will take a long time for this person to trust you again. Always feel free to approach your Jupiter boss with a problem.

COLLEAGUE

This Child of Jupiter will often spend a lot of time on the phone or fraternizing with buddies. It will be up to you to keep this person on track. Grousing and eye rolling aside, your Jupiter colleague will still come through in the end.

CHILD OF THE SUN

············· ❋ ·············

WITH CHILD OF SATURN

A Child of Saturn will always remind you of some teacher you once had. Even if you're just goofing around, this person will correct your pronunciation or point out the way you inadvertently raised an intriguing question. Everything is so serious! But once you get past the initial brush with authority, you'll come to appreciate how much this person truly values what you have to say. Your self-respect may even go up a notch as a result.

LOVE INTEREST

What impresses you most is how classy this person is. Your Saturn love interest is so sophisticated and well put together. Although it seems like this person will never relax, rest assured that he or she will eventually. The biggest question facing you as a couple is: are your work schedules compatible? If not, then you may go from hardly seeing this person to a phone call once a year on your birthday.

MATE

Work may come first with your Saturn mate, but that doesn't mean he or she is immune to fun. You just have to perfect the fine art of penciling in spontaneous outings. This is the perfect person to set up house and home with. But remember—the Sun and Saturn each symbolize the father, which means you can both have some pretty strong views about child rearing. Coordinate your approach beforehand so you don't confuse the kid.

CHILD

Your Saturn child won't have an easy go of it right away. He or she may be slow to make friends at school or may struggle to keep up in class. Saturn children can't help having difficult childhoods. It's just written into the script. However Saturn children grow younger over the years, and you'll be happy to see those early fumbling steps turn into easy strides.

PARENT

If you have a Saturn father, then he would have been as close to the classic TV dad—wise and good-humored—as you can get. He may even wear a cardigan sweater and smoke a pipe! Saturn mothers are a different story. She may have seemed unnecessarily critical and stern. Chances are this is more a reflection of her own upbringing. Over time she'll lighten up and will make a great friend and confidante when you're an adult.

SIBLING

You were predisposed to have a golden youth. It's a Solar thing. However Children of Saturn generally experience childhood as an unfavorable time. This may have created some friction—and being an optimist, it might have been hard to figure out why your Saturn sibling carried such an enormous chip on his or her shoulder. But once safely embarked on your adult lives you'll find that your brother or sister gets funnier with age.

FRIEND

It may constantly frustrate you the way your Saturn friend keeps picking apart your logic (not to mention your dreams), but in truth that's why you're friends. You're engaged in a constant debate as to whether the glass is half full or half empty. Though neither of you will win, you both benefit enormously from the other's perspective.

ENEMY

Watch your step if your Saturn enemy is in human resources or customer service. These Saturn types know how to play the system and can make your life miserable by letting the wheels of bureaucracy move even more slowly than they would normally.

BOSS

A Saturn boss is time conscious and cost-efficient—and will expect you to be the same. Though you will never be explicitly asked to, going the extra distance will always warm his or her heart. Expect scant praise, but that raise or promotion will be there when it counts.

COLLEAGUE

This person is apt to be better at your job than you. But don't worry. A Saturn colleague just feels more comfortable once he or she knows that all the bases are covered. You could learn a lot about success from hanging out with this person.

CHILD OF THE SUN

❋

WITH CHILD OF URANUS/SATURN

There's always something a little off about a Child of Uranus and Saturn. It isn't easy to pinpoint. This person is congenial, easy to talk to, and tremendously insightful. A Child of Uranus and Saturn may know more about the day-to-day running of your life than you do. Nevertheless there is still a lingering feeling that you don't know everything there is to know about this person. Which is true. It often takes years just to appreciate the full scope of a Uranus/Saturn Child's personality.

LOVE INTEREST

You will rarely meet someone this fascinating. The only problem is you may not feel like you're enough of a priority. Children of Uranus and Saturn are constantly busy, and getting your love interest to focus on just you can sometimes be an uphill battle. It may also be a little unnerving the way this person abruptly responds to you as if he or she has just been wakened from a dream or even met you for the first time. You may not know it—but you matter more than you think.

MATE

Chances are the two of you met at work and may even still work with each other. Uranian Children are often bound to others by a common cause, so taking on new projects and endeavors will be a constant in your life. Marry a Child of Uranus and Saturn and you marry everyone this person has ever known. Just tell your mate no phone calls after 11 P.M.

CHILD

Expect a lot of parent-teacher meetings. Your Uranus/Saturn child is super bright but scattered. Instead of trying to get your kid to sit down and focus (it will never happen), try short intense study periods. This will help stimulate interest and develop the attention span.

PARENT

Either your Uranus/Saturn parent was never around or you were dragged off to more boring adult functions than you care to remember. In any case, your parent may be better known to strangers than to you. However, there was bound to be a relative or friend who did some one-on-one intervention while you were growing up and kept the channels open so that the two of you might form a relationship of your own one day.

SIBLING

It may be hard to remember you both spring from the same parents—your personalities (and perhaps even appearance) couldn't be more different. Nevertheless there is a strong common bond if you choose to pursue it. But it would be up to you.

FRIEND

Children of Uranus and Saturn make good friends. There will be times when you see each other every day and times when you don't get together for years. A Uranus/Saturn friend will always keep in touch. This person may not be your "best" friend, but he or she will certainly be your truest.

ENEMY

There is almost no such thing as a Uranus/Saturn enemy. It's inconceivable. That said, you may wish this person would just relent and say that he or she doesn't like you. That way this person would stop trying to find new and different ways for you to get along.

BOSS

You may never spend much time together in person. Indeed, given your Uranus/Saturn boss's hectic schedule, you probably spend most of the time communicating by conference call or e-mail. The times when you actually do get together are full of urgency and tension. Things are always on edge, and business has to be taken care of lickety-split. That's why you always breathe a sigh of relief when he or she departs yet again.

COLLEAGUE

Buzz central. Your Uranus/Saturn colleague is on a first-name basis with everyone from the CEO to the boys in the mailroom. Follow this person around—not only does circulating throughout the office with him or her give you a chance to stretch your legs, but you also never know what you might overhear.

CHILD OF THE SUN

❈

WITH CHILD OF NEPTUNE/JUPITER

Children of Neptune and Jupiter are enigmatic. One moment they're funny and raucous and then suddenly they're quiet and reflective. Though you're intrigued by their deep feelings, you are also a little wary of them at the same time. How can someone stand to be so sensitive? As a Child of the Sun, you *identify* with what you feel. You're either happy or sad. But a Child of Neptune and Jupiter is in a constant state of flux—moving from one emotion to the next—not unlike the way the ocean changes color according to the clouds passing overhead.

LOVE INTEREST

You will find a Child of Neptune and Jupiter utterly captivating. You feel so comfortable and familiar that you may be tempted to move things along quickly. Don't. Despite the allure that a Neptune/Jupiter love interest projects (Neptune is the Planet of glamour), this person is still a person—which means you need to get to know each other and not let the romance go to your head.

MATE

A Neptune/Jupiter mate can still entice you after years of being together. Yet he or she doesn't have the same self-confidence you do. Being a Child of the Sun, you naturally aspire to be the best that you can be. Your mate may be afraid of not measuring up and will put aside his or her own dreams in order to support you in yours. This can foster a growing resentment over time. If you encourage your Neptune/Jupiter mate to realize creative pursuits then you'll both be happy.

CHILD

This is one kid you don't have to worry about amusing. A Neptune/Jupiter child can entertain himself or herself for hours. However encourage friendships from an early age. This keeps your little dreamer involved rather than tuning out all together.

PARENT

There's no doubt your Neptune/Jupiter parent adores you. But you may have felt like you didn't really bond. For people with Neptune powerful, the love they feel is so unconditional that they don't really make a distinction. Everything is equally important, which may have left you wondering what makes you any different from a loyal pet or favorite sweater? As a Child of the Sun, you need to feel special. Point this out. Your Neptune/Jupiter parent may even appreciate it.

SIBLING

You may have had little—if anything—to do with your Neptune/Jupiter sibling growing up. However when you get older, it becomes a different story. More often than not, you renew that family tie because of a crisis or being forced to share a burden. It may not be the most upbeat reason to get reacquainted, but the two of you will forge a very powerful and deep kinship.

FRIEND

You both have active imaginations, and when one of you gets started, it doesn't take much for the other to chime on in. You love to play, hang out, and discuss why things happen the way they do. However if you're both single, you shouldn't go to too many social events together. You'll get so wrapped up in talking with each other that everyone else will think you're a couple.

ENEMY

A Neptune/Jupiter enemy can turn from placid to tempestuous in an instant. If sufficiently enraged, he or she will keep pouring on the hostilities until they reach hurricane force. It's always best to beat a strategic retreat.

BOSS

Chances are you'll be making big decisions within months of coming on board. You have natural leadership ability, and your Neptune/Jupiter boss is more than happy to let you show off. But there's a reason why your boss got as far as he or she did—and that was by letting people like you believe that they were in charge . . . when they weren't.

COLLEAGUE

This person's eyes are often bigger than his or her follow-through, and this could translate into you coming to the rescue on numerous occasions. However, once firmly established, a Neptune/Jupiter colleague is always there for you.

CHILD OF THE SUN

.... ☀ ....

WITH CHILD OF PLUTO/MARS

You can sense this person's presence before he or she enters the room. If it's a good mood, everything immediately brightens up. If it's a dark mood, however, the temperature will drop considerably. You might even be able to see your own breath. Forget about keeping things light and breezy. A Child of Pluto and Mars will only call you on it. Although it can be a little daunting on occasion (as a Child of the Sun you don't like it when things get *too* heavy), the flavors in your life become that much more intense whenever you add a Pluto/Mars Child to the mix.

LOVE INTEREST

You love being the object of someone's affections. However Pluto is the Planet of obsession, which means that this person will monitor your every move. That may be more attention than you bargained for. If you're unsure about being in a relationship, then a Child of Pluto and Mars is not for you. If you're ready to hook up with someone who's every bit as dynamic as you—then you've found the right person.

MATE

Your marriage is the adventure of a lifetime. With a Pluto/Mars mate, you will share the sort of passion and drama that most people only experience at the movies. Though it won't always be smooth sailing, these ups and downs bring the two of you closer together in ways that neither of you could ever imagine. You are clearly the most important person in each other's life.

CHILD

No other kid in the room can compare to this one's single-minded drive and focus. Pluto/Mars children need to know the answer or grasp a solution. However this need to possess doesn't lend itself to give-

and-take, so expect stormy episodes to arise around the issue of sharing. Persevere. The sooner your Pluto/Mars child learns that sometimes you win and sometimes you lose, the easier it will be for him or her to accept that a disappointment doesn't mean the end of the world.

PARENT

Pluto/Mars parents are amazing until there's a shift in the balance of power. Equally proud (and stubborn), a Pluto/Mars parent will fight just as hard to maintain control as you will to assert yourself. Since neither of you will back down, it may be wise to part company for a while. Over time you'll find your way back into each other's lives again, and instead of bickering, you'll be staunch allies.

SIBLING

Your Pluto/Mars sibling is convinced you have it easy. It doesn't matter how hard you work to get to what you want in life, your brother or sister will still think you greased the palm of fate. Don't bother defending yourself. A Pluto/Mars sibling needs someone to envy, and being a Child of the Sun, you make a natural target. Nevertheless this person still loves you.

FRIEND

Pluto/Mars friends come into your life when you're on the brink of an extraordinary change. It's a good thing, too, because few people will stand by you when you're undergoing such an emotional upheaval. Afterward, when things return to normal, you'll discover a lighter, funnier side to this very complex person.

ENEMY

Not a good idea. Make up as soon as you can. You're simply out of your league with this one.

BOSS

You and your Pluto/Mars boss are perfectly suited. You both can get feisty without feeling like you have to apologize for it. But don't expect this person to open up right away. You have to prove your mettle and loyalty first.

COLLEAGUE

This one's your buddy. With everyone else you have to project that Solar confidence, but the nice thing about working with a Pluto/Mars colleague is that you can relax and say what's really on your mind without having to worry about the rest of the office finding out. Pluto/Mars Children make excellent confidants. They're also extremely gifted at working the system. This is the person to come to if you need a favor.

CHILD OF THE MOON

⋯⋯⋯⋯ ❋ ⋯⋯⋯⋯

WITH CHILD OF THE SUN

You are drawn to this person's dynamism and fire. A Child of the Sun positively radiates self-confidence. Inevitably some of that will rub off on you just by hanging out with this person. You know that the two of you would make a terrific team, but it's clear that a Child of the Sun needs to feel that he or she comes first. You don't mind that, because you know how to get your way by slipping in a subtle hint or a whispered suggestion.

LOVE INTEREST

Love at first sight. But you still have to decide whether getting serious about this person is really worth it. As a Child of the Moon, you have natural mothering instincts—even if you're a man. And seeing as the Sun rules youth and childhood, you could wind up with an overgrown Peter Pan or Heidi if you're not careful.

MATE

It's very easy to slip into clichés. You're the quiet Rock of Gibraltar while your other half is the showy entertainer. But just because certain roles come easily doesn't mean you have to typecast yourself. If you can find ways to play against type, then your Solar mate will follow your lead. Switching back and forth keeps your partnership fresh and alive.

CHILD

A Child of the Sun is the epitome of youthful innocence and humor. You never tire of the kid's antics and will probably accumulate enough video footage to open your own library. But things can get tense as your child grows older—especially if the child is the same sex as you. Remember: adolescence won't last forever.

PARENT

You may have felt more like the parent than the child. Although Solar parents always take their job seriously, they lack a certain follow-through—especially when it comes to the less glamorous aspects of being a mom or dad. As a Child of the Moon, you would have spotted what was missing right away and naturally filled in—perhaps even taking over certain chores like doing the laundry or shopping.

SIBLING

You've always been close. And in many ways, your Solar sibling looked up to you—even if you were younger. This bond continues into adulthood. You can always turn to this Child of the Sun for financial advice or to take the kids off your hands for the evening.

FRIEND

Children of the Sun see themselves as the animating spirit in everyone's lives. They'll happily grace you with their observations. Share a problem or a quandary and a Child of the Sun will tell you what he or she would do in your position.

ENEMY

Solar Children don't go out of their way to be nasty unless there's good reason for it. And oftentimes that reason is because their feelings have been hurt. A little time spent away from the arena—maybe invite this person out for a walk or a drink—usually results in getting to the bottom of the problem.

BOSS

You two are like a comedy team. Your Solar boss will get all blustery and bark commands while you stand behind him or her with arms akimbo, rolling your eyes and shaking your head. In truth, your boss knows how much time you spend doing damage control and even enjoys your wisecracks. This person also relies on you heavily for off-the-record advice.

COLLEAGUE

Solar Children don't always take the initiative, so be prepared to give some direction. If your Solar colleague is a guy, you'll have to prod him every step of the way. He's always convinced he's finished when you think he's only just begun. If your colleague is a gal, understand that once she's gotten an idea in her head it's almost impossible to get her to adopt another approach. Introduce your idea as an extension of hers—even if you know it's a stretch.

CHILD OF THE MOON

············ ❋ ············

WITH CHILD OF THE MOON

It's a relief not to have to spell everything out. You can rest assured that a fellow Child of the Moon gets you on your level. You can make all the elliptical remarks you want and this person will know *exactly* what you mean. The only thing to watch out for is that you can take on the other's mood without knowing it—leaving you wondering if that's really your funk you're in or somebody else's?

LOVE INTEREST

Since you are both accustomed to looking after the emotional needs of others, you may be bashful about expressing your feelings. Indeed the fact that you can predict what your Moon date is going to do next could make you self-conscious. Nevertheless you come from separate backgrounds and each have your own history. Enjoy getting to know the differences.

MATE

As Children of the Moon, you go through phases. But you don't necessarily go through your phases at the same time. For instance, your mate may be in a "full moon" phase: happy that matters are coming to fruition and getting ready to wind down, while you may be in a "new moon" phase, which is gung-ho and enthusiastic about getting a project or venture up off the ground. If you allow for a difference in clocks and rhythms, you'll always be there for each other, even if you're not reading from the same page.

CHILD

Your Lunar child brings out all of your protective instincts—whether or not this kid actually needs such close supervision. It's important to curb these tendencies. Not only because you'll worry yourself sick if you don't, but also because you want this child to be able to stand up on his or her own two feet one day. Moon children are extremely resilient.

PARENT

This is one of the most important people in your life. You two have always had more of a kinship than a parent/child relationship. Your roles are very fluid. In the course of a conversation you can move from the casualness of friends to the intimacy of siblings to the objectivity of business partners. This is one of the few people you'll accept criticism from, because you know it's based on something that your Lunar parent is also struggling to improve.

SIBLING

The two of you have always been—and always will be—close. The only bumpy period is when one of you starts dating or gets married. You don't like having to share your Moon sibling with anyone. After a while you will grudgingly accept this new face into the fold.

FRIEND

You run everything by each other—from decisions about your marriage to whether or not you want to switch laundry detergents. The only thing you want to guard against is becoming too dependent on this person's feedback. Think for yourself and you'll keep the friendship hearty. You don't want to wind up recycling each other's advice.

ENEMY

Since the dispute probably has to do with one of you horning in on the other's turf, you'll have to determine how far you're willing to go. If you're the one overstepping your bounds, then it probably isn't worth it. However if you're defending what's rightfully yours, then be prepared to put up a fight to the end.

BOSS

Even if you work at a corporation, it will still have the feel of a mom-and-pop store. That's because your Moon boss only wants to work with people who truly care about the product. However that same homey feeling can also bring some family dysfunction along with it. It's up to you to be professional.

COLLEAGUE

Sometimes the moods get in the way of work. You may get frustrated when your Moon colleague decides to be in a snit. It isn't easy to deliberately turn a blind eye, but it might be necessary if you want this person to get with the program.

CHILD OF THE MOON

.... ❉ ....

WITH CHILD OF MERCURY

A Child of Mercury gets you to see things more *intellectually*, while you prevail upon this cerebral person to give more credence to the emotions. This makes you perfect complements. But remember—what comes naturally for you is a stretch for this person. This will keep you from feeling hurt when he or she gets into an *ornery* mood. Mercury Children process thoughts out loud the way you process your feelings internally. Their words are just as mutable as your emotions are.

LOVE INTEREST

You probably have very different tastes. Your Mercury date may fail to appreciate the sentimental value of a favorite haunt, while you could find this person's home too austere. Thankfully you are both flexible and more than willing to see things from a different point of view.

MATE

You two are always on the go. There's no such thing as standing still when you have a Mercury mate. This person has boundless energy and can run you ragged if you're not careful, so don't be afraid to call time-out when you need it. One thing you may never resolve is the agenda issue. It drives you batty the way your Mercury mate constantly changes his or her schedule. In fact, the more you try to coordinate your schedules, the more this person will fuss with them. Simply do what you want, and this person will show up. A Mercury mate can't stand being out of the loop.

CHILD

A Mercury child will always ask questions. And it doesn't help to make up an answer if you don't know it. Your Mercury child will eventually find out and then ask why you pretended to know something when you didn't. Ironically, for a kid who does so much thinking, it may be nearly impossible to get him or her to concentrate on schoolwork. Believe it or not, loud music or the sound of the television helps. But be sure to examine the homework after it's been done. Mercury children are geniuses when it comes to pulling a fast one.

PARENT

Your Mercury parent was probably in and out of your life when you were growing up. But just because this person wasn't always around doesn't mean he or she didn't keep close tabs. Though you may still not spend much time together, it will always be high quality.

SIBLING

You probably couldn't stand each other when you were younger, and though you've made peace since the rubber-snake-in-your-lunch-box episode, it still doesn't take much to bring old suspicions back to the surface. Nevertheless this person adores you—although he or she will never tire of getting a rise out of you.

FRIEND

You probably blame your Mercury friend for all the crazy things you get talked into doing. But at the same time you should give your friend credit for opening your world and fostering your curiosity.

ENEMY

A Mercury enemy is a master at using your words against you. That's why it's best not to give this person any ammunition. If you have to communicate, do it in writing and keep all copies of your correspondence. It will come in handy later.

BOSS

Get used to the fact that your Mercury boss will always change the way you want to do something. It has nothing to do with you. It's simply Mercury's nature to fiddle with whatever it finds. Sometimes it's an improvement and sometimes it creates more work. That's why you never want to throw away any previous drafts until you're absolutely certain that everything's been finalized.

COLLEAGUE

The reason this Mercury colleague can fraternize so much and not get into trouble is because he or she can get the work done in half the time it takes everyone else. Needless to say, you are not like this. It's all right to visit, but keep an eye on the time.

CHILD OF THE MOON

※

WITH CHILD OF VENUS

A Child of Venus believes there are two sides to every story. This is different from your sympathetic approach to life. You often put yourself in someone else's shoes—asking yourself how you would feel if you were faced with a similar situation. Children of Venus put their emotions aside so that they can get a more balanced view of matters. You can learn a lot about people and the way they relate by being with a Child of Venus.

LOVE INTEREST

Courtship is very important to Children of Venus. It's how they decide if they want you in their lives or not. It may feel a little awkward having to "audition" for the role of paramour, but it's better than rehashing your family history yet again or talking about your plans for the future. The one thing you'll need to get used to is hearing all about your Venus lover's exes. They're still friends.

MATE

Your Venus mate wants to be out and about, making valuable professional or social contacts. At first you may be reluctant to follow along—as a Child of the Moon, you're ready to close up shop around 7 P.M.—but over time you'll come to appreciate these impromptu soirées.

CHILD

Good luck keeping up with your Venus child's ever-changing roster of friends. Play dates who appear one week may be passé the next. But what looks capricious is actually very well thought out. Children of Venus start networking early. Considering that this is just kindergarten, you can imagine what high school will be like.

PARENT

You may not have shared your Venus parent's preoccupation with appearances when you were growing up (you wanted to be comfortable, not chic), but you'll eventually come to realize what he or she was getting at. As a Child of the Moon, you have a strong inner life. You take things personally and agonize over job interviews and dates. Your Venus parent probably taught you that if you focused more on making the right impression, then you wouldn't have to worry so much about credentials or proving yourself.

SIBLING

Venus siblings act as if they don't know you in public, but they will confide everything in private. This can be a bit off-putting, but once you realize how your brother or sister regards these as two entirely separate spheres, then you won't mind it so much. Watch your back if you happen to make the acquaintance of someone who's attractive or well-to-do. A Venus sibling can be very competitive when it comes to love and money.

FRIEND

This is the person you turn to for coaching on how to ask for a raise, what to order on your first date, or where the most desirable neighborhood is. Conversely, a Venus friend will come to rely on your advice and support. It may never cease to amaze you how your Venus friend can be so naive about people's psychologies, but then that's why you're friends. You each add to the other's perspective.

ENEMY

You don't really have anything to fear from a Venus enemy. Venus makes love, not war. The only thing to watch out for is if you both have your eyes set on the same prize. This person is just as driven as you and twice as sneaky.

BOSS

Expect to do a lot of gruntwork while getting little credit for it. A Child of Venus sees his or her job as being out in the field making deals, generating contacts, and planting the seeds for future business. A Venus boss will then leave it up to others to do the follow-up calls or haggle over the fine print.

COLLEAGUE

Either this will be the most brilliant person you've ever hooked up with or dead weight. If your Venus colleague is a dud, refuse to help out with even the simplest task. It may seem harsh, but don't give an inch or this person will take a mile.

CHILD OF THE MOON

·········· ❊ ··········

WITH CHILD OF MARS

Children of Mars are passionate—which is something you understand. You feel things deeply, too. The difference is that a Child of Mars burns with an overwhelming urgency (everything must be done *now*), while you move with the current of events. A Child of Mars may regard you as too passive, while you see a Child of Mars as being too aggressive. Yet despite your contrasting temperaments, the two of you are perfectly suited.

LOVE INTEREST

Hopefully you like a love interest who comes on strong—because there won't be anything iffy about this person's intent. You, however, tend to vacillate. That's because your Birthday Planet is constantly changing its appearance in the sky. A Mars Child will relax as long as you can name a date when he or she can expect an answer. But don't keep this person hanging. A Mars Child has no patience.

MATE

Moon/Mars marriages aren't for the timid. It takes a while to work out the kinks. You may spend your first few years feeling terribly hurt, while your Mars mate might accuse you of emotional blackmail. But after all the angry silences, yelling, and tears (you're one of the few people who can make a Mars Child cry), you will eventually settle into a comfortable fit. Your Mars mate will gain a deeper appreciation for your feelings, while you'll develop a thicker hide.

CHILD

Mars children are accident-prone. They are always falling out of trees or not looking where they're going—it's enough to chill the blood of any Moon parent. However these little scrappers are tough and even love to show off their bruises and cuts. Since you'll never convince the kid to take it easy, prevail upon him or her to wear a safety helmet, knee pads, etc. Buy them in red or black so it looks cool.

PARENT

Your Mars mom or dad may not have been the easiest person in the world to please, but you would have benefited enormously from this person's can-do spirit. *No* just isn't a word in the Mars vocabulary. What you'll come to appreciate is that the reason your parent pushed you so hard wasn't in order for you to achieve—accomplishments come and go—but so that you would learn to never stop pushing *yourself.*

SIBLING

The troublemaker. The best thing a Mars sibling can do is move away as a young adult so that he or she can work out all that aggression in somebody else's backyard. When this person resurfaces, he or she is usually dramatically changed for the better. However if your Mars sibling stays close to home, then this person may take on the role of "black sheep." Don't even try rewriting the script.

FRIEND

Your Mars friend is in your life to galvanize you. Perhaps this person rekindles your creative spirit, challenges you to try for something you gave up on, or simply drags you to the gym three times a week. In any case, your self-confidence will improve courtesy of your Mars friend.

ENEMY

You don't want to go anywhere near the point of contention until your Mars enemy has calmed down. Once over it, this person would love to let bygones be bygones—as long as you agree that you're wrong. Stand your ground if you think you're in the right. This Mars Child will ultimately respect you for it.

BOSS

Mars bosses never think they're in charge, so you need to do everything in your power to make them feel like top dog. What you get in exchange is someone who will always go to bat for you. You'll also enjoy the rare experience of working for one of the best bosses you'll ever have.

COLLEAGUE

You couldn't work with anyone more clueless when it comes to handling day-to-day matters. However if it's an emergency, then this Mars colleague is decisive and focused. You'll marvel at the speed and dexterity with which he or she saves the day.

CHILD OF THE MOON

.... ❉ ....

WITH CHILD OF JUPITER

Something's always cooking when a Child of Jupiter (Planet of hospitality) and a Child of the Moon (Planet of hearth and home) hook up. Not only do you both love to be in the kitchen (eating as much as preparing food), but you also can't help setting a big table—which means friends will always be a part of your lives. As a child of the summer, you believe that no one should want for anything, and a Child of Jupiter will second that motion. However, this champion of munificence can be generous to a fault, so keep an eye on the till.

LOVE INTEREST

A Child of Jupiter is a true romantic. This person loves to be in love and will come rolling into your life and sweep you off your feet. However he or she is just as likely to go rolling back out again once the infatuation wears off. Clearly you'll need more than romance to keep this person's interest. Your willingness to share an adventure ensures your name remains uppermost in mind.

MATE

Once settled, a Jupiter mate is as true as they come. The only real difficulty you'll face is the money issue. Set up separate bank accounts. That way you won't be wiped out by the latest extravagance, and should this person overspend, he or she will have no choice but to adopt your shoestring budget.

CHILD

As far as your kid is concerned, the grass will always be greener on the other side of the fence. You'll never convince this Jupiter child otherwise, so instill the values of honoring obligations and taking responsibility as early on as you can. That way when he or she flies the nest (probably sooner rather than later) you can sleep at night, knowing that your kid can take care of himself or herself and isn't a cad.

PARENT

As warmhearted and good-natured as they come. Tempestuous perhaps (Jupiter is named after the god of storms), but you never felt intimidated or bullied. If anything, your Jupiter parent has always encouraged you to *express* what you feel and to not internalize so much.

SIBLING

It may have been hard to get to know your Jupiter sibling when you were younger, because this person was always trying to get out of things. Whether it was ducking out of chores or sneaking out the bedroom window late at night, it seemed like your brother or sister just didn't want to be around. However as an adult, it's often different. Jupiter may be the Planet of adventure, but he's also the Planet of tribes. A Jupiter sibling will always try to involve you more in his or her life.

FRIEND

You can always rely on a Jupiter friend to steal you away for an afternoon at the museum or a three-hour lunch at some out-of-the-way bistro. You may not see a lot of this person on a day-to-day basis, but when you do you're sure to come away half exhausted from laughing, your mind full of anecdotes, and at least three new must-read books to add to your list. But don't kill yourself trying to read them. Chances are this Child of Jupiter hasn't read them either.

ENEMY

It's difficult to make an enemy of a Child of Jupiter. Even if this person doesn't like you, he or she will always make a point of being pleasant in public. If there is a history of bad blood, it's probably due to you competing for the same job or love interest. Give it time and this Jupiter Child will get over it.

BOSS

They don't come much bossier. There's a lot of bluster that goes along with that authority. However, Jupiter Children take their leadership role seriously and will always exhibit sound judgment.

COLLEAGUE

If you're working on something exciting and fabulous, your Jupiter colleague will be there in body and spirit. If it's dull and tedious—you're on your own.

CHILD OF THE MOON

.... ❄ ....

WITH CHILD OF SATURN

Y ou're intrigued by this person's reserve. But it's not just the worldliness, the sophistication, or even the seriousness of purpose that draws you in. It may be a vague "lost" quality that's hard to pinpoint. You can sense the hidden emotional depth in a Child of Saturn that others often overlook.

LOVE INTEREST

Don't expect this person to open up right away. It takes Children of Saturn a while to decide if they're in or out. Even if you're laughing and carousing, you'll still sense that emotional distance. Part of this is due to their famously guarded nature, but the real reason Saturn Children take dating seriously is because they don't want to lead you on. Your feelings are in good hands with this person. You're better chaperoned than if your mom were sitting in the backseat.

MATE

This relationship just gets better with time. You may start off in opposite camps—you're probably too touchy-feely while your Saturn mate is huffy and stuffy—but you will gradually absorb some of each other's qualities. Perhaps the thing you love most is how nobody but you knows what your Saturn mate is *really* like.

CHILD

Telling your Saturn child to take it easy only makes him or her feel under more pressure to perform. Relax is a message that won't compute. You may wonder how this kid got to be so driven—even the word *okay* is interpreted as a criticism. It's just in their makeup. Saturn Children age backwards. They may start out as crotchety as a grandparent, but they become more youthful and delightful over time and at an age when you could really use a breath of fresh air.

PARENT

You may have resented how your Saturn parent was always interrupting your reveries to ask if you'd finished your chores or your homework. It may have seemed like your mom or dad was just lying in wait for your next relaxed moment before springing forward with something new to add to your to-do list. As a Moon Child, your downtime is when you do your best reflecting. Children of Saturn equate downtimes with depression or resignation. That drive to do may actually have been your Saturn parent's way of keeping you from slipping into a funk.

SIBLING

No matter what you do, your Saturn sibling will always zero in on what's missing. This critical intolerance may have gotten on your nerves when you were younger, and so you may have kept your thoughts and feelings under wraps. What you'll find as you get older, however, is that your Saturn sibling is probably the only other relative who takes family concerns as seriously as you do.

FRIEND

You're both moody but deal with it differently. If you feel down, you trust that in a few moments (or maybe even an hour), you'll come bobbing back up to the surface. Saturn Children are always skating on the edge of depression, so if they go into a downward spiral, you can rest assured it will take more than a few minutes for this person to resurface. The two of you can get quite intense, but there's no one you trust more.

ENEMY

Neither of you will back down. You're both convinced that if you acquiesce, you'll only be inviting a future attack. Talk clearly and unemotionally about what you need. Once this person realizes you're sincere, then he or she will find a way to make that happen.

BOSS

Saturn bosses don't think twice about burning the midnight oil. Indeed a Child of Saturn is proud of it. But don't worry. Your boss won't ask you to do the same.

COLLEAGUE

A Saturn colleague makes a great team player—as long as he or she is in charge. Let your Saturn colleague be the uncontested authority on anything from international law to changing the fax paper and this person will be happy.

CHILD OF THE MOON

·········· ❈ ··········

WITH CHILD OF URANUS/SATURN

A Child of Uranus and Saturn will always challenge you to grow as a person. It isn't easy being around this kind of energy. Yours is cyclical and rhythmic while this person's can seem abrupt. Sudden reversals and surprise twists are all part of the package. It takes a while to catch on to the fact that Children of Uranus and Saturn are actually following a cycle of their own—it's just so vast and elaborate that it's hard to grasp right away. But, like some forms of music, you will grow accustomed to it in time.

LOVE INTEREST

Children of Uranus and Saturn are so comfortable with objectifying the personal that they can come across as unfeeling. Everyone has feelings. Chances are the reason you're in this person's life is to flesh them out. Much of what you sense will only be hinted at, but thankfully, as a Child of the Moon, you're good at reading between the lines.

MATE

Children of Uranus and Saturn come with full-blown lifestyles, so it's easy to get overwhelmed by their schedules, friends, and demands on their time. Thankfully you are good at going with the flow and possess that wonderful Lunar ability to create your own personal retreat. What you'll find is that your Uranus/Saturn mate would rather spend time in *your* world. You're game—but only if he or she leaves all the craziness outside.

CHILD

You have a natural ability to visualize, while your child's talent is to conceptualize. Once you understand how different paths can arrive at the same destination, then you can work backward and figure out just how your Uranus/Saturn child actually *sees* the world. You may never understand it, but you don't need to in order to nurture it.

PARENT

You probably did a lot of moving around when you were younger. There's something about the mix of Uranian and Lunar energies that results in a frequent change of scene. The choices your Uranus/Saturn parent made may not have seemed sensible at the time, but given hindsight you'll come to appreciate the tough road this person traveled and how much of what you have is a result of it.

SIBLING

This is as close to a complete opposite as you're likely to find. If you're liberal, your sibling's conservative; if you've always been down-home in your taste, this Child of Uranus and Saturn is a roving bohemian. It's hard to believe you came from the same parents.

FRIEND

You probably met through bizarre circumstances. Uranus/Saturn friends usually blow into your life during times of upheaval and change. The wonderful thing about this person is how clear-eyed he or she is. If this Child of Uranus and Saturn sticks around, chances are many of your other friends won't. And it's not because of anything bad. It's just that once you start to see the world through a Uranus/Saturn friend's eyes, you'll never subscribe to conventional wisdom again.

ENEMY

You both have a blind spot when it comes to belief systems. You're emotionally invested in yours while a Child of Uranus and Saturn just assumes you are unenlightened. Most of the world gets by with an uneasy peace nowadays, and chances are you two can do the same.

BOSS

Your Uranus/Saturn boss can see so far down the road that you barely know what he or she is even referring to. But play along anyway. In about half an hour (or perhaps by day's end), you'll see exactly what this person was talking about. If it makes you feel any better—no one else understands your Uranus/Saturn boss either—although everyone recognizes the brilliance.

COLLEAGUE

It may take a while to figure out how this person got as far as he or she did. Uranus/Saturn colleagues often come across as spacey or hopelessly miscast. But like a high-fashion model whose everyday appearance can seem plain or bizarre, everything suddenly changes once it's time for work.

CHILD OF THE MOON

⁕

WITH CHILD OF NEPTUNE/JUPITER

Children of Neptune and Jupiter have such depth of feeling and breadth of imagination that you're in awe. Nevertheless your inner lives are very different. Yours is an integral part of you. Personal and intimate, your interior landscape fosters who you are as a person. Children of Neptune and Jupiter visualize all sorts of things, but there's no great need to fish them out of the stream of consciousness and make something of them. The imagination, as far as they're concerned, is like a wildlife preserve. Pristine in its beauty, it should be left untouched and admired at a distance.

LOVE INTEREST

Perhaps the most difficult thing to fathom is how your Neptune/Jupiter love interest can be so sensitive yet impersonal at the same time. Children of Neptune and Jupiter are elusive and hard to grasp. Some people enjoy this aura of mystery, but being a Moon Child, you need more of a bond. You will push to define matters right away. And if this person remains vague or noncommittal, you will let it slip—like so much water—through your fingers.

MATE

A Neptune/Jupiter mate makes you more affirmative. In a strange reversal of roles, you'll find that you're the one asking this person to express what he or she *really* feels. Don't let your mate defer to you. Make a point of empowering this person's right to choose. That way you won't get stuck returning half the things to the store that your Neptune/Jupiter mate agreed to only because he or she thought you really wanted them.

CHILD

Teach your Neptune/Jupiter child the value of setting personal boundaries. One's own sentiments needn't be open to debate. Helping your Neptune/Jupiter child to understand that a private life is a prerogative and not something to apologize for will keep him or her from blending into the woodwork.

PARENT

Your senses of justice, generosity, and charity all stream from this person. However your Neptune/Jupiter parent is more willing to sacrifice than you are. He or she is convinced that everything will be made right in the end. As a Child of the Moon, you are much too practical to swallow that one. This is why you're more likely to conserve resources and work with what you have than place your trust in a universe that supposedly gives back as much as it takes.

SIBLING

Neptune/Jupiter siblings often start out as emotional messes before evolving into beautifully graceful adults. The reason for this is that they're highly attuned to the family psyche. As your brother or sister develops a strong personality to contain (and shelter) all that raw feeling, then you'll begin to see someone who possesses good humor, judgment, and wisdom rather than an open channel broadcasting the things that people would really rather not be discussing.

FRIEND

Your Neptune/Jupiter friend is in your life to broaden your intellectual or spiritual horizons, so expect animated discussions and debates. This person gets you to see things on a "higher" level. Regardless of whether you adopt your friend's belief system or approach to life, what you'll gain is a new and refreshing way of examining your own.

ENEMY

Even if differences are irreconcilable, you are both so accommodating that you will find a way to get around the problem or to let the other bow out gracefully. Children of Neptune and Jupiter don't harbor grudges. They would rather make peace and move on with their lives.

BOSS

A Neptune/Jupiter boss always has an eye out for potential, and chances are the reason you got your job in the first place is because you've got what it takes to take over the business or start one of your own.

COLLEAGUE

This Child of Neptune and Jupiter makes a great confidante, but could be a less-than-efficient coworker. Everything is of equal priority. Show this person what needs to be done first and you'll ensure business gets taken care of.

CHILD OF THE MOON

.... ❋ ....

WITH CHILD OF PLUTO/MARS

Everything is so do-or-die with a Child of Pluto and Mars. Half measures are unheard of, as this person would rather risk it all than hold back. Nothing could be more contrary to your Lunar nature. However there's a part of you that simply can't resist the pull. You know you should probably avoid getting to know a Child of Pluto and Mars, but you'll race to catch up instead.

LOVE INTEREST

You were born during the height of summer, when crops are ripe and bursting with life. You trust in life's horn of plenty and see needs as wants that will ultimately be fulfilled. A Child of Pluto and Mars was born in the fall, when crops have already been harvested and gone to seed. It's a time of scarcity. This person doesn't see life as being especially copious. Indeed there's a constant feeling that everything is in short supply. This is what makes these love interests so intense. But then—that's why you fell for this person to begin with.

MATE

Anger is a source of strength with your mate. It's why he or she is often sore about something. This doesn't exactly square with your emotional approach to life. You want to comfort and smooth over the rough spots. Yet this source of tension also acts as an attraction. Ultimately a Pluto/Mars mate will empower you, while you will gradually teach this person that there is such a thing as living happily ever after.

CHILD

Your Pluto/Mars child is a born fighter. Even the choice of baby food was a bone of contention. Stop trying to make things nice and simply accept that this is your kid's way of announcing himself or herself to the world. Obviously you'd like it if things came easier, but children of Pluto and Mars have a sixth sense for choosing the roughest course possible. It toughens them up.

PARENT

Your Pluto/Mars parent loves you deeply, powerfully, and would do anything for you. However anxieties about money may have complicated your relationship. He or she places too much importance on finances—always seeing them as being out of reach. Once you realize that money is *not* the root of all evil—nor in the short supply you were led to believe—then it will cease to be the overriding preoccupation in your life. Your Pluto/Mars parent may even learn by your example.

SIBLING

You admire your Pluto/Mars sibling's guts. This person always did what he or she wanted to do—although you were also privy to much of the angst that went into it. Nevertheless, you learned to not back down to life's challenges. It's thanks to your Pluto/Mars sibling that you don't talk yourself out of half the things you used to.

FRIEND

You'll spend a lot of time discussing your love lives. And your Pluto/Mars friend will ask you all those personal questions that no one else would dare to. Be prepared to hear more about this person's date or spouse than you care to know.

ENEMY

Wave the white flag ASAP! Even if you don't think you did anything wrong, fess up. Your Pluto/Mars enemy will be merciful.

BOSS

Not a morning person! It doesn't matter when this person went to bed the night before, it just isn't a good time. However, once noon approaches, your Pluto/Mars boss is as chipper as can be: vivacious, funny, and full of inspiration. This is the best time to share problems or ask for things you'd be too afraid to otherwise.

COLLEAGUE

Make life pleasant for your colleague and he or she will return the favor. A Child of Pluto and Mars is low maintenance. Things only get tense when you actually have to *criticize* this person. Emphasize the good points and make it constructive—but don't sugarcoat anything. Then leave the matter alone. This person will incorporate what you suggested—one point at a time.

CHILD OF MERCURY

.... ❊ ....

WITH CHILD OF THE SUN

Your roles are set up from the start. A Child of the Sun sits on the throne while you clown around making fun. You know this person doesn't get half the jokes and wisecracks you send whizzing over the net, but the fact that he or she will laugh anyway warms your heart. It's extremely rare for you to *want* to impress anyone. But winning that stamp of approval from a Child of the Sun marks the high point of your day.

LOVE INTEREST

Not your first choice. A Child of the Sun usually opts for a yes-man (or woman) and though you'll play along, you'll eventually want to debate. If you hook up, it will probably be later in life or after you've both been married. At this point you can enjoy the special camaraderie you share free of all the romantic expectations (and stereotypes).

MATE

You two are a formidable team. Plus you're a lot of fun to be around. A Child of the Sun makes the perfect foil—not to mention "tough" cop to your "good" cop. You're happy to manage your day-to-day affairs, but whenever you have to bring in the big guns, you know you can always rely on your Solar mate to lay down the law with a recalcitrant kid or quarrelsome contractor.

CHILD

Your pride and joy. A Solar child is always game for the next adventure you have up your sleeve. Your only reservation, however, is with the way this kid always has to be right. As a Mercury parent, you should encourage your child to be more inquisitive. Anyone can be a know-it-all, but few people are clever enough to ask a really good question.

PARENT

In some ways you can't help feeling that your Solar parent shortchanged himself or herself. You're convinced that there's a potential yet to be realized. But you may be really talking about yourself. You're the one who doesn't want to accept convention, while your Solar parent is quite comfortable with it. Being happy in your life doesn't have to detract from your intellectual or creative pursuits.

SIBLING

You've always admired the way your Solar sibling could just step right up to the front of the line without once looking back. Clearly your Solar sibling is on to something, but what? It may take a lifetime to deduce the secret to this person's success.

FRIEND

A Solar friend is like a fire—vivacious and bright. But if that spirit burns low, you'll have to tend it. A Solar friend needs recognition along with the occasional pat on the back. Without it, the Child of the Sun will get sullen and mopey.

ENEMY

You could probably run circles around your Solar enemy, so you need to ask yourself if it's worth it. Children of the Sun are peace loving for the most part and really don't go looking for a fight. There's a good chance you can settle your differences even if you don't see eye to eye. However if properly provoked, your Solar enemy will retaliate.

BOSS

Your boss knows you're smart. That's why you were hired. However if you want to get anywhere, then you need to show some discretion to go along with that savvy. Otherwise you won't be trusted and subsequently will be kept on a short leash.

COLLEAGUE

A Solar colleague is instantly recognizable by his or her popularity. Chances are you'll hear about this person long before you meet. It's always worth getting to know this Child of the Sun because everyone comes to this person for the "real" scoop at review time. Don't make the mistake of assuming this person is just "one of the gang." Chances are your Solar colleague is your boss's cousin, married to a client, or happens to be drinking buddies with the floor manager.

CHILD OF MERCURY

.... ❋ ....

WITH CHILD OF THE MOON

Trying to get a Child of the Moon to talk about his or her feelings will only make this person clam up. But whistle a favorite TV theme from childhood or share a secret phrase that only you two know and this person's eyes will brighten. The Moon rules over memories and dreams, the soft underbelly of the human psyche. Children of the Moon are intensely private and always want things to be *entre nous*. This appeals to that side of you that loves to feel like you're "in" on something that others just don't get.

LOVE INTEREST

Don't be taken in by the easygoing manner. Your Lunar love interest can be just as evasive—and twice as elusive—as you. Every time you think you've got a Child of the Moon pegged, this person will let slip some remark or observation that suggests he or she may know more than you think. It's very hard for you to know what's on this person's mind—which is what keeps you coming back again and again.

MATE

You will never be allowed into that private place your Lunar mate guards so jealously. And if you're smart, you won't pry. Children of the Moon need their emotional space. It's not unlike what Virginia Woolf called "a room of one's own." So when your mate disappears behind a book, dons the earphones, or takes off for the weekend with friends—let this person be.

CHILD

One of the things you enjoy is how *physical* your Lunar child is. Your Birthday Planet rules the intellect and speech, but it also rules the five senses. You're naturally very tactile, so you'll treasure the way your kid will simply climb into your lap or hold your hand without saying anything. Your Moon child reminds you that there are other ways of communicating besides words.

PARENT

Your relationship may be more like siblings than parent and child. That's because your Lunar parent recognized how bright you were right away and often ran things by you to get your take on matters. It wouldn't be surprising if you two wind up in business together.

SIBLING

Despite your closeness, you may get the sense that your Lunar sibling doesn't disclose everything. That's because this person knows you don't always gauge what you say before you say it. Nevertheless the two of you are fast friends, and your Lunar sibling will eventually divulge all—though it's the juicy stuff you find out about last.

FRIEND

Your Lunar friend is the only one who will accompany you to that movie nobody wants to see or will read that book by the author whose name is a long string of consonants. And chances are the only reason you get all the way through that movie or book is because this person insists on finishing what you start.

ENEMY

A Lunar enemy will always be cagier than you. You may be a quick study, but a Child of the Moon is a shrewd observer. A favorite tactic is draining your reserves before closing in for the kill. There's a reason why this person's Ruling Planet was named after the goddess of the hunt.

BOSS

You'll impress your Lunar boss more by curbing that need to race ahead of the pack and working as part of a team. Children of the Moon are very tribal and keep a look out for what benefits the group as a whole. If you show you're a trouper, then this person will vote to keep you on the island.

COLLEAGUE

Children of the Moon will always do what's in the best interests of everyone—although they tend to be both subtle and conservative in their approach. If you want to know what's up at work, then a Lunar colleague is the person to ask. This is one of the few people who actually know what's up before you do.

CHILD OF MERCURY

·········· ❊ ··········

WITH CHILD OF MERCURY

What makes a fellow Mercury Child so intriguing is that this person will highlight the very qualities about yourself that you don't readily recognize. In many ways you're mirror opposites. You will always learn something new about yourself because of your involvement with another Child of Mercury.

LOVE INTEREST

Two peas in a pod—though you may be the last to recognize it. Chances are you met through friends who were sure you guys would hit it off. Although the attraction's mutual, it may take a while to warm to being a couple. You both recognize how this could be a dicey combination. Don't be surprised if you date on and off or maybe even see other people for a while. You know that once you commit, this will be it.

MATE

Yours isn't the sort of familiarity where you finish each other's sentences. Children of Mercury are never so predictable. It's more like you have each other's timing down pat. You know right where the other one is without having to turn around and look. You were built for collaboration. Understandably loved ones and friends will rally against you two pairing up for bridge or charades. You'll each review the other's performance and make helpful suggestions—even if you're on competing teams.

CHILD

Your Mercury child eats up everything you say and still wants to know more. You always wished you had someone to show you the ropes, so it will be wonderful to share your knowledge with someone who appreciates it. But just as you had to go your own way, your child will do the same. Let your kid go find himself or herself. Just think of how much you'll have to share when you meet up again!

PARENT

If Children of Mercury are supposed to be so bright, why is your mom or dad so slow on the uptake? Chances are your Mercury parent is brilliant—but in a way you don't (or won't) recognize. There are different types of intelligence, just as there are different types of personalities. In time you'll come to appreciate how your Mercury parent works.

SIBLING

Mercury is the Planet of sibling rivalry, so it wouldn't be surprising if things are tense between you. Nevertheless, you can't leave each other alone and will always be drawn back together—no matter how far you go in opposite directions. Indeed, yours is the type of relationship that flourishes best long-distance. It's when you get within proximity of each other that you get edgy.

FRIEND

Your best friend *and* your worst enemy—and not even you two are sure which is which half the time. You will bicker and fight one minute and then turn around and ask for advice about an intimate matter the next. You would do anything for each other—even if you're still not talking. You'd make wonderful business partners. That need to outdo each other ensures neither of you will rest on your laurels.

ENEMY

If this person is *truly* an enemy, then take it seriously. A Mercury enemy will exploit your blind spot. Yours may be the Ruling Planet of games, but bring this one to an end as soon as possible.

BOSS

Mercury bosses make excellent mentors. And it's because of this that you won't be working together long. Being a Child of Mercury means you're a quick study. But keep in touch. Not only is this person always there with advice and support, but he or she also makes an invaluable contact.

COLLEAGUE

The project is in good hands if you two are on it. Ideas volley back and forth with a fluency that baffles and mesmerizes your coworkers. It's because of this extraordinary repartee that you want to make a point of keeping people up to speed with what you do.

CHILD OF MERCURY

❋

WITH CHILD OF VENUS

If you ever consider a career in politics, then this is the perfect partner for you. As a Child of Mercury, you buzz from one conversation to the next. A Child of Venus, however, takes in the entire social landscape and then goes about making all the strategic contacts. You can learn a lot about how to get people to do things for you (instead of always doing for them) by hanging out with a Child of Venus. You'll also learn to tell the difference between the salad fork and the dinner fork.

LOVE INTEREST

Children of Venus aren't especially romantic. Like you, they prefer a light touch when it comes to dating and courting. But you'll have to know how to show your Venus love interest a good time. Read up on the latest movies, restaurants, and wine lists. But don't assume the burden of responsibility. A Child of Venus would love a chance to show off his or her own refined taste. Whatever you do—don't pretend to know more than you do about cultural matters.

MATE

This person takes your relationship very seriously. But where you tend to think in terms of "me" and "you," your Venus mate only sees "us." It's nice to be part of a united front, but sometimes it can be counterproductive—like when you want to point out how your mate may not be holding up his or her part of the bargain. Your Venus mate will agree—then ask what you can *both* do to make it better.

CHILD

Whether it's taking a bite of baby food to show how yummy it is or wading into the swimming pool to prove that it really isn't so cold, you'll have to go first if you want a Venus child to follow. It's best to introduce new things in a group setting. That way if the other kids are gung-ho, your Venus child won't want to be left behind.

PARENT

Your Venus mom or dad taught you the difference between what's fine and what's cheap. And if you had a particularly savvy parent, then you also learned how to make something cheap look fine. You have this person to thank for the ease and confidence with which you express yourself—as well as your extensive vocabulary.

SIBLING

If you were close in age, then you socialized together. Your friends were your sibling's friends and vice versa. You would have learned a thing or two about how to attract notice. To this day, the things that look best on you (be it makeup or a tie) were either picked out or given to you by your Venus sibling.

FRIEND

Children of Venus love to socialize just as much as you do, and your paths cross often and in a variety of milieus. Both Mercury and Venus are designed for collaboration, so there's an instinct for assessing how best to play off each other. If your Venus friend is quiet, you may be more talkative; if your Venus friend is charming and social, you may play escort.

ENEMY

Machiavelli was a Child of Venus. This should give you some idea of how mercenary your enemy can be. This person knows how to play the system even better than you, so as with anything Venusian, it's preferable to team up.

BOSS

Your Venus boss considers your working relationship to be a two-way street—except when it comes to your Venus boss. You'll be expected to give, but don't take. Or if you have to, be smart about it. Make your Venus boss look good and others will want to hire you away, so you can come do the same for them. And therein lies your bargaining chip.

COLLEAGUE

Not a hard worker, but a sharp dresser—and a fabulous networker. The advice this person has to impart may not do much for work, but it will certainly help you to climb the ladder of success.

CHILD OF MERCURY

········· ❋ ·········

WITH CHILD OF MARS

Children of Mars have conviction. They're just so *sure* of themselves. It's seductive to let yourself get carried away (and you often do), but eventually you realize that this person only has one answer or one approach to handling matters. As a Child of Mercury you like to keep your options handy so if plan A doesn't work you can always switch to plan B. Yet if you want to get those plans off the drawing board and into action, join forces with a Child of Mars.

LOVE INTEREST

This person will keep you on your toes—which is no small feat, considering how quick you are. Children of Mars tend to bring out the "machismo" in everyone they date—even if you're a woman. There's just something about their energy that challenges you to be tougher, stronger, and more aggressive than you are. It might be hard to figure out if you're really attracted to this person or not. Especially when your Mars love interest is daring you not to be.

MATE

Your Mars mate is early to bed and early to rise and greets each day as a chance to improve on what came before or as an opportunity waiting to be realized. At first you'll want to bury your head back under the pillows, but in time this person's gung-ho spirit rubs off.

CHILD

One thing you need to get straight with your kid is that there are different kinds of smarts—just as there are different kinds of people. Mars children never think they're bright enough. That's because they're more intuitive than analytical. They grasp things in the moment and thoughts translate to answers or actions with the immediacy of a reflex. But if asked to explain *how* he or she arrived at that conclusion, your Mars kid will start to mumble and fumble around for words. Help your child build a bridge from point A to point B without sacrificing that brilliant insight.

PARENT

A Mars parent is driven by the need to have an answer. You are motivated by curiosity. This isn't easy, as most parents are expected to be a guiding force in their children's lives. Yours may have reacted to your constant questioning as an undermining of his or her authority. It could take years to put this right, but once you do, you'll appreciate the differences in your approach.

SIBLING

When you were young you fought like cats and dogs. You just couldn't help pushing your Mars sibling's buttons. Nevertheless your admiration for your brother or sister's heroic spirit eventually won out. To this day your Mars sibling has a way of getting you to ask more from yourself than you would—given your druthers.

FRIEND

This is one active person. However the kind of action your Mars friend craves is usually of the high-wire variety. You enjoy an occasional spiritual crisis or down-to-the-last-minute thrill, but you also don't mind long rambling conversations that are mercifully free of earth-shattering consequences.

ENEMY

You enjoy having the last word or getting in that final dig. Mars energy is fueled by combat. If you don't want to be mired in a dispute that feeds on itself, then bring the matter to an end—pronto!

BOSS

Always take your cues from your Mars boss—even if you can see much further down the road (and being a Child of Mercury, that goes without saying). Acting like you're hearing an idea for the first time will make both your lives easier.

COLLEAGUE

You two click like nobody's business. The only thing to watch out for is when you both start to pick something apart. Neither of you will stop until all the flaws and deficiencies are laid bare—which is okay if you're fine-tuning a proposal, but a bit harsh if you're dealing with a person. It's up to you to get your Mars colleague to lighten up or back off.

CHILD OF MERCURY

………… ❋ …………

WITH CHILD OF JUPITER

Sometimes it seems like a Child of Jupiter is just asking to be swindled. Then something extraordinary happens—that lost cause is rescued in the eleventh hour or fortune smiles on an endeavor that looked like a lemon from the start. But it's more than just luck at work. It's something greater and more profound. Stick with a Child of Jupiter and even a skeptic like you will turn into a true believer.

LOVE INTEREST

Even places you've frequented for years take on new life when seen through this person's eyes. Maybe your Jupiter love interest notices something you overlooked or happens to be privy to a secret bit of history or fun fact. In any case, this person certainly knows the way to your heart. As a Child of Mercury, you naturally know a lot of things, but sometimes it takes being with a Child of Jupiter to *experience* them.

MATE

You place your trust in logic, and your Jupiter mate puts his or her trust in the power of faith. A Child of Jupiter needs to have something to believe in. Without it, this person wouldn't even get out of bed in the morning. It's tempting to poke holes in your mate's expectations, but you need to understand that a Child of Jupiter will always think BIG.

CHILD

Be ready to explain the higher purpose behind *why* things happen. A dry recitation of cause and effect just won't cut it. Your Jupiter child needs something to grab a hold of with his or her imagination. Otherwise this very important psychic muscle won't get exercised. Finding out there *isn't* a Santa Claus won't traumatize your Jupiter child, but never being told about him will. Jupiter children need magic in their lives. It's what allows them to dream those big dreams and make them come true.

PARENT

Hopefully you gave up on trying to figure out your Jupiter parent a long time ago. If not, quit while you're ahead. There is no such thing as *consistency*. Philosophies shift to take on the mood of the moment; convictions come and go according to who's arguing which side. And through it all your Jupiter parent will insist it's you who have changed *your* mind! Jupiter parents are big on participation. Your mom or dad always included you in things and naturally will expect you to do the same.

SIBLING

A Jupiter sibling will often upstage you. Your sibling will find some way to arrive late (causing everyone to worry) or blurt out something embarrassing. Do yourself a favor and skip the psychoanalyzing. There's no hidden agenda. It's just the way this person's wired.

FRIEND

Always willing to try anything once, don't come to this person if you think you need to be talked out of it. Not only will a Jupiter friend encourage you, he or she will also push you off the high dive. However a Jupiter friend makes the perfect traveling companion—whether it's a day trip or backpacking in Tibet.

ENEMY

Good-natured and fun loving, the Planet Jupiter was still named after the god of storms—which means this person can get LOUD. Your enemy's capacity to do harm lies in his or her talent for making a scene. And make no mistake about it. It will be mortifying.

BOSS

You do all the legwork—making phone calls, running back and forth, checking in on people—while your Jupiter boss does all the serious decision making. You complement each other perfectly because where you can be a little too staccato in your thinking, your Jupiter boss can immediately divine the link that joins all the pieces together, and where your Jupiter boss can get a little lofty with the grand view of things, you will subtly coax him or her back to earth.

COLLEAGUE

Between your psychoanalyzing and your Jupiter colleague's daydreaming, you guys could wind up spending a lot of time talking and getting very little work done.

CHILD OF MERCURY

.... ❋ ....

WITH CHILD OF SATURN

Children of Saturn take twice as long as you to do anything. They mull over decisions, weigh options, and ask tedious nitpicky questions. Yet everything changes when they're ready to act. Not only are they decisive, but they're also willing to do a lot more than is required. Chances are they've worked out contingencies you didn't even think about. Children of Saturn don't work moment to moment. They're life planners. That's why despite your impatience, you're all ears when they're ready to speak.

LOVE INTEREST
Don't be hurt if a Child of Saturn doesn't take you seriously right away. This person may have a hard time imagining why you would ever be attracted to him or her. You're light and breezy while a Child of Saturn can be heavy and serious. Nevertheless you both have a naughty sense of humor and love wordplay. Over time you may move this person from the "wonder what it would be like" to the "must have" column.

MATE
Although a Child of Saturn wants things to be established and orderly, he or she will never lose that edge. This person believes in always being just a little bit "hungry." Your Saturn mate is committed to being the best that he or she can be and will certainly support that in you. Hopefully you share that commitment. If not, then you could wind up in a frustrated love triangle with your mate and your mate's career.

CHILD
It may be tedious having to spell out *everything* to your Saturn kid, but it's also good exercise for you. It forces you to switch from speaking in shorthand to actually explaining what something means. If you outfit your child with the necessary facts and figures then when the kid grows up, he or she will be able to run with the ball.

PARENT
Clearly the worst form of punishment your Saturn parent could devise was to make you sit through another life lecture. You'd rather be grounded for a month! Despite the heavy-handed guidance, this is the first person you go to when you have to make any big decision. There's no disputing a Saturn parent's wisdom. But make sure you ask for advice over the phone. That way you can flip through some of your favorite magazines while your mom or dad goes on and on.

SIBLING

If older, then your Saturn sibling bossed you around; if younger—a snitch. However once safely embarked on adulthood, you could become the very best of friends. Your Saturn sibling gets a bit more devil-may-care with age, while you become more serious and analytical. It makes for a good balance.

FRIEND

You're Pinocchio—mischievous, clever, and easily distracted. Your Saturn friend is Jimminy Cricket—the voice of conscience. Pals from the get-go, you're in it together through thick and thin. But watch it with the banter. Sometimes the rib poking can get a bit much. You might grow tired of the constant criticism, and your Saturn friend may feel like you don't always show the proper respect. Occasionally you'll have to sit down and clear the air, but you'll always be best buddies.

ENEMY

Chances are you aren't enemies at all. You've just stepped over the line. Respect boundaries, honor obligations, and you'll never have cause to resent a Child of Saturn.

BOSS

Just do your job, don't waste his or her time with "trivialities," and you'll do fine.

COLLEAGUE

The best way to work with a Saturn colleague is to assign a job, clarify what you want, and then stay out of his or her hair. As a Child of Mercury you would prefer a constant exchange of information, but that's not how a Child of Saturn works. Saturn Children can't deal with interruptions or options in the abstract. That's why your colleague needs to actually produce something solid before he or she can be open to input. Otherwise this person just won't be able to think straight.

CHILD OF MERCURY

.... ❋ ....

WITH CHILD OF URANUS/SATURN

You'll never be bored with a Child of Uranus and Saturn. You won't be allowed to sit still long enough. This person is always on the go—physically and/or intellectually. Prepare to always be kept just a little bit off balance—and to enjoy every moment of it.

LOVE INTEREST

You will know whether this person is interested or not within the first five minutes of meeting him or her. Children of Uranus and Saturn don't believe in trial periods. They make up their minds right on the spot. This is often misunderstood as recklessness or passion. It's not. They just know what they want. Hopefully you're of the same opinion, because you'll never be able to convince this person otherwise.

MATE

Life with a Uranus/Saturn mate is blessedly free of neurosis—about the relationship. However when it comes to living with this person, you won't always be able to predict when he or she is in "Uranian" mode (which is coolly objective and seductively logical) or "Saturnine" mode (which is full of self-doubt and worry). This person swings so quickly from one to the other even you are not sure which one you're talking to. Then again, you may love being around someone who's even more screwy than you.

CHILD

Your Uranus/Saturn child is such an original that it hurts to think of him or her out there on the play-ground searching for true companionship. You know from experience how intolerant children can be of anyone who's different. Thankfully your kid has a natural talent for making friends, and you may even be surprised by their diverse backgrounds.

PARENT

You are your Uranus/Saturn parent's personal cause célèbre. There may have been one thing you did when you were growing up—perhaps it was something you drew for school or a poem you wrote—that convinced your mom or dad of your genius, and they have stayed convinced ever since. Whether or not you really are is anyone's guess—but it's still nice to know you will always have someone in your corner rooting for you.

SIBLING

A Uranus/Saturn sibling needs lots of room to grow, especially in adolescence, when the need to invent oneself is particularly strong. Your sibling would have spent very little time at home. Yet once this Child of Uranus and Saturn alights on who he or she is going to be, then you will be included in this person's life.

FRIEND

You tend to make Uranus/Saturn friends in faraway places, so chances are you do most of your communicating on the phone or by e-mail. It's fun corresponding with someone who enjoys writing notes and letters as much as you do.

ENEMY

It's very rare for a Child of Uranus and Saturn to be an enemy—unless this person has some heavy personal problems. Otherwise the only possible conflict would be over a violation of trust. A Child of Uranus and Saturn will forgive a lot, but being lied to is a capital crime. If it's a misunderstanding, then clear it up. This person will be fair-minded—even if he or she doesn't like you. If you really *did* lie, then apologize—and throw yourself on the mercy of the court.

BOSS

You two are so free and easy with each other that people will have a hard time discerning who's the boss and who's the employee. And that's the way your Uranus/Saturn boss likes it. The only thing you have to remember is to always show the proper respect. Although Uranus often defies convention, there's still a Saturn side—which means that this person believes in hierarchy.

COLLEAGUE

It may annoy you the way your Uranus/Saturn colleague always wants to dot all the *i*'s and cross all the *t*'s, but you could learn a thing or two about efficiency from this person. Take a tip from your colleague and do it right the first time.

CHILD OF MERCURY

❊

WITH CHILD OF NEPTUNE/JUPITER

A Child of Neptune and Jupiter is both inspiring and refreshing. This person isn't afraid of being vulnerable or giving. Indeed a Neptune/Jupiter Child's compassion for human weaknesses fills you with admiration. It's not every day when you meet someone who cares without expecting anything in return.

LOVE INTEREST

It isn't always easy to tell right away how a Neptune/Jupiter Child sees you. Are you a love interest or a lost cause? If you're a love interest, then just being near this person is intoxicating. If you're a lost cause, then your Neptune/Jupiter date will ask you all sorts of personal questions about your childhood, nod sympathetically, and then slip you the number of the local rehab center.

MATE

Continued exposure to your Neptune/Jupiter mate can't help but open your heart and soul. Instead of guarding your feelings, you'll come to accept them. You may get a little too warm-fuzzy for the old gang, but considering how they're still going home alone at the end of the night, you won't mind the trade-off.

CHILD

Your Neptune/Jupiter child could teach you a thing or two about the power of the imagination. At first you might just think your little dreamer is terribly clever until you begin to realize that he or she is drawing from a well of inspiration that's obviously deeper than what the kid could have possibly experienced so far. As a Child of Mercury, you're in a unique position to help your child develop that wonderfully mysterious imagination without losing touch with what everyone else considers "reality."

PARENT

You've always looked up to your Neptune/Jupiter parent. Though you've had your disagreements (you find this person's beliefs or politics to be hopelessly impractical), your mom or dad will never cease to be a source of inspiration. Chances are you inherited a certain talent and will either choose to follow in the same footsteps or go on to do something with it that's totally your own.

SIBLING

It seemed like just about everything you said made this person cry or get depressed. Your Neptune/Jupiter sibling is well versed in the martyr complex. Either things were blown out of proportion so that they bore little resemblance to your intent or your brother or sister absorbed all the blame and guilt like a sponge—making you feel like a culprit without a crime. Thankfully Neptune/Jupiter siblings usually outgrow this.

FRIEND

When your Neptune/Jupiter friend is on, there's no one you would rather be with. This person is funny, mischievous, and just a tad twisted. No one knows how to spin a yarn like a Child of Neptune and Jupiter. But when your friend is down then all life gets drained out of the room. Practice some psychic self-protection. If you're in the mood for propping up spirits, then go to it. But if you're not—skip it. There's no sense in you being dragged under, too.

ENEMY

Neptune is the Planet of the sea, so you'll want to be careful about getting drawn into any psychic undertows. If this person has a problem, then let him or her come to you with it. Otherwise, stay out of the water.

BOSS

A Neptune/Jupiter boss is totally unselfish—and that's the problem. Expect to spend a lot of time covering this person's bases and watching his or her back. It may often fall to you to do the firing or explain to a client or a customer that the fee that was too good to be true was indeed just that—too good to be true. The reason your boss still has a job is probably because of you.

COLLEAGUE

Watch it. Neptune/Jupiter colleagues are geniuses at dumping their obligations onto other people's plates, and given your work ethic, you could spend a lot of time cleaning up after them. Resist pitching in from the start. It's heartless, but the sooner this person's rid of a bad habit, the better.

CHILD OF MERCURY

❋

WITH CHILD OF PLUTO/MARS

This person positively mesmerizes you. The words have bite, the humor is wonderfully dark, and the mind is so fierce and uncompromising that no quip slips by unanswered. A Child of Pluto and Mars plays to all your fantasies of being naughty in public. The only thing that's hard to tell is how far this person is willing to go. Life with a Child of Pluto and Mars is not for the faint of heart.

LOVE INTEREST

If you don't like intensity then do yourself a favor and stay away. One can't separate the temperament from the artist, so don't even try to attempt something similar with this person. Either accept the entire package or skip it. But for those of you Mercury Children who don't mind the occasional chilly mood, you'll also get to experience life with a kick.

MATE

Each of you adds a dimension to the other. You bring levity where your mate brings depth. It's a nice combination. When your Pluto/Mars mate gets too intense, you're quick to demonstrate that this isn't the way the rest of the world thinks. It takes a while, but you will eventually prevail upon your mate to take in views other than his or her own and to not assume the worst.

CHILD

You're the perfect parent for this kind of kid. One of the most important things you can teach your Pluto/Mars child is that things *change*. Nothing is preordained or fated. Not only does this diffuse some of that famous Pluto fixation, but it will also lessen the impact of those childhood traumas (like unrequited puppy love or being chosen last for softball) that tend to leave such a lasting impression.

PARENT

You may still not feel that you understand your Pluto/Mars parent, but you admire the single-minded purpose. As an adult, you can see how your parent may have sabotaged his or her own efforts by issuing ultimatums or refusing to accept compromise. Nevertheless what your Pluto/Mars parent failed to learn you readily absorbed.

SIBLING

Someone should have hung a sign on your Pluto/Mars sibling's bedroom door that read: TREAD SOFTLY. PSYCHIC MINEFIELD. You may have resented how this person's temper dominated the household, but it takes time for a Child of Pluto and Mars to grow into his or her power—just like it takes time for you to learn *not* to say the first thing that comes to mind. Nevertheless, the two of you grow into a close and loyal friendship.

FRIEND

You can pull the wool over most anyone's eyes, but a Pluto/Mars friend will always bring you up short. This person sees past your "social butterfly" facade and will ask the questions that get you to really consider the consequences of your behavior. Sometimes you like it. Sometimes you don't. But you can always be yourself around this person.

ENEMY

Not worth it. Apologize, pay the fine, promise to wash the dishes—just do whatever it takes to get back into this person's good graces.

BOSS

Careful. Your Mercury curiosity could get you into trouble if you don't respect a couple of things. It's the nature of Pluto to treat everything like it's a secret—even if it's already public knowledge. You may want to expedite matters by doing some checking up on your own or going to your boss's boss. Don't. It will be interpreted as you going behind this person's back, which will effectively bring to an end the trust that is so important for working with a Pluto/Mars boss. Respect your Pluto/Mars boss's privacy and you'll get along fine.

COLLEAGUE

Children of Pluto and Mars are closet chatter boxes. They don't see themselves this way, but they're not fooling you. With that in mind, help this person out by keeping an eye on the time. You know that you can switch from visiting to work mode in an instant. Unfortunately the same can't be said for your colleague.

CHILD OF VENUS

·············· ✳ ··············

WITH CHILD OF THE SUN

Child of the Sun is wonderfully self-centered. But this doesn't mean selfish. Indeed few are so generous and giving. It's just that a Child of the Sun has no compunction about yawning loudly if he or she is bored or looking completely perplexed if someone fails to make a point. With a Child of the Sun, you'll learn that you don't have to play along so much with people and that you can express your own views without having to cushion everything you say.

LOVE INTEREST

Children of the Sun wear their hearts on their sleeves. If you're serious about this person, then you must act as if this is the first time you've ever been in love. Obviously your Sun lover knows better, but nothing will dampen the mood quicker than to talk about an ex or share a funny story from a previous date. As far as this person's concerned, his or her new life began when the two of you first met. If you want that luster to continue, then you'd best act as if the same goes for you.

MATE

Lions are ruled by the Sun, and your Solar mate will behave in a similar fashion. If your mate is male, than he will lounge around and let you do all the work. However when it comes to safeguarding his domain or making the really important decisions, then he is full of regal resolve that you find incredibly sexy and that never fails to take your breath away. If your mate is female, than she's a very hard worker and maybe even the breadwinner. But don't expect a free ride. She'll whip you into shape if need be.

CHILD

Every parent believes their child is gifted—however not every child believes he or she is gifted. A child of the Sun does. It's always amusing to watch your little prince or princess hold court. But what's amazing is how quickly other children will accept it. If there's artistic talent to go with that aplomb, then it's worth developing. Your kid could go far. Otherwise start the CEO training early.

PARENT

Your Solar parent always wanted to do all the "kiddy" things—like watch sci-fi movies and hang out with your friends—while you wanted to do all the "grown-up" things—like throw dinner parties and network with your parent's friends. One plus is that you always know who to call to come baby-sit your kids for the evening.

SIBLING

Hopefully you were opposite sex siblings. A Solar sibling can get very competitive when it comes to the looks department. Obviously this wouldn't have been a problem for you. Your Birthday Planet was named after the goddess of beauty, so you've never really had to try that hard.

FRIEND

Always walk *behind* your Solar friend. He or she needs to feel noticed and important. You don't need it as much, because people flock to you anyway. Solar friends give good money advice and have a head for figures, which helps, because you tend to focus more on the other kind of figures.

ENEMY

You don't make enemies with anyone and haven't the slightest idea of what this person is talking about.

BOSS

You two get along famously. Your Solar boss loves to be pampered and coddled as much as you enjoy making someone look and feel good. Flattery will get you everywhere, and though your boss knows perfectly well that he or she is being buttered up, you're just too irresistible. Your wish is this person's command. If you don't overstep your bounds then the give-and-take will flow freely between you.

COLLEAGUE

A Solar colleague always has to do things his or her way. Even if you know it's wrong, you're better off just indulging this person. Never underestimate a Child of the Sun's need for approval. It will always be your ace in the hole.

CHILD OF VENUS

########## ❋ ##########

WITH CHILD OF THE MOON

Children of the Moon work with what's already in place—subtly making alterations so that what emerges is a solution that makes everyone happy because it's organic and comes from with*in* rather than with*out*. Changes should be familiar enough so that people aren't turned off, but different so that they're also intrigued. You could learn a thing or two about harmony from a Child of the Moon.

LOVE INTEREST

Learning to read your Lunar love interest's signals will be the first order of the day. You may get the impression that you're being "tested." Actually, it's the waters that are being tested, not you. If your Lunar love interest feels like the mood is cool and distant, he or she will retreat. Whereas if the mood is warm and inviting, this person will surprise you by being enormously affectionate.

MATE

You place more importance on socializing than your Lunar mate does. But this doesn't have to be a problem if you allow for some downtime. It's how this person recharges his or her psychic batteries. If you've got a busy social schedule planned, then make allowances for a catnap or a quick bath. All this person needs is forty minutes.

CHILD

Moon children are notoriously moody. Clingy one moment, they can become aloof and distant the next. The biggest challenge will be in trying to get your kid to understand that what's okay at home isn't necessarily all right in public. Children of the Moon are natural mimics, so focus on setting a positive and consistent example.

PARENT

Your Lunar parent puts family first, while you put friends first. In no way does this reflect what you think of your family. You love your family and know that they will always be there, whereas a hot date or client who's only in town for a night may not be. Don't bother trying to explain or defend yourself. As long as you show up for family get-togethers and remember everyone's birthday, you'll be fine.

SIBLING

You two may have been much closer when you were younger—especially during high school. It's when both of you were in transition, and so you would have naturally clicked. As you get older, you may see your Lunar sibling as letting some things go (like personal hopes, dreams, or maybe even their figure) while you will always keep up with the latest trends. Though you may travel in different circles, you will always have that bond.

FRIEND

Children of the Moon make amazing friends. Because of your busy schedule, you can have a hard time staying in touch. But your Lunar friend will make a point of telephoning at least once every two weeks to see what's up and to make plans to get together. Seeing this person is always comfortable and easy. It's so relaxed and low maintenance.

ENEMY

A Lunar enemy can be very sneaky. You may weather an attack, think you're through the worst, but right when you least suspect it you get hit with a new maneuver aimed at making your life difficult. Make peace as soon as you can. This is one of the few people who can give you such a dressing-down that you're left trembling afterward.

BOSS

You may not work for this person very long. There's nothing wrong with your boss's personality. In fact you really enjoy each other. It's just that Lunar bosses are cheap, and you have extravagant tastes. You're also a bit more ambitious than your Moon boss, who tends to go with the flow.

COLLEAGUE

You can always rely on your Lunar colleague to cover for you. If you're running late or need to duck out of the office for an hour, this person will take care of everything. Make a point of rewarding him or her with a little something you picked up in your travels. It's the least you can do and will certainly go a long way.

CHILD OF VENUS

············ ❈ ············

WITH CHILD OF MERCURY

A Child of Mercury will never press you to make up your mind before you're ready. This person knows the benefit of keeping your options open and having an alternative handy. But where you tend to sit on your prerogatives, a Child of Mercury will put them into play. Mercury Children know that people pretty much fall into two camps: those who make choices and those who let their choices be made for them. You can learn a lot from a Child of Mercury about how to exercise your influence.

LOVE INTEREST

Chances are you started out friends, so it wouldn't be surprising if you went back to being friends after a romantic interlude. It's because you play so many roles in each other's lives—confidante, companion, business advisor, etc.—that "love interest" isn't necessarily more important than the rest. If something more definitive were to develop, it will probably be when you're both older.

MATE

You can't think of a better person to do things with. Your Mercury mate is just as eager as you to check out the new restaurant that opened or to test-drive the latest luxury car. Yet perhaps the best thing about your Mercury mate is that he or she always knows how to get the best deals. This is especially important given your refined tastes. You can always rely on your Mercury mate to find a way to enjoy the good things in life and not have to pay a fortune for them.

CHILD

Mercury is the Planet of the mind, and your kid's will develop faster than his or her peers. But you also want to impress upon your son or daughter the need for good manners and etiquette. There's a fine line between being witty and obnoxious and you won't let your kid cross it.

PARENT

It's a good thing your Mercury parent was always after you to improve your conversational skills, because as you've gotten older, you see for yourself how an extensive vocabulary, wide field of interests, and a solid grasp of current events can open doors that would have otherwise remained closed.

SIBLING

One of the best siblings you can have. You see eye to eye on just about everything. And if you don't, then it's always worth hearing what your Mercury sibling has to say. Your sibling has always been a reliable source of information ever since he or she first started telling you what to write in your book reports.

FRIEND

This person knows just about everyone, so your social circle will expand by virtue of association. Whenever you're about to go on a job interview or date, rehearse what you want to say with your Mercury friend first. He or she will tell you if you're being too desperate or holding back the good stuff.

ENEMY

A Mercury enemy can be formidable, because this person is a master at misinformation. He or she knows how to lay the trail of crumbs so that people arrive at the most damaging conclusions. That's why you want to strike first. Flood the channels with your version of events and your Mercury enemy will have no recourse but to come to you to make amends.

BOSS

It really depends on what kind of job you do. If it's something like PR, communications, or design, then you two will hit it off great. If it's something that requires organizational skills, your Mercury boss could become the bane of your existence by ceaselessly criticizing your typing and filing.

COLLEAGUE

You guys make a wonderful team. Each covers the other's weak point—sometimes a Mercury Child will put expediency before quality; whereas you can get so bogged down in refining just one idea that you forget about the rest of the picture. The sum of you together is clearly better than you apart.

CHILD OF VENUS

········· ❋ ·········

WITH CHILD OF VENUS

You and your fellow Child of Venus are simpatico. You both understand the need for symmetry and will immediately make the necessary adjustments so that yours is a seamless partnership. The only thing you have to watch out for is the Venusian habit of avoiding anything unpleasant. Since neither of you will bring it up, you can wind up supporting each other's tendency to procrastinate or sweep matters under the rug. Yet you are both fair listeners, so should one of you broach an unappealing topic, the other will make a point of hearing you out—and then thank you afterward.

LOVE INTEREST

One of you does the courting while the other one is always being courted. It's tempting to slip into these prefab roles, but introduce surprise twists from time to time. Not only will you keep your love interest guessing, but it will also be fun to see what he or she comes up with.

MATE

You and your Venus mate need to know that you're married to the most attractive person in the room. You two maintain your youth and vitality long after other couples have resigned themselves to the laws of gravity. However if you ever feel that your mate is taking you for granted, then just start flirting with someone else. That will get his or her attention pronto.

CHILD

The easy part about raising a Venus child is that you're familiar with all the tricks. You pulled most of them yourself. You're immune to the coaxing, cajoling, and staged snits. What's difficult is playing the heavy. Every child needs to learn the word *no*—*especially* a Venus kid. Without it your child will get used to things coming easily and will focus more on getting others to do for him or her. Self-sufficiency begins with being thrown back on your own resources.

PARENT

Not all Venus parents want to fool people into thinking you're siblings. Most are quite comfortable with being introduced as your mom or dad. Indeed your Venus parent has cultivated that sophisticated look that comes with age. The gray hair lends Dad a dignified air; the deeper voice makes Mom sound sultry. Better watch it. Or your Venus parent will wind up turning all the heads in the room.

SIBLING

Either you fought since day one—or you are best friends. If you two are always arguing, it's best to avoid each other's company. Chances are you don't even harbor any ill will; it's just that if one of you says something's black, the other will insist it's white. If best friends, then people light up when you two enter a room. You play off each other's humor and charm and delight everyone within reach.

FRIEND

Your friendship may have developed out of a business association that still continues to this day. As a Child of Venus you understand the importance of hooking up with the right people—as does your friend. You both bring something to the relationship that the other doesn't have.

ENEMY

Although a Venus enemy can be positively diabolical about getting his or her way, this same person can turn around and be generous just as quickly. Children of Venus believe in keeping friends close, but enemies closer.

BOSS

Never assume that things are peachy keen with a Venus boss. This person can tell you you're doing a fine job and then fire you the next day. The cloak-and-dagger tactics aren't meant to be malicious; they're simply indicative of how much this person *hates* confrontation. Always keep the line of communication open with your boss and make him or her feel comfortable about giving you feedback.

COLLEAGUE

Venus is the Planet of symmetry and will automatically seek its counterpart. Dissatisfaction with your colleague could actually make you more disciplined and expert in your work, whereas a chummy relationship may lead to goofing off all day.

CHILD OF VENUS

·········· ❉ ··········

WITH CHILD OF MARS

You two are flip sides of the same coin. Mars is the Planet of desire, while Venus symbolizes the object of desire, so you never have to worry about getting this person's attention. But defy convention (and expectations) by playing against type. If you take the lead then a Child of Mars will treat you like a comrade-in-arms instead of a damsel in distress.

LOVE INTEREST

Your Mars love interest will always be convinced you're not as into the relationship as he or she is. It's not a bad idea to keep this person guessing. If you make yourself too available, then you take away the challenge—and once that goes, a Mars Child's interest isn't far behind. At the same time, you don't want to be too blasé. Mars Children can get quite petulant if they don't feel that they're number one. Find the balance between fire and ice so that the temperature is just right.

MATE

You can't help but become more assertive living with a Mars mate. This person is always pushing to know what you think or feel, and after a while you'll just start volunteering it regardless of whether you've been asked. This candor will find its way into your other associations as well, and people will start to treat you like someone to be reckoned with. You'll also see your mate benefit from being around you. Though this person may never lose the rough edges, you'll notice how your mate phrases requests more politely, apologizes for being out of line, and even contemplates how actions in the moment affect consequences later.

CHILD

The best thing you can teach your Mars kid is how to win or lose gracefully. But instead of preaching the virtues of good sportsmanship (this simply won't translate) portray this as conduct befitting a champion. Mars children love a good role model and there are few challenges so worth pursuing as self-mastery.

PARENT

Mars parents can be demanding and provocative. This isn't because they're bad tempered; it's just that they thrive on friction. A criticism, argument, or fight keeps emotions percolating and assures your Mars parent of your attention, your loyalty, and your respect. You'll never convince this person to adopt a kinder, gentler approach. But as with a child or a dog, if you play with them for a while they'll settle down.

SIBLING

Your Mars sibling has always been very protective—racing to your defense if anyone was too critical or warily scrutinizing a date. Though flattering, it might have been awkward at times—especially if your brother or sister was much younger than you. The best thing you can do with a Mars sibling is to always make him or her feel needed.

FRIEND

Though you often have very opposite (and even heatedly opposed) reactions, you both want to hear the other out. You know this person is picking up on something you've missed. It's your Mars friend who prevents you from making compromises that might compromise yourself.

ENEMY

A Mars enemy won't recognize the merits of negotiation. Everything's win or lose. If the dispute doesn't matter all that much to you, throw in the towel. If it does, then try dealing with the people *around* your Mars enemy. They're more likely to see reason.

BOSS

You're probably the only person who can talk to your Mars boss—which is exactly how you both like it. Your Mars boss doesn't want to get bogged down in office politics or have to worry if a client feels coddled or not. You're more than happy to play guardian of the gate and keeper of the agenda.

COLLEAGUE

Get used to doing lots of damage control around your Mars colleague. This person can't help blurting out what he or she "really feels" or taking professional matters too personally. Yet it's that very same personal investment that makes your colleague's work so outstanding.

CHILD OF VENUS

.... ※ ....

WITH CHILD OF JUPITER

You both like to have a good time—and look good having it. You'll feel just as comfortable with this person at a backyard barbecue as you would at a black-tie event. Children of Jupiter are engaging, charismatic, and can switch from casual conversation to shop talk to current events all with the ease of a TV remote. Even if this person hasn't the slightest idea of what he or she is talking about, there's no cause for alarm. Everyone will still believe it anyway. What makes a Child of Jupiter so wonderful is that you really can take him or her anywhere!

LOVE INTEREST

You two enjoy each other's company so much that you may never get around to talking about future plans. But of the two, you'll be the one to bring it up. It irks you to have to show your hand first, but as a Child of Venus you're naturally more concerned about the relationship and where it might be heading. Don't expect your Jupiter love interest to help you out with that one. This person is as "free and easy" as they come. You may wind up having to issue an ultimatum to get this person's attention.

MATE

Jupiter mates still fantasize about the grass that's greener on the other side of the fence—long after they've settled down. It's all talk, but don't point that out. You'll only provoke a fight—or worse. Take lots of trips and outings instead. This will satisfy those wanderlust urges that he or she feels deep inside while demonstrating that the world as it *is* can often be more interesting than what one thinks it should be.

CHILD

You may be thrown off balance by the forcefulness of your kid's opinions. Children of Jupiter have an independent streak that's often reflected in their beliefs. This could put you at loggerheads—especially in adolescence, when neither of you thinks the other is right. However what eventually emerges is someone you admire and are more than just a little proud of.

PARENT

It drove you batty the way your Jupiter parent would just throw open the door to anyone who came knocking—regardless of the time of day or your state of dress. Other than that, your mom or dad was successful at getting you to lighten up around people and to not care so much about appearances—at least around your mom or dad. The only sore point is money. You each think the other is a spendthrift. In truth: you both are.

SIBLING

You may not mean to, but you will naturally follow in the footsteps of your Jupiter sibling. Whether it's moving to the same neighborhood or going into a similar line of business, your Jupiter brother or sister has an extraordinary influence over what you choose to do. But this isn't a copycat thing or even an attempt to win this person's approval. It's just that your Jupiter sibling happens to have really good ideas.

FRIEND

Favorite person to go shopping with or sit next to at the game. This person just won't say no to anything. Of course you wouldn't be caught dead wearing anything your Jupiter friend puts on (be it animal print leggings or face makeup done in the colors of the home team), but you always have a great time.

ENEMY

A Jupiter enemy needs a cause to be pumped up about in order to stay angry. Remove the cause and your enemy's ire dissipates with it.

BOSS

Treat your Jupiter boss like he or she is lord emperor (or empress) and you'll do fine. Flattery gets you everywhere; doing some work once in a while might also be a good idea.

COLLEAGUE

Your Jupiter colleague does things in broad strokes while you tend to fuss with specifics. If you can coordinate efforts, then this will prove to be a winning combination.

CHILD OF VENUS

·········· ✺ ··········

WITH CHILD OF SATURN

Children of Saturn will always pooh-pooh your extravagance and make fun of the way you put things, but that's because they secretly admire your style. If you want to win one over, then show this person something about his or her appearance that can be improved. Children of Saturn may start out unkempt, but they inevitably wind up becoming clotheshorses—and that's usually because there's a fashionista like you coaching them from the sidelines.

LOVE INTEREST

There's a difference between dating a Child of Saturn who's made it and one who hasn't. If your Saturn love interest is successful and well connected, then you'll need to bring something more than just good looks to the table. Introduce a little culture into your Saturn love interest's life and this person will worship the ground you walk on. However you'll want to be extra careful around Saturn love interests who are still "finding" themselves. They can be enormous mooches.

MATE

You two make a classic pair. Hopefully there's a social aspect to your Saturn mate's workaday world. If not, introduce one. Otherwise you may never see him or her. Partners in life, you'd also do well in business. Considering your partner's talent for making something out of nothing and yours for window dressing—you two have all the makings of a Fortune 500 company.

CHILD

A Saturn child craves structure and responsibility, so be prepared to assign chores—even if you have to make them up. Not only does this harness all that extra energy (which could result in nervous fretting if not channeled properly), but it also keeps your little worker bee from slipping into depression. If your Saturn child spends a lot of time on the computer, it might be worth it to give him or her a few bucks for on-line trading. It could save on student loans.

PARENT

Your Saturn parent has some pretty fixed ideas about what will make you happy. And many of them would probably make you miserable. Your parent is definitely a "fill-in-the-blanks" type. He or she wants things to be decided. That's why it's always best to tell this person about what you've got planned *after* it comes to fruition. It cuts down on the unsolicited advice.

SIBLING

You would have gravitated toward the "in" crowd, while your Saturn sibling hung out with the misfits. After years of pretending *not* to know each other, you may really enjoy getting acquainted as adults. Your brother or sister is very knowledgeable about people (your favorite subject), and you could teach your sibling a thing or two about hooking up with the right people who can make things happen.

FRIEND

You may have been instrumental in your Saturn friend meeting the love of his or her life, making a valuable contact, or moving into the apartment downstairs. Whatever the favor, this person has never forgotten it and will repay you a hundred times over. As far as you're concerned—it was nothing. But after seeing all the things your Saturn friend is willing to do to express gratitude, you'll never let on.

ENEMY

Like you, a Child of Saturn will never burn a bridge. Because a Saturn enemy will always take the high road, the only potential harm is what you would do to yourself. Resist the temptation to bad-mouth this person—even if he or she deserves it.

BOSS

A harsh taskmaster. Saturn bosses can't sleep nights unless they've found the fault in the merit. Sometimes this results in a real improvement and sometimes your boss is just creating more work for everyone.

COLLEAGUE

It isn't hard getting a Saturn colleague to do all your work. These types can't stand anything being left unfinished and will happily take on yours. However nobody knows how to guilt-trip better than a Child of Saturn. And that, in itself, is all the incentive you need to do your job.

CHILD OF VENUS

·········· ❈ ··········

WITH CHILD OF URANUS/SATURN

A Child of Uranus and Saturn makes your senses tingle. There's just so much richness to this person that it's impossible to label it all. Every time you think you've got a Uranus/Saturn Child pegged, he or she will confound your expectations. You could spend a lifetime just trying to figure out what makes this person tick.

LOVE INTEREST

Whether your Uranus/Saturn love interest knows it or not, the contrasting signals of "come closer" and "no stay away" has you hooked. But don't mistake these back-and-forth swings for playing hard to get. A Child of Uranus and Saturn doesn't play those games. What you regard as fickle and devilish may have more to do with this person figuring out the day's agenda or suddenly remembering an important phone call that's yet to be made.

MATE

Distance is built into their closeness, and though your mate will always tell you otherwise, the simple truth is that he or she needs a lot of elbow room. That's why this person is always on the road or works a job where he or she will be away for extended periods of time. This actually suits you fine, as it allows you to concentrate on matters of your own. Life only gets rough in the days before your mate leaves or has just returned home. It always takes a while to get back in sync with each other.

CHILD

Your Uranus/Saturn child always wants to do something exotic. And being a Venus parent—who are you to say no? However your spouse or in-laws may need some explanation as to why the kid wants to wear the tutu to school or go vegan at five. Teach your Uranus/Saturn child to introduce new ideas slowly and not to hit people over the head with them.

PARENT

Uncomfortable with showing praise, flattery, or special preference—all things you live for and can never get enough of—your Uranus/Saturn parent may have gone in the opposite direction by being too staid when it came to making you feel good about something you did. Children of Uranus and Saturn just get very uncomfortable around the issue of "ego" and tend to look down on the need for recognition and gratification. Translation? Look for it somewhere else—and know that this person can't stop singing your praises when you're out of earshot.

SIBLING

Incredibly bossy. Even if your brother or sister was younger, he or she just had a way of making you feel condescended to. Either you were made to feel as if you were slow or perhaps just a bit too *agreeable*. Nevertheless you do respect your sibling.

FRIEND

It isn't always easy to tell when your friend is going to play along or take you to task. Sometimes this person is feeling just as reckless and will even push the envelope much further than you ever would, and sometimes this person will simply look at you as if he or she doesn't even know you. That's a Uranus/Saturn friend—unpredictable.

ENEMY

The words *argument* and *fight* just don't compute. However the phrase "out of line" does, and a Uranus/Saturn enemy will do everything in his or her power to see that you either step back into place or are routed out all together.

BOSS

Although your boss will say there's no such thing as a "right" way of doing things and will even encourage you to find your own voice or style, you still have to contend with the Saturn side of this person. And that side is constantly watching two things: the clock and the money.

COLLEAGUE

Uranus/Saturn colleagues don't believe in titles. Work is a group collaboration. In fact, people should get together once a week to review their performances and to share insights and feedback. As a Child of Venus, you can see where this utopian vision is going. Do yourself a favor and just let this person take the lead. He or she is going to anyway.

CHILD OF VENUS

.... ❈ ....

WITH CHILD OF NEPTUNE/JUPITER

Both you and a Child of Neptune and Jupiter share a love of beauty, art, and people. Yet you two have markedly different points of view. A Child of Neptune and Jupiter gets you to look past the price tag or status symbol and to appreciate something's intrinsic value—like what does it say to you as a person? Whereas you will show a Child of Neptune and Jupiter that doing what you want in life doesn't mean becoming a starving artist or selling out. There is such a thing as having it all without losing yourself in the process.

LOVE INTEREST

It won't be easy to tell if you're on or off. Like you, a Child of Neptune and Jupiter makes distinctions between feelings and the relationship. But where your aim is to do what's in the best interests of the relationship, a Child of Neptune and Jupiter opts for what's best for feelings—which, at times, can become entirely too nebulous to decipher. Limit discussions about commitment to whether or not you're getting together for a movie tonight. You'll be happier.

MATE

This is your favorite person to be with. You're always intrigued by what your Neptune/Jupiter mate has to say and love getting glimpses of the world as seen through his or her eyes. However there's only so much profundity you can take, and thankfully your mate is just as comfortable in shallow water as in deep. The only thing that might get on your nerves is when your mate starts rhapsodizing about how he or she is just too sensitive or mystical to deal with the mundane concerns of a crass and trivial world. Remind this person that even the Dalai Lama has to pay bills.

CHILD

You couldn't ask for a more imaginative child. You love that this kid has such a creative inner life. With that in mind, encourage your kid to develop a strong social persona to go along with that private one. You'll help your Neptune/Jupiter child to feel at home in this world, too.

PARENT

Your Neptune/Jupiter parent imbued you with a powerful social conscience, so no matter how successful you are, you will always give something back. Not only does this do wonders for your karma, but it's good for tax breaks, too.

SIBLING

You probably think your sibling is so holier-than-thou, while your sibling considers you to be an opportunist. Once over the name-calling, you may come to see how—despite differences in approach—you actually have core values in common. You may even discover how each has something valuable to offer the other.

FRIEND

Chances are you met through some wild misadventure and you've been inseparable since. You two share *everything* with each other and won't make a move without bringing the other one up-to-date first. You may even be closer to this person than you are to your spouse. But there's no cause for alarm— especially considering how often your Neptune/Jupiter friend will take your spouse's side in an argument.

ENEMY

It doesn't matter if you're the one who's been wronged—your Neptune/Jupiter enemy will always have the sympathy vote. There's just something about this person's energy that elicits compassion. Settle differences without involving anyone else—you'll avoid the hazards of popular opinion.

BOSS

Your Neptune/Jupiter boss will ask what you would do if you were in his or her position. Volunteer an opinion with the expectation that this person will pick it apart and argue with you about it. Although you may see it as a lot of aggravation over nothing, it's actually your boss's way of getting the thought process moving.

COLLEAGUE

Both of you would rather be anywhere but work. With that in mind, you'll want to keep your focus on the task at hand. If anyone can bring out your gift for gab, lethargy, and fantasizing—it's a Child of Neptune and Jupiter.

CHILD OF VENUS

.... ❊ ....

WITH CHILD OF PLUTO/MARS

It can feel as if a Child of Pluto and Mars somehow gained access to your most private thoughts—he or she knows them so well. It's a nice feeling when you're getting along, but a less-than-pleasant experience when you're not. Few people can upset you so deeply and overpoweringly as a Child of Pluto and Mars, which creates the need for an absolute trust if you two are going to be a part of each other's lives.

LOVE INTEREST

Get within range of a Child of Pluto and Mars and you will immediately feel as if you can't live without this person. But spend a little time away and you'll begin to wonder what possessed you. Yet back in proximity with your Pluto/Mars love interest and all doubt evaporates. There's no in-between. Either this is the great love of your life or you'll need to keep your distance, because you won't be able to think of anyone else.

MATE

You'll find your Pluto/Mars mate is always convinced that you're holding out on him or her in some way. It might be questions about where you were, money you spent, or if you still feel the same after all these years. This can be unnerving because you adore your mate and don't know how to reassure this person. But don't worry about it. It's just the way this person is put together. If anything, you should be flattered. You will never be taken for granted. But sometimes the jealousy can get a bit much. That's when you have to look your mate squarely in the eye and just say, "Cool it."

CHILD

Be prepared to answer a lot of questions you would never have dreamed of asking when you were a child. At first you may be a little uncomfortable with the subject, but when you see how matter of fact your kid is about it, you'll lighten up. If your child is a boy, he can take forever to leave the nest. Encourage him to look for summer jobs so that he develops good work habits early. If your child is a girl, she may be a little *too* eager to be out and about. Keep her on a strict curfew through high school.

PARENT

Your Pluto/Mars parent will always be convinced you're too naive and innocent for your own good. It can sometimes be difficult being saddled with such an overprotective parent (especially when you have to introduce him or her to the person you're going out with), but no one will ever make you feel more cherished.

SIBLING

Not very good at sharing—whether it was toys or attention. And given your Pluto/Mars sibling's natural possessiveness, this person wasn't very good at sharing you either. But what may have been a bumpy start definitely improves with age. Children of Pluto and Mars are wonderful with *other* people's money. This person may not be able to rub two pennies together when it comes to his or her own finances, but when it comes to advice about yours—listen! This person has a knack for investments.

FRIEND

It may not be obvious, but your Pluto/Mars friend will always be at your beck and call. Don't make a request if you don't mean it, because this person will move heaven and earth to make it happen.

ENEMY

Not a good idea. You are certainly the superior strategist, but a Pluto/Mars enemy can always cut you to the quick—and will.

BOSS

There's only one right way to do things and that's the way your Pluto/Mars boss wants them done.

COLLEAGUE

Perhaps the best person you'll ever work with. Your Pluto/Mars colleague is thorough, resourceful, and doesn't take lip from anyone. This person is also fiercely loyal. Where others might sell you out for the sake of office politics, a Pluto/Mars colleague wouldn't think twice about coming to the rescue.

CHILD OF MARS

······ ❊ ······

WITH CHILD OF THE SUN

Y ou envy the way Children of the Sun can simply enjoy themselves. Their lives are mercifully
free of challenges in need of surmounting, skirmishes that must be fought, and actions that
require defending. A Child of the Sun can bask in the moment—like soaking up the rays of
the Sun—and just be. You may not be built for leisure (as a Child of Mars, you're too feisty), but a Child
of the Sun could certainly help you to lighten up.

LOVE INTEREST

It's not like you to actually want to *belong* to anyone—but you truly see yourself as being at your Solar
love interest's service. When you remember that Mars is the Planet of knights and the Sun is the Planet

of kings (and queens) then it doesn't seem so strange. You would probably do just about anything for this person—but draw the line at falling on your sword.

MATE

You'll drop everything to attend to a stopped-up sink. Otherwise you're busy scanning the horizon, looking for other problems to solve. But getting together only for emergencies isn't exactly your Solar mate's idea of any way to go through life. This person needs fun and laughter. Go ahead and unwind a bit. Isn't that why you married this person in the first place? Don't worry. You won't go soft.

CHILD

Your Solar son or daughter exudes self-confidence. The kid was just born with it. This isn't an easy concept to grasp, because for you self-confidence comes as a result of competition and proving your mettle. As a Mars parent you'll want to toughen up your kid, but, in trying to *build* confidence, you could inadvertently undermine it. No one's ever going to take your kid's confidence away. Like the Sun, it burns on its own energy.

PARENT

He or she came to all the games, competitions, and meets—no matter how far out of the way. Regardless of whether you won or lost you were still a champ in your Solar parent's eyes. You may feel like you have to do something to *earn* this kind of devotion—but you don't. That's your Mars talking. Solar love is bright and light and eternal. Like the Sun in the sky, you don't have to pay for it.

SIBLING

Your only criticism of your Solar sibling is that he or she doesn't show enough *gumption*. Solar Children like to be comfortable and aren't as willing as you to rock the boat. Though you like to stir things up, your Solar sibling learned that if he or she waited long enough, something good would eventually come along.

FRIEND

It doesn't matter how many times this person tells you to cool it or to bide your time, you will go ahead and do what you wanted to in the first place. And afterward, when you come back from the wars dragging your sword, your Solar friend will say: "I told you so." It would be nice if he or she dispensed with the smug expression. But that will probably only happen when you actually *listen* to this person's sensible advice.

ENEMY

A Solar enemy will get haughty and dismissive—which is tantamount to waving a red flag in front of you. Nevertheless it's up to you to hold back. Not only because you're "better than that," but also because this person really doesn't know what he or she is dealing with.

BOSS

The perfect working relationship. Your Solar boss loves to give orders and you love carrying them out. Work isn't just a "job" with you. Everything you do is top-notch and a matter of honor. Hopefully this person is worthy of your loyalty and trust.

COLLEAGUE

The perfect person to join forces with. But you both need to be careful about what you take on. Your willingness to go the distance can make you vulnerable to any manager or supervisor with a mind for exploiting it.

CHILD OF MARS

············ ❄ ············

WITH CHILD OF THE MOON

A Child of the Moon will just go with whatever mood you're in. But Moon children aren't passive. They're experts at "reading" feelings and responding to them, rather than talking about them. A Moon Child knows when to give you space and when to rein you in if you happen to be out of line.

LOVE INTEREST

Deeply feeling, Children of the Moon keep a tight lid on their emotions. The Moon was named after the goddess of the hunt, so your love interest is an expert at covering his or her tracks. Nevertheless there *are* signs of interest—if you know how to look for them. Always express joy at anything this person gives you, even if it's a tissue. You never know what may have sentimental value. The moment your Lunar love interest lends you something is when you know things are getting serious.

MATE

Neither of you is comfortable showing weakness. As a Child of Mars, you have a Spartan's response to pain—get over it and move on. Naturally secretive, your Lunar mate is more likely to try to solve a problem on his or her own before coming to you. You two aren't doing each other any favors by maintaining the stiff upper lip. Be the first to break the ice. The next time you stub your toe be really loud and obvious. Your Lunar mate's heart will jump at the chance of coming to your aid.

CHILD

Childhood is the only time a Moon child's feelings are so near the surface. You may feel the need to toughen the kid up. You know how mean-spirited other kids can be. But don't worry. Your Lunar child can take care of him or herself. A Moon child's strengths are different from yours. Just be there with a shoulder to lean on and a pep talk and you can't go wrong.

PARENT

If your Lunar parent is your dad, then he's low-key. A powerful presence in the household, he probably keeps to himself. Which is why you two got along so well. You know him better than anyone else. If your Lunar parent is your mom, then she's anything *but* low-key. Hopefully she has a good sense of humor and makes fun of her own outbursts. If not, don't antagonize her.

SIBLING

You were always intruding on your Lunar sibling's privacy. But then again, considering how much time your sibling spent on the phone or in the bathroom, it was hard not to. Relations improved once you both moved out and established your own households. However if either of you is visiting from out of town— don't tempt fate. Stay at a hotel.

FRIEND

This is the one person you can really talk to. He or she is so understanding and supportive. But make a point of asking how things are on this person's side of the fence. Lunar friends are very good at keeping their own concerns on the back burner.

ENEMY

You believe in just having it out. That's not the way a Lunar enemy operates. Lunar enemies take threats seriously and will go out of their way to avoid you. Let them. Trying to draw one out into the open is only asking for trouble.

BOSS

You hate how your Lunar boss changes moods from one day to the next. This person is impossible to predict! No other planet changes its appearance as dramatically as the Moon. This is something you want to remember about your Lunar boss. No matter how gruff or sullen he or she might get, given time, he or she will return to familiar good spirits.

COLLEAGUE

If anyone's going to pull your fat out of the fire, it's your Lunar colleague. Other people might get annoyed with having to explain things, but your Lunar colleague will always take the time to show you the ropes.

CHILD OF MARS

·········· ❋ ··········

WITH CHILD OF MERCURY

A Child of Mercury will always show you the quickest way to get from point A to point B—but it may not be by traveling a straight line. Sometimes you have to take a circuitous route or need to know the right people who can open certain doors. A Mercury Child is familiar with all the ins and outs.

LOVE INTEREST

It takes more than romance to woo a Child of Mercury. You have to have a love of people. At first it may bother you that your date's idea of a good time is to be out and about. You'd rather be in a dark corner getting more acquainted. But he or she wants to see how you interact in different environments and with certain mixes of people. If you're lively and fun—you're a keeper. If all you want to do is leave—then your Mercury love interest will happily show you the door.

MATE

You couldn't ask for a better team player. What may take some getting used to, though, is the way your mate will encourage you to come up with an idea or plan—and then ask if you really think it's any good. Mercury Children rarely introduce ideas of their own; their special talent is in taking an idea and making it *better*. And since you're so good at generating original concepts, it only makes sense that your mate would turn to you.

CHILD

You may feel that actions speak louder than words, but your kid believes it's the other way around. Don't expect to make a point unless you're willing to debate it. It won't fly if you just tell your Mercury kid not to think so much. Although this can get exasperating at times, it forces you to really consider the message you're sending. You can't help learning something new by raising a Mercury child.

PARENT

Your Mercury parent may have inadvertently turned you off to learning—probably because it meant so much to this person and it's your Mars nature to buck authority when you're young. Nevertheless you still absorbed what your mom or dad said, so it wouldn't be unusual for you to revisit education later. You may go back to school, study a subject on your own, or even pursue a career in academia—much to your Mercury parent's surprise and delight.

SIBLING

Mercury siblings have a way of mixing it up and then acting as if they haven't the slightest clue as to why you're so angry. Thankfully, with the passing of years, your sibling has less of a need for negative attention and more of a desire for the positive kind—which suits you fine.

FRIEND

You two probably share an activity or hobby that you both pursue with glee. There may even be a competitive element involved. But no one will applaud more loudly when you win. And if you lose, your Mercury friend always knows exactly what to say to boost your spirits.

ENEMY

No one is more devious. This person has a talent for using your words against you. Yet your Mercury enemy will eventually have to make a point or answer a question. And that's where you can pin him or her down if you're quick about it.

BOSS

As a Child of Mars you expect a strong hand when it comes to direction. You won't like the way your boss will ask anyone for input or consider possibilities that strike you as capricious or just plain silly. But Mercury bosses are very strategic and play their cards close to their chest. This person may have plans that you can't even begin to guess.

COLLEAGUE

A Mercury colleague is always there when you need him or her. You couldn't ask for better support. The only thing you have to watch out for is the way this person can egg you on without even meaning to.

CHILD OF MARS

.... ❋ ....

WITH CHILD OF VENUS

A Child of Venus will always arouse your interest—and your ire. You will never encounter so many obstacles to your happiness as you will with a Child of Venus. This person comes with more baggage and complications than anyone you've ever known. Making plans takes on all the twists and turns of an epic adventure. Yet whenever you've had enough and are ready to call it quits, a Child of Venus will make you feel like the luckiest person in the entire world. You two are meant to thwart as much as cavort.

LOVE INTEREST

Neither of you can anticipate how and when you come into each other's lives. For some reason you always seem to enter a Child of Venus's life right at the worst possible moment. Being gallant by nature (and that includes Children of Mars who are women), you don't mind. You like coming to the rescue. But though you might think your Venus love interest is playing hard to get, this person is actually just busy trying to put his or her affairs in order.

MATE

You naturally focus on your side of the relationship and trust that your mate will do likewise. A Child of Venus will do whatever he or she thinks is right for the relationship. At no point should you assume this reflects what this person wants or feels. Children of Venus keep that information to themselves. Don't mistake that obliging nature for passivity or subservience. Children of Venus love to be attached, but they don't want to feel beholden to anyone. Show respect and appreciation and you'll mate for life.

CHILD

If your Venus kid is a boy, prepare to fork out top dollar for the trendiest sneakers or the latest skate-board. If your kid is a girl, then the battle will be over makeup. Resistance is futile. But remember that Venus is the Planet of pledges. Build a relationship based on trust and your Venus kid will never betray it.

PARENT

Your Venus parent figured out a long time ago that you would either wind up being your own best friend or worst enemy, which is why he or she wisely stepped out of the line of fire. Once you settle into your own, you'll find your Venus parent emerging as more of a presence in your life—and you may even be surprised by your parent's strong and colorful opinions.

SIBLING

Your Venus sibling made everything look easy. The hair was immaculate, the clothes fit just right, even making friends appeared effortless. You, on the other hand, did everything the hard way. Once you catch on to the fact that there's an art to making things *look* easy, you'll change your mind about your approach and your sibling.

FRIEND

Your Venus friend can't help but take the opposite side of an argument. The more impassioned you get about your point of view, the more your friend will question it; the more blasé you are about doing something, the more your friend will try to pique your interest. If you want to get this person to agree with you, then practice a little reverse psychology. It works every time.

ENEMY

You don't become enemies with a Child of Venus until you realize you've been had—and then you get really mad. But you'll have only yourself to blame. Wait until you're in an objective frame of mind before discussing anything—especially finances. Otherwise your Venus enemy will fleece you every time.

BOSS

Your Venus boss will teach you that it's people who make good business, not money. There isn't a better person you could work for—or a more valuable mentor.

COLLEAGUE

Venus colleagues have perfected the art of "light and breezy," and you could learn a thing or two by treating certain things—like deadlines and money—as if they weren't a big deal.

CHILD OF MARS

········· ✻ ·········

WITH CHILD OF MARS

You never have to worry about this person's support or commitment. As soon as you put your shoulder to the wheel, a fellow Mars Child will do the same—and together you will surmount the most formidable obstacles.

LOVE INTEREST

For two passionate people, it's amazing how cool, calm, and collected you are around each other. The appeal isn't in the power of attraction but in the bond of friendship. As Children of Mars, you both know how your fiery desires flare and then smolder. And in truth, you don't trust them. But you do put your faith in camaraderie. Even if you and your Mars love interest don't remain an "item," you will always be friends.

MATE

You are the most important person in each other's life. If the two of you want to be alone, you have no compunction about canceling plans at the last minute. Subsequently if you're both in a fighting mood, you'll have it out right then and there—regardless of whether you're seated in the middle of a crowded restaurant. You two need to find a way to direct all that aggressive Mars energy so that it doesn't wind up taking a toll. Keeping yourselves busy with demanding work is key to your happiness.

CHILD

It's a good thing that your Birthday Planet makes you a natural coach. You know just when to push your kid and when to hold him or her back. One of the good things about raising a Mars kid is you can see where you were too hard on yourself. Teach your kid when to let him or herself off the hook and you will learn to do the same.

PARENT

Just because your Mars parent will always tell you to pick yourself up and jump back on the horse doesn't mean this person is insensitive to pain or looks down on weakness. Your parent knows that the best way to recover from a setback is to channel that anger and hurt into action right away. There's plenty of time to lick wounds later. Mars dads and Mars moms are extremely nurturing. Just like a coach in the boxing ring, they can be push-push one moment and then rubbing you down and whispering words of encouragement the next.

SIBLING

You couldn't help competing with each other. But where this would have brought out the nastier strains of sibling rivalry in most children, it actually creates a powerful bond between you. You know you can always count on your brother or sister to tell it like it is.

FRIEND

You are constantly in each other's business. People might mistake you for siblings or even lovers because of the familiarity with which you talk to each other and the way that neither of you will let the smallest thing slide. Whether it's one hair out of place or an off-color remark—your Mars friend will call you on it. And vice versa. It's nice to know that there's someone who cares about perfection as much as you.

ENEMY

If you and a fellow Mars Child are enemies then chances are the quarrel has nothing to do with you but involves a member of your family, a friend, or even the company you work for. Draw the necessary line in the sand, but leave an out. As long as you can both walk away saving face, then differences will be settled amicably.

BOSS

Hopefully this person handles authority well. If not, you will constantly challenge it until he or she leaves. If your Mars boss knows how to lead, then you know how to follow. Nothing makes you happier than to serve someone who deserves it.

COLLEAGUE

You two are always competing. If channeled positively your drive to outdo each other will result in work that just gets better and better. If it's negative then the entire office will become your battleground until one of you drives the other away.

CHILD OF MARS

·········· ※ ··········

WITH CHILD OF JUPITER

A Child of Jupiter brings out your fun side. But this person also brings a renewal of purpose. As a Child of Mars you can sometimes get stuck in a rut chasing after one prize and lose track of why you set off down this road in the first place. A Child of Jupiter shows you that life doesn't have to be contingent on whether or not you accomplish your goal.

LOVE INTEREST

Your Jupiter love interest is so worldly! You're just blown away by all the places this person has been and all the things he or she has done. You love all the highbrow references, the gossipy asides, and the general bonhomie that emanate from this person's life. You may wonder if you're interesting enough for this person. Don't worry. Jupiter Children haven't done half the things they say they have.

MATE

Your marriage is a work in progress. You may start out trying to adhere to the traditional roles, but over time you will reinvent them. You both treasure freedom *and* camaraderie, so in a good way this inspires you to be true to yourselves and subsequently to each other. The early years may be stormy. Mars and Jupiter are Planets of adventure, so the bonds between you are forged by the travails you go through together. Yet once over the hump, you couldn't ask for a better person to share your life with.

CHILD

You believe in setting goals. Jupiter can't help looking past them. Subsequently you may be satisfied with certain answers—or have confidence in things that have worked before—while your kid finds them limiting. This can result in conflict if you don't learn to step out of the way. It isn't easy giving your kid room to roam—especially when you're not convinced your kid even knows what he or she is doing. But the spirit of exploration lies at the core of any Jupiter child.

PARENT

Your sense of fairness, of leveling the playing field, and helping those who can't help themselves all come from your Jupiter parent. Your mom or dad taught you that the greatest trials aren't tests of strength, but tests of character. You have your Jupiter parent to thank for giving you your direction in life.

SIBLING

Your Jupiter sibling never settled for the easy answer or walked away from a matter of conscience. Your challenges often come in the form of obstacles and tests of will, whereas your Jupiter sibling usually faces moral dilemmas where the solution isn't always cut-and-dry. You may feel that this person brings it on himself or herself—but you always enjoy the philosophizing that follows.

FRIEND

If your friend got paid by the hour for all the Sturm und Drang he or she goes through, this person would be a millionaire! Nevertheless if you happen to be in the right mood, you enjoy listening to all the soul-searching. You know that the solution to your Jupiter friend's woes is less waxing poetic and more elbow grease, but you've said that already.

ENEMY

Your Jupiter enemy will project all of his or her intolerance, pettiness, and aggression on to you. Not all battles are won by contests; sometimes the person who puts the best spin on things wins them—so be careful that your actions don't play into the way your enemy portrays you.

BOSS

You're the person your Jupiter boss calls whenever something has to be enforced or a big mess needs to be cleaned up. You don't mind, but you wish your Jupiter boss would recognize some of your other talents. Don't sit around waiting for this person to get a clue. Show some initiative. He or she will make a point of giving you an opportunity to prove yourself.

COLLEAGUE

This person is in your life to brighten your workday. And to maybe even impart some words of wisdom that will stay with you long after you've moved on.

CHILD OF MARS

·········· ❀ ··········

WITH CHILD OF SATURN

Everything a Child of Saturn does is important. Children of Saturn often serve as personal role models. Whether it's an accomplishment that will go down in history or a decision that will affect the livelihood of others, they understand that their actions carry weight and will always take responsibility for them.

LOVE INTEREST

It may be hard to tell if you're really *into* your Saturn love interest or if getting this person's attention is such a challenge that you won't walk away until you've won it. Children of Saturn suffer from a chronic lack of time. That's why when you're on a date you'll sometimes feel as if the person's interviewing you for a job or making a sales pitch. Just remember—much of that frenetic intensity is a spillover from the workday. You don't mind someone having a busy schedule, as long as this person makes time for you.

MATE

Your marriage is a serious enterprise. It allows for both of you to do what you want. If one of you needs to go back to school, then the other will take on extra work to cover expenses. If the other is asked to relocate, then you will both sit down and review the pluses and minuses of the decision. Neither partner's priorities outweigh the other's. Nevertheless you can have your differences. As a Child of Mars, you take the short view of things while your Saturn mate takes the long view. But together you come up with a midpoint that serves you both well.

CHILD

Procrastination and delay are written into your Saturn kid's makeup. This is hard for you to understand—especially when you see how much your kid frets about it. Children of Saturn cling to anxiety, just as Children of Mars embrace action. Adhering to a day-to-day schedule, however, will help to give your Saturn child a sense of structure (always a plus) while cutting down on some of the existential crises.

PARENT

You're convinced that the newest idea is the best, which inevitably causes your Saturn parent to raise an eyebrow and ask what makes this one any better than what came before? Although you were often given the third degree, your Saturn parent always supported you once you could prove you were on the right track.

SIBLING

Saturn siblings carry a parental authority and have a way of putting things that makes what they say sound like written law. If you respect your brother and sister, then you don't mind this at all. If you don't think much of this person, then this is something that never fails to make you see red.

FRIEND

It's up to you to get the ball rolling. But once you've got a volley going, your friend will match you stroke for stroke. This person is every bit as committed and focused as you on having a good time or embarking on an endeavor.

ENEMY

Think twice before crossing swords with this one. A Saturn enemy doesn't really get mad. This person just doesn't want to have anything more to do with you. Severing ties might not seem like much at the moment—but given Saturn's ability to look further down the road, you may come to regret your actions.

BOSS

As far as you're concerned your Saturn boss would be a lot further along if he or she didn't take so long to make a decision. Yet the ironic thing is how many of those opportunities that seem "lost" either wind up not panning out or coming your boss's way yet again. Saturn is the Planet of time. And even if you think your boss doesn't act in a timely fashion, this person still has a remarkable sense of timing that never ceases to amaze and impress you.

COLLEAGUE

Even if you're equals, you need to decide who leads and who follows. If not you will bicker constantly and confuse everyone around you.

CHILD OF MARS

WITH CHILD OF URANUS/SATURN

Children of Uranus and Saturn are in even more of a hurry to get things done than you. But where you tend to focus on only one objective to the exclusion of everything else, Uranus/Saturn Children can't think straight unless they have a number of irons in the fire.

That way if one goes up in smoke, they can always switch to something else. A Child of Uranus and Saturn will show you you're capable of doing more than you know.

LOVE INTEREST

You'll know right away if this person's into you or not. If not, it will be glaringly obvious. If anyone does the pursuing, it will be your Uranus/Saturn love interest. You may find this a little off-putting. As a Child of Mars you like to take the initiative, but you might as well get used to the role reversals early on. Children of Uranus and Saturn always play against type.

MATE

No matter how long you've been together, there's still never a dull moment when this person's around. What can get difficult is when he or she is away—which is often the case, as your mate may travel in conjunction with work. It may surprise you to discover how much you rely (even depend!) on this person's presence. The flip side of this is that you'll do more traveling than you would normally. Your Uranus/Saturn mate opens your world.

CHILD

You can take this kid anywhere. He or she is amazingly adaptable and will inevitably wind up making friends with somebody. Yet every few months or so, your Uranus/Saturn child will refuse to do something that he or she has always enjoyed doing before. Don't fight it. It's just your kid's need to change his or her routine. Rearrange the order of things—like a bath *before* dinner instead of after—and your child will settle down again.

PARENT

It was never your Uranus/Saturn parent's intention to be confusing. It's just that this person never stopped looking for a better way to do things. And if that meant starting again halfway through the science project, then so be it. This taught you the importance of getting things right—no matter how long it takes.

SIBLING

At first you may have found your Uranus/Saturn sibling's inability to accept things "as is" hard to swallow. There was always something wrong or in drastic need of improvement. Over time, however, you developed an appreciation for this person's high standards and exacting eye.

FRIEND

Your Uranus/Saturn friend will always encourage you to say what's on your mind and to do what you think is best. As a Child of Mars, you follow orders. Your friend understands, but he or she also knows that if you don't stay true to yourself, then it doesn't matter how noble your actions are.

ENEMY

If there's a problem, it's probably the result of a miscommunication. It's always worth taking the time to straighten out. Lying is the only thing Children of Uranus and Saturn find unforgivable.

BOSS

Your boss will always push you to do more than you think you can. You have mixed feelings about this. On the one hand, you'd just rather be told what to do and you'll do it. Everything doesn't always have to be such a "learning" experience. There are times when you just want to do your job. Yet on the other hand, you're flattered that your Uranus/Saturn boss thinks so much of you that he or she wants you to do more. As long as this person keeps raising the bar, you'll keep striving to match it.

COLLEAGUE

Despite differences of opinion (which happen almost daily), you love working with your Uranus/Saturn colleague. Unlike others, you always know where you stand with this person.

CHILD OF MARS

※

WITH CHILD OF NEPTUNE/JUPITER

A Neptune/Jupiter Child is very good at getting you to examine someone else's side of a dispute. Though not always willing to give up a gripe, you eventually come around to seeing that there might be good reason for why others act the way they do. A Child of Neptune and Jupiter deepens your view of life and yourself.

LOVE INTEREST

A Neptune/Jupiter love interest almost always enters your life through the back door. There will be something clandestine about the two of you being together. One of you may be separated or in the process of getting a divorce. You could work for rival companies. Or you may come from wildly different backgrounds. Obviously this only fuels the ardor and intensity. Nevertheless at some point you are going to have to sit down and figure out the logistics of a future together. This may require an enormous sacrifice for both of you.

MATE

Prospects improve the longer you are together. Because you met during a time of emotional or financial stress, it's easy to believe things will always be this way. They won't. In time you'll surmount these obstacles and create a very solid foundation. Hardship brings you closer. Believe it or not—part of you will miss it when it's gone.

CHILD

The most important thing you can teach your kid is that dreams really can come true—but it's up to your kid to make them happen. Neptune/Jupiter children tend to assume that real life will never live up to what they can conceive of in their imaginations. By empowering your kid at an early age, he or she will learn that dreaming a dream is just the first step in a creative process. The rest is in trying to find a way to make it a reality.

PARENT

Your Neptune/Jupiter parent's tendency toward gloom and doom may have gotten on your nerves growing up. As far as you were concerned your mom or dad was much too willing to throw in the towel. Yet instead of undermining your confidence, these expressions of futility made you even more driven to win. This actually rekindles your parent's faith and optimism—although you may be the last to hear about it.

SIBLING

A continual source of inspiration. Perhaps it was your brother's or sister's quiet strength in the face of overwhelming obstacles; maybe it was simply this person's very unique and rich view of life—in any case your Neptune/Jupiter sibling was responsible for showing you that there's more to people (and life) than what you see on the surface.

FRIEND

You love to get this friend's "take" on things. It's always unique and insightful. It may frustrate you how your Neptune/Jupiter friend can be so talented yet leave so much of that potential untouched. But when you begin to see how truly rich and diverse this person's inner life is you'll be amazed that he or she is able to develop half the things on tap.

ENEMY

Chances are this person is already his or her own worst enemy. You don't need to do anything other than steer clear.

BOSS

It's always hard to figure out exactly how a Child of Neptune and Jupiter got to a position of authority. These types of bosses often come across as being hopelessly scattered and more than just a little clueless. However appearances can be deceiving. This person must have done something right to have gotten this far. Look and listen and you may learn a thing or two about how to get things done without having to show your hand.

COLLEAGUE

If your Neptune/Jupiter colleague is truly inspired, then you couldn't find a better role model. This person is so gifted and talented that everyone is in awe. This is someone who could truly transform the profession. However, if he or she is uninspired, then the complaining can get a bit much. You'll have to learn how to tune this person out.

CHILD OF MARS

·········· ☀ ··········

WITH CHILD OF PLUTO/MARS

Children of Pluto and Mars don't take disappointments lightly. That's because it's outrage—not love of the game—that provides the source of their willpower. There's an intensity to Pluto/Mars Children that you may find both intimidating and fascinating. There's no disputing they get results, and nobody messes with them. You also like how they've got guts.

LOVE INTEREST

You're not used to someone feeling things more powerfully than you do—but in truth, you like it. However, being a Child of Mars, you won't let on. You'll act tough and play hard to get—which of course keeps your Pluto/Mars love interest coming back for more. You won't have to worry about losing interest in this one. A Pluto/Mars love interest will keep your passions burning long after others have dwindled.

MATE

Pluto was named after the god of riches, so you'll notice your income increase with each passing year. A Pluto/Mars mate stokes the flames of your ambition and believes you're capable of more than you give yourself credit for. This person also happens to give really good financial advice. Even if all you want to do is basket weaving, your mate will know how to market it so that yours is the leading franchise. If you listen to your Pluto/Mars mate, you'll get to do whatever you want in life *and* never have to worry about how to make ends meet.

CHILD

Undoubtedly your Pluto/Mars kid will test your patience. Indeed tests of strength and willpower will be an ongoing theme in your relationship. If you find yourself in a situation where the more you push, the more your kid resists, then walk away from it. Don't hesitate to let your kid sit alone in his or her room until things cool down. Pluto/Mars kids are intensely self-reflective. One of the best things you can impart (as well as learn yourself) is that there's no shame in apologizing.

PARENT

Since kindergarten, your Pluto/Mars parent has been cross-examining you about what you did and who you talked to. Your mom or dad just can't help being in your business. You don't have to divulge everything. Just make your Pluto/Mars parent feel included. It's all he or she really wants.

SIBLING

Your Pluto/Mars sibling gets embroiled in situations you wouldn't go near. It may be a love interest who doesn't feel the same way or a job that your sibling says he or she can't stand. You're drawn to challenges, so that you can master them, whereas your sibling is drawn to ordeals that transform him or her just by suffering through them. As far as you're concerned these episodes are all pain and no gain, but for your Pluto/Mars sibling, they trigger a profound psychic metamorphosis.

FRIEND

You can always call your Pluto/Mars friend in a crisis. Not only will this person drop everything to rush to your aid, but you also know that he or she will do exactly what you would have done in the same situation.

ENEMY

Given that you two would battle each other to a draw (neither of you will relent), it will probably be up to you to signal your Pluto/Mars enemy that you're ready for a talk if he or she is. This person will take you up on it.

BOSS

Your Pluto/Mars boss is a real player and knows how to negotiate even if he or she holds the weaker hand. However your boss isn't very good at choosing his or her fights. There's a tendency to invest just as much energy in a trivial matter as in a crucial one. This is where you could be of great help. You know which battles to throw in order to win a war.

COLLEAGUE

You guys make a formidable team and won't take no for an answer—indeed you'll treat every ixnay as a challenge begging to be conquered. Sometimes a no really is a no, and you guys need to cool your jets.

CHILD OF JUPITER

❋

WITH CHILD OF THE SUN

A Child of the Sun will always bring things back to the here and now, which is good because you tend to get carried away with your impossible dreams and larger-than-life ideas. Happiness, for you, often lies further down the road, while for a Child of the Sun, happiness can be found at any given moment. Instead of focusing so much on the way things could be, you'll gain more of an appreciation for the way things *are* by spending time with a Child of the Sun.

LOVE INTEREST

Like you, Children of the Sun prefer to keep matters light and would rather spend time having fun than making any serious plans. This can give the mistaken impression that your Solar love interest is a free spirit. Actually, he or she will expect exclusivity while you're dating. Children of the Sun need to feel that they've got something everyone else wants. Sharing you with others depreciates your value.

MATE

You can do whatever you want—as long as you run it by your Solar mate first. For the most part your other half will be agreeable. After all, who could deny someone as vivacious and charming as yourself? However there will be times when this Child of the Sun will put his or her foot down. When this happens you must treat it seriously. Even if you know you could get your way by pushing, that's not what's at stake. Trust is. Children of the Sun must feel that their authority is respected—even if you're the one clearly in charge.

CHILD

Your Solar kid isn't quite the explorer you are. Indeed he or she is more than happy to just stay put, which means it's up to you to impart your love of exotica and adventure. If you're going to ask your little prince or princess to rough it (like going camping for the weekend), then make sure you bring along the latest in accoutrements.

PARENT

If you ever wondered where you got your own penchant for sermonizing, look no further. Your Solar parent *loves* to pontificate. Nevertheless this person also impressed upon you that each individual makes a world of difference and that you owe it to yourself (as well as to the people around you) to be the best person you can be. But this doesn't sound like such a cliché when you say it.

SIBLING

You may find your Solar sibling a little dull. Trying to get this person to accompany you anywhere when you were younger was like pulling teeth. This improves a little over the years, but not by much. However what your sibling may lack in worldliness, he or she makes up for with house and home. Your Solar sibling gets all the movie channels, has the coziest guest bed, and the best-stocked refrigerator.

FRIEND

The reason you get to do half the things you do is because of your Solar friend. You may be the one who gets the ball rolling with an idea to do this or that, but it's your Solar friend who will look up the movie times, keep extra cash on hand, or check to make sure that the country you want to visit isn't in the midst of a civil war.

ENEMY

Dealing with a Solar enemy will inadvertently reveal that you have an enormous ego, too. This is probably the one thing you resent the most, but your Solar enemy isn't telling you anything you didn't know before.

BOSS

Your Solar boss may think he or she is in charge, but you know it's really the other way around. Nevertheless, you're extremely generous by nature and will allow this person to continue under this mistaken impression. After all, your Solar boss needs the accolades more than you.

COLLEAGUE

You know you're a lot of fun to hang out with, but you don't want someone following you around all the time. It cramps your style.

CHILD OF JUPITER

.... ❋ ....

WITH CHILD OF THE MOON

You express yourself largely and dramatically. A bear hug, loud kiss, or a slap on the back broadcasts what you feel. Children of the Moon, however, are deeply private. More responsive than expressive, it's not always easy to tell where you stand with them. That's because much of their emotional life takes place on the inside. But as they get comfortable with you and open up, you'll come to appreciate and treasure your special bond.

LOVE INTEREST

Moon Children often come across as not being all that interested when you first meet, but if there's chemistry, you'll wind up conveniently "bumping" into this person fairly regularly. Children of the Moon never approach anything directly. Their Ruling Planet was named after the goddess of the hunt, so your love interest knows how to keep tabs on you without giving away the game.

MATE

You may be enterprising, but your Lunar mate's the one who has a head for figures. Even if you maintain separate bank accounts, this person will wind up managing your finances as well. You could do worse than let a Child of the Moon handle the investing and saving. This person usually knows which direction the interest rates will go before the Fed does.

CHILD

There are two types of Moon kids—hunters and gatherers. If your kid's a hunter, then he or she is either exploring in the woods or foraging through the malls. If your kid is a gatherer, then he or she will collect all the blankets and pillows within reach and settle down for a cozy afternoon in front of the TV or computer, or with a favorite book. The first type never comes home when you call—you'll just have to settle for whenever the kid shows up. And the second just won't leave the house.

PARENT

The stormier you got, the more placid your Lunar mom or dad became. But it's not like your parent was particularly Zen. This person simply tuned you out. Eventually you caught on to the fact that this behavior was *not* the way to your parent's heart. What you also learned was that it's the person who doesn't respond in kind who maintains the upper hand.

SIBLING

Your Lunar sibling remembers everything. But then what else do you expect from someone born under the Planet of memory? Be careful when you start in on one of those fish stories of yours. Your brother or sister won't think twice about correcting you on the spot—even if it means taking the punch out of your punch line.

FRIEND

This is one of the few people in your life who "gets" it. This person will gasp when you show him or her your favorite spot on a nature trail or cry just as heavily during the closing moments of a tearjerker. You never have to apologize for getting caught up in the moment when you're with your Lunar friend.

ENEMY

Once enraged, your Lunar enemy will just keep nipping at your heels no matter what. A Lunar enemy's ire is like a family feud. It can keep on going even if the original reason was forgotten long ago. The best thing is to never make enemies with a Child of the Moon. The second best thing might be to move out of state.

BOSS

Don't try to impress him or her with some big razzle-dazzle song and dance. Lunar bosses *hate* pitches. Simply map out your idea, leave a written copy on the desk, and wait for your boss to get back to you about it. If he or she does, then you know you've got this person's full support.

COLLEAGUE

You may often feel as if your Lunar colleague is always undermining your confidence. How did you get stuck with such a pessimist? Actually this person's a realist. There's a difference. A pessimist will tell you it's impossible, while a realist will show you the problems in your thinking.

CHILD OF JUPITER

.... ※ ....

WITH CHILD OF MERCURY

A Child of Mercury prompts you to question things. You might think this person's trying to pull a fast one or is just being clever for cleverness's sake. But after you start to analyze the way you think and your overall approach, you'll find that instead of losing faith in how life works, you actually gain more perspective and depth. Born under the Planet of the mind, a Child of Mercury's inquiries will always give you moment for pause *and* food for thought.

LOVE INTEREST

Children of Mercury don't wait on ceremony and think nothing of introducing themselves. Yet what you may find a little disconcerting is how much this person already knows about you. Children of Mercury always study their subject before making the first move. And of course the fact that someone would have gone through all the trouble in the first place gets your attention.

MATE

Neither of you will stand in line or do things by the book. As a Child of Jupiter, you haven't met a rule that can't be bent, and your Mercury mate has a special talent for locating loopholes. If you two don't wind up going into the snake oil business, then you might consider opening a law firm. You can coax, cajole, and bamboozle just about anyone—but each other. Your Mercury mate is the one person you trust most in the world and vice versa.

CHILD

There will come a day when your Mercury kid will catch you in a fib or confront you with one of the hundreds of contradictions you leave lying around. You might as well skip the excuses and the moralizing. They won't work. But you can take this opportunity to teach your kid a more valuable lesson. Sometimes you have to make slight adjustments in order to do what's right. This is the difference between following a law to the letter and honoring the spirit in which it was intended.

PARENT

Your Mercury parent made a lot of trouble for himself or herself by not leaving well enough alone. Sometimes the fuss was worth it and sometimes it wasn't. What you took away from this, however, was a self-imposed limit on how far you're willing to go (or how much you're willing to put up with) before you call it quits. Knowing when to wrap things up is just as important as knowing when to get them started.

SIBLING

Your Mercury sibling is always trying to steal your thunder. If your brother or sister isn't scrutinizing everything you say, then he or she is co-opting your ideas. Luckily you've got more brilliant ideas than you know what to do with, so you don't mind sharing the wealth.

FRIEND

Your Mercury friend is always game for what you have in mind—as long as it's not a repeat of what you did the other day. Children of Mercury hate doing the same thing twice. The only thing you have to watch out for is keeping this person waiting. Take any longer than fifteen minutes and your friend will move on to something else—leaving you in the lurch.

ENEMY

A Child of Mercury is more an opponent than an enemy. This person is a master game player and will outsmart you at every turn. Play fair and square, but if you lose, accept it graciously. You can always trust your Mercury opponent to do the same.

BOSS

The nitpicking gets on your nerves. But you have to admit that your boss has an eye for details. Dotting *i*'s and crossing *t*'s isn't a strong suit, but self-improvement is inevitable when you work for a Child of Mercury.

COLLEAGUE

A Mercury colleague may never *tell* you what to do, but after all the corrections, you'll eventually get the idea. You can't go wrong taking them to heart. Chances are your colleague's method really is more efficient.

CHILD OF JUPITER

·········· ❄ ··········

WITH CHILD OF VENUS

Children of Venus love people just as much as you do. Like you, they really see the best that humanity has to offer. All art, music, and culture are a celebration of the human spirit—whether it's an exhibit hanging in some posh museum or the way someone combines incongruous elements to create a "look." Venus Children always accent the positive. You won't hear anything jaded or disparaging come out of this person's mouth—unless something is tacky.

LOVE INTEREST

You like being seduced. And your Venus love interest knows just how to set the mood. Leading you on with come-hither looks and winsome smiles, this person knows how to play to your mind, your body, and your spirit. The only thing you're unsure about is your heart. But considering how that's the last thing a Child of Venus gives away, decide if you're serious or not about your future together before asking.

MATE

The funny thing is you may have seen more of each other when you were dating. That's because your Venus mate has a very active social schedule—as do you. Occasionally they intersect, but for the most part you travel in different circles. This keeps things fresh and lively, as you never fall into a rut and will always have something to talk about when you get together at the end of the day. One of your favorite games may be to show up at a social event, pretend not to know each other, and then start flirting.

CHILD

Venus kids can get a little precious—which is always your cue to bring your son or daughter down a peg or two. You don't want your child putting on airs or thinking he or she is better than anyone else. The kid's got enough grace, talent, charm, and good looks to not have to rub people's noses in it.

PARENT

Thank heavens your Venus parent taught you a little poise to go with that Jupiter rough-and-tumble. Otherwise you'd still be eating off other people's plates or carrying on at the top of your lungs. Behaving like a proper lady or a gentleman is not only classy, but you also carry it off so well. Where others appear stuffy or overly rehearsed, you wind up looking positively glamorous. Everyone treasures your thank-you notes.

SIBLING

You had to empty out the entire toy box before you could decide what you wanted. And even then you weren't too sure. But your Venus sibling always knew which toy was best and made a beeline straight to it. That difference continues to this day. You may be surrounded by a wealth of opportunities, but it's not easy for you to distinguish one from the rest. Not only does your sibling know how to do this, but he or she also happens to have good taste, too.

FRIEND

The jewel in your crown. Plus he or she always looks great! Your only reservation is that your Venus friend can be a little too fussy. But you don't mind loosening up this person a bit.

ENEMY

Venus enemies are masters of intrigue, so you never want to get talked into keeping things quiet or behind the scenes. Of the two of you, you're the more likable, so use your popularity to your advantage. You'll soon have your Venus enemy crying "uncle."

BOSS

As far as you're concerned your Venus boss plays it too safe. And for the most part, you're right. Children of Venus make better coordinators than innovators. But seeing as you will inevitably wind up doing your own thing one day, why not learn something new? It will prove invaluable later on.

COLLEAGUE

If your Venus colleague is the one out front greeting customers and handling orders, then things couldn't be better. But if this is the person you have to rely on for backup or follow-through—don't hold your breath. Venus colleagues are easily distracted by dust bunnies and broken nails.

CHILD OF JUPITER

❋

WITH CHILD OF MARS

A Child of Mars cuts right to the quick. It can be a little shocking for someone who likes to think about things as much as you, but it's also liberating. You can always rely on a Child of Mars for a push when you need it.

LOVE INTEREST

Your Mars love interest is certainly exciting to be around. But it's hard to imagine keeping up this kind of pace. Everything is so urgent and needs to be taken care of immediately! It's almost as if your personal trainer followed you home from the gym and is with you every waking hour—pushing you to go for the burn; reminding you to maintain good form. At a certain point, you're just going to want to relax and let it all hang out.

MATE

Your Mars mate can't help but see everything in terms of power structure. There are those who lead and those who serve. It will take a while to establish who's who, but in all likelihood you'll discover these roles change according to the situations you find yourselves in. Your Mars mate probably does best in emergencies or situations that require quick thinking, whereas you're good at looking beyond the heat of the moment and making decisions that prove cogent in the long run. No matter how bossy your mate gets, keep one very important thing in mind—Children of Mars love to take orders.

CHILD

Your Mars kid needs something to fight—it's how he or she builds up willpower. Since that means you'll be playing punching bag, infuse these little altercations with good humor and wit and your Mars kid will learn respect, the power of his or her own strength, as well as good sportsmanship. The more that you can show that there's a difference between a contest and a fight, the more your Mars child will develop a healthy attitude toward conflicts in general and won't take things so personally.

PARENT

The reason you accomplish as much as you do is because of your Mars parent. You might have bristled at the boot camp–style atmosphere of your early home life, but once you got those good habits drilled into you, then you never had to worry about slowing down. Children of Jupiter can be prone to laziness—but thanks to your Mars parent, you'll never know what that's like.

SIBLING

Your Mars sibling likes to fight. You can't stand it. But you're no patsy. You understand that the only way to resolve some conflicts is by taking a strong hand. But when you do it, it's because you've been *forced* to. In truth, your motives may not be so altruistic. Indeed your Mars sibling may serve as an uncomfortable reminder of an aggressive side that you're not at ease with.

FRIEND

If you're dealing with a problem that's straightforward, then your Mars friend is great, because he or she will come up with all kinds of solutions lickety-split. He or she may even offer to handle it for you. However if it's something that you're still trying to sort out, then your Mars friend may try to get a rise out of you by telling you you're thinking too much or that you're being too namby-pamby. At times like these you have to remember that your friend was born under the Planet of "actions speak louder than words."

ENEMY

You're not big on conflicts, so get someone else to do the fighting for you. Try another Child of Mars.

BOSS

It wouldn't be surprising if this person wound up working for you one day. Though Children of Mars make great leaders, they're not good developers—which is your strong suit. Nevertheless you could learn a thing or two from your Mars boss's hands-on approach—not to mention "don't-mess-with-me" attitude.

COLLEAGUE

Mars Children know how to throw their weight around—and will. Don't get between this person and an objective. You'll get mowed down.

CHILD OF JUPITER
·········· ❊ ··········
WITH CHILD OF JUPITER

The fish stories get bigger and the details more exaggerated when you and another Child of Jupiter get together. But facts aren't all that important. You understand what the other means—in spirit. And it's in the spirit of "creative license" that you both feel free to embellish or improvise on what the other has to say. Together you project so much cheer, volume, and bonhomie that you can't help but draw an audience.

LOVE INTEREST

You two are so social and fun loving that it's easy to forget you're supposed to be dating. When you go out, it's often in a group. On the rare occasions when you want to be intimate, one of you will inevitably wind up bumping into a friend at the restaurant or spotting an old pal while in line at the Cineplex. For this reason you may never get around to discussing your feelings. Unless there's a driving need to hook up, you could continue like this for months.

MATE

You are both equally temperamental and equally high maintenance—despite the fact you're convinced it's the *other* one who behaves unreasonably. As Children of Jupiter you are generous in all things—except when it comes to accepting responsibility for your actions. Rather than simply copping to a fault, you will react as if the mere insinuation of wrongdoing is the most unconscionable outrage, or you will be so overly heroic in your martyrdom that no one would doubt for a moment that you've been falsely accused. Somewhere in all the histrionics is the truth—though it may take the two of you years to find it.

CHILD

You may be the last on your block to know what your Jupiter kid is up to—although you were just as rascally when you were your son's or daughter's age. You believe in freedom and exploration, so you're reluctant to tie the kid down, but don't cover the kid's tracks with excuses and rationalizations. Freedom is more precious when there are limits imposed on it.

PARENT

You may differ with your Jupiter parent on approach, but you both share an unshakable faith in the human spirit. Perhaps your philosophy is more scientific, whereas your parent's is religious; you might put your faith in entrepreneurship while your parent is more the rugged individualist. The terminology may clash (you've had your fair share of heated debates), but scratch the surface and you'll find the moral fiber is the same.

SIBLING

Your Jupiter sibling may be the polar opposite of you—in temperament or outlook. When you remember that one of the functions of your Ruling Planet is to *broaden* your horizons, then you'll be able to see that even your sibling's obstinacy serves a higher purpose.

FRIEND

Although you have more best friends than you can count, your Jupiter friend is your *best* best friend.

ENEMY

You get along with most people, but if you and another Child of Jupiter have a falling-out—it's probably irreparable. The dispute, in itself, may not be a big deal, but you will both take the moral high ground, and neither of you will back down.

BOSS

Your boss is like a teacher or a guru. What you do is so much more than business. That's because it's so complex and multileveled. There's nothing wrong with you guys getting into long, windy, philosophical discussions—but you might want to save it for the end of the day. Otherwise you'll never get any work done.

COLLEAGUE

You and your colleague are probably the two loudest people in the office—which means you can't get away with anything. Duck out together and everyone knows something's up because it's eerily quiet. Hang out too long and the sound level gets so loud no one can think straight. You may have to save the socializing for company parties.

CHILD OF JUPITER

········· ❊ ·········

WITH CHILD OF SATURN

It may feel like you accent the positive, while a Child of Saturn dwells on the negative, but in truth you balance each other out. Saturn is the Planet of limits, so it's this person who will tell you that there's only so much money in the bank to finance what you want or remind you that your deadline's approaching, so you need to pick up the pace. You may resent the nagging and prodding, but you will always accomplish more with a Child of Saturn's help.

LOVE INTEREST

The pressure's on whenever you're dealing with a Saturn love interest. Things may seem fun and jovial on the surface, but this person will still try to feel out what you do for a living, how much you make, and what your plans are for the future. For a Child of Saturn, dates *are* job interviews. If you get called back right away, you're hired. If not—move on.

MATE

Jupiter and Saturn are patrician Planets. You invite loved ones, friends, and colleagues to rely on you as a *couple* and know that it's your union that gives them a sense of security and continuity. This adds to the personal bond that exists between you. Neither Children of Jupiter nor Children of Saturn were built for too much private life or self-analysis. You both have more important things to do with your time.

CHILD

Your Saturn kid never believed you when you said things would get easier. And though it may take your son or daughter longer than most to find the happiness you promised would be there, you know that he or she will eventually. Saturn kids never disappoint their Jupiter parents.

PARENT

Though you tuned out most of what your Saturn parent said when you were growing up (this person takes forever to get to the point!), you still absorbed the gist of it. There's no disputing your Saturn parent is wise, but the advice has its roots in a survivor mentality and doesn't take into account the lucky breaks, windfalls, and chance coincidences that frequent your life.

SIBLING

You two rarely agree (you both have strong opinions), but it's even more rare for you to fight. Your Saturn sibling is your equal, and no matter the age difference, you show each other the utmost respect. Your

Saturn sibling will always take your side in public—and you will do the same. Your family bond transcends any philosophical and/or political differences.

FRIEND

This is one of your oldest friends. And if not, then he or she might as well be, because it feels as if you've known each other forever. You've had your differences. Indeed you may be friends with this person's rival or ex—which would have caused no small amount of tension, since you're not going to let anyone decide who you associate with. Nevertheless, you will always feel protective about your Saturn friend—even if this person doesn't need it.

ENEMY

It's doubtful you're enemies. What's more likely is that you've had a falling-out, which means it might be a good idea to revisit the matter later when you're feeling less heated. Saturn Children often bring up the very flaw that you don't want to think about.

BOSS

You may see your job as a stepping-stone to your future, but your Saturn boss regards your job as something that needs doing pronto. Focus on the here and now, get things done in a timely fashion, and you'll never have cause for worry.

COLLEAGUE

Your Saturn colleague sees a block where you see an opening. You may never get passed this half-full/half-empty impasse, but if you do, then you would make an extraordinary team, because you will inspire your Saturn colleague to go further than he or she normally would, while your colleague will tell you when to turn right or left so that you don't keep walking into walls.

CHILD OF JUPITER

❀

WITH CHILD OF URANUS/SATURN

A Child of Uranus and Saturn isn't afraid to think big. It's very rare for you to come across someone whose concepts are grander than yours! Once you two get talking it's extraordinary the kind of brainstorming that goes on. World hunger, economic crises, and religious controversies are all solved in the blink of an eye!

LOVE INTEREST

Both of you tend to be erratic in your emotions—which has all the makings of a wild and passionate romance. However you both treasure your freedom and feel ambivalent about being tied down. One of you needs to be clear-cut about committing in order for the other to stay put. If you both question the idea, then there's no real glue to hold you together. However if you meet when you're older (or if there's a significant age difference) then you'll click right away.

MATE

Your relationship brings out the best in both of you. That's because you're both "team players" and won't think twice about making a personal sacrifice if it means doing right by everybody. Nevertheless there will be times when you get on each other's nerves—pet peeves include cutting the other off in midsentence and taking over a story in midtelling. You both love to talk and never hold back when it comes to voicing something you don't like. The secret to working out your differences is in respecting them. You never have to walk around on eggshells with your Uranus/Saturn mate. This person's feelings don't bruise easily.

CHILD

It's hard to remember that Uranus/Saturn children are children. They're so precocious and willing to take on challenges and responsibilities that are greater than their years. Nevertheless, they only go through childhood once, so the more you can introduce your kid to things that only children get to enjoy, the better. Seeing as how you've never been in a hurry to grow up, that won't pose too much of a problem.

PARENT

Sometimes it felt as if your Uranus/Saturn parent could read your mind. Your mom or dad knew just when to switch to something else because you'd been staring at the same page too long or how to pique your interest in an activity you wouldn't have gone near because it was supposed to be good for you. You will always value this person's hovering, yet benevolent, presence.

SIBLING

You may not have had much to do with each other when you were younger because you both lived such independent lives. That may even continue to this day. Nevertheless when you two do manage to hook up—during family get-togethers or on the phone—you're always amazed by how much you really enjoy each other's company. You'll spend hours catching up and filling each other in on the most telling (and humorous) details.

FRIEND

This is one of the few people you can see daily yet not find boring. You love your Uranus/Saturn friend's take on things, and because this person is always going through something funny and/or traumatic, you can't wait to get the latest scoop. You will always turn to each other for advice—and then not follow it.

ENEMY

Lightning to your thunder. Though you're louder and more intimidating, your Uranus/Saturn enemy knows just when to strike with the zingers. The remarkable thing is that after it's all over, the skies clear, and you're friends again—or at least back on civil terms.

BOSS

Your Uranus/Saturn boss is always interested in what you have to say. And since you're never short on insight (or opinions), you're happy to contribute. The truth is you're more interested in doing something creative or constructive than you are in jockeying for position. Your Uranus/Saturn boss sees that and appreciates it.

COLLEAGUE

You and your Uranus/Saturn colleague discuss everything in detail. If you like what's up, you'll see that it gets done. If you don't—you have your ways.

CHILD OF JUPITER

.... ❋ ....

WITH CHILD OF NEPTUNE/JUPITER

You feel right at home with a Child of Neptune and Jupiter. This person shares your love of romance, adventure, and spirituality. But where you look for these things in faraway places, a Child of Neptune and Jupiter searches within. Children of Neptune and Jupiter are convinced that our outer and inner lives exist in a reciprocal relationship. We may find things that intrigue and fascinate, but it's our inner lives that understand the meaning.

LOVE INTEREST

You are both so hopelessly romantic that you can get lost in each other's eyes and sighs and think nothing of letting all your feelings and sentiments gush forth in an uninterrupted flow. It's like falling in love for the first time! However, of the two, your well will run dry long before your Neptune/Jupiter love interest. Neptune was named after the god of oceans, so it's up to you to decide if you want to make the transition from infatuation to actualization. Otherwise you'll be lost at sea.

MATE

It could take years to truly get to know each other. There's just so much personality to both of you. Indeed your Neptune/Jupiter mate may clue you into sides of yourself you didn't even know existed. The wonderful thing about the two of you is that you never stop changing and growing. You are both committed to following the course of your lives wherever it may lead.

CHILD

Even you have to admit that your kid can sometimes get way out there. As a Child of Jupiter, you're reluctant to rope anyone in ("free to be you and me" is your personal motto), but if anyone can merge the wonder of the world with the wonders of the imagination: it's you. If you spend time in your kid's world then your kid will want to spend time in yours. Instead of popping in a video, read aloud from a picture book about faraway places.

PARENT

You admire your Neptune/Jupiter parent's sensitivity and compassion. You just wish it wouldn't be so overwhelming all the time. The best way to deal with your mom or dad when she or he starts in on the "Woes of the World" monologue is to simply nod and shake your head at the appropriate moments.

SIBLING

You're each convinced that the other is ducking his or her responsibilities. If you're truly interested in settling the matter, then spend less time with the blame game and more time coordinating efforts. Each of you really wants to help. But you both resent being bossed around.

FRIEND

What's so wonderful about your Neptune/Jupiter friend is that this person can tune into your state of consciousness. If you're feeling gung-ho, your friend is supportive and with you every step of the way. If you've had too much to drink, your friend will talk to you as if you make perfect sense—while making sure you get home safe and sound. This person will share your belly laughs and your saddest tears. You couldn't ask for a truer companion.

ENEMY

A Child of Neptune and Jupiter loves drama every bit as much as you and will stomp around slamming doors and shouting ultimatums. However, if there is little or no emotional display, then that means this person *really* doesn't like you. Watch your back.

BOSS

You two could discuss a situation's inherent potential until the cows come home, but in the end it's up to your Neptune/Jupiter boss to make sure that the work gets done. When he or she sets an agenda or decides on a deadline, then that's your cue to switch modes from building castles in the air to bringing it in for a landing.

COLLEAGUE

A Neptune/Jupiter colleague is an equal in every respect and will insist on being treated that way. This person is naturally adaptable and accommodating but knows when to draw the line if forced to.

CHILD OF JUPITER

.... ❅ ....

WITH CHILD OF PLUTO/MARS

You're the only one who can cheer up a Child of Pluto and Mars. Your capacity for optimism is as inexhaustible as their capacity for pessimism, and since they're not really all that invested in being glum (Children of Pluto and Mars are amazingly upbeat given half the chance), you inevitably win them over to your side.

LOVE INTEREST

You're exuberant. A Child of Pluto and Mars is passionate. This makes for an exciting and dramatic chemistry, but after a while the difference in temperaments will become clear. You see your love as free and flowing in abundance, while a Pluto/Mars Child regards it as a precious commodity. You don't mind shining a little light into some of those dark corners, but if you have to do it full-time, then you're out of there.

MATE

Despite your differences in temperament, yours is a union built to last. Over time, your enlivening spirit awakens the potential that lies buried within your Pluto/Mars mate, so instead of talking about what could be, he or she actively begins to make things happen. Subsequently your Pluto/Mars mate gives you a solid foundation, so instead of always traipsing off after something new, you learn to work with what you have. No one knows you as fully and completely as your Pluto/Mars mate. Though this person may often confound and infuriate you—when you fight it's loud and furious—you have the deepest respect for his or her brilliance and character. Though you will always see the positives in life, you can do that secure in the knowledge that your mate is keeping an eye out for the negatives. You are both spiritual *and* soul mates.

CHILD

Your Pluto/Mars kid is aggressive and intense. But as your son or daughter outgrows those early child-hood illnesses (for some reason they hit Pluto/Mars children harder than most, which is why they're always so physically uncomfortable), you'll start to see some good humor and sweet affection. Encourage it. Pluto/Mars children often regard their feelings as potential liabilities that need to be kept under wraps. You can teach your kid that though feelings can be easily hurt, they also rebound just as quickly.

PARENT

Not the easiest combination. The exacting, fixated nature of Pluto and Mars doesn't always blend well with the expansive, pioneering spirit of Jupiter. Plus you don't like being told no anymore than your Pluto/Mars parent appreciates being backed into a corner. However relations improve considerably once you're out on your own. But don't expect any sympathy when faced with raising a hellion of your own. Your Pluto/Mars parent will simply flash you a smile of triumph.

SIBLING

You and your Pluto/Mars sibling have always been close. But when you come across an obstacle or setback, you treat it as an opportunity to learn something new, while your sibling wants to just wallow in it. You'll never convince your brother or sister otherwise. Instead of upsetting yourself (as well as this person) with the philosophizing, why not adopt the attitude: to each his own?

FRIEND

It annoys you the way your Pluto/Mars friend always discovers the fly in the ointment. If it makes you feel better, your friend finds your hopefulness equally exasperating—and just as impossible to live without.

ENEMY

This won't last long. You can't stand to be around a poisonous atmosphere and will pull up stakes ASAP.

BOSS

You may never know it, but your Pluto/Mars boss really depends on you for a moral boost. You're like a personal lucky charm. Your unmitigated trust in the future is enlivening, and the way you make fun of enemies and revile critics always makes him or her smile. Your Pluto/Mars boss feels ready to take on the world as long as you're in his or her corner.

COLLEAGUE

For someone who's so brilliant and gifted, it's amazing how often this person winds up creating his or her own difficulties. When trouble's brewing, it's best to make yourself scarce.

CHILD OF SATURN

············ ✳ ············

WITH CHILD OF THE SUN

Y ou work hard to maintain your self-sufficiency, but a Child of the Sun knows you could always use a pat on the back and is only too happy to give you that vote of confidence.

LOVE INTEREST

Your Solar love interest is warm, glowing, and vital. But you're afraid that he or she may move on, so you hold back. Your tendency to play it safe may give off the wrong impression—that you aren't interested. If you don't want your fears to become a self-fulfilling prophecy then be up-front about what you feel. Children of the Sun love to be loved.

MATE

You make a perfect pair. Regal and stately on the outside, few would suspect how silly you can be in private. Nevertheless when you're on show, you're businesslike and responsible. You like to give to the community you belong to and are active in its affairs. You're both extremely busy, so when you rendezvous you're naturally very guarded about your time together. Family and friends know better than to interrupt.

CHILD

Solar kids are warm, affectionate, and trusting—all traits that you enjoy but that also make you nervous. Your Birthday Planet is cool and guarded, and with good reason. Childhood wasn't an easy time for you, and life didn't really improve until you got into adulthood. However just the opposite holds true for your kid. The Sun rules childhood, so this is a golden age for your little prince or princess. Curb your overprotective tendencies and you'll do fine.

PARENT

Your Solar parent couldn't understand why you had to do everything the hard way. But it's not as if you deliberately chose the most difficult path between point A and point B. What's at issue here is really just a difference in approach. Children of the Sun take life one day at a time, while Children of Saturn try to project how things are going to play out in the long run, so they can steer the best course. Your mom or dad will always believe you fret too much, while you will always believe your Sun parent doesn't fret enough. Thankfully you both have a good sense of humor about it.

SIBLING

You'll have to get used to your Solar sibling's skewed version of your childhood. As far as this person's concerned, he or she was the only one who understood you and heroically defended you when others were hard and unfeeling. It would have been nice had things actually been this way, but seeing as that's all behind you now and you've turned out no worse for wear—why burst your brother or sister's bubble?

FRIEND

Your Solar friend brings out the clown in you. This person also has the unique ability to make you see the bright side of a dreary prospect. And it's not because his or her advice is particularly savvy; it's just that everything seems less dark when your Solar friend's around.

ENEMY

If this person is in a position of power over you, then tread softly. Your Solar enemy can be imperious and—rather than sully his or her own hands—will get someone else to do the "dirty" work.

BOSS

Your Solar boss knows that he or she can depend on you, which is fine until you feel like you've outgrown your role or would like to try something different at work. Like the Sun, which is a constant source of heat and light, your boss doesn't welcome change or variance. Nevertheless, make a convincing case for what you would like to try (while demonstrating how your boss benefits) and you'll gain wholehearted support.

COLLEAGUE

As far as you're concerned this person's lazy and just doesn't realize how good he or she has got it. If half the energy spent complaining went into getting work done, then maybe your Solar colleague wouldn't feel so unappreciated.

CHILD OF SATURN

.... ※ ....

WITH CHILD OF THE MOON

Children of the Moon were born in the summer, when the Sun is strong and the earth is bursting with life. Subsequently they have an innate trust in things working out. This is different from you, who never takes anything on faith. But in some ways, a Child of the Moon is more practical. Where you tend to see life as a series of problems that need to be solved, a Child of the Moon moves along the current of events until it finds the circumstances that are most conducive to realizing its aims—then goes for it!

LOVE INTEREST

Children of the Moon like to nurture. Children of Saturn like to lecture. Accustomed to hooking up with love interests who need lots of love or guidance, it may take you two a while to realize you're dealing with an equal. Once that sinks in, you may find yourself at a loss as to what to do. If you explore the possibility of a relationship where the old roles (and rules) don't apply, then you won't be disappointed.

MATE

You're the breadwinner while your Lunar mate will inevitably wind up in charge of the household and/or kids. This holds true even if your Lunar mate is a man. Although these roles feel custom-made, you need to reverse them from time to time. You don't want to rob each other of the opportunity to grow. Besides, you want a chance to show off that one dish you know how to make to perfection.

CHILD

Your Lunar kid is extremely sensitive. But don't mistake feelings that hurt easily for weakness. Those emotions, which look so vulnerable, are the same emotions that will sustain your kid through the rough times and provide solace when nobody else can. Trying to tell your kid not to feel so much would be like someone trying to tell you not to take life so seriously.

PARENT

Either your Lunar parent smothered you with affection or made you eat too much. This comes from the fact that Children of the Moon interpret crossed arms as a cry for help and a thin figure as a sign of malnourishment. Since Children of Saturn are inclined to be lean and standoffish, you would have felt like your Lunar parent couldn't leave well enough alone. In time you'll establish a mutual respect of sorts.

SIBLING

It may not be until you're adults that you realize how much you have in common. Both of you are introspective, loyal, and see yourselves as long-suffering. However Moon Children are just as good with the guilt trips as Saturn Children, which is why you got on each other's nerves growing up. But once established with your own families and/or lifestyles, you'll turn to each other more for advice, support, and backup.

FRIEND

Your Lunar friend often surprises you with observations about yourself that are new to you. Normally this might make you feel judged or defensive. But your friend's manner is so casual and matter-of-fact that you don't mind. Indeed you even feel relieved there are some aspects of yourself that have eluded your own psychic censors.

ENEMY

A Lunar enemy goes for the weak spot. But this person doesn't fight to win; this person only fights to protect his or her home turf. A Child of the Moon is always open to finding a solution everyone can live with.

BOSS

You won't be working for this person very long. Either your Lunar boss runs the company like a mom-and-pop store (which goes against everything you learned in business school) or the vision is so singular (and the dynamics so personal) that you're tripping psychic wires without knowing it.

COLLEAGUE

You could work next to your Lunar colleague for years and never know the first thing about this person. But seeing as he or she is always professional and reliable in a pinch, you may not need to.

CHILD OF SATURN

·········· ❁ ··········

WITH CHILD OF MERCURY

C hildren of Mercury scrutinize everything. They listen for key words—which is why they can always parrot back what you've just said. While you will go off by yourself to do your *serious* thinking, Children of Mercury will kick around an idea, call up their friends to see what they think, and maybe even rustle up some lunch while they're at it. This haphazard jumble actually frees up the mind so it can do its most original thinking.

LOVE INTEREST

Between your reserve and a Child of Mercury's circuitous approach to anything dealing with matters of the heart, it will take a while to get your signals straight. Just because your Mercury love interest won't stop talking doesn't mean he or she is uninterested. It's just that when Children of Mercury get nervous (and you're one of the few who can make them nervous), they tend to talk a mile a minute. You may not believe it, but this person is actually shyer than you about making the first move. Steal a kiss and your Mercury love interest will take it from there.

MATE

You're both incredibly smart, proud of it, and get very snippy when you think you're being conde-scended to. Your Mercury mate wants you to hurry up, while you want your Mercury mate to slow down. Neither of you will ever understand the other's point of view, yet paradoxically you two are in perfect sync when you let your natures take their course.

CHILD

When your Mercury son or daughter asks a question, don't answer right away. Make a game of it instead. Come up with clever hints or intriguing clues that will lead him or her down the right path. That way when your Mercury kid figures out the answer, you can both enjoy the moment of discovery.

PARENT

It annoys you the way your mom or dad keeps changing the rules so that she or he is always right. What can you do but accept it as a parent's prerogative? But don't let this blind you to the remarkable judg-ment and insight. Your Mercury parent has a unique ability to switch channels from street-smart to philosophical to compassionate to analytical. You may never be able to pin this person down, but then your mom or dad wouldn't be a true Child of Mercury if you could.

SIBLING

Your Mercury sibling probably didn't know as much as he or she let on, but seeing as you were so willing to believe it, why say otherwise? Your chronic worrying often played right into this person's hands. Nevertheless your Mercury brother or sister adores you.

FRIEND

Your Mercury friend will always help you out of a jam—which makes up for all the times when he or she cancels at the last minute, wants to leave in the middle of a movie, or argues with you after asking for advice. Your Mercury friend is easily the most fascinating person you know. Hours fly by like minutes when you're together. Unfortunately minutes limp along like hours if you're waiting for this person to get off the phone.

ENEMY

A Mercury enemy is as crafty as you are strategic. This person can counter your every move. However, Mercury enemies aren't very good at making their own moves, so the best way to gain the upper hand is by not doing anything in the first place. Just wait them out. Their impatience gives them away every time.

BOSS

You can't help seeing the part of the equation your Mercury boss is missing—and vice versa. That's why you're really better suited as business partners. If there's a chance of that developing out of your current circumstances, then stick around. If not, you'll soon grow tired of cleaning up after this person's messes.

COLLEAGUE

Work out a hand signal for when you want to be left alone. Otherwise this person will talk your ear off, and being the long-suffering Child of Saturn, you'll put up with it.

CHILD OF SATURN

※

WITH CHILD OF VENUS

Whether it's climbing the ladder of success, scaling the social register, or putting the finishing touches on a project or bid—a Child of Venus can help you get to the next level. You work very hard and like to show off the blood, sweat, and tears. A Child of Venus knows you'll win people's hearts and admiration by using a softer touch. If you understate your accomplishments then people will not only be impressed with your achievements, but they'll also think you've got class, too.

LOVE INTEREST

You find this person enthralling—which is why you'll scurry in the opposite direction. But don't worry. Children of Venus don't bite—nor will they marry you for your money or lead you on before dumping you unceremoniously. The best way to flatter your Venus love interest is to let yourself be seduced. But play a little hard to get. You don't want to make it too easy.

MATE

Your Venus mate will insist that every decision be made together. Admittedly there will be times when your mate forces your hand by going out and buying something and pretending that he or she *thought* you wanted it; but for the most part everything is discussed and priced out beforehand. This will include your private life as well. Accustomed to being by yourself, you naturally treat your business like it's your business. Nothing could be more opposite from your Venus mate's way of thinking. At first you might feel self-conscious (not to mention awkward) about trotting out every single decision for review, but once you get into it you'll enjoy discussing the finer points of everything, from property values to toilet paper.

CHILD

Venus children aim to please and will urge you to tell them what you would like. Since you're a perfectionist and can always find something wrong, you could wind up sending the wrong message if you're not careful. Make a point of praising your Venus child and, if you see room for improvement, wait to introduce it another time. That way your kid won't associate improvement with approval and will naturally seek to make things better without feeling as if your affection depends on it.

PARENT

It's your Venus parent who taught you that one beautifully tailored suit was better than three cheap ones. And it's made all the difference. Given your druthers, you'd press your nose to the grindstone and just forge ahead. As a Child of Saturn you believe that hard work should pay off in the end. Thank goodness your Venus parent knows better, and it's this person you have to thank for lifting your sights. Ambition will only take you so far. After that—it's all finesse.

SIBLING

You were probably very critical of your Venus sibling's "agreeable" nature when you were younger, but with time you've come to appreciate your brother's or sister's talent for networking. You also understand that *agreeable* doesn't necessarily mean *pushover*. Much of your knowledge of people and politics is a result of watching your Venus sibling in action.

FRIEND

You have similar tastes yet rarely buy the same thing—which means you'll always admire (and secretly covet) what the other has. Venus friends always have a light touch, which is nice, considering how serious many of your other friendships can be.

ENEMY

Not a harsh word will be exchanged. You will both simply avoid each other's company.

BOSS

You usually don't like working for people, but a Venus boss is different. That's because this person recognizes a good thing when he or she sees it and won't spare the expenses. Your Venus boss will also praise your talents to the skies. Although you profess otherwise, you'll secretly eat up every word.

COLLEAGUE

Children of Venus are experts at getting others to do their work for them. You don't mind helping them if your Venus colleague happens to be good-looking or especially charming. Otherwise, you'll leave the pile of papers right where they are.

CHILD OF SATURN

·········· ❋ ··········

WITH CHILD OF MARS

Like you, a Child of Mars believes that challenges build character. Neither of you takes the easy way out or will back down from a fight. Since a Child of Mars spends more time wrestling with an opponent (whereas you wrestle more with your conscience), you'll find this person's approach to life to be exciting and invigorating. It's blessedly free of soul-searching. But expect to be on call to pull this person's fat out of the fire. Children of Mars love to push the envelope.

LOVE INTEREST

Children of Mars are wonderfully straightforward. However you may find this person's attitude toward dating to be a little too casual or even candid. But don't believe the swagger. That's just there for show. Mars love interests have lots of rough edges. That's why they need someone like you to give them that spit and polish.

MATE

The more you put on the brakes, the more your Mars mate floors the accelerator—and vice versa. There are times when this is a real turn-on, but there are times when it annoys you no end. You should remember that this is why you two hooked up in the first place. You want someone to push you, and your Mars mate wants someone who will control and direct. You're both evenly matched and equally fixed on doing things *your* way. If soldiers and athletes can get it together to work as a unit, so can you.

CHILD

The most valuable lesson you can teach your Mars kid is to finish what he or she starts. These little ones have no problem with getting something up and running. They're ambitious, determined, and even well organized—at first. But Mars, like Mercury, is a Planet of motion. Once the momentum fades, so does the interest. Mars kids are receptive to discipline. Show your kid that it's only when you get past the initial stage that the real contest begins and he or she will have no problem going the distance.

PARENT

Your Mars parent probably saw you as being too slow or too careful and, in typical Mars fashion, tried to provoke you into doing things faster by being curt or "in your face." Nothing could be more counterproductive for a Saturn Child. Nevertheless your mom or dad really does want the best for you—but you may still have to keep him or her on a short leash.

SIBLING

You may complain about your Mars sibling constantly, but the moment others chime in, you'll tell them off. You are very protective of your brother or sister—even if you think this person's making a mess of his or her life. Obviously your feelings are mixed, but like anything connected to Mars, they're strong.

FRIEND

Though your Mars friend always gives the impression of being unbreakable, you know how much that has cost. It takes a tough cookie to recognize a tough cookie. You're one of the few people that this person can unwind with, and your Mars friend appreciates it.

ENEMY

It's fire and ice when you two go at it. Though you ultimately have more lasting power, it's really not a battle worth fighting. A Mars enemy would much rather join you than try to beat you.

BOSS

A Mars boss is always dynamic and inspiring. Working for this person, you feel like you're ready to take on the world. But at some point decisions will need to be made that aren't so cut-and-dry, and this is where your Mars boss will prove if he or she has what it takes. If this person is too reckless, then chances are your Mars boss will no longer be boss.

COLLEAGUE

Children of Mars can't help but be competitive. Throw your colleague off the scent by acting as if you're interested in something else and this person will immediately chase after it—leaving you free to pursue what you *really* want.

CHILD OF SATURN

.... ✻ ....

WITH CHILD OF JUPITER

No matter how low it burns, a Child of Jupiter can always rekindle your faith. Maybe it's the indefatigable optimism, the sincere trust that there really is a higher purpose at work, or the simple way that this person's humor brightens your day. You may never escape your heavy burden of obligations and responsibilities, but being around a Child of Jupiter will certainly make them feel lighter.

LOVE INTEREST

You can tell when someone's not serious, and since Children of Jupiter make no bones about their restless spirits, you might pass—despite your feelings of attraction. But if you were to see each other regularly then things could click. It isn't easy for you to get past your fear of rejection—and your Jupiter love interest's carefree attitude certainly doesn't help. But given an opportunity to develop a friendship, you'll find that a Child of Jupiter has more staying power than you thought, and this person will realize that relationships don't have to begin and end in the same week in order to be romantic.

MATE

Your Jupiter mate is long on vision (whereas you tend to be too down-to-earth), and you're strong on invention (whereas your Jupiter mate tends to be too impractical). Together you two have what it takes to make those impossible dreams a reality.

CHILD

Your Jupiter kid is like a godsend—until he or she reaches adolescence. This is when all that affability and charm are replaced by a pain-in-the-derriere bent on contradicting your authority. Pick one or two rules to enforce and forget about the rest. Your son or daughter will need lots of elbowroom. But don't worry. When your Jupiter kid eventually reemerges, chances are he or she will go on to exceed even your greatest expectations.

PARENT

If you were in a bad mood, then your Jupiter parent had no patience. Take it outside. But if you had an ambition or a dream, then your Jupiter mom or dad would have done everything possible to help you realize it. If that meant driving long distances or scraping up the money to pay for lessons, then so be it. Your Jupiter parent taught you that there's no such thing as a dead end. No matter how many times that path diverges, it's all right as long as you keep going, because any road you take will lead to your destination in the end.

SIBLING

You started out more introverted, while your Jupiter sibling was the more outgoing one. However, if you were to move away, and your Jupiter sibling were to live near home, then you'd eventually become more gregarious and open-minded, while your sibling would get quiet and maybe even stodgy. It would then be up to you to help your Jupiter sibling get back in touch with that inner fire.

FRIEND

You may find that the only time you see your Jupiter friend is when he or she is going through a rough period. You don't mind. You like to feel needed. But your friend might appreciate it if he or she saw you at a time when life wasn't coming undone. Invite your Jupiter friend out to lunch once in a while, so he or she can see a different side of you.

ENEMY

Children of Jupiter hate to be on bad terms with anyone. And since they can't fake liking someone when they don't, they'll simply drop out of sight.

BOSS

There are at least a hundred things you see that your Jupiter boss could do if he or she was really serious about getting ahead in business. And if you're smart—you'll keep them to yourself.

COLLEAGUE

Your Jupiter colleague leaves everything until the night before and then does a mad dash in order to get a job done under the wire. Although this happens fairly frequently, it never loses its thrill. You might consider getting together an office pool.

CHILD OF SATURN

.... ❋ ....

WITH CHILD OF SATURN

Either you bring out the best in each other—or the worst. If you don't trust your fellow Child of Saturn, then you will both expend a lot of time and energy quoting rules and curtailing each other's efforts. However if you forge a bond of mutual respect, you will bring out capacities that neither of you knew existed. You will push each other to climb higher and progress further.

LOVE INTEREST

The only reason you would even talk to each other is if you're looking to settle down. Yet being born under the Planet of commitment, you tend to emphasize the points that look good on paper while glossing over the ones that are seated across the table from you. Be careful. They won't go away with time. If you decide to hook up with another Child of Saturn, then you must accept the entire package—warts and all.

MATE

You may start out stuffy and uptight, but like a favorite pair of shoes or a comfy old sweater, you relax with age—which makes sense, since you were both born under the Planet of time. This is one of the few unions where your mate really is your best friend. You share everything with this person—be it a life crisis or a funny moment. Expect lots of add-ons in your life. People feel most at home in your home. Don't be surprised if you wind up maintaining friendships with loved ones' ex-spouses or friends of friends. As a couple, you two are an invaluable source of wit and wisdom.

CHILD

In your attempt to give your kid the things you never had, you could be making matters worse. Childhood is rarely a good time for those born under Saturn—as you remember only too well. So instead of trying to make light of your son's or daughter's woes (you don't want to take away the kid's identity), show your little Sisyphus how to make something of them. Emphasizing a constructive approach over a critical one is the most valuable thing you could ever impart.

PARENT

You two locked horns fairly regularly. That's because your Saturn parent couldn't help correcting you—sometimes even *before* you had a chance to do what was being asked. Nevertheless, respect for your parent's authority is built in. What's nice is that over time this will change from deference to something you genuinely feel.

SIBLING

You two figured out each other's weak spots early on and have been exploiting them ever since. Hopefully this will lessen with age as you learn to control yourselves. There's no reason why you both can't be smart, talented, or good-looking. If the urge for one-upmanship proves too much, then you may want to avoid subjecting anyone else to this.

FRIEND

You both think the other one is an overlooked genius or an unappreciated artist. It's nice to foster such high opinions, but make sure the mutual admiration society doesn't get too exclusive. You two can become very critical of everyone else. If you don't want to wind up by yourselves in the corner, then lighten up.

ENEMY

You Children of Saturn don't back down from a fight and have a high tolerance for punishment, so you could both inflict a great deal of unnecessary damage. Don't let pride push you into acting recklessly. If you show that you're willing to talk, then your Saturn enemy will eagerly join you at the negotiating table.

BOSS

The best boss you may ever have. Expect to work hard for those accolades, because a Saturn boss won't give them away easily. Yet when you do win this person's respect and praise, it will feel like you've gone through a rite of passage.

COLLEAGUE

Hopefully this *isn't* one of those Saturn types who has to do everything a certain way. If so, then the persnicketiness will drive you crazy. Otherwise, this association could easily develop into a valuable and lasting friendship.

CHILD OF SATURN

.... ✳ ....

WITH CHILD OF URANUS/SATURN

A Child of Uranus and Saturn prevails on you to move past your limits. You're not used to looking at life in such independent terms. You accept obligations and responsibilities as your burden to bear. However a Child of Uranus and Saturn will show that you're actually free to rewrite the rules at any time.

LOVE INTEREST

You have to be at a certain place in your life to go out with a Uranus/Saturn love interest. If you're still struggling to make ends meet, then you probably won't have the energy or inclination. However, if you've been around the block, then you'll have the right mind-set for it. A Child of Uranus and Saturn will turn your world upside down. And you'll love every minute of it.

MATE

Your Uranus/Saturn mate can see what you're capable of and will push you to go for it. But this isn't done haphazardly. Your mate outlines goals that are very specific. Being a builder by nature, all you need is a life plan or blueprint and you'll take it from there. The flip side to making more money (an inevitable side effect to hooking up with a Child of Uranus and Saturn) is that your mate has expensive tastes. Don't believe it when he or she protests otherwise. While you're busy perusing the sale racks, your Uranus/Saturn mate is sitting down with that salesperson in the expensive-looking office, casually flipping through swatches while chatting over coffee.

CHILD

Your thinking is so alike that it's easy to forget that your kid has *two* Ruling Planets. However on that rare occasion when you hit upon a real difference of opinion, you will be reminded of this distinction—and in no uncertain terms. The challenge is in remaining as open-minded when you're kid is going *against* the grain as when he or she is being the very spirit of cooperation.

PARENT

Your Uranus/Saturn parent may not have been around much when you were growing up. The plus side is that you learned to rely on yourself—which is actually invaluable, considering how willing you are to bow to authority. The downside is you probably could have used more cheering up or a shoulder to lean on. But your Uranus/Saturn parent will more than make up for the absenteeism when you're an adult. You couldn't ask for a better friend.

SIBLING

You two see yourselves as being opposites. However loved ones and friends recognize the similarities right away. It may still annoy you the way your Uranus/Saturn brother or sister decides to buy the same car as you do or goes into a nearly identical line of work, but great minds think alike.

FRIEND

Your Uranus/Saturn friend plays both counterpart and complement. If you're too stuck in your ways, this person will encourage you to move things around in your life. If you're at loose ends, then this person is there for you—like a shelter from the storm. In turn you keep your friend's concerns grounded. This is extremely important, as Children of Uranus and Saturn tend to put personal priorities on the back burner.

ENEMY

If you're enemies, it's probably the result of how the alliances worked out—i.e., this person is friends with someone you can't stand or may even be going out with your ex. Given that, maintain a civil (even if frosty) manner.

BOSS

Expect to be treated like an equal in every way. Uranus/Saturn bosses are interested in redefining their field or industry, so they only work with high-caliber, talented people. But no prima donnas allowed.

COLLEAGUE

There are two types of Uranus/Saturn colleagues—team players and poseurs. If you're lucky to be working with a player, then this person will be right at your side every step of the way. If you're stuck with the second type—don't even give this wannabe the time of day.

CHILD OF SATURN

·········· ☀ ··········

WITH CHILD OF NEPTUNE/JUPITER

It's hard to be guarded when you're around a Child of Neptune and Jupiter. This person's effusive manner is just so disarming. Even if you've only just met, a Neptune/Jupiter Child will immediately treat you like the high point of the day. There's no standing on ceremony. A Neptune/Jupiter Child won't think twice about divulging a personal matter right there at the front door while asking you to hold the dustpan as he or she sweeps up the coffee grinds that spilled all over the floor. This person's candor and easygoing nature puts you at ease.

LOVE INTEREST

Sometimes your Neptune/Jupiter love interest acts as if he or she can't live without you, and sometimes this person forgets you were supposed to get together that evening. The difficulty with dating someone who has a strong Neptune side is that his or her heart is as wide and deep as the sea. You enjoy a little mystique, but in the end you may need a more solid idea of what you can expect.

MATE

You'll no longer see the world in nicely delineated categories. Your Neptune/Jupiter mate will convince you there's an underlying current running through the most disparate things. Issues at work echo issues at home, which may in turn bear an uncanny resemblance to events unfolding halfway around the world. This opens not only your mind but your imagination as well. You may start off as a down-to-earth type, but after prolonged exposure to your Neptune/Jupiter mate, you'll see how everything really is interconnected. It's deep. But draw the line at tie-dyed T-shirts.

CHILD

Your kid thinks visually, not logically. That's why he or she spaces out when you try to give a step-by-step explanation of how something works. However if you were to demonstrate it with whatever prop is handy or even tell it like a story, then you'll capture this kid's attention. You want to work with your son's or daughter's imagination, not against it. Many mathematicians and theoreticians are Children of Neptune and Jupiter.

PARENT

Your Neptune/Jupiter parent has never expected you to be anything other than what you are. This might have struck you as being *too* permissive when you were growing up (as a Child of Saturn you crave structure and discipline), but as you get older, you'll appreciate the enormous amount of confidence your dad or mom had in you. A Neptune/Jupiter parent can see the oak tree when it's still just an acorn.

SIBLING

This was probably the only person who could bring you out of those funks you got into from time to time as a kid. And though you probably have a much better handle on your mood swings, you know that if you're ever feeling down, your Neptune/Jupiter sibling is only a phone call away.

FRIEND

You feel like a child again when you're with your Neptune/Jupiter friend. You can playact, fantasize, even speak in a made-up language—and this person won't miss a beat. He or she is reading from the same page. The weird thing is it may even begin to make a strange kind of sense after a while.

ENEMY

Never underestimate this person's ability to poison the well. Neptune/Jupiter enemies are notorious gossips, and seeing as Neptune rules propaganda, you could find yourself on the outs with people you considered friends.

BOSS

Your Neptune/Jupiter boss is more than happy to leave you alone to do your own thing. But if you need this person to make a decision, then provide at least two, but no more than three, options. Like you, a Child of Neptune and Jupiter must be able to "see it" in order to decide—otherwise he or she will spend hours vacillating back and forth.

COLLEAGUE

Your Neptune/Jupiter colleague may be warm and affectionate, but that won't stop this person from using his or her affability as a smokescreen. Smile, nod, and then ask for the work you're expecting.

CHILD OF SATURN

.... ❋ ....

WITH CHILD OF PLUTO/MARS

Though you may never match the intensity of a Child of Pluto and Mars, you know exactly where this person is coming from. Like you, a Child of Pluto and Mars struggles to keep from becoming jaded or bitter and can find the humor in the bleakest situations. This person shares your steadfast commitment to doing whatever it takes to pick yourself back up again and turn a defeat into a triumph.

LOVE INTEREST

It's unlikely you two would hook up romantically unless there's a significant age difference. The reason for this is that you are attracted to "lighter" types of personalities who can counteract your heaviness. A Child of Pluto and Mars is more likely to commiserate with feelings of disappointment and futility, which is not what you need. However should you meet later on in life, you'll find someone who is earthy, sensual, and emotionally candid—all qualities that you enjoy.

MATE

Oddly enough, you're the upbeat one. That's because no matter how impossible the odds are, you will never give up. And it's this refusal to ever accept defeat that betrays you as the closet optimist you are. Your Pluto/Mars mate sees this and is greatly inspired by it. For two people who tend to emphasize the minuses over the pluses, it's amazing how much strength you bring out in each other. If channeled positively, that determination and willpower could transform your lives dramatically—and for the better!

CHILD

Your Pluto/Mars kid is a mini-networker. Pluto was named after the Greek god of wealth, and your little mover and shaker knows exactly where the money is. It won't really sink in until your son or daughter presents you with the birthday guest list. Who would have thought that such a shy and retiring kid would know so many influential people?

PARENT

This works best if it's an opposite sex parent. If so, then your Pluto/Mars mom or dad doesn't *identify* so strongly with your progress. But if your parent is the same sex as you, then you can expect a power struggle. Your Pluto/Mars mom or dad has some very fixed ideas about the way life works and is personally invested in you following these to the letter. Do yourself (and your parent) a favor and move out as soon as you can. The sooner you establish your own independence, the sooner this person will accept and respect it.

SIBLING

Children of Saturn and Children of Pluto and Mars make natural scapegoats. That's because you say what's on your mind, won't suffer fools gladly, and draw strength and power from rejection and hardship. This would have created a powerful bond of solidarity. Thankfully life gets easier with age, so the character of your relationship changes from bracing for the negative into welcoming the positive.

FRIEND

You two share more in-jokes, private nicknames, and secret glances than spouses who have been married for years. You confide just about everything—though your Pluto/Mars friend is always coaxing you to divulge more. Your Pluto/Mars friend has the ultimate thumbs-up or thumbs-down when it comes to your love life.

ENEMY

You can give as good as you get with a Pluto/Mars enemy, which will eventually beg the question: shouldn't you be on the same side?

BOSS

Your Pluto/Mars boss will always be in your corner. Don't be afraid to come to this person if you're struggling with a deadline or need a helping hand. Your Pluto/Mars boss loves to feel needed, and racing to the rescue is just the sort of thing that will make this person's day.

COLLEAGUE

Whether it's the fact that someone ordered the wrong kind of paper clips or the copy machine is on the fritz again, your colleague will immediately interpret it as a plot to make his or her life miserable. You'd love to tell this person that it's just another day in the life, but think better of it.

CHILD OF URANUS/SATURN

·········· ❋ ··········

WITH CHILD OF THE SUN

For Children of the Sun, there's only one way to do things—*their* way. This will bring out your argumentative side, because you can see at least three different ways of doing the same thing—and who's to say that any are better than the rest? Yet given your tendency to get lost in tangents, there's something reassuring about someone you know will never change his or her mind.

LOVE INTEREST

A Child of the Sun brings out your romantic side. Sometimes you can get so caught up in trying to make your life emulate your principles that you can forget you're a person who has feelings that are every bit as powerful as your thoughts. When you're born under two Birthday Planets (one that constantly looks ahead while the other sizes up what's behind), it's refreshing to encounter someone who's strictly present tense. Your Solar love interest will show you how a moment can last forever.

MATE

You know your Solar mate needs to come first, but it shouldn't be at the cost of your own identity. This is a tall order. On the one hand you're confident enough in your own individuality that you can walk behind your mate without feeling overshadowed. Yet because you tend to disassociate yourself from personal needs (the word *selfish* is practically a profanity with you), you can then go too far in the opposite direction, which is to define yourself solely in terms of your relationship. This would be a great disservice not only to yourself, but to your partner as well. A Child of the Sun is in your life to foster your individuality, not repress it.

CHILD

Uranus was named after the Greek god of the heavens. You have as many ideas as there are stars in the sky and can't help but take in the entire panorama. But your Solar kid needs to identify with one of those stars, not all of them. Without that sense of self, then your son or daughter will feel lost in space. Encourage your child's feelings of uniqueness, vitality, and entitlement. Once centered in who he or she is, your kid will be open to new ideas and higher realms.

PARENT

Your Solar parent is a kid who never grew up. Even if he or she is heralded as the quintessential authority on this or that, you know it's just this person pretending to act grown-up. In some ways you like how your dad or mom never lost that playful, guileless spirit; yet there are things that he or she did that were just too self-centered to be written off as naïve. Nevertheless this is the person who serves to remind you that we all have feet of clay.

SIBLING

Impossibly proud, boastful, and arrogant. Plus you could never quite figure out why you were always being lumped in with this person. Nevertheless you have a soft spot for your Solar brother or sister. You understand how beneath that self-assured demeanor lies a nest of insecurities.

FRIEND

A Solar friend will always remind you that you are the central figure in your own life. This is incredibly important, as there are times when you can lose sight of that—especially when you put the needs of the many in front of the needs of you. You can always rely on your Solar friend to come down squarely on your side.

ENEMY

You can run circles around this one. All you have to do is agree to everything and commit to nothing. Though fierce in the moment, Solar enemies have no follow-through.

BOSS

A little Napoleon. Nevertheless you only feel secure in your own authority when you can deride someone else's, so you may want to keep him or her around for show.

COLLEAGUE

Your experience with Solar colleagues is that they're lazy. However you do enjoy their sparkle and humor. Plus they're always going through some larger-than-life drama, which appeals to your love of soap operas.

CHILD OF URANUS/SATURN

·········· ✳ ··········

WITH CHILD OF THE MOON

Children of the Moon go with the flow. Like sea otters riding the waves, nothing deters them from going about their business. They eat, sleep, and raise their young while taking life's ups with its downs. Children of the Moon are remarkably flexible and can adapt to just about anything.

LOVE INTEREST

Starry nights are made all the more romantic by the glow of the Moon. You won't have to explain much to your Lunar love interest. This person instinctually picks up on many of the things you want to say but can't. Indeed he or she may even be able to read your emotions better than you. But don't expect this person to tell you about them. Children of the Moon *feel* their feelings; they don't talk about them. Hang around long enough and you'll develop a similar sensitivity and respect for the unspoken word.

MATE

At first it may bother you the way your Lunar mate puts everything in such banal, down-to-earth terms. You believe that there's more to solving life's problems than warming up some soup or serving milk and cookies. Yet there is also something to be said for keeping things firmly rooted on the ground. What matters most as far as your Lunar mate is concerned is *human* welfare with all its flesh and blood concerns. You're not going to do anyone any good if you're cranky because you didn't sleep well the night before or if you forced people to sit through a business meeting when they were famished. Given your own tendency to push your body to the limit, the reason you still function at full capacity is because you have a Lunar mate looking after you.

CHILD

Your Lunar kid brings out your earthy nature. Though your Uranus side can be abstract, your Saturn side is physical. This is the part of you that responds warmly to affection and the side of you that your son or daughter relates to most. Others may regard you as cool and austere, but your little Moon knows that beneath all that formality and poise you're just a big warm fuzzy.

PARENT

Your Lunar parent wants to see you get the opportunities that she or he never got. As a Child of Uranus and Saturn, the last thing you would ever want is for someone to make sacrifices on your behalf—especially a parent whom you adore. But when you understand how providing the resources to create your own success has always been your Lunar parent's personal ambition, then you'll be more than happy to do your part in making your mom or dad's dream come true.

SIBLING

Either your Lunar sibling thinks you're a kook or you think he or she is. At best yours has been a tolerant relationship, but as you've both gotten older and more set in your ways, there's less cause or reason to bridge the gap. However you should know that your brother or sister does boast about your accomplishments from time to time.

FRIEND

This person often sees the things that are right under your nose. You're fortunate to have someone in your life who never fails to take the simplest approach to a complex matter—and who possesses the humor and tact not to make you feel dumb about it.

ENEMY

Your Lunar enemy knows that it's the little things that can trip you up, so watch your minutiae if you ever go toe to toe with one of these meticulous types.

BOSS

You respect how hardworking your Lunar boss is, but after a while it becomes clear that this person works hard at working hard. You're not interested in getting stuck in a rut. You were meant to paint on a wider canvas.

COLLEAGUE

You can always tell when your Lunar colleague is upset with you because you'll get an e-mail about it. A positive working atmosphere is just as important to this person as it is to you.

CHILD OF URANUS/SATURN

·········· ❀ ··········

WITH CHILD OF MERCURY

A Child of Mercury can help unlock frozen mental wheels by asking questions, free-associating, or playing around with your sequence of ideas. Within moments you'll hit upon the key you're looking for. A Child of Mercury knows how to translate a concept into reality.

LOVE INTEREST

The very thing you have in common may also be the very thing that keeps you from getting romantically involved. Like you, Children of Mercury tend to be cerebral when it comes to their emotions. This can lead to plenty of discussions about what you'd like to see happen, but not a lot of action. However if you get together when you're older (or if there's a significant difference in age), then you'll form a comfortable fit.

MATE

You two are united by a common cause. You may work in the same field, share a particular passion, or your Mercury mate wants to start a family at the same time you do. Where as other people may fall out of love over time, your bond only grows stronger. Indeed it wouldn't be surprising if you actually fell in love after having been together for years. It's a bit unorthodox, but you are both unpredictable, capricious, and often need to find your own unique way of doing things. Not many people allow for that kind of latitude. Your Mercury mate will.

CHILD

Because your Mercury kid is such a fast learner, you may expect big results before he or she is ready. It's up to you to moderate your kid's pace. Children of Mercury are naturally clever, so they can fool you into thinking they know more than they really do. And if you're not careful, you could inadvertently encourage your kid to take shortcuts. Show your pathfinder all the different ways to explore a matter, and he or she won't be in such a rush to arrive at the answer.

PARENT

It's thanks to this person that you developed a business savvy to go along with that extraordinary mind of yours. That's because your Mercury parent didn't want you turning into one of those geniuses who can map out a genome but can't tie their own shoelaces. The combination of intellect and pragmatism makes you a double threat in the marketplace because you're not easy to pigeonhole.

SIBLING

You have a wonderful rapport. Though you may not see a lot of each other on a daily basis (you both have enormously busy lives), you can always pick up from where you last left off. At some point your paths will cross professionally, which gives you a wonderful excuse to spend some more time together.

FRIEND

Your Mercury friend's lightning reflexes rival your own. This is the only person who can provide some serious competition at tennis, golf, or computer games. Mercury friends are also perfect for moviegoing and/or shopping. No one knows how to negotiate the snack line or checkout counter like a Child of Mercury.

ENEMY

A Mercury enemy's favorite strategy for covering up his or her culpability is to saddle you with the blame—loudly and conspicuously. This is why you never want to lose your temper. It's what this person's counting on. Make this person seek you out and it will be on your terms. Born under the Planet of communication, Children of Mercury can't stand being stonewalled.

BOSS

This person will be open to new ideas if you can show the through-line that connects it to how things are currently done. If your ambitions are greater—like inventing a whole new way of doing things—forget about it. Mercury bosses are interested in expediency, not in making more work for themselves.

COLLEAGUE

If you want to find out how to do a job in half the time, ask a Mercury colleague. Not only will this person clue you into a shortcut, but he or she will also even show you how to erase your tracks.

CHILD OF URANUS/SATURN

············ ❋ ············

WITH CHILD OF VENUS

Children of Venus believe in putting people first. They take what someone has to offer—whether it's talent, resources, or connections—and then build on that. Since your expectations can sometimes exceed what people are capable of, a Child of Venus will give you a more realistic idea of what to expect. You may even be delightfully surprised when a Child of Venus comes up with something you never imagined.

LOVE INTEREST

Although you will profess otherwise, you have a great love of luxury. And if anyone shares your appreciation for the finer things in life, it's a Child of Venus. Indeed it's your Venus love interest who will clue you into some of the trends you might have missed. Whether or not you two ultimately get together romantically (money will be the deciding factor), you'll certainly have a marvelous time dating.

MATE

Your mate is the epitome of upwardly mobile. Even if it was never your intention to live more than just a modest lifestyle, you will see your material circumstances transform dramatically. Within years you'll go from scraping to get by to owning instead of renting. Your Venus mate always has something in the works. If this person isn't busy putting together a dinner party, then he or she is rethinking the color scheme of the house or reviewing the kids' schools for their curriculum *and* social contacts. Feathering the nest is a full-time occupation for your Venus mate.

CHILD

It's only natural for you to want to encourage your Venus kid to be his or her own person. Actually, nothing could be further from your son's or daughter's mind. Children of Venus are social animals. The only time they want to stand out is when they're surrounded by admirers, otherwise they frown on anyone who rocks the boat. But before you make any judgments, take a moment to watch this little smooth operator in action. Few people know how to work the system so well.

PARENT

Your Venus parent always recognized and respected your strong beliefs. And if your mom or dad wasn't as encouraging as you would have liked, it was because he or she was more concerned about the people whose convictions weren't as powerful as yours. That's why you were always told to tone it down or to try to see matters from someone else's point of view. You didn't need any validation. Your sense of being in the right was ingrained. What you needed was a fully developed sense of how you came across to others, so that when you were having your say, you weren't robbing anyone of the right to have theirs.

SIBLING

Your Venus sibling has always been the "nice" one. You can tell yourself it's because you refuse to compromise when it comes to your standards of excellence, but the truth is your Venus sister or brother figured out a long time ago that people are more willing to listen if you begin by pointing out what's right than by harping on what's wrong.

FRIEND

You should flip a coin when making plans for the evening, because by the time you two are finished reviewing particulars and weighing each and every pro and con it will be daybreak.

ENEMY

Watch it. Agreeing to everything (while committing to nothing) is your Venus enemy's tactic of choice. When you're dealing with someone born under the Planet of charm and persuasion, give up while you're ahead.

BOSS

Either your Venus boss can't make a decision or is impossibly stubborn. However, he or she will play a pivotal role in your career advancement. Though you may have done most (if not all) of the work, you will always be known as this person's protégé.

COLLEAGUE

Between your Venus colleague's attempts to get you to do his or her work and your attempts to teach this person a lesson, it's amazing that you accomplish as much as you do.

CHILD OF URANUS/SATURN

.... ❋ ....

WITH CHILD OF MARS

You can always rely on a Child of Mars to go the distance. This person won't give up before you do or leave you hanging in the lurch. If anything, Children of Mars are inspired by your breadth of vision. They never want it to come to an end. But you'll have to remember to tell this person when there's been a change in plans. If you forget, this energy dynamo will keep on going long after you've moved on to something else.

LOVE INTEREST

The attraction is instantaneous. And because Uranus and Mars are both such volatile Planets, it could burn out just as quickly. Nevertheless there are the makings of a deep and enduring relationship if one of you can slow things down. Given your Saturn side, that would be you. Remember that Children of Mars become more impassioned when something's kept from them.

MATE

One of the big issues you'll need to come to terms with is the anger problem. Anger is as natural to a Child of Mars as breathing. Asking this person to keep his or her temper in check would be analogous to someone telling you not to worry so much. It's just not going to happen. However that temper can be channeled in constructive ways. If your Mars mate feels free to curse up a storm, then that anger will burn bright and fast in the moment and go out. If your mate holds things inside, then that can be cause for concern, because this is when the anger becomes moody and petulant and you may feel as if you are walking around on eggshells. Anger, like any other emotion, is an energy that's meant to be expressed.

CHILD

It's easy to champion a fiercely individual spirit in the abstract, but it's quite a different matter when you have to deal with it day in and day out. At times your Mars kid's provocative edge can get to you and you may get irritable. That's allowed. It may even be desirable, in that Children of Mars like it when everything is put out on the table. They get very nervous around people who say they aren't angry when it's clear that they are.

PARENT

Though your Mars parent could be tough and demanding, he or she also had a great sense of humor. This taught you to focus on the task at hand, but not to get too bent out of shape if things didn't work out the way you wanted them to. Born under the Planet of contests, Mars parents know that if you don't win one round there's always next time. It's because of this person that you have such a healthy relationship to competition.

SIBLING

Hopefully each of you found your own place to shine when you were younger—otherwise it would have been nonstop one-upmanship. Nevertheless you have your Mars sibling's respect and (begrudging) admiration.

FRIEND

That back-and-forth repartee can get so fast and furious that total strangers can't help listening in—you two are just so funny. For two people who often take themselves too seriously, it's amazing what cutups you can be in each other's company.

ENEMY

You don't like bullies. Even if you aren't directly involved, you will not stand by and watch someone be strong-armed. As a Child of Uranus and Saturn, you outrank Mars in the cosmic scheme of things. If you stand your ground then this person will turn tail and run.

BOSS

You both have a deep respect for hierarchy, so your Mars boss won't abuse his or her authority any more than you would question it. This person wouldn't ask you to do anything that he or she isn't prepared to do as well.

COLLEAGUE

Always be specific when making a request, because your Mars colleague will take you literally. If you make a joke about asking for his or her firstborn, you just might get it.

CHILD OF URANUS/SATURN

.... ❊ ....

WITH CHILD OF JUPITER

You strive to emulate the ideal in your life. And if that means pushing yourself past what's comfortable or having to do without—then so be it. Children of Jupiter believe that people were the ones who made up those ideals in the first place, and that instead of looking for perfection at the top of our highest standards, we should look for it in the humor and incongruity of our everyday lives.

LOVE INTEREST

Chances are you're part of the same circle of friends. You enjoy each other's company, and because you almost always get together as part of a group, it may take a while before you realize your association could develop into something more. But nothing's ever simple when it comes to a Child of Jupiter. Don't be surprised to find yourself involved in a love triangle or some other complicated set of circumstances that flies in the face of just about every rule you adhere to.

MATE

Though the center of controversy when you were dating, as a couple you two are now practically the pillars of your community. You both have a great love of people and will throw open your doors to just about anyone in need. You also believe in helping others—especially young people—to develop their potential and talents. But don't take loved ones for granted. In your quest to ensure that everyone has a place at your table, the needs and concerns of your own children and/or close friends often get lost in the shuffle.

CHILD

It's because your Jupiter kid is such an independent spirit that you need to be hands-on. Otherwise your son or daughter will go from one pursuit to another without recognizing there's a through line. Your confidence that there is an underlying pattern to everything we do and that, given time, it will make itself known is both inspiring and reassuring.

PARENT

It may be hard to tell if your Jupiter parent was really as dogmatic as you remember. As a Child of Uranus you're predisposed to tipping sacred cows, and your Jupiter parent (with all of his or her talk of faith and morals) may have made an irresistible target. But once you got passed the heated arguments with their charges, countercharges, and fiery denunciations, you'll see that this person really does have your spiritual welfare uppermost in mind.

SIBLING

You've always felt your Jupiter sibling is just a bit too *accepting* of what others say. Conversely, your sibling thinks you like to stir things up just for the fun of it. Though you will always emerge from (and retreat to) opposite corners, there's plenty of common ground between you. This is one of the few people you feel comfortable debating with.

FRIEND

If this person isn't dragging you off to a weekend at the ashram, then it's a lecture or workshop. Ironically, it's not until you get around your Jupiter friend that you realize how close minded you can be. Though you both share a love of knowledge, this person is much more comfortable adopting a teacher or mentor. You tend to be self-taught. Thankfully your Jupiter friend gets you to lighten up and not view all figures of authority with such suspicion.

ENEMY

A Jupiter enemy can be just *as* unrelenting and hell-bent on getting his or her way as you—although this person will always say it's for the good of God or country or whatever else happens to come to mind.

BOSS

Your idea of showing how much you appreciate and respect this person is by doing the best job you can. However, Jupiter was named after the king of the gods in Greek mythology. In other words, your boss likes it when you wax poetic. Powers-that-be need ego stroking just like everyone else.

COLLEAGUE

A Jupiter colleague always knows the latest dirt and is more than happy to share. This is the person to go to if you ever want to know what's up.

CHILD OF URANUS/SATURN

WITH CHILD OF SATURN

A Child of Saturn has the other half of the equation you're looking for. You may be a font of brilliant ideas, but it's a Child of Saturn who can make them happen. Sometimes you'll be on opposite poles and other times you'll be in perfect agreement. Though a Child of Saturn can be a harsh critic, this person is also your biggest fan.

LOVE INTEREST

Usually you dazzle paramours with an astonishing fact or brilliant insight. But you'll have to work harder than that with your Saturn love interest—especially since he or she is at least as well read as you and will respond by testing your knowledge. The key to your heart is through your mind, so it could be love at first sight. It also doesn't hurt that this person knows how to dress and is well connected. This appeals to your elitist side.

MATE

You know you can be a handful. At times high-strung and temperamental, you can always rely on your Saturn mate to ground you. This person takes you seriously, but he or she won't indulge you. This is important because sometimes you'll get into a mode where you're just going to say or do everything opposite. But knowing that you've got such a strong anchor makes you feel more secure than if you had bundles of money in the bank. Although considering your Saturn mate's industriousness, that expectation isn't so far-fetched.

CHILD

It won't be easy to accept how shy your Saturn kid can be—especially given your ability to fraternize with all types. But give it time. Children of Saturn need to find their place in the social milieu before they feel comfortable. Introducing the little one to sports, dance, or music will help. Not only will he or she respond positively to learning a discipline, but talent also speaks more easily than words.

PARENT

The reason you question authority as much as you do is because you have a strong idea of what it should be. Your Saturn parent has always known this and wisely adopted a low profile when you switched from showing respect to looking for idols to topple. Nevertheless your mom or dad would have insisted that if you're going to knock something off its perch, then be prepared to replace it with something as good if not better; otherwise keep your opinions to yourself.

SIBLING

It doesn't matter how bossy, insensitive, or stuffy your Saturn sibling is—chances are you're contributing just as much to the one-upmanship. You both need to have the last word, and there's no limit to how far you'll go to get it.

FRIEND

Few people can get you to laugh at yourself. Your Saturn friend knows how to poke fun but not leave you feeling foolish. This is also the same person who will encourage you to pursue something you consider far-fetched or absurd. Your Saturn friend takes your aspirations more seriously than you do at times.

ENEMY

Chances are you're just on the opposite sides of a debate. If you respect your Saturn adversary's position then he or she will respect yours.

BOSS

If you're true blue, your Saturn boss will recognize it and invite you to become part of his or her inner circle. If not, then you'll never get past a certain point. If this continues to mystify you and you really want to know the reason, then your boss will tell you if you ask. But then be prepared to hear about some truths you are unwilling to admit to yourself.

COLLEAGUE

There are two types of Saturn colleagues—innovator and lackey. If you're lucky to be working with an innovator, then this person will not only raise your standards, but will also show you how to reach them. If you're stuck with the second type—see if you can't transfer somewhere else.

CHILD OF URANUS/SATURN

.... ❈ ....

WITH CHILD OF URANUS/SATURN

One of you will be pie-in-the-sky, while the other is squarely down-to-earth. But given how things are never formulaic where Uranus and Saturn are concerned, you can just as abruptly trade places. Yours is a powerful bond, and your relationship—always complex and multifaceted—grows with each passing year.

LOVE INTEREST

Dating is a tense time, as the attraction is electric and sensational, but you're also equally ambivalent. You will both be feeling out each other's strengths and weaknesses. The slightest "off" note—whether it's a passing comment, one phone call too many, or an untoward display of affection—may be all it takes to call it quits. One of the nice things about having Uranus as a Ruling Planet is that what goes around once inevitably comes around again. If you don't feel as if you really gave things a chance, then you can always look forward to round two.

MATE

You need something to sink your teeth into—whether it's starting a family, going into business, or taking on the restoration of your downtown's historic district yourselves. You are creative, industrious, and highly motivated. As a couple, you make an exceptional team. You like being busy, and though you'll often complain of how much you've got on your platter, you'll always make room for something new. You are both secretly proud of how much you accomplish together.

CHILD

Don't expect your Uranus/Saturn kid to fit cozily into your agenda. Even if you go to great pains to set things up just so, your kid will find something wrong with it and rebel. Take your cue from your little square peg. Not only will you save yourself a lot of time and trouble, but once your son or daughter fixates on an interest, he or she will fly with it. Uranus/Saturn kids are tremendously self-motivated.

PARENT

For someone who's constantly in your business, it's amazing how this person is never around when you really need him or her. But this has less to do with your dad or mom (who always means well) and is more a by-product of that slightly out-of-sync quality woven into the Uranus/Saturn dynamic. Though you may still receive presents originally intended for someone else or be surprised three days early because your Uranus/Saturn parent got the dates wrong, there's never a doubt that you are this person's pride and joy.

SIBLING

You alternate between singing each other's praises and disagreeing on the most trivial details. Yet this is the person you turn to whenever you're going through a tough time. Your Uranus/Saturn sister or brother may not tell you what to do, but she or he knows exactly what questions to ask to help you clear your mind or conscience.

FRIEND

You two are so devoted to each other that it's surprising how much *isn't* confided. That's because in the spirit of camaraderie, you will go the extra distance to not share anything that may cause the other one to worry. A little less stiff upper lip and some more heart-to-heart couldn't hurt.

ENEMY

Find a way to resolve your dispute and/or differences ASAP. You will both take up such opposite extremes that there is no hope of compromise. Any prolonged spat will result in heavy losses on both sides.

BOSS

Curb that impulse to change whatever is currently in place until you feel like there's a comfortable rapport between you and your Uranus/Saturn boss. At first this person will treat you warily—after all, he or she was once in the very same position you're in—but given time your energies will combine to do the most good.

COLLEAGUE

If you work closely together, you'll hardly exchange a word after hours. But if you're in different departments or if your work brings you into occasional contact, then you'll wind up becoming great friends. However, in the grand scheme of things, work always comes first.

CHILD OF URANUS/SATURN

············· ❋ ·············

WITH CHILD OF NEPTUNE/JUPITER

You see progress as constructive; a Child of Neptune and Jupiter sees progress as damage control. You strive to bring things to a higher level, while this person struggles to restore them to their original pristine state. At times contradictory, at times complementary, you are both inspired by your dream of a better world. Like you, a Child of Neptune and Jupiter sees everything in life as interconnected.

LOVE INTEREST

It's impossible to predict how your Neptune/Jupiter love interest is going to behave. He or she can switch from inflammatory debate one moment to cozying up beside you the next. Despite your own penchant for abrupt about-faces, you're not as quick to make the transition—and question if this person may not be trying to pull a fast one. Highly unlikely. A Child of Neptune and Jupiter's emotional life is as deep and mysterious as your mental life is vast and complex.

MATE

It would be easier if you just didn't see eye to eye on anything. Then you could simply respect each other's position and leave it at that. But it's because your differences often stem from the subtlest shade of gray that you can drive each other batty with the hair splitting. Loved ones and friends may fail to appreciate the discrepancy, but you two recognize how an enormous misunderstanding could result if it's not immediately put right. You're both stubborn when it comes to a philosophical debate, so you'll have to work out your differences point by point. It may seem like much ado about nothing, but it keeps your relationship lively.

CHILD

It's tempting to want to follow your little dreamer down the garden path, but someone has to keep things firmly rooted in reality. Nevertheless you can create moments of curiosity and wonder by transforming a lesson in how to tie shoelaces or reciting the alphabet into exercises of the imagination.

PARENT

Neptune/Jupiter parents are never quite convinced that they want to be doing what they're doing. There's a tendency to fantasize about the grass being greener on the other side of the fence, which is why they often talk about what life would be like if circumstances were different or if they were free of some thankless job or obligation. This is a chronic complaint that most adults find all too familiar—but it may have given you the impression that you were somehow to blame. It could take until you're an adult for you to realize that your Neptune/Jupiter parent was just talking out loud and that this person's love for you is never in doubt.

SIBLING

Your Neptune/Jupiter sibling is always hitting you up for money—even if he or she happens to make more than you. Though quick to pick up the tab for small things, this person will leave you holding the bag for the big expenses. You may have to limit get-togethers to once a year so you can afford it.

FRIEND

Stop harping on your Neptune/Jupiter friend to do something with all that creative potential. Talent may be inherent, but developing it is an entirely different matter. Whether or not your friend decides to pursue that is up to him or her. It's not why you are friends, so it certainly isn't worth fighting about.

ENEMY

Never declare war on a Neptune/Jupiter enemy before the check clears or if all personal property hasn't already been accounted for. Otherwise you can kiss it good-bye.

BOSS

Your Neptune/Jupiter boss is the visionary, so it's up to you to ensure that you get paid on time or are fully reimbursed for expenses. But what your boss lacks in managing day-to-day affairs, he or she more than makes up for with inspiration and infusing what you do with a sense of greater purpose.

COLLEAGUE

If this person spent half as much time *doing* the work as making excuses for getting out of it, then maybe something would get done.

CHILD OF URANUS/SATURN

·········· ❋ ··········

WITH CHILD OF PLUTO/MARS

You both know what it's like to be an outsider. A Child of Pluto and Mars is just as likely as you to follow the dictates of conscience—placing a higher value on what he or she feels is right than on what others expect. To a Child of Pluto and Mars, there is no such thing as a split between mundane and spiritual concerns. Indeed, the belief that what's highest in us is also reflected in our baser nature—and that we *must* work with both—is a fundamental tenet.

LOVE INTEREST

There's no denying the impact or the appeal. You find your Pluto/Mars love interest terribly exciting in a vaguely taboo way. However all of that could change after your first fight. Children of Pluto and Mars love to make war as much as they love to make love. That's why this person will refuse to compromise on the slightest point. This could rub you the wrong way. However if you were to treat this as just another form of horseplay, then you could get into it. These pairings work best if you get together after a first marriage or long-term relationship.

MATE

You admire your mate's emotional honesty. If this person doesn't like something then he or she will say so. Part of you longs to do the same, but as you're more political by nature, you worry about giving the wrong impression or stepping on someone's toes. Nevertheless your Pluto/Mars mate's candidness appeals to your subversive side, so you'll support it—until this person goes overboard. You may be a maverick, but you are not ill-mannered. And when your mate gets rude and insensitive, you won't think twice about upbraiding him or her right there on the spot.

CHILD

Pluto/Mars kids have an inability to let go. This flies in the face of everything you believe. Obviously you'll want to foster self-sufficiency, but taking something away from your kid just to prove a point is as bad as indulging every whim. Adopt a "win some, lose some" approach and you'll gradually set up an easy flow of give-and-take. Until then—be patient.

PARENT

This pairing works best if you and your parent are of the opposite sex. There's no feeling of resentment or like anyone's authority is being undermined when you disagree. However if your parent is the same sex as you, then this can bring out stubbornness and contrariness. Given time you'll bridge the gap and even establish camaraderie.

SIBLING

You look up to your Pluto/Mars sibling—even if your brother or sister is younger. You admire this person's passion and refusal to bend. You've learned a lot about courage and strength watching your Pluto/Mars sibling weather the various storms, but in truth you wouldn't have made half the decisions this person did. Your brother or sister seems hell-bent on charting the most difficult course imaginable.

FRIEND

You're as close as siblings ought to be—and without any of the infighting. Pluto/Mars friends always come into your life when you're undergoing a tremendous crisis. There aren't many people whom you allow to hold your hand, but a Pluto/Mars friend is there with the support, encouragement, and wisecracks every step of the way.

ENEMY

Neither of you will get loud. Nor will you raise your voice. You both just become eerily quiet. But of the two, you can last longer. Unlike your Pluto/Mars opponent, you really *can* turn off your feelings.

BOSS

This is the only person who can get you to compromise on principle or cover for a white lie. But considering how conscientious your Pluto/Mars boss is, you wouldn't be asked to do anything of the sort unless it was absolutely necessary.

COLLEAGUE

It all depends on whether your Pluto/Mars colleague wants to be there or not. If sufficiently motivated, then this person will bring out the best in everyone. If not, avoid him or her at all costs.

CHILD OF NEPTUNE/JUPITER

············ ❉ ············

WITH CHILD OF THE SUN

Children of the Sun *know* what they like. Everything they feel—even if it's distaste—is expressed immediately and unapologetically. You have strong feelings, too, but you're not always brave about them. A Child of the Sun will give you the confidence to say exactly what's on your mind.

LOVE INTEREST

Not everyone knows how to go on a date. But your Solar love interest does. Neither of you is shy about being romantic—you'll call each other several times a day and shower each other with gifts. Considering the wonderful time you're having, you're naturally reluctant about moving on to the next stage. Why spoil a good thing with talk about problems, old heartbreaks, fear of commitment, and all the other things that inevitably come up? Though maybe not as magical, those things can be romantic, too, because they allow you to bond on a deeper level. You can trust your Solar love interest to show you how.

MATE

You have a softening effect on your Solar mate—not unlike the way gauze is used to diffuse the glare of light so that it takes on an ambient glow. The reason this person is so tolerant, patient, and solicitous is because of you. This is why your mate will often acknowledge you as being the "better half." Loved ones and in-laws know this, which is why they come to you when they need something from your mate. Be careful about getting drafted into the role of go-between. It's up to you to remind everyone that you have a life of your own.

CHILD

Watching your Solar kid discover the world brings out the child in you. There are so many things you learn to appreciate all over again when seen through your son's or daughter's eyes. Cultivate that spirit of wonder. Show your little one that life only gets more marvelous as you go along and that the best is yet to come.

PARENT

Your dad or mom worked hard to provide for you. You had most of what you could wish for—except time with your Solar parent. This could leave you feeling like something's missing. But you would have had this feeling even if you got all the attention you required. One of the difficulties with being born under the Planet of unconditional love is that your emotional reservoir is so deep that you rarely feel the bottom beneath your feet. Be open to the feelings in the moment and you'll find your Solar parent swimming right alongside.

SIBLING

Your Solar sibling has his or her own corner of the world staked out. There's an answer for everything and everything has its place. You know that the world doesn't really work like this, but it's useless trying to convince your brother or sister otherwise. Accept this person's point of view for what it is and you'll get along fine.

FRIEND

This person is always encouraging you to be "yourself." It would be nice if you had a clearer idea of who that might be, but the truth is there are so many versions of you that not even you can keep track of them all. You like who you are when you're around your Solar friend.

ENEMY

Your Solar enemy is fair-minded and doesn't want to fight any more than you do. But if you're dealing with something *emotional*—watch out. Solar enemies don't forgive and they never forget.

BOSS

Your Solar boss is up-front; so don't expect this person to somehow be on the same wavelength as you. If there's something you want, ask for it. Either your Solar boss will say yes or no. It's as easy as that.

COLLEAGUE

If you're self-disciplined then you can hang out with your Solar colleague. But if you're not—steer clear, because this person can match you procrastination for procrastination.

CHILD OF NEPTUNE/JUPITER

········· ❋ ·········

WITH CHILD OF THE MOON

Children of the Moon get you. They are just as deeply feeling and sensitive. However, unlike you, they won't allow their emotions to run away with them. When things get too heavy or intense, Children of the Moon will remove themselves from the situation, so that they can get a clearer sense of what their reactions are. Safeguarding their personal boundaries is very important.

LOVE INTEREST

Children of the Moon like routine. That's why your Lunar love interest will end the evening by setting up a time for you to get together again. It's as much an automatic response as you hesitating because you want to keep things open-ended. Don't let different attitudes create a heated discussion where there doesn't have to be one. Simply volunteer a time and date that's good for you and this person will be fine.

MATE

For your Lunar mate, loved ones and friends come first. This is very important, as you can sometimes get too involved in the lives of people you don't know that well. One of the most valuable things you'll ever learn from your Lunar mate is how to screen your emotions. It's not unlike letting your answering machine screen your calls. If you picked up the phone every time it rang, you'd probably spend more time talking with telemarketers than you would visiting with someone you really care about. In the same way, if you were to respond to everyone who tugged on your sleeve then you wouldn't have any time for the people who matter most. Your Lunar mate will help you stake out your emotional turf—and defend it.

CHILD

Your Lunar kid needs a lot of one-on-one attention early on. Your little Moon will act out whenever he or she feels neglected. Childhood is the only time when your son or daughter will be this open and impressionable, so you don't want to miss your chance to create a deep and lasting bond.

PARENT

You get your love for history and the past from your Lunar parent. Whether it was a family story that first captured your imagination or a treasured piece of memorabilia that was passed on to you, your Moon mom or dad taught you that old things speak as clearly today as they did years ago. Much of your humor and earthy quality comes from your Lunar parent.

SIBLING

Chances are it was your sister or brother who turned you on to the great passion of your life. Maybe you followed this person to baseball practice or started taking piano lessons when your sibling decided to call it quits—in any case this person played a pivotal role.

FRIEND

The perfect person to go hunting or fishing with, as the Moon was named after the goddess of the hunt. This is also the ideal partner for antiquing, as your Lunar friend will never tire before you do. But your Lunar friend also knows how to just hang out. Like you, this person talks back to the TV.

ENEMY

If it's a dispute over property, quit while you're ahead. And if you're planning on skipping town or reneging on an agreement, you can forget about that, too. Your Lunar enemy will track you down *and* stick you with all the expenses. The best thing to do is settle your quarrel ASAP.

BOSS

It takes a while for a Lunar boss to warm up. Children of the Moon are slow to accept a new face. But once you've been there for a while (give it six months), this person will treat you like one of the family. You're lucky to be working for someone who's this supportive and encouraging.

COLLEAGUE

Children of the Moon are very sensitive to their environment and everything has to work just so or they won't be able to think straight. Seeing as you're not always the most organized of souls, you could probably benefit from being around this person.

CHILD OF NEPTUNE/JUPITER

·········· ❅ ··········

WITH CHILD OF MERCURY

You love a good joke or story, and few can make you laugh as heartily as a Child of Mercury. This person also shares your love of adventure and is just as willing as you to travel to some destination sight unseen because the name sounds good. Between your boundless wonder and a Child of Mercury's insatiable curiosity, you two will never run out of things to do.

LOVE INTEREST

Children of Mercury aren't always comfortable being swept off their feet. That's why you need to take things slow. Expect lots of hemming and hawing, last-minute cancellations, and long rambling monologues about what your Mercury love interest thinks he or she is feeling. What it comes down to is you have a more powerful impact than you know. Your love interest will get less awkward over time.

MATE

Your Mercury mate brings out your love of play. But this is more than just fun and recreation—though this person enjoys having a good time, too. Your mate gets you to question your feelings in ways you wouldn't normally do on your own. Like a Child of Mercury, you believe anything can be interpreted in a variety of ways—except when it comes to something you believe in. You can have an almost superstitious resistance to examining tenets you hold sacred. Nevertheless your Mercury mate will prevail upon you to rethink the world as well as your approach to it.

CHILD

Your Mercury kid is a handful. If this little monkey isn't busy getting into things that are clearly off-limits, then he or she is asking you questions that aren't easy to answer. Bone up on subjects ranging from who invented zippers to when is the universe's birthday. One day you'll be proud of the role you've played in your kid's thinking. It's thanks to you that he or she isn't afraid to see the fancy in a fact.

PARENT

You probably didn't appreciate your parent's skepticism when you were young. You may have even felt as if your Mercury mom or dad was somehow making fun of you. It's important to remember that Children of Mercury place their trust in thinking just like you place your trust in feelings—that's why they question, prod, and poke like they do. If anything, you may have inadvertently hurt your parent's feelings by accusing her or him of being callous. Thankfully all this gets ironed out when you get older.

SIBLING

Mercury rules the mind, so there's no disputing your sister or brother is a quick study. The problem is that you may have used this as an excuse not to develop your own brainpower. Each person has his or her own unique set of smarts. Don't make the mistake of underrating yours.

FRIEND

Your Mercury friend is always signing up for the latest fad—the more exotic and impractical, the better. You'll pooh-pooh this person and go on about the steep costs and the tremendous waste of time and energy. But that won't stop you from signing up, too.

ENEMY

Don't try to beat this person at his or her own game. Your Mercury enemy will only change the rules at the last minute. The sooner you go about your own business, the sooner this person will leave you in peace.

BOSS

Your Mercury boss may start off as a teacher or mentor, but this person isn't all that comfortable with the position. Either your boss will move on or you will. Nevertheless what you gain as a result of working for this person—the contacts, ins and outs, how to pique someone's interest in ten words or less—proves invaluable.

COLLEAGUE

Though a Mercury colleague is always quick to help out in a pinch, this person's idea of assistance may be very different from yours. Map out what you want from the start. Mercury colleagues are geniuses at doing just the bare minimum to get by.

CHILD OF NEPTUNE/JUPITER

WITH CHILD OF VENUS

Children of Venus always strive to keep the peace. This is why they go to such lengths to consider each and every point of view. As a Child of Neptune and Jupiter, you wish to erase people's differences so that everyone can get along. That's much too global and impractical as far as a Child of Venus is concerned. A genius at economy, this person knows that all it takes is converting one or two key players to establish harmony.

LOVE INTEREST

You believe that falling in love should be dreamy and poetic, so you could be caught off guard by how matter-of-fact your Venus love interest can be. He or she will size you up for suitability. Do you have good taste? Do you live in the right neighborhood? How much money do you make? It may seem a little insensitive, but when you consider how much time and energy is wasted on fumbling around to find the right match, you'll appreciate the way this person cuts right to the chase.

MATE

This person handles both the money *and* the social planning. You're more than happy to leave all that to your mate, as neither really interests you. But just as you insist that your mate respect your deep feelings and need to tune everything out, you have to at least act interested when he or she is crunching numbers and gossiping about friends—even if it is hard keeping all the names straight. Your partnership works like a seesaw. If one of you jumps off, then everything crashes to the ground, but if both of you are in your places, then life moves along smoothly.

CHILD

Your only downtime is when your daughter or son is at school. Once the afternoon bell rings, you'll be busy preparing snacks, taxiing friends back and forth, and taking phone messages. Your Venus kid loves to entertain, and whether you know it or not—you're the wait staff.

PARENT

Your Venus dad or mom always encouraged your creativity—as long as you could make money at it. Otherwise this person would have steered you toward a more practical vocation. If you truly want to pursue something artistic, then your parent feels like you're creative enough to find a way. If you don't, then it's best that you know how to support yourself.

SIBLING

Although more empathetic than your Venus sibling, you're also more likely to issue ultimatums when you don't get your way. The combination of Neptune and Jupiter gives you a stormy temperament. Your Venus sibling, however, knows it's never a good idea to burn a bridge, because no matter how good things turn out, you never know when you may need to cross back over it again.

FRIEND

You probably met when your Venus friend was going through a rough patch. Though you may not have thought much of it at the time, your Venus friend will never forget it. What you say carries a lot of weight with this person.

ENEMY

A Venus enemy knows how to use your weaknesses against you, so watch what you say. Given your tendency to see the negative in everything when you're feeling down or tired, this can leave you extremely vulnerable. One of your strongest weapons against a Venus opponent is that people will automatically take your side, but not if you come across as a downer.

BOSS

Your boss is an expert at taking credit for what others do while shifting the blame onto them whenever something goes wrong. It may seem unfair, but employees not only accept it—they expect it. Your Venus boss has an amazing ability to elicit loyalty. You could learn a lot about the politics of business by working for this person.

COLLEAGUE

Venus colleagues want to be friends. But for all the fun and laughter, business comes first. Miss a deadline or fumble an account and this person won't even pretend to know your name.

CHILD OF NEPTUNE/JUPITER

························ ❋ ···········

WITH CHILD OF MARS

Children of Mars are highly motivated. Though you may never share their single-minded drive (your energy fluctuates too much to sustain that kind of intensity), you are stimulated and excited by their presence. Like a first cup of coffee in the morning, just being around a Child of Mars gets you up and buzzing.

LOVE INTEREST

Getting together with this person is serious business. That's because there's always something at stake whenever Mars, the Planet of conflict, is concerned. But what makes for an exciting and impassioned romance may prove to be a bit much for your tastes. Give your Mars love interest a couple of months to settle down. If it starts to look like all this person does is go from crisis to crisis—you might want to skip it.

MATE

You have a positive influence on your mate. Over time, this person goes from being aimless and more than just a little reckless to someone who knuckles down and applies himself or herself in a way that loved ones and friends never expected to see. Your love and belief in your mate's potential for excellence give this person something to live for. Subsequently your mate has the equally positive effect of showing you that wishes really can come true—if you're willing to invest the elbow grease.

CHILD

This kid was born fearless. Your first inclination may be to rope in your little daredevil. After all, it's only natural for you to be protective. But try enrolling your son or daughter in martial arts, gymnastics, or ballet. Not only does this provide an outlet for all that energy, but the kid also acquires discipline as well. That way your son or daughter learns how to look after himself or herself. This will also cut down enormously on your worry.

PARENT

This person's answer to you feeling down or overwhelmed may be to start chanting "I know I can, I know I can." Focusing on mastering a steep challenge is the very thing that galvanizes your Mars dad or mom. However you have a different approach to surmounting difficulty. Oftentimes it means going in the opposite direction of your parent, because it's by losing your way that you wind up finding yourself. Just trust in the fact that when you return from your journey, its positive effect will be self-evident.

SIBLING

This person's solution to any crisis was to grab the bull by the horns and wrestle it to the ground. But don't underestimate your Mars sibling's ability to appreciate strength in all its different forms and expressions. Your sister or brother has always admired your quiet fortitude.

FRIEND

Given your tendency to wring your hands while lamenting the sorry state of the world, it's nice to have a Mars friend who will look you squarely in the eye and tell you to get over yourself. Succinct and to the point, this brings you right back to your senses.

ENEMY

Ironically, it may be your attempt to avoid a confrontation that's prolonging the hostility. Mars is the Planet of combat, so your enemy needs some excuse to fly into a rage. Try sticking out your tongue if you can't think of anything else. Once that rage is spent, your Mars enemy will leave you in peace.

BOSS

Your Mars boss is abrupt and gruff with everyone but you. For some reason you bring out this person's soft side. Colleagues are dying to know your secret, but the truth is there's nothing to tell. He or she just likes you.

COLLEAGUE

What makes you and a Mars colleague such a successful team is that you don't try to help. You're savvy enough to get out of this person's way and just let him or her do what comes naturally. But on those rare occasions when your Mars colleague is stymied—you're right there with a word of advice or moral support.

CHILD OF NEPTUNE/JUPITER

.... ☀ ....

WITH CHILD OF JUPITER

A Child of Jupiter is spirited—fiery and animated. This is very different from your disposition, which tends to be more soulful and reflective. You can always count on a Child of Jupiter to strike an upbeat note. This person believes that we are all bound by a higher purpose and that the reason we are in each other's lives is to help each other realize the best in ourselves.

LOVE INTEREST

You've heard the lines before. Many of the jokes and stories are as old as Nineveh. And it's easy to predict what this person is going to do next—you can see the "smooth move" from miles away. Your Jupiter love interest can be impossibly cheesy—a cross between a talk show host and a lounge singer. But none of that will stop you from falling deeply, passionately, and madly in love.

MATE

Although you have a lot in common—you're both spiritual, adventurous, and adore people—your perspectives couldn't be more different. Your Jupiter mate believes in the power of faith and can get very upset when you don't fall into step. It's hard for you to ignore the problems that a philosophy, creed, or self-help regimen will blithely sweep under the rug or explain away with a moralistic wave of the hand. This invariably sets you at odds, and since you were both born under Planets named after storm gods (Neptune's hurricanes are every bit as tempestuous as Jupiter's rolling thunder and lightning), you go at it full force. Nevertheless it's the drama and powerful conviction that drew you to each other in the first place. Disagreements broaden your horizons, and after the hail of words and tears, you always kiss and make up.

CHILD

Jupiter kids like labels. Knowing this is "good" and that is "bad" helps them navigate the ambiguities of the world. This may be hard to deal with at first because you believe we all carry the potential to be good *and* bad. But don't worry. Your Jupiter kid's belief system will mellow with age.

PARENT

Even if your Jupiter parent wasn't the type to fly into operatic rages, he or she didn't try to conceal a groan of disappointment or an exasperated sigh. Everything is expressed—spontaneously and without forethought. But what your Jupiter dad or mom lacks in discretion, he or she makes up for in love and humor.

SIBLING

Your Jupiter sibling gets all the attention. Whether she or he excelled at school and sports or became the bane of everyone's existence, this person is sure to be the talk of family get-togethers. It's no use competing. Ironically, your sister or brother would probably rather talk about you.

FRIEND

If you have strong feelings about something, then your Jupiter friend will urge you to take action— maybe do volunteer work, boycott products whose politics you deplore, or convert to solar energy. The fact that your Jupiter friend wouldn't follow through on any of these things is beside the point.

ENEMY

Children of Jupiter often overreact when they're upset. But for all the wind and fury, they are still fair-minded. You'll never make an enemy of a Child of Jupiter as long as you allow for a cooling-off period.

BOSS

Never believe it when your Jupiter boss says that something's in the bag. Chances are it all took place in his or her mind. Intentions don't always make the transition to actions when you're dealing with a Child of Jupiter, so you'll want to keep tabs. But be discreet about it. If your boss thinks you're checking up on him or her, you'll never hear the end of it.

COLLEAGUE

Your Jupiter colleague can sometimes *hear* what he or she wants to hear, so double-check with a higher-up. Otherwise you can wind up creating more work for yourself.

CHILD OF NEPTUNE/JUPITER

.... ❋ ....

WITH CHILD OF SATURN

A Child of Saturn makes the abstract concrete. This person will find a way to translate the most obscure ideas into easy-to-follow terms—and without sacrificing any of the poetry or profundity. This earthy approach also allows a Child of Saturn to address highly personal (and sometimes incendiary) issues with a confidence and calm that can be tremendously reassuring.

LOVE INTEREST

Your Saturn love interest comes highly recommended. You may be surprised to discover (after meeting on your own) that friends have been trying to set you up for weeks. But be careful about adopting a relaxed approach right away. That air of formality is there for a reason, and you'd best respect it.

MATE

Decorum is very important to your Saturn mate. There's a very good chance that your mate has to maintain a certain look when it comes to work. Maybe he or she is expected to appear buttoned-down and composed or even laid-back and sympathetic. In any case, it's not exactly what this person is like at home. Nevertheless, it's imperative that you maintain that awareness somewhere in the back of your head. If you keep private what's private and public what's public then you can't go wrong.

CHILD

Your Saturn kid demands a lot from himself or herself. No matter how you try to get this little perfectionist to lighten up, it won't work. That's why it's better to get behind what he or she wants to do than to stand in the way. But even if it's too much, your little Saturn often has to find out the hard way. It's how he or she learns to gauge when enough is enough. It also makes the eventual success all the sweeter.

PARENT

Your Saturn parent recognized in you his or her own tendency to withdraw, which is why this person was adamant about signing you up for extracurricular activities. Keeping you busy was your Saturn parent's solution to you getting mopey and depressed. However the by-product of all this running around is that you would have dabbled in a number of things you might not have discovered on your own. What began as a kind of impromptu therapy may have led to you discovering your true calling.

SIBLING

Your Saturn sibling was always willing to help shoulder the burden of responsibility—even if he or she was younger. Since you were equally committed to your family's well-being, you knew you had a natural ally. Life gets easier for both of you with age. No one appreciates what you've gone through more, which is what makes sharing the good times so gratifying.

FRIEND

Like you, this person is all too familiar with being handed the short end of the stick and knows that a modicum of self-pity is good for the soul. But your Saturn friend won't let you wallow in the mire. He or she also knows when enough is enough. When this person says to get over it, then you know it's time to move on.

ENEMY

When that wall goes up then it's best to gather your things and move on. A Saturn enemy never reconsiders and will remain completely unmoved by your entreaties.

BOSS

Your Saturn boss may think you're capable of doing more than you can, which could become a problem if you don't represent yourself accurately. Be up front. If anyone appreciates an honest assessment of abilities, it's your Saturn boss. Moreover this person will help you to develop them. Saturn is the Planet of the teacher, and your boss will regard your training as a long-term investment.

COLLEAGUE

Your Saturn colleague always keeps an eye on the time. That's why this person starts to get so fidgety if you take too long to get to the point. Don't be afraid to communicate in shorthand. Not only does your colleague follow, but she or he will also appreciate it.

CHILD OF NEPTUNE/JUPITER

WITH CHILD OF URANUS/SATURN

Children of Uranus and Saturn can turn on a dime. This isn't because they're flighty or capricious. Their abrupt about-face is often just as much a surprise to them as it is to you. But Children of Uranus and Saturn don't let things slide. If something's wrong, they won't rest until they get it right. Though this can sometimes prove inconvenient, circumstances usually bear them out in the end.

LOVE INTEREST

You two meet when you're both in transition. One of you may be winding down a relationship while the other is looking to finally settle down. Though this is bound to create tensions, this same out-of-sync quality allows you both to express sides of yourself that you might not have if you had met at any other time. Intense and absorbing, this could burn out as quickly as it begins or it may go on to become a long-lasting relationship.

MATE

Your penchant for letting things run their course acts as a calming and stabilizing influence. That's why it's a good idea for you to be the one to manage day-to-day affairs. But if you're facing a situation where a deadline is down to the wire or a number of decisions have to be made at the same time, then let your Uranus/Saturn mate take over. This person has a unique ability to size up complicated matters quickly and to bring wayward elements back into line. Playing to each other's strengths is the secret to your successful collaboration.

CHILD

It isn't easy raising an exception to the rule. Uranus/Saturn kids are either self-taught (automatically jumping ahead of the rest of the class) or interested in pursuing something so specialized it's unavailable in a regular curriculum. Though this means a lot of early mornings and late nights—not to mention running interference with your kid's teacher or principal—that extra effort always pays off.

PARENT

Things often had to fall apart before they could come together for your Uranus/Saturn parent. And though your mom or dad would have done her or his level best to spare you this, your Neptunian nature makes you highly impressionable, leaving you a bit shell-shocked. Thankfully you outgrow the nervousness and free-floating anxiety and with time find your own way of dealing with life's passages.

SIBLING

You and your Uranus/Saturn sibling always seem to have conflicting schedules. Thankfully when you finally do get a chance to relax and unwind, your time together is so special that you'll both never want it to end. This is good to keep in mind for when you have to go through all that hassle again.

FRIEND

If it weren't for you, your Uranus/Saturn friend would be scattered all over the place. But you know how to pull it all together. That's why this person comes to you for advice on everything from what to wear on a first date to fine-tuning a business proposal.

ENEMY

Not a good idea. Do what you can to resolve differences amiably. Given the turn-of-the-wheel nature of Uranus, you *will* meet again. And when you do, chances are this person will be in the driver's seat.

BOSS

Working for a Uranus/Saturn boss is really what you make of it. That's because this person won't be around much. He or she is always dashing off to some meeting or going on an overseas business trip. If you're self-disciplined and motivated, then this is perfect. You'll have a unique opportunity to really create your own job, and your Uranus/Saturn boss is always open to input and suggestions. But if you need more structure, then you may want to look for something else. These people don't slow down for anyone.

COLLEAGUE

Chaos seems to follow in the wake of your Uranus/Saturn colleague. Whether it's absentmindedly knocking a pile of papers off someone's desk or casually turning a simple procedure into an overly complicated exercise, your Uranus/Saturn colleague is in your life to ensure that no workday is event-free.

CHILD OF NEPTUNE/JUPITER

············ ❊ ············

WITH CHILD OF NEPTUNE/JUPITER

Qualities you have in common won't be recognizable right away. Indeed one of you could be poetic while the other is strictly matter-of-fact. Though you're both sensitive and dreamy, you have very different ways of showing it. It would be like introducing a classical guitarist to a heavy metal bassist and expecting them to hit it off right away. Part of the fun of getting to know a Child of Neptune and Jupiter is seeing familiar traits in a whole new light.

LOVE INTEREST

It wouldn't be impossible for you to conduct a mad love affair without getting to know the first thing about each other. Indeed given your soul-to-soul connection, you may not be all that interested in what this person is like outside of being with you. But should you opt for a more mundane, day-to-day existence, you'll find that your Neptune/Jupiter love interest loses none of his or her romance. There are always new depths to plumb.

MATE

You and your Neptune/Jupiter mate broaden each other's horizons. Perhaps you subscribe to two very different beliefs, come from opposite ends of the globe, or one of you grew up rich while the other was poor. Things that were kept hidden or buried come out because you both feel so comfortable around each other. Perhaps you discover that your mate is much funnier than how he or she originally came across or that this person went through tough times that you can barely begin to imagine. You may never know your Neptune/Jupiter mate completely. And you treasure that feeling. For you, it's a sacred mystery.

CHILD

Your Neptune/Jupiter kid is more resilient than you know. That's because your little empath has an instinctual feel for letting emotions run their course. As a parent, it isn't easy curbing one's protective instincts. But give your son or daughter room and privacy to work through his or her own feelings. Not only does it show respect, but it also encourage the kid to build psychic muscles.

PARENT

Your Neptune/Jupiter parent has very strong opinions about the ways of the world and how life works. This is great if you happen to be in agreement. You couldn't ask for better moral support. However if your ideas conflict, then your Neptune/Jupiter parent will simply tune you out. It's no use trying to point this out. Your parent won't get it. It would be like trying to confront someone with information that was divulged while under hypnosis. But in no way does this color the love that exists between you. This is one of the few people that you can still get along with even though you disagree.

SIBLING

One of you is considered the "wild" one, while the other is Goody Two-shoes. The truth is you're not really all that dissimilar until you get around each other. That's when you begin really playing up the differences.

FRIEND

Your psychic twin. You may even look alike. But if not, there's an unmistakable rapport that leads many to assume you must be related. Like twins, things aren't always so rosy. You can have enormous falling-outs and hold a grudge for years. However, in the end, you always make up, because no one gets you quite as deeply and completely as your Neptune/Jupiter friend.

ENEMY

One of you is freshwater; the other is salt, and never shall the two mix.

BOSS

Your Neptune/Jupiter boss comes into your life right at the time when you could use a helping hand. This person is instrumental in your success. However, be wary of those times when your

Neptune/Jupiter boss gets an uncontrollable compulsion to blame you for everything. Just because this person did you a favor doesn't mean you always have to take the heat.

COLLEAGUE

You always need to be a little careful around a Neptune/Jupiter colleague. If this person's feeling up— it's great. But if this person's feeling down, then everything's gloom and doom and you'll just be too bummed out for words.

CHILD OF NEPTUNE/JUPITER

·········· ✳ ··········

WITH CHILD OF PLUTO/MARS

Children of Pluto and Mars love mystery just as much as you. But where you will wisely accept that there are some things better left unknown, a Child of Pluto and Mars will seek to penetrate their hidden meaning. Children of Pluto and Mars are compelled to experience those things that no one will talk about openly.

LOVE INTEREST

The attraction is immediate and all-consuming. Your Pluto/Mars love interest is extremely intense and emotional (qualities you enjoy), but this person also tends to have a darker view of life. Moreover your Pluto/Mars love interest doesn't suffer fools gladly. But scratch beneath the surface and you'll find someone whose passion for life, although uncompromising, is incredibly exciting and invigorating.

MATE

Your Pluto/Mars mate relies on you for support and advice and would be lost without you. Your concern softens your mate's hard edges, and your gentle humor eventually prevails upon him or her to see things from a different point of view. However Pluto was named after the god of the Underworld and his Children can take great comfort in dwelling on life's underside. It keeps the infernal fires burning. Given your tendency to always make time for a loved one's troubles, there isn't much impetus for your mate to get over himself or herself. Commiseration isn't the same as compassion. Sometimes the most loving thing you can do is to be more economical with the water of life. That way your mate learns to consult his or her own conscience instead of always leaning on you.

CHILD

You draw strength from compassion while your son or daughter draws strength from outrage. In your attempt to soften life's blows, don't take away the survival mechanism your Pluto/Mars kid needs to withstand them. Show how the flow of emotions doesn't stop with having been wronged but eventually (like a river to the sea) leads to forgiveness. Your little one will learn to appreciate the validity of his or her reactions—as well as the validity of someone else's.

PARENT

Though you learned to temper your parent's heated reactions, there's no disputing your Pluto/Mars mom or dad has a point. Unfortunately that point can sometimes get lost due to this person's provocative way of raising it. You may not always share the sense of moral outrage, but the reason you're as upright as you are is because of your Pluto/Mars parent.

SIBLING

Hopefully you learned a long time ago *not* to tell your brother or sister to get over it. Those are fighting words to a Pluto/Mars sibling. For the most part this person is reasonable and can even laugh at himself or herself. But on those occasions when your Pluto/Mars sibling becomes impossibly obsessed, say something innocuous and get off the phone ASAP. Otherwise you'll be stuck listening to this broken record all day.

FRIEND

Never tell your Pluto/Mars friend that everyone goes through hard times. He or she is liable to hang up on you. As a Child of Neptune and Jupiter, you find solace in numbers. You like knowing that others feel as you do. Children of Pluto and Mars, however, find this idea trivializing and will respond by showing you just how *unlike* other people they can be.

ENEMY

In mythology, Jupiter, Neptune, and Pluto were all brothers. Seeing as two of those three siblings also happen to be your Ruling Planets—you outrank your Pluto/Mars enemy. When your enemy gives you the chill, tell this person to go try it somewhere else.

BOSS

You have a remarkable talent for getting this person to lighten up. No easy feat. You instinctually know what to say to deflate most tense situations. Your Pluto/Mars boss truly values you—more than you probably know.

COLLEAGUE

Give this person plenty of space. Once obsessed with a job or deadline, there's no talking to your Mars/Pluto colleague until it's in the bag.

CHILD OF PLUTO/MARS

········ ❋ ········

WITH CHILD OF THE SUN

Children of the Sun know better than to take on the weight of the world. That's why they're so good at assessing what they can and cannot do. If it's their responsibility, then they will shoulder it. But if something happens that doesn't directly involve them—no matter how close to home it may be—they will simply put it out of mind. This amazing self-possession is what allows them to sleep at night during the most stressful times. You'd love to be that impervious, but in truth worries tend to eat away at you. Letting yourself off the hook for the things you can't help is one of the most valuable lessons you could learn from a Child of the Sun.

LOVE INTEREST

You'll disagree on practically everything—which means, for you, it's love at first sight. Although your opinions clash, you and your Solar love interest can find more appealing ways to channel that combative energy. In matters of the heart and soul, you are simpatico.

MATE

Neither of you is low maintenance. You both demand a lot from each other in terms of patience and attention. But yours is the kind of partnership based on rising to the occasion. Your Solar mate may never stop complaining about (or reminding you of) all the things you put him or her through, but there's never a doubt that he or she would go through fire and water for you. Of course you'll never hear the end of it afterward.

CHILD

If anyone can get you down on all fours, talking baby talk, and pretending like you're a mythic creature from some faraway fairyland—it's your Solar kid. One smile from your golden prince or princess is all it takes and your dignity is out the window.

PARENT

It's hard *not* to put your Solar parent on a pedestal. Your dad or mom doesn't do anything halfway. If this person takes something on, then he or she will go the distance. It's almost as if your parent has no fear. That isn't an easy thing to live up to—especially when you question and worry and obsess as much as you do. But this person isn't in your life to overshadow you. Your dad or mom is here to galvanize and encourage you. You don't have to be anything other than who you are to earn this person's love.

SIBLING

You may start out bickering and fighting, but you'll grow into the best of friends. Having children of your own also helps. Family and kinship are important to both of you. Your Solar sibling is the only one who truly understands your obsession with the holiday season.

FRIEND

Whether it's a timely phone call that comes right when you're feeling down or an invitation to treat yourself to a day of shopping or a night at the movies, your Solar friend has a sixth sense for when you could use an upper.

ENEMY

Your Solar enemy is no fighter. But beware. A Solar enemy can nurse a grudge just as long as you and will retaliate when you least expect it.

BOSS

It doesn't matter how many times you change jobs or transfer departments, you will somehow wind up working for a Child of the Sun. Born under the Planet of kings and queens, your Solar boss is used to exercising authority. For a Child of the Sun, authority isn't about accomplishment or proving your mettle. It's about being a guiding light. If you accept that it's your Solar boss's job to lead and your job to follow, then you'll get along fine.

COLLEAGUE

This person runs everything by you first. Though your Solar colleague professes to only want to hear "good" things, she or he knows that you're the only one who will tell it like it is.

CHILD OF PLUTO/MARS

·········· ✳ ··········

WITH CHILD OF THE MOON

Children of the Moon put their faith in providence. They take the hard times with the good and trust that everything will work out in the end. Like the Moon, which has always been associated with cycles, Lunar types instinctually know prospects that look dismal one day can rally the next. Hang out with a Child of the Moon and you'll ease up on that all-or-nothing approach.

LOVE INTEREST

The attraction is unmistakable and it's clear you enjoy each other, but the deciding factor will be in how you negotiate your contrasting dispositions. Your Lunar love interest is looking for something comfortable, whereas you're looking for someone who can deal with your agony/ecstasy temperament. This requires a subtle kind of understanding which isn't always easy, given that you can both be so sensitive. There will be times when you have to rein in those emotional extremes and times when your Lunar love interest will have to ease up on being the buffer.

MATE

Your "take no prisoners" approach won't fly with your Lunar mate. And given your Plutonian tendency to act out first and ask questions later, you'll be glad your partner has the wherewithal to keep you in check. But don't expect an outright confrontation. Your mate knows you too well. Whether it's making sure you're sitting cozily by the fire before hitting you with some sobering news or canceling your credit cards if you refuse to live within a budget, your mate *will* bring you into line. It's your Lunar mate who introduces those moments of reflection that often keep you from doing something you'll regret.

CHILD

Your Lunar kid brings out all your nurturing instincts. You will be doting, solicitous, and overly protective. Trust that what looks so timid and vulnerable in childhood will strengthen and firm up with age. The best thing you can teach your little Moon is to express what's going on rather than to bottle it up inside.

PARENT

You've gone through some dramatic phases with your Lunar parent. When you were young, you worshipped the ground she or he walked on—soaking up every word of this person's philosophy. But after living on your own, you discovered how out-of-date many of these precepts were. This may have led you to look upon your Lunar mom or dad as hopelessly naive. But as time passes, you'll find that there's more than just a grain of truth to what your Lunar parent has to say. It may not always be apparent, but there's a consistency to the logic.

SIBLING

You will always be in each other's corner. When your Lunar sibling is doubtful, you're encouraging; if you're feeling overwhelmed, your sibling is comforting. Also, if something sounds suspicious or like it's a bit of a stretch, neither of you will hesitate to say so.

FRIEND

It takes forever to get your Lunar friend to divulge the juicy stuff. But after enough coaxing and prodding, you'll ferret it out. Your Lunar friend never disappoints. Just when you think you've heard it all, this person finds a way to outdo himself or herself.

ENEMY

Few people can make you feel so ashamed for being beastly—even if you're in the right! Guilt trips are your Lunar enemy's most effective weapon.

BOSS

If you're content to mosey along at a relaxed pace, then a Child of the Moon is the boss for you. This person will never push. But if you've got mountains to climb and ambitions to realize, then hook up with someone else, because this person is as slow as molasses.

COLLEAGUE

You could be getting ready to make a big pitch and this person will fret about whether his tie's on right or if she remembered to leave a note for the cleaning lady. Don't sweat it. Your colleague is right there with you. This is just his or her way of expressing nerves.

CHILD OF PLUTO/MARS

.... ❋ ....

WITH CHILD OF MERCURY

Children of Mercury see life as a series of turning points. To them, a fork in the road is an invitation to explore something new. And in keeping with their restless curiosity, they often choose the road less traveled. As a Child of Pluto and Mars, you set your sights on something, and that's what you want. Not only will a Child of Mercury convince you to remove the blinders and live a little, but this person may even show you how a diversion can turn into a destination.

LOVE INTEREST

You are drawn to this person's effervescence, while your Mercury love interest is intrigued by your intimidating presence. Each of you would like to have a bit more of what the other has. While you click right off the bat, both of you can be terribly contrary in your own way. Understanding and respecting the differences between you is the first step to bridging them.

MATE

Yours is a symbiotic relationship. With each passing year, your Mercury mate becomes tenderhearted as you become more open-minded and flexible. But this won't happen in any obvious way. Indeed it may be more apparent to people who have known both of you for a long time. Don't expect them to admit it. They wouldn't want to do anything to counteract the magical transformation taking place.

CHILD

Once you figure out that your kid's just asking questions to ask questions, then you won't be so invested in the answers. A favorite Mercury game is to ask the same question in a variety of ways to see if you get the same answer. It's how they play. Be patient. There aren't many times in life when one is free to *not* know one's own mind.

PARENT

As long as you were a kid, things were great. Your Mercury parent didn't need much prompting when it came to playing a favorite game or reading a bedtime story. It was like having a real-life imaginary friend. However as you get older, you'll notice that you're the one who matures while your Mercury parent remains eternally young. You will go through a period when you wish that she or he would act more age appropriate. But in time that will change, too, because you'll get less uptight and more accepting.

SIBLING

You could always count on your Mercury sibling to take the opposite side of the debate. Though this person claimed to just be playing devil's advocate, you knew he or she was doing it just to be a pain in the derriere. Over time you'll develop a warm affection and kinship. But your brother or sister will never lose that knack for telling childhood stories that make you cringe with embarrassment.

FRIEND

Your Mercury friend totally gets your sense of humor. You'll send each other cards, pictures, or obscure pieces of memorabilia that only the two of you would understand. When you're not trading in-jokes then its verbal jabs. Prickly and provocative, you two will spend hours arguing. Though you say you don't enjoy it, you're often the one who brings up the topic or refuses to back down. Nevertheless you trust your Mercury friend implicitly and know that what he or she is saying comes from the right place.

ENEMY

You may win the fight, but a Mercury enemy will always find a way to have the last word. If you're smart, you'll leave it at that.

BOSS

Your Mercury boss's inconsistency could drive you nuts. This person likes to explore as many tangents as possible. Most of the time, they're worth it. Sometimes it's pure whim. But use your own discretion. You don't have to worry about this person checking up on you. Mercury bosses aren't known for having long attention spans.

COLLEAGUE

Sometimes your Mercury colleague will make life easier and sometimes this person makes it harder. It really all depends on which side of the brain he or she woke up on.

CHILD OF PLUTO/MARS

❋

WITH CHILD OF VENUS

To you, a Child of Venus epitomizes all things beautiful. This person has the remarkable ability to make you forget yourself. Feelings of loneliness and scarcity slip away. You never feel so at peace as when you are around this person. A Child of Venus is your favorite obsession.

LOVE INTEREST

You evoke a powerful attraction from your Venus love interest—and equally strong feelings of ambivalence. Because it's in this person's nature to please, your Venus love interest will find it hard to say no to you. That's why, if you come on too strong, this person may respond by dropping out of sight for a while or being open-ended about committing. Any sign of hesitation makes you more resolute, and so you'll push even harder to firm things up between you. Rein in your passions and impatience. Your Venus love interest needs the freedom to make up her or his own mind.

MATE

There is no question that you two love each other deeply. However there is one matter you often fight over—and that's trust. Trust isn't a big deal for you, because you're suspicious of everybody. But that suspicion works against your mate's trusting you. For Children of Venus, trust isn't about fidelity. It's about *equality*. Your Venus mate's reaction to when you get too demanding is to be evasive and vague. This, in turn, stirs up your fears that something's amiss and you will tighten your hold on anything from finances to feelings. But if you relax your grip, you will find that instead of disappearing from sight, your Venus mate will come closer and even open up more. Letting down your guard is a tall order, but you've got to give to get.

CHILD

You could spoil this kid if you're not careful. And though it gives you immense pleasure, you may be setting a dangerous precedent. Not everyone will be as generous as you. Set up some kind of point system based on weekly chores or grades in school. That way your Venus son or daughter learns to work for the things that he or she wants.

PARENT

Your Venus parent doesn't mean to contradict you. It's just that you can get so fixed in your opinions that your dad or mom feels honor bound to represent the other side. The point of all this is to establish some kind of balance—which invariably lies somewhere in between.

SIBLING

You're still pulling your Venus sibling's fat out of the fire. It began with the breaking of Mom's favorite vase and continues to this day with the latest round of mismanaged finances or ill-conceived love affairs. You know your rescue efforts aren't doing a thing for your sister's or brother's sense of responsibility. But what can you do? It's family.

FRIEND

You will excuse things in your Venus friend that you wouldn't tolerate for a moment with anyone else. This person is helpless when it comes to doing certain things, and you can't resist lending a hand. Thankfully there's more to your relationship than call-and-response. Half the clothes in your closet once belonged to your Venus friend.

ENEMY

Given your predisposition to Venus types, you will put up with a lot before you retaliate. However once you've decided you've had all you can take, you'll quickly gain the upper hand.

BOSS

The examining and reexamining of every single detail can drive you crazy. Your Venus boss says it's about being thorough, but you know this person is really just trying to cover his or her backside. Don't let your frustration get the better of you. If you go ahead and act on your own, and it's wrong, your Venus boss won't think twice about hanging you out to dry.

COLLEAGUE

Expect to do all the grunt work. It's your forte. But if anyone knows how to apply the perfect finishing touch or ensure that the right people see your project—it's a Venus colleague.

CHILD OF PLUTO/MARS

········· ※ ·········

WITH CHILD OF MARS

Children of Mars are always on the lookout for a good challenge. They are drawn to situations that test their physical, mental, and spiritual fortitude. Whether they win or lose doesn't much matter as long as they can say that they've given it their all. Piquant and invigorating, a Child of Mars will fan the inner fire that you tend to keep on a low flame.

LOVE INTEREST

Your Mars love interest would do just about anything for you. This person tries to act otherwise (and you'd be well-advised to respect that tough demeanor), but the truth is she or he absolutely adores you. Strangely enough, this can be a bit of a letdown. That's because you have a history of falling for people you can't have. Check your first impulse (which is to move on) and give it time. You may find you don't know your heart as well as you think and that love needn't be such hard work after all.

MATE

You don't have to hold back with this person. You can let it all out. Though things may be dicey for the first few years (it takes a while to purge yourself of feelings you've been keeping inside), you'll find that your fights are actually few and far between. Indeed you'll be getting to know yourself in a whole new way, courtesy of your other half. Strength begets strength with Mars. Much of that moodiness and edgy temperament will burn away and be replaced by a potency and confidence that's always resided at the core of your being.

CHILD
Give that kid something to do. Although you're content to read, write, or be intensely reflective, your little powerhouse needs something active. Sports is the perfect outlet, as is dance or learning a discipline like chess or a musical instrument. Once properly situated, your little Mars will keep busy for hours.

PARENT
Your Mars parent is the epitome of the work ethic. Disciplined and motivated, this person always insisted you pay your own way. Much of your success and pragmatism comes from your Mars dad or mom. However things may get a bit tense if you surpass your Mars parent financially. This won't go over too well, as your business savvy doesn't really make sense to someone who's always taken the nose-to-the-grindstone approach. Keep in mind that the negativity is more a sign of discomfort than envy and you'll be able to express the generosity of spirit that should go along with all that prosperity.

SIBLING
You two always get a tad touchy around each other. Given your provocative energies (Mars is, after all, one of your Ruling Planets), you could be in a fighting mood without having anything to fight about. Altercations are about blowing off steam; it's rare when they stem from any real grievance. Your Mars sibling is fiercely devoted to you.

FRIEND
Most friends make light of your travails, but not your Mars buddy. This person will get just as peeved and heated as you—maybe even more so. There's something deeply satisfying about cursing up a storm with someone who's not afraid to get riled up. It's kind of like treating yourself to a nice juicy steak after weeks of healthy living.

ENEMY
Like pouring gasoline on a fire. Since you can maintain your cool in the heat of rage, it's up to you to bring things to a halt.

BOSS
The perfect person to work for if you're really into what you're doing. Indeed it's not so much a boss/employee relationship as it is a creative collaboration. Your Mars boss is interested in excellence, and given your tendency to raise the bar (and the standard) with just about anything you do, you'll find a worthy ally and supporter in this person.

COLLEAGUE

Like you, your Mars colleague doesn't do anything halfway. You might want to consider going into business together. There's no limit to what you could accomplish.

CHILD OF PLUTO/MARS

·········· ❄ ··········

WITH CHILD OF JUPITER

Things increase whenever you get near a Child of Jupiter. This can be anything from your income to your waist size. Like Pluto, Jupiter is also a Planet of riches, so the combination of energies is perfectly suited for any joint enterprise. However neither of you does anything in moderation. Seeing as you were born under the Planet of endings, it will be up to you to pull the plug when the good times go too far.

LOVE INTEREST

You are instantly smitten. And because you're afraid of rejection you may want to beat a quick retreat. But this spirit of bonhomie won't let you escape so easily. If you won't go to the party, then this person will bring the party to you. First meetings with a Jupiter love interest are often a bit nerve-racking. They usually take place in very public places and under the scrutiny of several people you don't know very well. This doesn't exactly gel with your more private Plutonian nature. But if you're going to date a Child of Jupiter, then get used to feeling as if there's a spotlight following you everywhere you go.

MATE

Your Jupiter mate brings out your grand style. For all of your preoccupation with not having enough money, the simple truth is you love luxury. You'll go from futon mattress on the floor to king-size sleigh bed complete with shams and bolsters—courtesy of your other half. But there's more at work than just maxing out your credit cards. By showing you how you can have it all, this person encourages you to live the life you want *now*. By pushing you to push yourself, your Jupiter mate gets you to develop that potential instead of just letting it lie dormant.

CHILD

Your Jupiter kid rekindles your faith. You're not always successful at keeping cynicism at bay, but that gushing enthusiasm and pervasive wonder that fills your Jupiter kid's soul gives you so much joy and uplift that you don't want anything to spoil it. Even if you don't believe that things work out for the best, you'll want them to for your Jupiter kid. And you'll devote your energies to making that happen.

PARENT

Not only does your Jupiter parent change his or her mind on a regular basis (and usually in accordance with the direction a current conversation is going), but this person will rewrite history as well. As a stickler for consistency *and* authenticity, this is unconscionable to you. Unfortunately your Jupiter dad or mom has such a "oh what's the harm" affability that others wind up regarding you as the sourpuss. A Jupiter parent is a master at reading audience response and using it to his or her advantage. You might as well keep the real facts to yourself.

SIBLING

Many of the sly stratagems that serve you successfully today were first tried out on your unsuspecting Jupiter sibling. One couldn't hope for a better mix of popular taste and gullibility. Your Jupiter sister or brother is still your favorite test subject.

FRIEND

Although your Jupiter friend will always vote thumbs-up while you vote thumbs-down, this won't stop the running commentary. If anything, you two take special delight in your contrasting opinions. Just keep it down when you're at the movies.

ENEMY

Not a good idea, because there's a good chance people will side with your Jupiter enemy over you. You may win the battle, but a coup d'état isn't far behind. Find one point where you agree and build on that.

BOSS

As long as you're in charge of the purse strings, everything will be fine. You'll make this person fiscally responsible. Otherwise keep an eye on the want ads. No one can bankrupt a company faster than a Jupiter boss.

COLLEAGUE

You're quick to poke holes in your Jupiter colleague's latest career maneuver or get-rich-quick scheme. But this won't stop you from secretly trying it out yourself.

CHILD OF PLUTO/MARS

·········· ☀ ··········

WITH CHILD OF SATURN

You know you've gone too far when a Child of Saturn raises an eyebrow. Just as driven, and twice as pragmatic, this person has an intuitive sense for avoiding those melees you often get mired in. You can always trust a Child of Saturn's judgment call.

LOVE INTEREST

You have to be at a certain point in your life to hook up with this type. That's because you like to obsess and a Child of Saturn just won't take it seriously. But after you get all that angst and heartbreak out of your system, then check out a Saturn love interest. Like you, this person is wry, to the point, and has no patience for fluff. Children of Saturn also get more attractive (and physically active) with age.

MATE

You're both relaxed and informal in each other's presence. Each of you instinctively knows when to chime in with just the right word or turn of phrase. The ironic thing is how much traveling and socializing you do. For two people who were regarded as such introverts before you got together, it's amazing how rarely you're at home. You always wanted to see the world. It's just that you didn't have the right person to see it with before your Saturn mate came along.

CHILD

There are some kids who will take criticism in stride, but not your little Saturn. She or he will soak up every word. Bear in mind that your Saturn daughter or son is just as demanding (maybe even more so!) than you, so limit yourself to one nit-picking comment. This puts the onus on you to find a more constructive way to impart information.

PARENT

Raising a family is serious business for a Saturn parent, which means that everything has to be done by the book. By the time you hit adolescence, though, your Saturn parent would have begun rewriting some of the rules, so that when you reach adulthood, your mom or dad is finally at a place where she or he can relax and enjoy a home life. Though your Saturn parent may not have been the most approachable person when you were young, she or he makes up for it by being a stellar grandparent.

SIBLING

You still turn to this person when you're in a bind. Whether it's a crossword puzzle that's got you stumped or a relationship problem, your Saturn sibling will help you find a solution. Just get off the phone before your brother or sister starts walking you through the thought process or you'll be sitting there for hours.

FRIEND

One of the best friends you could have. Not only will this person patiently sit through the umpteenth retelling of a love problem, but she or he will also help you carefully sift through what was said in order to get at the truth. Just remember, when this person says it's time to move on, move on.

ENEMY

Chances are you both have your sights set on the same prize, so try to adopt a more sporting attitude. After all is said and done, this person's allegiance will prove more valuable than anything you were fighting over.

BOSS

Your Saturn boss's high-handed manner may be a turnoff at first. Curt and to the point, this person's even more guarded than you. But give it time. Saturn bosses are notorious hard sells. There isn't a thing that goes on in your line of work that your Saturn boss isn't aware of. Do your work expertly and on time and this person will surprise you one day with a promotion or raise.

COLLEAGUE

Don't believe the self-effacing approach for an instant. Children of Saturn won't take no for an answer. Either you're part of the problem or the solution. If you fall in the problem column, then expect to be left out of the loop.

CHILD OF PLUTO/MARS

WITH CHILD OF URANUS/SATURN

Like you, a Child of Uranus and Saturn is a creature of extremes. Either something is right or wrong. There is no in-between. But where you rely on your gut feelings to show you the way, a Child of Uranus and Saturn turns to abstract principles and ideals to get a bird's-eye view. For two people who don't believe in compromise, you'd be amazed by how much common ground lies between your opposing camps.

LOVE INTEREST

Opposites attract, but you have to be at a certain place in life to make it work with a Uranus/Saturn love interest. If you're still learning how to harness your own emotional power, then things won't click. However if you feel comfortable with who you are, then you can appreciate the difference in your temperaments. Instead of trying to make this person fit into your world, you'll be able to spend time in hers or his.

MATE

Your Uranus/Saturn mate is always figuring out what to do next. This person must live according to a plan. It's fun (not to mention sexy) watching those mental wheels whirl as your mate scans the map or pores over a schedule. This person's mind is as swift and efficient as a computer. And like a computer, your mate can have off moments when he or she acts like a spaz. Nevertheless you can always bring your mate back on-line. You both know you're the one who has the final say.

CHILD

It would be nice if your kid were a little *less* independent, but that's not going to happen. Your little maverick has a mind of his or her own. Raising a Uranus/Saturn kid could turn you into a believer in past lives. It would certainly explain all the exotic ideas and references. Actually, Uranus/Saturn kids are like walking, talking antennae. They pick up everything. Which is why you want to be careful about what you say.

PARENT

Your Uranus/Saturn father may be hard to read. Dutiful and protective, there is still a peculiar sort of gentlemanly quality that isn't easy to penetrate. Spend enough time together and he becomes more relaxed. However next time you visit, you'll find that the demeanor is back up again. If you have a Uranus/Saturn mother, then she's very readable. Perhaps *too* readable. She'll carry on conversations for you—asking questions and answering them if you're not fast enough. She also takes a while to unwind, but when she does—she's a lot of fun.

SIBLING

Clear-eyed and fair, your Uranus/Saturn sibling has the ability to put aside personal feelings and examine a matter from all the different points of view. You caught on long ago as to how this seemingly impartial process conveniently proves your sibling is in the right—but you won't let on.

FRIEND

Don't expect a shoulder to cry on when going through a hard time. But considering your penchant for brooding, a cold splash of reality may be exactly what you need. Before you can even begin the "why does this always happen to me" lament, your Uranus/Saturn friend is busy making up to-do lists while phoning around to see what would be the best course of action for you to pursue. If anyone can get you to act in your own best interests, it's your Uranus/Saturn friend.

ENEMY
Not only is this a shrewd opponent, but a Uranus/Saturn enemy won't stop until you've been completely wiped out. Thankfully this person will only fight if provoked.

BOSS
Your Uranus/Saturn boss will always ask you to do more than you think you should. However given this person's farsightedness, you're probably being asked to nip a problem in the bud or line things up so they're ready to go before a project is slated to start.

COLLEAGUE
A real team player. Your Uranus/Saturn colleague can see what's missing in the current equation and will rush to fill it. Everyone can breathe a lot easier knowing that this person is on the job.

CHILD OF PLUTO/MARS

·········· ❄ ··········

WITH CHILD OF NEPTUNE/JUPITER

No matter how badly they've been wronged, Children of Neptune and Jupiter find a way to forgive and move on. This is something that baffles and intrigues you. What's the point of letting someone off the hook like that? Children of Neptune and Jupiter instinctively know that everyone will eventually reap what they sow.

LOVE INTEREST
You are completely enthralled. You just won't be able to resist your Neptune/Jupiter's siren song. Nevertheless, it's important to remember that there *is* an actual human being on the other end of all this fascination, so don't get too set in your expectations. However where most infatuations burn off like a morning fog, you'll discover that yours is even more beguiling in person.

MATE

You come first with your Neptune/Jupiter mate. You could get used to someone looking after your every need, but if you don't want to wake up one day to discover that your mate has left, then you need to ease up. As a Child of Pluto, you see everything from finances to feelings as being in short supply. This can make you psychically "hungry." For someone born under Neptune, the Planet of unconditional love, this is both appealing (Neptune's Children are drawn to people in need) and obligatory—because your mate will feel personally responsible for your happiness. This could create a voracious undercurrent where any attempt on this person's part to move away makes you pull even harder—believing, all the while, that this is what your other half wants. Take the initiative for your mate. Simple acts of sharing will go a long way toward creating a reciprocal flow between you.

CHILD

Your kid soaks up everything you feel. Since it's impossible for you to censor your emotions (that would be unhealthy for both of you), make a point of explaining your passions. For instance you might show how anger is your way of summoning up the energy to make a wrong a right, or that sadness is good because, like happiness, it also shows how much you care. Not only will your little one see that all emotions interact in some way with one another, but she or he won't be afraid to paint with such a rich palette.

PARENT

You hate to see your Neptune/Jupiter parent suffer. But this person can no more ration his or her sympathy than you could stifle your passion. For you—it's life's ordeals that are empowering. For your dad or mom, it's being there for others. No one can know why someone chooses the path they follow. But one person's trials may be someone else's spiritual awakening.

SIBLING

You could grow old waiting for your Neptune/Jupiter sibling to get it together. If you had a dime for every pipe dream, you'd be richer than Bill Gates! Don't bother trying to talk your sibling out of his or her fantasies. They're not doing any harm.

FRIEND

Avoid each other if you're both feeling frustrated or are in bad moods. That's because between the two of you, you could pack away more pints of ice cream or ring up more credit card debt than a small nation. Your Neptune/Jupiter friend may be your closest confidante, but this person also makes the perfect enabler.

ENEMY

Careful. This minnow can turn into a shark in the blink of an eye. And like a shark, your Neptune/Jupiter enemy can eat you up for breakfast.

BOSS

It's frightening to think of where your Neptune/Jupiter boss would be if you weren't around. But don't believe the helpless act for a minute. Children of Neptune and Jupiter are masters at being passive-aggressive. Nevertheless you think this person is brilliant and love to feel needed.

COLLEAGUE

Always check to make sure your Neptune/Jupiter colleague has followed through on what needs to be done—even if it's every fifteen minutes. You want to avoid any unpleasant surprises.

CHILD OF PLUTO/MARS

※

WITH CHILD OF PLUTO/MARS

Children of Pluto and Mars tend to avoid one another because of a fear that people as intense as yourselves shouldn't be left alone in the same room. Yet nothing could be further from the truth. Not only will another Child of Pluto and Mars totally get where you're coming from, but the nuances are so different that it's intriguing to see so much of yourself recast in the context of someone else's life.

LOVE INTEREST

This energy works best with young couples. That's because neither of you has really come into your own yet, so you won't be so uptight about who's in the driver's seat. Indeed you'll enjoy passing the reins back and forth. If you meet when you're more established (midthirties or later), then you'll need to take things slowly and give each other the benefit of the doubt. You'll both be wondering why the other never married or what's the real reason behind the divorce.

MATE

This is one of the strongest bonds that could exist between two people. However there will be many rough periods when you'll come close to calling it quits. You may have both been born under the Planet of ordeals and the transformations that arise from them, but that doesn't mean you'll undergo them at the same time. Yet no matter what, you'll stick together through thick and thin and slog your way through. You're Children of Pluto and Mars after all. And in the end, you'll be twice rewarded for all the travails you endure.

CHILD

It isn't easy watching someone make many of the same mistakes you did. But you need to remember that you were just as single-minded and inflexible when you were your son's or daughter's age. And like you, he or she will come out on the other side of this just fine.

PARENT

Emotional vulnerability to a Pluto/Mars parent is like nudity to anyone else. The first impulse is to cover it up. This is why your mom or dad would sometimes bark at you to get over yourself or discreetly change the subject if the issue hit too close to home. Yet despite the rough handling, you never stopped trying to connect—which becomes infinitely easier with adulthood. This person knows perfectly well that she or he didn't make life easy. Nevertheless hearing that said out loud will prove cathartic and bonding for you both.

SIBLING

You two couldn't be more dissimilar in appearance. If one of you is spiritual, the other one's materialistic. If one of you is bookish, the other's a jock. Yet beneath the surface you both know you have a lot in common and actually share many of the same views and opinions. In true Pluto/Mars fashion—it's your secret.

FRIEND

You love your Pluto/Mars friend deeply, but you have to be in the right frame of mind to get together. You can't help identifying with this person, and sometimes a "been there/done that" impatience creeps into your dealings with each other. When that starts, feelings are quickly stowed away, defenses go up, and the conversation comes to a standstill. But if you're both relaxed and comfortable, it's not unusual for you to spend days together at a time.

ENEMY

The greatest harm a Child of Pluto and Mars can do is to himself or herself. That would go double for you. Bearing in mind the law of diminishing returns, it might be better to skip the whole thing.

BOSS

This is one of the most profitable associations you can have. When you are promoted—as you invariably will be under your Pluto/Mars boss's aegis—make a point of turning to this person for advice. It's the greatest expression of gratitude you could show.

COLLEAGUE

Don't be surprised by the cool distance. As long as you're equals the potential of one day becoming rivals is never far from your Pluto/Mars colleague's mind.

AFTERWORD

So what does it mean that the first lunar landing took place in July, the month ruled by the Moon? Or that the first human being to set foot on her (in a modern reenactment of the alchemical marriage of Sol and Luna) was a Child of the Sun: Neil Armstrong? Or that Neil Armstrong's historic walk itself was the crowning achievement of the Apollo space mission, named after the Greek god of the Sun?

You are free to make of it what you will—which is the beauty of the Planets and their rulerships. There is no "right" answer, no one perfect way to live your life. If anything, there are at least ten ways of viewing any situation, and given all the potential combinations, there are countless more than even those. Whether you regard all of this as coincidence or proof of a higher order is up to you, the reader, to decide. But as you turned these pages you undoubtedly grew accustomed to the frequency of these coincidences, and hopefully they will tickle your curiosity and intrigue your imagination. And as you return to these pages, you will surely find things that didn't register before, and as you refamiliarize yourself with each Planet's realm, you will start to see how they work in the context of your own life.

There have been times in our world's history when a king wouldn't think of going to war without consulting the planets first or when a physician, upon hearing that a patient had fallen ill, would immediately cast a horoscope to determine not only the nature of the disease, but also the best way to treat it. Nowadays, it's different, but considering how much money is still spent on telescopes and satellites, it's clear that the planets haven't lost any of their allure.

Perhaps the most wonderful thing about the planets is that they each contain a world of meaning unto themselves. They exist simultaneously in our science and our mythology, our everyday references (who doesn't know that women are from Venus and men are from Mars?), and in our skies. At a time in our culture when religion and science are becoming more mutually exclusive, when technological advances reshape our lives before we've had a chance to psychologically catch up to them, and when our own planet has gone from being a wealth of resources to a severely limited one, it's comforting to know that the planets are still up there in the sky—following their orbits, as they have since time began. As both objects and symbols, they remain beyond our grasp—exerting their influence upon our minds and spirits and drawing our gaze ever upward.

ILLUSTRATION CREDITS

left: The Everett Collection, Inc.; top right: Bettmann/CORBIS; center right: Robert Nickelsberg/Timepix; bottom right: Henry Grossman/Timepix. **52** Top left: Picture Collection, The Branch Libraries, The New York Public Library; center left: Bettmann/CORBIS; bottom left: John Biever/SI/Timepix; right: Giraudon/Art Resource, NY. **53** Left: Mansell/Timepix; top right: Hulton-Deutsch Collection/CORBIS; center right: Bettmann/CORBIS; bottom right: Pix Inc./Timepix. **54** Left (all): Private Collection/Bridgeman Art Library; right: Scala/Art Resource, NY. **56** Bazuki Muhammad/Reuters/Timepix. **77** Image Select/Art Resource, NY. **78** Top left: John Zich/Timepix; center left: Alex Oliveira/DMI/Timepix; bottom left: Library of Congress; right: Artwork by Jamie Reid, courtesy of Sex Pistols Residuals. **79** Left: SEF/Art Resource, NY; top right: Mansell/Timepix; center right: Hulton Archive/Getty Images; bottom right: Stefano Rellandini/Reuters/Timepix. **80** Top: Library of Congress, Prints and Photographs Division; center: Simon Bruty/SI/Timepix; bottom: Neal Preston/CORBIS. **81** Left: Joffrey Ballet of Chicago, Calvin Kitten as the Chinese Conjurer. Photo: ©Migdoll '02; top right: PhotoDisc; center right: Library of Congress, Prints and Photographs Division; bottom right: Marion Curtis/DMI/Timepix. **82** Top left: Desmond Boylan/Reuters/Timepix; center left: Robin Moyer/Timepix; bottom left: AFP/CORBIS; right: Copyright©Agatha Christie Limited,

1920, Bonhams, London, UK/Bridgeman Art Library. **84** M. C. Escher's "Drawing Hands" © 2001 Cordon Art B.V. –Baarn-Holland, All rights reserved. **85** Scala/Art Resource, NY. **87** The Stapleton Collection/Bridgeman Art Library. **97** Private Collection/Bridgeman Art Library. **98** Private Collection/Bridgeman Art Library. **99** Top: Pix Inc./Timepix; bottom: Historisches Museum der Stadt, Vienna, Austria/Bridgeman Art Library. **100** Top left: Mansell/Timepix; center left: Mansell/Timepix; bottom left: Library of Congress, Prints and Photographs Division; right: Hulton-Deutsch Collection/CORBIS. **101** Left: Freud Museum London; top right: Bettmann/CORBIS; center right: Robin Platzer/Timepix; bottom right: Carl Sissac/Timepix. **102** Giraudon/Art Resource, NY. **103** Left: Mansell/Timepix; top right: Mansell/Timepix; center right: Jodie Gates and Doug Martin in The Joffrey Ballet of Chicago's production of Cranko's *Romeo and Juliet*. Photo: © Migdoll '02; bottom right: Allocca/DMI/Timepix. **104** Leonard Mccombe/Timepix. **105** Left: Alinari/Art Resource, NY; top right: Library of Congress, Prints and Photographs Division; center right: Eliot Elisofon/Timepix; bottom right: Vernon Merritt/Timepix. **108** Top: Mansell/Timepix; center: Mansell/Timepix; bottom: Marvin Lichtner/Timepix. **117** Victoria & Albert Museum, London, UK/Bridgeman Art Library. **118** Top: Mansell/Timepix; center: Library of Congress, Prints and Photographs

Division; bottom: William Philpott/Reuters/Timepix. **119** Left: John Iacono/SI/Timepix; top right: Library of Congress, Prints and Photographs Division; bottom right: Jerry Bauer/Pix Inc./Timepix. **120** Top left pair: (Bette Davis) Hank Walker/Timepix, (Joan Crawford) The Everett Collection, Inc.; center left pair: (Gloria Steinem) Library of Congress, Prints and Photographs Division, (Hugh Hefner) Bettmann/CORBIS; bottom left pair: Mansell/Timepix (both); right: The Pierpont Morgan Library/Art Resource, NY. **121** Left: Smithsonian American Art Museum, Washington, DC/Art Resource, NY; top right: Acey Harper/Timepix; center right: Frederick Brown/Reuters/Timepix; bottom right: Photofest, Inc. **122** The Pierpont Morgan Library/Art Resource, NY. **123** Top: Agence France-Presse; bottom: Scala/Art Resource, NY. **124** Top left: Picture Collection, The Branch Libraries, The New York Public Library; center left: Bettmann/CORBIS; bottom left: Marion Curtis/DMI/Timepix; right: © 2001 C. Herscoviei, Brussels/Artists Rights Society (ARS), NY/Giraudon/Art Resource, NY. **125** Tate Gallery, London/Art Resource, NY. **133** Grey Villet/Timepix. **134** Top left: Mansell/Timepix; center left: Bettmann/CORBIS; bottom left: Ian Cook/Timepix; right: Collection Kharbine-Tapabor, Paris, France/Bridgeman Art Library. **135** Left: Giraudon/Art Resource, NY; top right: Mansell/Timepix; center right: Pierre Boulat/Timepix; bot-

tom right: Ray Fisher/Timepix.
136 Top left: Picture Collection,
The Branch Libraries, The New
York Public Library; center left:
Mansell/Timepix; bottom left:
Library of Congress, Prints and
Photographs Division; right: Erich
Lessing/Art Resource, NY. **137** ©
2001 Artists Rights Society (ARS),
New York/ADAGP, Paris/Scala/Art
Resource, NY. **138** British
Library, London, UK/Bridgeman
Art Library. **139** Left: Yale University Art Gallery, New Haven,
CT, USA/Bridgeman Art Library;
center right: John Burgess/
Timepix; bottom right: Picture Collection, The Branch Libraries, The
New York Public Library. **140**
Top: Bettmann/CORBIS; center:
Library of Congress, Prints and
Photographs Division; bottom:
Bettmann/CORBIS. **141** Left:
Scala/Art Resource, NY; top right:
Mansell/Timepix; center right:
Library of Congress, Prints and
Photographs Division; bottom
right: Mansell/Timepix. **149**
Everett Collection, Inc. **150** Top
left: Charles Moore/Black Star/
Timepix; center left: Mansell/
Timepix; bottom left: Archive Photos/Timepix; right: Bibliotheque
Municipale, Rouen, France/Lauros-Giraudon/Bridgeman Art
Library. **151** Left: Scala/Art
Resource, NY; top right: Picture
Collection, The Branch Libraries,
The New York Public Library; bottom right: Popperfoto/Archive Photos/Timepix. **152** Top left: Library
of Congress, Prints and Photographs Division; center left:
CORBIS; bottom left: Dirck Halstead/Timepix; right: PEANUTS ©

UFS. **153** Art Resource, NY. **154**
Top: Library of Congress, Prints
and Photographs Division; center:
George Skadding/Timepix; bottom:
Laura Farr/Timepix. **155** Left:
Victoria & Albert Museum, London, UK/Bridgeman Art Library;
top right: Bettmann/CORBIS; center right: Picture Collection, The
Branch Libraries, The New York
Public Library; bottom right: ©
Tribune Media Services, Inc. All
Rights Reserved. Reprinted with
permission. **157** Left: Picture Collection, The Branch Libraries, The
New York Public Library; top right:
Al Fenn/Timepix; center right:
Bettmann/CORBIS; bottom right:
Bettmann/CORBIS. **158** Private
Collection/Portal Gallery Ltd/
Bridgeman Art Library. **165** Barry
Lewis/CORBIS. **166** Top left:
Mansell/Timepix; center left:
National Archive/Timepix; bottom
left: Library of Congress, Prints
and Photographs Division; right:
F. W. Wallace Collection, London,
UK/Bridgeman Art Library; **167**
Left: © 2001 Artists Rights Society (ARS), New York/ADAGP,
Paris/Artist's Collection/Bridgeman Art Library; top right:
Mansell/Timepix; center right:
Library of Congress, Prints and
Photographs Division; bottom
right: Diana Walter/Timepix. **168**
Top: David Rubinger/Timepix;
center: Picture Collection, The
Branch Libraries, The New York
Public Library; bottom: John
Biever/SI/Timepix. **170** Top left:
Loomis Dean/Timepix; center left:
Pierre Boulat/Timepix; bottom left:
Library of Congress, Prints and
Photographs Division; right:

Schalkwijk/Art Resource, NY.
171 Left: Scala/Art Resource, NY;
top right: Hulton Archive/Getty
Images; center right: Bettmann/
CORBIS; bottom right: Taro
Yamasaki/Timepix. **172** Top: Gjon
Mili/Timepix; center: Pix Inc./
Timepix; bottom: Hulton-Deutsch
Collection/CORBIS. **173** Scala/
Art Resource, NY. **179** Private
Collection/Bridgeman Art Library.
180 Top left: Mansell/Timepix;
center left: David Gahr/Timepix;
bottom left: Charles J. Peterson/
Timepix; right: National
Archive/Timepix. **181** Left:
Palazzo Barberini, Rome, Italy/
Bridgeman Art Library; top right:
Library of Congress, Prints and
Photographs Division; center right
pair: (Fritz Strassmann) Courtesy
of Max-Planck Society–
Gesellschaft, Munich, (Otto Hahn)
Ralph Crane/Timepix; bottom
right: Mansell/Timepix. **182** Top
left: Bettmann/CORBIS; center
left: Peter Stackpole/Timepix; bottom left: Ethan Miller/Reuters/
Timepix; top right: Private Collection/Bridgeman Art Library. **183**
Top: Timepix; bottom: Bill Bridges/
Timepix. **184** Kunstmuseum,
Basel, Switzerland/Bridgeman Art
Library. **185** Scala/Art Resource,
NY. **186** Top: Cynthia Johnson/
Timepix; center: Kevin Winter/
DMI/Timepix; bottom: David
Allocca/DMI/Timepix. **187** Top:
Library of Congress, Prints and
Photographs Division; center:
David Lees/Timepix; bottom: Bill
Eppridge/Timepix. **195** Werner
Forman/Art Resource, NY. **196**
Scala/Art Resource, NY. **197** Left:
Carlo Bavagnoli/Timepix; top

right: Charles H. Phillips/Timepix; center right: Brian Seed/Timepix; bottom right: Mansell/Timepix. **198** Top left: Bettmann/CORBIS; bottom left: Robin Platzer/Twin Images/Timepix; right: Scala/Art Resource, NY. **199** Left: James Keyser/Timepix; top right: Mansell/Timepix; center right: Ian Waldie/Reuters/Timepix; bottom right: Andreas Meier/Reuters/Timepix. **201** "The Insult That Made a Man Out of Mac®", "97 Lb weakling," and "Charles Atlas®" are the registered trademarks of Charles Atlas Ltd., P.O. Box D, Madison Square Station, New York, NY, 10159, USA, www.charlesatlas.com. **202** Top left: Bettmann/CORBIS; center left: Hulton-Deutsch Collection/CORBIS; bottom left: Ian Cook/Timepix; right: Scala/Art

Resource, NY. **203** Left: Scala/Art Resource, NY; top right: Picture Collection, The Branch Libraries, The New York Public Library; center right: Mansell/Timepix; bottom right: Loomis Dean/Timepix. **204** Top left: Library of Congress, Prints and Photographs Division; center left: Library of Congress, Prints and Photographs Division; bottom left: Library of Congress, Prints and Photographs Division; right: Pix Inc./Timepix. **206** © Estate of Ben Shahn/Licensed by VAGA, New York, NY.

PART III

Illustrations of "Sundials" by Tina Klem appear on the following pages:

213, 215, 217, 219, 221, 223, 225, 227, 229, 231, 233, 235.

Illustration of "Pluto" by Mike Costa appears on the following pages courtesy of Christopher Renstrom: **251, 289, 307, 331, 355, 379, 399, 406, 408, 410, 412, 414, 416, 417, 418, 420.**

All other illustrations in Part III, except for illustration of "Uranus," courtesy of Pictorial Archive of Decorative Renaissance Woodcuts by Jost Amman, Dover Publications Inc., New York.

PART IV

Réunion des Musées Nationaux/Art Resource, NY: **422** (cropped), **424, 442, 460, 460, 478, 478, 496, 514, 532, 550, 568, 586.**

604 Scala/Art Resource, NY.